X W9-CNQ-635

Introduction to Management in the Hospitality Industry

Introduction to Management in the Hospitality Industry

SIXTH EDITION

Tom Powers

PROFESSOR EMERITUS
SCHOOL OF HOTEL AND FOOD ADMINISTRATION
UNIVERSITY OF GUELPH

Clayton W. Barrows

ASSOCIATE PROFESSOR
SCHOOL OF HOTEL, RESTAURANT & TOURISM ADMINISTRATION
UNIVERSITY OF NEW ORLEANS

JOHN WILEY & SONS, INC.
New York | Chichester | Weinheim | Brisbane | Singapore | Toronto

This book is printed on acid-free paper. ♾

Copyright © 1999 by John Wiley & Sons. All rights reserved.

Published simultaneously in Canada.

No part of this publication may be reproduced, stored in a retrieval
system or transmitted in any form or by any means, electronic,
mechanical, photocopying, recording, scanning or otherwise, except
as permitted under Sections 107 or 108 of the 1976 United States
Copyright Act, without either the prior written permission of the
Publisher, or authorization through payment of the appropriate
per-copy fee to the Copyright Clearance Center, 222 Rosewood
Drive, Danvers, MA 01923, (508) 750-8400, fax (508) 750-4744.
Requests to the Publisher for permission should be addressed to the
Permissions Department, John Wiley & Sons, Inc., 605 Third Avenue,
New York, NY 10158-0012, (212) 850-6011, fax (212) 850-6008,
E-Mail: PERMREQ @ WILEY.COM.

This publication is designed to provide accurate and authoritative
information in regard to the subject matter covered. It is sold with
the understanding that the publisher is not engaged in rendering
professional services. If professional advice or other expert assistance
is required, the services of a competent professional person should
be sought.

Library of Congress Cataloging-in-Publication Data:

Powers, Thomas F.
    Introduction to management in the hospitality industry / Tom
Powers, Clayton W. Barrows.—6th ed.
      p. cm.—(Wiley service management series)
    Includes index.
    ISBN 0-471-25203-4 (cloth : alk. paper)
    1. Hospitality industry—Management. I. Barrows, Clayton W.
II. Title. III. Series.
TX911.3.M27P68 1999
647.94'068—dc21   98-30332

Printed in the United States of America.

10 9 8 7 6 5 4 3 2

*This book is dedicated to
the late F. Urban Powers (1898–1980),
a pioneer in the application of modern
management techniques
to the hospitality industry.*

From Student to Student

Welcome to the wonderful world of hospitality.

Introduction to Management in the Hospitality Industry is an excellent book to begin your journey into this profession. Although some of you may have already worked within the hospitality industry in one capacity or another, this begins your formal education into how industry standards and procedures have evolved. Whether working as a dishwasher, waiter, bus person, or parking attendant, some of you, myself included, have already enjoyed the excitement and adrenaline rush of busy guest service organizations. This book will validate and explain some experiences you may already have had, and introduce others.

As future hospitality managers, we must know a great deal about procedures and functions in order to make decisions and offer guidance at every stage of an operation. *Introduction to Management in the Hospitality Industry* is a resource to do so and a stepping-stone into the hospitality industry, because it was written with a commonsense approach to learning.

The objective of this book is to introduce hospitality management students to the primary resources associated with the industry: products, labor, and revenue. As a student in the introductory course, it was great to have the background of so many large hotel chains and quick-service restaurants at my fingertips. I knew at that point that it was true what they say about the people who choose this business: "It gets in your blood." This book helped me complete the first in a series of steps that will allow me to reach the top.

The authors have included some helpful features in the book that will complement what you are learning in class.

◆ The case histories are designed to give you information and a real-world look at how organizations are constantly evolving to achieve greater success.

◆ The Review Questions at the end of each chapter can be used as a study guide to assess your comprehension of the chapter. The questions truly tested my ability to apply and place all the information into perspective. I knew that, if I could answer the Review Questions, I would score well on the test. If you don't believe me, try it for yourself.

◆ The Chapter Summary provides an overall view of the most important and useful information in the chapter. Let me tell you, this feature saved me from those unexpected "pop quizzes." There were times when taking just a few minutes to read the chapter summary before class was the best decision I could make. I know my GPA would agree.

Finally, thank you for taking the time to read my comments. I trust this book will give you a strong foundation in the hospitality industry, as it has given me, and allow you to start building a successful professional career.

Pamela Dowden is a Hotel Restaurant Management student at Johnson & Wales University, Charleston, South Carolina, campus. She writes: "After working in a number of jobs that didn't make me happy, I started researching schools in the hospitality industry, because I was the best bartender you could find, and loved it. My long-term goal is to become the owner and operator of a jazz restaurant."

Preface

This sixth edition of *Introduction to Management in the Hospitality Industry* features a host of changes in both format and content. Some were made as a result of feedback obtained from hospitality students and professors, in an effort to make the textbook more user-friendly while maintaining the strengths for which it has become known. Other changes reflect our need to present a current overview of the hospitality industry.

Perhaps the most significant change is the introduction of a new co-author to this edition, Clayton Barrows. Clayton brings 25 years of experience in the hospitality industry and in hospitality education. His contributions to the new edition have been invaluable, and his vision for this textbook and for hospitality education is one that will serve students well.

Some other important new features in this edition include additional career information for students, more international examples, extensive industry notes and case histories, and exercises requiring students to research on the Internet.

GOALS AND PURPOSE

Through all of these changes, however, a basic commitment to five principles has remained constant. In this text, we strive to:

- ◆ Present hospitality as a single, interrelated industry

- ◆ Emphasize problem-solving tools rather than pat answers

◆ Focus on industry-wide trends rather than bare facts and figures

◆ Emphasize the importance of learning through experience by providing a framework for students' field experiences and observations

◆ Finally, and most fundamentally, help students see that whether they are working in the largest company in the industry or a small independent company, they are in business for themselves, building their reputation, skills, and know-how, which are the principle assets of their business and the cornerstones for a successful professional career.

$\mathcal{C}$ONTENT CHANGES

To develop an industry-wide perspective, the text is divided into six major parts: career concerns and the factors that underlie growth and change in the hospitality industry; the food service sector of hospitality; the lodging business; travel and tourism; the fundamentals of management; and the concept of service.

Part 1, "Perspectives on Careers in Hospitality" begins developing an industry-wide perspective for students with a general discussion of careers in hospitality. A chapter on demographic trends, the demand for hospitality services from various consumer segments, and the supply of labor has been moved forward to become Chapter 2 and has been expanded to encompass the entire hospitality industry.

Part 2 takes an in-depth look at food service. Chapter 3 looks at the restaurant business and contains a discussion of restaurant types. The subjects of restaurant operations (Chapter 4), restaurant organization—independent, chain, and franchise (Chapter 5), health and environmental concerns (Chapter 7), and competition in food service each merit their own chapter. In Chapter 6, we have used the concept of **marketing mix** to frame our discussion of competition so as to offer an introduction to some key marketing concepts as well as an insight into competitive practice in food service. Institutional food service (Chapter 8) has unique characteristics and opportunities that set it apart from the rest of the industry. Clayton Barrows has drawn upon his experiences in the institutional sector to craft a revised and updated chapter.

Lodging, too, has evolved into specialized forms of operation serving different market segments. Part 3 looks at the lodging industry. The products developed for various lodging segments are examined in Chapter 9, using the typology developed by Smith Travel Research. Hotel and motel operations are the subject of Chapter 10, which concludes with a section on specialized career fields in the lodging industry. In the past few years, new modes of financing hotel expansion have resulted in a growth in supply that is equal to or greater than the growth in demand for many lodging segments. Understanding the basis of the financial trends driving this expansion and the economic context within which hotel competition operates has an important bearing on the career decisions that hotel management professionals will be making in the coming years, and is the subject of Chapter 11. Similar to food service, Chapter 12 on hotel competition uses a marketing mix framework to analyze competitive practices in lodging.

Tourism, the world's largest industry, and one of the fastest growing, is vital to hospitality businesses of all kinds and is the subject of Part 4. Chapter 13 looks at the growth of tourism, its economic and social impacts, its importance to the U.S. balance of trade, along with updated travel information, ecotourism, and contemporary trends in the airline and travel agency businesses. Chapter 14 identifies major categories of destinations and discusses the types of businesses and activities that drive each destination sector.

Part 5 on management in the hospitality industry provides an introduction to the tools that managers use to help them achieve their goals. Using theory, examples, and new case histories, the chapters portray the management function as an active force for solving the problems that hospitality organizations face. These chapters also introduce students to some basic managerial terms and concepts that they will encounter in future courses, as well as in their own careers.

Service has been recognized on all sides as the most important factor for success in today's business world. How much more true this must be for the hospitality service industry. The final chapter of the book is devoted to this vital topic.

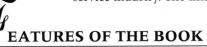 EATURES OF THE BOOK

Several pedagogical features have been developed for this textbook to help students understand the material more easily and to help bring the world of hospitality alive.

◆ *The Purpose of This Chapter* introduces the chapter to students and discusses the significance to the hospitality industry of the topics covered.

◆ *This Chapter Should Help You* lists specific learning objectives at the beginning of each chapter to help students focus their efforts and alert them to the important concepts discussed.

◆ *Industry Practice Notes* appear in almost every chapter. These boxes take a closer look at specific trends or practices in the hospitality industry, from booking reservations over the Internet (Chapter 13) to the changing roles for women in food service (Chapter 2).

◆ *Case Histories* support the chapter discussions by highlighting examples from today's hospitality organizations and associations.

◆ *Global Hospitality Notes* have been added to give students an international perspective to their studies. The boxes cover topics as diverse as career opportunities overseas (Chapter 1) and ecotourism in other countries (Chapter 14).

◆ The *Careers in Hospitality* icon appears throughout the book in the margin of the text to alert students to specific discussions of career opportunities in the hospitality industry.

◆ The *Summary* provides a concise synopsis of the topics presented in the chapter.

◆ Throughout the chapter, *key words* are highlighted in boldface, generally when they are first introduced and defined. A list of key words and concepts appears at the end of each chapter.

◆ The *Review Questions* test students' recall and understanding of the key points in each chapter. Answers are provided in the *Instructor's Manual.*

◆ New to this edition are a series of *Internet Exercises*, which are research exercises and projects, developed to familiarize students with the different ways in which the hospitality industry is using the World Wide Web. Answers are included in the *Instructor's Manual.*

$\mathscr{S}$UPPLEMENTARY MATERIALS

An *Instructor's Manual* (ISBN 0471–33028–0) with test questions accompanies this textbook. The *Manual* includes sample syllabi, chapter overviews and outlines, teaching suggestions, answers to the review questions and Internet exercises, transparency masters of selected tables and illustrations, as well as the test questions and their answers. The test questions are also available in electronic form on a *Microtest,* which is available to course instructors upon request.

$\mathscr{A}$CKNOWLEDGMENTS

First of all, it is my pleasure to welcome Clayton Barrows as co-author. Researching and writing this text is an immense task, and, as much as I enjoy it, I am relieved to have someone with whom to share this responsibility. Moreover, his presence gives assurance that this text will, indeed, be around for a long time.

We would also like to acknowledge many people who have helped in shaping this book, even at the risk of inadvertently overlooking some of the friends and colleagues who have helped us. My wife, Jo Marie Powers, who is also a colleague in HRI, is the source of many ideas found in this text—not all, I'm afraid, properly acknowledged. Her advice and critical reactions have been vital to developing the text over the course of earlier editions, and it continues to be true with this one. She also has made major contributions to the test bank developed for this edition and has served as editor and co-author of the *Instructor's Manual.*

Student Involvement

To shape the current edition, we solicited feedback from hospitality students throughout the United States who had used this textbook in their introductory courses. Their comments and suggestions have added a new dimension to this revision, and we are grateful for their participation. They are:

Pamela Dowden, Johnson & Wales University

Cheryl Inskeep, Indiana University-Purdue

Lawrence Slade, Colorado State University

Roberta Taylor, Northwestern Business College

Christine Toth, Westchester Community College

Saskia Villamil, Northern Virginia Community College

Faculty Input

We are especially indebted to two individuals for their contributions to this edition. Dr. Richard Patterson of Western Kentucky University drew upon his extensive knowledge of the World Wide Web to develop the Internet exercises at the end of each chapter. He also provided Internet addresses for the organizations and associations discussed in the case histories. His commitment and enthusiasm have been invaluable. My thanks also to Choon-Chiang Leong, Professor and Director of the MBA program at the Nanyang Business School, Nanyang Technological University in Singapore, for suggesting expanded attention to the international dimensions of hospitality and tourism, and for making numerous helpful suggestions regarding this revision.

The authors also wish to acknowledge Dr. Gary Vallen for his assistance in the revision of Chapter 10 on Lodging Operations.

Colleagues from the School of Hotel and Food Administration at the University of Guelph have provided us with numerous insights that have shaped this text in important ways. We must acknowledge especially Jim Pickworth, who has an eagle eye for information that is important to updating the text and is generous in providing it.

We are also grateful to the professors who reviewed the previous editions and early drafts of this edition. Their comments and suggestions have helped us immensely in the preparation of this revision:

Patricia Agnew, Johnson & Wales University

James Bardi, Penn State University-Berks Campus

James Bennett, Indiana University-Purdue

John Courtney, Johnson County Community College

John Dunn, Santa Barbara City College

Susan Gregory, Colorado State University

Choon-Chiang Leong, Nanyang Technological University, Singapore

Kathryn Hashimoto, University of New Orleans

Lynn Huffman, Texas Tech University

Frank Lattuca, University of Massachusetts-Amherst

Brian Miller, University of Massachusetts-Amherst

Paul Myer, Northwestern Business College

Daryl Nosek, Westchester Community College

Howard Reichbart, Northern Virginia Community College

Randy Sahajdack, Grand Rapids Community College

Andrew Schwarz, Sullivan County Community College

Industry Support

The research published by the National Restaurant Association forms, as always, an important part of the food service chapters of this book and, indeed, has influenced other portions of the text in important ways as well. We are especially indebted to Krista Lindhard and her colleagues in the information specialists group at the NRA who have helped us time and again, when information or a vagrant citation went astray. The Institutional Foodservice Manufacturing Association (IFMA) has also been most helpful in permitting us to quote from the Chain Operator's Exchange (COEX) Proceedings. As always, at ARAMARK, Joel Katz has run interference for us and has helped us locate information in the rich bank of ARAMARK practice. Joan Rice and John Wannenberg of ARAMARK Public Relations have provided invaluable help in lining up information sources for the industry practice notes, drawing on that company's experience. A final note of thanks at ARAMARK goes to Mary Jo McLaughlin, who gave generously of her time and knowledge to help us develop a concrete example of the work of a manager and a leader.

There are more than a few footnotes to identify specific points of information that have been taken from the work of John Rohs and Warren Gump of Schroder and Co., but these alone do not give adequate credit to their influence on our discussion of lodging. John Rohs is owed a special debt for his generosity over many years and several editions of this text for providing insight into the economics of the hotel business and sometimes—with considerable patience—for explaining what should already have been clear.

People at Smith Travel Research (STR) and especially Randy Smith, the founder and CEO of STR, have gone out of their way to make available facts, figures, and analysis that draw on the depth and breadth of their research. Steven Rushmore and Carolyn Malone at Hospitality Valuation Services (HVS) have also generously made portions of their research available to us. At Chervenak, Keane and Company, Larry Chervenak and Joan Christmas, Editor of the *CKC Report*, have helped us keep up with lodging's ongoing technological revolution.

The Hospitality Industry Investment Conference, held Annually in New York City, has provided yet another key to understanding changing hospitality institutions. The conceptual underpinnings of this text owe a great deal to the speakers at that conference over many years. We would particularly like to thank our colleagues at New York University, Sandra Dove-Lowther and Ruthe Davis, Director of Professional Development Programs at NYU, for their help. They have extended many courtesies to us.

At Cornell University's Nestlé Library, HOSTLINE provides scholars with helpful assistance in locating and accessing documents not in their own library. Erik Nesbit of HOSTLINE deserves special thanks for help that went beyond the call of duty.

As always, Wiley's editors have been most helpful. Claire Zuckerman was the Senior Editor with whom we began working on this revision. Following her much lamented early retirement, JoAnna Turtletaub ably took over. Their advice and encouragement have been a great support in our efforts.

A special word of thanks must go to Matt Van Hattem, a developmental editor at Wiley, whose editorial and substantive insights have had a major impact on this edition. Matt became both a colleague and a friend as the revision proceeded. Finally, Donna Conte was the production editor who was responsible for shepherding an unwieldy typescript, rough illustrations, and a lot of pictures into the book you hold in your hand—and she has done so with grace, patience, and charm.

Tom Powers	Clayton Barrows
Moon River, Ontario	New Orleans, Louisiana

September 1998

Contents

Chapter 6   Competitive Forces in Food Service   **146**

Chapter 10   Hotel and Motel Operations   274

Chapter 11   Forces Shaping the Hotel Business   308

Part 4   TRAVEL, TOURISM, AND THE HOSPITALITY INDUSTRY 377

Chapter 13   Tourism: Front and Center   378

Chapter 14   Destinations: Tourism Generators   408

Part 5   MANAGEMENT IN THE HOSPITALITY INDUSTRY   447

Chapter 15   Management: A New Way of Thinking   448

Chapter 16	**Planning in Hospitality Management**	**474**

Chapter 17	**Organizing in Hospitality Managment**	**496**

Part 1

Perspectives on Careers in Hospitality

Chapter 1

Courtesy of Four Seasons Hotel, Mexico, D.F.

The Hospitality Industry and You

The Purpose of This Chapter

Your own career choice is probably the most important management decision you'll ever make—at least from your point of view. This chapter has been designed, therefore, to help you analyze a career in the hospitality industry and correlate that analysis with your field experiences while in school. It will also help prepare you for the first career decision you make just before or after you graduate. This chapter discusses the career decisions ahead of you over the next three to five years.

This Chapter Should Help You

1. Know what kinds of businesses (and other establishments) make up the hospitality industry

2. Know why people study in hospitality management programs—and what advantages these academic programs may have for you

3. Think of your career decision in terms of a life's work not just a job

4. Start planning your field experiences—again, not just as jobs but as crucial parts of your education

5. Relate your education—both class and field experiences—to your employment goals at graduation

6. Evaluate the employment outlook in the various sectors of the hospitality industry, and learn where the "hot spots" and "soft spots" are

WHAT IS HOSPITALITY MANAGEMENT?

When we think of the hospitality industry, we usually think of hotels and restaurants. However, the term has a much broader meaning. According to the *Oxford English Dictionary*, hospitality means "the reception and entertainment of guests, visitors or strangers with liberality and good will." The word hospitality is derived from hospice, a medieval "house of rest" for travelers and pilgrims. A hospice was also an early form of what we now call a nursing home, and the word is clearly related to hospital.

Hospitality, then, includes hotels and restaurants. It also refers, however, to other kinds of institutions that offer shelter or food or both to people away from their homes. Moreover, these institutions have more than a common historical heritage. They also share the management problems of providing food and

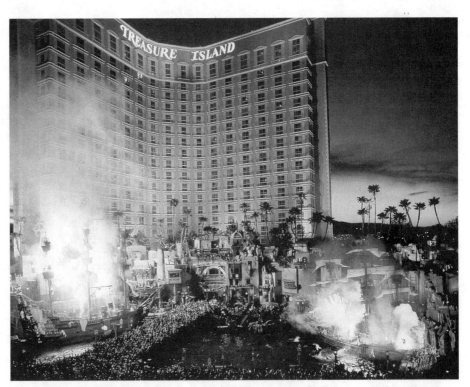

Some of the attractions prepared for the guests of the Treasure Island Hotel and Casino are really mind-boggling. Here the *HMS Britannia* and the pirate ship *Hispaniola* battle to the death—as they do every half hour in front of the hotel.
Courtesy of Treasure Island, Mirage Resorts

shelter—problems that include erecting a building; providing heat, light, and power; cleaning and maintaining the premises; and preparing and serving food in a way that pleases the guests. We expect all of this to be done "with liberality and good will" when we stay in a hotel or dine in a restaurant, but we can also rightfully expect the same treatment from the dietary department in a health care facility or from a school lunch program.

The hospitality professions are among the oldest of the humane professions, and they involve making a guest, client, or resident welcome and comfortable. There is a more important reason, however, that people interested in a career in these fields should think of **hospitality as an industry**. Today, managers and supervisors, as well as skilled employees, find that opportunities for advancement often mean moving from one part of the hospitality industry to another. For example, a hospitality graduate may begin as a management trainee with a restaurant company; complete the necessary training; and, in a short time, take a job as an assistant manager in a hotel. The next job offer could come from a hospitality conglomerate, such as ARAMARK. ARAMARK provides food service operations not only in plant and office food services, but also in such varied areas as recreation centers, college campuses, health care facilities, airline food services, community nutrition centers, and gourmet restaurants. Similarly, Holiday Inns is in the hotel business, but it is also one of the largest food service companies in the United States.

The point is that the hospitality industry is tied together as a clearly recognizable unit by more than just a common heritage and a commitment to "liberality and good will." Careers in the industry are such that your big break may come in a part of the industry entirely different from the one you expected. Hospitality management is one of the few remaining places in our specialized world of work that calls for a broadly gauged generalist—and the student who understands this principle increases the opportunity for a rewarding career in one of the hospitality industries.

THE MANAGER'S ROLE IN THE HOSPITALITY INDUSTRY

As a successful manager in the hospitality industry, you must exhibit many skills and command much specialized knowledge, but, for now, let's discuss three general kinds of hospitality objectives:

1. A manager wants to make the guest welcome personally. This requires both a friendly manner on your part toward the guest and an atmosphere of "liberality and good will" among the people who work with you in serving the guests. That almost always means an organization in which workers get along well with one another.

2. A manager wants to make things work for the guest. Food has to be savory and hot or cold according to design—and on time. Beds must be made and rooms cleaned. A hospitality system requires a lot of work, and the manager must see that it is done.

3. A manager wants to make sure the operation will continue to provide service and make a **profit**. When we speak of "liberality and good will," we don't mean giving the whole place away! In a restaurant or hotel operated for profit, portion sizes are related to cost, and so menu and room prices must be related to building and operating costs. This enables the establishment to recover the cost of its operation and to make enough additional income to pay back any money borrowed, as well as to provide a return to the owner who risked a good deal of money—and time—to build the establishment. (This situation is surprisingly similar to subsidized operations such as most school lunch programs and many health care food services. Here the problem is not to make a profit but to achieve either a break-even or zero-profit operation, or a controlled but negative profit—that is, a loss covered by a subsidy from another source.) The key lies in achieving a controlled profit, loss, or break-even operation. A good term to describe this management concern is conformance to budget.

Managers must be able to relate successfully to employees and guests, direct the work of their operation, and achieve operating goals within a budget.

*W*HY STUDY IN A HOSPITALITY MANAGEMENT PROGRAM?

One way to learn the hospitality business is to go to work in it and acquire the necessary skills to operate the business. The trouble with this approach, however, is that the skills that accompany the various work stations (cook, server, etc.) are not the same as those needed by hospitality managers. In earlier times of small operations in a slowly changing society, hospitality education was basically skill centered. Most hospitality managers learned their work through apprenticeships. The old crafts built on apprenticeships assumed that knowledge—and work—were unchanging. However, this assumption no longer holds true. As Peter Drucker, a noted management consultant, pointed out, "Today the center [of our society's productivity] is the **knowledge worker**, the man or woman who applies to productive work ideas, concepts, and information."[1] In other words, studying is a necessary part of your preparation for a career as a supervisor or manager.

Many people argue that the liberal arts provide excellent preparation not only for work but also for life. They're quite right. What we've found, however, is that many students just aren't interested in the liberal arts subject matter. Because they are not interested, they are not eager to learn. On the other hand, these same people become hard-working students in a career-oriented program that interests them. There is no real reason for educational preparation for work to be separate from preparation for life. We spend at least half our waking hours at work. As we will learn shortly, work lies at the heart of a person's life and can lead directly to "self-discovery."

Business administration offers a logical route to management preparation. Indeed, many hospitality managers have prepared for their careers in this field. Business administration, however, is principally concerned with the manufacturing and marketing of a physical product in a national market. By contrast, the **hospitality industry** is a service industry, and the management of a service institution is different. Food is a restaurant's product, but most of the "manufacturing" (often all of it) is done right in the place that offers the service. The market is local, and the emphasis is on face-to-face contact with the guest. Hospitality operations are also smaller; so the problems of a large bureaucracy are not as significant as are the problems of face-to-face relationships with employees and guests. Moreover, the hospitality industry has a number of unique characteristics. People work weekend and odd hours. We are expected by both guests and fellow workers to be friendly and cheerful. Furthermore, we are expected to care what happens to the guest. Our product, we will argue in a later chapter, is really the guest's experience. Some would argue that hospitality has a culture of its own. An important task of both schooling and work experience, then, is that of acculturating people to the life of the hospitality industry.

Our point is not that there is something wrong with liberal arts or business administration. The point is that hospitality management programs are usually made up of students who are interested in the industry that they are studying. There is a difference between the hospitality service system and the typical manufacturing company—between the hospitality product and the manufacturer's product.

Why do people want to study in a hospitality management program? Perhaps the best answer can be found in the reasons why students before you have chosen this particular course of study. Their reasons fall into three categories: their experience, their interests, and their ambitions. Figure 1.1 lists the various reasons that students cite, in order of frequency. Many students become interested in hospitality because a job they once had proved particularly attractive. Others learn of the industry through family or friends working in the field.

One important consideration for many students is that they like and are interested in people. As we just saw, working well with people is a crucial part of a

EXPERIENCE
    Personal work experience
    Family background in the industry
    Contact with other students and faculty in hospitality management programs
INTERESTS
    Enjoy working with people
    Enjoy working with food
    Enjoy dining out, travel, variety
AMBITION
    Opportunity for employment and advancement
    Desire to operate own business
    Desire to be independent

Figure 1.1 The reasons that students select hospitality management programs.

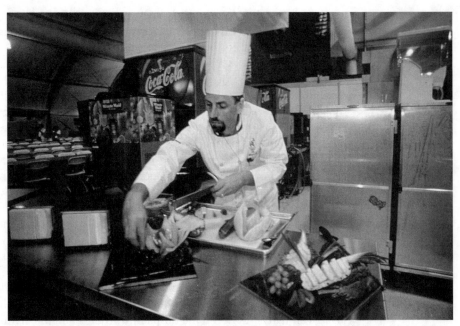

Luxury food service relies on a highly skilled team, made up of people in the front and the back of the house.
Courtesy of ARAMARK.

manager's job in our industry. Many students, too, have a natural interest in food, and some are attracted by the natural glamour of the hospitality industry.

Employment Opportunities

In addition, the employment outlook is solid in most segments of the hospitality industry, particularly for managers. Many people are attracted to a field in which they are reasonably sure they can secure employment. Others feel that in a job market with more opportunities than applicants, they will enjoy a good measure of independence, whether in their own businesses or as company employees. Many students are drawn to the hospitality industry because they want to get into their own business. One way to do that is through franchised operations, in either food service or lodging. Others, with good reason, suspect there are opportunities for innovation off the beaten track of the franchise organizations. There are many successful examples of the latter throughout the hospitality industry.

Many young entrepreneurs have chosen catering as a low-investment field that offers opportunities to people with a flair for foods and careful service. Catering is a fast-growing segment of food service and is also a business that students sometimes try while in school, either through a student organization or as a group of students setting up a small catering operation.

In the lodging area, one enterprising young couple expanded in an ingenious way the services of a small country inn. Once they and their tiny inn had been established in the community, they arranged to represent a large number of rental-unit owners in the area, offering marketing services to the owners and providing "front office" and housekeeping services for their guests in some 50 units, ranging from one-bedroom condominiums to larger condos and even houses.[2] The biggest appeal to being in business for yourself, cited by two-thirds of entrepreneurs, was not money but being your own boss.[3]

There are many other opportunities, as well. For instance, people with chef's training may open their own business, especially if they feel that they have a sufficient management background. In the health care area, home care organizations are expanding in response to the needs of our growing senior citizen population and offer a wide range of opportunities to entrepreneurs. This interest in independent operations reinforces the need for studying hospitality management.

Whether you're studying hospitality management because you want to start a business of your own or because you found your past work experience in the business especially interesting—or perhaps just because the need for managers in the area makes the job prospects attractive—management studies are an important preparation for budding entrepreneurs. Hospitality management students tend to be highly motivated, lively people who take pride in their future in a career of service.

𝒫LANNING A CAREER

Why Do We Work?

We all have several motives for going to work. We work to live—to provide food, clothing, and shelter. Psychologists and sociologists tell us, however, that our work also provides a sense of who we are and binds us to the community in which we live. The ancient Greeks, who had slaves to perform menial tasks, saw work as a curse. Their Hebrew contemporaries saw it as punishment. Early Christians, too, saw work for profit as offensive. By the time of the Middle Ages, however, people began to accept **work as a vocation**, that is, as a calling from God. Gradually, as working conditions improved and work became something that all social classes did, it became a necessary part of maturation and self-fulfillment in our society.

Today, workers at all levels demand more than just a job. Indeed, work has been defined as "an activity that produces something of value for other people."[4] This definition puts work into a social context. That is, it implies there is a social purpose to work, as well as the crude purpose of survival. It is an important achievement in human history that the majority of Americans can define their own approach to a life of work as something more than mere survival.

Work contributes to our self-esteem in two ways. First, by doing our work well, we prove our own competence to ourselves. Psychologists tell us that this is essential to a healthy life, as this information gives us a sense of control over both ourselves and our environment. Second, by working, we contribute to others—others come to depend on us. Human beings, as social animals, need this sense of participation. For these reasons, what happens at work becomes a large part of our sense of self-worth.

Education for such a significant part of life is clearly important. Indeed, education has become essential in most walks of life. There is, moreover, a clear connection between education and income. According to *American Demographics,* "college graduates earn twice as much annually as do high school graduates"—and the difference is growing.[5] The evidence, then, is that your commitment to education will pay off.

The next section explores career planning in regard to employment decisions that you must make while you are still in school. We will also discuss selecting your first employer when you leave school. If you've chosen the hospitality industry as your career, this section will help you map out your job plans. If you are still undecided, the section should help you think about this field in a more concrete way and give you some ideas about exploring your career through part-time employment. A large number of readers of this text already have significant work experience, many in hospitality fields. Because not everyone has such experience in his or her background, however, this is a subject that does need to be covered. Perhaps those with more experience will find this a useful opportunity to review plans they've already made. A fresh look at your commitments will probably be worthwhile.

It's hard to overstate the importance of career planning. Young people, particularly in high school, find that their career plans change constantly. By the time they've graduated from high school, their career plans may have begun to take definite shape, but there still may be more changes. For example, people who start out studying for a career in the hotel business may find the opportunities they want in food service. Others may begin preparations for the restaurant industry only to find they prefer the hours offered in contract food service. This kind of change in plans will be easier to cope with if you have a plan that can guide you until your experience enables you to judge the "fit" between yourself and the available opportunities. As a prospective manager, give at least as much time and attention to planning for decisions that affect your career as you expect to give to decisions you will be making for your employer. Remember that no matter for whom you work, you're always in business for yourself, because it's your life.

*E*MPLOYMENT AS AN IMPORTANT PART OF YOUR EDUCATION

Profit in a business is treated in two ways. Some is paid out to the owner or shareholders as dividends (returns on their investment). Some of the profit, however, is retained by the business to provide funds for future growth. This portion of profit that is not paid out is called retained earnings. We need a concept of retained earnings to consider the real place of work experience in career development.

Profiting from Work Experience

The most obvious profit you earn from work is the income paid to you by an employer. In the early years of your career, however, there are other kinds of

Hospitality takes many forms and is always changing. One of the fastest growing areas in food service is off-premise food, such as take-out and delivery.
Courtesy of Domino's Pizza, Inc.

benefits that are at least as important as income. The key to understanding this statement is the idea of a lifetime income. You'll obviously need income over your entire life span, but giving up some income now may gain you income (and, we ought to note, enjoyment, a sense of satisfaction, and independence) just a few years later. There is, then, a **job-benefit mix** made up of both money and knowledge to be gained from any job. Knowledge gained today can be traded with an employer for income tomorrow: a better salary for a better qualified person. The decision to take a job that will add to your knowledge is, thus, a decision for retained earnings and for acquiring knowledge that you can use later.

Every job, therefore, has to be weighed according to its benefit mix, not just in terms of the dollar income it provides. A part-time job as a supermarket stock person (well, it is a "food-related" job in a way) might seem attractive because it pays more than a job busing dishes does. However, if you think about the learning portion of the benefit mix and your total income, including what you learn, your decision may—and probably should—be for the job that will add to your professional education.

There is another important point to consider about retained earnings and the benefit mix. Often, the only part-time job in the industry available to students is an unskilled one. Many people find these jobs dull, and they often pay poorly. If you think about these jobs in terms of their total income, however, you may change your perspective. Although the work of a busboy or a dishwasher may not be very challenging, you can improve your total profits from such a job by resolving to learn all you can about the operation. In this way, you can build your retained earnings—the bank of skills and knowledge that nobody can ever take away from you.

Learning Strategies for Work Experience

When you go to work, regardless of the position you take, you can learn a good deal through careful observation. Look first at how the operation is organized. More specifically, look at both its managerial organization and its physical organization.

Managerial Organization. Who is the boss? Who reports to (or works directly with) him or her? Is the work divided into definite departments or sections? Is one person responsible for each department? To whom do the department staff members report? If you can answer these questions, you will have figured out the formal organization of the operation. Indeed, most large companies will have an organization chart that you can look at. If your employer doesn't have such a chart, ask him or her to explain the organization to you. You'll be surprised at how helpful to hospitality management students most employers and supervisors are.

While you're thinking about organization, it is also important to notice the **informal organization** or the "social organization" of the group with whom you are working. Which of the workers are influential? Who seem to be the informal leaders? Why? Most work groups are made up of cliques with informal leaders. After you identify this informal structure, ask yourself how management deals with it. Remember that someday the management of these informal organizations will be your problem; in time, you will be helping to manage the organization, and you will need their cooperation. In the meantime, this first-hand experience will help you both in your studies and in sizing up the real world of work.

The Physical Plant. You can learn a great deal about a **physical plant** by making a simple drawing of your workplace, such as the one shown in Figure 1.2. On this drawing, identify the main work areas and major pieces of equipment. Then begin to note on it where you see problems resulting from cross traffic or bottlenecks. For example, if you're working in the back of the house, you can chart the flow of products from the back door (receiver) to storage and from there to preparation. You should also trace the flow of dishes. Dirty dishes come to the dishroom window and go to the clean-supply area after washing. How are they transported to the cooler or to the pantry people for use in service? If you are working in the **back of the house**, you will be looking mostly at the flow of kitchen workers and dishes from the viewpoint of the kitchen, dishroom, or pantry. A similar flow analysis of

Figure 1.2   A sample layout.

guests and servers (and plates) can also be made from the **front of the house** (i.e., the dining room).

A study of guest flow in a hotel lobby can be equally enlightening. Trace the flow of room guests, restaurant guests, banquet department guests, and service employees arriving through the lobby. Where do you observe congestion?

These simple charting activities will give you some practical experience that will be useful for later courses in layout and design and in food service operations and analysis.

Learning from the Back of the House. Things to look for in the back of the house include how quality is assured in food preparation, menu planning, recipes, cooking methods, supervision, and food holding. (How is lunch prepared in advance? How is it kept hot or cold? How long can food be held?) How are food costs controlled? For instance, are food portions standardized? Are they measured? How? How is access to storerooms controlled? These all are points you'll consider a great deal in later courses. From the very beginning, however, you can collect information that is invaluable to your studies and your career.

Learning from the Front of the House. If you are busing dishes or working as a waiter, a waitress, or a server on a cafeteria line, you can learn a great deal about the operation from observing the guests or clients. Who are the customers, and what do they value? Peter Drucker called these the two central questions in determining what a business is and what it should be doing.[6] Are the guests or clients satisfied? What, in particular, seems to please them?

Employees in the hospitality industry derive personal satisfaction from pleasing the guests. So be sure to find out whether or not your job will allow you this satisfaction. Would you change things? How?

In any job you take, your future work lies in managing others and serving people. Wherever you work and whatever you do, you can observe critically the management and guest or client relations of others. Ask yourself, "How would I have handled that problem? Is this an effective management style? In what other ways have I seen this problem handled?" Your development as a manager also means the development of a management style that suits you, and that is a job that will depend, in large part, on your personal experience.

$\mathcal{G}$ETTING A JOB

Hospitality jobs can be obtained from several sources. For example, your college may maintain a placement office. Many hospitality management programs receive direct requests for part-time help. Some programs maintain a job bulletin board or file, and some even work with industry to provide internships. The "help wanted" pages of your newspaper also may offer leads, as may your local employment service office. Sometimes, personal contacts established through your fellow students, your instructor, or your family or neighborhood will pay off. Or you may find

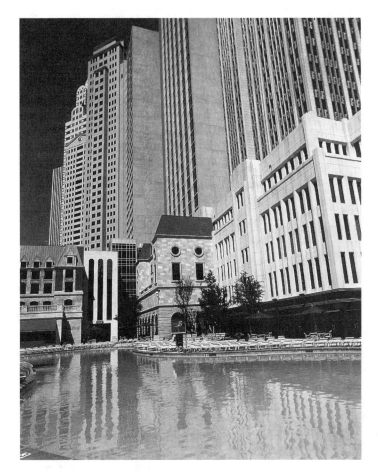

To give guests a thrill, the New York, New York Casino Resort Hotel in Las Vegas is built to capture the look and feel of the real Manhattan.
Courtesy of New York, New York, Las Vegas, Nevada

it necessary to "pound the pavement," making personal applications in places where you would like to work.

Some employers may even arrange for hospitality management students to rotate through more than one position and even to assume some supervisory responsibility to help them gain a broader experience.

Getting in the Door

It is not enough just to ask for a job. Careful attention to your appearance is important, too. For an interview, this probably means a coat and tie for men, a conservative dress or suit for women. Neatness and cleanliness are the absolute minimum. (Neatness and cleanliness are, after all, major aspects of the hospitality product.) When you apply for or have an interview for a job, if you can, find out who the manager is; then, if the operation is not a large one, ask for him or her by name. In a larger organization, however, you'll deal with a personnel manager. The same basic rules of appearance apply, regardless of the organization's size.

Don't be afraid to check up on the status of your application. Here's an old but worthwhile adage from personal selling: It takes three calls to make a sale. The number three isn't magic, but a certain persistence—letting an employer know that you are interested—often will land you a job. Be sure to identify yourself as a hospitality management student, because this tells an employer that you will be interested in your work. Industry Practice Note 1.1 gives you a recruiter's eye view of the job placement process.

Learning on the Job

Let's look at some ideas about learning on the job. One key is your attitude. If you are really interested and eager to learn, you will, in fact, learn a great deal more, because you will naturally extend yourself, ask questions, and observe what's going on around you.

Many hospitality managers report that they gained the most useful knowledge on the job on their own time. Let's assume you're working as a dishwasher in the summer and your operation has a person assigned to meat cutting. You may be allowed to observe and then perhaps help out—as long as you do it on your own time. Your "profit" in such a situation is in the "retained earnings" of increased knowledge. Many job skills can be learned through observation and some unpaid practice: bartending (by a waitress or waiter), clerking on a front desk (by a bellman), and even some cooking (by a dishwasher or cook's helper). With this kind of experience behind you, it may be possible to win the skilled job part-time during the year or for the following summer.

One of the best student jobs, from a learning standpoint, is a relief job, either day-off relief or vacation relief. The training for this fill-in work can teach you a good deal about every skill in your operation. Although these skills differ from the skills a manager uses, they are important for a manager to know, because the structure of the hospitality industry keeps most managers close to the operating level. Knowledge of necessary skills gives managers credibility among their employees, facilitates communication, and equips them to deal confidently with skilled employees. In fact, a good manager ought to be able to pitch in when employees get stuck.[7] For these reasons, one phrase that should never pass your lips is "that's not my job."

Other Ways of Profiting from a Job

In addition to income and knowledge, after-school part-time employment has other advantages. For example, your employer might have a full-time job for you upon graduation. This is particularly likely if your employer happens to be a fairly large firm or if you want to remain close to the area of your schooling.

You may choose to take off a term or two from school to pursue a particular interest or just to clarify your longer-term job goals. This does have the advantage of

*I*ndustry Practice Note 1.1

An Employer's View of Job Placement[1]

What do you look for?
We look for the perfect walk-on-the-water, charismatic, fire-eating, miracle-inducing human specimen. And we always settle for less. A motivated, articulate, results-oriented, technically competent, value-centered candidate can usually name his or her price (within reason).

What's your favorite question, the one you ask to get the best "read" on a person?
"If you were a vegetable on the salad bar of life, which one would you be and why?" I've never really used it but do get a big kick out of it. My best question really is a well-placed follow-up question when I think a candidate is being intentionally vague. These open-ended follow-up questions, such as "Can you explain that in more detail?" are worth their weight in gold.

How much does Daka depend on formal testing and how much on personal interviews?
We're 90% personal interviews and 10% tests and assessments now, but moving quickly to a 50–40 approach. Testing and assessment tools are *the* hot ideas. Get used to them.

What is the quickest way for an interviewee to take him- or herself out of the running?
Get caught in an exaggeration, lie or withhold important information. When that happens, the ballgame's just about over.

What skills do today's recruits have that those of 10 years ago didn't?
Above all, a love of, an affinity for, an addiction to *technology,* specifically computers and related technology tools. Don't even think about crossing into the new millennium if you haven't read an issue of *Wired.*

Do most candidates still have a poor perception of the foodservice industry? Why or why not?
No, most candidates like the potential of good income, fast upward progression, and lots of accountability that comes with this field. Pepsi-Co, Marriott, Outback, Daka—of course—and others have helped immensely in delivering on the promise of fast-track, high-visibility, great-income careers in foodservice.

1. The article quotes Lou Kaucic, senior vice president of human resources at Daka International, Danvers, MA.

Source: Restaurants and Institutions, June 1, 1996.

giving you more than "just a summer job" on your résumé—but be sure you don't let the work experience get in the way of acquiring the basic educational requirements for progress into management.

Wherever—and for however long—you work, remember that through your employment you may make contacts that will help you after graduation. People with whom you have worked may be able to tell you of interesting opportunities or recommend you for a job.

Global Hospitality Note 1.1

Career Opportunities Overseas

Companies hire North Americans to work in hospitality positions abroad for several reasons. Some countries do not have a large enough source of trained managers. Moreover, particularly in responsible positions, a good fit with the rest of the firm's executive staff is important—and often easier for an American firm to achieve with someone from North America. The relevant operating experience may not be available to people living outside the United States and Canada.

North American employees, however, are more expensive to hire for most companies than are local nationals because their salaries are usually supplemented by substantial expatriate benefits. Cost is not, however, the only reason for hiring people from the host country. Local people have an understanding of the culture of the employees in a particular country, to say nothing of fluency in the language. Local managers, moreover, do not arouse the resentment that is directed at a foreign manager. For many of the same reasons, foreign-owned firms operating in the United States seek U.S. managers and supervisors in their U.S. operations.

A final point to consider is that many North American firms are using franchising as the vehicle for their overseas expansion. In this case, the franchisee is most often a local national whose local knowledge and contacts are invaluable to the franchisor. Not surprisingly, however, the franchisee is most likely to prefer people from his or her own culture if that is possible.

Although most positions in operations outside the United States *are* filled with people from those countries, many American companies offer significant opportunities for overseas employment. One of the first obstacles to immediate employment over-

seas is the immigration restrictions of other countries (similar to the restrictions enforced in the United States). Employment of foreign nationals is usually permitted only if the employer is able to show that the prospective employee has special skills that are not otherwise available in the country. It is not surprising, therefore, that many employees who do receive overseas assignments have been employed by the company for a few years and, thus, have significant operating experience.

Another major problem facing Americans who want to work overseas is a lack of language skills. In fact, many hospitality programs are now encouraging students to select the study of at least one foreign language as part of their curriculum. The ability to adapt to a different culture is also important and probably the only way to get it is to have some experience of living abroad.

Summer or short-term work or study abroad not only gives students experience in living in another culture but also may offer them the opportunity to build up contacts that will help them in securing employment abroad upon graduation. Opportunities to study abroad are plentiful in summer programs offered by many hospitality programs. Some institutions also maintain exchange programs with institutions in foreign countries.

Obtaining work abroad is more difficult because work permits are required to be legally employed in a foreign country and these are usually not easy to come by. Some colleges and universities have begun to arrange for exchange programs for summer employment but, unfortunately, many do not yet have such a program.

As a student seeking overseas work, you should begin with your own institution's placement office and international center. The consulate or embassy of the country you seek to work in may be aware of exchange programs or other means to obtain a work permit. Probably the best source of information is other students who have worked abroad. Talk with students at your own institution or those you meet at regional or national restaurant or hotel shows. They know the ropes and can give practical advice on getting jobs and what to expect in the way of pay and working conditions. Whether you are interested in overseas work as a career or not, work, travel, and study abroad can all be unique educational experiences that broaden your cultural background, increase you sophistication, and enhance your résumé.

Don't underestimate a recommendation. Even if your summer employer doesn't have a career opportunity for you, a favorable recommendation can give your career a big boost when you graduate. In addition, many employers may have contacts they will make available to you—perhaps friends of theirs who can offer interesting opportunities. The lesson here is that the record you make on the job now can help shape your career later.

*E*MPLOYMENT AT GRADUATION

Graduation probably seems a long way off right now, but you should already be considering strategies for finding a job when you finish your formal education. Clear goals formed now will direct your work experience plans and, to a lesser degree, the courses you take and the topics you emphasize within those courses. If you have not yet decided on a specific goal, then this question deserves prompt but careful consideration as you continue your education. You still have plenty of time.

Global Hospitality Note 1.1 offers some information you may find helpful if you think you might like to work overseas.

The rest of this section offers a kind of "dry run" postgraduation placement procedure. From this distance, you can view the process objectively. When you come closer to graduation, you may find the subject a tense one: People worry about placement as graduation nears, even if they're quite sure of finding a job.

*G*OALS AND OBJECTIVES: THE STRATEGY OF JOB PLACEMENT

Most hospitality management students have three concerns. First, many students are interested in such income issues as starting salary and the possibility of raises and bonuses.

Second, students are concerned with personal satisfaction. They wonder about opportunities for self-expression, creativity, initiative, and independence. Although few starting jobs offer a great deal of independence, some types of work (e.g., employment with a franchising company) can lead quite rapidly to independent ownership. Students also want to know about the number of hours they'll be investing in their work. Many companies expect long hours, especially from junior management. Other sectors, especially institutional operations, make more modest demands (but may offer more modest prospects for advancement).

Third, many students, particularly in health care food service, want to achieve such professional goals as competence as a registered dietitian or a dietetic technician. Professional goals in the commercial sector are clearly associated with developing a topflight reputation as an operator.

These three sets of interests are obviously related; for example, most personal goals include the elements of income, satisfaction, and professional status. Although it may be too early to set definite goals, it is not too early to begin evaluating these elements. From the three concerns we've just discussed, the following are five elements of the strategy of job placement for your consideration:

1. *Income.* The place to begin your analysis is with the issue of survival. How much will you require to meet your financial needs? For example, your needs will be greater if you plan to support a family than if you need to support only yourself. If your income needs are modest, you may decide to forgo luxuries to take a lower-paying job that offers superior training. Thus, you would make an investment in retained earnings—the knowledge you hope someday to trade for more income, security, and job satisfaction.

2. *Professional status.* Whether your goal is professional certification (as a registered dietitian, for example) or a reputation as a topflight hotelier or restaurateur, you should consider the job's benefit mix. In this case, you may choose to accept a lower income (but one on which you can live and in line with what such jobs pay in your region). Although you shouldn't be indifferent to income, you'll want to focus principally on what the job can teach you.

3. *Evaluating an employer.* Students who make snap judgments about a company and act aggressively during an interview often offend potential employers, who, after all, see the interview as an occasion to evaluate the student crop. Nevertheless, in a quiet way, you should learn about the company's commitment to training. Does it have a training program? If not, how does it translate its entry-level jobs into learning experiences? (Inquiries directed to your acquaintances and the younger management people can help you determine how the company really scores in these areas.) Because training beyond the entry-level basics requires responsibility and access to promotion, you will want to know about the opportunities for advancement. Finally, you need to evaluate the company's operations. Are they quality operations? Can you be proud to work there? If the quality of food or service is consistently poor, can you help improve things? Or will you be misled into learning the wrong way to do things?

4. *Determining potential job satisfaction.* Some students study hospitality management only to discover that their real love is food preparation. Such

students may decide, late in their student careers, to seek a job that provides skill training in food preparation. Other students may decide they need a high income immediately (to pay off debts or to do some traveling, for example). These students may decide to trade the skills they have acquired in their work experiences to gain a high income for a year or two as a waitress or waiter in a topflight operation. Such a goal is highly personal but perfectly reasonable. The key is to form a goal and keep moving toward it. The student who wants eventually to own an operation will probably have to postpone his or her goal while developing the management skills and reputation necessary to attract the needed financial backing.

5. *Accepting skilled jobs.* Students sometimes accept skilled jobs rather than management jobs because that is all they can find. This happens, quite often, especially during a period of recession. Younger students, too, are prone to suffer from this problem for a year or two, as are students who choose to locate in small communities. The concept of retained earnings provides the key to riding out these periods. Learn as much as you can and don't abandon your goals.

A final word is in order on goals, priorities, and opportunities. Hospitality students' preferences for work upon graduation are summarized in Table 1.1.[8] Hotels are clearly the favored sector of the hospitality industry and luxury operations are preferred over mid-market or midscale operations among this sample of students. Interestingly, fast food (quick-service restaurant, QSR) and contract and noncommercial food service are at the bottom of the list. There is an old saying, *De gustibus non disputandem est* (In tastes, there is no disputing)—and that certainly should apply to job preferences. Still, the researchers speak of "how fulfilling and

Table 1.1   Hospitality Graduates' Career Preferences Ranked in Order of Preference

Rank	Industry Segment
1	Luxury hotels
2	Clubs
3	Mid-market hotels
4	Fine dining/Upscale
5	Midscale/Family
6	Contract/Noncommercial
7	Economy hotels
8	Quick-service restaurants

Source: Robert H. Woods and Michael P. Sciarini, "Where Hospitality Students Want to Work," *Journal of Hospitality and Tourism Education,* vol. 9 no. 2, 1997, Table 3, p. 7.

rewarding careers in the QSR industry can be" and suggest that, "Perhaps more than any other [this segment] provides an opportunity for hospitality students to 'fast track' to the top." On the other hand, later in this text, we will point out that, although work in institutional management is not any "easier," its hours are more regular and its pace more predictable.

Luxury hotels and luxury restaurants are undoubtedly more glamorous than many other operations—or at least seem so—and it does appear that they are attracting the largest number of graduates as applicants. In the supply–demand equation, they have a plentiful supply of applicants and yet they are relatively smaller sectors of hospitality employment (as are clubs). That is to say, they have less demand for people than many other sectors. In economics, you may recall, a large supply met by a modest demand is generally expected to yield a lower price. Of course, there are no dollar signs on job satisfaction and these are highly personal choices. Still, the truth is that no job offers *everything*. You have to decide what your highest priorities are and then choose the opportunity that suits you best. If career advancement, achieving a substantial income, and gaining responsibility—or perhaps just having a manageable work life—are priorities for you, you may want to consider at least interviewing with some of the companies that are on the bottom of everybody else's list.

THE OUTLOOK FOR HOSPITALITY

Over the past two generations, the hospitality industry has evolved to accommodate explosive growth, radically changing consumer demand, and a substantially different social and economic environment. We will examine some of the basic forces driving these changes in Chapter 2. The following brief summary points will alert you to some of the key trends discussed in the balance of this text. We can begin with trends closest to the industry and move outward to broader societal developments.

Polarization in Hospitality Service Organizations

Hospitality companies are grouping themselves, to a very large extent, either as limited-service organizations or as service-intensive operations. In lodging, although there are price point divisions—budget, economy and midscale, upscale and upper upscale—the most basic division is between *limited-service* and *full-service* properties. In later chapters, we will be concerned with the possibility of overbuilding and future excess capacity in all but the luxury segment of lodging.

In food service, simpler operations specializing in off-premise service to guests—take-out, drive-through, and delivery—have provided most of the growth in restaurant sales in recent years. Fast food, too, continues its healthy growth trend. Table service restaurant growth in the more economical family restaurant segment has flattened, but within the table service group a more service-intensive format—casual restaurants—has shown healthy growth.

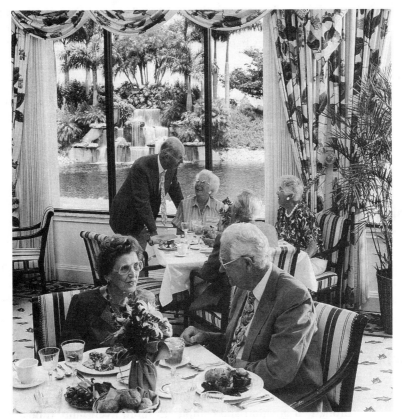

Bentley Village, a Classic Residence by Hyatt, offers luxury accommodations to senior citizens in one of hospitality's most promising growth sectors.
Courtesy of Hyatt Corporation

Restaurants and hotels, then, are tailoring themselves to specialized markets, a practice often referred to as target marketing.

Accelerating Competition

One of the major reasons hotels and restaurants are increasingly targeting specific market segments is that, in most markets, there is more than enough hotel and restaurant capacity to go around. Competition will be even tougher in the years ahead. In food service, operators are adapting their operations by opening new restaurants and bringing them closer to the customer, that is, making them more convenient. Lodging capacity, as we have already noted, offers a highly competitive outlook for all but the luxury sector. The growth in competition makes tightly controlled operations especially important to survival. We will consider those issues for restaurants in Chapter 4 and for hotels in Chapter 11.

Service Is the Difference

As competing firms expand their menus and amenities and dress up their operations, all operations at a given price level tend to become more like one another. The crucial differentiation becomes service—and usually personal service. Understanding service and how to manage it is so vitally important that the last chapter of this book is devoted to it. In the world of today and tomorrow, service will be the difference between barely surviving (or worse) and achieving success.

Value Consciousness

An educated, sophisticated customer base is placing increasing emphasis on the value of goods or services received in relation to the price paid in the marketplace. This trend probably originates in the baby boom generation. The best educated generation in history has become a generation of careful shoppers. With an intensely competitive industry vying to serve them, consumers are in a position to demand good value for their money.

Technology

Another driving force the industry has wrestled with for some years is the explosion of technology. Technology has already changed the way work is done in operations through automation and computerization. Even more fundamental, however, are the changes in marketing and management made possible by technological advances. Lodging marketing, already shaped by a global computerized reservation network, is likely to undergo yet another revolution as the Internet expands the communication capacity of operators, their competitors, and the guest. Restaurants, too, are maintaining web sites, many of which are already interactive rather than simply informational. Some take-out operations are experimenting with taking orders via the Internet. With greatly improved communication and computerized financial and operational reporting, the hierarchy of organizations is collapsing and a flatter organization structure is emerging.

Empowerment

As a direct result of the reduced numbers of middle management, employees and managers at all levels are being asked to assume more responsibility. For example, they are being empowered to solve many of the guest's service problems on the spot. This is an outgrowth not only of improved communication but of a more educated generation of employees. Bright, well-educated people want to do their own problem solving—and generally are able to do so effectively.

Diversity

The face of North America is changing. Whereas the white male has always been the dominant force in the labor market, the majority of people entering the workforce for the foreseeable future will be women and minorities such as African Americans, Hispanics, and Asians. Managers will need a broad background and an openness to many kinds of people and cultures to prosper in the time ahead.

Concern with Security

People are concerned with security on two levels. Broadly, as the incidence of *perceived* violence increases, people worry about their personal security—and so we see a proliferation of private security forces in hotels, restaurants, and other public places as well as high-tech security measures such as "keyless" electronic locks in hotel rooms. Security has become a commodity that some people are willing to pay for—and that hospitality establishments must provide.

Concern with Sanitation

The incidence of food-borne illness has increased as the food service system has become more complex as the number of operations have expanded. One case of "food poisoning" can seriously injure a restaurant's reputation. More than one can endanger an operation's survival. The level of food safety demanded by consumer and regulatory agencies alike has escalated in the light of recent cases of food poisoning. That escalation will continue in the years ahead.

Globalization

With the falling of trade barriers such as that brought on by the North American Free Trade Agreement and the European Economic Community, borders have become less important. The ease of financial transactions and information flow means that some of the largest "U.S. firms" are owned abroad—and that U.S. firms are major players overseas, as well. Burger King and Holiday Inn, for example, are owned by British companies and Motel 6 by a French firm. On the other hand, McDonald's is the largest restaurant chain in Europe, and Pizza Hut has restaurants in more countries than any other food service company in the world.

With all of the dynamism that the hospitality industry offers, an exciting future beckons as you begin this study of the industry and what makes it tick.

 UMMARY

As we have seen, the hospitality industry includes hotels, restaurants, and other institutions that offer shelter and/or food to people away from home. A manager in the hospitality industry, therefore, must keep in mind the following three objectives: (1) making the guest welcome personally, (2) making things work for the guest, and (3) making sure that the operation will continue to provide service and meet its budget.

We mentioned the many reasons for studying in a hospitality program, including past experiences working in the field, interests in the field, and ambitions in the field.

We also discussed why people work and how to get the most from a job, including weighing both retained earnings and the job-benefit mix. We pointed out that in the hospitality industry you can learn a lot from studying the physical plant and from how the front and the back of the house are managed.

We then turned to ways to get a job—including preparing for an interview—and how to gain the most from whatever job you do find. We also talked about what you should consider in regard to a more permanent job: income; professional status; your employer; potential job satisfaction; and accepting an interim, less-skilled job. We noted, as well, that supply and demand work in the job market as they do elsewhere, suggesting that what is most popular in terms of employment may not necessarily translate into the best opportunity.

Finally, we began our book-long discussion of the outlook for the hospitality industry, which we found to be bright but full of change and competition.

◆ *K*EY WORDS AND CONCEPTS

Hospitality	Job-benefit mix
Manager's role	Managerial organization
Profit	Informal organization
Knowledge worker	Physical plant
Hospitality industry	Back of the house
Work as a vocation	Front of the house
Work experience	Strategy of job placement

◆ *R*EVIEW QUESTIONS

1. What kinds of institutions or establishments does the hospitality industry include?

2. What is the role of a manager in the hospitality industry?

3. Why did you choose to study in a hospitality management program?

4. What are some of the reasons that people work?

5. What is retained earnings in the context of this chapter?

6. Describe the job-benefit mix. Give examples from your experience or from that of your classmates.

7. What are some things to learn from the front of the house? The back of the house?

8. What kinds of things can you learn from a part-time or summer job that are not strictly part of the job?

9. What are three principal concerns in regard to a job after graduation?

10. What are the five elements of the strategy of job placement?

◆ NTERNET EXERCISES

1. **Site Name:** *The Educational Foundation of the National Restaurant Association*
   URL: http://www.edfound.org/
   Background Information: The Educational Foundation of the National Restaurant Association is a not-for-profit organization committed to developing, promoting, and providing education and training programs for the restaurant and hospitality industry. It delivers the tools that empower people to build satisfying and lasting careers in the industry.

   EXERCISES:

   a. What certification courses does the Educational Foundation provide that are very important to the restaurant industry?

   b. What professional programs are offered for career development to high school and college students?

   c. Describe why the Educational Foundation is important to hotel, restaurant, and tourism management students.

2. **Site Name:** *The Foodservice Connection*
   URL: http://www.foodservice.org/
   Background Information: This site is dedicated to the food service industry and provides information on employment, links to professional associations, industry information, a shopping expo, etc. It has a search engine to help in locating information.

Site Name: *Tripod's Internship Center*
URL: http://www.tripod.com/jobs__career/intern__visa/
Background Information: One of the best ways to investigate a career and to find a job is to participate in an internship program. At this web site, you can find internship opportunities tailored to your needs, by choosing either a location area, a field of study, or both. This site lists internships in food and beverage, restaurant management, and hotel/motel management, as well as many other fields.

Site Name: *The Monster Board Job Search*
URL: http://www.monster.com/
Background Information: This site allows you to search through over 50,000 jobs worldwide, many of them in the hospitality industry. This site not only lists job opportunities but internship opportunities, as well.

Site Name: *Job Search Websites*
URL: http://www.wku.edu/~hrtm/job-srch.htm
Background Information: This page lists many of the major job search web sites on the Internet. It can be used as a launchpad for a job and/or internship search. Choose a web site and search for hospitality jobs.

Site Name: *International Association of Convention & Visitor Bureaus*
URL: http://www.iacvb.org/iacvb.html
Background Information: This site provides information for both meeting professionals and tour operators. Consumers planning business and leisure travel will also find valuable information at this site. Convention and visitor bureaus can provide brochures and information about special events and attractions. Use this site to identify job opportunities in the convention and visitor bureaus as well.

Site Name: *Hospitality Net*
URL: http://www.hospitalitynet.nl/
Background Information: This web site is based in The Netherlands and has information on news, trends, facts, job opportunities, events, vendors, etc.

EXERCISE:

Visit at least one of the preceding web sites. Go to the career opportunities section for hospitality/tourism jobs. Look through all of the hospitality jobs to become familiar with the jobs that are available. Describe a job opportunity in a hospitality area that you might be interested in if you were graduating and looking for a job.

◆ OTES

1. Peter F. Drucker, *The Age of Discontinuity* (New York: Harper & Row, 1968), p. 264.
2. *Lodging*, September 1984, pp. 68–71.
3. *Nations Restaurant News*, October 15, 1990, p. 14.
4. *Work in America* (Cambridge, MA: MIT Press, n.d.), p. 3.
5. *American Demographics*, February 1994, p. 20.

6. Peter F. Drucker, *Management: Tasks, Responsibilities, Practices* (New York: Harper & Row, 1974), pp. 80–86.

7. If they get stuck too often, of course, management must find out why and correct the problem. If a manager has to pitch in frequently, it can be a sign of inadequate organization.

8. Robert H. Woods and Michael P. Sciarini, "Where Hospitality Students Want to Work," *Journal of Hospitality and Tourism Education,* vol. 9, no. 2, 1997, pp. 6–10. The study was based on responses to a questionnaire administered to students at 20 four-year programs, which had a wide geographic distribution.

Chapter 2

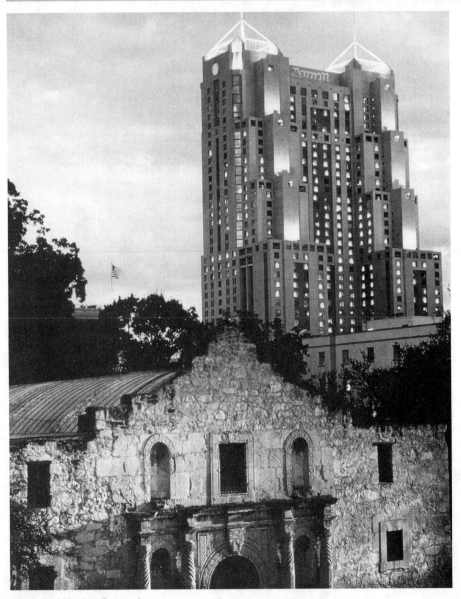

Courtesy of Marriott Corporation

Forces for Growth and Change in the Hospitality Industry

The Purpose of This Chapter

The hospitality industry, as it is today and will be tomorrow, is the result of the interaction of basic market forces. In this chapter, we will look at two of the most basic of these forces. The first is the *demand* for hospitality services from consumers. Second, we must consider the *supply* of those things required to provide service, such as land and its produce, food, as well as labor. We begin by considering demand; it is the fundamental factor that gives rise to business activity. For this, we must learn about the customer. We will then consider the supply of the factors of production used by hospitality service companies.

This Chapter Should Help You

1. Understand the impact of the changing demographics of the North American population on the demand for hospitality services

2. Assess the impact of the baby boomers on demand and the changes in demand that are likely to come about as a result of their aging

3. Recognize the opportunities and challenges inherent in North America's increasing diversity

4. See how changes in the proportion of women working and alterations in family structure affect consumers and the markets for hospitality services

5. Identify the key factors of supply required by hospitality organizations and become familiar with trends that are changing their relative cost

6. Understand how hospitality service companies are responding to changes in the labor force

EMAND

Demand, ultimately, means customers. We will look at customers from three different perspectives. First, we need to understand what the population's changing age patterns are and second, how they affect the demand for hospitality products. Finally, we will look at other patterns of change, such as the increase in the number of working women, the transformation of the family structure, and changes in income and spending patterns. **Demographics** is the study of objectively measurable factors in our population, such as the trends mentioned above. As we review this statistical material, however, it is important to keep in mind another perspective, the human face behind the numbers. To do that, we will want to consider what the facts mean in terms of our *customer base*. The material in this section is vital to understanding the most basic force driving the hospitality industry's development—demand; that is, customers.

The Changing Age Composition of Our Population

The central factor necessary to understanding the changing population of North America is the baby-boom generation, and then to set it in the context of other major population segments. We begin by describing just what the baby boom is. We will then turn to the key population segments that follow the boomers.

Beginning with the Great Depression, the birth rate fell dramatically and remained low throughout the 1930s. Then came World War II, which also produced a low birth rate. After the war, however, servicemen came home and began to get married in very large numbers. Not surprisingly, between 1946 and 1964, the number of births rose as well. The boom in births was out of all proportion to anything the country had experienced before. The resulting **baby boomers**, that is, people who were born between 1946 and 1964, have, as a generation, had an unprecedented impact on all facets of American life, ranging from economics to social change.

In 1997, there were 77.8 million baby boomers ranging in age from 33 to 51 and constituting nearly one-third of the U.S. population. Although the number of *native-born* baby boomers was at its highest in 1964 at the end of the baby boom, immigration has increased the size of the boomer cohort by significantly more than deaths have decreased it since that time.

By the mid-1960s, most of the boomers' parents had passed the age when people have children. Furthermore, just at that point, the smaller generation born during the Depression and war years reached the age of marrying—and child bearing. Because there were fewer people in their child-bearing years, fewer chil-

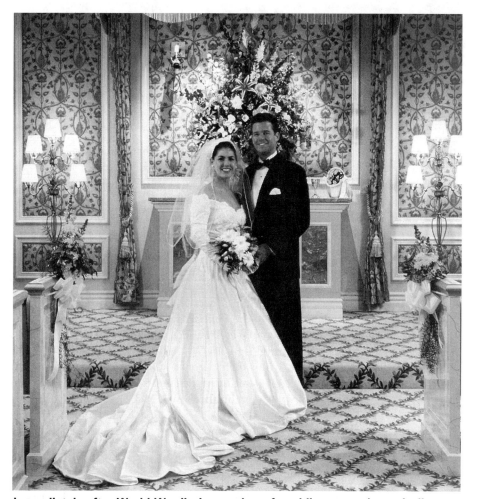

Immediately after World War II, the number of weddings rose dramatically, resulting in a tremendous number of births from the mid-1940s through the mid-1960s.
Courtesy of Treasure Island, Mirage Resorts

dren were born. The result was the "birth dearth" generation born between 1965 and 1975.

Labeled **Generation X**, this group ranged in age, in 1999, from 24 to 34. This generation began to come of age as the growth of the 1980s flattened into the recession of the early 1990s. The GenXers have lived through the downsizing years and face a much more competitive job market. Not surprisingly, they have a reputation for being worldly wise and pragmatic. Their tastes in food service distinctively favor the informal and casual—and their relative youth dictates a modest average income and a consequent price consciousness.[1]

Industry Practice Note 2.1

Demographics in Practice

Two Chicago area Italian restaurants—both owned by the same family—surveyed their patrons to determine the difference between the clientele of the two operations. One was suburban and the other a downtown unit. At the suburban location, patrons were, on average, older. They were more likely to be married and had higher incomes than downtown patrons.

The qualities important to customer satisfaction were different in the two patron groups. In the suburbs, customers placed high value on quality of service, employee friendliness, and value. Downtown patrons also considered price and value important but placed greatest emphasis on quality of food and timeliness of service.

Source: Adapted from the *Cornell Hotel and Restaurant Administration Quarterly,* August 1997, p. 56.

Food service makes a perfect case history for assessing the impact of generational change on hospitality. Fast food grew up to feed the boomers when they were children and when their parents, still young, had limited incomes and needed to economize. Then, starting in the late 1950s, the boomers, as young people, began to have money to spend on their own. McDonald's, Burger King, and other fast-food operations suited their tastes and their pocketbooks. In the late 1960s and early 1970s, however, the boomers were becoming young adults—and Wendy's, among others, developed an upscale fast-food operation to meet their moderately higher incomes and more sophisticated tastes. Similarly, in the early 1980s, as a significant number of boomers passed the age of 30, the "gourmet hamburger" restaurant appeared, accommodating their increasing incomes and aspirations. Industry Practice Note 2.1 gives another example from food service of the impact of differences in age on guest preferences.

The baby boomers have also had a significant impact on lodging. Kemmons Wilson's first Holiday Inn was built when the oldest boomers were 6 years old. Holiday Inns began as a roadside chain serving business travelers, but the big profits came in the summer days of 100 percent occupancy, with the surge in family travel that accompanied the growing up of the boomers. Later in the 1980s, about the time boomers began to move into their middle years, all-suite properties began to multiply to meet a surging demand for more spacious accommodations. Boomers, on a short holiday, make up a significant portion of the all-suites weekend occupancy, and much of the all-suites weekday trade is boomers on business. Moreover, it seems reasonable to assume that the growth of midscale limited-service properties is related, at least to some degree, to the boomers' tastes for informality and their desires for value.

In the mid-1970s, we saw the boomers themselves come into the family forma-tion age. The increase in the number of children born during the late 1970s has been referred to as the "echo" of the baby boom. As the huge generation of boomers entered their child-bearing years, births rose simply because there were more poten-tial parents. The **echo boom**, however, was somewhat smaller because the boom-ers chose to have smaller families than their parents had had.

The baby boom is a tide that is bound to recede as boomers age and death takes it toll. In fact, 1997 was the first year in which the number of boomers—including immigrants—has actually declined. By 2010, the U.S. Census Bureau projects the size of the baby boom will have fallen to 74.6 million and, by 2020, to 69 million.[2] In the near future, however, boomers will be especially important not only because they are numerous but because they are in their middle years, a time normally associated with high average earnings. In fact, the 45- to 54-year-old age group spends 17 percent more per capita than the average household.[3] Significantly, the total amount as well as the proportion of the food budget spent on food away from home rises as household income rises, as does the propensity to travel. Households headed by people aged 35 to 54 spend more *total dollars* on dining out than younger patrons, although, because of their higher average incomes, they spend a lower *proportion* of their income on restaurant purchases.[4]

Even while the boomers occupy center stage, we have noted that another generation has begun to edge toward the limelight. The "echo boomers," children of the baby boomers, born between 1976 and 1994, were aged 3 to 21 in 1997. By 2010, this generation will have nearly overtaken the boomer generation in size, numbering 73 million compared to the boomers' reduced numbers of about 75 million.

Figure 2.1 shows the trend in population by age group from 1997 to 2010. Table 2.1 highlights the relative change of each age group resulting from births, deaths, and immigration. There will be a modest growth in the *number* of children, supporting a continuing emphasis on services aimed at families with young children such as special rates, accommodations, and services for families in lodging and children-friendly services like playgrounds, games, and children's menus in restaur-ants. One food service chain that puts real emphasis on targeting children is T.G.I. Friday's. Its children's menu, described as having a "Disneyesque approach to tak-ing care of kids," won *Restaurant Hospitality*'s 1997 award for children's menus. The company's frequent-diner program partnered with Toys "R" Us so that children can earn awards for frequent visits to the restaurant.[5]

The number of teenagers and young adults will be expanding over the period to 2010, which is good news for the purveyors of inexpensive, no-frills food service such as QSRs. Adolescents have an average income of $64 a week, which amounts to over $3300 a year. Their impact, however, is greater than this because of the substantial influence they have over family buying decisions[6]—including where to go on vacations and what lodging to use on family trips.

The number of people aged 25 to 34 and 35 to 44 will decline between now and 2010. This has implications for labor supply, which are discussed in a later section. The baby boomers' move into their middle years will mark a major shift in the

Table 2.1   U.S. Population to 2010[a]

	1996	Percentage of Population[b]	2010	Percentage of Population[b]	Percentage Change 1996–2010
All ages	265,253		297,716		12.2%
Under age 5	19,403	7.3	20,012	6.7	3.1
5 to 13	34,809	13.1	35,605	12.0	2.3
14 to 17	15,167	5.7	16,894	5.6	11.4
18 to 24	24,616	9.3	30,138	10.1	22.4
25 to 34	40,374	15.2	38,292	12.9	−5.2
35 to 44	43,311	16.3	38,521	12.9	−11.1
45 to 54	32,341	12.2	43,564	14.6	34.7
55 to 64	21,360	8.1	35,283	11.8	65.2
65 and older	33,872	12.8	39,408	13.2	16.3
85 and older	3,747	1.4	5,671	1.9	51.3

[a]Projected U.S. population by age, 1996–2010, and percentage change, 1996–2010, number in thousands.
[b]Totals do not add to 100 percent due to rounding.
Source: U.S. Census Bureau.

(millions of American adults aged 25 to 74, by age group, 1997, 2005, and 2010)

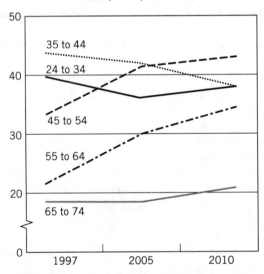

The young-adult market will fall and rise as the baby-bust and baby-boomlet generations move through their 20s. The preretiree market will steadily grow as the baby boom continues to fill it.

Figure 2.1   Population trends by age group, 1997–2010.
(*Source:* U.S. Census Bureau, *American Demographics,* July 1997, p. 14.)

Emphasis on services for families with children will continue to be important to all kinds of hospitality operations.
Courtesy of Four Seasons Hotels

population, as middle-aged people (45 to 54) increase by 35 percent and preretirement-aged people (55 to 64) grow by 65 percent. As we have noted, these age groups are normally associated with the relatively high incomes of peak earning years. Growth of this population segment is likely to support a continuing increase in demand for upscale food service and other hospitality products such as lodging and travel.

The slow but steady growth in the over-65 age group will be a preview of the trend toward growing demand for services of all kinds for retirees, which will explode after 2010 as the baby boomers move into retirement.

Diversity and Cultural Change

We need to consider four other basic structural changes that will shape the demand for hospitality services in the 21st century. These are an increasingly diverse population, the proportion of women working, changing family composition, and a changing income distribution.

A moment's reflection suggests the relationship of these factors to the hospitality industry. One of the factors accounting for the success of ethnic restaurants, for instance, is America's already great diversity. Working women move from being competitors of the restaurant business to being its customers. A family with two working spouses finds it easier to schedule the shorter vacations that have become increasingly popular in North America. More children (or fewer) means a difference in the kind of hospitality service concepts that will succeed—and much the same can be said for more (or less) income.

Diversity of the U.S. Population.   According to Census Bureau projections, African Americans, Asians, Native Americans, and Hispanics will achieve a majority of the U.S. population shortly after 2050. In less than one life span, non-Hispanic whites will go from being the dominant majority to a minority status. This shift in the balance of North America's ethnic makeup has already taken place in New Mexico, Hawaii, and many large cities. California will reach the point where minorities achieve a collective majority in 2000, as will Texas in 2010.[7]

By the year 2005, the U.S. population of Hispanics and African Americans will be about equal[8] and Hispanics are expected to become the largest of the minority groups shortly thereafter. The Hispanic population is increasing rapidly because of a higher birth rate and also because of immigration, both legal and illegal.

"Hispanics," we should note, is a convenient term but one that hides substantial differences. Most U.S. Hispanics (64 percent) are of Mexican origin, but two-thirds of these were born in the United States. The Census Bureau says that 10 percent of Hispanics are of Puerto Rican origin but *American Demographics* says this reflects less than half the true Puerto Rican market. Most Puerto Ricans on the U.S. mainland were born in the United States. All Puerto Ricans are U.S. citizens. Four percent of Hispanics are of Cuban origin. Hispanic Americans also include a significant number of people from other Latin American countries. Over 6 million people claim Hispanic ancestry.[9]

During the decade from 1990 to 2000, the U.S. population of African-American extraction is projected to increase from 29.4 million to 34 million in 2001. In that year, African Americans will still be the largest minority in the United States. The proportion of African Americans living in the southern United States was 90 percent in 1900 but is now only 53 percent, a proportion that is projected to remain constant until 2010.[10]

Asian Americans will number 10.9 million in 2001, up a remarkable 50 percent from the 1990 level of 7.3 million. "Asian Americans are overwhelmingly urban but they are the least segregated minority group . . . . Today many Asians are ready to assimilate. They speak English and have been exposed to the culture." Their median household income, at $40,600 in 1995, was substantially higher than the non-Hispanic white household average of $37,200.[11]

We will be discussing the topic of diversity again in a later section on the hospitality workforce. At this point, we can note that the shift toward the popularity of ethnic foods almost certainly reflects a change in demand resulting from the increase in America's present diversity. Another example of diversity's present impact is the number of Convention and Visitor's Bureaus all over North America that are targeting African-American groups. As our population increases in diversity, firms will have a heightened need to adapt product and service to the tastes of the growing "majority of minorities."

*Female workforce participation rates prior to 1947 are estimates by the U.S. Census Bureau. From 1947 to 1994 the rates are those published by the U.S. Bureau of Labor Statistics and the rates from 1995 to 2005 are estimated by that agency.

Figure 2.2   Female workforce participation rate, 1900–2005.

We have been discussing ethnic diversity but this is by no means the only way in which the population mix is changing or diversity is expressed. The gradual aging of the boomers means that our population will soon have a much larger senior population. Students of demographics speak of a "dependency ratio" to express the relationship between people in certain age groups who are, for the most part, working and people in other age groups who have not yet begun to work or have retired. One study cited in *American Demographics* estimates that the "elderly dependency ratio" (proportion of retired to those still in the workforce) will increase 42 percent between 1996 and 2020, whereas the youth dependency ratio will decline 11 percent.[12]

Another form of diversity has developed in the last two generations as women's presence and roles in the workforce have changed, a topic to which we now turn.

Working Women.   During the past century, the changes in our views of women and the family have had an enormous impact on the hospitality industry in general and especially on food service. Figure 2.2 shows the change in women's employment over the past century—and the Bureau of Labor Statistics (BLS) projection of that employment to the year 2005. In the early part of this century, women working outside the home were the exception. Until the start of World War II, less than a quarter of women were in the workforce; that is, they either had a job or were looking for one. World War II saw that rate increase to nearly one-third of women. Over the next five years, the rate rose until, in 1980, over 50 percent of women were at work away from home and, in 1997, just short of 60 percent.

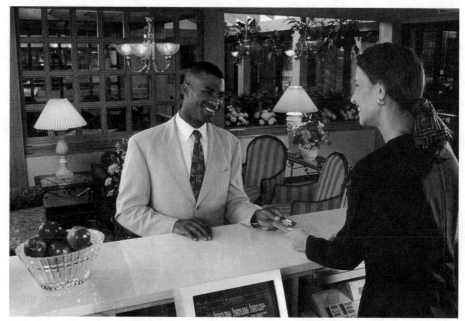

Women are playing an increasingly prominent role in lodging.
Courtesy of Marriott International

This is a change of major proportions in a relatively short period of time. It has resulted in significant changes in many aspects of our society—including, of course, the hospitality industry. Moreover, we have moved from a time when, in 1947, it was unusual for mothers to work outside the home to a world in which the unusual mother is the one who is not also a wage earner. In 1994, roughly three-quarters of the women in their prime child-bearing years (20 to 44) earned a wage. Estimates indicate that, although the trend toward more wage-earning women will continue, the largest part of this change is behind us.

One result of the changes in the majority of women's lifestyles—for food service—is that many more women are mid-day food service customers. In families in which both spouses work, moreover, cooking dinner at the end of a day's work is likely to be easy to give up for a restaurant meal, and two incomes make that quite affordable. As we have already noted, working women and **two-income families** are also major contributors toward the trend in shorter vacations. You will recall, too, that these same families make up the bulk of the all-suites weekend market.

It seems likely that the statistics we have cited actually *understate* women's work roles. Women enter and exit the workforce more frequently than men to accommodate other life changes such as marriage and childbirth. Counted as non-participants are many women who are not working *at the moment* but who expect to return to work shortly. In fact, *American Demographics* has estimated that 90 percent of women aged 18 to 49 are in the workforce sometime during a two-year period.[13]

The change in the status of women is certainly reflected in the hospitality industry. The National Restaurant Association (NRA) reports, based on 1992 census data, that women owned 37 percent of eating and drinking places and that their operations employed one out of three eating and drinking place employees.[14] In addition, as highlighted in Industry Practice Note 2.2, the roles of women in other food service areas are changing, too. Although women in hotel management have not progressed in large numbers into the executive ranks above the property level, women are playing a more prominent role as general managers and in other key areas of lodging.

Family Composition. The largest segment of households in the United States today is the 25 million households with children under age 18. Between 1995 and 2010, however, *American Demographics* projects the number of households *without* children under 18 will grow faster than average, increasing 29 percent to 37 million. Married couples with children under 18 are expected to *decrease* 10 percent to 23 million as the baby boomers' children continue to grow up and leave home.[15] One significance of these population changes is that couples without children to support spend more than any other household. They spend more on take-out food, for instance, than they do on groceries. A recent survey showed that 90 percent of

Couples without children spend more than any other household.
Courtesy of Caesar's Palace, Las Vegas

Industry Practice Note 2.2

Changing Roles for Women in Food Service

During the past 10 years, women have made notable advances in the food service industry. According to the Bureau of Labor Statistics (**http://www.bls.gov/**), of the total number of women employed in food preparation and service occupations in 1985, only 6 percent were supervisors. In 1995, the number of females holding supervisory positions increased 34.5 percent to top 260,000, accounting for 68.9 percent of all food preparation and service supervisors.

Women have also made gains in some other traditionally male-dominated food service occupations. In 1985, only 47.9 percent of bartenders were women; in 1995, nearly 70 percent of bartenders were women. Those occupational gains are noteworthy because they are high-paying food service positions.

Occupations traditionally filled by women, such as waitstaff, have seen a decrease in female representation. In 1985, women represented 84 percent of all waitstaff positions; by 1995, that number had decreased more than six percentage points. Another traditionally female-dominated food service labor category—food counter workers—also decreased five percentage points between 1985 and 1995.[1]

The fact remains, however, that, in the industry's top ranks, women are woefully underrepresented. Why is this true? Some argue that there is a "glass ceiling"; in effect, top-ranking men want others around them and as their successors who are like them. Moreover, "old boy networks" have existed for years and provide sources for mentoring as well as valuable contacts. "Old girl networks" are emerging but they are still new and limited in size.

The glass ceiling argument is countered by some, however, who point out that women have been a numerically important factor in managerial ranks only in recent times and, not surprisingly, women began at the same entry-level positions men did. It takes some years to advance through the ranks for most people. Accordingly, women are more and more likely to be seen in the top ranks as the large number now in middle management continue their progress. The large female enrollment in many hospitality management programs argues, too, for a gradual improvement in the balance of top management between the sexes.

Which of these two positions is right? A brief poll of your classmates will undoubtedly reveal many on both sides of this argument. As with so many complex problems, there seems to be some truth in both points of view. It is hard to deny that there is prejudice against seeing women as equals on the part of many hospitality executives. On the other hand, social change of the scale involved in the changing roles of women in our society *does* take time—just as acquiring the experience needed for top management takes time.

Many successful women executives argue that women have to be better than their male competitors. And the fact is, many are. One thing seems absolutely clear: Men who cannot work with women or for women are doomed to a limited career in the hospitality world of the 21st century.

1. Data from *Restaurants USA*, June–July 1996, p. 17.

empty nesters aged 45 to 59 eat out at least twice a week—and 58 percent eat out four or more times a week.[16] They are also avid travelers.

Another change in family structure is the growth in **single-person households**, and here the trends are different for men and women. Male singles are younger, whereas women living alone tend to be older widows, reflecting the tendency for wives to outlive their husbands. Males have higher incomes, and their per capita spending ($20,000) is a third larger than women's ($15,000). Men spend twice as much of their annual food budgets ($1577) on food away from home as do women ($763). Although exhibiting different trends, both single-person households are good potential customers and, as women's incomes continue to rise, they are likely to resemble one another more.[17]

One of the reasons for the growth in single-person households is that people are marrying later. Much of this development can be explained by increasing levels of education. The proportion of high school graduates who go on to college increased from 45 percent in 1960 to 63 percent in 1993. Seventy-two percent are continuing their education to make more money and 77 percent to get a better job.[18] And, apparently, they are delaying marriage until their education is finished.[19]

Single parents, on the other hand, are a group who have relatively lower incomes. Single parents, for instance, eat out 25 percent less often than the average American. They are less likely to be hotel customers because their budgets do not permit them to travel as freely as other groups. Eighty-five percent of single parents are single mothers. the size of this group has been growing rapidly. *American Demographics* projects that this segment of the population could increase 50 percent by the year 2010.[20]

Changing Income Distribution

In the 1980s, the **middle class** decreased in size with more people leaving it than entering it. In general, the "winners" have been college-educated people, retirees with investment income, and women with full-time jobs. Women's average income, adjusted for inflation, has increased. The men's average, on the other hand, (in all age groups except 45 to 54) has declined.[21]

In the 1990s, it appears that the middle class has taken a further jolt from restructuring. It is white-collar workers and middle managers who have been hardest hit by the efforts to increase efficiency in many large firms. Industry Practice Note 2.3 discusses the issue of the size of the middle class further.

Figure 2.3 shows that the higher a household's income, the more frequently its members are likely to dine out. Many guests eat out, out of necessity, and so many who have moved down the economic ladder have not been lost entirely to food service. In lodging and travel, however, this is much less true because these are almost entirely discretionary expenditures. Although the large numerical growth in lower-income families discussed in Industry Practice Note 2.3 probably indicates a growing number of customers for lower-check-average restaurants, it almost certainly denotes a group that is effectively less able to participate in the travel market.

It is important to recognize that not all factors affecting demand can be as

*I*ndustry Practice Note 2.3

Is the Middle Class Shrinking?

Most North Americans think of themselves as middle class, whatever their actual income is. In the short term, people's incomes are growing. After years of salary stagnation in the early 1990s, the typical American household's income rose by 1.2 percent in 1996 to $35,492—but that household was still 3 percent worse off than it was in 1989. Over a longer time period, from 1984 to 1994, the average household's income increased only 1 percent. These averages, however, conceal trends that reveal something of the fate of the middle class. The average income of the poorest fifth increased by only one-tenth of a percentage point, whereas that of the top fifth increased 20 percent.

DEFINING MIDDLE CLASS

American Demographics (**http://www.demographics.com/Publications/AD**) proposes three definitions of middle class: (1) those with incomes ranging around the national average ($25,000 to $50,000); (2) a broader group, with incomes of $15,000 to $75,000; and, finally, (3) households with incomes between 75 percent and 125 percent of the median. Although the numbers that emerge from these three categories differ, they all point to a similar conclusion: The *proportion* of the population that is middle class is decreasing but, with a growing total population, the absolute number of middle-class household's is increasing.

Table 1 shows an increase in the number of U.S. households with incomes in the middle range of $25,000 to $74,999 of nearly a third. Note, however, that it also shows a decline of 7.1 points or 13 percent in the *proportion* of households in the middle category.

The real dynamics seem to be in the two far right-hand columns. Here, we see the *number* of households more than tripling and their proportion of total doubling. This suggests a growing number of people

---

Table 1   The Middle Class Is Growing in Number

Income Year	Less than $25,000		$25,000 to $74,999		$75,000 or more	
	Number (000,000)	Percentage (%)	Number (000,000)	Percentage (%)	Number (000,000)	Percentage (%)
1970	25.3	39.1	35.0	54.1	4.4	6.8
1975	29.4	40.3	38.0	52.1	5.5	7.5
1980	32.5	39.4	42.1	51.1	7.8	9.5
1985	34.4	38.9	43.9	49.6	10.2	11.5
1990	35.3	37.4	46.5	49.3	12.5	13.3
1994	39.0	39.4	46.5	47.0	13.5	13.6

Income in constant 1994 dollars.
Source: U.S. Census Bureau, *American Demographics,* October 1996, p. 32.

are stretching the definition of "middle class" by becoming wealthier. To balance that view, however, it is worth remembering that the *number* in the lower-income category in Table 1 (far left-hand column) increased by 13.7 million households, a jump of over 50 percent, although the *proportion* remained essentially the same. The Census Bureau reported that somewhere between 10 percent and 13.7 percent of Americans (depending on whether noncash benefits such as food stamps are included) had poverty level incomes.

Sources: Elia Kacapyr, "Are You Middle Class?" *American Demographics,* October 1996, pp. 31–35. "Better off, But Not Much," *The Economist,* October 4, 1997, p. 35.

numerically specific as the demographics we have been reviewing. Industry Practice Note 2.4 discusses how people's different patterns of activities, interests, and opinions, sometimes called **psychographics**, affect the demand for food service.

Households in the upper-income groups frequently represent dual-income families where both spouses are working. These families experience great time pressure, which, undoubtedly, explains the rapid growth in both take-out sales and the upscale, casual category, a haven offering a quick moment of fun and relaxation to these busy people.

SUPPLY

The key factors of supply that concern us are land and its produce, food, and labor. Capital is a third factor of production, but we will reserve discussion of it until the

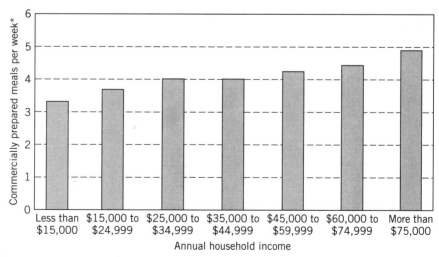

*Average per individual.

Figure 2.3   Higher income equals more dining-out occasions.
(*Source:* Meal Consumption Behavior—1996, National Restaurant Association.)

Industry Practice Note 2.4

Lifestyle and Demand for Hospitality Services

The vast majority of North Americans have sufficient money to meet their most immediate needs. Increasingly, however, they do not have enough time. Although some studies suggest people are actually working fewer hours,[1] there is no question that most people feel more pressed for time. As a result, people are rearranging their lives to try to provide the time they need for essentials beyond work. "By the year 2005," one authoritative study suggests, "many Americans will have never cooked a meal from basic ingredients."[2] That study suggests that consumers will choose services that fill certain needs. "Demographics and changing lifestyles are driving a strong national desire for convenience, fun, family friendliness, health, variety and value in food service."[3]

A recent study by the National Restaurant Association (**http://www.restaurant.org/**) reveals that "frequent-diner customers are responsible for an overwhelming 74 percent of all dinner occasions when the meal is purchased outside the home." In fact, frequent-diner customers purchase dinners away from home about four times per week versus just once a week for other dinner customers.

The NRA study asserts that eating out becomes a habit, with frequent guests falling into the five categories set out in Figure 1. *Note that all of the categories relate to lifestyle.* The categories, "Too Tired to Cook" and "Busy Parents" should need no further explanation. "Care Seekers" are identified as older adults and empty nesters. "Urban Sophisticates" are younger urban professionals. "Flavor Seekers" choose a restaurant for dinner based on what they have a taste or craving for.

1. Geoffrey Godbey, "Time, Work and Leisure: Trends That Will Shape the Hospitality Industry," *Hospitality Research Journal,* Vol. 7, No. 1, 1993.
2. McKinsey and Company, "Foodservice 2000" Executive Summary, *Proceedings of the 24th Annual Chain Operators Exchange,* Orlando, March 2–5, 1997 (Chicago: International Foodservice Manufacturer's Association, 1997).
3. Ibid.

Frequent-Diner Groups	Purchasing Pattern	Percent of All Dinner Occasions
Busy Parents	Fast-food carryout, especially drive-thru	21
Care Seekers	On-premises, inexpensive sit-down, buffet, fast food	22
Too Tired to Cook	Variety of carry-out sources	13
Urban Sophisticates	Higher-priced restaurants	9
Flavor-Savorers	Moderately priced sit-down and delivery	9

Figure 1 Five customer groups and their purchasing patterns. (*Source: Restaurants USA,* September 1997, p. 29.)

High-traffic locations, such as the famed Strip in Las Vegas, are always in demand by hospitality operators.
Courtesy of Las Vegas News Bureau

lodging chapters. The patterns of access to public markets discussed there can, however, be applied to the hospitality industry in general.

Land and Its Produce

Land and the things that come from the land are classically one of the major "factors of production" in economics. In hospitality, we are concerned with land itself, as well as with a major product of the land, food.

Land. Because hospitality firms need land for their locations, certain kinds of land are critical to the industry. Good **locations**, such as high-traffic areas, locations near major destinations, or locations associated with scenic beauty, fall into this category.[22] Furthermore, they are becoming scarcer with every passing day for at least two reasons: the existence of established operations and environmental pressures.

To deal with the first of these, the simple fact is that most of the best high-traffic locations are already occupied. What creates good locations are changes in the transportation system and changes in population concentrations. The building of new highways has slowed greatly compared to the time when the interstate highway system was under construction. As a result, fewer "new locations" are being created in this way. Moreover, population mobility has decreased significantly in recent years; that is, people are moving somewhat less and so they are creating fewer new locations.[23]

In recent years, we have seen restaurant chains acquired by other restaurant chains principally in order to obtain their locations for expansion. One of the factors that led QSR chains to seek locations in malls some years ago was the very shortage of freestanding locations we are discussing.

A second reason for the growing scarcity of locations is **environmental pressure**. Location scarcity is especially severe in scenic locations such as seashores, which are often zoned to prevent building—especially commercial building—in scenic or environmentally sensitive locations. Environmental pressures do, however, go beyond scenic locations. Restaurants, particularly QSRs, are meeting more resistance because of the noise, traffic, odor, and crowding that can accompany such operations. Restaurants have been "zoned out" of many communities or parts of communities.

On balance, the greater pressure comes from the impact of present locations being occupied, but, for both reasons discussed previously, land in the form of good locations is a scarce commodity.

Food.   Although the cost of food may vary from season to season, for the most part these variations affect all food service competitors in roughly the same way. Food service price changes would have to reflect any change in raw food cost. **Food supply** conditions do not suggest any major price changes in North America in the foreseeable future, although a premature frost or dry summer can always drive up some prices temporarily. We should note, however, that major climatic changes, such as those that could be brought on by the greenhouse effect and the earth's warming, do pose a longer-term threat to world food supplies.

Labor

The Bureau of Labor Statistics has developed a long-term forecast of the demand for labor extending into the next century.[24] That forecast predicts a growth in the U.S. workforce of about 14 percent from 1994 to 2005. People interested in careers in hospitality management can take encouragement from the fact that demand for food service and lodging managers is projected by the BLS to grow at more than twice the rate of the total workforce or 33 percent from 1994 to 2005. The BLS expects there will be 192,000 *new* management positions and a total, including turnover, of 313,000 management openings to be filled during that period.[25]

The growth in food service employment is projected at 14 percent, and so employment prospects appear to be about average for food service compared to the economy as a whole. What makes that outlook somewhat more difficult, however, is the relatively high turnover in the industry, highlighted in Tables 2.2 and 2.3. This high turnover magnifies the demand for labor because it takes a relatively larger number of people to keep positions filled.

The BLS estimated that in the 12 years between 1994 and 2005, there would be over a million new positions in food service but, owing to turnover, the total *number*

Table 2.2 Employee Turnover in Food Service

Restaurant Type	Employee Type	
	Salaried Employees	Hourly Employees
Full service		
Average check under $10	43%	97%
Full service		
Average check over $10	40%	80%
Fast food	50%	121%

Source: 1997 Restaurant Industry Operations Report, National Restaurant Association.

of positions to be filled in that time would be 3.5 million.[26] The National Restaurant Association predicts a substantially higher number, 3.9 million positions in the 10 years from 1996 to 2005.[27]

Among the skilled positions in the food service business, bakers and waiters and waitresses are projected to grow two to two and a half times as fast as the labor force as a whole. Food preparation workers are listed by the BLS as one of the occupations with the largest job growth with a rate of growth 50 percent faster than that of the workforce as a whole.[28]

It is more difficult for us to make projections for the lodging workforce because, in the BLS categories, lodging workers are often merged into other, larger categories, as, for instance, with "baggage porters and bellhops" where bellstaff are considered, with a number of other, somewhat similar jobs in transportation. Similarly, people working in housekeeping are included in the category of "janitors and cleaners, including maids and housekeeping cleaners." One category of lodging worker that is projected separately, however, is desk clerks, which are expected to increase 20 percent.

Two categories related to the travel industry are travel agents, slated to grow 23 percent, and flight attendants, a group projected to increase by 28 percent. To reflect

Table 2.3 Top Seven Reasons for Industry Exit by Former Food Service Employees

1	More money
2	Better work schedule
3	More enjoyable work
4	Pursue current occupation
5	Advancement opportunity
6	Better employee benefits
7	To go to school

Source: Restaurants and Institutions, May 1, 1997, p. 108, based on the *Industry of Choice* study of the NRA Educational Foundation.

the growth in tourism generally, it is interesting to note that "amusement and recreation attendants" are projected to grow 52 percent, nearly four times as fast as the workforce as a whole.

Growth means there will be opportunities. However, in the preceding discussion, wherever you see a growth figure higher than the average of 14 percent for the workforce as a whole, you may wonder how the industry will go about attracting more than its "fair share" (i.e., proportionate share) of workforce growth to that category of worker. Of course, it is the managers who will have the job of finding people to fill these fast-growing needs. Moreover, competitive industries, such as retailing and health care, are growing rapidly. Retailing employment is likely to grow at half again the rate of the total workforce, and health care *service* occupations (those that are most directly competitive with hourly hospitality jobs) will be growing at nearly three times the average rate.[29] As an industry, then, we can expect to face stiff competition for workers. Hospitality managers have their work cut out for them.

What means *is* the industry likely to use to fill these positions? Already, in many markets, starting food service workers are receiving well above minimum wage. According to a survey conducted by the Society for Human Resource Management, 39 percent of companies of all sizes are using bonuses to encourage hourly employees to stay with their company, a further enhancement of wages. In some labor markets, Burger King is supplementing wages with transportation passes and commuter tickets.[30]

Companies are "target marketing" segments of potential employees. Some operations, for instance, have held free breakfasts for seniors to get them interested in jobs.[31] The evidence is that "fewer and fewer people are actually retiring these days." The number of people drawing pension income who are still working grew substantially between 1984 and 1993. One authority dubbed them "restless retirees."[32]

Another source of labor will be **immigrants**, both legal and illegal. The non-Hispanic white labor force will grow by 8 percent between 1994 and 2005, but the number of Hispanic workers will increase over four times as fast at 36 percent. The number of Asian workers will grow 39 percent in the same period.[33]

Illegal immigration is like floodwater around a dike, always there and always seeking entry through any hole in the structure. Repeated crackdowns, like temporary repairs to a dike, staunch the flow for a time. However, as long as the employment outlook in the United States is better and wages several times higher than in Latin America, it is likely that immigrants will continue to be an important source of labor in the regions to which immigrants move.

Finally, **part-time workers**, who have always played a major role in food service, will continue to be important. Interestingly, a BLS study indicates that 85 percent of women and nearly 75 percent of men who are working part time are doing so *voluntarily*. In fact, the proportion of part-time workers who are involuntarily part-timers is at a 20-year low.[34] This suggests the part-time labor pool is not made up of disgruntled people who can't get full-time work but of people who have other claims on their time and need to supplement their income. This makes them an attractive source of labor.

*W*ORKFORCE DIVERSITY

Historically, the main component of the workforce has been the white male. Even with the increasing female workforce participation rate, in 1991 almost 50 percent of those entering the workforce were white males. African Americans in the labor force, however, are increasing nearly twice as fast and the Hispanic workforce four times as fast as the white male workforce. Because female employment is also growing faster than male employment, we can forecast a dramatic change in the people entering the workforce. Compared with 50 percent in the early 1990s, white males will account for only 12–15 percent of *new entrants* to the workforce by the year 2000. **Workforce diversity** is a permanent fact of life in North America. Because a large part of the growth will occur among minorities, which have historically had lower incomes than average, an even larger component of workers will probably come from disadvantaged backgrounds with poorer educational preparation.

The components of diversity include ethnic background and place of birth (i.e., immigrants), education and skill level, income level, gender, age, differing abilities, and sexual orientation.[35] Organizations have generally tolerated diversity and tried to regulate it. With growing diversity, however, close students of organizational dynamics call for an approach that goes beyond tolerating diversity to valuing it, seeing people for the contribution they can make rather than their surface differences:

> [Organizations are coming] to hire women and minorities because of the benefits of having different types of people in the workforce . . . . Within the hospitality industry, the ability to attract and retain the highest quality employees, improve responsiveness to consumer needs, enhance creativity and innovation, and continually improve operating efficiencies is becoming essential for survival. Companies that value diversity will best be able to meet this challenge.[36]

*T*HE IMPACT OF LABOR SCARCITY

The evidence we have suggests it is food service that will experience the tightest pressure in the hospitality industry from trying to keep up with the demand for workers. It is important, however, to keep in mind that nearly 40 percent of U.S. hotels are full-service operations and so have a commitment to food service, some of them—resorts, luxury operations, and convention hotels—a very extensive commitment. Accordingly, the hotel industry will not escape unscathed by a shortage of labor.

Food service faces high levels of employee turnover and increasing competition from other industries. Moreover, the number of food service workers needs to grow faster than the workforce as a whole. The interaction of those forces, in good times when competition from other employers is sharp, almost certainly spells higher prices. Even in slower times, it suggests hiring and retaining workers, especially in the skilled and supervisory categories, will be difficult. The food service industry has

Food service faces a labor crisis, and efforts to recruit and retain skilled workers have become critical to operators.
Copyright Robert Fried, 1992

recognized the labor crisis for some time, however. In addition to raising wages, many operators have enhanced benefit programs and instituted support services such as more generous family leave policies. On-the-job efforts to recognize supervisor performance and to provide career ladders for successful people are becoming a more conscious and purposeful force in food service. Attracting good people and keeping them once they are in place is simply cost-effective management of human resources.

$\mathscr{S}$UMMARY

Demand, ultimately, means customers. We looked at how one customer group, the baby boomers, has changed the hospitality industry. Our customer's average age is increasing as the boomers move into their middle years. We also looked at two other cohorts, the GenXers and the echo boomers. Family travel continues to create demand for child-friendly hospitality. The slow but steady growth in the over-65 population foreshadows the explosion in that age group in 2010 when boomers start to turn 65. We discussed four other demographic changes: diversity, working women, changing families, and changing incomes.

Working women are an established workforce fact. Seventy five percent of women in child-bearing years work and as many as 90 percent work at some time during the year. Two-income families mean more demand for food service and for travel but more pressure on time, making shorter vacations popular.

Families without children—empty nesters and those who chose not to have children—have higher disposable incomes and comprise a fast-growing group. Families *with* children, however, are still the largest segment. The growth in single-person households is partly the result of a later marriage age because of longer times spent in education. Another single-person household group is widows, as wives tend to outlive husbands.

In the changing income trends, we find the "winners" are college-educated people, affluent retirees, and women in full-time work. The number of middle-class households is increasing, but their *proportion* is declining as upper- and lower-income groups increase more rapidly.

The factors of production we considered are land and its produce and labor. Available locations are a category of land that is important to all segments of hospitality as they continue to become scarcer. Environmental pressures add to the difficulty of finding new locations. Although food supply is expected to be adequate, short-term weather problems or a major change in the climate could lead to scarcity and higher cost food.

The other factor of production we considered, labor, offers good news and bad news. There will be plenty of jobs for people who seek hospitality management careers—but the challenge of keeping the operation staffed that will be theirs is going to be difficult. The industry's growth and high turnover continues to require a greater share of a slow-growing workforce. Moreover, there will be stiff competition from other industries for the workers we seek.

To fill the demand for workers, wages are rising at many hospitality firms as are fringe benefits and bonuses. Sources of labor supply are being targeted such as "restless retirees." Immigrants and part-timers will continue to be an important part of the hospitality workforce.

◆ $\mathcal{K}$EY WORDS AND CONCEPTS

Demand	Two-income families
Demographics	Empty nesters
Baby boomers	Single-person households
Generation X	Middle class
Echo boom	Psychographics
Diversity of the U.S. population	Activities, interests, opinions
Working women	Land and its produce
Family composition	Locations
Income distribution	Environmental pressures

Food supply   Part-time workers
Immigrants   Workforce diversity

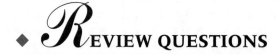

◆ REVIEW QUESTIONS

1. How would you define demand? What critical changes in demand do you foresee in the future? Why?

2. Why are the baby boomers so important? What impact do you see them having on the hospitality industry in the next few years? In the longer-term future?

3. Besides the baby boomers, what other significant age groups were discussed in the chapter?

4. Trace the impact of the boomers on the hospitality industry. What impact do you think your age group will have on food service? On lodging?

5. What are the main elements of diversity discussed in this chapter? What are the major trends related to diversity? What are their likely effects?

6. Discuss the growth in the proportion of women working. What changes have working women caused as they relate to the hospitality industry? What does the future appear to hold regarding women in the workforce?

7. What is the largest household type? What are some rapidly growing household types? What kinds of customers are each of these groups for hospitality?

8. Is the middle class shrinking? Which income groups are growing in absolute numbers? In proportionate share of population?

9. What categories of land as a factor of production are important to the hospitality industry? What is likely to affect the cost and availability of those factors?

10. The food service workforce is expected to grow at about the pace of the total workforce. In spite of this, what factors make the need for food service workers problematic? How does this affect the hotel business? What are some sources of supply that can be tapped?

◆ NTERNET EXERCISES

1. **Site Name:** *FedStats*
   URL: http://www.fedstats.gov/
   Background Information: More than 70 agencies of the federal government produce statistics of interest to the public. The Federal Interagency Council on Statistical Policy maintains this site to provide easy access to the full range of statistics and information produced by these agencies for public use.

   EXERCISES:

   a. List at least five federal agencies that might produce statistics or demographic data of interest to the hospitality industry. Describe, in detail, how these data may be of assistance/interest to the hospitality manager.

   b. Do a search for restaurant manager. What documents are available under that topic?

   c. Do a search for women and employment and/or minorities and employment. What information is available that may be of interest to the restaurant manager?

2. **Site Name:** *Nations Restaurant News*
   URL: http://www.nrn.com/index.htm
   Background Information: This is the on-line journal of the National Restaurant Association

   EXERCISES:

   a. Review the articles on the web site. What trends or forces do you see that are changing the restaurant industry?

   b. Are there any mergers of Chapter 11 actions?

   c. Search the archives for a force shaping food service as discussed in the textbook. Lead a class discussion on the information found at this web site.

◆ OTES

1. "Generation X; Consumer Profile," *Restaurants and Institutions*, May 1, 1996, pp. 116–118.
2. Shannon Dortch, "Rise and Fall of Generations," *American Demographics*, July 1996, pp. 6–7 and 43.
3. Cheryl Russell, "The Ungraying of America," *American Demographics*, July 1997, p. 12.
4. "A Booming Business," *Restaurants USA*, August 1996, p. 40.
5. *Restaurant Hospitality*, June 1997, p. 47.
6. *Restaurants and Institutions*, February 15, 1997, p. 57.
7. Brad Edmondson, "The Minority Majority in 2001," *American Demographics*, October 1996, p. 17.
8. Ronald E. Kitscher, "Summary of BLS Projections to 2005," *Monthly Labor Review*, November 1995, p. 4.

9. Brad Edmondson, "Hispanic Americans in 2001," *American Demographics,* January 1997, p. 17.

10. Brad Edmondson, "Black America in 2001," *American Demographics,* November 1996, p. 15.

11. Brad Edmondson, "Asian Americans in 2001," *American Demographics,* February 1997, p. 17.

12. Brad Edmondson, "Work Slowdown," *American Demographics,* March 1996, pp. 4–7.

13. Horst H. Stipp, "What Is a Working Woman?" *American Demographics,* July 1988, pp. 24–25.

14. Karen Gardner, "You've Come a Long Way," *Restaurants USA,* June–July 1996, pp. 45–47.

15. *American Demographics,* April 1997, p. 27.

16. Kimberly Lowe, "Empty Nests, Full Pockets," *Restaurants and Institutions,* May 15, 1997, pp. 116–118.

17. Patricia Browne, "Sex and the Single Spender," *American Demographics,* November 1993, pp. 28–34.

18. Ibid.

19. *American Demographics,* January 1997, p. 11.

20. "The Future of Households," *American Demographics,* December 1993, pp. 27–40.

21. Peter Francese, "Income Winners," *American Demographics,* August 1992, p. 3.

22. For a fuller discussion of the importance of locations in the hospitality industry, see Tom Powers, *Marketing Hospitality,* 2nd ed. (New York: John Wiley & Sons, 1997), especially Chapter 10.

23. Tom R. Troland, "Outlook on Shifts in Demographic Markets," Presentation to the TIA Marketing Outlook Forum, October 5–7, 1997. According to Mr. Troland, the mobility of the U.S. population fell from 21.2 percent in 1951 and 18.6 percent as recently as 1986 to 16.6 percent in 1994.

24. "The Workforce in 2005," *Monthly Labor Review,* November 1995, pp. 3–84.

25. George T. Silvestri, "Occupational Employment to 2005," *Monthly Labor Review,* November 1995, p. 70. Statistics in this section are drawn from the U.S. "moderate growth scenario."

26. Ibid., p. 64.

27. Nicole Castagna, "Help Wanted," *Restaurants and Institutions,* May 1, 1997. Ms. Castagna is quoting from the NRA Educational Foundation's study *Industry of Choice.*

28. Silvestri, "Occupational Employment to 2005," p. 81.

29. Ibid., pp. 67 and 70.

30. Ann Stone, "Retention Span," *Restaurants and Institutions,* August 1, 1997, p. 70.

31. Ibid.

32. Anne Fisher, "What Labor Shortage?" *Fortune,* June 23, 1997.

33. Edmondson, "Work Slowdown," p. 6.

34. Gene Epstein, "A Small Scale Revolution," *Barrons,* August 11, 1997, p. 42.

35. Julia Christensen, "The Diversity Dynamic: Implications for Organization in 2005," *Hospitality Research Journal,* Vol. 17, No. 1, pp. 69–84.

36. Ibid.

Part 2
Food Service

$\mathscr{C}$hapter 3

Courtesy of the Four Seasons Hotel, London

The Restaurant Business

The Purpose of This Chapter

After an overview of the restaurant business, the chapter focuses first on two basic markets served by restaurants: the dining market and then the eating market. Under dining, we are concerned with the "casualizing" of fine dining and the growth of upscale casual food service.

The fastest-growing part of the eating market is in off-premise operations, such as take-out and delivery. We will also look at the contemporary popular-priced restaurants that are the largest segments of the existing restaurant industry: fast-food and midscale operations such as family restaurants. This discussion of the major components of the restaurant industry closes with a look at restaurants in retailing in areas such as malls and truck stops.

This Chapter Should Help You

1. Estimate the relative and absolute size of the major components of the food service business and recognize the economic impact of food service

2. Describe and contrast the major kinds of restaurant operations in the dining market and the eating market

3. Learn why some restaurant types are growing and others are declining

4. Become familiar with how changing consumer preferences lead to change in restaurants

5. Describe the principal types of casual restaurants and their special appeals

6. Become aware of the increasing significance of the off-premise market

THE VARIED FIELD OF FOOD SERVICE

The word "restaurant" covers a broad range of food service operations. The term comes from the French word *restaurant,* meaning "restorers of energy." The term was used as early as the mid-1700s to describe public places that offered soup and bread. Today, any public place that specializes in the sale of prepared food for consumption on or off premise can be described as a restaurant.

Food service is a basic part of the North American way of life. Americans spent over one-third of their food budget on **food away from home** in 1995. Most of that amount is spent[1] in commercial restaurants. Virtually everyone in North America has eaten in a restaurant, and roughly half the population eats in a restaurant at least once in any given month. Food service's share of the food dollar has increased steadily over the last 35 years. All the growth in *food* expenditures is accounted for by the growth in food service. This growth has come at the expense of food sales in grocery stores and other retail food outlets.[2]

Seventy percent of the food and drink purchased away from home is sold in restaurants, cafeterias, and taverns. Hotel and motel restaurants account for another 5.2 percent. Sales in restaurants located in other retail establishments, such as department stores and drugstores, account for over 5.5 percent. Thus, slightly more than $8 out of every $10 spent for food service is spent in commercial operations.

Contractors and caterers (who serve food in places such as industrial plants and office buildings, health care facilities, and schools and colleges) generate 7.8 percent of food sales, whereas 9.1 percent is sold by institutions that operate their own food service. Just over 2 percent of sales are made through vending machines. Nearly 20 percent of food-away-from-home expenditures are accounted for by the institutional market. These estimates are summarized in Table 3.1.

The shares of the market held by the segments identified in Table 3.1 tend to be stable from year to year. Such seeming stability, however, hides important evolutionary processes that are going on *within* each category. In fact, the industry is in the throes of change.

Although food and drink sales overall grew 4.4 percent between 1995 and 1998, some areas have actually decreased. Bars and taverns, for instance, are down 3.0 percent, probably reflecting health concerns as well as increased public concern—and outrage—regarding DWI (driving while intoxicated) and tightened dramshop laws. Within the lodging category, hotel restaurants have shown an increase (4.3 percent) in food service sales, but motor hotel and motel restaurants have had a modest decrease (4 percent).[3] This decrease probably reflects the growth of lodging segments that deemphasize food service (see Chapters 9 and 11). These properties either offer no food service or provide only a complimentary continental breakfast.

Table 3.1   The Major Areas of Food Service, 1998

Category	Food and Drink Sales	
	1998 Sales (Billions of $)	Percentage Sales of Total
Restaurants, cafeterias, and fast food	222.8	66.5
Bars and taverns	10.9	3.2
Food service in lodging	17.6	5.2
Food service in retail stores	15.2	4.5
Vending and nonstore retailers	7.6	2.3
Recreation and sports	4.6	1.4
Contractors and caterers	26.0	7.8
Institutions operating own food service	30.5	9.1
TOTAL	335.2	100.0

Note: Dollar amounts and percentages shown are based on estimates for 1998 made by the NRA in *Restaurants USA,* December 1997, p. F6.
Source: National Restaurant Association.

For some years, the biggest growth in food service has been in operations like take-out, drive-through, and delivery, which we will call "off-premise sales." In fact, off-premise food service accounted for the lion's share of the growth in total restaurant sales since the late 1980s.[4] On-premise (i.e., in-restaurant) sales actually declined in 1992 and have increased by only 1 or 2 percent since, compared to the much healthier growth in off-premise sales shown in Figure 3.1.

During the 1960s and 1970s, fast food altered dramatically the meaning of what a restaurant was. The trend toward off-premise consumption, which is now well established, suggests that another fundamental change in the business definition of restaurants may be evolving.

Another set of changes involves fine dining, for years the mainstay of the upscale restaurant segment. By and large, fine dining, with its trappings of formality, has been declining in relative importance, whereas casual dining has been growing very rapidly. In 1996, higher-check upscale operations continued this trend with a decline of 1 percent. To some degree, fine dining's decline appears to be a result of consumers' apparent interest in value in food service and a sensitivity to the relatively high prices fine dining must charge. Food tastes are changing as well. There has been a continuing concern about healthy eating, although that appears to have moderated recently.

Many of the changes in food service result from changes in the age composition of North America's population. The huge generation that was born in the 20 years following World War II, the baby boomers, are entering middle age. As they do so, their lifestyles are changing. They were raised with fast food and prefer an informal ambience. Now, as parents, they find a casual atmosphere more comfortable for the whole family.

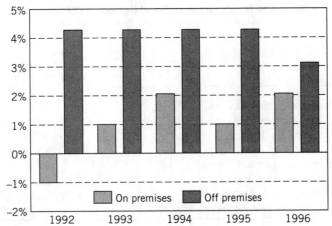

Figure 3.1   On- and off-premise traffic growth, 1992–1996—percent change from previous year.
(*Source:* NPD/CREST, 1996, National Restaurant Association.)

Quick-service restaurant (QSR) sales continue to rise, by 4 percent in 1996 over 1995. Furthermore, as we noted, sales in casual dining restaurants are rising rapidly, too—up 5 percent in 1996. Finally, we should note that institutional sales have also shown healthy growth, with contractors and caterers (private companies providing food service to institutions) growing at nearly 5 percent and institutions that provide their own food service growing at just over half that pace (2.6 percent). Institutional food service, contract companies and institutional operations, are discussed further in Chapter 8.

The Outlook for Food Service

One authoritative study suggests that "by the year 2005, many Americans will have never cooked a meal from basic ingredients."[5] People are apparently less willing to spend the time to cook their own food, which suggests growing business for those of us in the business of providing food to people away from home.

As Figure 3.2 indicates, gains in restaurant traffic are outpacing population gains by a significant factor. Figure 3.3 suggests a major reason for that healthy growth: Customers are generally pleased with the value they receive at restaurants. Quick-service restaurants achieved a 64 percent satisfaction rate for value received, whereas higher-priced restaurants pleased 67 percent and moderately priced operations achieved an 82 percent approval rating.[6]

The study cited earlier concludes that changes in demographics and lifestyles will combine to produce "the greatest decade of growth the food service industry has ever known."[7]

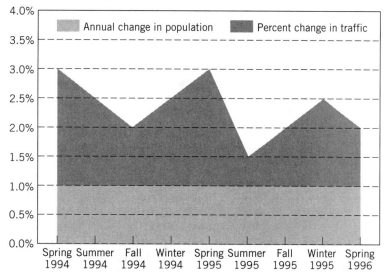

Figure 3.2 Traffic gains outpacing population — percent change from same period previous year.
(*Source:* NPD/CREST, 1996, U.S. Bureau of the Census, NRA.)

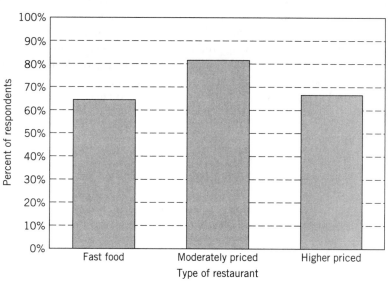

Figure 3.3 Satisfaction with value — met or exceeded consumers' expectations, 1995.
(*Source: Tableservice Restaurant Trends—1996,* National Restaurant Association.)

𝒯HE RESTAURANT BUSINESS

Describing the restaurant business is like trying to hit a moving target: The restaurant market is constantly changing. Moreover, there are so many and varied types of restaurants that it is difficult to devise a model to fit them all. Nevertheless, we need some basic terminology to describe the field, even generally.

First, we need to consider the basic distinction between the dining market and the eating market. We will look at dining operations such as fine dining and casual, upscale restaurants, and, at the other extreme, we will discuss the rapidly growing off-premise operations, such as take-out and delivery, which are imparting major growth to the eating market. In the next major section of this chapter, we will consider contemporary popular-priced restaurants that are the largest segments of the restaurant business today. These include the quick-service restaurants and midscale operations such as the family restaurant. The chapter will conclude with consideration of restaurants as part of larger institutions.

𝒯HE DINING MARKET AND THE EATING MARKET

One of the 20th century's most innovative restaurateurs, Joe Baum, summed up the challenge of food service in this way: "A restaurant takes a basic drive—the simple act of eating—and transforms it into a civilized ritual involving hospitality and imagination and satisfaction and graciousness and warmth."[8]

Restaurants serve both our social and our biological needs. We can divide restaurants into those serving predominantly our social needs—the **dining market**—and those serving our biological needs—the **eating market**. Nearly all meals eaten in the company of others have a social dimension, just as the most formal state dinner has its biological aspect. The main purpose, however, is usually clear.

Dining Well

People dine out for a variety of reasons, including to escape from boredom, to socialize, to avoid drudgery, to be waited on, to have foods different from those served at home, and for convenience.

Because dining (as opposed to eating) is predominantly a social event, service is important. Research on what consumers value in service[9] revealed that the server in a good restaurant is expected to anticipate the guests' needs and to be attentive, but not disruptive. At lunch, and to a lesser degree at dinner, guests value promptness and efficiency. At dinner, the service needs to be both timely (no long waits) and well timed ("when I'm ready"). The servers are expected to be friendly, as signified by a warm smile, and accurate. The role of the server is, therefore, much more than a mechanical one. (Service is discussed in more detail in the final chapter of the book.)

In the relatively expensive restaurants serving the dining market, the operation that falls short on significant measures of service is likely to lose customers quickly.

Fine dining offers the experience of luxury. It enhances the importance of special occasions.
Courtesy of The Plaza

The demographics of such customers, as always, are important. The guest who dines in a fine restaurant is usually older, well educated, has a higher than average income, and is accustomed to dining out and to traveling.

Fine-Dining Restaurants. Most full-service, fine-dining establishments are small, independent operations, some seating fewer than 100 guests. Despite their modest capacities, these restaurants succeed because of their excellent quality. Many are staffed by trained professional chefs who have brought with them a craft tradition that dates back to the Middle Ages. Many other operations provide excellent food prepared by American staffs who are often less rigidly trained.

Excellence is the absolute prerequisite in **fine dining** because the prices charged are necessarily high. An operator may do everything possible to make the restaurant efficient, but the guests still expect careful, personal service: food prepared to order by highly skilled chefs and served by expert waiters or waitresses. Because this service is, quite literally, manual labor, only marginal improvements in productivity are possible. For example, a cook, waitress, or waiter can move only so much faster before she or he reaches the limits of human performance. Thus, only moderate savings are possible through improved efficiency, which makes an escalation of prices inevitable. (It is an axiom of economics that, as prices rise, consumers become more discriminating.) Thus, the clientele of the fine-dining restaurant expects, demands, and is willing to pay for excellence. In fact, less than 1 percent of table service restaurants fit into this category.

These distinguished operations generally require a "critical mass" of three kinds: a large market, skilled workers, and devoted management. First, because of the high prices they must charge, most are located in or near large population centers or in major tourism areas where there is a sufficiently large number of people with high incomes to ensure a satisfactory sales volume. Only about 4 percent of the total U.S. population are fine-dining customers.[10]

A second requirement of these restaurants is chefs and service personnel with highly polished skills. It has been, until quite recently, difficult to find this kind of staff but the growth in culinary education and training programs has reduced the shortage somewhat. People with these skills are most likely to be found in large metropolitan areas.

A third and most important requirement for successful fine-dining restaurants is a special devotion from the key operating personnel, especially their owners. The hours tend to be long, and the owners, although amply compensated, generally devote their lives to their work.

As we have already noted, fine-dining sales have been falling since the late 1980s and continued that decline in 1996. Although some part of this decline may be due to price sensitivity and health concerns about rich foods, there seems to have been a basic shift in consumer service preferences as well. Older patrons have been accustomed to the kind of service rituals that characterize these operations. As younger customers progress in income and age to the point where they might be customers for fine dining, they are put off by overly formal fine dining. They prefer an upscale experience that is less "stuffy."

As Charles Bernstein, a long-time observer of the fine-dining scene, put it:

> Operating a quality restaurant has never been easy, but often has been rewarding personally and financially. But that feeling is changing. The personal time commitment and investment dollars are causing fine-dining owners to question whether it is all worth the mind boggling effort. [The closing of] a number of landmark restaurants [has] sent shockwaves through the industry. [Some operators have] decided not to continue if they had to "downscale" and relax their impeccable standards.[11]

The decor of casual restaurants is light and cheerful, and encourages guests to relax and have fun.
Courtesy of Nero's Restaurant, Caesar's Palace, Las Vegas

Casual Upscale Dining. The fastest-growing segment of food service is **casual dining**. Close observers of the restaurant business have summarized the competitive position of casual dining in this way: "Casual dining offers popular foods in a setting that is more appealing than most midscale restaurants and more of a value than fine dining."[12]

The movement of the baby boomers into their peak earning years explains the growth of casual dining. As consumers age and more restaurant options are available to them, taste preferences become increasingly sophisticated. Customers have little trouble distinguishing between excellent food and average food and which restaurant experiences represent excellent value.[13]

Excellence in food is one of the appeals of casual restaurants. Another is top-flight service. Although less time consuming and elaborate than in more formal and higher-priced restaurants, successful casual restaurants provide service that employs a very professional and attentive approach.[14]

Most casual restaurants have a unifying theme that is pervasive in the design of their menu, interior decor, and often the exterior of the building. Menu specialties are highly varied. Many casual restaurants have an ethnic theme; the two fastest-growing themes are Mexican and Italian. A theme serves to augment the diner's

A restaurant theme serves to augment the diner's surroundings and creates an exciting experience.
Courtesy of Rainforest Café

experience and to create an atmosphere that imparts a sense of adventure to a night out. Richard Komen, president of a leading casual restaurant company, Restaurants Unlimited, points out that dining in an upscale environment has a "significant component of emotional satisfaction" because "dining is a highly charged emotional experience." Understanding the emotional needs of guests "separate[s] upscale dining from just eating . . . . Upscale restauranting is the business of making guests feel good."[15] Other motifs that are used to provide operations with a theme include sports—as in sports bars—and specialty preparation techniques such as barbecue. Casual steakhouses are also popular and often adopt a regional theme such as "Mortons of Chicago" or the "Lone Star Steakhouse."

Multiple-concept chains such as Brinker International play an important role in casual dining. Brinker's operates Chili's and has begun an active franchising program for Chili's brand, which already operates well over 300 units in the United States. That company also operates several other rapidly growing concepts: Grady's American Grill, Romano's Macaroni Grill, On the Border Cafes, Cozymel's, and Maggiano's Little Italy. Darden Restaurants (Red Lobster and Olive Garden) is another example of a multiple-concept chain. Concepts for a new chain operation are

Case History 3.1 Top Denver Restaurant Faces Hard Decision

On its 10th anniversary, Zenith American Grill in Denver was named Colorado's No. 1 restaurant by the Zagat Survey and received its fourth diamond from the American Automobile Association. Then it closed.

The final honors were the latest in a string of achievements for chef/owner Kevin Taylor. Critical acclaim, however, doesn't guarantee financial success, and kudos alone couldn't keep the 240-seat upscale restaurant afloat.

"The market changed," says Taylor, who realized that local interest in the restaurant had peaked. "We've had a huge influx of steakhouses in Denver. Until the end, we still had a great out-of-town clientele, but the locals aren't eating like that anymore. They are going back to meat and potatoes."

Taylor doesn't blame food alone. "Zenith was a very '80s-style restaurant, very architectural, very cold, and it was cutting edge when it opened," he says, "but people don't want to sit in big, open rooms anymore. We had to face the fact that we either invest $200,000 to change the decor or do a different concept." Taylor opted for the latter. He's already opened two casual restaurants this year and has a third on the way. After that, he plans an intimate, fine-dining restaurant in a boutique hotel.

Source: Restaurants and Institutions, August 15, 1997, p. 21.

developed through extensive market research, tested in one or more pilot operations, and, once proven, "rolled out" to the regional or national market. Sometimes, rather than developing a concept themselves, multiconcept chains purchase a promising independent operation, fine tune the concept for a wider market, and then roll it out to regional and national markets. In contrast to the QSR and mid-priced segments with their breakfast–lunch focus, casual restaurants cater to the higher-check-average lunch and dinner day parts. Naturally, this results in a higher level of dollar sales. Casual upscale unit sales are also helped by the addition of alcoholic beverages, which usually adds a higher-profit category of sales.

Many fine-dining restaurants have made the decision to move to meet the market demand for a more relaxed atmosphere and more reasonable prices. One restaurant in Detroit, Sebastian's, spent $300,000 to remodel and become Sebastian's Grill. The average check fell from $38 to $24 but customer counts rose—and the average age of customers fell by 30 years.[16]

The impact of changing tastes, it turns out, can be more powerful even than first-rate operations. The operator of the Zenith American Grill in Denver, whose story is discussed at more length in Case History 3.1, closed a very successful four-diamond restaurant—and opened three casual restaurants.

Eating Market Dynamics

Fast food, which we will look at in more detail in a moment, is patronized by nearly every household. Two-thirds of households patronize fast food frequently; that is, some member of those households buys fast food three or four times a week. Nearly half of households visit midscale restaurants (such as a family restaurant) on average once or twice a week.[17] These fast-food and midscale restaurant customers are the heart of the eating markets. Midscale operations, however, are in mature segments of the industry where growth, over the long run, is about that of the economy as a whole. Fast food, as we noted earlier, is continuing rapid growth, at a compound annual rate of 5.8 percent from 1994 to 1997. Off-premise dining is also a segment of the restaurant business that is in a rapid growth stage.

The three main players in **off-premise dining** are take-out, drive-through, and delivery. Each of these has maintained roughly the same share of the off-premise sales for some years. The largest part of off-premise sales is take-out with nearly two-thirds of the traffic and volume. Drive-through is the second most frequent with just short of one-third of the business. Delivery is the smallest with roughly 10 percent.[18] The off-premise segment is often referred to as *home meal replacement* (HMR). Over half of the food purchased for off-premise consumption was eaten at home. The other most common places people eat take-out food is at work or in the car.

The bulk of on-premise sales are fairly evenly divided between lunch and dinner. For off-premise sales, the highest volume is at dinner. Dinner and P.M. snacks account for over half of off-premise transactions, but the noon meal still achieves nearly one-third of off-premise sales.

Take-Out. Take-out is an old established part of food service, but its recent rapid growth has increased its prominence. Consumers have indicated their interest in take-out with their growing patronage. Not surprisingly, operators have responded to this consumer interest. Nearly all fast-food operations offer take-out meals, and fast-food operations account for the lion's share of take-out sales. The vast majority of midscale table service restaurants also offer take-out, as do many upscale operations. Thus, increased sales of take-out food are fueled not only by consumer preference but by the wide availability of take-out food service.

Drive-Through. Initially, **drive-through** service was introduced as a part of an existing fast-food restaurant and that is still an important use of the drive-through. The drive-through came into its own, however, with the introduction of the double drive-through. These operations enjoyed the advantage of low capital costs because of the small building and relatively small size lot on which they could be fitted. Highly simplified menus gave them an operating cost advantage, too, and fast delivery times appealed to many customers.

It quickly became apparent to QSR operators that the double drive-through

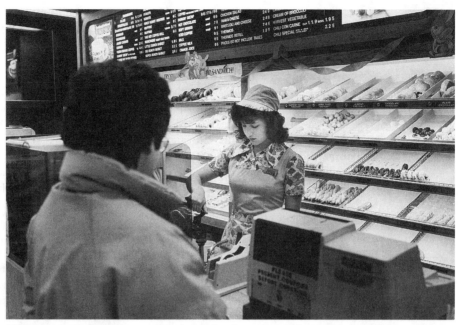

Take-out is a growth component of food service. It is popular with customers and widely available.
Jack Spratt, New York Times

was a serious competitive threat and the competitive response was not long in coming. Existing QSRs improved their drive-through facilities and used their powerful brands in a promotional push. Many QSRs that lacked drive-through facilities added them. In the shakeout that followed, a number of double drive-through chains, which had been growing rapidly, went out of business. Some survived but these now serve a specialty niche and the dominant force in the drive-through market is the branded QSRs such as McDonald's and Burger King.

Delivery. Delivery operations do not fit well in the same unit with table service operations. Not only does demand peak just when the dining room is busiest (as is also true with take-out), but the parking lot and its aisles are jammed with customers' cars just when delivery vehicle traffic in and out is at its peak. Moreover, the skills of the service staff are different. A person who is very effective as a server in face-to-face service will not automatically be effective in the telephone contact that is the typical start of a delivery transaction, at least not without specific training and an operating system designed to handle delivery. For these reasons, many companies have found it best to limit delivery operations to separate delivery units. Delivery-only units have cost advantages, too, in that they can be located on less expensive real estate.

Many delivery chains use a single number for all units. Often, a catchy phone number is used as a handy focus for promotion. Take, for example, Pizza Pizza. Its Toronto number, 967–11–11 (try saying it rhythmically), has become so widely known that Canadian immigration officials sometimes use it as a quick check on the authenticity of people claiming residence in Toronto.

The single number is much more than a promotional trick, however, At the central answering facility, employees take calls working at computer terminals. When a customer places an order, the operator asks for his or her phone number and address. Using this information, the order is passed to the nearest unit for dispatch. At the same time, the customer's name and order goes into the computerized guest history system. Then, on subsequent calls, the operator is able to call up the customer's record, using his or her phone number. Thus, when John Doe calls, the operator can say, "Good to hear from you again, Mr. Doe. Would you like to have your usual pepperoni and mushrooms? Shall we deliver it to the side door again?" The single-number system is spreading and is being used not only for pizza but for a wide variety of other food service delivery products.

One of the problems encountered by delivery companies is driver safety. Delivery units have been denied licenses because of local concern about speeding delivery drivers. Domino's dropped its 30-minute delivery guarantee at company units after a jury awarded $78 million to a woman hit by a Domino's delivery driver. Franchised units, however, may continue to offer the guarantee if they so choose.[19]

CONTEMPORARY POPULAR-PRICED RESTAURANTS

Contemporary restaurants refer not only to restaurants that are in operation today but those that are likely to continue to be an important force in the industry into the next century. We have already discussed the casual upscale restaurant, off-premise operations, and home meal replacement. In this section, we will discuss the on-premise business of the two largest segments of today's popular-priced restaurant business: the QSR and midscale operations such as family restaurants and pizza operations.

Quick-service restaurants account for slightly more than half of restaurant sales (compared to 28 percent in 1970) and nearly three-quarters of customer traffic. Full-service restaurants, including both midscale and upscale, with a much lower share of traffic still achieve roughly half of restaurant dollar sales because of their higher check average.

The QSR concepts experienced healthy growth, but the results for full-service operations showed wide variation. In 1996, for instance, casual dining rose by 5 percent, but higher-check, upscale establishments continued a decline that began in the late 1980s, falling another 1 percent in 1996. Traffic at midscale operations fell 2 percent in 1996, continuing a trend that has resulted in a lower share of the market.

In Figure 3.4, the various types of restaurants are compared in terms of their

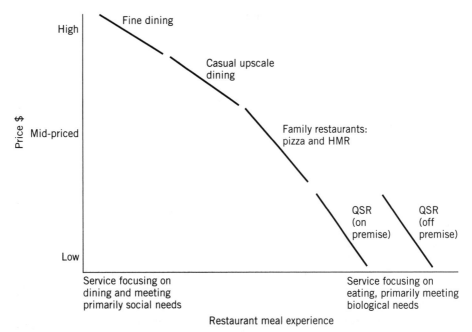

Figure 3.4 Factors bearing on meal experience include time available; importance of convenience, utilitarian as opposed to social event; and degree of subordination to other activities.

price level and the meal experience that is provided. The meal experience includes the services and amenities provided, as well as such factors as the time available, the importance of convenience (as in location), the degree to which the meal is utilitarian (i.e., a "biological event"), and the degree that it is tied to other activities. Utilitarian meals (a hurried lunch during the working day) where convenience and speed are essential would be at one end of the dining experience scale. A special occasion, perhaps a wedding anniversary celebration, where a couple might drive 50 miles to visit a unique restaurant and spend two or three hours dining would be at the other end.[20]

Midscale restaurants have somewhat higher prices (about $4.50 to $7.00 compared to $2.00 to $4.50 for QSRs). Home meal replacement (HMR), a mid-price take-out concept, has a higher social content than other take-out operations because, even as a take-out option, it is often a family-centered occasion. Its on-premise offerings, too, provide a public place for celebration or entertaining similar to that of a family restaurant or other mid-priced operation. Fine-dining prices begin at the top of other categories and range much higher. With this overview in mind, let us now turn our attention to a more detailed consideration of the basic restaurant groups identified.

Table 3.2   Productivity in Food Service Establishments

Food Service Type	Direct Labor Hours per 100 Guests
Luxury restaurants	72.3
Family restaurants	20.7
Cafeterias	18.3
Fast food	10.5

Source: Agricultural Research Service.

Quick-Service Restaurants

All of the **quick-service restaurant** (QSR) operations tend to simplify their production processes and use self-service. The result is a drastic reduction in labor in both the front and the back of the house, as Table 3.2 shows. Because fast-food restaurants (or QSRs—we use the term interchangeably) require less labor, they can pass on their savings to the customer in the form of lower prices. Furthermore, these operations, even with their lower prices, have historically earned profits substantially higher than those of other operations.

Fast Food: The Classics.   Fast-food restaurants are the product of a long evolution dating back to the late 1940s. McDonald's, for instance, began as a drive-in, selling inexpensive hamburgers, french fries, and milk shakes to be consumed in the car or taken away. From a small production unit, McDonald's expanded the food "pickup" area in the front of the store slightly to provide a limited amount of seating. This worked well enough that a larger seating area was added to one side—and then to both sides—of the production unit. These units were still quite simple with plain white walls for simplicity in housekeeping. The early units had a utilitarian air about them. Gradually, however, decoration was added to the seating area, very simply at first and then more extensively. Today, McDonald's restaurants are generally attractively decorated and some units are quite elaborate.

The decor and physical plant were certainly not the only things that evolved. The early, very simple menu was gradually expanded. To attract people who wanted something other than a variety of hamburgers, chicken and fish were added. To attract an increasingly health-conscious public, salad and decaffeinated coffee were added. To meet demand for service earlier in the day, breakfast was added. Although the menu still remains quite simple, the choice of hamburgers—or not—of the early days has been replaced by much wider variety.

McDonald's has periodically faced difficult internal and external challenges, including crowded markets, well-heeled competitors set on taking away its customers, and disgruntled franchisees. Nevertheless, with $31 billion in annual worldwide sales, McDonald's is the best-selling food service brand in the world, with sales

The quick-service restaurant (QSR) offers a quick, easy stop for people in a hurry.

Self-service speeds service and, with a simplified menu, offers the guest real savings.
Courtesy Arby's Restaurants

over three times that of the next largest brand.[21] Apparently, the evolution can be considered a success, to date.

This evolution of menu and plant was matched in a general way by other fast-food giants and their competitors. Gradually, fast-food menus offered a wider selection until they were affording enough choice to make them a serious threat to family restaurants because of their lower prices.

The key to the success of fast food, nevertheless, is its simplicity. A key simplification remains fast food's limited menu. Each item on the menu has been "engineered" to simplify and standardize its purchasing, production, and service. Simplification of the production process permits the use of unskilled labor. The fast-food operation is, in many ways, more like a manufacturing enterprise than a traditional restaurant. One management scholar put it this way:

> McDonalds has created a highly sophisticated piece of service technology by applying the manufacturing mode of managerial thought to a labor-intensive service situation. If a machine is a piece of equipment with the capability of producing a predictably standardized, customer-satisfying output while minimizing the operating discretion of its attendant, that is what a McDonalds outlet is. It produces, with the help of totally unskilled machine tenders, a fairly sophisticated, reliable product at great speed and low cost.

> McDonalds represents the **industrialization of service**—applying through management, the same systematic modes of analysis, design, organization and control that are commonplace in manufacturing. These more than anything account for its success.[22]

Fast Food's Unique Characteristics.   Tim Zagat, editor of a prestigious newsletter on fine restaurants, surveyed his regular subscriber list to find out what they knew about fast food. He discovered that even his upper-crust clientele was very knowledgeable about QSRs and that they had formed definite preferences among fast-food restaurants—in addition to their fine-dining preferences. As Mr. Zagat remarked, "Eating in fast-food chains is an undeniable part of the American lifestyle."[23] The presence of fast-food operations in every market of any size is a key characteristic of fast food and one of the main factors supporting the growth of fast food over the past 25 years. Because of their many locations, they make eating out convenient. That convenience reinforces patronage.

We have already noted that simplified menus and operations that use unskilled labor result in a price that is very attractive to the consumer. This simple operating format results in fast service and has earned fast food its name. Self-service is built into the operating format, reinforcing both speed of service and lower cost, especially in the absence of any tipping.

Fast food is **dominated by chains**, which introduces an interesting note of complexity into what appears to be a fairly simple operation. Although the operation of any single QSR unit is relatively straightforward compared with other, more service-intensive restaurants, the operation of the restaurant chain as a whole—

that is, as a system of interactive parts—is highly complex. With over 12,000 restaurants in the United States alone, for instance, McDonald's requires a huge management structure to make all the parts of the system function together in a consistent fashion that the consumer can depend on.

An interesting illustration of this complexity can be found in the area of purchasing. When the corner restaurant adds baked potatoes or chicken to the menu, the whole process can be accomplished by changing the day's menu and instructing the cook. In a complex system, however, much more is involved. When Wendy's first added baked potatoes to its menu, for instance, the entire U.S. potato market was disrupted by the huge new demand. Similarly, when Burger King introduced the bacon cheeseburger, those three strips of bacon (times millions of customers) so increased the demand for bacon that it disrupted the national commodities market in hog bellies.

Although we have asserted that a fast-food unit is a relatively simple operation, it is not true that managing one is in any way a simple task. Managing the very tight quality and cost controls on which QSR operations depend is, indeed, demanding. Very high sales volumes and extreme peaks and valleys of demand throughout the day require managers to hire numerous part-time employees whose schedules vary from day to day and week to week. Keeping this crew properly trained and motivated is a major task. Given the costs associated with turnover, such as lost training time as well as the management time required to hire and train new employees, maintaining staff morale is also a major factor in controlling payroll costs. That means real leadership skills are needed.

Fast food, as we have noted, is dominated by chain and franchise organizations. This is probably true because there are real economies of scale available to operations that are—within a given chain—virtually "clones" of one another. These economies are achieved not only in purchasing raw product but in advertising and marketing and in the development of operating skills. A person new to the business must necessarily follow a learning curve in which he or she begins with ignorance of food service and only gradually develops sufficient know-how to operate successfully. A management trainee or franchisee of a successful chain can use the systems developed by the organization to begin well ahead on the management learning curve and to move more quickly along that curve.

Another reason for chain dominance is the highly standardized product. How much difference is there, really, between one hamburger and another or between fried chicken products? With such a simple and narrow product line, it is difficult for an independent in this segment to achieve a viable basis for product differentiation. Whatever differentiation the independent may achieve, it must then withstand the blast of advertising deployed by its chain competitors. For all these difficulties, smaller regional chains, however, can, and do, compete successfully against the market leaders—in their own regional markets.

Fast food is a vital North American social institution and one that has been adopted by many countries around the globe. In Table 3.3, we summarize its most significant distinguishing characteristics.

Table 3.3   What Makes Fast Food Different?

Location strategy (they are everywhere!)
Highly limited menus
Sales volume: very high and highly variable
Fast service: high degree of self-service
Numerous part-time employees with various schedules
Use of unskilled labor—and highly skilled management
Key role for unit managers
Highly competitive prices
Chain domination
Simple unit: complex system

**Some operations, such as this buffet restaurant, feature self-service, which
provides a lower cost operating format and permits competitive pricing.**
Courtesy of Buffets, Inc.

Fast Food's Continuing Evolution.   We noted at the beginning of this section that fast food today was the product of 50 years of evolution—and that process continues. Profit-oriented companies sometimes make mistakes but they quickly correct them if they want to survive.

One of the positive aspects of fast food's evolution was the upgraded unit's physical plant and decor. Because of the high capital costs (such as depreciation and interest on borrowed capital), however, the cost of building a unit has a major impact on its cost structure. As investment costs began to mount in the 1980s, they drove costs out of line. New smaller prototype units, however, have now been developed that reduced this investment.

New product development has been a vital force in rejuvenating fast-food concepts. Whenever a Wendy's concept has become dated in consumers' minds—and sales have begun to fall—the company has redefined its business with new products. Beginning with salad bars and baked potatoes and, more recently, its popular food bars, the company has regained its earlier popularity—and done so repeatedly.

Fast food's business is concentrated in the breakfast and lunch day parts and, to a lesser degree, in snack periods. All of these day parts have in common a relatively smaller check average than dinner and most firms are continually seeking to enter the higher-check-average dinner day part.

Distribution: Expanding Points of Distribution.   **Distribution** refers to the marketing problem of gaining a presence in many markets. Fast-food chains and other food service operators have begun to expand the number of markets they can serve by developing not just downsized units but special limited versions of their concepts suitable for offering some of the company's product line in locations such as college and university student centers, shopping malls, hospitals, and the like. The smaller **points of distribution** (or PODs) can be located almost any place that there is consumer traffic. The large unit in which a POD is located is called a **host**. Hosts provide **venues** for PODs. Venues are analogous to a restaurant location, but they denote not only a place but also a particular category of guests that the host's premises provide: students at colleges, shoppers in a department store, or workers in an office complex. Hosts and food service operators benefit each other. Food service enhances the host's operation by providing additional service and another revenue stream (rent). The host's venue provides a profitable location to the food service company. The theory behind PODs has been dubbed "intercept marketing," in that the idea is to offer product wherever the consumer is, intercepting them in work or play. The other side of a firm's successful distribution is *consumer convenience*.[24] Points of distribution are proving a major vehicle for the continuing growth of fast food[25] and will be discussed further in Chapter 6.

The Future of Fast Food.   Perhaps the most difficult challenge that QSRs face is the shift in the composition of the population, that is, the aging of the baby boomers. Baby boomers played a major role in creating demand for fast food when they were children and for its gradual upscaling as they entered their teens and twenties in the years just before and after 1970. In 1995, the youngest baby boomer turned 30. As they leave their youth behind and enter middle age, baby boomers' tastes are naturally changing. They are able to afford a more expensive restaurant and prefer a more upscale environment and more extensive service. Although fast-food operators have made every effort to adapt to changing tastes, the QSR may no longer fit their needs as well as it did when they were younger.

On the other hand, there is a large group of younger customers who have come along—and will continue to do so—to replace the boomers. Moreover, fast food, as we noted earlier, is a part of the harried American lifestyle. At whatever age they may be, when speed or cost are especially important, fast food is the easiest choice. Fast-food management opportunities continue to be promising.

Indeed, with so many units in operation and with healthy growth, there is a need for large numbers of new managers to replace those who are promoted or leave the business. There is, moreover, a persistent shortage of qualified managers. Quick-service restaurants are likely to continue to offer attractive opportunities. They give significant responsibility to new managers and generous compensation to those who can deliver results. Their many units mean many opportunities for advancement.

Midscale Restaurants

Although midscale restaurants may not look like fast-food operations, the heart of all their operating systems closely resembles the QSR format. Their back-of-the-house production system has been simplified by a specialized menu that reduces skill levels, thus holding down wage costs and speeding service. Midscale restaurants might, therefore, be called "moderately fast food." Although the customers in these operations are prepared to wait a bit for food, they will not have to wait much longer than in a QSR. We will discuss three of the most numerous specialty restaurant types: family restaurants, HMRs, and pizza operations.

Family Restaurants: A Step Up. **Family restaurants**, such as Denny's, Shoney's, or Big Boy, are table service restaurants that compete principally with QSR operations and have more in common with these lower-priced operations than with upscale units. Although they provide table service, they often offer self-service in the form of salad bars, breakfast bars, and dessert bars. Family restaurants usually offer breakfast, lunch, and dinner and, like QSRs, have their largest business at lunch and dinner.

Menus at family restaurants offer a wider variety of selection and in this they resemble their upscale cousins more than QSRs. This resemblance to full service is, however, deceiving. First, the preparation staff is limited to one or more short-order cooks. Almost everything is prepared to order, sometimes from scratch (as with the sandwiches and breakfast items that give the menu much of its variety) and sometimes from frozen or chilled prepared foods that are reheated to order. The production process is really almost as straightforward as the fast-food process.

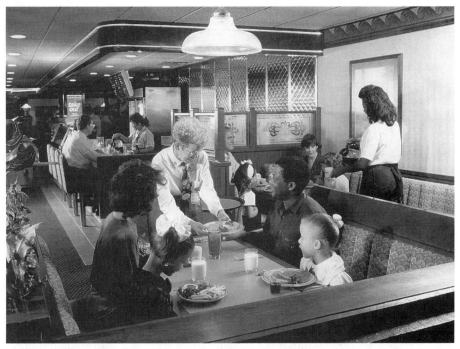

Family restaurants offer table service at reasonable prices in a pleasant atmosphere.
Courtesy of Denny's, Inc./Flagstar

Furthermore, the service the customers receive is anything but elaborate. Place settings usually consist of paper placemats and a minimum of china and silver. Most meals consist of a choice of soup or salad, an entrée with rolls and butter, and perhaps a dessert. This reduction in courses simplifies service. Platters, sandwiches, and salads are the mainstay of the menu, all attractively but simply served. Breakfast is the largest meal for some operators and a significant one for most others. Snacks and coffee breaks are also an important source of business, particularly for family restaurants that combine a bakery with their unit. Table 3.4 shows the 10 leading family chains. In this segment, chains dominate with over three-quarters of the market.

The relatively straightforward operating format of family restaurants helps keep the cost of training new service employees manageable. In addition, the flexible menu permits operations to drop menu choices when their food costs advance too rapidly, substituting less costly items.

The guests who visit a family restaurant want to be waited on and, in choosing a family restaurant, they are opting for an informal, simple, relatively inexpensive style of service. These operations generally offer a pleasant, modern restaurant located near high pedestrian or vehicular traffic and convenient to shoppers and suburban family diners.

Table 3.4 Ten Largest Family Restaurant Chains

Denny's	
Shoney's	http://www.shoneys.com/
Boston Market	http://www.boston-market.com/
Big Boy	http://www.bobs.net/
IHOP (International House of Pancakes)	http://www.ihop.com/
Cracker Barrel	http://www.crackerbarrelocs.com/
Coco's	
Perkins Family Restaurants	http://www.perkinsrestaurants.com/
Friendly's Restaurants	http://www.friendlys.com/
Bob Evans Farms	

Source: Restaurants and Institutions, July 15, 1997.

Family restaurants, with their more varied menus, table service, and modest price level, offer considerable appeal to the aging baby boomer. For families, children's menus are available that often cost less than feeding the same child at a QSR. Another strong market for family restaurants is 55- to 64-year-olds, a segment of the population that will be in a growth phase beginning in 1995. Many family restaurants offer budget menus or special selections for seniors. To appeal to all these market segments, family restaurants are offering expanded menus featuring selections that are lighter and healthier.

Family restaurants have been losing market share to their competitors, casual restaurants and QSR operations. On the one hand, their customers can choose a QSR that offers less menu choice and service but lower price and an ambience that is frequently equal to that offered by a family restaurant. At the other extreme, family restaurants face competition from casual, full-service restaurants, some of which offer prices that are not much higher. Like any operation in the middle, family restaurants have to watch out for price competition from those below and value competition from those on the next rung up. You may recall that Figure 3.3 showed substantially greater satisfaction with the value received by customers in family restaurants than with QSRs or higher-priced restaurants. This suggests that customers recognize the quality of the mid-priced operations but perhaps their real preference is for something more upscale—or else they are pressed financially and must choose the lower-cost alternative. They recognize value in the mid-priced segment but the greater growth goes to their up- and downscale competitors. Whatever is going on in the guests' minds, family restaurants seem to be caught in a competitive middle ground.

Home Meal Replacement.   Operations such as Kenny Rogers Roasters and Boston Market have pioneered a new kind of take-out–eat-in operation, featuring a different kind of food than the burger, sandwich, and pizza that have dominated the take-out market. **Home meal replacement (HMR)**, as this segment is called, features American "comfort foods" such as chicken, turkey, and ham prepared in a way that consumers might prepare it themselves at home. Home meal replacement food not only tastes good but fits the image of family food and is often referred to as home cooked. ("Truth in menu" suggests it should be called "home-*style* cooking" and in some jurisdictions advertising "home cooking" in a restaurant could lead to criminal charges under the laws covering fraud.)

Boston Market was a real growth phenomenon, expanding from a single operation to 1200 units in six years. There is evidence, however, that the chain needed a pause in its meteoric growth. The company has been closing marginal units more recently and has called a halt to expansion. Another well-known operator in this segment is Kenny Rogers Roasters. This chain is named after a famous country singer and the decor features reproductions of his record awards and the music played in the dining room is, logically enough, by Kenny Rogers. Grocery store and delicatessen chains have long featured variants of the HMR concept and they, too, are expanding their take-out offerings aggressively. We should recognize, as well, that take-out operations of all kinds are competitors with HMR operators. A number of new HMR concepts have entered the field, some featuring colocation with an existing brand. Industry Practice Note 3.1 offers some details on the demand for HMR.[26]

Pizza Restaurants.   Pizza is big business. Among the major chain concepts studied by *Restaurants and Institutions* in its annual chain restaurant study, "The Top 400 Restaurant Concepts," the pizza segment ranks second in size with total segment sales of $15.6 billion. (Hamburger chains are first with $54.8 billion.) Thirty-one pizza brands rank among the 400 largest-selling restaurant brands.[27]

Pizza restaurants once depended almost exclusively on a single item. In recent years, however, pizza restaurants have extended their product lien to appeal to more customers. New items include the deep-dish, Chicago-style pizza; pizza with thick or thin crust; specialty two-crusted pizza; and, at lunch, individual-sized pizzas. All have added variety and choice to the pizza menu. In addition, many operations have added other Italian dishes and, at lunch, submarine sandwiches. Despite all their menu and service expansion, however, these operations are still principally pizza restaurants. The cost of their food product itself is relatively low, and these operations also have low labor costs.

Pizza is an interesting product in itself and would merit our attention on that basis. The pizza segment of the industry, however, is especially interesting for having pioneered home delivery. Domino's was the first to show on a national scale that delivery was an economically viable concept.

There are numerous other midscale restaurants featuring, for instance, seafood, Mexican food, and Asian food. They generally fit the pattern already described: limited menus, highly efficient productivity, limited service, and a product characterized by a relatively low food cost.

Industry Practice Note 3.1

Demand Growing for Alternatives to Home Cooking

◆ Off-premise use of restaurants grew to an all-time high 64 visits per capita in 1995, according to NPD Group.

◆ The top three reasons customers give for a carry-out dinner are "pressed for time" (29 percent), "no energy/fatigue" (27 percent), and "want home cooking" (16 percent), according to the National Restaurant Association study "Dinner Decision Making—1996."

◆ Even "traditional" families have warmed to the restaurant take-home trend. A *Better Homes and Gardens* survey of readers showed that 76 per-

cent take home prepared food to eat at least once a month, up 36 percent just since 1992.

◆ The heaviest users of restaurant take-home meals are DINKS (double income, no kids), but low- and middle-income families have doubled their use of restaurant take-home in the last decade, according to NPD.

◆ Singles at all income levels are lighter users of restaurant take-home then marrieds.

Source: Paul Moomaw, *Restaurants USA*, November 1996, p. 23.

High-Check-Average Restaurants

Fine dining, if it is defined as an elaborate ritual of service combined with a European-style kitchen, appears to be in decline. If it is defined, however, simply as restaurants with a check average over $30, fine dining in a new "casualized" version is still very much with us. In fact, according to an NRA study focused largely on the late 1980s, restaurants with a check average over $30 were the fastest-growing category of table service restaurants during that period. Still, these high-check-average restaurants account for less than 4 percent of restaurant sales and 1.5 percent of table service restaurant establishments.[28]

High-check-average operations are primarily found in large cities, such as New York, Chicago, or Los Angeles. These operations are also associated with a high per capita income.[29] West Palm Beach and Boca Raton, Florida, for instance, with a combined population of less than 1 million people, have 163 high-check-average establishments, over one-third more than Chicago, which has a population of 8 million. A third factor that supports demand for this kind of operation is tourism. A tourism center, such as New Orleans, had 66 restaurants with a check average over $30, despite Louisiana's relatively low per capita income. In tourism centers, visitors can create a demand local people might not be able to sustain.

One substantial reason for the growth in high-check-average restaurants—but one that doesn't show up in the statistics—is the great expansion in programs preparing skilled culinarians. Programs such as these are supplying a native-born cadre to an industry that, a generation ago, relied mostly on Europe for skilled cooks.

Casual Restaurants

Casual restaurants are a place where you can "relax and enjoy familiar—yet interesting—food that tastes good but doesn't over extend your budget."[30] One of the major contributions of the baby-boom generation to the North American way of life is an increasing acceptance of casual dress and behavior. This preference is expressed in many aspects of the culture, most noticeably in food service. We will discuss three popular categories of casual restaurants: specialty restaurants, ethnic restaurants, and "eatertainment."

Specialty Restaurants. **Specialty Restaurants** featuring a specific *kind of food* constitute a significant component of the casual restaurant segment. Most of these offer a theme related to the food specialty. With a slightly more relaxed view of diet than prevailed just a few years ago, customers are flocking to steakhouses, for instance. Some of the *Restaurants and Institutions* 400's (hereafter R&I 400) fastest-growing concepts are steakhouse chains such as the Lone Star Steakhouse and Saloon. Many steakhouses feature a Western decor that adds a themed element to the dining experience.

Seafood restaurants can combine a healthy-low-fat image with a popular food product. The sea offers plenty of nautical themes for an ambience to enhance the diners' experience. Pasta is also proving its continuing popularity, offering not only a healthy, low-fat product but one that has a relatively low cost.

Several of the R&I 400 chains are *Brewpubs,* which feature a combination of food and beer made in the operation's own microbrewery. Although alcohol consumption is down significantly—about 11 percent from 1990 to 1995—beer continues to be a popular beverage and accounted for 88 percent of all alcoholic beverages consumed in the United States in 1995. During the period from 1994 to 1995, *craft-brewed beer* sales grew 51 percent and that growth rate has been over 30 percent in each of the five years from 1991 to 1995.[31]

Microbrewed and local beers are used to a greater extent at higher-check-average operations. Whether beer or some other kind of beverage, most casual specialty restaurants do offer alcoholic beverages as a part of their dining experience.

Ethnic Restaurants. **Ethnic restaurants** offer a cuisine and theme that combine to provide a "get-away" experience. The most popular ethnic themes are Italian, French, and Mexican. Many ethnic cuisines offer not only taste uniqueness but also appeal to guests who want to keep their fat intake down. This can be particularly true of Italian and Mexican restaurants.

The popularity of ethnic restaurants, such as the Mexican restaurant pictured here, arises in part from America's diversity.
Copyright Robert Fried, 1992

"Eatertainment." For the specialty restaurants discussed earlier, the focus of the guests' experience is the food, often enhanced by a related ambience. Ethnic restaurants, too, feature a specialized food with a matching ambience playing a somewhat larger role. There are, however, theme restaurants in which the diner's experience is centered in the entertainment provided by the restaurants' stage-set-like decor. Here, the food is an important but secondary consideration. One of the best known of these operations is the Hard Rock Cafe, which pioneered the concept of combining entertainment and eating in 1971.

Larry Levy, the chairman of the company that runs DIVE!, a chain of submarine-themed restaurants, defines these entertainment-centered operations in this way: "They are high-visibility restaurants with a major physical presence and they have a great big idea with an entertainment component behind them."[32]

These operations offer movie quality special effects, professional actors, and audio-anametronic creatures like talking ghosts to create their atmosphere. The

Repeat business in theme restaurants such as the Rainforest Café is dependent on excellence in both food and service.
Courtesy of Rainforest Café

economics of theme restaurants call for big investors. The operators of "Dave and Buster's" spend $10 million dollars on each unit, which includes not only restaurants and bars but computer and virtual reality games. In addition to food sales, these units offer alcoholic beverages and sometimes charge an entrance fee. Sales of branded merchandise such as T-shirts, caps, and sweaters are also a major source of revenue. Rainforest Cafe's president notes that a large staff as well as heavy investment combine to make a 200-seat restaurant the minimum size feasible. Many are much larger.

The *experience* offered by the restaurant is the center of the concept. At Rainforest Cafe, thunderstorms regularly pass through the restaurant, but operators agree that the "WOW" factor is good for only the first visit—or perhaps one or two more. After that, the quality of food and service becomes critical. The danger of obsolescence is a real problem for these high-investment operations unless food and service are excellent—and perhaps even if they are. Accordingly, these operations are located in high population areas and major tourist attractions where there is a high audience turnover. Not every concept will make it, but the idea of a popular restaurant featuring entertainment and food—as well as liquor—has been validated by Hard Rock Cafe's 25 years of successful growth.

ℛESTAURANTS AS PART OF A LARGER BUSINESS

Thus far, this chapter has examined freestanding restaurants—separate and distinct operations. A substantial part of the food service industry is, however, made up of operations that are the food service units of larger centers. A major area that we should consider briefly is restaurants in retailing. Some of these are located in department stores and truck stops. Others are found in shopping centers. It is interesting to see how trends in these catering establishments match those in the restaurant business elsewhere.

Restaurants in Retail Stores

Restaurants in department stores and drugstores were originally built as a service to shoppers. A shopper, after all, who had to leave the store for lunch might resume shopping in some other store. The restaurants, therefore, helped keep the shoppers in the store and often helped attract them there in the first place. Increasingly, in-store restaurants are themselves becoming worthwhile businesses in that they often generate higher profit margins than do the store's other retail sales. In fact, if properly merchandised, restaurants can bring shoppers into the store, not just keep them there.

The economics of restaurant operations that gave rise to the QSR are now at work in retailing. Retailer-housed restaurants are being pressed to adopt QSR service patterns to hold costs in line and to meet the customers' demand for speed.

Indeed, many retailers have brought in franchised concepts to operate food service in their stores. Such, for instance, is the case with Wal-Mart and McDonald's.

Restaurants in Shopping Malls

Thirty years ago, Americans did 5 percent of their shopping in malls. Today, malls account for well over half of nonautomotive retail sales. Malls have become a place to relax, as well as shop. Insulated from the weather, with excellent security, they are a clean and comfortable place to stroll. Malls have been thought of as "places to buy," but they are also "places to be." One of the major purposes that consumers give for visiting malls is browsing. Furthermore, one of the major attractions of the larger malls is their food service establishments.[33] The food court idea, first developed in malls, offers the consumer significant choice, yet gives each operator a chance to specialize and achieve high productivity because of the large volume of customers provided. In fact, the food court concept has been adopted in a number of other settings, such as hotels, casinos, hospitals, and expressway food service.

The composition of mall food service is quite similar to the restaurant industry as a whole. Quick-service restaurants capture about two-thirds of visits; midscale restaurants about one-quarter; with the balance going to more upscale table service concepts. Mall locations have been growing faster than the rest of food service for several years. Less traditional units and ethnic units have fared the best in malls. The dominant food service operators are independents and small chains.[34] This is probably true because the mall provides a basic volume of visitors, and the smaller operator does not have to support major advertising expenditures. About three-quarters of mall food service customers are shoppers. One-quarter are mall employees.[35]

Restaurants at Truck Stops

Another significant set of operations that are part of a larger system are located in truck stops and other roadside complexes that serve the interstate highway system and road travelers in general. Restaurant operations in truck stops generally feature a family restaurant or a coffee-shop style of operation that offers travelers a break in their journey—a chance to eat and to sit for a few minutes in a comfortable atmosphere. In addition, these operations usually provide special sections for truckers who need superquick service. Many truck stops have installed individual telephones in each booth in the truckers' section to cater to their need to call in or call home. As this segment of the business continues to develop, theme truck stop restaurants are on the increase, with steamboat themes, as well as American colonial and wharfside, all proving attractive to customers.

The truck stop restaurant is almost always part of a larger service package that includes gas and diesel fuel, truck repair facilities, gift and sundry shops, and often a motel. Originally intended as an ancillary service, truck stop restaurants have grown to the point where they do about a tenth of the dollar volume of all truck stop business.

$\mathscr{S}$UMMARY

Food service is an integral and vital part of the North American way of life. Table 3.1 summarizes the major components of the food service business. Gains in restaurant traffic have outpaced population growth in recent years and experts are forecasting continuing growth. Food service can be divided into the dining market and the eating market. Fine-dining restaurants require a large market, skilled workers, and devoted management. Fine-dining restaurant sales have been falling since the late 1980s, probably as a result of some combination of changing tastes, price sensitivity, and health concerns about rich foods. Casual upscale restaurants, on the other hand, have become very popular.

The most dynamic part of the eating market is the off-premise segment made up of take-out, drive-through, and delivery. Other contemporary popular-priced restaurants are fast-food (QSRs) and midscale restaurants such as family restaurants and the mid-price take-out operations referred to as home meal replacement (HMR). Quick-service restaurants are characterized by wide distribution, limited menus, and the use of unskilled labor. Other characteristics are summarized in Table 3.3. Even wider distribution is made possible by the development of PODs, downsized units that can provide food service in a host's venue, following a strategy of intercept marketing and a philosophy of maximum convenience for the customer. Midscale restaurants use a simplified menu and production system that resembles fast food, but these operations offer table service. Family restaurants are in a difficult competitive position, caught in the middle between fast-food and casual restaurants. Pizza restaurants are a large component of the midscale restaurant scene but are also noted as the originators of large-scale food service delivery.

Fine dining, which has defined itself to fit contemporary customers' preferences for casual restaurants, includes specialty restaurants, ethnic restaurants, and "eatertainment" operations, which combine food with various kinds of entertainment.

Some restaurants are part of a larger enterprise, such as a department store, a mall, or a truck stop. Their success is usually dependent on the success of the larger unit.

◆ KEY WORDS AND CONCEPTS

Food away from home
Dining market
Eating market
Fine dining
Casual dining
Off Premise dining
   Take-out
   Drive-through
   Delivery
Quick-service restaurant (QSR)
   Industrialization of food
     service
   Simple unit/complex system

Dominance of chains
Distribution
   Points of distribution (PODs)
Family restaurants
Home meal replacement (HMR)
Pizza restaurants
High-check-average operations
Casual restaurants
   Specialty restaurants
   Ethnic restaurants
   "Eatertainment"
Restaurants in retail stores

◆ REVIEW QUESTIONS

1. How do the dining market and the eating market differ?

2. What kinds of restaurants are included in each market?

3. What are the growth concepts in the dining market and the eating market?

4. Do you agree or disagree that fast food is a part of the American lifestyle?

5. What is the outlook for the QSR?

6. How are midscale restaurants different from QSRs? How are they similar?

7. What are the risks inherent in "eatertainment"? How can these be dealt with?

8. What are the prospects for fine dining?

9. What larger businesses do restaurants serve?

◆ *I*NTERNET EXERCISE

1. **Site Name:** *Chilis Grill and Bar*
   URL: http://www.chilis.com/
   Background Information: Chili's has over 570 fun neighborhood places to eat, drink, hang out, and laugh with friends all over the world.

   Site Name: *Wendys*
   URL: http://www.wendys.com/
   Background Information: Wendy's is a quick-service restaurant that has over 5000 stores. It serves old-fashioned hamburgers and a variety of other items.

   Site Name: *Olive Garden Restaurant*
   URL: http://www.olivegarden.com/
   Background Information: The Olive Garden is a multiunit chain that is currently operated by Darden Restaurants, Inc. It currently has over 460 restaurants.

   EXERCISES:

   a. Most casual restaurants have a unifying theme that is pervasive in the design of their menu, decor, and web site. Identify the theme for each of the restaurants listed above.

   b. Which of the above companies provides a means for applying for jobs via their web site?

   c. Which of the above companies provides information regarding their menus and plans for new menu items?

   d. After viewing all three web sites, choose the site that has the most useful information and discuss why you chose that web site.

◆ *N*OTES

1. U.S. Bureau of Labor Statistics, Consumer Expenditure Survey, 1995.

2. McKinsey and Company, "Foodservice 2005," Executive Summary, *Proceedings of the 24th Annual Chain Operators Exchange,* Orlando, March 2–5, 1997 (Chicago: International Foodservice Manufacturers Association, 1997).

3. *Restaurants USA,* December 1997, p. F7.

4. This statistical information and that in the next two paragraphs is taken from the "CREST Year End Report, 1996," *Restaurants USA*, April 1997, p. 44.

5. McKinsey and Company, "Foodservice 2005."

6. *Restaurants USA*, March 1996, p. 40.

7. McKinsey and Company, "Foodservice 2005."

8. *Restaurants and Institutions*, February 5, 1986, p. 16.

9. Ron Dimbert, "An Evaluation of Service Requirements," *Proceedings of the 12th Annual Chain Operators Exchange*, Miami, February 17–20, 1985 (Chicago: International Foodservice Manufacturers Association, 1985).

10. George D. Rice, "Meeting the Challenges of the 90s," *Proceedings of the 21st Annual Chain Operators Exchange*, Orlando, February 27–30, 1994 (Chicago: International Foodservice Manufacturers Association, 1994).

11. Charles Bernstein, "Fine Dining: Overwhelming Challenges," *Restaurants and Institutions*, April 1, 1993, p. 12.

12. John F. Rohs and Wayne Daniels, *Restaurant Industry Update, Security Analysis* (New York: Wertheim Schroder & Co., 1994), p. 16.

13. Michael G. Mueller, "Restaurant Industry Trends and Analysis" (San Francisco: Montgomery Securities, 1994), p. 10.

14. Ibid., p. 53, describing Landry's Seafood Restaurants.

15. Richard Komen, "Upscale Restauranting in the 1990s," Burtonshaw Lecture, April 1990. The Burtonshaw Lecture brings an industry leader to the Washington State University campus to discuss a key contemporary topic with students, faculty, and industry executives.

16. *Restaurant Hospitality*, January 1992, p. 90.

17. Rice, "Meeting the Challenges of the 90s."

18. Ibid.

19. *Wall Street Journal*, December 22, 1993, p. B1.

20. I am indebted to Professor James Pickworth for developing the conceptual scheme that underlies the horizontal, dining experience dimensions of this figure and for helping me to think through the relationships presented.

21. *Restaurants and Institutions*, July 15, 1997, pp. 62–118.

22. Theodore Leavitt, "Management and the Post-Industrial State," *The Public Interest*, Summer 1976, p. 89.

23. *Wall Street Journal*, October 5, 1988, p. B1.

24. This is a somewhat simplified statement of the problem of distribution. For a more extended discussion, see Tom Powers, *Marketing Hospitality*, 2nd ed. (New York: John Wiley & Sons, 1997), especially Chapter 9.

25. The discussion of PODs and intercept marketing is based on presentations by Ira Blumenthal, "Brands on the Run" and "Snapshots of Branding," *Proceedings, of the 21st and 22nd Annual Chain Operators Exchange* (Chicago: International Foodservice Manufacturers Association, 1994 and 1995).

26. The preceding discussion of HMR draws on Paul Moomaw, "HMR Finds Its Place at the Table," *Restaurants USA*, November 1996, pp. 22–26.

27. *Restaurants and Institutions*, July 15, 1997, p. 113.

28. "Metros Focus on Fine Dining," *Restaurants USA*, September 1996, pp. 43–35. The information contained in this section is taken from that article unless otherwise noted.

29. *Restaurants USA*, December 1995, p. 18.

30. Kimberly D. Lowe and Erin Nicholas, "Growing Casual," *Restaurants and Institutions*, July 15, 1997, pp. 101–110.

31. Karen Gardner, "A Toast to Tradition," *Restaurants USA,* February 1997, pp. 31–34.

32. Much of the discussion of "eatertainment" is drawn from Cheryl Ursins, "Theme Restaurants Play to Diners' Appetites for Fun," *Restaurants USA,* August 1996, pp. 24–29.

33. John Marinovich, "The Malling of America," *Proceedings of the 17th Annual Chain Operators Exchange,* Orlando, February 25–28, 1990 (Chicago: International Foodservice Manufacturers Association, 1990).

34. "Leveraging Non-Traditional Opportunities," *Proceedings of the 17th Annual Chain Operators Exchange,* Orlando, Manufacturers Association, 1990).

35. Ibid.

$\mathscr{C}$hapter 4

Courtesy of University of Nevada, Las Vegas

Restaurant Operations

The Purpose of This Chapter

The best opportunities for advancement in food service are in operations. Staff specialists, such as marketers, accountants, and human resources people, all play an important role in food service chains, but most restaurant chains (and institutional operations) have operations people in the top jobs. An independent restaurant operator is, first and foremost, an operations executive who often does most of the staff specialist work as well. Indeed, many senior executives boast of having started at the bottom in food service operations. Although their time spent washing dishes or performing other unskilled jobs may have been only a few months—perhaps during a summer vacation—many executives feel that that kind of operational experience helped them understand the work of the employees they lead.

In this chapter, we want to develop an overview of the all-important topic of restaurant operations. The opening section reviews the key responsibilities in major operational areas and describes a typical day in the life of food service. This should help you to start thinking about the paths to advancement that best suit you.

The chapter concludes with a section on profitability in food service operations and a summary of the financial statements. These statements are used to track operating results, that is, income, expenses, and profit.

This Chapter Should Help You

1. Form an overall impression of what people do in food service operations

2. Provide a basis for your own observation of food service (Whether your work is for a summer, part time while in school, or full time, learning from your work should become part of your professional life.)

3. Identify the main divisions of activity in food service, what work is done in each, and what the main responsibilities and jobs are

4. Identify the major approaches to making a profit and the major means of keeping score in food service operations

RESTAURANT OPERATIONS

The best way to become familiar with operations in a restaurant or other food service organization is to work in one. The following discussion, however, should give you useful background and a framework for thinking about your experiences. We will focus on three areas of the restaurant: the front of the house, the back of the house, and "the office." Within each section, we will look at the principal responsibilities of each area, the tasks that are performed there, and the kinds of roles played in the food service drama by employees working in that area. Finally, we will look at the general supervisory and managerial positions typical of that area.

Because our concern is with the whole range of restaurants, from QSR to fine dining, the amount of detail we can deal with will be limited. In general, we'll take as our model a medium-priced, casual table service restaurant. Where there are substantial variations in fast food or fine dining, we'll note those, however,

The Front of the House

This is the part of the operation with which everyone is familiar because they can see it. It is more complex, however, than it at first appears. The **front of the house** is at once an operating system, a business place, and a social stage setting. As an operating system, it is laid out to provide maximum efficiency to workers and ease of movements to guests. As a business, it is a marketplace that provides an exchange of service for money, which requires appropriate controls. Finally, it is a social place where people not only enjoy their meals but enjoy one another's company, good service, and a pleasing atmosphere.

Responsibilities. Probably the key responsibility of the front of the house is **guest satisfaction,** with particular emphasis on personal service. Chapter 21 on the role of service in the hospitality industry discusses service in more detail, but here we can just note that service goes beyond the mechanical delivery of the food to include the way the guest is served by the people in the restaurant.

The kind of service that should be delivered has a great deal to do with what the guest wants and expects; that is, in a fast-food restaurant, guests expect economy and speedy service at the counter and self-service—even to the point of discarding their own used disposables after they are finished eating. Although there is emphasis on speed and economy, the guest is entitled to expect a friendly greeting, accuracy in order filling, and a cheerful willingness to handle any problems that occur. In midscale restaurants, the table service provided raises the level of interaction

In the front of the house, personal service and guest satisfaction are the most important responsibility.
Courtesy of Buffets, Inc.

with the guest. Although speed of service is still usually expected, the success of the guest's experience is more dependent on the server's personal style. A grouchy waiter or waitress can ruin a good meal: A pleasant manner can help out even when things go wrong.

In casual and fine dining, guest satisfaction and service requirements have a considerably different frame of reference. As a rule, casual dining implies a leisurely meal and that is even more true for fine dining. Accordingly, speed is not always as important as the timely arrival of courses, that is, when the guest is ready. The higher price the guest pays raises the level of service he or she expects. A server in a coffee shop may serve from the wrong side or ask who gets which sandwich without arousing a strong reaction. Errors should not happen there, either, but when the price is modest, guests' expectations are usually modest. On the other hand, when people are paying more for a meal, they expect professional service and a high degree of expertise on the part of staff.

Although service is the most obvious job of the front of the house, those who work there share in the responsibility for a quality food product. This means food isn't left to get cold (or baked dry under heat lamps) at a kitchen pickup station. If there is an error in the way food is prepared, the front of the house is where it is likely to show up in a guest complaint. People in the front of the house, therefore, need to be ready to deal with complaints. This requires at least two things. First, there must be a willingness to listen sympathetically to a guest's complaint. Second, a system must be in place that permits the server or a supervisor to correct any error promptly and cheerfully. In other words, employees must be empowered to satisfy guests' needs. (Empowerment, which is discussed in the final chapter of the book, refers to an approach to managing people that gives employees discretion over as many decisions as possible affecting the quality of the guest's experience.) An unhappy guest is much more expensive than a lost meal. Customers represent potential future sales and powerful word-of-mouth advertising.

The front of the house is the place where food product and service are sold and a lot of money changes hands. **Control** aspects of the operation that are important involve **check control** and **cash control.** Guest check control—being sure that every order taken is on a guest check—prevents servers from "going into business for themselves." An unscrupulous server might take orders, serve the food, and pocket some or all of the money. Today, point-of-sales systems make this kind of scam much more difficult, but there are still ways around even the most scientific system. Because money is the most valuable commodity, ounce for ounce, that a person can steal, extreme vigilance is called for in controlling cash.

Tasks.   From the preceding description of responsibilities, you can see the kinds of tasks performed in the front of the house:

Greeting the guest

Taking the order

Serving the food

Removing used tableware

Accepting payment and accounting for sales, charge as well as cash

Thanking the guest and inviting comments and return business

Roles.   The tasks are performed quite differently in different levels of restaurants. The hostess or host (in very upscale operations, the headwaiter or—waitress or maître d'hôtel) greets the guests, shows them to their table, and, often, supervises the service. Some large, very busy restaurants separate greeting and seating, with hostesses or hosts from several dining rooms ("seaters") taking guests to their table after the guests have been directed to them by the person at the main entrance, sometimes called "the greeter." At the opposite end of the scale, in QSRs, the counterperson is the greeter, thus making the smile and personal greeting there more important than casual observation might suggest.

The cashier's main duty is taking money or charge slips from guests and giving change when the check is paid. In some smaller operations, however, the cashier doubles as a host or hostess. The cashier is also sometimes responsible for taking reservations and making a record of them.

In table service operations, the food server takes the order and looks after the

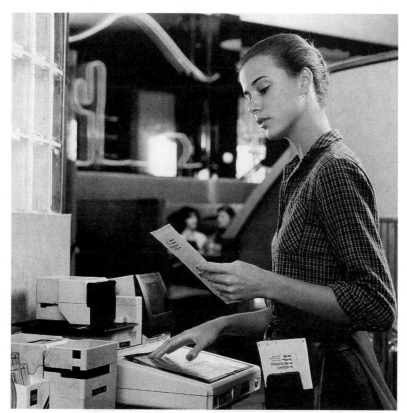

The cashier's role in cash control is critical to profit.
Courtesy of NCR Corporation

guest's needs for the balance of the meal. The server spends more time with the guest than any other employee. What the guest expects regarding service is based on the type of operation. More elaborate service, potentially longer interactions as a result of consultations on choices of food and wine, and highly expert behavior on the part of the server are all expected in more expensive operations. In family restaurants and fast-food operations, although the length and intensity of interaction are much lower, the guest is entitled to expect a genuine interest in the customers on the part of the server, a friendly and cheerful manner, and competence in serving the right food promptly to be minimum—and reasonable—expectations. At all levels of restaurant service, excellent service is crucial to success in an increasingly competitive market.

Servers are generally assigned to a specific group of tables, called a station. In some restaurants, servers work in teams to cover a larger station, often with the understanding that only one of them will be in the kitchen at a time so that at least one of them will be in the dining room and available to the guests at all times. In

European dining rooms and those in North America patterned after them, a *chef de rang* and *commis de rang*—effectively, the chief of station and his or her assistant—work together in a team. In less formal operations, food servers are supported by a busperson who clears and sets tables but provides no service directly to the guest except, perhaps, to pour water or coffee. The busperson's job is basically to heighten the productivity of the service staff and to speed table turnover and service to the guest. Their personal appearance and manner, however, are a part of the guest's experience.

Supervision. Front-of-the-house supervision is ideally exercised by the senior manager on duty. Most managers should be expected to devote the majority of their time to the front of the house during meal hours to ensure that guests are served well. This also enables the manager to greet and speak with guests. In this sense, the manager is expected to be a public figure whose recognition is important to the guest—"I know the manager here." At the same time, she or he can deal with complaints, follow up on employee training, and generally assess the quality of the operation. In some cases, of course, the manager finds it necessary to spend more time in the back of the house if there are quality or cost problems there.

In larger operations, a dining room manager is delegated responsibility from the general manager to manage service in a specific area or in the whole front of the house. In many operations, the job of host or hostess includes supervisory responsibility for the service in the room or rooms for which he or she is responsible.

In addition to supervising service, managers in the front of the house have responsibility for supervising cleaning staff and cashiers, and for opening and closing procedures in the restaurant. Opening and closing duties are sometimes discharged by a lead employee.

The Back of the House

In many ways, the **back of the house** is like a factory. Some factories are assembly plants. Others manufacture goods from raw materials. A similar distinction can be made regarding restaurants. Some are really an "assembly operation," where food is simply finished and plated by kitchen staff. This is true of operations that use a lot of prepared foods such as portioned steaks or a sandwich operation such as a QSR. In others, the product is actually "manufactured" on premise or, as we more commonly say, cooked from scratch.

Responsibilities. The principal responsibility of the back of the house is the quality of the food the guest is served. This is a matter not only of food taste but also of food safety and **sanitation.** Sanitation, then, is also an extremely important responsibility. Finally, cost control with respect to food, labor, and supplies is a make-or-break responsibility of the back of the house. Because prompt, timely service is dependent on being able to get the food out of the kitchen on time, the kitchen has a major responsibility in service.

There are varying skill levels for cooks, but the guest's demand for a high standard of quality applies to all of them.
Courtesy of Domino's Pizza, Inc.

Tasks. Food production stands out as the predominant work done in the back of the house. Controlling quality and cost are usually parallel activities. In other words, standardized recipes and carefully thought-out procedures, used consistently, will produce food that has the correct ingredients, thus ensuring both quality and cost.

An important dimension of cost control is portion control. Say a sandwich that calls for 2 ounces of ham has 2½ ounces. Although "only" a half ounce overweight, that is 25 percent additional meat and probably represents an increase of 20 percent in cost. Portion control has a quality dimension, as well. Assume two guests order fish and the planned portion is 8 ounces. One receives a 7-ounce portion and the other 9 ounces. Although the average is the same and, therefore, cost won't be affected, the guests are likely to notice the discrepancy. Portions should be the same for a guest at every visit—and they should be the same for every guest.

Dishwashing and pot washing are not skilled jobs, but they are certainly important work. Anyone who has been in a restaurant that ran out of clean dishes in the middle of the meal or pots during a heavy preparation period can testify to this. These are activities that use a significant amount of labor in any operation that serves food on permanent ware and has a varied menu (i.e., most operations outside of fast food). Labor cost control is, therefore, an important element in planning ware washing. Because detergent is a commodity that restaurants use in large quantity, the costs of supplies are a significant concern. Quality work, which relates not only to the workers' performance but to adequate water temperatures and soap solutions, is absolutely essential.

Cleanup work is important in both the front and the back of the house, but, because it is more clearly related to sanitation, back-of-the-house cleanup is especially significant. Although in most operations workers clean up as they work during the day, the heavy cleanup is usually done at night when the restaurant is closed.

Roles.   Cooks come not only in all sizes and shapes but also with varying skill levels. In fine dining, cooking is generally done by people with professional chef's credentials, received only after serving a lengthy apprenticeship. The much talked about "hamburger flippers" of fast-food operations are at the other end of the scale. It is not surprising that the "flipper's" work can be learned quickly, because the operation has been deliberately designed to reduce the skill requirements. In between these extremes lie the short-order cook, the grill person, the salad preparation person, and many others who have a significant amount of skill but in a narrow range of specialized activities. Whatever the skill level, it is crucial to the success of the operation that this work be done well.

Dishwashers are often people who have taken the job on a short-term—and often part-time—basis. Because the job is repetitive, monotonous, and messy, it is not surprising that it has a high turnover. We ought to note, however, that an inquisitive, observant person working in the dishroom—or on the pot sink—is in a position to learn a lot about what makes a restaurant run.

Some operations employ people with disabilities in dish and pot work, as well as in salad and vegetable preparation. Mentally handicapped employees often find the routine, repetitive nature of the work suited to their abilities. Not surprisingly, they find that their dignity as individuals is enhanced by their success in doing an important job well. As a result, employers, such as Marriott, which have developed successful programs for disabled workers, have experienced a significantly lower turnover among this group of workers.

An important role we haven't touched on yet is that of the receiver. One person may be responsible for this function or the job may be shared by several employees. It is the receiver's responsibility to accept shipments to the restaurant and to check them for accuracy in weight or count, as well as quality. In most operations, the receiver will also check to be sure that goods received were ordered in the number and quality delivered.

In large operations such as hotels and clubs, the receiver may report directly to the accounting department because the work relates to control. The receiver needs a good working relationship with the kitchen staff, whatever the formal reporting procedure. In most operations, the receiver has duties closely involved with kitchen operations, such as storing food and keeping storage and receiving areas clean and sanitary. Some restaurants distribute the tasks of the receiver among two or more people. In a hotel one of the authors ran, for instance, counting and weighing of goods received was done by the pot washer, whereas verifying quality was the responsibility of the restaurant manager on duty.

Supervision.   Because a variety of titles are used in different organizations, we will focus on three functional areas: food production, ware washing, and cleanup and closing. Food production is headed by a person carrying the title of chef, executive chef, or food production manager. In smaller, simpler operations, the title may be head cook or just cook. In these latter operations, the general manager and her or his assistants usually exercise some supervision over cooks, so it is important that they have cooking experience in their own backgrounds.

Dishwashing, pot washing, and cleanup in very large organizations, particularly hotels and clubs, is supervised by a steward. In smaller organizations, the manager on duty takes on this responsibility.

Closing responsibility is very much related to these activities but deserves separate discussion because of its importance in relation to sanitation and security. The closing manager is responsible for the major cleanup of the food production areas each day (and probably has the same responsibility in the front of the house). This person also oversees putting valuable food and beverage products into secure storage at the end of the day and locking up the restaurant itself when all employees have left. The job is not a very glamorous one but it is clearly important.

The "Office"

We have put "office" in quotation marks because it has many organizational designations, from "manager's office" to "accounting office." The functions relate to the administrative coordination and accounting in the operation.

Responsibilities and Tasks.   **The office** has as its first task administrative assistance to the general manager and his or her staff. The office staff handles correspondence, phone calls, and other office procedures. These activities, although routine, are essential to maintaining the image of the restaurant in the eyes of its public. Ideally, managers should not be bogged down in this time-consuming work. It is essential to have office staff to free managers to manage.

A second major area of responsibility is keeping the books. Often, the actual books of account are kept in some other place (a chain's home office or an accountant's office for an independent), but the preliminary processing of cashier's deposits, preparation of payrolls, and approval of bills to be paid are all included in this function. Prompt payment of bills is very important to a restaurant's good name in the community; so whether this is done in house, at a home office, or by a local bookkeeping service, it deserves careful and prompt attention. Either on premise or off, regular cost control reports must be prepared, usually including the statement of income and expenses (which is discussed in the closing section of this chapter).

Roles.   The manager's secretary or administrative assistant often functions as office manager. Independent operators commonly employ a bookkeeper or accoun-

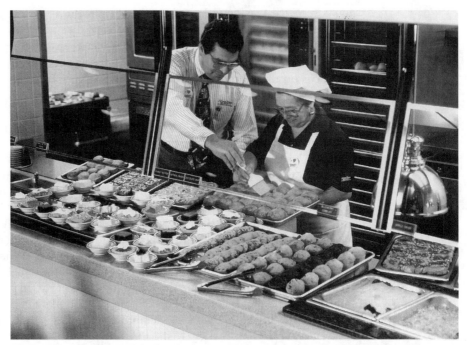

The work of managers in food service puts a high priority on people skills.
Courtesy of Buffets, Inc.

tant full or part time or use an outside service. On the other hand, chains handle most accounting centrally. Often, the secretary/office manager is responsible for filling out forms that serve as the basis for the more formal reports.

Supervision.   As noted previously, the person who supervises on-premise clerical work usually reports to the general manager, as does any in-house accountant. We should note, however, that there are many smaller operations whose low sales volume will not support clerical staff. In these cases, the clerical and accounting routines are usually handled by the managers themselves. In chains, particularly fast-food chains, there has been an extensive effort to automate reporting systems. Here, most reports are prepared from routine entries made in the point-of-sales register and transmitted directly to the central accounting office automatically over the phone lines.

General Management

We should now add one additional category to our framework for observing a restaurant, that of the general managers and their assistants. It is essential that there be someone in charge whenever an operation is open. One possible schedule is as follows: An assistant manager comes in before the restaurant opens and oversees all the opening routines. These include turning on equipment, unlocking storage areas, and seeing to it that all of the crew has shown up and that all the necessary stations are covered. The general manager arrives in midmorning and stays at least through the evening meal rush. The closing manager arrives sometime in the afternoon and is usually the last person to leave, locking up for the night. The schedule just described fits a restaurant in which the major meals are lunch and dinner. Checklists are often used as reminders and are a good way to document tasks. An operation with different hours of operation would have a different schedule in some of the details, but the essential functions identified here would all have to be covered in some way. The key point is that someone in the unit is in charge at all times.

In talking about management, we have really been describing **management presence.** We may not always see the title "manger" used, however. Many of the duties of management are carried out by supervisors. In fast-food and smaller restaurants, managers and their assistants are often supplemented by crew chiefs and lead employees.

We have used the title "general manager" in this section but should note that this is a title used principally in larger operations. The function of overall direction, however, is the same even if the title used is unit manager or simply manager. Because the general manager can't be present every hour of the day, her or his assistants, whatever their titles, stand in for the manager when he or she cannot be physically present. A key point is that managers act as a team to give direction to the unit, to maintain standards (quality and cost), and to secure the best possible experience for their guests.

Daily Routine.   As we have already mentioned, **opening and closing** a restaurant require specialized work. The highest levels of activity, of course, occur during the meal periods. Between the rush hours, a lot of routine work is accomplished. The following is a look at the major divisions of a restaurant's day.

Opening.   Somebody has to unlock the door. In a small operation, it may be a lead employee; in a large operation, it will probably be an assistant manager. As other employees arrive for work, storage areas and walk-ins must be unlocked. If a junior-level supervisor was in charge of closing the night before, it is especially important that the first manager on duty inspect the restaurant and especially the back of the house for cleanliness and sanitation.

In larger restaurants, a considerable amount of equipment has to be turned on. Sometimes this process is automated, but, in other operations, equipment is turned on by hand, following a carefully planned schedule. One element of a utility's charge relates to the amount of power used, but another relates to the peak demand level. If someone throws all the electrical panel switches, turning on air conditioners, lights, exhaust fans, ovens, and so forth all at once, this will create a costly, artificially high demand peak. Schedules to phase in electrical equipment over a longer period may be followed by the person who opens up to avoid this problem.

As noted earlier, it is important to be sure that all stations are covered, that is, that everybody is coming to work. If an employee calls in at 6:30 A.M. to say he or she can't make it, or if somebody just doesn't show up, appropriate steps must be taken to cover that position. This could mean calling the appropriate supervisor at home to let that person know of the problem. Alternatively, the opening manager might also handle it more directly by calling in someone who can cover the position.

Before and After the Rush. Much of the work done outside the meal period is routine. Probably the most important is "making your setup," that is, preparing the food that will be needed during the next meal period. In a full-menu operation, this will likely involve roasting and baking meats, chopping lettuce and other salad ingredients, and other food preparation tasks. In more specialized operations, it may involve slicing prepared meats or simply transferring an appropriate amount of ready-to-use food from the walk-in to a working refrigerator. It is essential that safe food-handling procedures always be followed to prevent food contamination. In some QSRs, a key portion of the setup actually occurs just as the meal period is about to begin, when product is prepared and stored in the bin, ready for the rush that is about to commence. The key element in making the setup is to do as much as possible before the meal to be ready to serve customers promptly.

Sidework is another important activity done by waitresses and waiters on a regular schedule. Sidework includes such tasks as cleaning and filling salt and pepper shakers, cleaning the side stands, and, in many restaurants, some cleaning of the dining room itself. This is work that can't be done during the rush of the meal hour. The front of the house has a sidework setup for every meal period, too. Side stands must be stocked with flatware, napkins, butter, sugar packets, or whatever guest and food supplies might be needed during the coming rush.

Other routine work, such as calling in orders, preparing cash deposits and reports on the previous day's business, and preparing and posting work schedules, are all tended to by management staff or under their supervision. It is important that this routine work be done during off-peak hours so that managers on duty can be available during rush hours to greet guests, supervise service, and help out if a worker gets stuck. When you see a manager moving through the dining room pouring coffee, that manager is (or should be) using that work as a way of greeting guests and helping busy servers rather than covering a shortage in the service staff.

The Meal Periods. Not every meal is a rush in terms of the restaurant's seating capacity. Employees are scheduled, however, to meet the levels of business, so there should be no extra help around. Accordingly, those who are there will probably experience most meal periods as a rush. Each meal has its own characteristics—probably somewhat different in different operations—and the service offered needs to be adapted to that style. In a hotel one of the authors ran, breakfast guests came from the hotel. They were slightly distracted, thinking about the day ahead, and were more interested in their newspaper or breakfast companion than in visiting with dining room staff. Lunch was mostly local businesspeople on a business lunch with clients or in a party of co-workers. The emphasis at both breakfast and lunch was on speed and efficiency. Most guests had to go somewhere else on a fairly tight schedule.

In contrast, dinner was a more relaxed meal. The day was over and people were not in as much of a hurry. There were more single diners, and many were quite happy to visit for a few minutes with staff.

Closing. We have already discussed the importance of the housekeeping, sanitation, and security duties involved in closing activities. We might just note, in addition, that there is guest contact work, that is, easing the last few people out of the restaurant without offending them or waiting until they're ready to leave, depending on house policy. Special care must be employed, in operations serving alcohol, with guests who may be intoxicated to avoid liability for the operation for any harm they might do to themselves or others. There should be written house policies covering this contingency.

Life in the Restaurant Business

Whether or not to work in the restaurant business is really a decision about the kind of life you want to lead. Weekend and holiday work is common, and work weeks of 50 and 60 hours are, too, especially while you are working your way up in management. The work is often physically demanding because you are on your feet, under pressure, and in a hurry for most of the working day.

On the other hand, it is an exciting business. It involves working with people—both employees and guests—in a way that is very rewarding. Every day—every meal—is a new challenge, and there are literally hundreds of opportunities to make people feel good. Few things are as pleasant as the end of a meal when a restaurant crew can take satisfaction in the success of its joint efforts.

Salary Levels

According to the National Restaurant Association, the median range for managers' salaries in 1995 was between $24,000 and $37,500. The salary level depended on the operation, the region of the country, and the sales volume. For instance, the median earnings for a unit manager in an operation with annual sales of less than $500,000 was $26,000, including a $2000 bonus. On the other hand, the median for a unit manager of an operation with sales of $2 million was $45,000 (including a bonus, on average, of $5800). The typical requirement for a unit manager position is between two and five years of experience.

Employers tend to view the assistant manager's position as an entry-level management position, according to the NRA study. The typical experience requirement for this position was between one and three years. The median salary for people filling the position of assistant manager was between $21,400 and $25,100.[1]

Chefs' earnings ranged from $25,570 (including an average bonus of $570) for pastry chefs to $41,000 for executive chefs (including, on average, a bonus of $3000).[2]

The average salary for owners was $44,000 and for chief executive officers $56,000, but this does not include profit in the case of owners or bonuses in the case of chief executive officers.

As we are dealing with averages, there are many people earning both more and less than these amounts. There is a considerable range in earnings because pay depends on the size of the operation, profit levels and the responsibilities involved. Nevertheless, the figures give benchmarks that you may find useful.

*M*AKING A PROFIT IN FOOD SERVICE OPERATIONS

Restaurants have three basic stakeholders. One is the customers. Another is the employees, who seek a good place to work and a decent living. At bottom, though, the purpose that underlies the logic of any business is to make a profit. Without profit, funds to renew the business—to remodel, to launch new products or services, to expand to serve a changing market—and keep employees on the payroll are just not available. Moreover, the third stakeholder, the owners, like all of us, need some reward for their effort and risk. Profit, then, serves a vital role in any business.

There are two basic approaches to increasing profit. One is to increase sales; the other is to reduce costs. Most commonly, operators try to do both to the limits of what will make sense for the other stakeholders.

Increasing Sales

The two basic approaches to **increasing sales** are to sell to more people or to sell more to your present customers—or to do both. Increasing the customer base is usually thought of as the job of advertising and promotion. A superior operation that achieves a good reputation may build its customer base through word-of-mouth referrals.

Another approach is to increase sales to the customers you now have, that is, to increase the check average. One obvious way to do this is simply to raise prices. Unless the price level of the competition is also going up, however, this will most probably result in a loss of customers. Effective approaches to increasing the average check are menu redesign and suggestive selling.

One of the most common menu redesign strategies is the combination meal. Several items that are sold separately—for instance, a hamburger, french fries, a soft drink, and dessert in fast food—are sold together for a price that is less than the price of each sold separately. If this is a good value to the customer, it is likely to persuade a certain percentage to buy more than they might otherwise have done. In a table service restaurant, this kind of combination is referred to as a complete dinner (or lunch) or table d'hôte. The higher check average results in an increase in sales. Another result is likely to be a slightly higher food cost percentage because the selling price is reduced but the food cost remains the same. On the other hand, because total dollar sales have increased and, almost certainly, no additional labor has been scheduled, the labor cost percentage will be lower. The intent would be to have the higher food cost more than offset by the reduced labor cost percentage.

Suggestive selling is another effective technique for increasing sales. Common

Cost Group	Technique	Example of Measurement
Food	Yielding	Dollar cost or weight per portion served
Labor	Productivity standards	Number of guests served per waitress hour or per dollar of service payroll
China, glass, and silver	Breakage/loss counts	Guests served per broken/missing piece
Supplies	Usage monitoring	Gallons/pounds of soap used per 100 guests

Figure 4.1   Some common cost control techniques.

targets for increased sales are appetizers, side dishes, wine, desserts, or after-dinner drinks. The service staff is crucial to this effort: "May I suggest something from our wine cellar? A bottle of Pommard would complement the roast beef perfectly." Operators often offer prizes or bonuses for the server most effective in selling.

Reducing Costs

Just as raising prices faster than the competition will drive off customers, so will cheapening quality through the use of inferior ingredients or smaller portions. Thus, **reducing costs** must result from improved efficiency, which is a fit subject for not one but several books. We will content ourselves here by noting that some of the most common techniques for reducing costs in food service involve more careful scheduling of employees; improved portion control; and more careful monitoring of the issue and use of supplies such as soap, paper goods, and other disposables. Generally, the key to reducing costs is a careful review of the operation to find places where waste can be reduced without loss of quality. Following such a review, realistic standards are set and performance is monitored against those standards. Figure 4.1 shows some common techniques for monitoring cost performance with examples of the kind of measurement used.

Provided that reduced costs come from improved efficiency rather than cheapening quality, it will have a greater impact on profit. A dollar saved in cost, after all, is a dollar more profit. An increase in sales, however, will be accompanied by some increased cost—the variable cost, such as food cost, for instance—and so will not produce as much profit.

$\mathcal{K}$EEPING THE SCORE IN OPERATIONS: ACCOUNTING STATEMENTS AND OPERATING RATIOS

A discussion of operations is not complete without a brief review of the common score-keeping methods used in the field. Elsewhere in your hospitality curriculum, you will undoubtedly study the subject of control at more length. As part of your introduction to the hospitality field, however, this section will discuss briefly some key food service control terms, accounting statements and operating statistics.

Cost of Sales

The **cost of sales** refers to the cost of products consumed by the guest in the process of operations. The principal product costs include:

◆ *Food cost.*   The cost of food prepared for and consumed by guests

◆ *Beverage or bar cost.*   The cost of alcoholic beverages and other ingredients, such as juices, carbonated water, or fruit, used to make drinks for guests

Note that these (and all other) costs are customarily stated both in dollar amounts and as a percentage of sales. For example, if your food cost is $25,000 and your food sales are $75,000, then the food cost percentage will be $25,000/$75,000 or 33.3 percent. Although dollar costs are essential to the accounting system, the percentage of the cost (i.e., its size relative to the sales level) is more useful to managers because the percentages for one month (or for some other period) can readily be compared with those of other months, with a budget, and with industry averages.

Controllable Expenses

Controllable expenses are costs that may be expected to vary to some degree and over which operating management can exercise direct control. Controllable expenses include:

◆ *Payroll costs.*   Payroll costs are the wages and salaries paid to employees.

◆ *Employee benefits.*   Employee benefits include social security taxes, workers' compensation insurance, and pension payments.

◆ *Other variable costs.*   Other costs that generally vary with sales are laundry, linen, uniforms, china, glass and silver, guest supplies, cleaning supplies, and menus. Some costs in the category of controllable expenses have both a fixed and a variable component (utilities cost), but others are fixed by management decision, which is subject to change (advertising and promotion, utilities, administrative and general, and repairs and maintenance).

Capital Costs

This group of costs varies with the value of the fixed assets, usually land, building, furniture and fixtures, and equipment. The higher the value, for instance, the higher the property taxes or insurance. The same is true of depreciation, which is a bookkeeping entry to write off the cost of a capital asset. Interest varies, of course, with the size of the debt and the interest rate.

By categorizing cost information in this way, we focus attention on the operation's key variables. The cost percentages also reflect the efficiency of various seg-

Table 4.1   Comparison of U.S. Restaurant Operating Statistics

	Quick-Service Restaurants	Full-Service Restaurants, Average Check Under $10	Full-Service Restaurants, Average Check $10 and Over
Food cost[a]	31.8%	34.0%	35.5%
Beverage cost[b]	—	29.3	30.2
Product cost[c]	31.8	32.8	34.3
Payroll and related costs[d]	29.5	34.3	33.2
Prime cost[e]	61.3	67.1	67.5
Other operating costs	22.1	20.2	20.6
Occupancy and capital costs[f]	12.2	9.3	8.5
Profit before income taxes	6.9	3.0	3.1

[a] Food cost as percentage of food sales.
[b] Beverage cost as percentage of beverage sales.
[c] Total food and beverage cost as percentage of total food and beverage sales.
[d] Includes employee benefits.
[e] Total of product cost and labor cost.
[f] Includes occupancy costs, depreciation, and interest expense.
Source: Restaurant Operations Report (Washington, DC: National Restaurant Association, 1997).

ments of an operation. Food costs reflect management pricing and the kitchen crew's efficiency. Labor costs reflect efficiency in employee scheduling and the adequacy of sales volume in proportion to the operation's crew size. Results can be improved by either reducing employee hours or increasing sales.

Two key operating statistics are covers and check averages. The number of **covers** refers to the number of guests. (Guest count is an alternative term.) The **check average** can be what it sounds like, the average dollar amount of a check. Because parties (a group of guests seated together) vary in size, however, the check average is usually quoted as the average sale per guest. This figure is found by dividing the total dollar sales by the number of guests served during the period and is sometimes referred to as the average cover.

Figure 4.2 shows an example of a restaurant statement of income and expenses (also called an operating statement or a profit-and-loss statement). This statement shows the relationship of the costs we have just discussed and also how the check averages are computed.

As a final way to compare and contrast differing restaurants, Table 4.1 presents selected average operating ratios for the kinds of restaurants we described in the previous chapter.

UMMARY

A good way to structure your observation of food service is around the major divisions of the front of the house, the back of the house, and the office or the

**STATEMENT OF INCOME
AND EXPENSES
Suburban Restaurant
Year Ending December 31, 20xx**

SALES			
Food	$962,400		80.2%
Food	237,600		19.8
Total sales	1,200,000		100.0
COST OF SALES			
Food	$348,400		36.2%
Beverage	66,100		27.8
Total cost of sales	414,500		34.5
CONTROLLABLE EXPENSES			
Payroll	$338,400		28.2%
Employee benefits	62,400		5.2
Direct operating expenses	64,800		5.4
Music and entertainment	3,600		0.3
Advertising and promotion	22,800		1.9
Utilities	38,400		3.2
Administrative and general	46,800		3.9
Repairs and maintenance	21,600		1.8
Total controllable expenses	598,800		49.9
INCOME BEFORE CAPITAL COSTS	$187,200		15.6%
CAPITAL COSTS			
Rent, property taxes, and insurance	$ 84,000		7.0%
Interest and depreciation	46,800		3.9
Total capital costs	130,800		10.9
NET PROFIT BEFORE INCOME TAXES	$ 56,400		4.7%
Number of covers served		74,918	
Food check average		$12.85	
Beverage check average		$ 3.17	
Total check average		$16.02	

Figure 4.2   Restaurant statement of income and expense.

administrative function. Guest satisfaction, personal service, and accounting for sales are the major responsibilities of the front of the house. Food quality as well as food safety, sanitation, and food cost control are crucial in the back of the house. The office staff provides administrative assistance to managers and handles routine accounting and cost control functions. It is vital to ensure that there is some kind of management presence whenever an operation's employees are at work. The food service day revolves around opening and closing routines and rush periods at meals. Food service operations can be made profitable by increasing revenues or decreasing costs. Sales can be increased by selling more to existing customers or by broadening the customer base. Costs must be reduced through greater efficiency, rather than by cheapening the product and service. In operations, the effectiveness of results is measured with financial statements, particularly the statement of income and expense, and in operating statistics and ratios.

◆ KEY WORDS AND CONCEPTS

Front of the house	Opening and closing
Guest satisfaction	Increasing sales
Check control	Reducing costs
Cash control	Cost of sales
Back of the house	Controllable expenses
Sanitation	Covers
The office	Check average
Management presence	

◆ REVIEW QUESTIONS

1. What are the most important elements of quality in food service? How are they attained?

2. What is meant by management presence? Why is it important? Have you seen it provided in operations in which you have worked?

3. What characteristics do you think are important in a person who chooses to work in food service operations?

4. What pitfalls can you see in the attempts to increase sales? To reduce costs?

5. What are the major approaches to increasing profit? Which is the best way? Why? What are its dangers?

6. What are the main controllable costs? Why are they called controllable?

◆ *I*NTERNET EXERCISES

1. **Site Name:** *Food Safety Project, Iowa State University Extension*
   URL: http://www.exnet.iastate.edu/pages/families/fs/homepage.html
   Background Information: Iowa State University Extension believes that resources are needed for consumers, educators, and students to access research-based, unbiased information on food safety and quality. The goal of the Food Safety Project is to develop educational materials that give the public the tools they need to minimize their risk of food-borne illness.

   EXERCISES:

   a. What information is included on this site and how can it help food service professionals?

   b. The web site talks about FAT TOM. Who is FAT TOM?

2. **Site Name:** *Outback Steakhouse*
   URL: http://www.outback.com/home.htm
   Background Information: The Outback Steakhouse is a multiunit chain that features steaks on the menu as well as a variety of other items.

   EXERCISE:

   Go to the Outback web site and find the following information:

   a. Food cost percentage

   b. Labor cost percentage

   c. Total revenue

   d. Net income

3. **Site Name:** *National Restaurant Association*
   URL: http://www.restaurant.org/
   Background Information: The National Restaurant Association is the business association for the restaurant industry. With more than 30,000 members representing over 175,000 restaurants, NRA membership includes table service restaurants, quick-service outlets, and cafeterias, as well as professionals and academic institutions associated with the restaurant industry.

   EXERCISES:

   a. If you were planning a new restaurant or reviving an old one, what studies are provided by the NRA that might assist you in the decision-making/planning process?

   b. If you wanted to compare the success of your operation with that of your competitors and/or those with similar operations, what information is provided by the NRA that might be helpful to you?

   c. The NRA lists several food-borne illnesses on its web site. What illnesses are covered and what information is provided?

◆ NOTES

1. Hudson Reihle, "Unit Manager Salary Ranges," *Restaurants USA,* May 1997, pp. 42–45.
2. Hudson Reihle, "Region, Responsibility Ingredients in Chef's Compensation," *Restaurants USA,* April 1997, pp. 43–44.

Chapter 5

Courtesy of Rainforest Café

Restaurant Industry Organization: Chain, Independent, or Franchise

The Purpose of This Chapter

This chapter is concerned with the relationship between the form of ownership of the restaurant and the likelihood of success. Chains have many advantages but so do independents. The advantage—or disadvantage—often depends on the situation: Factors such as location, type of operation, and the operation's relationship to the community all have a bearing.

Somewhere between private ownership and chain ownership is the franchised operation. Franchisees have some of the independence of ownership but agree to give up much of it for the right to be a part of a successful concept. Because franchises play such an important role in food service, it is essential for you to assess this means of organizing ownership, too.

This Chapter Should Help You

1. Compare the relative advantages and disadvantages of chains and independents on six significant dimensions

2. Identify and assess the independent's imperative, as well as its unique advantage

3. Distinguish between product franchising and business concept franchising and identify which of them is most commonly used in the hospitality industry

4. Differentiate the services the franchisor offers the new franchisee and those offered the established franchisee

5. Assess the advantages and disadvantages of franchising to both the franchisor and the franchisee and determine if a franchised business might be of interest to you

We sometimes hear that the days of the independent restaurant are past. Although this is certainly not true, the role of the independent restaurant in the industry is changing. Chains have advantages in some industry segments, but independents have strengths that are hard to match in others. It is useful, therefore, to discuss the competitive advantages of both independents and chains. Most restaurant chains include owned units as well as franchised units. Franchised units have some aspects in common with chain operations and others in common with independents. For that reason, the chapter concludes with a discussion of franchised restaurant systems.

CHAIN RESTAURANT SYSTEMS

Chains are playing a growing role in food service. Moreover, they are prominent among the companies that recruit graduates of hospitality programs. Both factors make them of interest to us.

One of the advantages of a major franchise is a well-known brand name.
Copyright Burger King Corporation.

Chains have strengths in six different areas: (1) marketing and brand recognition, (2) site selection expertise, (3) access to capital, (4) purchasing economies, (5) centrally administered control and information systems, and (6) personnel program development. All of these strengths represent economies of scale: The savings come, in one way or another, from spreading a centralized activity over a large number of units so that each absorbs only a small portion of the cost but all have the benefit of specialized expertise or buying power when they need it.

Marketing and Brand Recognition

More young children in America recognize Santa Claus than any other public figure. Ronald McDonald comes second! Because McDonald's and its franchisees spend well over 2 billion dollars on **marketing** and advertising, it's no wonder more children recognize Ronald than, say, Mickey Mouse, Donald Duck, or the Easter Bunny. Indeed, McDonald's has created a generic item—the Big Mac. The company has done for the hamburger what Coke did for cola, Avon for cosmetics, and Kodak for film. The reasons for this success are threefold: simplicity of message, enormous spending, and the additive effect.

The message of modern advertising is affected by the form in which it is offered: 10-, 30-, or 60-second television commercials, for instance. Even in the print media, the message must be kept simple, because an advertisement in a newspaper or magazine has to compete with other ads and news or feature stories for the consumer's casual attention. The message of the specialty restaurant resembles its menu. It boils down to a simple statement or a catch phrase. In fact, marketing people generally try to design a "tag line" that summarizes the benefits they want an advertising campaign to tell the consumer. Some years ago, Wendy's used the slogan, "Ain't no reason to go any place else." Although this slogan set off a letter-writing campaign complaining about the grammar (apparently organized by high school English teachers), Wendy's officials judged it effective in "breaking through the clutter." Of the many other advertising messages that assail the consumer, you will remember classic tag lines of the past that are still revived from time to time:

"We do it all for you."

"You deserve a break today."

"Finger lickin' good."

Television advertising, even at the local level, is very expensive. National or even regional television advertising is so expensive that it is limited to the very largest companies. Chains can pool the advertising dollars of their many units to make television affordable. Few, except the largest independents, however, can afford to use televison.

In all categories, independent restaurants tend to spend less than chains on marketing. Chains have a need to establish and maintain a brand name in multiple markets and to maintain a presence in the regional and national media. In Table 5.1, however, it is noticeable that the level of marketing spending for independent

Table 5.1 Marketing Expenditures in Food Service

Restaurant Type	Level of Marketing Expense[a]		
	Lower Quartile (%)	Median (%)	Upper Quartile (%)
Table service—check average under $10			
Single-unit independents	0.7	1.7	3.1
Multiunit company operated	1.9	3.7	4.0
Multiunit franchise operated	2.7	3.0	3.5
Table service—check average over $10			
Single-unit independents	1.1	2.2	3.7
Multiunit company operated	1.2	2.0	3.3
Multiunit franchised	—[b]	—	—
Quick-service restaurants			
Single-unit independents	1.1	3.0	4.7
Multiunit company operated	2.9	5.1	7.5
Multiunit franchised	3.7	4.7	6.9

[a] Ratio to total sales.
[b] Insufficient data.
Source: 1997 Restaurant Industry Operations Report (Washington, DC: National Restaurant Association, 1997).

and chain table service restaurants with check averages of $10 or more are fairly comparable. In the lower-check-average table service group and QSRs, however, independents spend much less than chains. Quick-service restaurants with their relatively simple product line have a need to differentiate themselves in the consumer's mind and so it is not surprising that these operations spend more than table service restaurants on marketing. Quick-service company-owned and franchised chain units are fairly close to one another in spending on marketing.[1]

All this advertising will be effective only if consumers get exactly what they expect. Therefore, chains concentrate on ensuring consistency of quality and service in operations. Customers know what to expect in each of the units and, in an increasingly mobile society, that is important. For those on the go such as tourists, shoppers, or businesspeople, what is more natural than to stop at a familiar sign? If that experience is pleasant, it will reinforce the desire to return to that sign in the local market or wherever else it appears.

A standard exterior appearance gives franchise operators, and company-owned brands such as Cracker Barrel, a high recognition value.
Courtesy of Cracker Barrel Old Country Store, Inc.

Site Selection Expertise

The success of most restaurants is also enhanced by a location near the heart of major traffic patterns. The technique for analyzing location potential requires a special kind of knowledge, and chains can afford real estate departments that possess that expertise.

Access to Capital

Most bankers and other money lenders have traditionally treated restaurants as risky businesses. Therefore, an independent operator who wants to open a restaurant (or even remodel or expand an existing operation) may find it difficult to raise the needed capital. However, the banker's willingness to lend increases with the size of the company: If one unit should falter, the banker knows that the company will want to protect its credit record. To do so, it can divert funds from successful operations to "carry" one in trouble until the problems can be worked out. Although franchisees are not likely to be supported financially by the franchisor, franchise companies regard a failure of one unit as a threat to the reputation of their whole franchise system and often buy up failing units rather than let them go under. In any case, failure is much less common among franchised restaurants than among independent operations. Not surprisingly, banks not only make capital available to units of larger companies, and to franchised units, but they also offer lower interest rates on these loans.

Publicly traded companies, whose stocks are bought and sold on markets such as the New York Stock Exchange, can tap capital from sources such as individual investors buying for their own account, as well as mutual funds, insurance companies, and pension funds that invest people's savings for them. Hospitality companies with well-known brand names and well-established operating track records enjoy a wide following among investors and their activity is important enough to the industry that *Nations Restaurant News* carriers a weekly section, "Financial News," which features a summary of the 120 publicly traded restaurant stocks. In addition to funds raised through stock sales, companies can sell bonds through public markets, raising larger sums than are typically available through bank loans.

Purchasing Economies

Chains can centralize their **purchasing** either by buying centrally in their own commissary or by negotiating centrally with suppliers who then deliver the products, made according to rigid specifications, from their own warehouses and processing plants. Chains purchase in great quantity, and they can use this bargaining leverage to negotiate the best possible prices and terms. Indeed, the leverage of a large purchaser goes beyond price. McDonald's, for instance, has persuaded competing suppliers to work together on the development of new technology or to share their proprietary technology to benefit McDonald's. In addition, chains can afford their own research and development laboratories for testing products and developing new equipment.

Control and Information Systems

Economies of scale are important here. Chains can spend large sums on developing procedures for collecting and analyzing accounting and marketing information. They can devise costly computer programs and purchase or lease expensive computer equipment, again spreading the cost over a large number of operations. Daily reports often go by phone line overnight, from the unit's computerized point-of-sales (POS) system to the central-office computer. There they are analyzed, problems are highlighted, and reports are sent to area supervisors, as well as to the unit. This means follow-up on operating results can be handled quickly. Moreover, centrally managed inspection and quality control staff review units' efficiency and quality regularly.

Personnel Program Development

Some restaurant chains have established sophisticated **training programs** for hourly employees, using audiovisual techniques such as films, tapes, and slide shows to demonstrate the proper ways of performing food service operations. An increasing number of interactive computer-based training programs are being developed and special training exercises are also now available to subscribing companies through closed-circuit television. The standardized procedures emphasized in company training programs, in turn, lower the cost of training and improve its effectiveness. This saving is especially advantageous in semiskilled and unskilled jobs, which traditionally experience high turnover rates and, therefore, consume considerable training time.

Management training is also important, and large food service organizations can usually afford the cost of thorough entry-level management training programs. ARAMARK, for instance, estimates the first-year direct costs for training a management trainee fresh out of college to be $15,000. This includes the trainee's salary while in training, fringe benefits, and travel and classroom costs, with an additional $4200 estimated as the cost of the manager's time to provide on-the-job training. In effect, this company spends as much as or more than a year of college costs on its trainees, a truly valuable education for the person who receives it.[2]

Because of their multiple operations, moreover, chains can instill in beginning managers an incentive to work hard by offering transfers, which involve gradual increases in responsibility and compensation. In addition, a district and regional management organization monitors each manager's progress. Early in a manager's career, he or she begins to receive performance bonuses tied to the unit's operating results. These bonuses and the success they represent are powerful motivators.

A well-landscaped site and contemporary building help draw guests into a restaurant.
Courtesy of Denny's, Inc.

Table 5.2   Market Share of 100 Largest U.S. Restaurant Chains

Year	Percentage of Sales
1972	30.2
1978	40.2
1983	44.7
1989	46.6
1992	46.4
1996	49.3

Source: Data from Technomic Consultants, Chicago.

Chains' Market Share

As Table 5.2 suggests, chains have dramatically increased their share of sales over the past 25 years. Chains have nearly half the restaurant sales in the United States (49.3 percent), up from 48.8 percent in 1995 and less than 33 percent in 1972.[3] What is interesting, though, is that the **chains' market share** growth seems to be slowing, increasing only 1 percent in the most recent year reported.

Because successful chains usually have "deep pockets" (i.e., adequate financial reserves), they are able to ride out recessions. Indeed, some larger chains look on a recession as a time when they can purchase smaller or less successful chains having trouble weathering the economic storm. Although most experts agree that the concentration of chains will continue, fierce competition from regional chains, shifting consumer preferences, and competitive patterns will ensure that few, if any, players, will establish anything resembling market dominance except on a local or temporary basis.

*O*PERATING ADVANTAGES OF THE INDEPENDENT RESTAURANT

Although chains undeniably have advantages in the competitive battle for the consumer's dollar, **independent restaurants** also enjoy advantages that will ensure them a continuing place in the market, a different place from that of the chains, perhaps, but a significant place nevertheless.

We can use the same method to analyze the strengths of the independents that we used to examine the chain specialty restaurants. The advantages of the chains derive basically from the large·size of their organization. The advantages of the independent derive from a somewhat different common core. The independent's flexibility, the motivation of its owner, and the owner's closeness to the operation affect its success.

In a large organization, a bureaucracy must grow up to guide decision making. Although this is a necessary—and in some ways healthy—development, it does mean a slower and more impersonal approach to problem solving in larger organizations.

To survive and prosper, the independent must achieve differentiation: The operation must have unique characteristics in its marketplace that earn consumers' repeat patronage. Flexibility and a highly focused operation, then, are the independent's edge. Differentiation is the independent's imperative.

Although the following analysis does not deal directly with the issue, we should note that economies of scale are also important in the independent restaurant. The small operation, the mom-and-pop restaurant, finds itself increasingly pressed by rising costs. We cannot specify a minimum volume requirement for success, but National Restaurant Association (NRA) figures show that, in each size grouping, the restaurants with higher total sales achieve not only a higher dollar profit but a higher percentage of sales as profit.

Marketing and Brand Recognition

Ronald McDonald may be a popular figure, but he is not a real person. The successful restaurant proprietor, however, is real. In fact, successful restaurateurs often become well known, are involved in community affairs, and establish strong ties of friendship with many of their customers. This local celebrity can be especially effective in differentiating the operation in the community, "standing on the door," greeting guests by name as they arrive, moving through the dining room recognizing friends and acquaintances, dealing graciously with complaints, and expressing gratitude for praise. "Thanks and come back again" has an especially pleasant ring when it comes from the boss—the owner whose status in the town isn't subject to corporate whim or sudden transfer.

Although the chain may have advantages among transients, the operator of a high-quality operation enjoys an almost unique advantage in the local market. Moreover, word-of-mouth advertising may spread his or her reputation to an even larger area. The key to recognition for the independent is more than just personality; it is, first and foremost, quality.

Chains clearly have the advantage when it comes to advertising because of their national or regional advertising. In contrast to chains, however, many independents spend relatively little on paid advertising, relying instead on personal relationships, their reputation, and word of mouth. Moreover, independents begin with an advantage that chain units must work very hard to achieve, their local identity.

Site Selection

The chain operation continually faces the problem of selecting the right site as it seeks new locations for expansion. It may seem that site selection would not be a problem for an independent operation because that operation is already "in place." On the other hand, successful independents sometimes expand by adding locations. These may be full-scale operations or, quite commonly in recent years, scaled-down versions such as the PODs discussed in Chapter 3. Another occasion when independents need to make location decisions is when evolving urban patterns and real estate values change a location's attractiveness. In some cases, a neighborhood goes into decline, bringing a threatening environment that is unattractive to guests. Alternatively, a restaurant may have a lease (rather than outright ownership) in an area that has become too attractive—at least in terms of rising rents. When the lease comes up for renewal, the owner may decide to move.

When the topic of relocation or adding a location arises, however, the independent operator begins with her or his own knowledge of the area and can add to that by hiring one of the consulting firms that specialize in location analysis. This can be an expensive service, but such services are generally available and the added expense will probably be worthwhile.

Access to Capital

In most cases, the chain will have the most ready access to capital. Sources of capital, however, are available to small businesses. As noted earlier, banks are often hesitant to lend to restaurants because they are viewed as high-risk enterprises. On the other hand, if an operator has a well-established banking relationship and a carefully worked out business plan covering a proposed expansion, the local bank may be happy to make the loan.

The bank, however, is more likely to become involved if the operator can gain support from the U.S. **Small Business Administration (SBA).** Participation by the SBA does not eliminate risk for the banks, but it reduces it by guaranteeing a percentage of the loan against loss. An SBA loan is likely to be for a longer period, thus lowering the monthly payments required from the borrower. Industry Practice Note 5.1 discusses how operators can gain SBA participation.

SBA loans vary widely, from $5000 to $2 million, according to the NRA. In fiscal year 1995, the SBA guaranteed over 6000 restaurant loans with a value of $940 million. The average was for $152,000.[4] The SBA has developed a "Low Doc" program, which cuts paper work and waiting time for approval for amounts of $100,000 or less.

Attracting outside equity capital involves giving up a share of ownership in the business by selling stock. Although such sales are generally limited to small chains, an independent with a concept that can form the basis of a viable chain may be a candidate for equity investment through a venture capital group. Industry Practice Note 5.2 discusses reasons for obtaining additional equity (i.e., ownership) capital.

Venture capital groups are made up of wealthy individuals who pool their funds under the direction of a manager with financial experience and expertise. A venture capital group will expect to have a considerable voice in the running of the business and may take a significant share of ownership in the company without necessarily increasing the value of the owner's equity in the way that a stock offering normally does. **Initial public offerings (IPOs)** involve the sale of stock through an underwriting firm of stockbrokers. An IPO would be very difficult for any but the largest independent. This method does, however, apply to successful independents that have expanded to the point where they are now small chains. Well-known restaurant companies that achieved their early expansion through

Working with the SBA

The key to securing an SBA loan is being prepared and finding the right lender. Know your needs and be able to explain how you arrived at the amount you are requesting.

A successful loan application package will provide a financial history of the restaurant. It will also include a narrative background on the operation, the principals, and goals for the restaurant. Personal financial statements and tax returns for the owners will be required. Most important are monthly cash flow projections. However, the SBA counsels that if you can obtain a conventional loan, that's what you should do. The SBA is only authorized to back loans where credit is not available on the same terms without a guarantee. The SBA recommends that business owners seek a loan from a bank with which they have already established a relationship.

There are certain things about the loan process you can control; the amount of preparation and how you approach a bank are two of them. The SBA recommends contacting your bank and asking what elements it requires in a loan request package. Once you have pulled together all the necessary materials, deliver the package to your banker a few days in advance of your meeting, so that there will be adequate time for him or her to review your request. That way, the banker is ready to respond to your request. The following are four common criteria used to determine the viability of a loan request: previous management experience, net worth, collateral, and cash flow projections.

Whatever you, as a borrower, can bring to the table to calm the fears of the lender and show that you are well prepared to run your own business helps. That includes training, education, and experience. Knowing the business is not all it takes to be successful; you also need to have management and financial skills.

One successful borrower contacted four banks in his hunt for financing and spent nearly two years preparing his business plan. The plan included recipes, sample menus, equipment prices, and sources of supplies.

If your banker doesn't handle SBA-guaranteed loans, call the SBA district office in your area to locate banks in your state that are approved SBA lending sources. To find the district office's telephone number, consult the Small business Administration listings under United State Government in the telephone book, or call the SBA at (800) 8ASK-SBA or 827–5722, or consult their web site (**http://www.sba.gov/**).

Source: "The SBA," *Restaurants USA,* November 1996, pp. 16–17.

Industry Practice Note 5.2

Why Go Public?

"There are really only two strong reasons for restaurant companies to go public," says Barry M. Stouffer, a restaurant analyst for J.C. Bradford of Nashville, Tennessee. "You go public to raise capital or you go public for liquidity reasons, [meaning] you go from private to public ownership so that investors can get better valuation and can readily sell some of their interest."

The beginning of this decade saw a surge of public restaurant offerings. One of the most dynamic restaurant IPOs of the decade was Boston Chicken (**http://www.bostonchicken.com/**). The stock soared 143 percent the day it opened in November 1993—jumping from $10 to $24¼. One year later, however, the stock had settled at $13½. In June 1998, the stock was selling for around $4½.

Initial public offerings did generate excitement early in the 1990s, including those of the Lone Star Steakhouse and Outback Steakhouse (**http://www.outback.com/**).[1] "But restaurant offerings really tailed off after 1993," says Stouffer.

Although the decision to go public is usually premised on the need to raise capital or to provide an exit strategy for private investors (i.e., a way to convert their ownership in a private corporation into stock that can be sold for cash if they wish to leave the business), public offerings do provide other competitive advantages for companies. Customers often feel more comfortable doing business with a public company, banks are more likely to make loans to interested franchisees, and management can add stock option plans to its arsenal of employee incentives.

Source: Adapted from David Belman, "Is It Time to Go Public?" *Restaurants USA,* June–July 1996, pp. 29–33.

1. For a comprehensive list of restaurant chains, go to **http://www.wku.edu/~hrtm/hotlrest.htm.**

IPOs include Boston Market, Rainforest Café, Lone Star Steakhouse, and Outback Steakhouse.[5]

Purchasing Economies

The chain enjoys substantial advantages in its purchasing economies. The independent's problem, however, may differ somewhat from the chain's. Because of the importance of quality in the independent operation, the price advantages in centralized purchasing may not be as important as an ability to find top-quality products consistently. Thus, long-standing personal friendships with local purveyors can be an advantage for the independent.

Control and Information Systems

Chains can use centralized cost control systems. These systems also yield a wealth of marketing information. This practice is, in fact, essential to companies operating many units in a national market. Increasingly, however, independents are able to purchase POS systems that have standardized but highly complex software, which will generate management reports that are on a par with those available in chains. Moreover, the complex menu of the single, independent, full-service restaurant lends itself to the operator's subjective interpretation, impressions, and "hunches" about the changing preferences of the guests.

Cost control procedures may be more stringent in the chain operation, but if an owner keeps an eye on everything from preparation to portion sizes to the garbage can (the amount of food left on a plate is often a good clue to overportioning), effective cost control can be achieved even when a POS system to fit the operator's needs is not available or when the cost of such a system is prohibitive. By using the uniform system of accounts and professional advice available from restaurant accounting specialists, independents can readily develop control systems adequate to their needs.

This description of the independent operator suggests what has become a food service axiom: Anyone who cannot operate successfully without the corporate brass looking over his or her shoulder will probably be out of business as an independent in a short time.

Personnel

The independent proprietor can, and usually does, develop close personal ties with the employees, a practice that can help reduce turnover. Even though "old hand" employees can act as trainers, the cost of training new workers tends to be higher for the independent because of the complex operation and because he or she lacks the economies of a centralized training program.

Although advancement incentives are not as abundant in independent operations as in the chains, some successful independents hire young people, train them over a period of several years to become effective supervisors, and then help them move on to a larger operation. Often, too, the independent finds key employees whose life goals are satisfied by their positions as chef, host or hostess, or head bartender. These employees may receive bonus plans similar to those offered by the chains.

Independents have a special attraction for employees who are tied by family obligations or a strong personal preference to their home community. The problem of being transferred is unlikely to arise with independents. With chains, however, the probability is that advancement is dependent on a willingness to relocate.

The Independent's Extra: Flexibility

One strength that the independent boasts is the flexibility inherent in having only one boss or a small partnership. Fast decision making permits the independent to adapt to changing market conditions. In addition, because there is no need to maintain a standard chain image, an independent is free to develop menus that take advantage of local tastes. Finally, there are many "one of a kind" niches in the marketplace, special situations that don't repeat themselves often enough to make them interesting to chains. Yet these situations may be ideally suited to the strengths of independents.

The Independent's Imperative: Differentiation

One element of the independent's differentiation, as we have seen, is the personal identity of its owner and another is its reputation as a local firm. Strategically, it is important to choose a concept, that is, a menu, service style, ambience, and atmosphere, that is fundamentally different from what everybody else is doing. Ninety percent of hamburger sandwich sales are made by the major chains. Logically, then, the fast-food hamburger market is not one for an independent operator unless it has a unique advantage. There is a good chance that KFC's brand appeal will be more powerful than any product differentiation an independent can achieve in a fried chicken take-out unit. Instead, independents must present a menu and dining experience that is uniquely their own. Independents rely on the differentiation provided by unique foods, outstanding service, pleasing ambience, and personal identity to achieve clear differentiation and consumer preference.

Between Independent and Chain

Between the independent and the chain lie at least two other possibilities. First, some independent operations are so successful that they open additional units, without, however, becoming so large as to lose the "hands-on" management of the owner/operator. *Nations Restaurant News* refers to these as "independent group operators." They are not exactly chains but, because of their success, they are no longer single-unit operators. The other possibility, and one that is pursued by thousands of businesspeople, is a franchised operation.

*F*RANCHISED RESTAURANTS

A conversation with a franchisee is likely to yield this contradiction: The franchisee clearly thinks of himself as an independent businessman but is likely to refer to the franchisor in the course of the conversation as "the parent company." As one report suggested, "Many franchisees do not really wish to be independent at all but are tempted by the opportunity to be part of a large group, sharing in its successful image, and yet also maintaining an 'individual identity.'"[6]

Roughly half of restaurant sales in the United States are made by franchised units. Fast-food restaurants featuring hamburgers comprise the largest category of franchised units. Pizza, steak, and full-menu operations and restaurants featuring chicken also constitute a large number of franchised operations.

There are two basic kinds of franchising: product or trade name franchising and business format franchising. Trade name franchising such as a soft drink or automobile dealership franchises confer the right to use a brand name and to sell a particular product. The type of franchising found in the hospitality industry, however, is

Franchised restaurants offer independent operators the use of an established brand name and a familiar product.
Courtesy of Bonanza Restaurants/Metromedia Restaurant Group

called business format franchising. **Business format franchising** "includes not only the product, service and trademark, but the entire business format itself—a marketing strategy and plan, operating manuals and standards, quality control, and continuing two way communication."[7]

The franchisee has a substantial investment (ownership of the franchise and very possibly of land, building, furniture, and fixtures or a lease on them). Beyond that, he or she has full day-to-day operating control and responsibility. For instance, franchisees are responsible for hiring employees, supervising the daily operation (or managing those who do that supervision), and generally representing themselves in the community as independent businesspeople. The degree of franchisee control over key issues varies from one franchise group to another, but many franchisees share considerable freedom of advertising, choice of some suppliers, and additions to and renovations of the physical plant. Although some aspects of the unit's budget are governed by the franchise agreement, the franchisee retains significant budgetary discretion under most agreements and, in practice, exercises even more.

On the other hand, the essence of almost all franchises in the hospitality industry is an agreement by the franchisee to follow the form of the franchisor's business system in order to gain the advantages of that business format. The franchisee has, indeed, relinquished a great deal of discretion in the management of the enterprise and is a part of a system that largely defines its operation. The restaurant franchisee's relationship is neither that of an employee nor that of an independent customer of the franchisor.

The most common characteristics of a **franchise agreement** are as follows:

1. A contractual relationship sets forth the rights and responsibilities of each party.

2. The purpose of the arrangement is the efficient distribution of an entire business concept.

3. Both parties contribute resources to establish and maintain the franchise.

4. The contract describes the contribution of each party and the specific marketing and operating procedures.

5. The franchise is a business entity that requires the full-time business activity of the franchisee or his or her representative.

6. The franchisee and franchisor participate in a common public identity.

7. There is customarily a payment of an initial franchise fee, continuing royalties, and usually a required contribution to a common advertising fund.[8]

Services provided the franchisee can be divided into those that are especially important to the new franchisee and those that are offered on a continuing basis.

The New Franchisee

The franchisor offers to an investor, who often has no previous experience, a proven way of doing business, including established products, an operating system, and a complete marketing program.

A well-developed franchise minimizes risk, but this may not be true of a new, unproven franchise concept. Moreover, a franchise cannot guarantee a profit commensurate with the investment made—nor even guarantee any profit at all. Small Business Administration studies indicate that somewhere between one-fourth and one-third of all businesses fail during their first year, and 65 percent fail within their first five years. The International Franchise Association estimates failure rates among franchise units at 5 percent.[9] On the other hand, studies conducted at Wayne State University and UCLA indicate much higher failure rates of 25 to 35 percent.[10]

In addition to an overall concept, the franchisor provides a number of specific services to the newcomer.

Screening. Being screened to see whether you are an acceptable franchisee may not seem like a service. A moment's reflection, however, will show that careful franchisee selection is in the best interests not only of the company and other, existing franchisees, but of the prospective franchisee, as well.

Site Selection and Planning.   Franchisors maintain a real estate department staffed with site selection experts. The franchise company also has its pooled experience to guide it. Given the importance of location to most hospitality operations, the availability of expert advice is important. The physical layout of the operation, from the site plan to the building, equipment, and furnishings, and even a list of small wares and opening inventory, will be spelled out in detail.

Preopening Training.   Virtually all franchise organizations have some means of training the franchisee and his or her key personnel. This service ranges from McDonald's Hamburger University to simpler programs based on experience in an existing store.

Operations Manuals.   The backbone of the operating system is typically a set of comprehensive operations manuals and a complete set of recipes that cover all products on the menu. The operations manual sets forth operating procedures from opening to closing and nearly everything in between. All major equipment operations and routine maintenance are described in the operations manual or in a separate equipment manual. Industry Practice Note 5.3 outlines questions a prospective franchisee should keep in mind when assessing a franchisor.

Continuing Franchise Services

Once a unit is open and running, the first year or two of advice and assistance is the most crucial. Even once a franchisee is sufficiently experienced to manage his or her unit without close assistance, the advantages of a franchise are still impressive. These services relate to operations and control and to marketing.

Operating and Control Procedures.   The franchisor strives to present operating methods that have control procedures designed into them. For instance, McDonald's not only specifies the portion sizes of its french fries but also has designed packages and serving devices that ensure that the portion sizes will be accurately maintained. Similarly, Long John Silver's specifies a procedure for portioning fish to minimize waste.

The essential ingredient in a successful franchisor's "proven way of doing business" is not just a great idea but an operational concept. The concept works and is accepted by customers, and its results can be tracked so that its continuing success can be measured and assessed. We should note here, too, that the product and service that underlie the franchise must be continually redeveloped to remain current in the marketplace. Franchisor services in several specialized areas related to operations and control are discussed next.

Industry Practice Note 5.3

Interested in Becoming a Franchisee?

Here are seven basic questions for a prospective franchisee:

1. Is the company itself reasonably secure financially, or is it selling franchises to get cash to cover ongoing expenses?
   ◆ Is the company selective in choosing franchisees?
   ◆ Is it in too big a hurry to get your money? Is this deal too good to be true?

   Today, sweetheart deals are few and far between.

2. Does the company have a solid base of company-owned units? If it does,
   ◆ It is in the same business as its franchisees.
   ◆ It is in the company's interest to concentrate on improving marketing and operating systems.

   If your primary business is operations and the company's is selling franchises, the system is headed for trouble.

3. Is the system successful on a per-unit basis? To find out, look at several numbers:
   ◆ Comparable average sales of stores that have been open longer than one year (sometimes first-year sales are very high and then drop off).
   ◆ Unit-level trends: What is really needed are sales data adjusted for inflation or, better yet, customer counts at the unit level.

   A business is really only growing when it's serving more people.

4. Is the franchisor innovative across all parts of its business?
   ◆ The company should be working on operating and equipment refinements.

◆ Ask what it is doing in purchasing, recruiting, training, and labor scheduling. Is anyone working to make uniforms more attractive, durable, and comfortable, for instance?

The best companies are consistently trying to upgrade every component of their business.

5. Does the company share sufficient support services with its franchisees?
   ◆ In general, the company should provide guidance and strategic direction on marketing and excellent operations training. In addition, every franchisee should have contact with a company employee whose primary responsibility is a small group of franchised restaurants.
   ◆ There are some services that a company can't provide, such as setting prices. In addition, others are risky, such as getting involved in franchisee manager selection.

Support services must be shared in such a way that they respect the franchisee's independence.

6. Does the company respect its franchisees?
   ◆ In addition to formal publications, there should be regular informal forums or councils in which selected franchisees meet face to face with top management to discuss both problems and opportunities.
   ◆ Corporate staff should collect ideas, test them, and, if they look good, involve franchisees in expanded testing.

Franchisees should actually participate in the development of any change that will affect their units.

7. Does the franchisor provide long-term leadership for the entire system?

- Franchisee participation is no excuse for franchisor abdication of its leadership responsibilities. Somebody has to make the formal decisions, and that must be the franchisor.
- A primary function of the franchisor is to protect the value of each franchise by actively and aggressively monitoring operations, demanding that each unit live up to system standards.

Perhaps a necessary long-term decision is not popular. Making tough decisions and following through may be the best real test of leadership.

Source: Adapted from Don N. Smith, Burtenshaw Lecture, Washington State University.

Information Management. Accounting systems furnished by franchisors normally integrate the individual sales transactions from the point-of-sales terminal with both daily management reports and the franchisee's books of account. This makes current management and marketing information available in a timely way and helps hold down the cost of accounting services. This system also provides the franchisor with reliable figures on which to compute the franchisee's royalty payments and other charges such as the advertising assessment.

Quality Control. Inspection systems help keep units on their toes and provide the franchisee with an expert—if sometimes annoying—outsider's view of the operation. Quality control staff use detailed inspection forms that ensure systemwide standards. Inspectors are trained by the franchisor and their work is generally backed up by detailed written guidelines.

Training. In addition to the opening training effort, franchisors prepare training materials such as videotapes and CD-ROMs that cover standardized ways of accomplishing common tasks in a unit. The franchisor's training department also prepares training manuals and other training aids.

Field Support. There is general agreement on the importance of field support: "It is the quality of field support that ultimately determines how good a franchise system is."[11] The backbone of field support is an experienced franchise district manager. One of the most serious problems with unsuccessful franchise systems is a lack of field staff or field staff lacking in expertise. One experienced franchisee commented on a failing franchise system, "We started to get pretty annoyed when we found we had to train the franchisor's field staff if we wanted to keep them from messing things up."

Purchasing. Most franchised restaurant companies have purchasing cooperatives. The co-op offers one-stop shopping for virtually all products required in the operation: food, packaging, and equipment, and often insurance programs. In addition, the co-op periodically publishes a price list that the units can use in negotiating prices with local distributors. The co-op may also publish a newsletter containing information on pricing and trends in equipment, food products, and supply.

Although attractive price and the convenience of one-stop shopping are important purchasing franchisee benefits, particularly with the co-ops, perhaps the most important advantage in the purchasing area is quality maintenance. The lengthy product development process includes careful attention to each product ingredient and the development of detailed product specifications. Often, the franchisor will work with the research department of a supplier's company to develop a product to meet these specifications and to anticipate market fluctuations. Moreover, it is common for franchisors to maintain a quality control staff in a supplier's plants and maintain rigorous inspection systems that monitor the product from the fabrication plant to regional storage centers and then to the individual operating unit.

Marketing. Second only in importance to providing franchisees with a unique way of doing business is provision of a well-established brand and the ongoing development and execution of the system's marketing plan. Although franchisees usually are consulted about the marketing program, the executive responsibility for developing and implementing the system's marketing program lies with the franchisor's top management and marketing staff.

Advertising. In addition to developing and executing a national or (for smaller chains) regional advertising program, most franchisors assist in operating advertising co-ops that are funded with franchisees' advertising contributions. National advertising co-ops typically provide copies of the company's television and radio commercials to franchisee members for a nominal price as well as mats for both black-and-white and color newspaper ads. Co-ops also develop point-of-purchase promotional materials such as window banners and counter cards. Regional and local co-ops devote their efforts to media buying and to executing the advertising program in their area. The pooling of media buys at the local level yields substantial savings, makes advertising dollars go further, and secures a frequency of advertising that heightens effectiveness. Local and regional co-ops also often coordinate local promotional programs such as those using coupons, games, or premium merchandise.

New Products. The marketplace changes constantly, and it is the franchisor's responsibility to monitor and respond to those changes. The company's marketing department carries out a program of continuing market research. When a new product emerges, from research or from suggestions from franchisees, the company develops the new product in its test kitchens and tests it for consumer acceptance with taste panels and for fit with the operating system in a pilot store or stores. If test marketing in selected units is successful, the product will be "rolled out" systemwide with standard procedures for operation and extensive promotional support.

New Concepts. Some franchisors have developed or acquired entirely new concepts. Sometimes this effort is undertaken to offer existing franchisees opportunities for new store growth without moving outside the franchisor's system. Increasingly, however, new concepts are used to build volume in an existing store much the same way as adding a new product to the menu. These more major changes in the franchisor and franchisee's product line are achieved through colocation of two or more concepts. Wendy's, for instance, acquired a doughnut chain, Tim Horton's, clearly a noncompetitive product line for Wendy's main brand.

The Tim Horton's menu draws many customers in the morning, when the Wendy's menu isn't even offered. The concepts work synergistically. By each occupying half the space, Wendy's and Tim Horton's save about 25 percent on building and site costs at each equally shared site.[12] In some locations, Tim Horton's products are offered at a kiosk adjacent to the Wendy's operation. Although the saving on site costs is important, the greatest benefit is incremental sales. These are achieved, first of all, through the new concept. Equally important, however, is the exposure, in the preceding example, of Tim Horton's breakfast customers to a Wendy's as a possible lunch site and, of course, letting Wendy's lunch and dinner customers know where they can get a quick breakfast.

CKE Restaurants, a southwestern hamburger chain, offers "Green Burrito" brand Mexican food at many of its units under license from BG Foods Corporations. Sales in these units have increased 25 percent. KFC has added Taco Bell Mexican food to its menu in a large number of units and has even begun to experiment with Pizza Hut products.[13] (KFC, Taco Bell, and Pizza Hut are all owned by Tricon Global Restaurants.)

Drawbacks for the Franchisee

Some of the more obvious drawbacks of obtaining a franchise have been implicit in our discussion: loss of independence and payment of substantial advertising assessments and franchise fees. If the franchisee has picked a weak franchising organization, field support and other management services may be inadequate.

Franchising is not risk free. The franchisee is generally completely dependent on the franchisor not only for marketing but often for purchasing and other operations-oriented assistsance. If a franchise concept is not kept up to date—as many argue was the case some years ago for Howard Johnson's Restaurants, for instance—or loses its focus, it is difficult for the franchisee to do much about it.

What happens when things really go wrong is illustrated by the case of Arthur Treacher's Fish and Chips. A successful and growing franchise in the mid-1970s, Treacher's then had serious difficulties that ended in bankruptcy. Its national marketing efforts virtually ceased. Its product quality control system broke down, yet the franchisees were contractually obligated to purchase only from approved suppliers. The franchisees also were required to pay both advertising fees and royalties but claimed they received little or no services in return. Many franchisees withheld payment of fees and royalties and then became involved in lengthy lawsuits that were expensive in both executive time and attorney's fees. Although some Treacher's franchisees weathered the series of setbacks, virtually all suffered serious losses, and many left the field. Although the Treacher's franchise system has begun to grow again, the turnaround took a number of years.

Through expansion, franchise companies can increase their presence in the marketplace, improve their geographic coverage, and offer customers convenient access to their products.
Courtesy of Domino's Pizza, Inc.

The Franchisor's View

The franchisee makes most—often, all—of the investment in a new unit. As a result, franchising gives the franchisor the means to expand rapidly without extensive use of its own capital. By expanding rapidly, the franchising organization achieves a presence in the marketplace that is, in itself, an advantage. Moreover, the more units a company has in a market, the more advertising media it can buy. In addition, the better geographic coverage there is, the easier it will be for people to visit often; the restaurants are simply closer and more convenient. Finally, continuous exposure of all kinds—seeing television commercials, driving past the sign and building, as well as actually visiting the restaurant—contribute to "top-of-mind awareness," that is, being the first place that comes into people's minds when they think of a restaurant. Being in place in a market is a crucial advantage and one more readily secured quickly through franchising.

The franchising organization gains highly motivated owner/managers who require less field supervision than owned units do. A district manager supervising owned units is usually responsible for four to eight units. A supervisor (or consultant, as they are sometimes called) overseeing franchised units is likely to cover somewhere between 15 and 30 units.[14] This permits a large company like Mc-Donald's to operate with a much smaller organization than would be possible if it had to provide close supervision to all of its thousands of units.

Franchising companies also draw on franchisees as a source of know-how. According to Don N. Smith, president of Perkins Pancake Houses, input from the grass-roots level "creates a check and balance that enables the corporate functional support groups to keep a proper perspective on the business." Smith also stressed the value of practical ideas that franchisees running daily operations can bring to the solution of operating problems:

> A simple example is the sour cream gun at Taco Bell. Everyone in the Taco Bell system knew it was needed for better portion control and faster speed of service. After spending several years and several hundred thousand dollars with no practical solution in sight, the company gave up. Finally, a franchisee showed them how it should be done. On a much larger scale, breakfast at McDonald's had been tried without success until a franchisee came up with Egg McMuffin.[15]

Franchising Disadvantages to Franchisors

The bargain struck with franchisees has its costs to franchisors. Although their experience varies, many franchise companies find that their owned stores yield higher sales and profit margins. In addition, if the company owned all its units—if it could overcome the organizational difficulties of a much larger, more complex organization—the profits earned from the same stores would be higher than the royalties received from a franchised store.

From time to time, franchising companies are struck by the amount of profit they are "giving up." In the late 1980s and early 1990s, PepsiCo embarked on an ambitious repurchase program in its restaurant divisions, then made up of KFC, Taco Bell, and Pizza Hut. The effect, however, was to tie up a lot of capital without improving returns enough to justify the investment. PepsiCo and then Tricon Global Restaurants, the company that now owns KFC, Taco Bell, and Pizza Hut, have more recently followed an aggressive program of refranchising the units they purchased earlier.

We should note that not all franchise royalty income is profit. Usually, 2 percent of sales is needed to service a franchise system. Because of start-up costs for a new franchised unit for the franchisor, it may be three years before the royalties begin to contribute to the franchisor's profit. In addition, the franchisor will already have made a considerable investment in legal and accounting costs, as well as executives' time.

Franchisor–Franchisee Relations

We have said that franchisees are independent in some ways and yet subordinate in other ways. It is hardly surprising that this somewhat contradictory relationship sometimes leads to problems. To secure better communication between the parties,

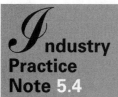

Industry Practice Note 5.4

Conflict in Food Service Franchising

Conflict between franchisors and franchisees has been expressed in a growing number of franchisees' organizations, which are independent of and sometimes opposed to particular franchisors. Franchisees and their associations are filing lawsuits against franchisors and engaging in lobbying before legislative and regulatory bodies for more protection. Four principal sources of conflict are inaccurate financial information, encroachment, conflict of interest on the part of a franchisor/supplier, and problems with franchise renewal.

Inaccurate Financial Information

Although regulated by both federal and state agencies, franchisor financial information is claimed by some franchisees to be unduly rosy. For instance, 26 franchisees of Cajun Joe complained in an arbitration proceeding that sales were overestimated and costs "grossly underestimated" so that profit projections were overstated.[1]

Encroachment

Encroachment refers to the practice of locating franchises closer to one another than franchisees think is appropriate if an adequate profit is to be made. It raises the question of how large a protected territory a franchisee requires. In 1993, a group of KFC franchisees successfully lobbied for a bill in the Iowa legislature that prohibits a franchisor from locating a new franchise within three miles of an existing franchise.[2] The result, reportedly, is that major franchisors slowed or halted the granting of franchises in that state.

Some franchise expansion is taking place in the form of downsized units. Franchisors argue that, even if these locations are near existing franchisees, they constitute an entirely different market of store or shopping mall patrons who would not go outside to eat a quick lunch, anyway. Franchisees argue that (1) the small unit downgrades the image of the franchise and (2) people who have already eaten at a sub shop or hamburger chain or some other restrictive concept are less likely to patronize the franchisee later that day or in the near future.[3]

One McDonald's franchisee who had five new stores built close by, with a resulting drop of 35 percent in sales, summed up his view of encroachment, "Remember the franchisor is in the business of maximizing his revenues, even if that means saturating your market with competing stores."[4]

Conflict of Interest

The franchisor's ability to require product purchases from its own distribution center is somewhat limited by antitrust laws. Nevertheless, there is a gray area in practice, which relates to supplies provided for the purpose of maintaining quality. Eleven Domino's franchisees have filed a lawsuit under the antitrust laws, alleging that they are overcharged for raw dough and that the franchisor, which must approve all suppliers, is acting in a manner that discourages alternate suppliers from entering the market. A similar suit was filed in 1993 by a group of Little Caesar's franchisees.[5]

Franchise Renewal

Most cancellations of franchises are for unpaid costs and relatively few disputes arise, considering the huge number of franchises there are in operation. Nevertheless, as franchisors try to tighten operations in the face of growing competition, franchisees become concerned. McDonald's "Franchising 2000" business plan indicated it would tie franchise renewals to grades on franchisees' performance. In response, 200 franchisees have formed an independent association. A spokesperson expressed their concern that regional staff might not be fair and consistent in grading units. "We're going to monitor [the process]. We're going to try to make sure it's done fairly."[6]

1. *Nation's Restaurant News,* December 20, 1993, p. 3.
2. Andrew E. Serwer, "Trouble in Franchise Nation," *Fortune,* March 6, 1995, pp. 115–129.
3. Rupert M. Barkoff and W. Michael Garner, "Encroachment. The Thorn in Every Successful Franchisor's Side," Paper presented to the American Bar Association Forum on Franchising, October 20–22, 1993, Dallas.
4. Serwer, "Trouble in Franchise Nation." p. 118.
5. *Nations Restaurant News,* July 10, 1995, pp. 7 and 115; September 11, 1995, p. 3.
6. *Nations Restaurant News,* April 1, 1996, pp. 1 and 96.

most franchisors have a "Franchisee's Council"—KFC calls it a "Service Council"—made up of representatives elected by the franchisees. This council meets with the franchisor's top management to discuss major marketing and operational issues.

Still, problems do arise in the best run companies. In 1997, McDonald's chief executive officer took an early retirement, the company was reorganized, and many top-level managers were reassigned. *Restaurants and Institutions* concluded that one factor in this shakeup was that "the burger colossus needs to get closer to its disgruntled franchisees."[16] At about the same time, *Restaurant Business* cited one of the major strengths of David Noval, chief executive officer of KFC and Pizza Hut, as his ability to straighten out a poor relationship between the company and its franchiseees.[17]

Conflict between franchisors and franchisees is discussed further in Industry Practice Note 5.4.

Franchising: A Middle Way

The franchisee is not fully independent but neither is he or she as much at risk as the independent. Taking part in a larger organization that provides vital services while still allowing a considerable measure of financial and managerial independence has much to say for it. A person who is unable to work within a tightly prescribed system would be uncomfortable as a franchisee. Those who can live within such a framework, however, can reap significant rewards with less risk than they would have in their own business.

 UMMARY

Restaurants are organized into groups in chains or franchise organizations or stand alone as independents. Chains and independents can be compared on the basis of brand recognition, site selection, access to capital, purchasing economies, information and control systems, and personnel programs. Chains' strengths come largely from economies of scale. The independent's advantages lie in flexibility and the closeness of the owner/manager to the operation. To be successful, however, independents must differentiate their operation so that they stand out from the crowd.

Franchising offers operators a degree of independence but requires a willingness to work within a defined operation. Franchisees must give up some control over the operation but, in return, their risks are lowered dramatically. Franchisees generally pay a development fee, a royalty fee, and an advertising assessment. The franchisor provides a proven system of operation and expert field staff, as well as a marketing program.

Services that are especially helpful to new franchisees include screening, site selection and planning, preopening training, and a complete documentation of the operating concept in an operations manual. The chapter identifies 10 areas of support to continuing franchisees: operating and control procedures, information management, quality control, training, field support, purchasing, marketing, advertising, new products, and new concepts.

There are positive and negative aspects of franchising for both partners in the arrangement. Franchisees gain a proven format and the assistance described previously but give up much of their independence and are required to pay substantial fees. Moreover, the franchisee is completely dependent on the franchisor. The franchisor is enabled to expand rapidly, largely on the franchisee's investment and organization, and has, in the franchisee, a highly motivated manager and a rich source of innovative ideas. On the other hand, company stores often yield higher sales and better profits, which the franchisor must give up along with a significant degree of operational control. Given the close and somewhat ambiguous nature of their relationshp—neither that of employee and employer nor that of independent partners—there is often conflict within the franchise community, which franchisors are moving to contain with franchisee councils.

◆ KEY WORDS AND CONCEPTS

Marketing	Independent restaurants
Brand recognition	Small Business Administration
Site selection	(SBA)
Access to capital	Venture capital
Publicly traded companies	Initial public offering (IPO)
Purchasing economies	Independent's extra
Control and information systems	Independent's imperative
Training programs	Business format franchising
Chains' market share	Franchise agreement

◆ EVIEW QUESTIONS

1. How do you rate the advantages of the chain and independent on the six factors cited in the text? What other factors should be considered?

2. What is the trend in chains' market share in food service? Where do you think independents are likely to be strongest?

3. What are the major services provided by the franchisor to the new franchisee? Contrast them with the continuing services provided to established franchisees.

4. How do you assess your prospects as a franchisee? What characteristics do you think would be important to being a successful franchisee?

5. What does the franchisor gain from franchising? What advantages does the franchisor give up by franchising instead of owning units?

◆ 𝓘NTERNET EXERCISES

1. **Site Name:** *FranNet—The Franchise Connection*
   URL: http://www.frannet.com/content/articlesdirectory.html
   Background Information: The nation's largest group of franchise consultants that assists investors in finding the right franchise. The group provides a wealth of free information to visitors of the site.

   EXERCISE:

   Choose an article from this site that is of interest to you. Read the article and lead a class discussion on how your chosen topic would be of benefit to an individual seeking to purchase a restaurant frachise.

2. **Site Name:** *American Association of Franchisees and Dealers*
   URL: http://www.aafd.org/htdocs/buying/roadmap.htm
   Background Information: This is a professional association that is dedicated to helping investors choose the right franchise. It provides free information to the public as well as more in-depth information to members.

   EXERCISE:

   Compare the "8 Things to Look for in a Franchise" on the web site with the "seven basic questions for a prospective franchisee" (see Industry Practice Note 5.3). What are the similarities and differences? How does the franchisee's bill of rights [http://www.aafd.org/htdocs/billofrights.htm] support these two documents?

3. **Site Name:** *Small Business Administration*
   URL: http://www.sba.gov/
   Background Information: The Small Business Administration (SBA) was created by Congress in 1953 to help America's entrepreneurs form successful small enterprises. Today, SBA's program offices in every state offer financing, training, and advocacy for small firms. These programs are delivered by SBA offices in every state, the District of Columbia, the Virgin Islands, and Puerto Rico. In addition, the SBA works with thousands of lending, educational, and training institutions nationwide.

   EXERCISES:

   a. Surf the SBA web site and identify how the SBA could help you if you were to start a small hospitality business.

   b. What are the criteria to qualify for help from the SBA?

4. **Site Name:** *Metromedia Restaurant Group/Ponderosa Restaurants*
   URL: http://www.bonanzarestaurants.com/franbon.htm
   Background Information: In 1989, Bonanza Restaurants, a brand of steakhouses begun in the 1960s, joined the Metromedia Restaurant Group (owners of Bennigan's, Steak and Ale, and Ponderosa) to benefit from the synergy of shared resources. Today, there are 118 franchise stores throughout the United States, Canada, and Puerto Rico.

   EXERCISE:

   List and describe the services Metromedia Restaurant Group offers to new franchise operators. How much would the initial investment be to open a Bonanza Restaurant?

 ◆ ○○ₒ○NOTES

1. *1997 Restaurant Industry Operations Report* (Washington, DC: National Restaurant Association, 1997).
2. Personal communication, Joel Katz, Director, Organization and Management, ARAMARK, January 1998.
3. 1996 Technomic Top 100 (Chicago: Technomic Consultants, 1996).
4. The information in this section is taken from Jenny Hedden, "The Buck Starts Here," *Restaurants USA*, November 1996, pp. 13–16.
5. David Belman, "Is It Time to Go Public?" *Restaurants USA*, June–July 1996, pp. 29–33.
6. E. Patrick McGuire, *Franchised Distribution* (New York: The Conference Board, 1971).
7. Andrew Kostecka, *Franchising in the Economy* (Washington, DC: U.S. Government Printing Office, 1986), p. 3.
8. Ibid.
9. Personal communication, International Franchise Association, August 1997.
10. Andrew E. Serwer, "Trouble in Franchise Nation," *Fortune*, March 6, 1995, pp. 115–129.
11. McGuire, *Franchised Distribution*, p. 93.
12. *Wall Street Journal*, October 16, 1996, p. B1.

13. Ibid.
14. Don N. Smith, Burtenshaw Lecture, Washington State University, Fall 1985.
15. Ibid.
16. Daniel P. Puzo, Editor in Chief, "Viewpoint," *Restaurant and Institutions,* August 1, 1997, p. 12.
17. *Restaurant Business,* May 1, 1997, p. 57.

$\mathscr{C}$hapter 6

Pizza Hut and the Pizza Hut logo are registered trademarks of Pizza Hut, Inc., and are used with permission.

Competitive Forces in Food Service

The Purpose of This Chapter

In this chapter, we will look at the all-important subject of competition from three points of view. We will be concerned first with how competitive conditions in food service have evolved over the recent past, as consumer tastes and industry conditions changed. Then, using the marketing mix of product, price, place, and promotion as a framework, we will examine current competitive practices. Finally, we will look at competitors outside the industry such as convenience stores, supermarkets, and the home, which also compete for the food service customer.

This Chapter Should Help You

1. Understand the changes that have taken place in food service competition

2. Assess the competitive conditions in the food service business

3. Describe the food service marketing mix

4. Define the food service product and discuss the role of new products in food service competition

5. Recognize the advantages and disadvantages of competing on price and the times when it is most appropriate

6. Relate the concepts of distribution to the development of PODs and define intercept marketing

7. Explain the major forms of paid marketing communication in food service

8. Discuss the specialized media for reaching the increasingly diverse restaurant customer base

9. Describe the major forms of sales promotion

10. Assess the strengths and weaknesses of other industries with which food service must compete

COMPETITIVE CONDITIONS IN FOOD SERVICE

Competition in food service has always been intense. There are many buyers and many sellers, a condition that makes it hard for any company to achieve control over the market—that is, over prices and other competitive practices. The nature of the competition, however, has changed from the heady days of the growth of new chain concepts in a rapidly expanding market—roughly from 1950 to 1975—to a time today when established food service giants struggle with each other over a much more slowly growing market.

During the period from 1950 to the early 1980s, the industry grew rapidly. As more women went to work, more families could afford to eat out—and were pressed by time to do so. In spite of intense competition, firms had lots of opportunities in an expanding market.

Moreover, the competition between *new chain concepts* was largely to fill unmet demand. The challenge was to grow rapidly enough to snap up the available locations in existing territories and expand into new territories ahead of the competition.

Although there was competition between new concepts for both customers and locations, newer operations were competing, to a large extent, for the customers' attention and patronage principally against outmoded, independent operations. It was relatively easy for new, well-advertised, low-priced operations to take business from old, tired units that had high labor costs and usually indifferent, expensive service.

In the 1980s, however, conditions began to change. During the 1970s, it had already become harder to find good locations. Moreover, the marketplace changed from one that was anxious to try a new concept to one already saturated with restaurants constructed during the past 10 or 15 years. Competition now was more and more between established operations with sophisticated marketing and a proven, accepted operating format. In hamburgers, for instance, competition had gone from Joe's Diner versus McDonald's to McDonald's versus Burger King versus Wendy's versus Hardee's—all struggling aggressively for market share. Nevertheless, the industry continued to expand in numbers of units. Between 1985 and 1987, 40,000 restaurants opened. By the end of the 1980s, the leading chains were growing more rapidly in numbers of units than in real (inflation adjusted) sales.[1]

Some companies have left the field—or a substantial part of it. Marriott, for instance, sold off most of its restaurants and fast-food divisions, as well as, more recently, its institutional food service. Basically, the reason for these decisions ap-

Food service has become a mature market, with many established brands in competition.
Courtesy of Fulton County, Georgia Department of Planning

pears to have been limited food service profits in a crowded industry and competitive pressures that were likely only to get worse. The established players had a dominance that even a company as large and accomplished as Marriott could not challenge.[2]

Although our discussion above (and throughout this chapter) has characterized chain operations, we should note, too, that many independent operations have withdrawn from the market and many of the remaining independents are either very large operations or operators that dominate a small or very specialized market. The independents' role in food service remains a vital one but their share of the market has fallen steadily for some years. Success appears to come mainly to those who have a very distinct way of differentiating themselves from their competitors.

Heightened competition—and food service firms' reactions to it—have created a situation that is sufficiently different that fundamentally new competitive strategies are emerging or have emerged that are changing the face of food service.

THE MARKETING MIX

A good frame of reference for examining these strategic changes is to review what is happening in food service *marketing*. Marketing is a mix of activities that deals with the *product* itself, the product's *price*, the *place* (or *places*) in which it is offered, and *promotion* of the product.[3] The "4Ps" are referred to as the **marketing mix** and, among them, they cover the major areas of competitive activity. The marketing mix is a fundamental tool of analysis, widely used in the hospitality industry. It is important to realize that marketing is a *mix* of activities. Marketing activities, in the examples that follow, may emphasize one element of the mix but two or three others are usually involved, either explicitly or implicitly.

Product

A useful way of looking at the hospitality **product** is that it is actually the **guest's experience.** In a restaurant, this involves not only the food served but the way the server and guest interact and the atmosphere of the place. This is not to argue that the physical product (food) is unimportant but it needs to be seen in the context of

The hospitality product is the guest's total experience.
Courtesy of Caesar's Palace, Las Vegas

the overall *concept* of the operation that determines the guest's total experience. Our discussion of product will, therefore, cover *food products* and *restaurant concepts.*

The importance of good food hardly needs to be discussed. Guests simply *assume* the food is acceptable. What is acceptable, of course, varies from operation to operation. Wendy's creates a different product expectation in guests than does the Waldorf Astoria or the Four Seasons. Product acceptability requires that guest expectation be met or exceeded. It is clear that all elements of this service product are essential. A grouchy server or a dirty dining room can spoil the best experience.

New Products.   **New products** are often a key part of a campaign to revitalize sales in a well-established chain. New products add a note of excitement for customers. As one authority put it, "It is our belief that menu enhancement is one of the most potent strategic weapons available to restaurant marketers."[4] New products are also used to target new market segments. Some years ago, for instance, Wendy's noted that it had a mainly male customer base. To target women, Wendy's introduced the baked potato as a main meal dish and installed salad bars. Both products—salads and baked potatoes—had the effect of increasing Wendy's market share among women. Interestingly, Taco Bell later introduced its large-portion tacos and burritos to increase its market share among men.

The evidence suggests that a majority of QSR guests are very interested in new products and this is even truer of guests selecting a full-service restaurant. Although not *all* products need to be new, it is clear that, to achieve and maintian "good menu variety," the excitement of new products is required from time to time—and on a regular basis.

The term *new product* can mean products that are a genuine innovation—that is, a product that has not been served before commercially. These are sometimes referred to as "new-to-world." Examples are the Egg McMuffin and Chicken McNuggets, products that set off major sales growth for McDonald's when they were introduced. Other new products, often introduced defensively, are referred to as "new-to-chain" and are essentially an imitation of a successful new product offered by another operator. KFC's chicken nugget product is an example of this category. KFC introduced it as a defensive measure when the McNugget had made McDonald's the biggest "chicken chain" in North America.

Many successful new products appear to follow a **life cycle** similar to that for products in fashion-dominated industries. Figure 6.1 (which depicts industry-wide sales) shows new product sales increasing rapidly during the introduction and growth stages. At the peak of the cycle, total sales of the product are at their highest, largely because everybody is competing to sell it. Many new products can't maintain the consumer's interest when everybody else is offering the same or similar products. Consumers tire of them as the novelty wears off.

Figure 6.2 shows that maturity doesn't necessarily mean the death of a concept. In fact, most products we all use are at the mature stage of the life cycle, but marketers have learned to spice up an existing product with changes in its marketing mix. This is equally true not just of individual products but of entire concepts.

When a concept goes unchanged too long, it does become dated. Chic Chi's was

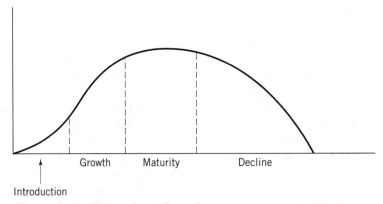

Figure 6.1 The product life cycle.

one of the first chains to offer casual dining as the heart of its concept. That concept, however, remained essentially unchanged for 21 years. As a result, Chi Chi's had several years of declining sales but, in 1997, the chain began working to bring restaurant decor and menu design up to date—and supported these *product* changes with a new advertising campaign.[5] Another casual chain, Chili's, responded to decreasing sales by changing 60 percent of its menu items and adding 24 new

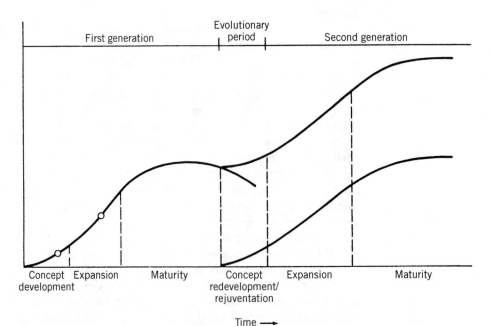

Figure 6.2 Restaurant concept life cycle.
(*Source:* Adapted from Technomic Consultants.)

products to its menu. By the end of 1997, Chili's sales had gone from a decline to nearly a 6 percent increase. Although much of the improvement came from stronger pricing, in spite of higher prices, customer traffic increased 1.5 percent, as well.[6]

Addition of services and changes in decor can be crucial in the competitive struggle. Drive-through restaurants found themselves trapped in price-oriented, 99-cent "sandwich wars." Two of the leaders in that segment decided to sidestep this no-win strategic trap by changing the concept (i.e., product) and adding indoor seating. Although conversion costs were as high as $200,00 per store, increased traffic counts, sales, and profits justified this move.[7]

Typically, new menu items are introduced to improve sales. Two West Coast chains, Jack in the Box and Carl's Jr., saw an opportunity to increase sales where both of them had a weak day part, at breakfast. Jack in the Box introduced "combo meals," which bundled several products in an attractively priced package. Carl's Jr. introduced a proven breakfast menu from Hardee's, a chain recently purchased by CKE, Carl's Jr.'s parent.[8] In each of the preceding cases, the company sought to rejuvenate its concept to achieve the rebound depicted in Figure 6.2.

Concept Blur.   In some ways, food service companies are changing the nature of their product by seeking to serve entirely new markets. This may ultimately change the way the public perceives them but, thus far, it has resulted in increased sales. Fast-food products, for instance, are increasingly turning up in in-flight meals. Fast-food chains are partnering with gasoline companies, offering food service along the highway in gas stations. In addition, many food service companies are packaging their product for distribution through retail stores. Taco Bell, for instance, has sold the rights to its brand name and entered into partnership with food manufacturers that will handle development of the manufactured product and its distribution. Growing customer demand for Chef Paul Prudhomme's spices finally led him to develop a line of packaged seasonings, which are now available nationally. Other famous food service names associated with retail products are as varied as White Castle, Wolfgang Puck, Charlie Trotters, and Bob Evans Farms.[9]

A development that is in the forefront of **concept blur** is the introduction of downsized units with limited versions of a franchise brand's menu. These seem to be popping up everywhere, in carts or other portable units. We will return to this topic when we discuss *place* later in this chapter. Case History 6.1 gives an example of one company's "blurring" through deliberate product evolution.

Branding.   **Branding** is considered a *product* characteristic because the brand is used to heighten awareness of the product in the consumer's mind. The uses of branding in food service are on the increase today and industry practice is highly varied. It can involve branding of individual menu items, as with the Big Mac, to give them greater prominence, or it can involve using a manufacturer's name on an operation's menu such as Haagen Dazs ice cream in a Burger King.[10]

Sometimes it is not just one product but an entire concept that is adopted in a joint location. Miami Subs needed a way to strengthen its weak day parts. Rather

ℭase History 6.1 — Concept Blur and the Great American Hot Dog

Nathan's Famous has come a long way from where it started in 1916, selling hot dogs on Coney Island in New York. The company has moved into the HMR market with plans to sell its branded hot dog through supermarkets. Other new products to be sold in family-sized containers: mashed potatoes, creamed spinach, ham, turkey, and chicken strips.

In order to take the company's brand outside its established territory in the northeastern United States, the company has also franchised its brand to operators of turnpike rest stops, retail stores, Las Vegas hotels, and college campuses. Nathan's has also contracted to have its hot dogs sold at 17 different fast-food chains.

Source: Adapted from *Restaurants and Institutions,* March 1, 1998, p. 20.

than invent and promote a new product of its own, the company added Baskin-Robbins ice cream and frozen yogurt, which sold well in the otherwise slow late afternoon and late evening day parts. Baskin-Robbins has executed successful dual-concept agreements with Subway, Blimpies, and White Castle.[11]

Finally, *product improvements* can center around more tightly *controlled operations.* The leader in the home meal replacement market, Boston Market, announced in mid-1997 that it would be closing nearly 50 restaurants during the remainder of the year to focus on *improving unit performance* at its best restaurants.[12] Similarly, fast-food leader, McDonald's, sought to fight falling sales volume with improvements to existing products, resolving to stop microwaving sandwiches and reintroduced toasted buns for its sandwiches. New products were also being planned to liven McDonald's familiar menu. In addition, another familiar name, Pizza Hut, announced plans to roll out four to six new pasta dishes as a part of its campaign to boost sales.[13]

Price

The restaurant industry was reminded of the power of price competition by Taco Bell in the mid-1980s when experiments with lower prices proved so successful that they were adopted as a major strategy of the company. **Value pricing,** as it came to be called, drove sales increases of 60 percent from 1987 to 1990.[14] Some of the hazards of leading with price came home to roost roughly 10 years later. John Martin, widely recognized as one of the most talented restaurant executives of a generation, after a 10-year run of value pricing, was replaced as president of Taco Bell. Not long thereafter, Taco Bell was reported to be shifting away from low prices and upgrading to higher quality with higher prices in a move code-named "Project

A brand name helps to heighten the guest's awareness of the product.
Courtesy of Rainforest Café

Gold."[15] The problem with value pricing proved to be that eventually competitors adopted new pricing strategies to counter it. Then what was left was a lower profit margin for everyone.

One way of effectively reducing prices temporarily is by offering coupons that entitle the bearer to a special discount, a practice called **couponing.** Although this does affect price, it is generally treated as a *promotional* tactic and so we will treat it under that topic later in the chapter. We should note here, however, that couponing and other price-cutting tactics are sometimes likened to an addiction. It is easy, even pleasant, to start. Sales go up; customers are happy with a bargain; and, with rising sales, things look brighter for the operation. At the end of a prolonged period of discounting, however, the favorable impact on sales is usually eroded. Moreover, profit margins decrease immediately unless the increase in customer traffic offsets the price reduction. Direct, noticeable competition on price in food service occurs, but it is the exception rather than the rule just because its result is generally to depress everyone's margins. Price competition is most common in the off months (usually January through March) when market leaders seek to maintain volume at or above break-even levels at the expense of their smaller competitors.

There is a risk in price reductions, namely, that the lower price will denote a cheapened product to the customer. On the other hand, in the late 1980s and early 1990s, many fine-dining establishments rewrote their menus when customers rebelled against upscale operations with very high menu prices. The new menus featured foods that had a lower food cost and, hence, could be offered at an attractive price. This led to a turnaround for many of these operations. As with virtually all marketing activities, the key is to keep prices in line with customer expectations and to offer products that are perceived to be a good value to the customer.

Pricing: Strategic Implications.   Pressure on prices, we should note, has implications for other elements of the marketing mix. A period of rising prices can mean a favorable climate for competition through innovation. The cost of upgraded decors, new product development, more extensive preparation equipment, and more preparation labor—all could be passed on to the consumer in higher prices. In the future, however, the test for innovation may be stiffer. Changes will have to create savings or major increases in sales volume. If innovations don't pass these stricter tests, they may have to be dropped, because their cost cannot be passed on in ever-higher prices.

Place — and Places

In marketing, place refers to the **location,** the place where the good or service is offered. The great hotelier, Elsworth Statler, said of hotels that the three most important factors in success are "location, location, and location." This has often been repeated regarding many other retailers and is certainly true of food service.

A good location provides access to customers.
Courtesy of Domino's Pizza, Inc.

Food service chains are now concerned, however, not just with place but with *places*. They are seeking to achieve wide **distribution** of their product and so are developing tactics to multiply the number of *places* in which their product—or some version of it—can be offered.

Indeed, one of the most dramatic changes since the introduction of fast food is now under way as multiunit companies change their strategy regarding location. One authority refers to the process as "intercept marketing" in response to what he calls the American public's growing preference for "intercept eating," that is, eating on the run.[16]

Today's customers live harried and hurried lives. Whether members of a two-working-spouse family or a single-parent family, adults today see themselves as increasingly rushed.[17] The tendency is to fit meals in wherever they happen to be, to "grab a bite" as the phrase has it "on the run." Wide distribution, then, is achieved by locating an outlet wherever consumers might go in any numbers.

Restaurant companies have developed new, downsized units for places where a traditional unit won't fit. These units often take the form of a kiosk or mobile cart requiring minimal investment. The name given these new units is **points of distribution** (PODs).

To take just one example, Little Caesars, a pizza chain, had over 500 in-store restaurants in K-Mart stores across North America in late 1997 when the two companies announced their intention to expand this number by another 1000 units, 800 of which would be downsized "Pizza Express" units. The remainder, mostly in larger stores, would be "Pizza Station" outlets offering the traditional Little Caesars menu.[18]

In the language marketers have developed to talk about PODs, a *host* is any establishment, such as K-Mart, where high traffic is likely to offer potential high-volume sales. Examples include retailers, colleges, airports, manufacturing plants, or theme parks. The host offers a food service operator access to the host's traffic. The advantage to the host is that its establishment is enhanced by the additional service; the food service company, on the other hand, gets increased access to customers and sales. Host locations are referred to as *venues*. A venue includes not only a place but assurance of a particular kind of traffic associated with the location such as shoppers, students, or office workers.[19]

The expansion of food service chains via PODs has stirred considerable controversy. Other franchisees are concerned that the downsized units will dilute brand image, threaten quality, and create competition for existing franchisees. As one Little Caesars franchisee said, "I'm totally against it. . . . If a customer goes in and has a 6 inch pizza for lunch, that woman, if she is the one making the meal decision that night, will not choose to buy pizza from a Little Caesar's Restaurant."[20]

The expansion of downsized units is not limited to QSRs. Casual restaurants, including independents, have jumped on the bandwagon of multiplying the *places* where their food service is offered, often in downsized units with restricted menus. What PODs of all kinds offer the consumer is an advantage highly valued in this fast-paced, hurried age: the convenience of a handy location.

Contract companies have become franchisees of restaurant companies and have also developed their own proprietary brands such as ARAMARK's "Itza Pizza." Restaurant companies now find that they face competition from contract companies that have begun to operate units in retail stores and malls. Contract companies, on the other hand, face competition from restaurant companies in the institutional market. Restaurant companies are franchising "hosts" to operate units as part of their own food service operation. For instance, Subway Express units are springing up on campuses; Baskin-Robbins kiosks and carts are found not only on campuses but in hospitals, factories, airports, and tollway plazas. Pizza Hut, too, delivers its product for resale in institutions such as hospitals and schools.

Promotion

Table service restaurants spend 2.5 percent of sales on marketing, whereas QSRs spend 5.7 percent.[21] The food service industry is one of the largest advertisers in the United States. Spending on marketing was close to $9 billion in 1997.[22] Major forms of paid promotional activities, or marketing communication as it is often called, are advertising and sales promotion.[23] We will discuss each briefly.

Advertising.   **Advertising** is used as part of a long-term communications strategy and is often intended to create or burnish an image. Advertising campaigns are generally made up of many different ads and commercials tied together by some common theme. In late 1997, McDonald's announced a campaign whose platform for new ads uses the slogan "Did somebody say McDonald's?" All the commercials in this campaign follow a theme depicting consumers experiencing contagious cravings for the global giant's products.[24] As media become more crowded, themes come and go and are adapted depending on consumer reaction. However, one thing that stands out clearly is the very generous spending on advertising. In introducing a new dual-patty product, the "Big King," for instance, Burger King budgeted $30 million.

Responding to a Diverse Market.   To reach a diverse market, specialized advertising directed at particular ethnic markets is becoming common practice. Both advertising agencies and specialized media have evolved to reach Hispanic and African-American consumers, who make up markets of 28 million and 34 million, respectively.[25] Industry Practice Note 6.1 discusses some pointers from the National Restaurant Association on marketing to Hispanic Americans.

The most common media for mass communication in food service are the electronic and print media, billboards, and direct mail. Figure 6.3 shows the breakdown of the major components of each and characteristics frequently associated with each.

The Internet in Food Service Promotion.   A new medium for restaurant advertising is the Internet, where a growing number of operators are developing a presence. Although the use of the Internet in food service marketing is still in its infancy, there are plenty of examples available to illustrate the direction in which

Industry Practice Note 6.1

Food Service Advertising and Diversity

We already noted in Chapter 2 the growing population of Hispanic Americans in the United States, and how this growth will affect future demand for food service. How could a food service company market its products to the Hispanic population?

Marketing and advertising experts say the most important thing to remember is that, although Hispanics speak Spanish, there are different ethnic groups that make up the Hispanic market. In Miami and New York City, most Hispanics are Caribbeans from Puerto Rico or Cuba; they tend to listen to salsa music and use words such as "carro" for car and "mesonero" for waiter. In Texas and Los Angeles, however, the Hispanic population consists largely of Mexicans and Central Americans. This group typically prefers traditional ranchera music and foods such as enchiladas and tacos; they use words such as "coche" for car and "camarero" for waiter.

Experts recommend that operators consider hiring a full-service Spanish-language advertising agency. "Many ad shops have bilingual capabilities, but a two-person Spanish-speaking division that translates an ad into Spanish from English won't work," says one expert. She suggests finding an agency with a staff that understands the culture and has a proven track record in Hispanic advertising. "Too many companies think they can reach the Hispanic market effectively by marketing in English—and that doesn't work," she adds. "Advertise in Spanish, since Spanish dominates most Hispanic households."

Spanish-language ads should be created from scratch. "A general-market campaign with a voice-over won't work and may be insulting." In addition, slogans or ideas in English do not often translate exactly into or have the same meaning in Spanish. An example of an advertising campaign that failed because of direct translation was Chevrolet's 1970s unveiling of its Nova model in Latin America. The problem with the Nova was not the car, but that in Spanish "no va" means "will not go"—not a good motto for an automobile company.

Source: "Sending the Right Message," *Restaurants USA,* January 1997, p. 18.

Medium	Characteristics
BROADCAST MEDIA	
Television	Large audience, low cost per viewer but high total cost. Combines sight, motion, and sound.
Radio	Highly targetable, lower cost than TV.
Cable TV	Highly targetable, fragmented market.
PRINT MEDIA	
Newspapers	Limited targeting possible. Printed word is regarded as credible by many.
Magazines	Targetable, generally prestigious, high-quality reproduction of photos.
ROADSIDE	Excellent for directions. Message limited to about eight words.
DIRECT MEDIA	Excellent targeting but costly per prospect reached. Good coupon distribution vehicle.

Figure 6.3 Advertising media and their characteristics.

the industry is moving. Home pages on the World Wide Web are used primarily as sources of information. Many, however, provide links to E-mail addresses, so users can communicate directly with the operation. On-line service providers such as America on Line (AOL) and CompuServe feature information about and for food service professionals. An "E-zine" or electronic magazine called the *Electronic Gourmet Guide* targets principally home cooks but is developing features that relate to restaurants.[26]

Papa John's Pizza began testing on-line ordering for take-out and delivery in late 1997 with a sample of 40 stores located in markets that have a large number of Internet users. Availability of Internet ordering service is promoted through more conventional media such as television and radio, as well as in-store signage.[27]

Sales Promotion.   **Sales promotion** consists of activities other than advertising that are directed at gaining immediate patronage. The most common forms of sales promotion are "deals," which include coupons, games, and promotional merchandise. Deals are intended to enhance the value of the product offered—and to stimulate immediate purchase.

Coupons.   Coupons are often offered in connection with very low product cost fountain drinks (a product cost as low as 2 or 3 percent). As a result of their low cost, couponing these items has a limited impact on the operation's profit margin. During the off season, however, coupons discounting main meal items are more common.

Games.   Games cost considerably less than couponing main meal items. They enhance value by offering a little excitement—the *possibility* of an all-expenses paid vacation in some exotic locale, for instance. Moreover, lots of small prizes (french fries, a free soft drink) make the possibility of winning fairly likely—and winning anything is usually a pleasant experience.

Promotional Merchandise.   Promotional merchandise such as toys or glassware are often called "self-liquidators" because the merchandise is usually sold at cost, limiting the impact of the deal on the promotional budget. Typically, merchandise comes in sets of three or four to encourage repeat patronage: "Collect All Four!"

As Figure 6.4 makes clear, deals are becoming an increasingly common inducement to customers.

In more upscale operations, special events are a common form of promotion. Special ethnic menus or celebrations of holiday events such as Valentine's Day or Mother's Day fit this category.

An increasingly common form of highly targeted sales promotion involves frequent-guest programs. These programs offer rewards to good customers and encourage repeat patronage. Frequent-guest programs increase guest loyalty and yield valuable information on customers, which can be used in future marketing programs.

Figure 6.4 Deal use rising—percent of restaurant occasions where a deal was used, 1990 to 1995.
(*Source:* "NPD/CREST Annual Household Report," *Restaurants USA,* March 1996, p. 47.)

$\mathcal{C}$OMPETITION WITH OTHER INDUSTRIES

It is an axiom of economics that people's wants will expand indefinitely but that their resources are limited. Most people would like a new car, a vacation in Europe or the Caribbean, as well as the latest in VCR, stereo, and computer equipment. They would also like to dine in the finest restaurants. The problem is, however, as few can afford all of that, most must choose. Give up dining out in the best the local restaurant scene has to offer for the next year or so and you may have the price of that vacation. Forgo lunch at your favorite restaurant and brown-bag it for six weeks and you can probably save the price of a new VCR and two or three video rentals. Thus, food service is, in a very real way, in **generic competition** with all other industries, especially those providing leisure services and conveniences.

Some industries, however, challenge food service on its own turf, offering directly competitive products. We will concentrate our attention on these retailers here. Convenience stores offer their own variety of fast food and from locations that are so numerous that they seem to be "just around the corner" from wherever you may be. Supermarkets are not as numerous as convenience stores, but they *are* conveniently located and virtually everyone visits them in the course of a week. Both are formidable competitors for food service.

Convenience Stores

Although their most frequent customers are males under age 35, C stores, as they are often called, are visited once or twice a month by most of the adult population. A significant part of C store sales are directly competitive with food service sales, especially beverages and sandwiches. Because nearly all C stores have microwave equipment and offer prepared foods, these retail units can compete for more than the snack market. Many offer a service deli and a variety of QSR foods. Some C stores have a point of distribution from one of the major QSR chains located in the store. Although food service is relatively more labor intensive than other C store products, it offers a higher contribution to overhead and profits—roughly 60 percent as compared with 30 percent for other products.

Interestingly, after 7-Eleven and Circle K, the largest operators of C stores are oil companies. Oil companies have four distinct advantages over many other C store operators. First, because of their large gasoline sales, they can afford prime corner locations. Second, they have the backing of cash-rich corporations. Third, they are able to sell gas at lower prices. Finally, consumers can use their gasoline credit card to make their purchase, which is a major convenience. Oil companies have solid motives to expand operations. They want to make their petroleum products as widely available as possible. We can expect, therefore, continuing expansion and growing competition from these new industry leaders, as well as from the more established 7-Eleven and Circle K.

Supermarkets

Restaurateurs and retailers selling food for consumption at home have always been in competition. For some years, restaurants' share of that market has been increasing. That struggle is intensifying as a result of sharpened competitive practices in the grocery business and changing patterns in leisure-time usage. We will discuss the grocery business in this section and look briefly at the changing patterns in leisure in the next section. Clearly, the two developments are interrelated.

Supermarkets have customers from 100 percent of households over a 52-week period, that is, in effect, everybody.[28] With this kind of exposure, they are formidable competitors for the food dollar. A state-of-the-art store today emphasizes food service and many grocery stores are adding food courts and full-scale restaurants, including ethnic-themed operations as well as brand name QSRs. McDonald's, Burger King, Pizza Hut, and Taco bell all operate units in supermarkets, and contract companies such as ARAMARK have developed branded programs for supermarkets. We discussed the development of more numerous *places* earlier and here we can see it as a part of the blurring of concepts. When is a restaurant "sort of not exactly" a restaurant? When it's part of a grocery store offering food service. Or, perhaps, we should just say, grocery stores are a very significant part of the ever-increasing competition for the consumer's food dollar.

Supermarkets are endangering restaurants' home meal replacement market share. In a survey conducted in 1997 by the Food Marketing Institute, a grocery trade industry organization, 22 percent of consumers questioned said they used supermarkets as their main source of take-out food, up from 11 percent in 1988.[29] Supermarket take-out food is generally less costly to the consumer than restaurant take-out food and grocery stores offer wider variety. The convenience of picking up a few staples—milk or bread for breakfast—while picking up dinner is undeniable.

Fast food has a tough competitor in convenience stores, which offer meals as well as snacks.
Courtesy of Southland Corporation.

Restaurants, however, have the advantage of a service culture and higher-quality food. Supermarket managers are often rooted in a retail mind set. As one supermarket executive put it, "They tried to apply [the retailing mind set] to rotisserie chicken. They'd set out all the chickens at 8:00 A.M. and wait until they were sold. You'd never see that in a restaurant."[30]

By partnering with food service operators—or hiring managers and chefs away from restaurants—supermarkets are making efforts to improve their performance. The competition between food service and supermarkets promises to continue to be stiff. Industry Practice Note 6.2, which looks at the impact of this competition on food produce manufacturers, suggests just how intense this competition is.

The Home as Competition

As the baby boomers move into their middle years and greater family responsibilities, the attractions of staying at home increase. When asked which of a dozen items says the most about who you are, Americans 30 years and older put home as number one, ahead of jobs, hobbies, travel, and various personal possessions.[31]

The number of meals purchased at restaurants is growing, according to a leading market researcher, but an increasing proportion of these meals are take-out.[32] Indeed, the home is emerging as an entertainment center. Television watching is the number one leisure activity. A substantial majority of people own a video

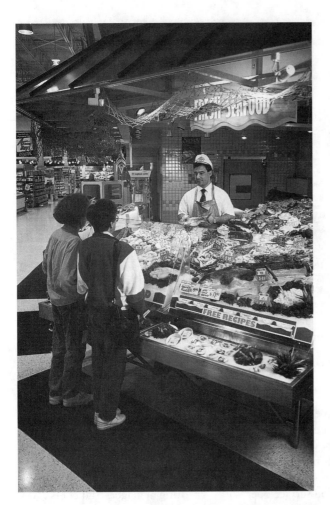

Grocery store deli departments are working hard to increase their share of the food service market.
Courtesy of Publix Super Markets

cassette recorder and make significant use of it. Americans spend 30 percent of their free time watching television and television options are about to explode.[33] Television signals will become digital impulses that can be compressed to send an hour of television in a 5-second squirt of energy. This will enable cable companies to greatly expand consumer choices of entertainment. Cable companies can also offer options such as home shopping and similar services.[34]

The home computer's capabilities are being expanded by manufacturers. On-line computer services such as Prodigy and CompuServe offer functional services such as stock market news and the ability to book your own travel reservations. These services also provide a variety of "chat lines" and other entertainment options.

"The pleasure of leisure," as one authority described it, "is control, and consumers have lost a lot of control in recent years."[35] The home is an environment that

Competition Between Food Service and Grocers Spurs New Product Development

Industry Practice Note 6.2

Food service sales are strong and to food product manufacturers that means a demand for new products from both food service and its competitors. A survey of food product manufacturing executives undertaken by *Prepared Foods* indicated that the shift of consumer food dollars from grocery to restaurant is making the development of new products more urgent.

Over 50 percent of those responding to the survey said that food products for food service operations offer the greatest potential for growth for their companies during the upcoming year. In addition, however, 55 percent said they saw the food service department of supermarkets as an important growth area. Growth in both areas can be attributed to the continuing growth in demand for prepared meals, convenience foods, ready-to-eat, and ready-to-heat items.

Source: Adapted from *Restaurants and Institutions,* March 15, 1998, p. 24.

maximizes consumers' control. It is *their* territory. The pattern of activity that emerges suits itself well to staying home with somebody's take-out meal. It is not surprising that plenty of competitors exist for that business.

The combination of frozen or chilled foods from the supermarket and the microwave offer simple and cost-effective competition with restaurants. The number of households that have a microwave has increased from about 25 percent in 1982 to over 80 percent in 1992 and the principal use of the microwave is for warming food. The growth in take-out and delivery is clearly the restaurant business's response to this freezer case competition.

The future probably offers only more encouragement for "cocooning," as some call the practice of staying at home. *American Demographics,* for instance, predicts that "telephone technology will replace television as the dominant medium worldwide."[36] Although that development will occur gradually over the next few decades, it will undoubtedly be an important part of broadening home entertainment even further.

SUMMARY

In competitive terms, food service chains are operating in a *mature* market characterized by established operations with sophisticated marketing and proven operating formats. Successful independents compete by differentiation or by dominating small specialized markets. In spite of increasing chain market share, the food service market remains a highly competitive one characterized by many buyers and many sellers.

We used the marketing mix to characterize competitive activity in food service. As Product is essentially the guest's experience, all the elements of the operation are important. Food quality is absolutely essential and new food products are a major way of stimulating guest interest and renewing an operation. The product life cycle concept does not mean that established products or concepts die out but, rather, that concepts need to be reinvigorated.

Low Price has been used as a lead variable in the marketing mix but, eventually, competitive prices develop. Consequently, long-term competition is usually focused on nonprice variables. Temporary price cutting, as with coupons, can be effective in the short run, particularly in the off season. Although price reductions risk cheapening the product in the guests' eyes, sometimes market conditions dictate a long-term reduction in price *levels,* as in the case of fine dining at the end of the 1980s, when guests' perceptions of value changes.

Place denotes two somewhat different ideas. *Place* as location involves factors such as traffic and population density and closeness to major attractions. On the other hand, *places* refers to the concept of distribution and of intercept marketing. This involves having operations, sometimes downscaled PODs, available wherever customers choose to go in large numbers.

Promotion is a critical element in the food service marketing mix. Food service is one of the largest advertisers in the United States and advertising is often built around themes that are used in several ads or commercials. Figure 6.3 reviews the major media used, whereas the Internet constitutes a new medium of growing importance. Sales promotion is used to stimulate immediate purchase. Some of its principal tools, usually called deals, are coupons, games, and promotional merchandise. In upscale operations, sales promotion often takes the form of special events. A highly targeted form of sales promotion is aimed at a company's present customers in frequent-guest programs.

Food service must compete with all other consumer products and services but faces particular competitive challenges from C stores, supermarkets, and the comforts and conveniences of home.

◆ KEY WORDS AND CONCEPTS

Marketing mix	Concept blur
Product	Branding
Price	Value pricing
Place	Couponing
Promotion	Off-season pricing
Product as guest's experience	Price cutting as addiction
New products	Location
Life cycle	Distribution

Points of distribution (PODs)
Advertising
Internet
Sales promotion

Competition with other industries
Generic competition
The home as competition

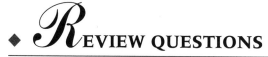

◆ REVIEW QUESTIONS

1. How has the competitive climate changed?

2. What do you mean when you say that the food service product is the guest's experience?

3. What is the role of new products in a competitive strategy?

4. What are the stages of the restaurant life cycle?

5. What are the benefits and risks of value pricing?

6. How is the concept of distribution being used in food service competition?

7. How is the Internet being used in food service competition? What new developments do you anticipate in the use of the Internet in food service competition.

8. When is sales promotion used? What are its principal elements?

9. Discuss the significance of each element of the marketing mix in food service competition in your city. What recent developments strike you as significant in the local competitive scene?

10. What competitive practices have grocery chains in your area engaged in that will affect food service? How do you rate local C store competition against fast food?

11. What factors support the home as an effective competitor?

◆ INTERNET EXERCISES

1. **Site Name:** *McDonalds, Burger King, Taco Bell, Wendys*
   URL: http://www.mcdonalds.com/
   http://www.burgerking.com/
   http://www.tacobell.com/
   http://www.wendys.com/

Background Information: All four major quick-service restaurants (QSRs) have web sites that promote their restaurants.

EXERCISES:

a. Which QSRs advertise promotional merchandise on their web sites?

b. How effective do you believe promotional merchandise is in attracting customers?

c. Which of the major QSRs are running a promotional game?

d. Which QSRs are merchandising new products? If so, how are the new products being merchandised?

e. Do you believe these advertising strategies really work as they are intended to do?

2. **Site Name:** *Foodservice Connection*
   URL: http://www.foodservice.org/
   Background Information: The Foodservice Connection provides a search engine to obtain food and supplies over the Internet. Click on the Online Expo to find the search engine.

EXERCISE:

You are a food service operator who is looking to purchase pies on line. Find three vendors that can provide you with unbaked pies.

 ◆ *N*OTES

1. Ron Paul, "The Squeeze Is On," *TRA Abstracts,* December 1989, p. 2.

2. For an extended discussion of Marriott's decision to leave the restaurant market, see Christopher Muller, "The Marriott Divestment: Leaving the Past Behind," *Cornell Hotel and Restaurant Administration Quarterly,* February 1990, pp. 7–13.

3. The marketing mix is a convenient frame of reference for discussing current competitive practices. Some would argue, however, for other, different definitions and, in fact, the definition we employ evolves from a simple "4Ps" approach to something a bit more complicated. For a brief discussion and critical assessment of the marketing mix, see Christian Gronroos, *Service Management and Marketing* (Lexington, MA: Lexington Books, 1990), pp. 134–136.

4. Nancy Kruse, "Winning the Battle for New Products and New Profits: Strategies and Tactics for New Product Development," *Proceedings of the 18th Annual Chain Operators Exchange* (Chicago: International Foodservice Manufacturers Association, 1991).

5. *Restaurant Business,* May 15, 1997, p. 49.

6. *Nations Restaurant News,* August 18, 1997, p. 8.

7. *Nations Restaurant News,* September 1, 1997, p. 3.

8. *Nations Restaurant News,* September 29, 1997, p. 6.

9. Nicole Castagna, "To Market, to Market," *Restaurants and Institutions,* August 15, 1997, pp. 89–98.

10. The example is taken from Ira J. Blumenthal, "Snapshots of Branding," *Proceedings of the 22nd Annual Chain Operators Exchange* (Chicago: International Foodservice Manufacturers Association, 1995).

11. Melanie Crosbie, "Dual Branding Makes Its Mark," *Restaurants USA,* February 1997, pp. 22–27.

12. *Nations Restaurant News,* August 18, 1997, p. 5.

13. *Advertising Age,* July 21, 1997, p. 1.

14. Roger Hallowell and Leonard A. Schlissenger, *Taco Bell Corp.* (Boston: Harvard Business School, 1991).

15. *Nations Restaurant News,* February 10, 1997, p. 1.

16. Ira J. Blumenthal, "Brand on the Run," *Proceedings of the 21st Annual Chain Operators Exchange* (Chicago: International Foodservice Manufacturers Association, 1994).

17. Geoffrey Godbey, "Time, Work and Leisure: Trends That Will Shape the Hospitality Industry," *Hospitality Research Journal,* Vol. 17, No. 1, pp. 49–58, especially pp. 52–54.

18. *Nations Restaurant News,* October 6, 1997, pp. 3 and 18.

19. Blumenthal, "Snapshots of Branding."

20. *Nations Restaurant News,* October 6, 1997, p. 18.

21. *1997 Restaurant Industry Operations Report* (Washington, DC: National Restaurant Association, 1997).

22. Ibid., pp. 6 and 11.

23. Another form of marketing communications, which is not discussed here, is public relations. This is particularly important to upscale operations.

24. *Nations Restaurant News,* October 13, 1997, p. 2. This theme, according to a company spokesman, targets the "inner child."

25. Jay Iwonoski, "Translating Your Marketing Message," *Restaurants USA,* January 1997, pp. 19–21.

26. Jean Smith, "Feeding Your Face in Cyberspace," *Restaurants USA,* March 1996, pp. 34–36.

27. *Nations Restaurant News,* October 13, 1997, p. 20.

28. *TRA Foodservice Digest/Supermarket Business,* March 1992, p. 25.

29. *Nations Restaurant News,* October 13, 1997, p. 4.

30. Jacqueline Dulen and Kimberly Lowe, "Finding the Perfect Solution," *Restaurants and Institutions,* October 15, 1997, pp. 87–102.

31. *American Demographics,* January 1997, p. 26.

32. Dulen and Lowe, "Finding the Perfect Solution," pp. 88–89. They are quoting Harry Bolzon, a vice president of NDP Group.

33. Jim Spring, "Seven Days of Play," *American Demographics,* May 1993, p. 50.

34. Rebecca Piirto, "Taming the TV Beast," *American Demographics,* March 1993, p. 34.

35. *Wall Street Journal,* November 22, 1989, p. B1.

36. Cheryl Russell, "The Fifth Medium," *American Demographics,* October 1989, p. 2.

Chapter 7

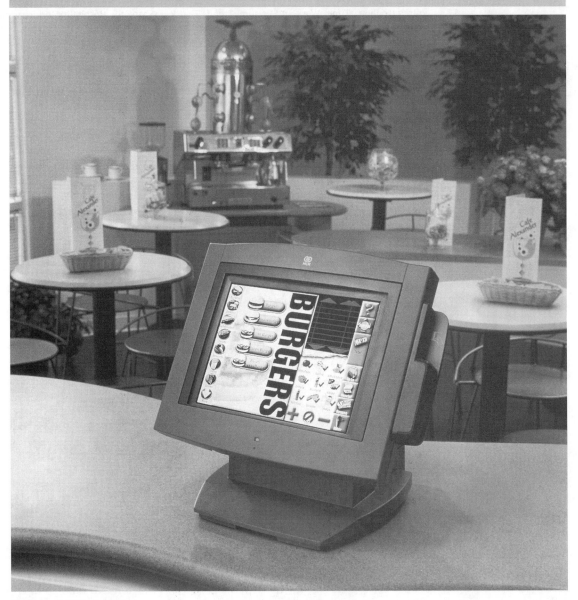

Courtesy of NCR Corporation

Issues Facing Food
Service

The Purpose of This Chapter

This chapter continues our discussion of the factors shaping the food service business. We will consider food service's reaction to a number of pressing issues. Once again, we will begin with the consumer and consumer concerns, such as nutrition, and with the closely related consumerist movement. We will then turn to the impact on food service of rising consumer concern—as well as growing government action—related to the environment. Akin to the environment in many ways is the topic of energy scarcity and energy management. Finally, we will look at the challenges posed by technology and the technological responses to cost and quality problems with which food service now has to contend.

This Chapter Should Help You

1. Recognize consumer concerns for health and nutrition as part of the challenge of planning food service operations

2. Understand the basis of the consumer movement and identify the major issues it raises with regard to food service

3. Become familiar with a rising operational and environmental concern in food service, that of solid waste management, which you are bound to encounter for the rest of your career in the hospitality industry

4. Identify the major impacts of technology on food service from guest ordering and payment to food production and information management

171

*C*ONSUMER CONCERNS

During the 1980s, health, diet, nutrition, and exercise were prime topics of concern for food service customers. Although consumers are still concerned about these topics, the level of concern appears to have declined. Participation in exercise and strenuous activity, for instance, has declined slightly since 1992, while the percentage of people who reported no physical exercise increased moderately.[1]

A study by the American Dietetics Association suggests that it is taste, not health, that motivates the eating habits of a majority of Americans. Seventy-nine percent of those in the survey acknowledged that nutrition had a major impact on health, but only 39 percent of that group said they were doing all they could to eat healthily. Furthermore, only a third said they take care to eat a balanced diet.[2]

A "fat replacement technology" has been developed for some foods, substituting ingredients that simulate the taste of fat in products such as ice cream. Consumer reaction to this product suggests the market is much more interested in "real" taste. Operators report the product is limited to a special health-conscious niche and is not widely accepted by the public. McDonald's low-fat hamburger, "McLean Deluxe," was only kept alive by corporate policy. Sales were so poor that it was dubbed "McFlop"; in 1993, it accounted for only 2 percent of sales.[3] McDonald's kept the "McLean" around until 1996, but similar products were dropped by competitors a year or two after their introduction because of a lack of demand.[4]

Nutrition

We Americans are given to extremes, and periodically the Puritan in our character seems to take over. The heightened concern with health and nutrition may have hit an extreme in the 1980s, but there is still a substantial awareness of these issues. For instance, a 1996 survey showed that an overwhelming majority of 85 percent of survey respondents said they believed that people who exercise regularly live longer; almost 75 percent said exercisers are happier and 71 percent felt they are more attractive than nonexercisers.[5] On the other hand, *Restaurants and Institutions* says many experts speculate that people are just tired of all the nutritional doomsday warnings and have figuratively thrown up their hands and adopted an "I just don't care" attitude.[6]

Whatever the state of Americans' minds may be, *American Demographics* reports that "overweight has become more prevalent among all age groups. Americans seem to be losing interest in weight loss diets." Former Surgeon General C. Everett Koop, best known for his long battle against cigarettes, said that if he had stayed in office longer he "would have launched the same assault on obesity" that he did on cigarettes.[7]

The percentage of Americans who have been on a weight loss diet decreased between 1986 and 1996 from 10 percent to 8 percent for men, and from 20 percent to 16 percent for women. Some suggest that women have gone from trying to manage their weight—an extremely frustrating business—to managing their "body image" and accepting more realistic ideals of body image.[8]

The evidence suggests that some of the message on healthy eating is getting through to Americans. Beef consumption fell 14 percent (although it now seems to be increasing in popularity again). The consumption of chicken—a lower-fat alternative—jumped 37 percent to 46 pounds per capita in the 10 years ending in 1994. Fruit consumption increased 12 percent and vegetable consumption rose 14 percent; experts expect those healthful patterns will continue for the next 10 years. It seems, however, that Americans may just be eating more of everything, both "good for you" and otherwise.

Some part of the overweight problem relates to the way in which our society is developing. The way we live is physically less demanding than it was a generation or two ago. From automobiles to TV remotes, we consume fewer calories in our everyday living. There are fewer physically demanding jobs and more jobs that involve sitting in front of a computer screen or at a desk. In addition, more and more of our foods are refined and require less energy to digest. The biggest villain is fat. Americans eat more french fries than they do fresh potatoes! Moreover, as we noted at the beginning of this section, there hasn't been an increase in recreational exercise to make up for a more sedentary lifestyle. Under the circumstances, the increase in obesity, however distressing, is not particularly surprising.

Dietary Schizophrenia.   Customers talk a good game but do not always follow their commitments in practice. When a salt-free soup was brought out, for instance, it failed initially for lack of consumer acceptance. We live in a time when, whatever people say, consumer behavior actually supports the rapid growth of stores specializing in high-butter-fat ice cream and when doughnut stores have become a major fast-food category. As one observer put it,

> While healthful food habits can contribute to a better life for young and old alike, for many consumers, there appears to be a disconnect between attitudes and behavior . . . professing great interest in healthy eating, but not following healthful food behavior in real life at least not in their purchases of food away from home.[9]

Perhaps we can best sum up the symptoms of **dietary schizophrenia** by saying that consumers are concerned about their health—and about pleasing themselves. Sometimes they act on their concerns—and sometimes on their need for pleasure. Accordingly, food service operations must be ready to serve either interest.

Industry Response.   Restaurants are not in the preaching business and so consumers do tend to get what they want. Just as salad bars and low-fat foods were developed in response to heightened dietary concerns in the 1980s, today operators are responding to customers, particularly the younger ones, who want more to eat. Wendy's Big Bacon Classic weighs in at 700 calories. Harvey's introduced a new sandwich in 1995, the Monster Burger, which provides 970 calories and 67 grams of fat. Burger King sells about 4.6 million Whoppers daily—each with 730 calories and 24 grams of fat. In contrast to the fat-heavy burgers, Taco Bell introduced a new line of low-fat tacos and burritos in 1995, spending $20 million on advertising the new line and giving away 8 million samples of the product. It was the biggest product launch in Taco Bell's history. The original eight products were quickly cut to three and when the chain's overall sales began to drop, the company abandoned the campaign.[10]

Restaurants and Institutions summed up one aspect of the restaurants' situation in this way: "Hardees, McDonalds and other chains have learned the hard way, that people may pay lip service to eating low fat food but most customers still opt for what tastes good. And what tastes good usually contains more fat."[11]

On the other hand, there are still plenty of people who are concerned about nutrition. As one operator put it, "You've got to leave alternatives. We don't want a group of people in our office, for example, getting ready to go to lunch and someone saying 'We can't go there. They don't have anything I can eat.' "[12]

Efforts such as the McLean Deluxe, which relied on substituting a seaweed derivative for fat, have been replaced by a strategy of offering products such as chicken and potatoes that are, in themselves, low in fat. Although Harvey's Monster Burger has a brisk demand, the company also offers a no-fat side dish of gravy and mashed potatoes that fits well with its skinless chicken product. Wendy's, too, offers a skinless chicken sandwich and baked potatoes—with or without fat-rich toppings—as an alternative to french fries.

> Restaurants follow consumer preferences wherever they lead—which often means they go in different directions at the same time. "The issue for the large majority of consumers," however, as a leading market researcher put it, "is clearly taste and flavor."[13]

Consumerism. Many of the concerns of individual consumers, such as health, fitness, and nutrition, are shared by lots of consumers. Some of these concerns have been selected by organized interest groups as important to consumer education, to raise the consumer's consciousness: This is **consumerism.** American consumerism has been around since the mid-19th century, and can be defined as follows:

> Consumerism is, first of all, a social movement. It is a movement by which society, through representative groups and individuals, seeks social change. Consumerism has as its specific objective to achieve a balance of power between buyers and sellers. It is an effort to equalize the rights of buyers with the rights of sellers.[14]

In view of its increasing size and visibility, the hospitality industry attracts plenty of attention from consumer groups. A sampling of hospitality issues typically raised by consumerists may lead to a better understanding of how consumerism can affect the food service field. Our discussion will include complaints about junk food, labeling, truth in dining, problems related to sanitation, and alcohol abuse.

Peter Drucker called consumerism "the shame of marketing." Consumerism, he feels, reflects business's almost exclusive emphasis on selling (which begins with "our product" and how to sell it) instead of on "marketing," which begins with the consumers' needs and expectations and moves toward supplying products that meet those needs.

Consumerism is also the opportunity of marketing. It will force businesses to become market focused in their actions as well as their pronouncements. Developing a positive response to consumerist sentiment is probably more effective than resentment and resistance. There is truth in the old adage, "If you can't fight 'em, join 'em."[15]

Junk Food and a Hectic Pace

One of the principal indictments by consumerists against food service (and especially against fast food and vending) is that it purveys nutritionless "junk food." Although fast food does pose some nutritional problems, the junk-food charge is just not true. The charge may say more about American food habits than about the nutritional adequacy of the food itself.

A typical meal at McDonald's—a hamburger, french fries, and milk shake—provides nearly one-third of the recommended dietary allowance (RDA), or the equivalent of what a standard school lunch provides, with, however, a deficiency in vitamins A and C. The deficiency in these two vitamins can be remedied somewhat if the customer switches from a hamburger to a Big Mac, which contains the necessary lettuce and tomato slices. If the customer chooses to have a salad, the dietary deficiency is no longer a problem.

Consumer demand is what drives food service growth. Delivery services provide one method of meeting the public's need for convenience.
Courtesy of Domino's Pizza, Inc.

Some critics just don't seem to like fast food at all. They charge that "fast foods, with their abundance of useless calories and sugar" (the junk-food charge) are really a part of the problem of Americans' poor diet. Their description:

> Meals should be taken in a leisurely way, with personal interaction. . . . [People who opt for fast foods are being] dehumanized—they are becoming more like automobiles driving up to a gas station and being refilled. . . . The ubiquitous multimillion dollar advertising campaigns, particularly the millions spent on television advertising, has greatly influenced the public in the direction of fast foods.[16]

Two problems here go beyond the junk-food issue. These critics believe they know what is good for people (which, in a medical sense, they may), and they resent the fact that people choose to disregard their expert advice. The main criticism, however, is really of Americans' poor eating habits, notably "the quick pace inherent in our society."

Whatever else is true, the duty of the American restaurant business in a market economy is to serve consumers not to reform them. It is difficult, however, for the hospitality industry to deal with this kind of criticism, in which the industry becomes a scapegoat for the annoyance that some feel at a simple economic reality: The food service within the reach of most pocketbooks uses food service systems that are not (and cannot be) labor intensive. They use preparation methods that are quick and unskilled, hence, inexpensive. Fast food is fast because, all in all, that is what many consumers want.

The second problem raised is that of the effect of advertising on consumer behavior. This issue reflects an old and complex debate in the general field of marketing. From our earlier discussion of contemporary menu patterns, it is clear that restaurants are interested in offering only what the guests want, not in forcing something on them. For example, notice that the decor and atmosphere in specialty restaurants have been growing warmer and friendlier to meet earlier criticisms of coldness and austerity. In addition, salad bars and packaged salads were added because that is what consumers wanted. That is, the weight of consumer opinion is usually felt in the marketplace. Change in business institutions comes, of course, more slowly than consumerists would like; particularly, in competitive industries such as food service, change comes only when it is clear that the consumer wants it. To some degree, the consumerists' demands for quick change reflect an antibusiness bias, which some consumerists seem to have. Their background is often in government or academic life, and maybe they don't understand how businesses really operate. Many seem to prefer a command economy (with their preferences ruling) to a market economy where, in the long run, consumers' preferences rule.

The junk-food criticism will not just go away, however. Field studies suggest that many guests do not follow the Big Mac–fries–milk shake meal profile referred to earlier. For instance, to save money or suit their tastes, many customers replace the milk shake with a soft drink, and the result is a meal with less than one-third the recommended dietary allowance. In addition, although they appeal to a minority of customers, salads are clearly not the number one seller in fast food. Moreover, a number of chains are under fire from consumerists for continuing to use beef fat (which is rich in saturated fat) for some products, especially french fries. We should note, however, that, in response to consumers' concerns, most chains have shifted to vegetable shortening for most frying.

Nutritional Labeling

The **Nutrition Labeling and Education Act** (NLEA) was passed in 1990, but the restaurant industry was largely exempted from it by the **Food and Drug Administration (FDA)**. In 1996, however, the Center for Science in the Public Interest (CSPI) was successful in a suit in federal court against the FDA. Consequently, as of May 1997, restaurants are covered by the NLEA. The NLEA applies only to menu listings that make nutrient or health claims.

> Nutrient claims make a statement about a specific nutrient or food component of a menu item or meal. A nutrient claim typically includes such words as "reduced," "free" or "low." Claims such as "low in fat" or "cholesterol free" are common nutrient claims. In addition, using the word "fresh" is considered a nutrient claim because there is a strict definition of what constitutes a "fresh" food item.[17]

Table 7.1 shows a listing of words that might be part of a **nutrient claim.** Significantly, use of symbols such as a heart or an apple to signify healthful menu items are also covered by the regulation.

A **health claim** ties the food or meal with health status or disease prevention. A health claim usually relates to and mentions a specific disease. The government has approved only the seven health claims described in Industry Practice Note 7.1, which the FDA has determined to be scientifically documented.

Notice that one way a restaurant can avoid this regulation is simply by avoiding nutrient or health claims on its menu. Moreover, if a claim is made, the restaurant need not publish the information on the menu. It must, however, have a "printed

---

Table 7.1 Language of Nutrient Claims

You need to have documentation if your menu uses any of the following words or symbols representing these words:

- Free
- Low
- Reduced
- Light/Lite
- Provides/Contains/Good Source of
- High/Excellent Source of/Rich in
- Lean/Extra-Lean
- Fresh
- Natural
- Healthy

Source: Restaurants USA, October 1996, p. 38.

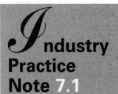

Defining Health Claims

Industry Practice Note 7.1

The following seven food and health/disease connections are the only ones for which the government allows health claims to be made. In order to make health claims on menus, restaurateurs must follow specific guidelines as to wording.

◆ Fiber-containing fruits, vegetables, and grains in relation to cancer-prevention claims

◆ Fruits and vegetables in relation to cancer-prevention claims

◆ Fiber-containing fruits, vegetables, and grains in relation to heart-disease-prevention claims

◆ Fat in relation to cancer

◆ Saturated fat and cholesterol in relation to heart disease

◆ Sodium in relation to high blood pressure (hypertension)

◆ Calcium in relation to osteoporosis

Source: Restaurants USA, October 1996, p. 38.

backup that the staff can refer to quickly."[18] Finally, the only thing that must be documented is the claim on the menu. Thus, if a claim is made as to the number of calories, that claim must be documented but there is no need to document other aspects of the menu item such as the number of grams of fat or the amount of salt.

The restaurant is required to have a "reasonable basis" for its belief that the claim made is true. Restaurants can use computer databases, U.S. Department of Agriculture (USDA) handbooks, cookbooks, or other "reasonable sources" to determine nutrient levels.

Although the Center for Science in the Public Interest (CSPI) views the NLEA as a good first step, a spokesperson for the Center notes what CSPI regards as several weaknesses in the present legislation.[19] In manufactured food products, all labels must contain the standard ingredient and nutrient information, but in a restaurant, the customer must ask for documentation. Otherwise, the restaurant need not provide it. As a practical matter, however, most restaurants make this information continually available in a pamphlet and have for some years. The requirement did, however, place a new burden on independents.

A second problem the CSPI cites is the narrowness of the regulation. As noted earlier, the information made available need relate only to *claims made* rather than providing a complete nutrient profile for the item. This can result in "weak and misleading" information. Moreover, the "reasonable standard" is very loose in the CSPI's view. Simply adding up the ingredients in a recipe—which may or may not be followed closely—is not enough in their view.

Finally, the FDA has made it clear that it will not be involved in enforcement of the NLEA in restaurants. It will leave enforcement to state and local authorities. Given the huge number of restaurants and the FDA's limited resources, this is hardly a surprising decision but it does suggest the strong possibility of somewhat uneven enforcement.

The official position of the CSPI remains that stated by its executive director, Michael Jacobsen, in 1993: "Every diner has a right to know as much about the foods they eat in restaurants as those they buy in grocery stores."[20] Although this is still the CSPI's formal position, it is not a current priority in regulatory or legislative lobbying by the Center. The composition of Congress in the last half of the 1990s makes such a goal impractical—for the moment.

Almost certainly, however, the industry has not heard the last of this issue. Should the composition of Congress or the climate of official opinion change, the CSPI will undoubtedly be pressing once again for stricter disclosure standards for restaurants.

Sanitation

As with so many consumer issues, **sanitation** involves government regulations—in this case, as embodied in public health officers and inspectors. With the increasing use of off-premise, prepared foods, the incidence of food poisoning in public accommodations has been rising steeply. The kinds of sanitary precautions associated with food service systems that prepare food, freeze or chill it, and then transport it elsewhere. First, the risks of thawing and spoilage are high. Second, the food is handled by more people. Some operators resist the increased emphasis on sanitation but most have accepted—many enthusiastically—the need to upgrade sanitation practices and to establish and enforce high sanitation standards. The Educational Foundation of the National Restaurant Association has pioneered the development of sanitation educational materials and programs and has trained several million workers and certified over 800,000 managers.[21]

It is quite clear that, for the most part, the industry and those calling for the highest standards of sanitation are in the same camp. This is not surprising because, as one industry leader put it, "a single mention of an incident in an evening news broadcast can shake public confidence in a national chain or a hometown restaurant."[22] Sizzler Restaurants, for instance, had just three instances of food-borne illness—in restaurants that were well run and scored well on sanitation inspections. The resulting bad publicity led to a loss in sales of 30 percent and, ultimately, the closing of 40 restaurants. Moreover, the advertising budget was increased by $4 million to try to counteract the unfavorable publicity.[23] Restaurants have a real survival stake in good sanitation.

Hazard Analysis and Critical Control Points. The best comprehensive approach to sanitation programs reflects a shift in thinking about sanitation from an inspection system that is largely reactive to one that takes a systematic approach to the prevention of food safety problems. In one sense, **hazard analysis and critical**

control points (HACCP) is just the application of good common sense to the production of safe food. The elements of an HACCP program are: (1) Possible avenues of hazard are identified; (2) appropriate preventive controls are designed and installed; (3) the controls are monitored and records kept to ensure that the system is working properly; and (4) when problems occur, they are identified and promptly corrected.[24]

The HACCP approach is at the heart of both "Servsafe," the sanitation training program developed by the Educational Foundation of the NRA, and the inspection system for food products developed by the Food and Drug Administration. Consumers rely on food safety in restaurants as a basic article of faith. It takes hard and continuing effort to fulfill that trust.

Alcohol and Dining

The many fatal accidents that have been attributed to driving under the influence of alcohol have given the hospitality industry a wide-ranging set of problems. In many jurisdictions, restaurants and bars that sell drinks to people who are later involved in accidents are now being held legally responsible for damages. The result has been, among other things, a great rise in liability insurance rates. Laws have been proposed—and in many jurisdictions passed—making illegal the "happy hours" and other advertised price reductions on the sale of drinks. In addition, in a less strictly legal sense, operators have been concerned about the image of their operations and the industry in general.

The industry's response has generally been swift and positive. One idea is "designated driver" programs. Designated drivers agree not to drink and to drive for the whole group they are with. Many operators recognize designated drivers with a badge and reward them with free soft drinks—and a certificate good for a free drink at their next visit. Alcohol awareness training—teaching bartenders and servers how to tell when people have had too much to drink and how to deal with them—is also becoming more common. If you work in an operation that serves alcohol, be sure to find out what the establishment's policy is regarding service to intoxicated guests—or those who might be intoxicated. You should do this not only because you will want to follow the house policy but because it will help you to understand better the industry's response to a complicated problem.

Consumers are drinking less, and this has posed problems for many operators. Because sales of alcoholic beverages usually carry a much higher profit than food sales, reduction in alcohol consumption has seriously affected profitability. The marketing response that has helped many operators is the development of a whole line of colorful and tasty "mocktails," which are made without alcohol. Featuring "lite" beers and wines also caters to the guest's desire to hold down caloric and alcohol intake and helps maintain sales. There has been a 900 percent increase in per capita consumption of bottled water since 1976, when bottled water was thought of as something to drink in a foreign country. Bottled water replaces not only alcoholic beverages but is often drunk instead of coffee. In 1994, consumers drank almost half as much bottled water as they did coffee (2.1 gallons per capita).[25]

Alcoholic beverages are a high-profit item, but alcohol-related accidents have also made them a high-risk product.
Courtesy of NCR Corporation

$\mathcal{F}$OOD SERVICE AND THE ENVIRONMENT

"Saving the environment" generates a great deal of concern and enthusiasm—and rightly so. Our purpose here, however, is to think about the impact of the environmental movement on food service. The view we will adopt, not surprisingly, is that of the business community, which looks at environmental proposals in terms of costs and benefits.

It can be difficult to discuss the environment because the concept is so broadly defined. For some, it includes water conservation, elimination of aerosols (which damage the earth's atmosphere), avoidance of animal testing by manufacturers of guest amenities, use of foods that have been naturally fertilized and have not been grown using pesticides, planting trees, and saving the rainforests. All of these activities are doubtlessly meritorious and praiseworthy, but it is hard to see individual operations having a great impact in such broad contexts. Not only that but a notion of the environment that is so broad and multifaceted makes it difficult to focus on the problems where food service can make a really strong contribution to the struggle to save the environment. We certainly cannot afford to be indifferent to the problems of the environment as it is more globally defined. In this chapter, however, we want to examine and understand problems that are a threat and need to be dealt with at the unit level.

Restaurants and food service in general are basically a clean industry rather than a polluting one. It is true that in some settings restaurants are faulted for creating traffic or noise problems. A few neighborhoods have objected to cooking odors coming from kitchen exhausts. These, however, are exceptional rather than everyday concerns. There are areas, however, in which food service faces, at the unit level, a serious environmental problem. Along with other businesses and every household in America, **solid-waste disposal**–otherwise called garbage—is a problem whose time has come. Garbage is not only an environmental problem but an operational problem, as well. The cost of conventional waste disposal is rising and, because of the scarcity of landfills, is more than likely to continue to increase.

Thinking about Garbage: From Dump to Waste Stream

Not very long ago, garbage was taken to the dump—and dumped—and nobody thought much about the management issues involved. As the pressure of population, an ever richer economy, and a "throwaway society" interacted, however, problems of groundwater contamination, rodent infestation, toxic substances, and smell, to name a few, gave rise to a concern over the safety of what we now call a **sanitary landfill.** A first-class dump—that is, a sanitary landfill—costs something over $500,000 an acre to build. Specialized facilities designed to handle toxic substances, such as ash from incinerators, cost even more. To prevent groundwater contamination, a sanitary landfill is lined with clay or a synthetic liner and is equipped with a groundwater monitoring system. Because rotting garbage produces an explosive gas, landfills have methane collection systems. To keep down the smell as well as the insects and rats, the day's garbage is covered with a layer of dirt each night.[26]

Sanitary landfills are expensive to build and maintain. More important, it is now hard to find new dump sites because communities really don't want them in their own backyards. In fact, in recent years, the number of landfill sites has dropped dramatically.

Americans generate about 3½ pounds of garbage per person every day (from 50 to 100 percent more than other countries with similar standards of living). That is about 100 pounds a week for a family of four, or 2½ tons per year. The pressure not only from businesses but from households puts an increasing load on a declining number of landfills. The "tipping cost" (the cost to tip the contents of a garbage truck into a landfill) has doubled in a number of cities, and the Fresh Kills landfill, at 2.8 billion cubic feet of waste, has become the highest point of "land" on the East Coast and threatens to displace the Great Wall of China (3.6 billion cubic feet) as the world's largest structure.

The Fresh Kills Landfill is the largest man-made "structure" on the Eastern seaboard. It takes New York City's trash and is almost filled to capacity.
Courtesy of AP/Wide World

Just at the point where the demand for landfill space is rising and the supply of such space is declining, another complication arises—public attitudes. The American public views environmental issues as one of the key issues of the day. Environmentally concerned citizens are also food service customers, and their strong views need to be taken into account. In fact, opinion surveys show that environmentally concerned people make up about half the population—and they are both the highest in income and the best educated. Restaurants' interest in the solid-waste problem, then, is driven by a concern to be responsible citizens, by the concerns of their best customers, and by exploding waste-removal costs. As a result, we have replaced the concept of the dump, where things are dropped and forgotten, with that of a waste stream, which needs to be managed.

Managing the Waste Stream

A study conducted at the University of Wisconsin–Stout gives us a good idea of the composition of the food service **waste stream.** Institutional food service and table service restaurants generate about 1 pound of waste per meal served, whereas fast food generates roughly 1⅓ pounds per meal.[27] Table 7.2 shows the types and proportions of waste generated by the major categories of food service.[28]

As we set out to consider how the waste stream is to be managed, a word of caution is in order. The public perception of environmentally effective action is not necessarily consistent from year to year. In some cases, popular environmental views don't always make physical sense. "In 1976, when McDonald's switched from paper to polystyrene packaging for its burgers," for instance, "it was hailed as an environmentally wise decision. The public was worried about cutting trees and the energy that paper production consumed."[29] When McDonald's switched back to paper 15 years later, it was hailed as an environmental victory; but the case for this being so is subject to debate. Public perception, then, as well as scientific fact, needs to be taken into consideration.

The techniques available to deal with the **waste stream** can be summarized in three words: **reduce, reuse, and recycle.** These are the ideal solutions, but the facts of life require our list to be expanded to include composting, incineration, and the use of landfills. Figure 7.1 summarizes these techniques and we will examine each of them briefly.

Table 7.2 Contents of the Food Service Waste Stream by Food Service Type

Type of Waste	Proportion of Waste Stream for		
	Institutional	Table Service	Fast Food
Paper	40%	44%	65%
Plastic	23	16	17
Food	23	21	5
Glass	5	12	4
Tin	8	3	6
Aluminum	1	4	3

Source: Data adapted from Peter A. D'Souza and Leland L. Nicholls, "Waste Management: The Priority for the 1990's," Technical Paper, University of Wisconsin–Stout, n.d.

1. **Reduce**
2. **Reuse**
3. **Recycle**
4. **Compost**
5. **Incinerate**
6. **Landfill**

Figure 7.1 Techniques for managing the waste stream.

Reduce. Increasingly, the public is glad to be offered the possibility of receiving a product without wrapping or a bag, and some fast-food companies are offering customers sandwiches without their customary paper wrapping. Often, it is possible to switch to a less bulky form of packaging—from cardboard to paper, for instance. Companies are also insisting that suppliers provide product in packaging that minimizes waste.

McDonald's switch back to paper reduced the volume of packaging waste by 90 percent. We need to note, however, that the plastic-laminated paper it now uses is likely to decay only very, very slowly, if at all, in a landfill.

Thus, although a reduction in bulk was realized by McDonald's decision, it is questionable whether the overall environmental impact has been positive or not. In fact, the president of McDonald's USA at that time indicated the switch took place not because the plastic form of packaging was an inferior material but because customers "don't feel good about it."[30]

Reuse. Another seemingly appealing strategy for many operations is a switch from disposables to permanent ware (reusable china or plastic dinnerware). This would reduce dramatically paper and plastic waste. The problems this "solution" creates, however, suggest once again how important it is not to oversimplify. Restaurants built to rely on disposables have no space to locate a dishroom or china storage. If they remodeled to put it in, the cost would be exorbitant, and space would probably have to come from customer seating—with reduced sales as the result. A heavy expenditure resulting in reduced sales would bankrupt many restaurants. Even if we assume, implausibly, that such a development could take place, the result of all the additional water discharged would cause the city sewage system, quite literally, to "explode." A dishwasher, after all, requires from 70 to 500 gallons of water per hour to operate. Such an increase in dishwashing would also result in thermal pollution of rivers from the hot water and chemical pollution from the very strong soaps used in dishwashing.

Other forms of reuse are more practical. Products can be bought in containers that can be returned to the manufacturers for reuse or reused in the operation. Instead of discarding skids in a warehouse or commissary, most are now being built to stand up to reuse.

The major opportunities available from a strategy of reducing and reusing appear to lie with changes in the way products are purchased. Minimizing unnecessary packaging, eliminating the use of toxic dyes or other substances that make a

Source separation is a first step in recycling.
Courtesy of Mobil Chemical Corp.

package hard to recycle, and using recycled products or recycling containers all contribute to a reduction in the total waste stream.

Recycle.   A substantial amount of recycling is already going on in food service. Metal, paper cardboard, and glass are already established as recyclables. We should note, however, that, in recycling, all metals are not equal. Steel cans can be and are usefully recycled, but the advantages are nowhere near as great as they are for aluminum cans. In fact, it's now cheaper to recycle aluminum than it is to mine bauxite, the ore from which aluminum is extracted.

The key factor in recycling is its economics. True, the materials in the waste stream have some value, but the basic driving force is the rise in landfill costs. Although some communities still have adequate landfill space, the evidence suggests that waste trucked in from distant cities will, in time, fill these. Overall, landfill costs, as we noted earlier, are rising; and for large metropolitan areas, landfill availability is literally disappearing.

Recycling, however, requires considerable effort. Think about the case of fast-food waste. If we want to recycle, it will be necessary to sort the waste into recyclable categories. Some operators, particularly institutions, are using consumer sorting. Consumers may be asked to use different bins for glass, paper, plastic, and food waste. Let us assume that we decide to persuade our customers to sort paper, plastic, and food waste into separate containers. New bins—taking up additional floor space—must be installed and a suitable "training program" set up for our guests. This educational effort would almost certainly include special signage showing the guest what was expected, and tray liners and posters explaining why we're

The SPI plastic coding system is a method of labeling all plastic containers with a code which identifies their primary resin. The purpose of the code system is to help in sorting plastic products by resin for recycling. Not all plastics are the same, so for recycling of plastic to be successful, they must be sorted by resin in order to be reused in the manufacture of products. The plastic codes most often will be located on the bottom of the product. There are seven different resin codes.

PLASTIC MATERIAL CODE SYSTEM

PETE	**HDPE**	**V** (3)
Polyethylene Terephthalate	High Density Polyethylene	Vinyl or Polyvinyl Chloride
LDPE (4)	**PP** (5)	**PS** (6)	**OTHER** (7)
Low Density Polyethylene	Polypropylene	Polysytrene	All Other Resins and Multiple and Blend Resins

The SPI coding is a national system which is necessary to maintain consistency throughout both the plastics manufacturing and plastics recycling industries. Regional recyclers must have the confidence that the coding symbol on the bottom of a container always means the same thing.

Figure 7.2 Society of the Plastics Industry (SPI) coding system.
(*Source: Environmental Issues* (Norwalk, CN: James River Corporation, Dixie Product Business, September 1990).)

undertaking this effort. At least during the start-up period, some personal "assistance" to explain the process—and solicit people's support—would probably be required. The trash will then very likely have to be resorted either by an employee, by the waste hauler, or by the recycler. Thus, sorting, alone, requires considerable time and effort. Plastics, moreover, will need to be further sorted according to resin type, using the codes shown in Figure 7.2.

The storage we presently have is probably a dumpster with perhaps a second container for corrugated boxes. Under the new regimen, however, we will need separate containers for several categories of waste. They certainly won't fit into the present back of the house so they will almost certainly have to be crowded into the loading dock area, which may require some redesign to make everything fit and still have room for delivery trucks.

This is not the end of the complications. We probably at present have only one

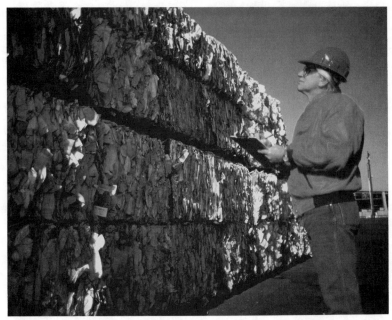

Once separated, trash can be baled and sent to the recycling facility.
Courtesy of Mobil Chemical Corp.

hauler—"the garbage truck." That company does everything for us with one truck. Under the new arrangements, different haulers might be required: one for paper, another for metal, and so forth. Even assuming one company does all of the work, the truck that does the hauling will have to have multiple compartments, or possibly the hauler will have to use more than one truck, each designed for different parts of the waste stream. Because the technology of sorting garbage is changing rapidly, it may be that much more of the sorting will be done at recycling centers in future years. This could significantly reduce the restaurant's labor cost in sorting and make recycling more attractive.

As we have noted, the advantage to the restaurant of recycling is financial—the hauling fees for recycling are less than the tipping fees at the landfill. A further major advantage is that of public relations. Customers are concerned about the environment and are likely to react favorably to firms that are leaders or solid performers in the environmental arena.

Compost. **Composting** refers to the collection and processing of food trimmings, scraps, and leftovers. Small-scale composting has been going on in rural areas (and backyards) for centuries. However, as a large-scale movement affecting all of society, it is still in its infancy.

Because of the wet, dense nature of food waste, it must be combined for composting with a bulking agent such as leaves, wood chips, or shredded paper to allow for air circulation. The material is placed in rows and, in most present-day applications, a front-end loader is used to turn the material periodically to maintain exposure to the air. More mechanized plants to manage the composting process will undoubtedly become common in the future. Finished compost can be used as potting soil or to enrich a garden or the soil around trees or bushes. Thus, the revenues derived are likely to be modest. Nevertheless, test programs report a reduction in garbage removal costs of 50 percent and more because of costs saved by avoiding landfill fees.[31]

Incinerate.   **Incineration,** unfortunately, creates environmental problems of its own. One principal concern is air pollution; however, it does appear that technical advances in scrubber systems and combustion control make it possible to overcome these problems in properly managed systems.[32] As no management system is perfect, what this means is that, in practice, air pollution control may not be perfect. Because the air pollutants can include heavy metals, acid that leads to acid rain, and poisonous dioxin, this is no small issue.

A second problem is that 25 percent of the product remains as ash after incineration and must be placed in a landfill. Because the ash contains toxic pollutants, the danger of eventual leaching into groundwater is a serious one.[33] Specialized landfill sites with extra protection against leaching are needed.

A further concern put forward by environmentalists is the contribution that incineration can make to the greenhouse effect. Where the only alternative to incineration is dumping in a landfill, this concern is misplaced. Landfills generate methane, which traps heat radiation and, hence, contributes more to the greenhouse effect than would the gases given off by incineration. If, however, the alternative to incineration is recycling, recycling would be preferred both because of its environmental impact (air quality and elimination of ash) and because of its significantly lower cost to the community and to individual businesses.[34]

Landfill.   The least preferred, but most commonly used method of disposal is the **landfill.** They are costly to construct and maintain and are potentially long-term environmental hazards. They hide rather than dispose of the trash, which decays only very slowly and imperfectly under the landfill's conditions of lack of oxygen and moisture. As noted, they can contribute to a worsening of the greenhouse effect. It appears that the scarcity of landfills may eventually drive the cost of this method of disposal beyond what most operations can afford.

Fortunately for food service operators, residential recycling programs being set up by municipalities and other governmental agencies may eventually create the channels of collection, redistribution, and processing necessary to make large-scale recycling work. As our discussion makes clear, moving toward recycling is no simple matter. Managing the waste stream will almost certainly be a concern that touches your career, so it is good to have a broad understanding of it.

𝒯ECHNOLOGY

Some years ago, a researcher looked into the future of food service, and this is what he saw:

The restaurant of the future will be automated. One individual will be capable of running a 10,000-meal-a-day commissary. Computer-controlled, automated equipment will run the food processing operation from storeroom to cleanup as well as take care of inventory control and the reordering process. In addition, the computer will handle all records, write all necessary business reports (including the annual report), forecast requirements, and perform all cost accounting duties.

Customers will dine in a computer-manipulated environment of aromatic and visual stimuli. They will stand before lighted menus picturing various entrees and punch out selections at order stations. Within 2½ minutes, they will be served the meal via conveyor belt running with the wall and stopping at the proper table. Dish busing commences upon the customer arising from the seat. Dirty dishes move onto a conveyor belt within an adjacent wall. The dishwashing process is completely automated. A 200-seat restaurant will require four employees and a manager.[35]

If technology can put an astronaut on the moon, it can surely bus tables. However, it's not what is technically possible that counts; it's what makes economic sense. In the foreseeable future, even in the face of steeply rising wages, the 10,000-meal-a-day commissaries that come into use will require a good many more employees, because it will make economic sense. Although a computer-operated food production, storage, and cleanup system is theoretically possible, it would be like using a computer just to add up a grocery bill. Less-expensive methods are available.

On the other hand, touch screen ordering stations, such as the one pictured at the beginning of the chapter, have become a reality, although they are more commonly used for servers to place orders than by guests. Even where they are available for use by guests, an alternative interpersonal ordering system is also available.

We hear reports of "six-armed robots" being designed for use in food service; but even if this six-armed fellow replaced three full-time workers, it would take five years for the savings to pay for the investment—if the repair bills were not too high. Moreover, how will people feel about giving their order to a robot out of a science fiction film, taking their food from it, and having it clean up after them? As a novelty, it sounds interesting—but for steady diet, people may need quite a lot of time to get used to it, much less like it.

Although the computerized environment described previously or a fully automated food production system are unlikely to emerge in the foreseeable future, labor costs give mechanization and automation an appeal to operators. Much of the change in equipment is incremental, that is, small improvements that make the kind of equipment we presently use even better. These applications of technology include better energy control and more mechanization of existing equipment to make control of the production process easier. Examples include timers on fryers and moving belts in ovens. In addition, in almost every area of food service, the potentially revolutionary elements of technological change loom larger than they did just a few years ago. We will look briefly at developments in customer ordering and payment systems, food production, alternative unit designs, and information systems.

Enhancing Customer Service

Guest Ordering.   Although we are not likely to see customers being waited on by anything resembling a robot, the ability to serve people is being enhanced by electronics and computerization. Handheld computer terminals are used by wait-resses and waiters to take orders at tableside automatically and instantly convey the order to the kitchen. Computers speed service, give servers more time to spend with guests, or permit servers to serve more guests. Computer terminals are especially helpful where the service area is remote from the kitchen. Whatever kind of order-ing terminal is used, whether a handheld unit or a stationary touch screen used by several servers, they generate legible guest checks, avoid errors in addition, speed service, and improve productivity.

Another application of technology that affects the way customers use restaur-ants is a video-equipped, drive-through, order-taking system that permits a more personal interaction between order taking and guest. Evidence suggests that the system also improves transaction speed. Single-telephone-number systems in deliv-ery firms use computerized guest histories to facilitate order taking. These computer-ized systems also enhance customer convenience for take-out and delivery and offer economies of scale, as well as insight into customer ordering patterns through guest history computer files. The fax machine has also proved a boon to take-out and delivery operations.

Guest Payment.   Credit cards are convenient to the guest. Moreover, a study at one QSR chain showed that credit card customers spent well over 50 percent more than cash customers. Bank debit cards are also being used in some restaurants.

The credit card represents an important social technology supported in a num-ber of ways by electronics. Credit cards are widely used in table service restaurants. Their increasing use in fast food is an important service improvement that offers greater convenience to the customer and improvements in sales and efficiency to the operator.

From order to payment, customer interaction is being facilitated by technology. We can turn our attention now to how the *production process* is being improved.

Technology in the Back of the House

Food Production.   Individual pieces of equipment are being improved by enhanc-ing their energy efficiency both in terms of their cooking and in terms of their effect on ventilation requirements. The technologies that underlie these developments are impressive, but the impacts are in marginal improvements in cost and opera-tion. Some new equipment, such as the combination steamer/oven, add flexibility to the kitchen because it can be used in more than one process. Another innova-tion, the two-sided griddle, reduces cooking times by one-third to one-half or more and also reduces shrinkage in the product.

The use of conveyors in ovens speeds cooking but, more importantly, improves control over the process. Setting the belt speed correctly ensures that the product will not be over- or undercooked because an employee's timing was off.

Refrigeration.   In the 1950s, frozen prepared foods were introduced into restaur-ants. Frozen entrées simplified delivery and inventory problems and reduced skill levels while broadening the range of menu items that could be used in a kitchen lacking skilled cooks. The freezing process, however, has adverse effects on quality.

Ice crystals that form at the time of freezing cut tissue in the product, which changes the consistency of some products. Also, when products are reconstituted, they lose flavor-filled juices.

The next advance in the use of refrigeration was the development of chilled prepared foods. Foods are held in the latent temperature zone, from 28 to 30 degrees Fahrenheit (−1 to −2 degrees Celsius). In this temperature range, holding characteristics, in terms of both flavor and microbiological quality, remain at the level of the fresh product's quality.

There are two methods of chilling a product: tumble chill (cooked food is packaged in plastic and chilled in cold circulating water) and blast chill (food held in pans is chilled by exposure to high-velocity, convected cold air). Foods chilled by cold water have a shelf life of up to 21 to 45 days, depending on the type of food product. Foods chilled by convected air have a shorter shelf life, up to 5 days, including the day of preparation and the day of use.[36]

A major advantage of this new storage technology is in the scheduling flexibility and productivity it gives the operation. Skilled cooks can be brought into a central facility to work from nine to five, Monday through Friday, preparing products to be held in inventory. Less skilled employees can be used during all the hours of operation to reconstitute a varied menu of high-quality products that have not lost flavor through the freezing process.

The applications of cook and chill range from cruise ships offering "24 hour food service and high volume, high end cooking"[37] to the state of Tennessee where "a single commissary unit provides 70,000 meals a day to all the state's prisons and mental health facilities."[38]

Technology, the Internet, and Food Service Marketing

The Internet is an advertising medium of great power and more and more restaurants are taking advantage of it. The most common approach to using the Internet is to establish a web site on the World Wide Web (WWW). "In general, restaurant sites tend to be easy to comprehend with a single level main or home page."[39] The web site can offer electronic couponing, frequent browser promotion, and an on-line review of menu offerings. "Providing a communications channel between a restaurant and web surfers creates a pipeline for feedback. Web sites featuring customer email sections and correspondence links to company management have become relatively commonplace."[40]

> Although Internet commerce is in its infancy, there are clear indications that the Internet is moving from simple provision of information to becoming a transaction vehicle. Restaurants offering home delivery service are appearing on the net with increased frequency. Web sites typically use a shopping cart metaphor to allow surfers to browse product lines, select products for purchase, and complete payment.[41]

Technology and Banquet Sales.   Automatic sales and catering software makes it possible to combine management of an individual customer account with the overall management of group sales and catering. These systems are both accurate and more efficient in their use of people's time. A typical computerized sales and catering system would include a daily function summary showing space bookings

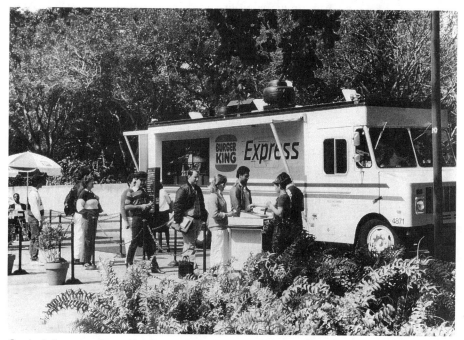

Scaled-down units make it possible to provide limited food service in many locations that could not have been served in the past.
Courtesy of Burger King

for every day of the year, details on each function such as room setup and menu, and timing of meals and breaks. When the booking is complete, a contract reflecting the customer's requests is prepared automatically by the system. Where the restaurant is a part of a hotel or conference center, group rooms control is also provided.[42]

Technology and Management

Computerized point-of-sales (POS) systems not only make the service process easier for employees, they save managers work by preparing routine reports; tracking inventory, stock levels, and costs, and determining which items are producing a profit. Some companies are linked directly to their suppliers' computers and ordering is done automatically as product is used. Red Lobster's management system prepares a daily food use forecast that is adjusted by unit managers and used as a basis to bring product from locked storage to the preparation area for the day. The same usage report is transmitted to the chain's Orlando headquarters, where it is translated into orders to suppliers. These are transmitted from Orlando to suppliers across the United States and Canada. Notice that this process not only increases control chainwide but saves a good deal of time for unit managers.

The banquet sales system referred to previously not only handles the space commitments and the details of booking a function but provides complete management and marketing information. Management information, for instance, includes reports summarizing financial results and sales forecasts. Marketing reports show contact history by individual account and summarize lost business in a report that helps highlight problem areas.

$\mathcal{S}$UMMARY

Although there is a concern about nutrition among consumers that cannot be overlooked, there is an even stronger preference for taste. Operators try for balance with menu offerings to suit both preferences. Consumerists criticize food service for not following what consumerists see as the path of virtue, but restaurants know that they cannot force consumers to behave in a certain way despite all their advertising. Marketing does best when it follows the lead of the guest.

The NLEA limits the health claims restaurants can make and requires them to provide information on any nutrient or health claim they make. Although enforcement of the NLEA is very uneven, most restaurants were in compliance with the act before it was passed.

Sanitation is a major concern to the restaurant industry and the Educational Foundation of the NRA has certified several million workers and nearly a million managers in courses on that topic. The industry's interest is explained, in some part, by self-interest. Bad publicity about sanitation can destroy a restaurant. The best approach to developing a sanitation program is to follow the principles and procedures of HACCP.

Environmental concerns about waste management can be acted on effectively at the unit level. The shrinking availability and mounting costs of sanitary landfills give a pragmatic basis for this concern as do the sentiments of our customers who are concerned about the environment. The six ways to deal with solid waste discussed were: reduce, reuse, recycle, compost, incinerate, and landfill. Choosing cost-effective solutions is complicated by program costs, availability of support channels, and unwanted side effects.

Technology is playing a growing role in food service, but it is still subject to economics and customer acceptance. Technology is being used to enhance guest services and to control costs. The chapter discussed the uses of technology in the following areas: guest ordering and payment, food production and refrigeration, marketing (specifically on the Internet), managing banquet and catering departments, and management control and communication.

◆ $\mathcal{K}$EY WORDS AND CONCEPTS

Healthy eating
Nutritious food and consumer
    demand
Overweight and obesity
Dietary schizophrenia
Consumerism

Nutrition Labeling and Education
    Act (NLEA)
Nutrient claim
Health claim
Food and Drug Administration
    (FDA)

ZHONG
312193737
Score: 47 of 64 points (73%)

Scores [Individual]

	Resp [Ans]	Points Rcvd		Resp [Ans]	Points Rcvd		Resp [Ans]	Points Rcvd		Resp [Ans]	Points Rcvd
x 1.	A[D]	0 of 1	17.	D[D]	1 of 1	33.	A[A]	1 of 1	49.	A[A]	1 of 1
2.	A[A]	1 of 1	18.	B[B]	1 of 1	34.	C[C]	1 of 1	50.	B[B]	1 of 1
3.	A[A]	1 of 1	19.	B[B]	1 of 1	x 35.	B[A]	0 of 1	x 51.	A[B]	0 of 1
4.	C[C]	1 of 1	20.	A[A]	1 of 1	x 36.	C[A]	0 of 1	52.	B[B]	1 of 1
5.	C[C]	1 of 1	x 21.	B[A]	0 of 1	x 37.	A[B]	0 of 1	53.	A[A]	1 of 1
6.	C[C]	1 of 1	22.	D[D]	1 of 1	x 38.	B[C]	0 of 1	54.	A[A]	1 of 1
x 7.	D[C]	0 of 1	23.	B[B]	1 of 1	39.	B[B]	1 of 1	55.	A[A]	1 of 1
8.	A[A]	1 of 1	24.	C[C]	1 of 1	40.	D[D]	1 of 1	56.	B[B]	1 of 1
x 9.	D[C]	0 of 1	25.	B[B]	1 of 1	41.	B[B]	1 of 1	x 57.	A[B]	0 of 1
10.	C[C]	1 of 1	26.	C[C]	1 of 1	42.	B[B]	1 of 1	x 58.	A[B]	0 of 1
11.	A[A]	1 of 1	x 27.	C[D]	0 of 1	43.	A[A]	1 of 1	59.	A[A]	1 of 1
12.	A[A]	1 of 1	x 28.	D[B]	0 of 1	44.	A[A]	1 of 1	x 60.	B[A]	0 of 1
13.	B[B]	1 of 1	x 29.	D[C]	0 of 1	45.	A[A]	1 of 1	61.	B[B]	1 of 1
14.	B[B]	1 of 1	30.	D[D]	1 of 1	x 46.	A[B]	0 of 1	62.	A[A]	1 of 1
15.	A[A]	1 of 1	31.	A[A]	1 of 1	47.	A[A]	1 of 1	63.	B[B]	1 of 1
16.	A[A]	1 of 1	x 32.	C[A]	0 of 1	48.	A[A]	1 of 1	64.	A[A]	1 of 1

Sanitation

Hazard analysis and critical control
points (HACCP)

Solid-waste disposal

Sanitary landfill

Waste stream

Reduce, reuse, and recycle

Composting

Incineration

Landfill

Technology

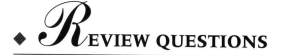

REVIEW QUESTIONS

1. What is meant by dietary schizophrenia? What does it arise from? What do you think of the way the industry is responding to it?

2. Which of the consumerist issues discussed in this chapter have you encountered as a customer or employee of food service? What are your views on these issues?

3. Do you view the typical QSR menu as junk food? How would you respond to a charge of junk food against fast food?

4. Should restaurants be required to identify foods that were not prepared on premise?

5. What is the status of landfill availability and cost in your community? What is its outlook? What is the outlook for recycling and composting in your area?

6. Using as an example an operation with which you are familiar, describe the steps necessary to make recycling possible in that unit.

7. What problems hinder the use of technology? What technological innovations do you think operations should be seeking? What problems do you think might arise from those innovations?

INTERNET EXERCISES

1. **Site Name:** *National Restaurant Association*
   URL: http://www.restaurant.org/
   Background Information: The NRA provides information on consumer studies, trends in restaurants, and press releases that identify trends and issues confronting the industry.

   EXERCISE:

   Identify and discuss the current trends/issues confronting the restaurant industry.

2. **Site Name:** *Center for Science in the Public Interest*
URL: http://www.cspinet.org/
Background Information: The Center for Science in the Public Interest (CSPI) is a nonprofit education and advocacy organization that focuses on improving the safety and nutritional quality of our food supply. The CSPI seeks to promote health through educating the public about nutrition and alcohol; it represents citizens' interests before legislative, regulatory, and judicial bodies; and it works to ensure that advances in science are used for the public's good.

EXERCISES:

a. Identify and discuss a current issue that is being pursued by the CSPI and how it will impact the restaurant industry.

b. Discuss your feelings on whether this issue is justified and why.

3. **Site Name:** *CSPI Booze News*
URL: http://www.cspinet.org/booze/index.html
Background Information: In 1981, the CSPI launched the Alcohol Policies Project to reduce the health and social consequences of drinking. The project's prevention-oriented policy strategy is aimed at curbing alcohol-related problems.

EXERCISE:

Identify the current project initiatives that are part of the Alcohol Policies Project. Describe how you feel the initiatives will impact the restaurant industry.

◆ OTES

1. Shannon Dortch, "America Weighs In," *American Demographics,* June 1997, pp. 39–43.

2. *Nations Restaurant News,* September 22, 1997, p. 32.

3. *Wall Street Journal,* April 15, 1993.

4. Ann Stone, "Lean? No Thanks," *Restaurants and Institutions,* May 15, 1997, pp. 102–115.

5. George D. Rice, "Meeting the Challenges of the 90s," *Proceedings of the 21st Annual Chain Operators Exchange* Orlando, Feb. 27–30, 1994, (Chicago: International Foodservice Manufacturers Association, 1994).

6. Stone, "Lean? No Thanks," p. 110.

7. Dortch, "America Weighs In," pp. 39–40.

8. Ibid., p. 43. Dortch is quoting Rocehlle Udell, Editor, *Self* magazine.

9. Rice, "Meeting the Challenges of the 90s."

10. Stone, "Lean? No Thanks," p. 110.

11. Ibid.

12. Ibid.

13. Rice, "Meeting the Challenges of the 90s."

14. Robert L. Blomstorm, "The Hospitality Industry and the Consumer Movement," *The Institute Journal,* April 1973, p. 9.

15. Peter F. Drucker, *Management Tasks, Responsibilities, Practices* (New York: Harper & Row, 1974), p. 64.

16. *Nations Restaurant News,* November 10, 1974, p. 4. Although the quote is dated, it still captures very succinctly the attitude of many consumerist social critics, contemporary as well as past.

17. Catherine Brochier, "Decoding the New Menu-Labelling Regulations," *Restaurants USA*, October 1996, p. 36.

18. Ibid.

19. Personal communication, Leila Farzani, Senior Staff Attorney, Center for Science in the Public Interest, November 1997. I am indebted to Ms. Farzani for her helpfulness.

20. Michael F. Jacobsen, "Restaurant Nutrition in the 1990s," Address to COEX 93, March 2, 1993.

21. Personal communication, Kate Sisslin, Education Foundation of the National Restaurant Association, December 1997.

22. Michael Grisanti, "Food Safety . . . Staying out of the Limelight," *Proceedings of the 21st Annual Chain Operators Exchange* (Chicago: International Foodservice Manufacturers Association, 1994).

23. Richard Brimingham, President and CEO, Sizzler Restaurants, Remarks during a panel discussion at COEX 94, February 28, 1994.

24. Michael R. Taylor, Deputy, Commission for Policy, U.S. Food and Drug Administration, "FDA's Food Safety Initiative," Address to COEX 94, February 28, 1994.

25. *Restaurants USA*, March 1997, p. 45.

26. *Wall Street Journal*, May 1, 1990, p. A4.

27. Peter A. D'Souza and Leland L. Nicholls, "Waste Management: The Priority for the 1990's," Technical Paper, University of Wisconsin–Stout, n.d. Only the figure for institutions is given in the report. The fast-food figure can readily be derived, using the check average given and a waste per 1000 pound figure. The table service figure, however, was estimated assuming an average of four chair turns per day for a seven-day week against an average of 25 pounds for family restaurants and 30 pounds for fine-dining operations.

28. The report uses the term "fine dining" where I have used "table service." The category found in the report for fine dining has a check average of $4 to $13. For the sake of consistency of usage in this text, I have changed this table. The authors note that the study was undertaken in a midwestern city and may differ somewhat from other regions.

29. *Fortune*, February 1990, quoted in *Foodservice and Hospitality*, October 1990, p. 30.

30. *Nations Restaurant News*, November 19, 1990. p. 4.

31. Tom Watson, "Food Waste Composting: Institutions Get a Taste," *Resource Recycling*, November 1990, pp. 45–47.

32. Moira Marx Nir, "Implications of Post-Consumer Plastic Waste," *Plastics Engineering*, September–October 1990, p. 3.

33. Ibid., p. 10.

34. Ibid., p. 10.

35. *Institutions/Volume Feeding*, October 1975, p. 47.

36. Nicole Castagna, "Know Your Cook-Chill," *Restaurants and Institutions*, November 1, 1997, p. 84.

37. Beth Lorengini, "Cruise Control," *Restaurants and Institutions*, September 1997, pp. 84–86.

38. Castagna, "Know Your Cook-Chill."

39. Michael L. Kasavana, "Restaurants and the Web," *Computers, Food Service and You*, May–June 1997, pp. 5–8.

40. Ibid., p. 6.

41. Ibid., p. 7.

42. I am indebted to Hodges Technology of St. Clair, Michigan, for providing me with the information on group bookings.

Chapter 8

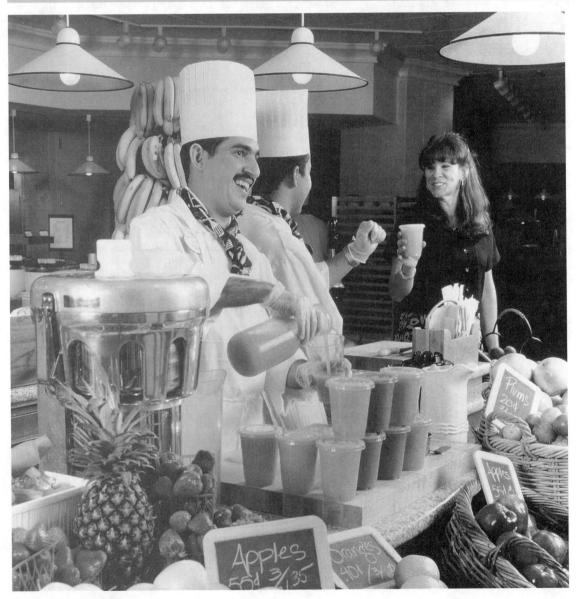

Courtesy of ARAMARK.

Institutions and Institutional Food Service

The Purpose of This Chapter

This chapter discusses these important and significant segments of the food service industry, which, taken together, account for roughly a quarter of total food service sales. Some of the characteristics of this component of hospitality are unique. Yet the increasing emphasis on marketing and use of brand names in the institutional sector would suggest that the lines between institutional food service and other segments are becoming blurred. Moreover, this is a segment that offers excellent compensation, good opportunities for advancement, and often more stable working hours. Because many companies operate in both the commercial hospitality industry and the institutional or noncommercial sector, it is an area that you may come into contact with even if your plans now are to work in hotels or restaurants. It is, in short, an area of the industry that deserves careful examination.

This Chapter Should Help You

1. Become familiar with the four major segments of institutional operations and the kinds of opportunities each offers

2. Understand the differences between self-operated institutional food service and that managed by contract companies

3. Understand the important distinction between client and guest

4. Identify the major government food service programs and the clients they serve

5. Explore the growing retirement housing community market and the involvement of hotel companies in it

6. Recognize the importance of other institutional segments in which contract companies and other firms have a large stake, such as recreation and in-flight food service

7. Recognize the role that private clubs play and understand the many career opportunities for students in this segment

8. Understand the important functions of vending in serving guest and client needs

9. Recognize some of the elements that are common to the different lines of business in this segment

COMPARING INSTITUTIONAL AND COMMERCIAL FOOD SERVICES

Any discussion of the institutional sector, to those more familiar with traditional restaurants, requires that one expand his or her preconceptions of what the food service industry encompasses. Even the terminology used to describe this segment tends to be different. For instance, there are several different terms used to describe this segment—*on-site* being one of the more current terms in use. Also, the sector is so broad and encompasses so many different types of operations that to attempt to group all of these different businesses under one umbrella does the sector a bit of an injustice. This will become clear as the different subsegments are discussed. Another reason that discussions of this segment require looking beyond the traditional restaurant model is because of the different types of companies that operate within the segment. For instance, an important distinction within institutional food service is between **contract management companies** (hereafter, contract companies) that manage a food service facility for a third party and institutional organizations that operate their own food service (hereafter, **institutional operations** or **self-ops**).

Finally, dividing food service into commercial and institutional (or noncommercial) segments is somewhat artificial and misleading, as some of the same firms that profit from providing institutions with food services also operate in other areas of the hospitality industry. ARAMARK, for instance, operates hotels in national parks and has a line of business that supplies uniforms. Sodexho Marriott Services is a part of Marriott International, which is a major hotel operator in the United States (and operates restaurants on expressways, among other endeavors). Morrison's Health Care, Inc., another large contractor, is part of the same company that operates a number of full-service concepts such as Ruby Tuesdays and Tia's. As one quickly discovers, there are numerous companies that operate in sometimes completely different food service environments simultaneously, as evidenced by the preceding examples.

Returning our focus to the institutional, or on-site, sector, there are significant differences that exist between restaurants and institutional food service with which students should be aware. One important difference is that, where institutional food service once represented a "captive market," restaurant customers have always had a range of choices, including choices of facilities and menus. This distinction still exists but to a much lesser extent. Institutional food service providers, both self-operated and managed, have found that, with certain exceptions, guests do have a choice in the long run. As a result, food service operators have found that a marketing approach that views patients, company employees, and students as *guests* and focuses on their preferences is an approach that tends to win more friends than the old "eat it and like it" institutional attitude.

Success is measured by the **participation rate** of the guests. College students who don't like the food withdraw from board plans, patients who have a choice of hospitals often choose the institution with superior food service, and even inmates find ways to assert their food preferences. In an age of consumerism, moreover, even guests who can't "vote with their feet" and go someplace else don't hesitate to complain. Therefore, competition among the various food service contractors is often decided on the basis of marketing techniques, as well as management skills.

Another major difference between traditional restaurants and institutional services relates to their primary functions. Even though many companies provide both restaurant and institutional food services and use similar marketing and managerial techniques in both areas, the major difference between the two markets is that the food service in institutions is a small part of a larger operation with a greater purpose of overriding importance—health care, education, or manufacturing, for instance. In a commercial restaurant, the challenge is to please the guest. In the institutional environment, it is necessary to meet the needs of both the guests and the *client* (i.e., the institution itself).

The distinction between client and guest is important. The client is the institution along with its managers and policymakers. These are the people who ultimately award the contract or, when the institution operates its own food service, hire and fire the food service director. Pleasing the guest (i.e., the individual diner, patient, student, resident, or inmate) is important, but the client must be pleased, as well. Some years ago, the president of ARAMARK put it this way, "Today, you take a blank yellow pad, find out what the client wants, and try to institute a formula that works. It's really the client's operation, not the contractor's."[1] The evidence suggests that the same formula still applies today.

There may be a substantial difference in an institutional setting between the needs and wants of the guest and those of the client. In school food service, for instance, the client's (i.e., the school's) goals are providing not only adequate meals but also nutrition education by showing the students what a nutritionally balanced meal is like. The goals of a young school child may obviously be quite a bit different.

If the institution's food service is operated by a contract company, the two parties must agree upon the type of contract to be followed, as well as negotiate the terms of that particular contract. Contracts can take a variety of forms. Contracts sometimes call for the institution to essentially allow the contractor to operate on a break-even basis and to pay the contractor a fee every period for the management of the operation. Other contracts allow the contractor to operate solely on a profit-and-loss basis where the contractor covers its own expenses and manages the

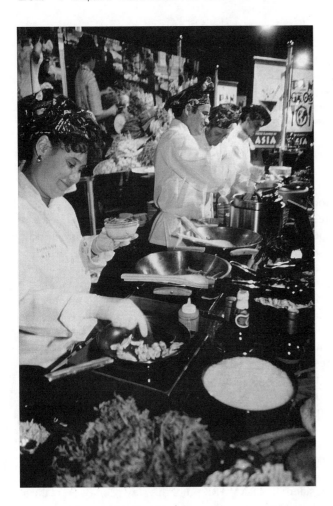

Institutional food service operations can plan the number of meals served and portion sizes with more certainty than commercial restaurants.
Courtesy of ARAMARK.

revenues, taking sole responsibility for the profit (or loss) at the end of each period. Other contracts might be a hybrid of these two, depending on the scope of the operation. However, in most segments, the movement seems to be more toward profit-and-loss-type contracts. Whether the operation is subsidized, break-even, or for-profit, however, there is always some budgeted performance target that must be met regardless of who operates the service. Even for self-operated institutions, the trend is for them to become more self-sufficient with a greater degree of fiscal responsibility.

Finally, the two segments (commercial and institutional) have very different operating challenges. For example, the number of meals and portion sizes are much easier to predict in institutional operations. Because of this greater predictability, institutional food service operations often operate in a less hurried atmosphere than that in restaurants, in which customer volume and menu popularity often fluctuate. Moreover, although managers tend to work long hours in commercial food service, the working hours in institutional food service are usually shorter, or at least more predictable. This is particularly true in environments that have discrete operating periods such as colleges and most businesses.

On the other hand, although a guest may visit a restaurant frequently, few of them eat as regularly in their favorite restaurant as do the guests in institutional operations. Thus, varying the menu for a guest who must eat in the same place for weeks, months, or even years at a time can be a demanding task. Further distinctions are discussed next.

$\mathscr{I}$NSTITUTIONAL OPERATORS

Many institutions see no need to pay the overhead and profits of a contract company. This attitude is perhaps most prevalent in primary/secondary school feeding and in health care where many institutions still operate their own food service. Operating on the assumption that their own employees can manage as efficiently as a contract company can, these institutions choose to keep the overhead and profit they otherwise would have to pay to an outside company. These institutions can control their operations, and, to some extent, they can limit the staff turnover traditionally associated with contract companies, which frequently promote or transfer their employees. "If we like a person," said one university official, "we might lose him to a contract company. In our own operation, if we treat him right we have a good chance of keeping him—of maintaining staff stability."

$\mathscr{C}$ONTRACT MANAGEMENT COMPANIES

Contract companies, on the other hand, feel that their method of operation offers advantages to operators of all sizes. True, unit managers may be transferred. We should note, however, that a contract company provides the client with two kinds of managers: the unit manager and the regional and district managers who train, evaluate, and supervise the unit manager's work and ensure management continuity. That continuity is an important offset to the possibility of transfer. Perhaps even more important, the transfer is a part of a process of career progression. People who want to advance are drawn to that kind of opportunity. Thus, a contract company is likely to attract aggressive managers. Managers who choose to stay with institutional operators are likely to have less opportunity for advancement although they will have other advantages, such as stability in where they live.

Another area in which contract companies offer advantages is that of purchasing. Selection of the best, most cost-effective purveyor offers major potential for savings. So does knowledgeable negotiation on the client's behalf by national buyers with broad experience. Contract companies conduct audits of cost-plus suppliers' books to ensure accurate billing, an expenditure of effort and money that might not be practical for an individual client. Finally, because contract companies buy on a regional or national scale, they can consolidate purchasing for several clients, thus achieving significant economies. In recent years, however, institutional operators

Global Hospitality Note 8.1

International Perspectives

Although the discussion of institutional food service in this chapter is primarily limited to examples in the United States, this should in no way imply that such operations are limited to this country. Companies, hospitals, colleges, and so on in every part of the world have provided food service to their associates/students/customers for a very long time. One look at the top food service management companies in this sector indicates just how truly international this market is. Current leaders, in order of sales, are Sodexho Marriott Services, Compass Group, and ARAMARK. Sodexho (**http://www.sodexho.com/**), which recently merged with Marriott, is a French-based company that has had a presence in the United States since the mid-1980s. Marriott (**http://www. marriott.com/**) is well known in the United States and continues to expand into new countries. Compass Group (**http://www.compass-usa.com/**), which oper-

ates several subsidiaries including Canteen and Chartwells, is based in England and operates in over 45 countries worldwide. Finally, perhaps the best example of ARAMARK's (**http://www.aramark.com/**) international expertise is its long involvement with providing food service for the Olympics. ARAMARK also manages a variety of services around the globe.

What does the future hold? Without a doubt, further international expansion for the larger companies in this segment. This may occur in the way of outright expansions, mergers and acquisitions, and international partnerships. One recent example of the latter was the merger of Marriott Management Services with Sodexho, a move that catapulted the new company to the number one position in the field.

Note: Additional institutional food management companies can be found at: **http://www.wku.edu/~hrtm/hotlrest.htm**.

have made moves that can offset this advantage by forming cooperative buying groups and passing the volume discount advantages on to the member institutions.

Contract companies also offer to their clients, at cost, extensive facilities planning services. These services include operational design (equipment), interior design, procurement, supervision of construction, and equipment installation. Specialized accounting and market-planning services may also be offered to clients.

Finally, contract companies offer the collective experience of management and marketing in many markets. Marketing programs can be tailored to individual clients, for instance, yet also draw on national marketing programs developed by the contractor. This has proved especially helpful in areas such as nutritionally oriented marketing programs.

Pros and Cons of Contract Management

To all of this, the large institutional operator will likely respond that a large institution (medical center, university, or school district) is large enough to achieve most

Table 8.1   The Institutional Food Service Market, 1995

	Estimated Size of Total Market (Number of Accounts)[a]	Degree of Penetration by Contract Companies[b]
Business and industry	36,367	80–85%
Colleges and universities	3,541	50–55%
Hospitals	6,806	40–45%
Primary and secondary schools	84,422	10–15%
TOTAL	131,136	

[a]*Source:* International Foodservice Manufacturers Association.
[b]*Source:* "Managed Services Companies," *Cornell Hotel and Restaurant Administration Quarterly,* June 1997.

or all of these advantages on its own. A smaller institution might add that voluntary buying co-ops and judicious use of consultants can also achieve a good part of these effects. Both would emphasize that the institution retains full control over the operation, which reports directly to the institution's top management.

No doubt, contract companies would make responses to each of these points. Our purpose is not to settle the issue in any final way. There really is no one answer to the debate. What we want is to suggest the outlines of the competition between institutional operator and contract company for consideration by the reader.

The contract companies' share is substantial and growing in most segments. Although exact figures are difficult to determine, Table 8.1 indicates some reasonable estimates and shows that contract food service companies currently manage a significant number of institutional food services. Health care is one area in which contract companies have relatively low market *penetration,* but even this area is increasing as a result of health care facilities wishing to **outsource** their food service, and other support services, in an effort to focus on their core functions—care for patients. Contract companies have also had success with public schools in recent years. The two areas in which the contract companies are well established are colleges and universities and business and industry.

Each of the four major divisions within institutional food services have unique characteristics. Moreover, the factors that affect the outlook for each vary. We will consider each of them briefly.

ℬUSINESS AND INDUSTRY FOOD SERVICE

Business and industry (B&I) food service provides food for the convenience of both the guest (the company associates) and the client (the employer). The client wants inexpensive food with enough variety and quality to satisfy the associates, as the client knows that food can directly affect morale. Quick service is also important, because the time for coffee breaks and lunch is limited. Finally, it is in the best interest of most companies to keep their employees on the premises during food service breaks.

Two of the underlying forces that drive the B&I market are the size of the workforce and the level of employment. The size of the workforce affects the long-term outlook. When it was growing, the workforce was a strong positive force, during the years when the baby boomers were leaving school and entering employment. Now that the surge is over, however, the Bureau of Labor Statistics estimates that the workforce will increase at a more modest rate. Within the workforce, the trend is toward an economy increasingly dominated by service industries that employ more office and white-collar employees. The volume of food service in commercial and office buildings is growing at a significantly faster pace than it is in manufacturing plants. In periods of low unemployment, such as is the case currently, B&I volume may rise. On the other hand, B&I is especially sensitive to downturns in employment.

Recent downsizings have caused companies to take a close look at their food

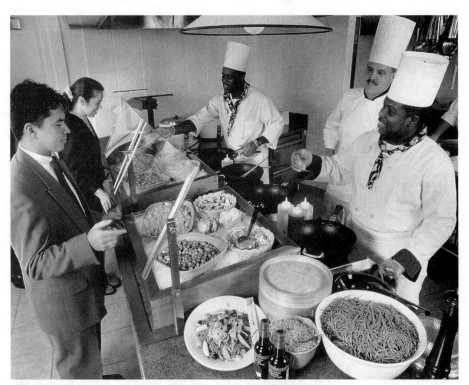

Institutional food service in commercial and office buildings has grown in the 1990s.
Courtesy of ARAMARK

service operations and to take the necessary measures to streamline them and, increasingly, outsource them. The National Restaurant Association indicates that business and industry sales (managed by contract companies) experienced significant growth between 1995 and 1998, while independent operators experienced negative growth during that same period.[2]

The food service that is offered in the industrial setting is increasingly feeling the effects of outside competition from restaurants. Even with the limited time available, employees may choose to go off site for their meals. Almost 10 years ago, the chairman of ARAMARK put it succinctly when he said that ARAMARK's competition is "fast food, dial a fax, the supermarkets, the vending truck and brown baggers."[3] The same holds true today, only more so.

Each of the institutional segments is combating these competitive forces in its own way, but the B&I segment has been one of the most aggressive. One very effective strategy that contract management companies, in particular, have adopted has been to develop food service concepts or **brands** of their own or to use established commercial franchise brands. ARAMARK's strategy has been to develop its own brands such as Gretel's Bake Shop, Itza Pizza, El Pollo Grande, and Leghorn. Brand name units are themed much like any other chain operation, and the brand is promoted within the client's establishment. ARAMARK finds a high level of consumer acceptance for these brands as evidenced by large increases in sales in units where they are established. The other advantage is that no franchise royalties are paid. This results in savings that can be passed on to both guest and client. ARAMARK also makes extensive use, however, of major national franchise brands, as does Sodexho Marriott Services. Marriott, for instance, has partnered with franchise brands such as Pizza Hut and Nathan's Famous. Other brands in use at contract companies include Wendy's, Little Caesars, Dunkin Donuts, I Can't Believe It's Yogurt, Chick-Fil-A, and Starbuck's.

The advantages of the brand name specialty restaurant format, whether the brand is proprietary or franchised, are startlingly similar to the advantages that food service has in the commercial restaurant business.

◆ The operation has an identity that helps secure patronage from an increasingly brand-conscious food service customer.

◆ The facility is simpler to build than is a full-menu concept, and the investment required can be significantly less.

◆ Operating costs are lower, too, because of the simpler menu and because customers are accustomed to self-busing in fast food.

◆ Fast food is fast—in-plant feeding at General Motors plants takes only 3 minutes, compared with 12 minutes under earlier formats.

One of the most important considerations when introducing a branded concept, whether a national or proprietary brand, is the expected increase in the participation rate (or capture rate). Marriott, before its merger, introduced a new

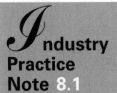

Measuring Guest Participation

Industry Practice Note 8.1

In the commercial food service sector, most activity is driven by sales and vice versa. In on-site food service, whether self-operated or overseen by a management company, the critical factor is the participation (or capture) rate. If company associates, college students, and so forth choose not to "participate" in the on-site food service, neither the client nor the food service operator will be satisfied. This holds true whether the facility is located in a hospital, ballpark, university, or industrial park.

Food service operators go about managing the participation rate in a variety of ways. One thing is for certain, however—more and more, the strategies that managers are employing closely resemble those used by managers of commercial operations. New services, positioning, branding, focusing on quality, attractive pricing, providing innovative menus, and merchandising are but a few of the ways that managers attempt to influence the participation rate of guests.

Not too long ago, it would have been hard to imagine being able to order upscale Chinese food in the company cafeteria, find a food court in a hospital, or order a microbrewed beer at the ballpark. Yet with operators focusing ever-more attention on customizing their products and services to meet the desires of customers, the battle over participation rate will rage on.

brand, Crossroads Cuisines, in 1996. The concept was developed specifically for the B&I market and incorporates elements of traditional restaurant dining. The average sales increase, after introducing Crossroads Cuisines, across accounts, was 14 percent.[4] Other techniques for increasing the participation rate are described in Industry Practice Note 8.1.

The purpose of employee food service operations changes, however, with different employee levels. Many companies maintain executive dining rooms boasting fancy menus and elegant service. Such dining rooms are often used to entertain important business guests—customers, prospective employees, the press, and politicians. Executive dining room privileges can also be an important status symbol among managerial employees. Further, even though recent tax law changes have generally lowered the rate at which business meals may be deducted (to 50 percent), meals served to employees at their place of work remains 100 percent deductible under certain conditions. Clearly, there are several legitimate reasons that speak to providing meals to line employees as well as executives.

In summary, changes continue to occur in the B&I segment: More aggressive marketing, more streamlined operations, increasing usage of branded concepts, addition of innovative menus, decreasing employer subsidies, and greater penetration by contract companies are all changing the image of this segment.

COLLEGE AND UNIVERSITY FOOD SERVICE

The **college and university food service** segment is very different from B&I. To understand college food service, one must first understand the **board plan.** Students eating in residence halls may be required to contract for a minimum number of meals over a term or semester. The food service operation benefits from this arrangement in two ways. First, the absentee factor ensures that some students will miss some meals they contracted for, which permits the food service operation to price the total package below what all the meals would cost if every student ate every meal there. This makes the package price attractive.

Second, and more important, the board plan provides a predictable volume of sales over a fairly long period—a term, a semester, or a year. At the start of that period, the operator can closely estimate what the sales volume will be. Because attendance ratios and the popularity of various menu items are fairly predictable, the operator can also estimate how much food to prepare for each meal.

Full board plans were once the rule rather than the exception, particularly on purely residential campuses. Although some colleges still offer only a full board plan (three meals a day, seven days a week while school is in session), flexible board plans have become more and more popular. For example, some plans exclude breakfast, whereas others drop the weekend meals. With a flexible plan that invites students to contract for only the meals they expect to eat, the absentee rate goes down and the average price charged per meal goes up, because of the lower absentee rates. Nevertheless, in plans that drop a significant number of meals, the total price of the meal contract also drops. In any case, both the full board plan and the flexible plan generally charge students on the basis of the average number of meals they consume.

Some schools, such as New Mexico State University (operated by Chartwells) don't have a mandatory board plan and instead allow students to use their campus identification card to purchase food anywhere on campus. The use of such cards is becoming more common. With most card programs, students contract for some minimum dollar value of food service and receive a cash card with the amount they have paid credited to the card. As they use the card, the card is scanned and the amount of each item (or full meal) is electronically deducted from the balance. Students usually receive the food purchased through their card at some discount from what competitive commercial operations charge and so it is still a bargain. The contracts, on the other hand, give the operator a basis for projecting the demand for the school year for scheduling, purchasing, and general budgeting, and they also guarantee some minimum level of sales volume. Some schools are even experimenting with allowing students to use these same cards at off-campus locations.

As in the B&I segment, colleges and universities are also trying to market their services more. Flexible board plans and the use of cash cards represent just a small part of a total marketing approach, which adapts the services available to the guests' needs and preferences. Only about one-fifth of college and university students, however, live on campus. Roughly half live off campus, and the remaining students live at home with their parents. The need to attract off-campus students as customers heightens the competitive nature of college food service.

The use of brand names and franchised concepts has also taken hold in college and university food service. The acceptance of students' preferences for fast food and the use of familiar branded concepts has achieved major improvements in sales. At San Diego State University, for instance, while enrollment fell nearly 25 percent, food sales actually rose from $4.3 million to $4.8 million when 10 branded concepts were introduced. One-third of colleges and universities now offer branded options and brand franchisors are becoming more flexible in reducing menus, adapting hours of operation, and reducing the amount of space required as they seek to get their brand "in place" in institutions. The use of brand names is by no means limited to contract companies, however. Institutions that operate their own food service have had success with that tactic, too. In fact, the National Association of College and University Food Service (NACUFS) has been instrumental in assisting self-operated institutions to capitalize on the branding trend. NACUFS has developed a series of brands for use by its members. Institutional operators can and do have national franchise brands as a part of their operation, as well.

The management companies have been very effective with branding in colleges and universities. ARAMARK has recently introduced a new concept called Pan Geos on 44 college campuses. This new concept is based on a cluster design offering various international cuisines. In the short time that the concept has been in place, various units have experienced higher customer counts, increased check averages, and lower food costs.[5] With the success of Pan Geos, it can be anticipated that more management companies will develop similar offerings. One final note with regard to branding—where the national brands were once limited to larger campuses, they are starting to appear at smaller institutions, some having as few as 400 students!

College Students as Customers

College students are generally pleasant to deal with, but at times they can be very demanding. They need to be consulted in planning, and patient attention to complaints is important, too. An unhappy group of college students—with a natural bent for boisterousness—can be a difficult group to deal with. College food service operators stress the need for a strong communications program between the food service staff and the students. All agree that, in addition to good food and tight cost controls, a successful college food service operation must have "people skills"; that is, it must be able to deal effectively with the guests.

The 16- to 24-year-old portion of the population declined between 1990 and 1995 but is expected to increase through the year 2010.[6] In addition, college and university enrollments are expected to increase over the next decade, albeit modestly (between 1 and 2 percent annually).[7] The average age of the college population continues to climb, as well. Adult participation in higher education is expected to continue to increase perhaps, in part, because of increased competition in the job

The introduction of concepts such as Pan Geos has successfully increased sales in college and university food service outlets.
Courtesy of ARAMARK

market. In California, for instance, 40 percent of college food service customers are over 25. Older students are more likely to live off campus, which means retaining their business on campus is a more competitive proposition. The trend in this segment has been for colleges and universities to outsource their food service to food service management companies. In fact, the National Restaurant Association estimates the growth rate for management companies in this area will reach 7.7 percent in 1998.[8]

In summary, the college and university segment appears to be a healthy one, although students continue to become more demanding and sophisticated, suggesting greater challenges ahead for food service operators. As a result of increased participation rates and a growing population group, however, college and university food service seems likely to be a growth segment for nearly a generation to come. In addition, nontraditional opportunities are beginning to surface for food service operators. These opportunities might include extending food service responsibilities (such as to arenas, research parks, or catering services) and/or taking on a wider range of responsibilities across college campuses, including the management of mail services, campus bookstores, and facilities management.

In short, just like the other segments, the entire food service environment is changing on college campuses. As Charlie Liming, district manager for campus services at ARAMARK, put it, "The local mall is being moved to college campuses."[9]

ℋEALTH CARE FOOD SERVICE

CAREERS IN HOSPITALITY

As changes are occurring in both B&I and colleges and universities, changes are perhaps occurring at an even greater rate in the health care environment. This section will discuss some of these changes, as well as provide a general overview of this unique food service segment.

Health care facilities can be divided into three general categories: large hospitals (over 300 beds), small to medium hospitals, and nursing homes. In all three of these settings, health care professionals—*dietitians,* along with such paraprofessionals as *dietetic managers* and *dietetic technicians*—play important roles. Some of the key positions in hospital food service operations are described next.

The Dietetic Professional

"The dietitian," according to an authoritative study of the profession, "is a 'translator' of the science of nutrition into the skill of furnishing optimum nourishment. The word translator is used in its familiar context of 'translating ideas into action.' "[10]

The largest group within the profession is made up of **clinical dietitians** concerned principally with the problems of special diets and with educating patients who have health problems that require temporary or permanent diet changes. **Administrative dietitians** are concerned principally with the management of food service systems, for the most part in health care. (Dietitians also work in education and in nonhealth care food services, and their commitment to community nutrition is growing rapidly, as well.)

Dietitians who complete a bachelor's degree program and a supervised practice program (either in an internship program or in a coordinated program that combines both academic classwork and supervised practice) and who pass a national registration examination are considered registered dietitians (RDs) by the Commission on Dietetic Registration (CDR), which is the credentialing agency for the American Dietetic Association (ADA). Registered dietitians are required by hospital accreditation standards and government regulations to supervise health care food services either on a full-time basis or as consultants.

Large hospitals generally employ a number of clinical dietitians whose primary responsibility is the provision of medical nutrition therapy (MNT) for inpatients as well as outpatients. Medical nutrition therapy is the nutrition therapy component within the medical treatment and management of disease. An important part of the dietitian's work is planning and implementing the nutrition therapy so that the patient and family are able to continue the treatment after discharge.

In a smaller hospital or in a nursing home, the food service manager is somewhat less likely to be a registered dietitian. In such cases, however, a consulting registered dietitian will provide professional guidance.

The Dietetic Technician

A somewhat newer role in health care is that of the **dietetic technician.** Qualification for this designation requires completion of an appropriate associate degree program. Technicians occupy key roles in medium and large hospitals, working under the direction of registered dietitians. Dietetic technicians screen and interview patients to determine their dietary needs or problems and, in large hospitals, often have supervisory responsibilities. In smaller hospitals, technicians may run dietary departments under the periodic supervision of consulting registered dietitians. One of the most important areas of opportunity for dietetic technicians is in life care facilities, such as nursing homes, where technicians serve as food service managers under the supervision of a consulting registered dietitian. Technicians must take a registration exam, and fully qualified technicians are registered as DTRs, that is, dietetic technicians-registered.

The Dietary Manager

The **dietary manager** also has an important role in health care food service. Dietary managers must have had a considerable amount of on-the-job experience and must also have completed a course of instruction covering subjects such as food service management, supervision, and basic nutrition. A separate organization, the Dietary Managers Association, provides for their education and certification as certified dietary managers (CDMs). Certified dietary managers are not credentialed by the CDR and are not members of the ADA. Dietary managers are employed principally in nursing homes. Some dietary managers have completed the dietetic technician's more extensive two-year course of instruction and may use either title.

Dietary Department Organization

The organization of the dietary department should be considered in the context of the overall health care facility organization. However, presenting an organization chart of a "typical" hospital would be self-defeating because hospitals vary greatly in size, are organized differently, and are currently in the midst of wholesale restructuring. Readers should be aware of two trends, however, in the organization of hospitals: (1) Organizations are generally becoming flatter and (2) more and more support services are being outsourced. With this being said, the food service department must fit in with what tends to be a large and complex organization. Other functions and professional services in a hospital would include nursing, laboratories, X-ray services, ambulance services, environmental services, fiscal services, administrative services, and pharmacies, among others. The dietary department would probably be found in the general services division along with other support services, such as plant engineering and housekeeping. The fiscal services division includes functions such as accounting, receiving, and storage. Thus, in some hospitals, receiving and storage may be carried out for food service by another support unit. Administrative services include the personnel and purchasing functions. Here again, note that another division may

Figure 8.1 **Functional organization of the dietary department.**

assume these functions for the dietary department. This already-complex organization is further complicated by the medical and surgical staffs—the professionals on whose services the entire institution is centered.

Work in hospital food service is fast paced, and many employees find the medical atmosphere exciting. The organizational complexity and need for nutrition care (the provision of special therapeutic diets) as a separate concern makes a career in health care food service one of the most complex and demanding of the food service careers.

The organization of the dietary department will vary in its assignment and reporting relationships according to the size and function of the hospital. The main functions appear in Figure 8.1.

The same kitchen usually prepares the food for all the employees, house diet patients, and visitors. Some hospitals maintain a separate diet kitchen; others allow the same crew to prepare the special diets following appropriate recipes. Patient food service personnel deliver the food to the floors and return dishes and other equipment to the kitchen after the meals. One trend that is occurring in patient feeding is perhaps best illustrated by what ARAMARK is doing in some of its accounts, such as at the Tulane University Hospital and Clinic in New Orleans. There, in an effort to develop a more efficient system, ARAMARK has modified its patient meal plan by moving more toward the airline feeding model. It has all but eliminated written menus and instead offers patients a choice of two items, which are brought up to the floors and held in warming boxes. Patients then indicate their choice and the meal is brought into the room immediately. Although last-minute modifications can still be made and special diets accommodated, the average patient is fed in a much more efficient manner, resulting in fewer late trays and higher levels of patient satisfaction.

In addition to patient feeding, hospitals may have a variety of other food service outlets: Cafeterias serve the staff, visitors, and, in some cases, ambulatory patients. There may also be special dining areas limited for use by the doctors and/or senior staff. Additionally, many hospitals provide catering for in-house events while some are even branching out and doing off-premise catering for nonhospital-related events.

Nursing homes, smaller hospitals, and extended-care facilities (discussed in a later section) perform these similar functions on a smaller scale. Thus, such an institution may employ only a consulting dietitian and may combine food production and patient food service. Or the cafeterias in some nursing homes may be expanded to serve all ambulatory patients, often in traditional dining rooms.

Trends in Health Care Food Service

In the past, health care was a "recession-proof" food service segment with a strong growth potential. Although health care is still less sensitive to economic conditions than are many other food service segments, regulation by government agencies, which reimburse hospitals for many health care expenditures, complicates administration. Regulators have capped costs by limiting the length of stay that is covered. Private health insurance plans have established similar limits. As a result, hospital occupancy and revenue were limited, too. Hospitals are reacting in several ways including developing networks, affiliations with other hospitals, and their own health maintenance organizations (HMOs). Health care, in general, has had to learn to live with less. This has had a dramatic impact on dietary departments. Because there are fewer patient meals to be served, the number of staff has often been reduced. Because the development of a government-mandated health care program is still under consideration, it is difficult to foresee what its impact on health care will be if and when it is enacted beyond noting that by making health care more accessible it is likely to increase demand.

So far, lower hospital occupancy levels have led to greater competition for patients, and the dietary department often plays a key role in this competition by offering special services and frills. Hospitals have also found ways to reduce costs and boost revenue. These often include taking a marketing-oriented approach and building sales.

Lowering Costs. With skyrocketing daily charges for hospital rooms and pressure from government and insurance companies for shorter hospital stays, hospitals have developed alternative arrangements for those patients needing less-intensive care. Hospitals have converted facilities to hotel-type accommodations or developed arrangements with nearby hotels to house discharged patients who still need to remain near the hospital. These alternative accommodations are more affordable for the patient and, where in-house space is used, provide revenue to the hospital.

Another strategy for cost reduction involves consolidation of food production facilities. One large unit takes on responsibility for basic production for several nearby facilities. This centralized location may then employ a *cook-chill* food production system. Most hospitals that operate their own food service also purchase supplies, including food service products, through cooperative purchasing organizations or **group purchasing organizations** (GPOs). Pooled purchasing volumes, often in the hundreds of millions of dollars, secure lower unit costs. In addition, hospital food service, like all other food service organizations, has carefully examined its employee scheduling practices and product use to ensure maximum effi-

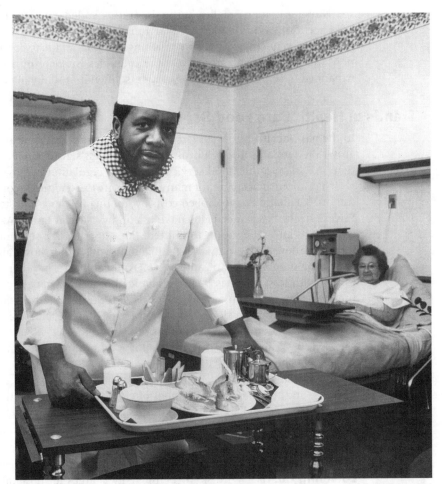

Institutional operators have the dominant role in health care food service, although contract companies are capturing an increasing share of the market.
Courtesy of St. Luke's/Roosevelt Hospital Center

ciency. One hospital specializing in short-stay elective surgery, for instance, converted completely to frozen prepared foods, eliminating its production kitchen entirely. The production activity is limited entirely to reconstituting frozen foods and portioning prepared salad greens for distribution to the floors.

Enhancing Revenue. Most hospitals serve more nonpatient than patient meals. Not surprisingly, therefore, the nonpatient side of hospital food service has offered major opportunities for increasing sales. Hospitals have upgraded their public dining facilities to attract more business from staff and visitors in the hospital. Like colleges and universities, some hospitals are adding national brands to their offerings, although not to the same extent. These not only offer greater market appeal to customers but lower operating costs.

Hospitals have also broadened their food service activities to target customers outside the hospital. For instance, Windham Hospital, a 120-bed hospital in Connecticut, has begun an off-site food delivery program. The program targets anyone in the area who needs upscale meals delivered to their homes for any short period of time.[11] Other programs and services currently being offered by hospitals include Meals on Wheels and providing meals to day care centers.

Additionally, some hospitals offer what is, in effect, commercial catering—handling weddings and other functions both on and off premise. Hospital bakeries offer fresh baked breads and pastries, including wedding cakes, to the public. Others offer regular take-out meals, delicatessens, even on-premise convenience stores. In general, hospitals are becoming very creative in adding revenue-enhancing services. One New Orleans area hospital, East Jefferson General Hospital, has recently added meeting and conference space to its facility in an effort to capitalize upon a perceived need in the local market.

In summary, health care institutions have been subject to cost pressures that result from both government regulation and from competitive pressures. Health care institutions have responded with efforts to contain costs and to enhance revenues with a better mix of services aimed at a broader spectrum of customers, that is, with an improved marketing program. Much of the burden has fallen on the food service directors of these facilities who are taking on more and more responsibilities through expanded roles and increased services. We should end this section by noting, in addition, that health care is expected to be one of the fastest-growing areas in the economy well into the 21st century.

$\mathcal{S}$CHOOL AND COMMUNITY FOOD SERVICE

The fourth major segment of the institutional sector is **school and community food service.** This segment is quite different from the previously discussed segments in several ways, including the high degree of self-ops, the goals and objectives of the segment, and the challenges that the segment is currently facing (e.g., tight budgetary constraints). This section will focus on the unique aspects of the segment.

The earliest government food service programs began around 1900 in Europe.[12] Programs in the United States date from the Great Depression, when the need to use surplus agricultural commodities was joined to concern for feeding the children of poor families. During and after World War II, the explosion in the number of working women fueled the need for a broader program. What was once a function of the family—providing lunch—was, in effect, shifted to the school food service system. From the end of World War II to the early 1980s, funding for school food service expanded steadily. With the coming of a more conservative administration, however, school food service (along with many other social service programs) was cut back drastically during the 1980s. Still, the basic functions of the program remain substantially the same.

The first function is to provide a nutritious lunch to all students; the second is to provide nutritious food at both breakfast and lunch to underprivileged children. If anything, the role of school food service as a replacement for what were once family functions has been expanded.

The U.S. Department of Agriculture (USDA) regulations have, for many years, required that school lunches conform to a basic pattern. A recent change now means that schools that receive federal subsidies must establish their meal plans based on the calorie, nutrient, and fat content of foods instead of on the food group, as was the previous practice. This change went into effect beginning with the 1996/1997 academic year. Changes are based on the new dietary guidelines developed by the USDA.

A significant portion of the cost of school food service is met by subsidies in cash and kind provided by federal and state governments and the local school board. Children who qualify according to a means test receive a free lunch and breakfast. The majority of children participating in the school breakfast program qualify as disadvantaged.

Funding restrictions, however, have presented difficulties for school food service programs. The most obvious response to reduced government funding is to raise prices, but this often results in reduced participation rates. In conversations with school food service managers, as well as the American School Food Service Association, it would appear that the operating premise that many managers abide by is that, for every cent that the student costs increase, participation drops 1 percent. School districts have reacted to reduced funding in much the same way that other institutions have, by increased marketing activity and, to a lesser degree, by diversification of activities to gain more revenues.

An additional challenge facing school food service programs has been the requirement of nutritious selections. The most successful response to this has been to develop menu offerings that closely resemble fast-food menus yet meet the USDA guidelines. Pizza, Mexican foods, chicken nuggets, and popular sandwiches such as hamburgers and hot dogs play a major role in such menus. In effect, these menus give the consumers what they want. They are often criticized, however, for not doing the educational job of teaching students what they should eat. Nevertheless, given pressure to sell food at higher prices to maintain their economic viability, schools have had to embrace a marketing approach to survive.

School food service districts have also expanded their operations to outside customers. Efforts to build sales volume include catering and selling take-out items, including fresh baked goods, as well as selling prepared foods to other institutional customers in the community.

Marketing efforts are not limited to menu and format alterations. To meet the need to communicate with customers, student advisory councils are formed in schools. School lunch dining areas are upgraded and remodeled to make them more attractive. Self-service speeds service while reducing cost and gives the customer a feeling of having a choice. Food bars, buffets, and scramble systems are seeing greater utilization in schools. An example of how one school combined marketing with service to increase participation is exemplified in the Cleveland school system, which uses mobile breakfast kiosks that can be moved directly to individual classrooms![13]

The School Food Service Model

The accumulated experience of school food service suggests a model for public sector food service programs. The first element in that model is that it meet clearly defined social needs that attract broad public support. School food service provides nutritious meals to needy children who might otherwise go hungry, and it helps make well-balanced meals available to all students.

The second element in the **school food service model** is that it pools subsidies. The federal subsidy usually requires matching state or local funds. Because the subsidies from the various levels of government are pooled, the result constitutes a "bargain." The student's lunch, even if he or she paid the full price, is less expensive than it would be if purchased anywhere else—even if it were brought from home.

The attractiveness of this bargain encourages participation, and participation ensures the third element of the model, a high volume. This high volume makes the meal program more efficient, and it results in further economies. In short, it improves the bargain.

The pattern of administration is the fourth and final element. There is general monitoring of the fairly broad guidelines at the national and state levels, but most

Centralized preparation of food in many school systems permits significant economies of scale.
Courtesy of Sky Chefs, Inc.

operational decisions are made entirely at the local level. Technical advice is always available. Thus, the model encourages adaptation to local tastes and conditions.

The "bargain" that school lunches offer to young consumers and their families never has been completely dependent on federal subsidies. Both state and local governments (and, in some communities, charitable organizations) have contributed to the cost of school lunches in direct subsidies of varying amounts.

Increasingly, the school is being seen not just as an educational institution but as a social agency in the community that can use its physical plant—buildings, kitchens, dining areas—and its other resources, such as experienced administration, skilled cooks, and backup custodial staff, to serve a variety of population groups. Schools around the country are now getting involved with the feeding of seniors, day care centers, off-site feeding such as at public parks during the summer, and various other community support services.

Contract Companies in School Food Service

A relatively new market for contract companies is the school market. The lowest penetration of contract companies among the four segments is in school food service. Many school boards, however, facing tighter budgetary restrictions, are finding it advantageous to bring in a company with specialized food service expertise to take on what is, for them, an activity only indirectly related to education, which is the school system's principal mission and expertise. Because such a high percentage of the market is "self-op" (i.e., operated by the school system), there is a huge market for contract companies to pursue. Although its profit margin is not as high as for some other institutional sectors, school food service is a logical addition to a contract company's operations. Contract companies do not just take over one or two schools when they receive an account. Rather, the numbers can run into the 100s as was the case in Chicago where the number of school programs under the control of contract companies is 370.[14] In addition, in many cases, the contract company finds it can serve a school board not only with food service but also in other areas, such as grounds maintenance and custodial services.

In an interview in which she discussed career opportunities with contract companies in the school food service area, Beth Tarter, human resources manager for Sodexho Marriott Service, pointed out that there are a number of advantages to this area. Because it is growing, there are numerous opportunities for advancement. The excitement of a very large account—$5 or $6 million—is more likely to come at an earlier stage than in other areas of food service. School food service also has quality-of-life advantages. This is an area that offers a professional career in food service with a five-day week. Night and weekend work occurs occasionally, usually in connection with a special event at a school, but such an event is the exception. Moreover, many people in school food service have 10½-month contracts that give them their summers off. One manager whose main joy in life is sailing pointed out that he could find no better job to match his professional expertise and his leisure interest. He spends his summers on a sailboat. Clearly, there are some advantages for students who might choose this segment of the industry.

Service Programs for the Aging

One of the fastest-growing segments of our population for the foreseeable future will be people over the age of 65. Although many people in this age bracket are healthy and active, not all of them are. Similarly, many but not all of the people over the age of 65 are comfortable financially. Although retirement incomes for most are not as high as for working people, neither are financial needs. Many live in homes already paid for and have significant savings to draw on. On the other hand, not all elderly are affluent. Many must live on their social security checks and limited savings. People over 75 are more likely to fall into this category. They are more likely to be financially needy and to require assistance to survive. The rapid growth of this group is one reason for the increasing demand for government supportive services for the elderly.

People over 65 commonly have disabilities related to their age. By age 65, for instance, over two-thirds of individuals have a least one chronic condition. Of the individuals between the ages of 65 and 74, only 20 percent need assistance in performing their daily activities. However, once they reach the age of 85 or older, almost one-half experience some difficulty with daily activities such as bathing or dressing.[15] Disabilities such as these tend to be concentrated among those in the latter age group.

The Census Bureau predicts continuing growth for those in both the 65 and older age group and the 85 and older age group. Their predictions suggest that, by 2050, the elderly population will increase more than twofold. Those aged 85 and older will constitute 5 percent of the population.[16] Certainly, this is a population group that will be growing for the foreseeable future and one that has a set of unique needs. We will look briefly at programs to meet the needs for food service in this section. We will also examine the growing life care institutional segment in which hotel companies such as Marriott and Hyatt figure prominently.

Community-Based Services

The ideal arrangement for the elderly is to live independently in their own homes. As their physical and mental abilities deteriorate, however, they begin to require assistance. Many Americans provide help to elderly friends or family members without pay. Community agencies have come into being to provide help to people living independently and to families who are helping an elderly relative or friend.

Approximately 123 million **congregate meals** were provided to 2½ million elderly in 1995, while another 119 million meals were delivered to almost one million people through Meals on Wheels, according to the Administration on Aging (AOA).[17]

The national nutrition program for the elderly is designed to provide older Americans, particularly those with low income, with low-cost, nutritionally sound meals. Emphasis is given to providing these meals in group settings. The nutritional projects provide at least one hot meal a day (meeting one-third of the daily nutritional requirements) five days a week to older citizens (60+) and their spouses of any age.

Although participants would be given an opportunity to pay for their meals, "no means test will be made and no one will be turned away on the basis of their inability to pay for a meal." Congregate meals are funded by the Administration on Aging and by state and local agencies.

Meals on Wheels and similar programs also receive direct and indirect support from all levels of government and from local private agencies, as well. The programs deliver meals to people living in their homes who have difficulty getting out. In addition to funding from governmental and private agencies, these programs often rely on local volunteers to assist in fulfilling their mission.

Retirement Housing Communities

A number of firms, including hotel companies like Marriott International and Hyatt, have become active in providing housing, and, in some cases, a mix of additional services, to affluent senior citizens. Some seniors want to live in a community that can provide the independence of apartment living along with the security of having health care and professional services available without having to move to another facility. Others desire to live in an environment that provides them with a higher level of assistance with daily activities. Such facilities obviously provide much more than just food service and, in fact, incorporate many components of various hospitality services discussed in this and other chapters.

Different levels of accommodations and services are provided in retirement communities. These are often categorized as follows:

Independent living. Private apartment living where residents enjoy an independent lifestyle, with the security of knowing that whatever services or professional assistance they may need are readily available.

Assisted living. Private apartment living for residents who can maintain an independent lifestyle, but need limited assistance with day-to-day activities such as dressing, grooming, bathing, or monitoring of medication.

Personal care. Personal care takes assisted living a step further by providing a greater level of hands-on assistance in performing daily activities, while allowing residents to maintain as much independence as possible.

Licensed nursing facility. Private and semiprivate rooms are available for residents who need long-term or short-term intermediate and/or skilled nursing care and supervision.

These describe the four basic models under which many retirement communities may operate, although an individual operation may fall anywhere along this continuum. In addition, there is currently a movement in the industry toward developing **continuing care retirement communities (CCRCs).** Companies providing this level of services offer a wide range of life care services, all under one roof. Seniors typically pay one price and are guaranteed different levels of life care as they age and as required.

Marriott Senior Living Services operates over 80 retirement communities in all. Their Brighton Gardens line of communities represent their assisted-living segment. In these communities, seniors receive, in addition to housing and meals, housekeeping services and various social programs. They also offer additional health care services in some of the communities.

Hyatt Corporation, another hotel company active in this field, operated 10 high-end retirement communities in 1998 under the Classic Residence banner. Negotiations are in progress for acquisition and further development, indicating a major corporate commitment to the field. Hyatt facilities offer a range of services and, in some cases, are CCRCs. Earlier in the decade, Penny Pritzker, president of Classic Residence by Hyatt, pointed out that such residences are principally a need-driven service business catering to people 75 years of age and older. Most people, she noted, would prefer to stay in their own home, but events such as the death of a spouse or problems of health that make going up stairs or driving a car difficult or impossible require them to choose a lifestyle that provides more assistance. Further, Ms. Pritzker noted that retirement housing is a marketing-intensive business in which referrals based on success with your present residents are crucial. "The business," she said, "is psychology as much as service." The successful operator combines the ability to deal professionally with the resident with an ability to deal compassionately and to recognize that your operation is your resident's home.[18]

Classic Residences by Hyatt offer luxury accommodations to senior citizens.
Courtesy of Hyatt Hotels Corporation; Photo by Stan Ries

As with every other segment discussed in this chapter, food service plays a major role in senior living centers, serving utility, social, and pleasure functions. In support of this, a survey of Marriott Senior Living Services notes that 91 percent of seniors responding said food quality was an important factor in choosing a retirement center.

There are many other service companies that operate in this unique segment, including ServiceMaster and others. However, in addition to the major companies involved with the management of retirement communities, there are also many independently operated facilities. An example of an independently operated facility, would be Woldenberg Village located in New Orleans. The Woldenberg "campus" consists of The Living Centre (nursing home) and The Villas (a 60-unit facility), which is described as an independent-living facility with services. Residents of Woldenberg are essentially able to live independently and, if desired, choose from the various service packages available to them. As opposed to the "one-size-fits-all" philosophy, residents can choose from among the various packages available and pay on an à la carte basis.

In the early 1990s, this sector of hospitality was characterized by high business failure rates. Some of the problems experienced by operators included lack of operating know-how suited to the specific market, poor location choices, overrapid expansion, a nursing shortage, and increasing regulation. Since that time, new companies have entered the market and failed projects have been absorbed. As a result, industry analysts view this segment very favorably leading into the next decade. The only question that remains is whether supply can continue to meet the ever-increasing demand.

OTHER INSTITUTIONAL FOOD SERVICE SEGMENTS

In addition to the four institutional segments already discussed, there are a variety of other segments that are sometimes less visible than their higher-profile counterparts yet are still deserving of attention. Unfortunately, it is beyond the scope of this chapter to cover all of the different types of businesses that could conceivably fall into this category but some very important types of services are discussed next. As evidenced by the large size of the organizations in these sectors, each of them is an important element in the food service (and related) industries.

Recreation

Recreational food service is one of the widest reaching of all the segments discussed thus far. This segment can include food service in such diverse facilities as stadiums and arenas, convention centers, zoos and aquariums, and even fairs and expositions, among others. As with other segments, facilities may be managed or self-operated.

One contract management company, ARAMARK, has its own division devoted to this segment. ARAMARK's Sports and Entertainment Services division presents a profile of a company with involvement in a variety of recreational activities. In 1998, ARAMARK operated food service at 18 convention centers; 75 stadiums, arenas, and racetracks; and a variety of state and national parks.[19] In addition, ARAMARK has been responsible for the food service at virtually all Olympic and Pan American games since 1968. Another company, which specializes in stadium and arena feeding, is Sportservice, a division of Delaware North.

More and more, companies seem to be recognizing this segment for its dynamic operating environment, as well as for the opportunities it affords. Recreation feeding plays the enviable role of complementing some of life's pleasures such as a day at the ballpark or the state fair. In fact, it seems that entertainment is nearly as important to stadium operators as a winning team, so we see more and more of a Disneyland kind of format that emphasizes enjoying the experience of coming to a ball game as much as the sport itself. Hospitality service, particularly food service, has an important role to play in delivering the experience.

As in other institutions, brand names are becoming increasingly important. National names like McDonald's are prominent in stadiums but often local or regional brands are represented as well. Although hot dogs, soft drinks, and beer are still the most popular items, ballparks and other recreation sites are expanding their menus to include more upscale foods (the tiramisu at the FleetCenter in Boston is rumored to be very good). As the entertainment and recreation sector continues to thrive, so too should the food services associated with it.

Private Clubs

A segment not totally unrelated to the recreation segment is that segment consisting of private clubs. *Private clubs* are just that—recreational, social, and/or dining facilities available for the exclusive use of their members. Clubs are characterized by their independence, exclusivity, and unique qualities. In fact, it has been said many times that no two clubs are exactly alike. This segment includes city clubs (which tend to focus on dining services), yacht clubs, swimming clubs, tennis clubs, golf clubs, and country clubs (which tend to be full service), among others. In reality, there may be a club devoted to just about any activity that you may think of but, more often than not, food service constitutes a large part of what they offer to their members. Clubs provide a home away from home for their members and, as a result, they are often characterized by a high level of personal service.

Clubs may be owned by their members (in which case the club usually hires a professional manager). These types of clubs tend to be run on a not-for-profit basis. Clubs may also be owned independently or by a corporation, in which case they would be operated on a for-profit basis. Finally, as with other segments within the larger institutional sector, there are companies that specialize in the management of clubs (such as Club Corporation of America).

Although the majority of successful club managers have extensive food and beverage experience, students should be aware that, in order to be successful, a manager must be a jack-of-all-trades. Managing a large club usually means overseeing many different types of departments requiring a unique level of expertise. Clubs truly combine all of the best things that the hospitality industry has to offer, all under one roof.

Transportation

In the United States, *transportation food service* is usually synonymous with airline (or **in-flight**) food service. Of course, there is food service associated with other forms of transportation, including rail and ferry, but the industry is dominated by food service geared to air passengers. As with other segments, there are companies that operate their own food service (such as United Airlines), as well as companies that specialize in in-flight feeding (Dobbs International). Many of these companies are quite large and regularly appear on lists of the largest food service companies.

The airline food service business is fast paced and requires people who work well under pressure. The uncertain number of passengers on an outbound flight, sudden cancellations or additions to the airlines' flight schedules, and the various equipment configurations used in different aircraft make in-flight food service a challenging field. Add to this that the production area is often located some distance away from the airport and one can imagine some of the challenges associated with this type of food service.

As with every other segment, however, airline food service is changing. There seems to be no clear trend indicating how the different companies are implementing these changes and, more specifically, modifying their services. Some are cutting back their services, some are eliminating their food service entirely, while others are putting a greater emphasis on their food service. Those companies that are putting a greater emphasis on food are hiring high-profile chefs as consultants and partnering with other companies (e.g., United Airlines and Starbucks). What is clear is that one decision that every airline must make involves food.

Perhaps one of the biggest changes taking place in transportation food service is happening on the ground. Specifically, food service in airports is becoming big business. Airports around the country now offer a selection of products and services once unimaginable. T.G.I. Friday's, Samuel Adams Brewpubs, Au Bon Pain, Cafe du Monde, Starbucks, and a variety of other recognizable food service providers have begun targeting airline terminals. Even theme restaurants can be found in airports. One recent example is The Encounter, a restaurant with a space theme, located at Los Angeles International Airport.

Although different companies may sometimes manage in-flight food service and airport food service, the two are irrefutably linked. As more passengers travel by air, they will expect to be able to have the same choices that are available to them elsewhere. Research is also indicating that travelers are now expecting something more than the usual quick-service outlets. The evidence suggests, however, that some of the more dynamic changes in the industry are occurring in this segment.

VENDING

Vending is not really a segment of institutional food service but a method of delivering food service that is used in all segments. Vending is most common in the college and university and business and industry segments; it is least common in schools. Although vending is used in institutions, it is also used in many other settings such as hotels and retail stores. At $7.2 billion,[20] vending is a major factor in

Case History 8.1 Vending Meets One Building's Food Service Needs

An office building housing some 2500 employees was built in the heart of a large city. The designers refused to incorporate a restaurant because kitchen facilities and storerooms would take up space destined for other uses. Dishrooms and the necessary plumbing and air ducts required for a kitchen would also have added to the cost of the building.

In addition, the building's management did not feel qualified to operate its own food service and had heard that leased restaurants often took up much of the building manager's time. Finally, management felt that a restaurant would also create traffic problems at the loading dock, with the numerous deliveries and garbage and trash removal.

Although captial expenses and operating complications argued against a restaurant, the designers wanted food service available in the building as a convenience to the occupants. Consequently, they designed vending restaurants that would provide an ample menu selection, including not only sandwiches but also scrambled eggs, sausage, and pancakes for breakfast, and fried chicken, french fried potatoes, Salisbury steak, and other traditional entrées for lunch and dinner. Although entrées such as these currently account for only a small percentage of food service vending sales, their presence constitutes an important service for the guest.

The food (including sandwiches, which make up some three-quarters of vended food service sales) is prepared at the vendor's commissary. The food is delivered before the building's regular operating hours, to avoid congestion.

food service, accounting for over 2 percent of the 1997 national total. Beyond vending's aggregate size, we need to consider vending here briefly to understand its function for clients and the advantages (and disadvantages) it presents to guests.

Most vended food falls in the snack and beverage categories. A significant portion, however, constitutes main meal service, particularly breakfast and, to a lesser degree, lunch. Technological advantages are improving the variety and quality of product offered through vending. New products include pizza, pastas, and upscale beverages such as cappuccino. In addition, the snacks and beverages are commonly used to supplement main meals brought from home. Vending, therefore, plays an important role in the overall food service business, as is indicated in the following example.

A professional building accommodating about 500 people opened a small table service restaurant just off the lobby. The occupants of the building were unhappy with the quality of the operation, however, and the operator finally went out of business. Its eight employees were replaced by a vending restaurant that offered a variety of specialty sandwiches prepared in the vendor's commissary and heated by the customer in an on-site microwave oven. The operation required one attendant on duty from 8:00 A.M. to 4:30 P.M. on weekdays.

Guests are rarely enthusiastic about vending restaurants, but their impersonality can be reduced by attended vending, which provides a specially trained host or hostess who makes change, gives refunds, and handles complaints. Still, vending remains primarily a mechanical, self-service process.

On the positive side, vending restaurants are convenient, can solve economic and operational problems for building and plant managers, and can increase food service variety. Most food service vending operations are found in public buildings, plants, factories, and offices in which the clientele is too small to justify a full-fledged food service operation and too far from other restaurant facilities for the employees to reach them easily on their lunch hours. Case History 8.1 describes how a vending restaurant proved to be the ideal solution in one office building.

The variety of products that vendors sell is growing and improving. About half of the companies offering vended food services have their own commissaries, and their vending outlets usually are equipped with microwave ovens.

Vending is clearly a part of the eating market, as defined in Chapter 3, rather than the dining market. Vending companies have found that if they offer manual vending (i.e., a cafeteria staffed by "real, live" people) during some of their hours of service, all of their products are more likely to be accepted. One vendor speculated that this is true because the personal touch allows the guests to associate the vended food with the people who provide food services in the more traditional cafeterias.

Vending offers the hospitality industry a means of extending food service hours to meet the convenience of guests and to provide acceptable service where it would be economically impossible to provide full manual food service.

UMMARY

It should be clear at this point that the institutional sector is a wide-reaching and incredibly varied segment with many unique qualities. Although the institution has a greater hold on its market because of convenience, restaurants provide a lively alternative and plenty of competition for most institutions. In addition, institutional food service must serve the needs of both the client institution and the individual guest. Contract companies have the largest market share in business and industry and college and university food service. Institutional operators have the dominant role in health care and school food service, although contract companies' share of those markets has been increasing. Brand name concepts and aggressive marketing are important in all sectors of institutional food service.

The largest food service program is school food service. Its long experience in serving young people and their families suggests a model for other public-sector activities. That model is based on acknowledged social need, pooling of subsidies, concentration of activity to achieve high volume, and flexible administration that permits local initiatives.

Retirement housing communities provide affluent older people with as much independence as they can manage but also afford them support, such as health care, without requiring them to move to another place. Other areas discussed were recreation, transportation (mainly airline), and a somewhat unique segment—private clubs.

Vending is an important method of delivering food service, particularly in places that are not large enough to support a full food service operation or where the investment in facilities and operating support needed by food service cannot be made.

The principal arguments regarding the choice between an institutional operation and a contract company involve questions of scale, control of operations, and management expertise.

◆ 𝒦EY WORDS AND CONCEPTS

Contract management companies
Institutional operations
Self-ops
Participation rate
Outsource
Business and industry (B&I) food service
Brands
College and university food service
Board plan
Health care food service
Clinical dietitians
Administrative dietitians

Dietetic technician
Dietary manager
Group purchasing organizations (GPOs)
School and community food service
School food service model
Congregate meals
Continuing care retirement communities (CCRCs)
In-flight
Vending

◆ 𝓡EVIEW QUESTIONS

1. What do institutional and commercial food services have in common? How are they different?

2. How do guest and client interests differ? What interests do they have in common?

3. Who operates the food service in your institution? Do you think an institutional operator or a contract company will do the best job of providing for the needs of the guest? Of the client? Why?

4. What characteristics are important to each of the four major divisions of institutional food service?

5. What opportunities do you see for extending hospitality services to the elderly? What facilities are available in your community for independent living for the aging?

6. What are some of the factors that have caused airport food service to become so dynamic?

7. What do you think might be some of the challenges associated with the management of a member-owned club?

8. What are the advantages and drawbacks of vending for the client? For the guest?

◆ 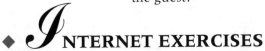NTERNET EXERCISES

1. **Site Name:** *ARAMARK Managed Services*
   URL: http://www.aramark.com
   Background Informaton: The world's largest managed services company, ARAMARK manages operations that support its customers' businesses with everything from food to uniforms to health care.

   EXERCISES:

   a. Surf the web site and identify the managed services that ARAMARK provides.

   b. Describe how an individual would determine job vacancies with ARAMARK and how you would apply for a position with ARAMARK.

2. **Site Name:** *Dietary Managers Association*
   URL: http://www.dmaonline.org/index.html
   Background Information: The Dietary Managers Association (DMA) is a not-for-profit association established in 1960 that today has over 16,000 professionals dedicated to the mission: "to provide optimum nutritional care through food service management." DMA members work in hospitals, long-term care facilities, schools, correctional facilities, and other noncommercial settings.

   EXERCISE: What are the benefits of belonging to the Dietary Managers Association?

3. **Site Name:** *American Society for Healthcare Food Service Administrators*
   URL: http://www.ashfsa.org/
   Background Information: Since its beginning in 1967, the American Society for Healthcare Food Service Administrators (ASHFSA) has continued to provide members with quality education, networking, and opportunities for professional growth. It is one of 15 personal membership societies of the American Hospital Association.

   EXERCISES:

   a. Surf the ASHFSA web site. What are the benefits of belonging to this association?

   b. What is the mission and vision of this organization?

OTES

1. *Nations Restaurant News,* December 17, 1990, p. 48.

2. *Restaurants USA,* Vol. 17, No. 11, December 1997, p. F19.

3. *Nations Restaurant News,* December 17, 1990, p. 58.

4. Marriott Management Services Press Release, October 17, 1996.

5. *Food Service Director,* October 15, 1997, p. 12.

6. *Restaurants USA,* Vol. 17, No. 11, December 1997, p. F16.

7. Chronicle of Higher Education Almanac, 1997–1998.

8. *Restaurants USA,* December 1997, p. F7.

9. Charlie Liming, District Manager, Campus Services, ARAMARK, Personal communication, February 11, 1998.

10. *The Profession of Dietetics: Report of the Study Commission on Dietetics* (Chicago: American Dietetic Association, 1972).

11. *Food Service Director,* October 15, 1997, p. 1.

12. For an authoritative, extended treatment of the school food service program, see Gordon W. Gunderson, *The National School Lunch Program: Background and Development* (Washington, DC: Food and Nutrition Service, U.S. Department of Agriculture, n.d.).

13. *Foodservice—A Segmented Industry* (Chicago: International Foodservice Manufacturers Association, 1995).

14. Janice Matsumoto, "Giant Strides," *Restaurants and Institutions,* August 15, 1997.

15. *American Demographics,* July 1997.

16. U.S. Census Bureau, "Sixty-Five Plus in the United States," May 1995.

17. Administration on Aging web site (**www.aoa.dhhs.gov**), March 26, 1998.

18. Penny Pritzker, Remarks made during a panel discussion, "Hospitals and Congregate Living Centers," 12th Annual Hospitality Industry Investment Conference, New York, June 3–5, 1990.

19. ARAMARK web site (**www.aramark.com/services/sports.htm**), March 8, 1998.

20. *Restaurants USA,* December 1997, p. F7. The figure given is for vending and nonstore retailers.

Part 3

Lodging

$\mathcal{C}$hapter 9

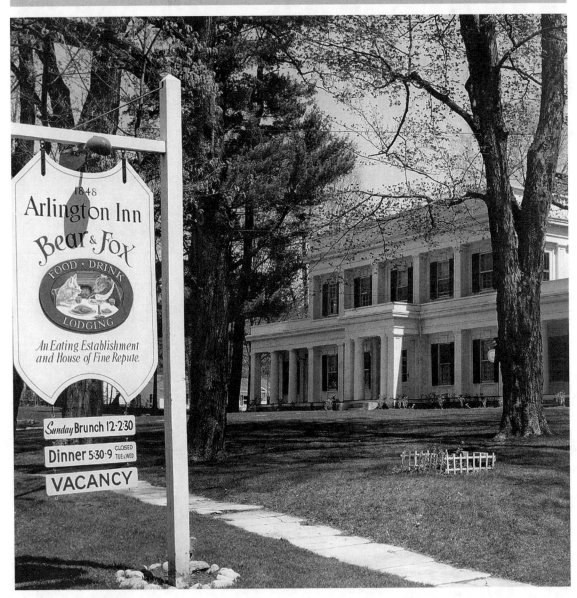

Courtesy Vermont Travel Division

Lodging: Meeting Guest Needs

The Purpose of This Chapter

In this chapter, we look at lodging as a set of products and services that have evolved out of guest needs and preferences. We begin with the evolution of lodging to fit transportation and destination patterns and individual guest preferences. To develop an understanding of our guests, we look at trends and guest preferences in business travel, leisure travel, and international travel. With an understanding of the broad outlines of who our customers are, we will consider the six rate and service level–based categories of lodging and then lodging types that are based on function rather than price and service level.

This Chapter Should Help You

1. Trace the recent evolution of lodging and relate it to changing patterns of transportation, destinations, and guest needs

2. Identify the principal customer types served by the hotel industry

3. Discuss trends in business travel and the possible reasons behind them

4. Understand the needs and preferences of business travelers

5. Characterize leisure and personal travel in terms of its importance to the lodging market and its outlook

6. Explain the importance of international travel and the steps that are being taken by operators to develop this source of business

7. Differentiate between full-service and limited-service properties and trace those differences to guest preferences

8. List the six rate and service level-based lodging categories and discuss the prospects for each

9. Identify property types that are based on function rather than rate and service level and describe the function of each

*T*HE EVOLUTION OF LODGING

The lodging business has always followed the **patterns of transportation and destinations** of its time: caravansaries, inns along Roman roads, posthouses, and so forth. It has responded, too, to changes in destination patterns. Toward the end of the 19th century, North American hotels grew up to serve the rail traveler. Often the hotel was physically connected to the railroad station. A few of these hotels still survive, and some, such as Toronto's Royal York, remain thriving centers. Of the hotels built during the first half of this century, those not physically connected to the railroad station were usually convenient to it and to the major destinations in the downtown sections of cities.

In the past, although differences in quality and price existed, most hotels provided products and services for the entire market. Now, however, lodging responds not only to changing transportation and destination patterns but also to the varying specialized needs of travelers, producing distinctively different products for different market segments.

The two principal determinants of the location of a hotel, the transportation system and the destination, were themselves greatly changed in the period of economic expansion that followed World War II. As a result, several waves of hotel and motel building have altered the face of American innkeeping.

The Motel

Although a few "Mo Hotels," or **motels,** were to be found in the Southwest even in the late 1920s, and "tourist courts" began to appear in the 1930s, the big wave of motel building followed World War II.

The end of the war released a pent-up demand for automobiles. During the 1930s, depressed economic conditions prevented many people from buying a car; then during the war, automotive production concentrated on military needs. The explosive growth in auto travel that followed the end of the war brought people into the travel market, as both buyers and sellers.

The first motels were small, simple affairs, commonly with under 20 units (or guest rooms). These properties lacked the complex facilities of a hotel and were generally managed by resident owners with a few paid employees.

They were built at the edge of town, where land costs were substantially lower than downtown. The single-story construction that typified motels until the late 1950s (and even the two-story pattern of later motor hotels) offered construction that was significantly less expensive, compared with the downtown high-rise properties that were built on prime real estate. Capital costs, such as land and building, represent the largest single cost in many lodging establishments, and so lower land and building costs and the lower capital costs that resulted gave motels significant advantages. These savings could be, and generally were, passed on to the guests in the form of lower rates.

Probably more important, motels offered a location convenient to the highway. Because the typical guest traveled by car, he or she could drive to any local destination during the day, returning to the accommodations in the evening. Meanwhile, inexperienced travelers, who had always been put off by the formality of hotels, with their dressy room clerks, bellhops who had to be tipped, and ornate lobbies, preferred the informal atmosphere of the motel, a "come as you are," atmosphere in terms of both dress and social preferences. In the motel, they might be greeted by the owner working the front desk. Motel operators were proud of their informality. The personal touch they offered guests and the motel's convenience and lower prices were their stock in trade. Few motel operators had formal training, and many would gladly tell one and all that their lack of professional training was the very secret of their success.

The Motor Hotel

For a few years, it appeared that hotels (in general, the relatively large downtown properties) and motels (usually the small properties located at the edge of town) would battle for the new mobile tourist market. Unhappily for both the hotel and the mom-and-pop motel, the situation was not that simple.

In 1952, Kemmons Wilson, a Memphis home-building and real estate developer, took his family on a vacation trip. He was depressed by the dearth of accommodations to meet his family's and the business traveler's needs. He returned to Memphis with a vision of a new kind of motel property that combined the advantage of a hotel's broad range of services with a motel's convenience to the auto traveler. That insight, which came to be known as the **motor hotel,** revolutionized the lodging industry.

Motels became larger and began to offer a wide range of services. Dining rooms or coffee shops, cocktail lounges, and meeting rooms appealed to the business traveler. Swimming pools became essential to the touring family. Room telephones, usually present in hotels but generally absent in motels, became the rule in motor hotels, thus requiring a switchboard and someone to operate it. Whereas hotels and motels had offered coin-operated radios and television, free television and then free color television became the rule.

Although there were experiments with smaller inns, having 50 to 75 rooms, most lodging companies determined that generally a 100-unit facility was the smallest that made economic sense. That size permitted full utilization of the minimum operating staff and provided a sufficient sale size to amortize the investment in such supportive services as pools and restaurants. However, with the advent of the limited-service hotel, which does not include a restaurant, smaller properties in small cities are once again feasible.

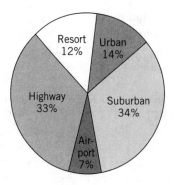

Figure 9.1 Room supply by location.
(*Source:* John Rohs and Warren Gump, *Lodging Industry Annual Review,* February 25, 1998; Smith Travel Research.)

The number of highway hotels and motels increased by nearly 1 percent in 1996 and almost 2 percent in 1997, while demand for these properties declined slightly.[1] As Figure 9.1 indicates, roughly one-third of U.S. hotel rooms are highway hotels and well over half of the country's economy properties have highway locations.[2] In 1997, highway hotels had an average daily rate (ADR) of $55, an occupancy of 60.8 percent, and, as a result, revenue per available room (RevPAR) of $34. Table 9.1 summarizes the performance of hotels classified by the hotels' location.

The Airport Motor Hotel. In the 1950s and 1960s, as air travel became more and more common, a new kind of property appeared, designed especially to accommodate air travelers. Even though these travelers arrive by air, they rent cars often enough to justify a lodging design similar to that of the motor hotel. The principal distinction of the airport property is its location. **Airport hotels** offer most of the facilities of a downtown hotel, although at a somewhat more moderate rate. They tend to emphasize small- to medium-sized meeting room capacities, because of the preponderance of business meetings at these properties. An important "extra" service provided by almost all airport hotels is the courtesy van, which offers guests

Table 9.1 Location Market Performance Rankings

Rank by 1997 Data	Revenues ($B)	Room Supply (millions)	RevPAR[a]	Occupancy	ADR
Suburban	$20.9	1202 (1)	$48 (4)	65.9% (4)	$72 (4)
Urban	14.9	509 (3)	$80 (1)	69.8% (2)	$115 (1)
Highway	14.0	1145 (2)	$34 (5)	60.8% (5)	$55 (5)
Resort	12.2	419 (4)	$80 (2)	69.7% (3)	$115 (2)
Airport	4.8	240 (5)	$55 (3)	70.5% (1)	$78 (3)

[a]Revenue per available room. This ratio is often taken as the best single measure of the utilization of assets.
Source: John Rohs and Warren Gump, *Lodging Industry Annual Review,* February 25, 1998; Smith Travel Research.

transportation between the property and the airport. Seven percent of U.S. hotels have airport locations. In 1997, airport hotels achieved an average rate of $78 and an occupancy of 70.5 percent.

The Downtown Hotel

Although the older **downtown hotels** faced new competition on the edge of town, they had little competition from the downtown market areas because new properties there were scarce. At about the same time that U.S. cities began their urban renewal, however, the interstate highway system began to penetrate the downtown areas. The downtown renewal area, with its new office and shopping complexes, often revived interest in hotel construction designed to serve these new destinations. Urban renewal, coupled with the limited-access interstate highway, opened up the city to the nation's travelers.

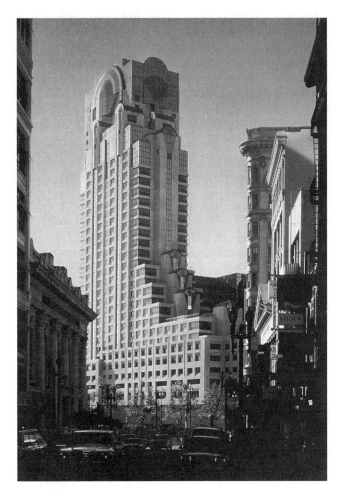

Downtown hotels like the San Francisco Marriott are almost always high-rise properties. The high cost of land requires a large number of rooms to cover the investment.
Courtesy of Marriott International

Downtown properties have many advantages. They are near the large office complexes and retail stores; by day, they are near business destinations; and by night, they are close to many of a large city's entertainment centers. Although the downtown property generally depends less on "off-the-road" travelers than do the motor hotels, their guests arrive often enough by automobile (and use rented cars often enough) to justify ample facilities for automobiles. These facilities commonly include a motor entrance and on-premise parking accessible to a guest without assistance from (and tips for) the hotel staff. Many well-located older downtown properties have also been remodeled to include most of these facilities. Although on-premise parking has not always been feasible, reasonably convenient off-premise parking with valet service to pick up and deliver the car is common. Thus, nearly all first-class downtown properties are reasonably "auto friendly" in their design. According to Smith Travel Research,[3] 14 percent of U.S. hotels are urban hotels (i.e., downtown). They achieved an occupancy of 68.8 percent and an average rate of $115. The higher rate is needed to offset the higher land cost and the fact that many downtown hotels have more extensive public facilities (i.e., banquet and meeting space) to service very large meetings.

𝒮ERVING THE GUEST

In the past, one could speak in terms of a few hotel types related mainly to location and style of construction, as we have just done. Today, however, this product orientation has been fundamentally altered by the logic of marketing. Although product and location still matter, putting the customers' needs and preferences first has resulted in a segmented hotel market made up of several quite different kinds of lodging. Before we can understand hotels, therefore, we must review the principal customer types.

People traveling on business account for nearly a third of the trips of over 100 miles taken by Americans. As Figure 9.2 shows, business travelers account for 31 percent of hotels' patronage. Group meetings provide another 26 percent. Thus, over half of hotel guests are either on business or attending a meeting, conference, or convention.[4]

Notice how different the needs of customer segments can be. The family on a vacation is usually looking for fun and relaxation while the business traveler needs speed and efficiency to maximize the use of his or her time. For the business group,

Business 31%
Leisure 23%
Other 20%
Conference/ Group 26%

Figure 9.2 Lodging customer mix breakdown, 1996.
(*Source:* American Hotel and Motel Association.)

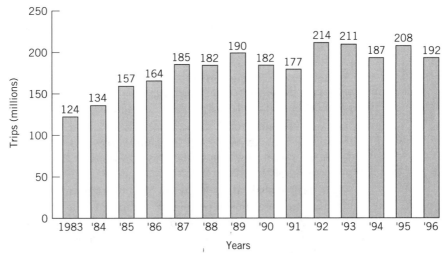

Figure 9.3 U.S. resident business travel.
(*Source:* 1996 Survey of Business Travel.)

meeting room facilities and service are key while large meeting capacity is needed by most conventions. Government travelers usually travel on a strictly limited scale of reimbursement called *per diem* (i.e., per day) and so are often quite rate sensitive.

Business Travel

Business travel grew rapidly in the 1980s until 1989. As Figure 9.3 indicates, business travel fell during the recession and recovered in 1992. Since that time, however, business travel has stagnated or even fallen in spite of an unprecedented economic boom. Business and convention travelers account for nearly one-third (32 percent) of all travel in the United States but, as we have already noted, 57 percent of hotel industry sales. The stagnation in business travel, accordingly, is an important and potentially threatening development for lodging.

What Is Happening to Business Travel?   One factor that may account for a considerable portion of the reduction in business travel may be a temporary one. Undiscounted airline fares rose nearly 40 percent between 1996 and 1997.[6] Moreover, they are expected to continue to rise at the rate of 5 to 6 percent in 1998.[7] Most business travelers cannot meet the restrictions on discounted tickets. Although fares may eventually slow their skyrocketing rise, they have served as a strong force, inducing companies to prune travel budgets.

Another factor was summed up by Peter Yesawich: "Technology is not our friend."[8] Businesses are meeting communication needs with telephones, teleconferencing, video-conferencing, faxes, and E-mail. John Rohs points to the World Wide Web as a long-term threat to business travel, citing the Web's ability to facilitate the accumulation and dissemination of information and to enable face to face, "live" contact across town or across the globe . . . [which] should produce a more discernable impact on lodging over the next five years than tele- and video-conferencing have over the past fifteen.[9]

To end this discussion of trends in business travel on a more positive note, however, there are factors that underline a strong, continuing need for business travel. One of these is the need for "in-the-flesh," face-to-face meetings. Consider the case of the director of market research for a large travel publishing company: "I work for somebody who is in England who works for somebody who is in New Jersey who works for somebody who is in Holland. Every now and then, we need to get together."[10]

In fact, globalization is one of the major growth factors in business travel. Overseas frequent-business travelers are much more often international travelers than are American travelers and a substantial portion of their travel is to the United States. Another positive factor is the need for constant retraining that arises from technological progress. People have to travel to be trained—and people have to travel to give that training.[11]

What Do Business Travelers Want? Figure 9.4 reminds us of the advice of the pioneering hotelier Elsworth Statler who said that the three most important things

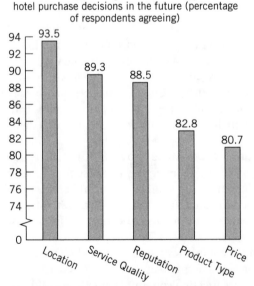

Statement: The following item will strongly influence hotel purchase decisions in the future (percentage of respondents agreeing)

Figure 9.4 Important factors for guests in choosing a hotel.
(*Source:* Data, *Lodging Hospitality,* August 1996.)

about a hotel are "location, location, and location." Clearly, however, the figure also raises questions about Mr. Statler's priorities because it shows four other factors that score in the 80 percent range of agreement as important in influencing hotel stay decisions. Although location is a clear first at 93.5 percent, service quality ranks a close second at 89.3 and reputation, at 88.5, is not far behind. Clearly, product type—whether it be luxury, midscale, or economy—is also important. Finally, although price is clearly not irrelevant, it does lag in fifth place.[12]

The *Official Airline Guide* (OAG) "Business Travel Lifestyle Survey" polled over 5000 frequent business travelers to determine their preferences in hotel amenities. Sixty percent ranked satellite/cable television as the most important hotel amenity. Just under half said 24-hour room service was a priority for them and a third cited a fitness facility.[13]

A survey of Courtyard by Marriott guests revealed the importance of computers to business travelers. Nearly 60 percent of the Marriott study respondents reported traveling with a laptop. Apparently, it's not *all* work because 70 percent of these kept "games loaded and ready to play."[14] The OAG study cited previously, using a broader sample, confirmed the importance of the laptop, although only 25 percent of its respondents had taken a PC with them on a trip. Still, 95 percent of those who did so made use of their PC in their hotel room.

Marriott was among the first to develop a guest room especially designed for business travelers and other companies have quickly adopted a similar pattern in their executive rooms. Marriott's room, dubbed "The Room That Works," has the following features[15]:

1. A mobile writing desk as well as a large console table

2. Two power outlets and a modem jack mounted in the console top

3. A movable task light

4. A fully adjustable ergonomic chair

To meet the needs of business travelers, business centers in hotels offer such services as photocopying and fax machines, desktop publishing software, computer workstations, laser printers, dictaphones, and clerical staff on call 24 hours a day. Such special targeting of business travelers is not limited to upscale properties. One budget chain offers "work processors" to its business guests, including free faxes and photocopies (up to10 of each), assistance with pickup and delivery of overnight packages, and help finding clerical assistance around the clock.

Business travelers operate on dramatically varying budgets. Some are quite cost conscious while others have more generous expense accounts. Accordingly, business travelers are found in all price levels of the hotel business.

Today, 40 percent of business travelers are women and that market segment is still growing, albeit slowly.[16] Many argue women travelers have distinct needs and preferences. Those who can afford the higher rates prefer suite hotels because they have a room separate from their bedroom in which to conduct business; Embassy Suites, most of whose hotels' atriums are surrounded by hallways, argue that women find the open hallway areas more secure. Indeed, *many operators believe*

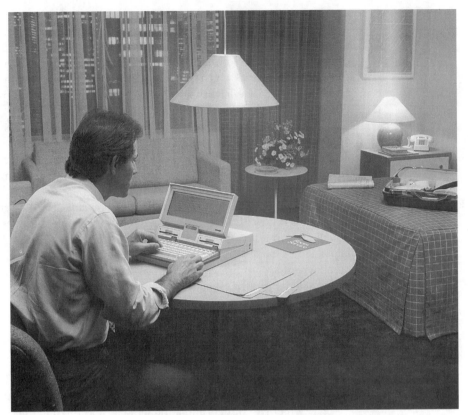

Most business travelers expect to work in their hotel room.

that women tend to be more security conscious. Some chains offer special services and amenities in the room for women. For instance, market research at Westin indicated that women wanted irons, hair dryers, full-length mirrors, and coffee makers. High-quality makeup mirrors are now standard at Crown Plaza properties.[17] Others argue that women want the same basic hotel services that men do and resent being treated differently. No doubt, as women travelers continue to increase in number, the competitive nature of the industry will continue to drive the search for effective ways to serve them better. Novotel's experience of some differences between men and women quests is summarized in Industry Practice Note 9.1.

Leisure and Personal Travel

Leisure and personal travel account for roughly 68 percent of the trips taken by Americans[18] but many of these travelers don't stay in hotels. The American Hotel and Motel Association reports that 23 percent of hotels' customers are on vacation and 20 percent are traveling for "other reasons."[19] The lodging industry's biggest

Industry Practice Note 9.1

Demystifying Gender Differences Among Hotel Guests

For the past five years, management at the Novotel New York has accumulated interesting year-end data that help demystify many of the differences between male and female guests.

Of 311 guests who locked themselves out of their rooms in 1997, 197 were men, including about 83 who were in some state of undress.

Male guests keep their bedrooms colder and their bathrooms dirtier, request more smoking rooms, order more adult movies and room service, and fre-quent the lobby bar and the hotel fitness center more often than their female counterparts.

Women are the best tippers, use more towels, make more phone calls, use hotel laundry and pressing services more often, utilize more drawers and closet space, and are more likely to bring children along on a business trip.

Male and female hotel guests do share one habit; neither make their beds.

Source: Hotels, April 1998, p. 24.

competitor for this personal and leisure travel segment is "staying with friends and relatives" (50 percent of personal travelers), followed by camping and recreational vehicles (3 percent) and owned or rented cabin or second home (5 percent).[20]

A number of factors make industry observers optimistic about the future of personal travel. Over the past decade, leisure trips have grown at nearly twice the rate of business trips (2.9 versus 1.6 percent).[21] The arrival of the baby boomers in the peak travel years (i.e., middle age) should be bullish for lodging. Another growing travel segment is made up of senior citizens. Hotel chains are offering discounts and other inducements to attract this market. More cost-conscious, senior travelers are more likely to travel during off-peak seasons, when hotels need the business.

The International Traveler

As easy transportation and instant communication shrink our world, more and more businesses here and abroad are investing in international markets. As a result, business travel has become international. At the same time, as incomes have im-proved in Europe, Asia, and South America, each of these regions provides the United States with a growing number of tourists. By one knowledgeable estimate,

Total international travel accounted for over 10 percent of lodging room night demand in 1997 and 13 percent of room revenues. . . . If we allow for [food and beverage and other

Resort hotels such as the Luxor in Las Vegas use architecture to convey the desired image of the property.
Courtesy of Luxor Casino Hotel, Las Vegas

expenditures] the international visitor's share of the total lodging industry revenue is probably 14–15 percent. . . . Moreover, with international travel forecast to grow at twice the pace of domestic travel at least through the year 2000, we estimate that the international market could represent 16–19 percent of industry revenue by the turn of the century.[22]

Hotels reports that, by the year 2000, the seniors' market in Europe will number about 100 million, many of whom will doubtless be avid international travelers.[23]

Not surprisingly, North American hotel companies are anxious to pursue the **international travel** market. American brands are expanding rapidly abroad. Much overseas travel takes place within the traveler's own region (i.e., most Asians travel within Asia, South Americans within South America, etc.). Overseas travelers, however, are more likely to visit the United States than other destinations when they travel outside their own area. To take part in the growth of international travel, companies have to have properties in those markets. Moreover, the best way to publicize a chain at the points of origin of international travel is to have a property in the country. This makes local people familiar with the brand.[24]

The usefulness of being represented in overseas markets is illustrated by a sales program of Motel 6. Although Motel 6 operates in North America, it is owned by the European company Accor, which also operates several international hotel chains and a network of travel agents. Working through its European travel agent affiliates, Motel 6 offers European travelers vouchers at one set price that can be used for a night's stay in any of the company's 770 properties throughout the United States. The result is that "Each year, Europeans purchase several hundred thousand dollars worth of vouchers for rooms at Motel 6 properties, assuring a single room rate and avoiding currency hassles."[25]

Attempts to attract foreign travelers are certainly not limited to overseas expansion. In North American hotels, multilingual staffs are becoming more important, as are signs and menus printed in more than one language. A number of hotels in areas where many Japanese visit have developed menus featuring traditional Japanese foods. Many North American hotels offer Japanese breakfasts.

𝒯YPES OF LODGING

Figure 9.5 illustrates the proportionate share of room supply provided by the six major property types based on room rate and service level in 1997 and 1991.[26] Table 9.2 shows those property types with examples of the kinds of chains found in each in 1997. In the sections that follow, we will first discuss the recent performance of each of these property types briefly. Next, we will consider property types that are not limited to just one of the categories found in Table 9.2, such as all-suite hotels,

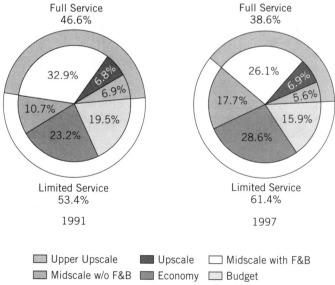

Figure 9.5   Total U.S. hotels by chain scale. Percentage of hotels in each segment, 1997 and 1991.
(*Source:* Adapted from *Lodging Outlook,* February 1998.)

248 ◆ Chapter 9 LODGING: MEETING GUEST NEEDS

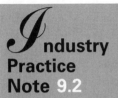

*I*ndustry
Practice
Note 9.2

Where Have All the Independents Gone?

At the beginning of 1987, 56.7 percent of U.S. hotels were independents. By the beginning of 1997, the number of independent hotels had decreased by nearly 900 properties, while the total number of hotels in the industry had increased by over 4800, or 22 percent. Some of the decrease in share of independent properties, then, is accounted for by the fact that the industry grew while independents didn't. In fact, the 976 independent hotels that closed their doors during the 10-year period accounted for 73 percent of all hotel closings during that time. Newly opened independent hotels (851) accounted for only 12 percent of new openings.

Another factor is conversions. Although 3010 hotels converted from chain to independent, during the same period, 3745 independent hotels joined a chain or franchise group. Thus, independents netted a loss of another 735 hotels.[1]

Figure 1 measures the decrease in demand (i.e., room night sold) over the past 20 years and here the picture is even less encouraging. Nearly half of all hotel stays in 1980 were spent in an independent hotel but less than a third were in 1997 and the projection is for a further decline by 2000.

A review of operating results of chain and independent hotels by Smith Travel Research shows that

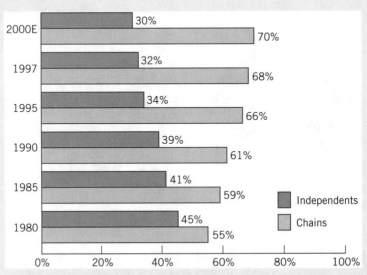

Figure 1 Hotel stays at independent hotels have fallen over the past 20 years, while stays at chain hotels grew. (*Source:* Smith Travel Research; John Rohs and Warren Gump, *Lodging Industry Annual Review*, February 25, 1998.)

independents had higher expenses per room as a percentage of revenue. Food and beverage profit margins were weaker for independents. Payroll was higher. Independents spent 10 percent less as a proportion of sales on marketing. Smith Travel Research concluded that its study "reveals many areas where improvement in the control of operating expenses could improve the bottom line."[2]

We should note, however, that the real weakness in the independents' performance may be not in expense control but in generating revenue. Recall that, because costs are expressed as a percentage of sales, there are two ways to improve percentage performance: increase sales or lower costs. Although some of the inefficiency in independents' performance may arise from poor cost control, a lot of it may be due to poor sales performance, which could arise from the lack of a known brand name. Low marketing expenses would simply make that situation worse.

1. The preceding figures are taken from "Special Analysis: Industry Expansion 1987–1996," *Lodging Outlook*, June 1997, Table 1.
2. Chuck Ross, "Strong and Independent," *Lodging,* December 1996, pp. 47–48.

extended-stay lodging properties, resort hotels, and convention hotels. We discuss changes in the status of independent hotels in Industry Practice Note 9.2.

Full-Service Properties

Full-service properties provide a wide variety of services but the single factor that separates them from limited-service properties most clearly is the availability of a full food service operation. Between 1991 and 1997, the proportion of full-service hotels declined eight percentage points. A decline such as this—nearly 17 percent in market share in the span of only seven years—suggests a shortage of full-service

Table 9.2 Lodging Chains by Price and Service Level

Segment[a]	Examples of Companies
Upper upscale	Four Seasons, Ritz Carlton, Hyatt, Hilton, Marriott
Upscale	Radisson, Doubletree, Residence Inn, Crowne Plaza, Rennaisance
Midscale with food and beverage	Holiday Inn, Best Western, Ramada, Quality Inn, Howard Johnson
Midscale without food and beverage	Hampton Inns, Holiday Inn Express, Comfort Inns, La Quinta
Economy	Days Inn, Super 8, Travel Lodge, Fairfield Inn, Red Roof
Budget	Motel 6, Econolodge, Knights Inn, Microtel, Sleep Inns

[a]There are all-suite and extended-stay brands to fit every segment.
Note: A comprehensive list of lodging chains can be found at: **http://www.wku.edu./~hrtm/hotlrest.htm.**

The hotel room must offer the guest more than just a place to sleep; it must offer comfort and utility.
Courtesy of Caesar's Palace, Las Vegas

rooms in some markets. It also signals a major change in direction in lodging, toward a market that is more segmented by service levels. The full-service property categories discussed next are upper upscale, upscale, and midscale properties with food and beverage.

Upper Upscale Hotels.   An **upper upscale property** is one that is in the top 15 percent of a market's rate structure. We adopt this rate-oriented definition of the "top of the line" because it is the industry standard, set by Smith Travel Research, and observed by most industry analysts. Upper upscale properties had an average daily rate of $130.92.[27]

We ought to note, however, that "Truly luxury properties are those which have an average daily rate of $175 and up and are very distinctive, one of a kind assets."[28] Chains or brands whose properties are generally in the luxury category include Four Seasons and the Ritz Carlton. Many luxury properties are independents such as "The Mansion at Turtle Creek" (Dallas), the Broadmoor (Colorado Springs), or the Del Coronado (San Diego). Properties in this category would typically carry a five-star rating by Mobil or a five-diamond rating by AAA.

The upper upscale segment includes luxury properties but it also includes four-star properties such as those operated by Hyatt, Hilton, or Marriott. Upper upscale hotels, as a group, have the highest occupancies and, of course, the highest average rates. One of the reasons for their high occupancy is that newly built competition has been slow to develop. The reasons for this involve recent industry history.

In the 1980s, many buyers, frequently from overseas, paid inflated prices for so-called "trophy" properties. The result was a number of upper upscale properties that could not earn an adequate return. During the bottom of the lodging downtrend in 1991, some distress sales took place. At that time, a few properties changed hands at 47 percent of their replacement value and one property reportedly was sold for 15 cents on the dollar. Indeed, even in 1997, luxury properties were being sold at 61 percent of their replacement value.[29]

It is reasonably clear that if you can buy a property for less than it costs to build the same kind of property, it makes sense to buy instead of build. Accordingly, although some luxury hotels have changed ownership or affiliation, very few new properties have been added in this category. Expert opinion, however, is that luxury room supply will begin to expand in 1999 and onward. That is when the impact of conversions of well-located structures such as office buildings to hotels as well as some new hotel construction will begin to take effect.[30] Nevertheless, occupancies in the luxury segment are expected to continue to lead the industry for the foreseeable future.[31] In 1997, these hotels had an average occupancy of 74.4 percent and achieved an average rate of $130.92. Revenue grew at a healthy 8 percent.

Upscale Hotels.   These hotels have a full range of services and aspire to a luxury image but their service is not as intensive as in luxury or upper upscale hotels nor is their physical plant as extensive. In 1997, **upscale hotels** achieved an average rate of $89.15. Supply growth in this sector has been driven by a large number of conversions of hotels from the level above and below this one as properties were repositioned during the 1990–1991 recession. Between 1998 and 1999, supply is expected to continue to grow at 3.5 to 5 percent driven by aggressive franchising while demand is expected to grow by only 3 to 4.5 percent. Revenue grew in 1997 at a rate of about 6 percent.[32]

Midscale Hotels with Food and Beverage.   These properties are often caught in the middle. They are competing with the segment above, which have more and better services and facilities, and with the segment below, which are newer and yet have lower prices. The properties, many of them 20 to 30 or more years old, are dated and often show their age. Even when upgraded by renovation, they often remain at a competitive disadvantage with the newer limited-service properties and more luxurious upscale hotels. Midscale hotels with food and beverage had an average rate of $64.45 and an occupancy of just over 61 percent.

Midscale hotels with food and beverage are not, however, without their advantages. Long established, they have powerful brand names such as Holiday Inns, Ramada, and Best Western.[33] Moreover, having been "in place" for many years, they often have excellent locations and valuable client relationships. Moreover, properties located in smaller cities are often *the* leading hotel in town—because more upscale hotel groups cannot afford to build in smaller markets. These properties have a significant advantage in their locale.

Still, many midscale properties have been converted to other brands in other segments. Indeed, in Holiday Inns' case, a limited-service brand, Holiday Inn Express, has been established largely as a conversion vehicle for Holiday Inns and other mid-market properties that do not want a food and beverage operation. Holiday Hospitality's upscale brand, Crowne Plaza, has also been used as a conversion vehicle.

Limited-Service Properties

The absence of food and beverage (F&B) facilities would once have condemned a property to the very lowest rate groups. Food and beverage service requires extensive physical plant, including dining rooms, cocktail lounges, and meeting and banquet rooms along with the back-of-the-house facilities necessary to operate

Limited-service properties such as Fairfield Inn are usually located near a full-service restaurant and offer guest room accommodations that are competitive with full-service hotels.
Courtesy of Marriott International

these facilities. Thus, food and beverage add a major investment burden to full-service hotels. In addition, they create a significant payroll cost. Because the F&B operation does not create a profit commensurate with either investment or cost, **limited-service properties** have important cost and investment advantages over their full-service competitors. One of the reasons that these properties *can* satisfy guests without having restaurant facilities is their location in centers of development, which have many restaurant chain and independent operations in the immediate neighborhood.

Growth in limited-service properties has proceeded at a rapid pace. As one leading real estate consulting group put it,

> The limited service segment accounted for over 73 per cent of total [new rooms] industry wide. . . . Limited service supply increases are expected to outpace demand and occupancies are expected to continue to decline during [1998]. . . . The construction of limited service hotel rooms is pushing a number of markets around the country dangerously close to being overbuilt.[34]

In addition, Smith Travel Service had this to say about the two lower-priced limited-service segments:

> The portion of industry wide room revenue produced by economy/budget hotels in 1997 was 25 percent less than that attributable to those price-level groups in 1987. That number is disproportionate to the drop in share of both supply and demand. Hotels in the economy lodging segment have lost market share to new, limited-service, mid-price properties of comparable size opened in the suburban and highway locations favored by economy/budget operators.[35]

We will discuss three limited-service segments: midscale hotels without food and beverage, economy hotels and motels, and budget hotels and motels.

Midscale Hotels Without Food and Beverage.

Although the number of midscale properties with food and beverage have decreased by seven percentage points, those without food and beverage have increased by the same seven percentage points. The growth from just under 11 percent of properties in 1991 to nearly 18 percent in 1997 is an increase in *share* of properties of nearly two-thirds. Between 1998 and 1999, supply is expected to increase from both new construction and conversion of older full-service properties to limited-service brands. Although construction and conversion activity is high in this sector, demand has also shown healthy growth. With supply and demand advancing at roughly the same pace, revenue growth has maintained a steady pace of growth of between 3.5 and 4 percent.[36] Midscale hotels achieved an occupancy level of 67 percent in 1997 and an average daily rate of $60.08.

Economy Hotels and Motels.

Supply has been growing in this sector as fast or faster than demand since 1994. Between 1995 and 1997, **economy properties,** which represent 12 percent of total hotel rooms, had 37 percent of industry growth. Between 1998 and 1999, supply is expected to outpace demand growth by 1 to 2

Properties and brands are growing rapidly in the economy sector.
Courtesy of U.S. Franchise Systems

percent. With an average rate of $48.68 and an occupancy under 60 percent, revenue is growing at the rate of only 1 percent, the slowest pace of any of the segments discussed. The economy sector has been characterized as "the weakest in the hotel business—with little reason for that to change."[37]

The outlook for the economy lodging group, however, is not entirely bleak according to one industry expert:

> A combination of significantly lower fixed charges (especially interest expense), continued room rate increases greater than inflation, and improved operating efficiencies should help this segment—with its strong operating margins—to achieve favorable bottom line profits despite weakening occupancies and eroding market share. These hotels can still be profitable with less than glamorous "top-line" numbers.[38]

Budget Hotels and Motels.   **Budget properties** achieved an average rate of $37.06 in 1997 and an occupancy rate of 61.0 percent. The most dramatic growth in this segment is the result of growth in the budget extended-stay chains, which will be discussed later in this chapter. Growth is expected to be at the rate of 8 to 11 percent, which is well above historical levels, but demand is also growing at record rates of 6 to 10 percent. The average room rate was $37.06, while occupancy was 61 per cent. Because of the average rate growth, revenue growth is projected to rise 2.5 to 3 percent between 1998 and 1999, despite a possible marginal decline in occupancy.

The operating statistics for each segment are summarized in Table 9.3. Global Hospitality Note 9.1 chronicles the growth of the economy and budget sectors in

Table 9.3 Operating Performance of Hotels by Price Segment

	Occupancy	Average Daily Rate	RevPAR[a] Growth
Upper upscale	74.4%	$130.92	7.7%
Upscale	72.1	89.15	5.6
Midscale with food and beverage	61.3	64.45	3.8
Midscale without food and beverage	67.0	60.08	4.1
Economy	58.4	48.68	1.0
Budget	61.0	37.06	2.9

[a]Revenue per available room.
Source: John Rohs and Warren Gump, *Lodging Industry Annual Review,* February 25, 1998.

two major overseas markets. Industry Practice Note 9.3 explores an aspect of the diversity of owners of hotels in the United States.

All-Suite Hotels

Smith Travel Research defines **all-suite hotels** as follows:

> All-suite hotels are properties in which each guest unit consists of a bedroom and a living room. Traditionally, these hotels have limited public space and services. The term is broadly used and may include hotels which have some suites or a hotel with partial dividing walls in the bedroom.[39]

The categories of hotels we have been discussing are divided into categories by rate and service level. All-suite hotels, however, have entrants in every category. Thus, "all-suite" is really in many ways as much an architectural designation as it is a hotel type.

When all-suite hotels were introduced, they stirred a great deal of controversy in the industry. Proponents pointed to high occupancies and rates as evidence of strong consumer demand while critics noted that the higher construction costs mean higher capital costs. The critics charged that capital costs were large enough that the advantage of rate and occupancy would be offset by higher depreciation. Darryl Hartley-Leonard, then president of Hyatt Hotels, has called all-suite hotels "one of the worst economic propositions this industry has ever seen."[40] On the other hand, Severyn Ashkenazy, one of the first all-suite hotel operators, suggested that the all-suite hotel represents the next step in the development of the luxury hotel.[41]

There seems to be little doubt about the financial performance of all-suites. As Table 9.4 shows, all-suites have maintained a five-point lead in occupancy over the industry average in spite of an increase in capacity over twice the rate of increase of

The Economy Sector Flowers Overseas

Global Hospitality Note 9.1

Shanghai-based Jin Jiang Group (**http://www .chinats.com/center.htm**) is China's leading hotel company. In 1997, the company

opened the first of a planned 300 property chain of no frills, 1 star hotels. . . . Franchising the brand throughout the nation, Jin Jiang will itself build and operate 20 of the properties on the rim of Shanghai, demonstrating its confidence in its own product. These basic 85 to 100 room hotels will offer what the booming domestic market needs, safe, sanitary and affordable lodging. Each hotel will cost about $1.3 million, can be built to simple plans in a few months and importantly to China's municipal entrepreneurs, offers almost immediate returns. The first hotel opened in Shanghai in the summer of 1997 with a pleasing 85 per cent occupancy. Even with room rates pitched at $18, that means a solid 40 per cent annual cash flow on investment.[1]

On the other side of the world, the budget sector is soaring in Great Britain:

In 1997, the U.K. budget hotel segment added 82 hotels and more than 4,500 rooms. Plans call for more than 900 budget hotels and 53,000 rooms by 2002, or nearly 20% annual growth. The success of the budget sector in motorway service areas or along main arterial roads inevitably will lead operators to seek sites in traditional hotel territory—primarily city and town centers, where the conversion or development of vacant office blocks, government buildings or old hospitals has become commonplace. Budget rates that continue to climb faster than the U.K.'s rate of inflation ultimately may create opportunities for a super-budget product.[2]

1. *Hotels,* April 1998, p. 54.
2. *Hotels,* March 1998, p. 8.

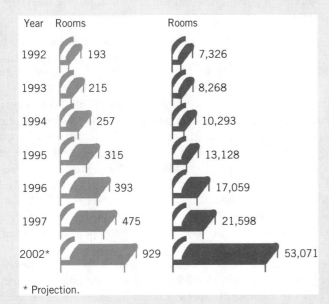

Year	Rooms	Rooms
1992	193	7,326
1993	215	8,268
1994	257	10,293
1995	315	13,128
1996	393	17,059
1997	475	21,598
2002*	929	53,071

* Projection.

Figure 1   U.K. budget hotel growth, 1992–2002. (*Source:* Deloitte & Touche, Hospitality and Leisure Consulting, *Hotels,* April 1998.)

✐ndustry Practice Note 9.3

Diversity in Lodging Ownership: The Asian American Hotel Owner's Association

Fifty years after the first Indian immigrant opened a hotel in the United States, the Asian-American presence in the North American hotel industry is an imposing one. As to how it all got started, however, H. P. Rama, chief executive officer of JHM Enterprises and secretary of the AH&MA, remarked that,

We are the sons of farmers from India, accidental hoteliers. We have not received any formal training in how to run a hotel business. If we can achieve with no money, no technical skill, and poor communication, think what [the next generation] can achieve.[1]

The Asian American Hotel Owner's Association (AAHOA) represents more than 18,000 hotel properties and 5000 owners. "Asian American hoteliers operate 50 per cent of the industry's economy segment and 35 per cent of all properties."[2] Although there are Chinese, Korean, and Taiwanese hoteliers, 90 percent of Asian-American hotel operators are of Indian descent and virtually all of them can trace their ancestry to one Indian state, Gujarat, in the northwest of India.[3]

According to *Lodging* magazine,

Much is made of hospitality being an innnate part of the Indian tradition. But there are other cultural reasons so many Indian immigrants—and people of Indian descent who came to this country from other, mostly British or African nations—gained such a strong and fast foothold in lodging. Signifi-

cant among them are strong family and communal ties and a pronounced entrepreneurial bent.

"It is also part of our culture to be our own boss," says Mike Patel, now 34 and President of Diplomat, which owns 12 hotels in the Southeast. "We say life is too short to work 9 to 5". . . .

As with most immigrant groups, few Indians arrived in this country with venture capital. Instead, they relied on a large, loyal network of relatives and friends to teach them the business and—with most institutions sceptical about extending them loans—lend them the money to buy a property of their own. . . . Dr. Margaret Simms, director of research programs for the Joint Centres for Political and Economic Studies, says the willingness of Indian Americans to lend and borrow capital among themselves—often without charging interest—provides access to business opportunities "that are beyond the capabilities of most native borns."[4]

The goals of AAHOA, according to its president, Mike Patel, are to provide a forum for its membership, to assist its members in their relationships with franchisors, to promote education among Asian-American hotel operators, and to encourage women and youth from the Asian-American community to make careers in hospitality.[5]

1. Harry Lister, "Accidental No More," *Lodging,* December 1996, pp. 54–58.
2. *Hotel and Motel Management,* March 18, 1988, p. 6.
3. H. Lister, "Accidental No More," p. 58.
4. Ibid., pp. 54–58.
5. Personal communication, March 1998.

Table 9.4 Occupancy of All-Suite Hotels and Industry Average, 1992–1997

	Industry Average	All-Suite Hotels
1992	62.7	68.4
1993	63.6	70.1
1994	64.9	71.3
1995	65.2	70.7
1996	65.1	70.5
1997	64.6	69.8

Source: Smith Travel Research.

the industry. Moreover, the average rate per occupied room has consistently remained at least 38 percent higher than the industry average.[42]

Transient All-Suite Market. Embassy Suites, a market leader in the transient all-suite market, offers guest accommodations about 20 percent larger in total square footage than a conventional hotel room. This space, however, is divided into two rooms, separated by the bathroom and a kitchenette. The properties (excepting a few conversions) are built around an atrium. The living room of the suite overlooks the corridor and atrium and the bedroom has an outside view.

The target customer for weekday business is an upper-level executive, while families are good weekend customers. The living room couch pulls out to make a double bed, allowing children and parents to both have some privacy on a weekend minivacation. Figure 9.6 shows a floor plan of a typical Embassy Suites guest unit. Each suite includes a telephone and remote-control television in both rooms, a

Figure 9.6 A typical guest unit at Embassy Suites.
(*Source:* Embassy Suites.)

minirefrigerator, electric coffee maker with a complimentary supply of regular and decaf coffee, a microwave oven, and a wet bar. The rooms do not, however, include a full kitchen.

Some all-suite properties have restaurants and bars as well as limited meeting space, but it is common to limit food and beverage service to a complimentary breakfast. Embassy Suites usually offers more extensive restaurant service but generally leases the restaurant operation to another company. The emphasis in the all-suite property is on the guest room. Food and beverage, where available, are provided as a supporting service, generally with restricted hours of operation.

Extended-Stay Properties

There are some who would argue that **extended-stay properties** are more like apartment houses than they are hotels, but the fact is that most large hotel chains have an entry in the extended-stay market. Accordingly, we will treat these properties as hotels. Interestingly, the extended-stay market grew out of the all-suite market. The first chain of extended-stay properties was Residence Inns. Now operated by Marriott International, it is the largest extended-stay chain with 254 hotels and over 30,000 units. Figure 9.7 shows the floor plan of an upscale extended-stay brand, Homewood Suites.

The most dynamic area of growth in lodging in 1998 is the economy and budget sectors of the extended-stay market. The first budget extended-stay chain was Villager Lodge, founded in 1989 by a group of investors who purchased a budget motel, added simple cooking facilities, and changed the rate structure to favor week-long stays. The chain's growth strategy has been to convert underperforming motels in areas suitable for extended-stay business. These include high-population-density areas and areas with significant office or commercial development. Properties must have access to major roads or intersections. Because of its strategy of acquiring

Figure 9.7 An upscale extended-stay suite.
(*Source:* Promus Companies.)

Extended-stay properties such as Residence Inns offer accommodations especially designed to meet the needs of guests who will be staying more than a day or two.
Courtesy of Marriott International

underperforming properties, Villager can keep its capital costs down through low acquisition costs.[43] Uniquely, Villager is a 100 percent conversion chain. Villager Lodge has 100 properties and 6400 rooms in 32 states. The largest budget extended-stay chain is Extended Stay America, with 114 properties and 13,678 rooms—and another 73 hotels and 8390 rooms under construction in 1998.

The Extended-Stay Customer.   Rohs sums up the sources of demand for extended-stay properties. With the increasing trend in American business, toward outsourcing and the use of consultants in lieu of in-house staff, the extended-stay market has evolved to fill a need for longer-term, business-related stays ranging from a few days to several months. For the consumer, the extended-stay product is more cost efficient than traditional hotels or corporate apartments and offers amenities such as kitchenettes, laundries, room decor, and more appeal to a customer in search of a temporary home away from home. Figure 9.8 profiles the extended-stay customer.

The Resort Hotel

The hotel accounting firm of Pannel Kerr Forster defines a **resort hotel** as one that is "usually located in a suburban or isolated rural location, with special recreational

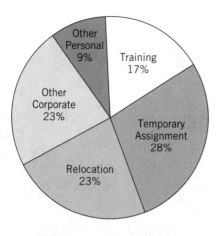

Figure 9.8 **The extended-stay customer: purpose of travel.**
(*Source:* John Rohs and Warren Gump, Lodging Industry Annual Review, February 25, 1998.)

facilities to attract pleasure seeking guests." Resorts are destinations for travel that invite a guest to spend as much as a week or more and provide the extensive leisure facilities a vacationer expects. Accordingly, most resort guests are willing to pay higher rates for these services.

According to Chuck Ross, vice president of Smith Travel Research, there were 1807 properties with 375,000 rooms in resort markets.

> In 1996, that group of properties had an occupancy of 70 percent, an average daily rate of more than $110 and room revenue in excess of $10.5 billion. Although resort hotels represent less than 5 percent of lodging properties, they account for an estimated 21 percent of pretax income.[44]

Some destination resorts offer a mix of activities suited to the sports enthusiast. The Homestead in Hot Springs, Virginia, for instance, offers in its advertising:

> horseback riding, woodland walking, trout fishing, mineral spa, swimming, three 18-hole championship golf courses, tennis, buckboard and surrey driving, skeet and trap shooting, ten pin and lawn bowling, loafing, and skiing.

The Greenbrier in White Sulphur Springs, West Virginia, describes itself as "a 6,500-acre estate secluded in the beautiful Alleghenies." In addition to sports, the Greenbrier, like most such "adult resorts," offers extensive meeting and convention facilities: "The new conference center includes ballrooms, auditoriums, theatre, exhibit hall and 25 meeting rooms fully equipped with the latest audiovisual equipment. Capable of serving groups of 10 to 1,100."

A quite different kind of "adult destination" (where, as in the Homestead and the Greenbrier, children are always welcome) is found in Las Vegas. The number one hotel city in terms of hotel sales, Las Vegas is famous for its gambling, but its resort hotels offer much more (including, sometimes, features for the whole family). For example, the Las Vegas Hilton advertises itself as the place

> where the real superstars play in Las Vegas. Now the largest, most complete resort in the world. Incredible dining in eight unsurpassed restaurants, including the spectacu-

Much of the competition in the luxury resort business is international.
Courtesy of Four Seasons Resort, Nevis, West Indies; Photo by Jeremy Ferguson

lar Japanese Fantasyland, Benihana, Village! Plus an 8½-acre outdoor recreation deck and even a unique "youth hotel" for the youngsters alone.

These adult-centered resort hotels do, of course, welcome children, but other destination complexes are designed primarily with the family, and especially children, in mind. The most famous of these is Walt Disney World. Although the resorts we described include many other activities, we can accurately say that, at Disney World, several hotels are integrated within a larger entertainment center. That center includes not only the three theme parks for which Walt Disney World is best known but also all varieties of water sports on a large lake, a sophisticated campground sporting its own entertainment centers, three golf courses, and the customary amenities and luxuries available at each hotel.

The Meeting and Convention Market

Two quite different types of properties serve the group market. **Conference centers** serve smaller meetings and are often used by companies for specialized training classes. **Convention hotels,** on the other hand, serve larger groups such as conventions and trade shows.

Conference Centers.   A conference center is a lodging facility where 60 percent or more of total occupancy is generated by conferences and which offers a full-package plan, including guest rooms, meals, and a full-service conference room, as well as skilled staff trained to serve meeting planners and attendees. Conference centers are operated by some very large corporations, such as General Motors and the telephone companies, to provide facilities for training their own employees. Other centers are operated by universities. Finally, private companies operate conference centers that offer a resort-like atmosphere to companies, associations, and other groups for extended seminars and training sessions. Facilities include meeting rooms that are designed to be comfortable places to spend long hours of concentrated effort and that provide state-of-the-art audio and visual support. Outside the meeting, these resort-style properties include spacious lobbies and dining areas, golf courses, tennis courts, as well as health club facilities. The argument in favor of a conference center for a meeting is that any meeting represents a major outlay and the object must be to achieve productivity from the expenditure. Conference centers, then, argue that they may cost more but they offer more bang for the buck.

Sales at all kinds of conference centers have improved since the depths of the recession in 1991. Profits at executive conference centers, which specialize in holding business meetings, tripled from 1991 to 1995. Although colleges and universities had the greatest increase in occupancy, low rates held down their profit growth somewhat but they still managed to double their operating profit in the same five-year period.[45]

Convention Hotels.   These larger properties provide facilities and services geared to meet the needs of large group and association meetings and trade shows. Typically, these hotels have in excess of 400 guest rooms and contain substantial amounts of function and banquet space flexibility designed for use by large meeting groups. They often work in concert with other convention hotels and convention centers to provide facilities for citywide conventions and trade shows.

Morris Lapidus, an architect who has designed convention hotels, provided an interesting and colorful description of the convention hotel and its function some years ago that is still apt today:

> The convention hotel is a new form of American hybrid. All of us are familiar with the great American convention, where an organization or corporation gathers as many members as it can in one particular place and fills up a horrendous agenda with lectures, meetings, group discussions, film shows, workshops and lots of drinking. The main reason for all this endeavor is to conduct a forum for ideas, to keep members apprised of what the parent organization has been doing, and to get everybody's idea of where they are going and how they should get there. It is also a nifty tax write-off.

> The convention hotel should be a ceremonial hotel, so far as meeting areas are concerned. This is the place where the "tribe" honors the chiefs, hands out the awards to diligent warriors, and welcomes the initiates. The organization's brass must look and sound good on the platform of meetings and banquets. The warriors—and the warriors' spouses when present—should be equally seated and treated. And the novitiates, for whom it is an honor just to be there, must have an opportunity to feel part of the inner circle.

Hotels that seek to compete in the meeting and convention market must provide first class meeting facilities and service.
Courtesy of the Mayflower Hotel

The conventional hotel must also have super-suites for the chiefs and many comfortable but similar rooms for the warriors. The novitiates may be housed more economically although this is seldom the case. They may share rooms and not be permitted to bring along their spouses until they're full-fledged warriors.[46]

Lapidus also observed that the guest rooms at conventions are often social centers where friends or business associates come for a drink or an informal meeting. These rooms, thus, should be spacious and should separate the dressing area from the living quarters. The best arrangement, Lapidus declared, is to provide one double bed and a couch that can become a second double bed in larger rooms. Of course, there is a need for more modest single rooms for "warriors and novitiates," to use his analogy.

Other Specialized Segments

Condominiums. **Condominiums,** or "condos" as they are often called, generally offer the features of an apartment building—multiroom apartments with full kitchens—sometimes combined with those of a hotel, such as on-premise food and beverage service. The units, however, are usually sold to individual owners, but the overall property is operated by a management company. Condos that service the vacation market are most commonly located in resort areas.

Two kinds of condo ownership are available. Some condos are sold outright, and their owners have the right to year-round occupancy. Another, increasingly common practice is to sell **time-shares,** the right to occupy the condo for a limited and specific time, with others having that right for other time periods. The price of a time-share usually depends on the desirability of the particular time period, with less attractive time periods costing substantially less than peak periods do.

Time-share developers have become more and more flexible in the kind of product they offer. It is now possible to purchase split-week segments, which "allow [the] owner to stay three or four days at one time and the remaining days at a later time." Even greater flexibility is provided by vacation clubs that offer time-shares on a point system. "A buyer can use the points for one vacation or take smaller intervals throughout the year. Major hotel companies such as Disney, Marriott and Hilton offer the point system."[47] In 1996, time-share sales in the United States were $2.3 billion for 22,000 intervals. The average price of a time-share travel interval was $10,325.[48] Although a number of well-known lodging companies are involved in the time-share market, 90 percent of time-share resorts are owned by independents, "leaving the door wide open for branded hotel companies to consolidate the industry."[49]

Time-shares had a somewhat shady reputation in their early days but the entry of well-known hotel companies in the mid-1980s has helped to give the product a greater respectability. The typical customer is 45 to 50 years old and has an annual income of $65,000 to $70,000 a year and an above-average education. Typical employment is in managerial and professional positions.[50]

Time-shares were started as an alternative to hotel rooms, as a way to save money on hotel stays, but as major hotel companies move into the business, they are, in some ways, a complimentary product for hotel companies. In fact, mixed-use properties, which offer hotel accommodations and time-share accommodations, as well as food, entertainment, and shopping, are becoming more common. Although similar to hotels in some ways, the time-share business is a quite different business. The transaction with the customer is much more complex, involving credit, financing, and legal dimensions that exceed anything found in hotels. The length of time of the commitment—a night or a few nights in contrast to 10 to 40 years of perpetual ownership—is a key difference. Another contrast is the cost structure of the deal. Marketing costs range from 30 to 40 percent of the purchase price of a time-share, including sales commissions that range from 12 to 20 percent. The product itself represents 20 to 30 percent of revenue and administration ac-

Industry Practice Note 9.4

Innkeeping Insights

The following are words of wisdom from bed and breakfast operators for you to ponder before you open a bed and breakfast:

◆ Kay Owen, LaCorsette Maison Inn, Newton, Iowa: "Know your business before you get into it. There are so many people getting into this business and then getting right out. It's the professional inns that are making it. Study it as a profession before you invest one penny."

◆ Mark Carter, Carter House/Hotel Carter (**http://www.moriah.com/carter/index.html**), Eureka, California: "Innkeeping is a good thing. It can be a profitable thing. But remember, it will tie you down more. You're not going to be on five days and off two."

◆ Ned Shank, Dairy Hollow House, Eureka Springs, Arkansas: "In innkeeping you have unexpected things come to you when you're already busy, things that guests need, or things that break."

"I work all the time. That's it, in a nutshell," says LaCorsette Maison's Owen. "A lot of people think they love to have people in, so they'll open a bed-and-breakfast. They don't realize how grueling it is."

Source: Restaurants USA, October 1997, p. 34.

counts for another 7 to 10 percent. A hotel background in accounting, management, and rental is useful in gaining entry into this field.[51]

Bed and Breakfast.   With the escalation of transient rates at hotels, an opportunity has been created to serve a more price-sensitive market. One response is the economy lodging segment we discussed earlier. Another is the provision of accommodations in a private home or the conversion of a residential property to accommodate transient guests. The **bed and breakfast (B&B)** market has grown to be a $2.2 billion business in the United States. The number of B&Bs has increased from fewer than 1000 in 1980 to more than 25,000 in 1998.[52] The owners of B&Bs often provide all the necessary labor but some employ full- or part-time help. Although many B&Bs are operated as a sideline, a source of extra income, an increasing number are really small-scale resorts that represent a major investment. Bed and breakfasts are also beginning to cut into the business travel market, offering people traveling on business not only an attractive rate but a home away from home. The highly personal style of the B&B—being a guest in someone's home—appeals to many travelers, both business and leisure.[53] In Industry Practice Note 9.4, some B&B operators share insights gained from their experiences.

$\mathcal{L}$ODGING AS A COMMUNITY INSTITUTION

You may have seen the following slogan behind the counter in some businesses: "This is a nonprofit business. We didn't plan it that way; it just happened!" To a greater degree than in many other industries, that not-so-funny joke applies to hotels and motor hotels, except that the meager profits may not be all that unexpected. To see why, we need to shift our attention from the purposes of the individual guest to those of the community.

In many small towns, the hotel or motel is more or less a public institution. It is a gathering place for local leaders and provides hospitality for visitors to the city's principal businesses. Because of these community benefits, some small-town hotels have been built more or less as nonprofit operations, with both ownership and even capital loaned without any real expectations of much profit. The benefits to the community—and to its principal institutions—are seen as sufficient to offset a lack of profit. This may not be the rule, but it is far from uncommon.

In practice, however, most hotel operators discover that an unprofitable hotel is also an unsuccessful hotel. The need for operating subsidies, or the simple absence of sufficient financial return, makes the property lose its luster and eventually become downright unattractive. The owners grow reluctant to pay adequate executive salaries and to spend the funds necessary to maintain the physical plant. Gradually, the plant decays, the organization loses its enthusiasm, and eventually the hotel closes its doors.

The community need for hotel services, however, often leads real estate developers to promote hotels as part of real estate developments in large cities. A developer acquires the rights to a large tract of land and plans a complex of office buildings, department stores, and other retail establishments. The development may be situated downtown; it may work with urban redevelopment; or it may settle at the edge of the city as part of an office park or an industrial park consisting of offices, light manufacturing, or warehousing and distribution centers. Although the development's overt purpose is suggested by its title (urban redevelopment, office park, industrial park), one of the first buildings to go up will probably be a hotel or motor hotel. The developer's hope, of course, is that the hotel will earn a profit, but he or she builds it mainly because of its importance to the overall development.

The developer may not be particularly interested in entering the hotel field, but the development surely needs the hotel. Visitors with business in the area need a place to stay. Headquarters units need space for sales meetings and other technical conferences. Those with offices or who are otherwise working in the area need a place to eat lunch, get a snack, meet for a drink, and perhaps entertain out-of-town guests at dinner at the end of the day.

Most development projects are preceded by a feasibility study of the project's economics. Two extracts from such feasibility studies, conducted in a medium-sized

Hotels provide a focus and services for community activities.
Courtesy of the Arkansas Department of Parks and Tourism

city (Middleton) in a basically rural area and a large metropolitan center (Bigton), suggest some of the developers' underlying motives. (Because these are confidential documents, the identity of the cities has been disguised.)

> [This is] one of a series of studies dealing with the proposed Middleton Square development in the Washington Street Urban Renewal Project area in Middleton.

> The urban renewal area covers six city blocks between the existing downtown area and the shore of Lake Washington. The proposed Middleton Square development contemplates a comprehensive, integrated development of new office structures (one of which is already under construction), adequate automobile parking, a full range of retail facilities including a major full-line department store, and the 300-room hotel which is the subject of this analysis. All of these facilities are expected to *upgrade and modernize Downtown Middleton.*

In a study conducted in a Bigton hotel development under consideration, the following information came under the heading of "Impact and Location":

> A new, large, and spectacularly designed hotel in Downtown Bigton would have a *significant impact on Bigton.* Properly promoted, the proposed hotel would not only *focus more attention on Bigton as one of the nation's great metropolitan centers,* but the hotel

would also substantially improve the inventory of transient lodging accommodations in the downtown area, and thereby strengthen that area's competitive position in the lodging market. If the hotel is as successful as predicted in this analysis, it will attract comparable competition to the downtown area—further *reinforcing that area's position in the local lodging market.*

The function of a hotel property, then, sometimes involves what economists call **externalities**—benefits external to the hotel itself, such as community development, the enhancement of property values in the area in general, and service to people who need food and lodging and would not visit the area without them. It's hardly surprising, then, that many new hotel properties have financial difficulties. This is particularly true for properties built during waves of real estate speculation such as those that occurred in the late 1920s, the early 1970s, and the 1980s. For sophisticated hotel operators, however, this kind of situation creates real opportunities to purchase properties cheaply on the low end of the cycle.

SUMMARY

Lodging follows the patterns of transportation and destinations of the times. Downtown hotels once served railroad passengers and still serve the needs of travelers who have business or entertainment interests in the center city. Motels and motor hotels serve people traveling by car as airport hotels do air passengers.

Business travel has been flat in recent years as companies react to rising travel costs and better means of communication. Business travelers value location convenience highly but they are also interested in service quality, a hotel's reputation, the type of hotel, and, finally, price. Hotels that want to serve business guests must accommodate their need to work on the road with conveniently arranged, comfortable rooms. Although business travel has flattened, leisure and personal travel continues to grow steadily. Aging baby boomers are a good leisure market. International travel is growing faster than domestic travel and U.S. chains are expanding overseas to gain their share of that market.

There are six categories of properties that are based on rate and service level: upper upscale, upscale, midscale with F&B, midscale without F&B, economy, and budget. Upper upscale properties have the most promising outlook because there is a shortage of rooms in this category and it takes time and capital to develop new upper upscale properties. Upscale and midscale properties are threatened with overcapacity in some markets and the economy and budget markets are already overbuilt in many areas.

All-suite hotels are represented at all levels of price and service intensity. These properties continue to outperform the industry in terms of rate and occupancy. Extended-stay properties are the fastest-growing group of properties, particularly in the lower price category. Resort hotels cater to pleasure-seeking guests. Although small in number of properties, resort hotels have excellent profit performance. Meeting and convention properties have participated in the upswing in the hotel business in recent years with revenue growing steadily and profits growing at an even faster rate. Condominiums have some similarities to hotels but involve a much different type of transaction in terms of time and amount. The time-share market makes it possible to own a condo for a specific time period and vacation clubs permit a guest to purchase a specified value of vacation time and to use it in three- or four-day periods. Finally, bed and breakfasts serve all segments of the market with accommodations in homes or in small inns.

Because hotels often fill the needs of the community or a real estate development, they are sometimes built without regard to profit outlook. Experience shows, however, that an unprofitable hotel is usually unsuccessful as an operation in serving the guest.

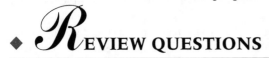

KEY WORDS AND CONCEPTS

Patterns of transportation and
   destinations
Motels
Motor hotel
Airport hotels
Downtown hotels
Business travel
Leisure and personal travel
International travel
Full-service properties
   Upper upscale property
   Upscale hotels
   Midscale hotels with food and
     beverage
Limited-service properties

Midscale hotels without food
   and beverage
Economy properties
Budget properties
All-suite hotels
Extended-stay properties
Resort hotel
Conference centers
Convention hotels
Condominiums
Time-share
Bed and breakfast (B&B)
Lodging as a community institution
Externalities

REVIEW QUESTIONS

1. How does transportation affect the hotel business?

2. What travel trends are favorable to lodging? Which are not? What do you think will be the best market segments for lodging in your community?

3. What are some means for hotel companies to increase sales to international travelers?

4. What are the two major divisions of lodging accommodations?

5. Name the five location markets discussed in the chapter. How do you assess their performance?

6. Name the six different rate and service level categories of hotels. What are the occupancies for each? Average rate? Outlook for future growth?

7. Identify the seven functional lodging types discussed in the chapter. What market does each serve?

8. What motives besides profit cause people to develop hotels? What is meant by externalities? What do you think the prospects are for hotels that are built mainly to serve those kinds of needs (i.e., externalities)?

◆ *I*INTERNET EXERCISES

1. **Site Name:** *American Hotel & Motel Association Online*
   URL: http://www.ei-ahma.org/webs/ahma/ahmahome.htm
   Background Information: The American Hotel and Motel Association (AH&MA) is the voice of the $80 billion U.S. lodging industry. The AH&MA, with headquarters in Washington, DC, offers communication, governmental affairs, marketing, hospitality operations, educational, convention, risk management, technology, information, and member relations services to hotels, motels, and lodging facilities throughout the world.

   EXERCISES:

   a. Describe what HITIS is and its impact on the hospitality industry.

   b. Using the AH&MA web site, describe the typical lodging customer.

2. **Site Name:** *Choice Hotels*
   URL: http://www.hotelchoice.com/cgi-bin/res/webres?chaininfo.html
   Background Information: Choice Hotels is a conglomerate of seven hotel brands under one corporate umbrella. The brands repersent each segment of the market.

   EXERCISE: Identify each of the seven brand names of Choice Hotels and, based on the information on the web site, determine which lodging category they might fit (full service, economy, etc.).

3. **Site Name:** *Motel 6*
   URL: http://www.motel6.com/
   Background Information: Beginning in 1962 with one property in Southern Caifornia, Motel 6 is now the largest company-owned and -operated lodging chain in the United States. Motel 6 began the concept of a nationwide economy chain—where travelers can find consistent quality at prices lower than all national brand name properties.

   EXERCISES:

   a. What is the average daily rate for Motel 6?

   b. How many rooms does the typical Motel 6 have?

   c. What is the Motel 6 concept?

◆ ✐**N**OTES

1. *Lodging Outlook,* November 1997 and January 1997.

2. *Lodging Outlook,* December 1997.

3. Smith Travel Research is the leading source of statistical information on hotel demand, supply, and financial and operating performance.

4. *1996 Lodging Industry Profile* (Washington, DC: American Hotel and Motel Association, 1997).

5. *1996 Survey of Business Travel* (Washington, DC: Travel Industry Association of America, October 1997).

6. *New York Times,* January 11, 1998, p. 1.

7. Remarks by Erik Altschul during a panel discussion on the Outlook for Business Travel at the TIA Marketing Outlook Forum, Cleveland, October 7, 1997.

8. Peter C. Yesawich, Remarks during an address to the National Outlook Forum, October 18, 1996. Mr. Yesawich is president of Yesawich, Pepperdine and Brown and has written widely on the travel industry.

9. John Rohs and Warren Gump, *Lodging Industry Annual Review,* February 25, 1998, p. 16. John Rohs is a managing director of Schroder and Co., Inc., a member of the New York Stock Exchange. He has been a security analyst specializing in the hospitality industry for many years and is a frequent speaker at industry leadership meetings.

10. Victoria Driver, Remarks during a panel discussion on the Outlook for Business Travel at the TIA Marketing Outlook Forum, Cleveland, October 7, 1997.

11. Ibid.

12. Roger S. Cline, "A View to the Millennium," *Lodging Hospitality,* August 1996. This article summarizes a joint study by Arthur Anderson and Company and New York University, *Hospitality 2000: A View to the Next Millennium.*

13. *Hotel Business,* June 21–July 6 1997, p. 2.

14. *Hotel Business,* January 7, 1997, p. 3.

15. David J. Bretl, Marriott Corporation, 1995.

16. Driver, Outlook for Business Travel.

17. *Lodging,* April 1997, p. 123.

18. *1998 Outlook for Travel and Tourism, Proceedings of the Travel Industry Association of America's 23rd Annual Marketing Outlook Forum,* October 5–7, 1998, Cleveland (Washington, DC: Travel Industry Association of America, December 1997). Leisure travel can be thought of as vacation travel, whereas personal travel includes personal or family non-vacation concerns and special events.

19. *Lodging Industry Profile* (Washington, DC: American Hotel and Motel Association, 1997).

20. *National Travel Survey* (Washington, DC: Travel Industry Association of America, 1996). The figures are based on travel from January to June.

21. Rohs and Gump, *Lodging Industry Annual Review,* p. 16.

22. Rohs and Gump, *Lodging Industry Annual Review,* p. 17.

23. *Hotel,* March 1994, pp. 20–21.

24. J. T. Kuhlman, President, America's Inter Continental Hotels, Remarks during a panel discussion, "Chains: Foreign Based," International Hospitality Investment Conference, New York, June 7, 1994.

25. *Lodging,* March 1998, p. 49.

26. These categories are those used by Smith Travel Research (STR). One problem, however, is that STR uses rate relative to the local market rate structure exclusively. As a result, as pointed out in E & Y Kenneth Leventhal's *1998 National Lodging Forecast*, the STR categories "may include [lesser] upscale properties in the [highest] rate category" because they qualify in that particular market area, although they might not in a larger market. Thus, for instance, the STR "upper upscale" had an average rate of $129 in 1997 but Leventhal points out, "truly luxury properties are those with an average daily rate of $175 and up and are very distinctive, one of a kind assets" (p. 8). The reader should be aware that, in using the STR numbers, we are probably overstating the size of "luxury" properties, if that word is used in the sense that Leventhal uses it.

27. Statistics in this section, unless otherwise noted, are taken from Rohs and Gump, *Lodging Industry Annual Review*. Rohs and Gump, in turn, generally credit Smith Travel Research for their data.

28. *1998 National Lodging Forecast*, E & Y Kenneth Leventhal Real Estate Group, Earnst and Young LLP, p. 8.

29. Rohs and Gump, *Lodging Industry Annual Review*, p. 11.

30. *Hotels*, November 1997, p. 22.

31. Leventhal, *1998 National Lodging Forecast*, p. 8.

32. Rohs and Gump, *Lodging Industry Annual Review*, p. 18.

33. Best Western operates mid-market properties that have food and beverage and some that do not. The latter are generally smaller properties.

34. Leventhal, *1998 National Lodging Forecast*, p. 6.

35. Chuck Ross, "Budget Returns on Economy Properties." *Lodging*, January 1998, p. 62.

36. *Lodging Outlook*, February 1998, chart 2.

37. Rohs and Gump, *Lodging Industry Annual Review*, p. 20.

38. Chuck Ross, *Lodging*, January 1998, p. 62.

39. *The Host Study: 1997* (Smith Travel Research), p. 33.

40. *Hotels*, January 1990, p. 34.

41. Severyn Ashkenazy, Remarks made during a panel discussion, Hospitality Industry Investment Conference, New York, June 1991.

42. Data from Smith Travel Research.

43. Villager Lodge Franchise System Profile, March 1998.

44. Chuck Ross, "Destination: Continual Profitability," *Lodging*, April 1997, p. 49.

45. David Arnold, "Conference Centers Coming of Age," *Lodging*, February 1997, p. 17.

46. Morris Lapidus, "How Architects Design Rooms Differently," *Cornell Hotel and Restaurant Administration Quarterly*, May 1974, p. 69.

47. Paula Morabito, "Coming of Age," *Lodging*, July 1997, pp. 35–36.

48. *Hotels*, August 1997, p. 24.

49. Robyn Taylor Parets, "Getting Their Share," *Lodging*, February 1997, p. 44.

50. This profile is based on discussions during workshops on Timeshare and Condo Hotels at the International Hospitality Industry Investment Conference, June 6, 1994.

51. *Lodging*, June 1993, pp. 25–28.

52. Data provided by the Professional Association of Innkeepers International, an association of Bed and Breakfast and Country Inn operators.

53. A free packet of information on starting a B&B is available from the Professional Association on Innkeepers, P.O. Box 90710, Santa Barbara, CA 93190. A text, revised in 1996, *So You Want to Be an Innkeeper*, by Davies, Hardy, Bell and Brown, is published by Chronical Books.

Chapter 10

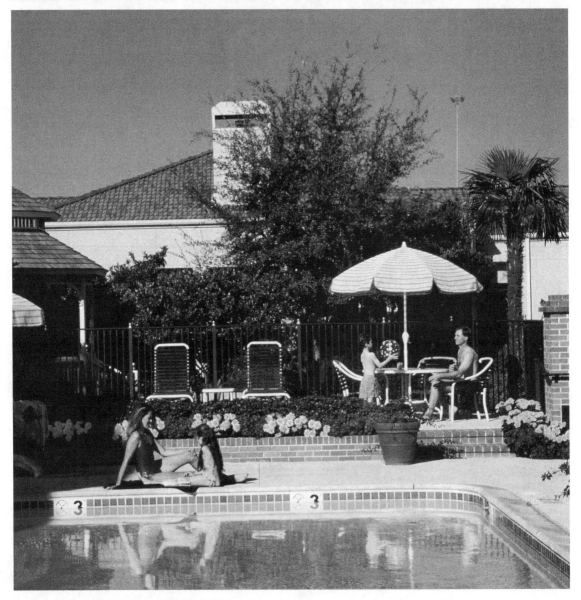

Courtesy of Courtyard Inn, Marriott International

Hotel and Motel Operations*

The Purpose of This Chapter

It is impossible to teach someone how to "run a hotel" from a book. Only practical experience can teach a subject so complex. This chapter is intended, however, to help you learn more quickly from experience by making you familiar with: (1) the major operating and staff departments in a hotel, (2) the information flows that tie a hotel together and how they are handled, and (3) the patterns of income and cost that affect hotel operations. Finally, this chapter outlines the major hospitality career entry points and the paths available for advancement.

This Chapter Should Help You

1. Name the major functional departments in a hotel and explain how they relate to one another

2. Trace the general flow of work accomplished in the major departments and their key subunits

3. Explain why the food and beverage department, although not the principal source of profit, is so important to some hotels' success

4. Relate the principal sources of income and expense to the appropriate department according to the uniform system of accounts for hotels

*The authors wish to acknowledge the assistance of Prof. Gary Vallen in the revision of this chapter.

5. Define the role of yield management in hotel industry pricing

6. Understand the technical and managerial responses to security problems in hotels

7. Explain how accounting statements can be used to measure the performance of key executives and department heads in a hotel

8. Define and use the key operating ratios and terms that describe an operation

9. Explain the relationship of the financial structure of a hotel to its cost of operations

Hotel properties range in size from tiny to huge. Although large properties such as Chicago's Hilton and Towers or the Excalibur in Las Vegas catch the public's imagination, the majority of properties offer between 100 and 250 units. Because most students will encounter these kinds of properties in their work, the examples in this chapter will assume a motor hotel in the 100- to 250-unit range.

Surprisingly enough, most properties perform basically the same functions, but the way in which they accomplish them varies with the property size. When there are significant variations in routine practices in larger properties, we will note them.

Hotels, large or small, perform the same basic functions. However, the way those functions are carried out varies with the size of the property.
Courtesy of Cendant Corp.

Our emphasis, however, will be on the similarities found throughout the hotel business rather than on the variations.

MAJOR FUNCTIONAL DEPARTMENTS

Figure 10.1 shows the basic functional areas of any hotel or motor hotel. This figure includes elements not found in some operations, as some hotels lack food and beverage departments and many do not have a gift shop or garage. Our purpose, however, is not to draw a chart that represents all properties inclusively; that would be impossible. Rather, we have outlined the major activities usually present in most properties.

A large property may employ a general manager under whom an executive assistant manager assumes responsibility for day-to-day operations. There is often a resident manager who supervises several departments, usually on the rooms side of the house, and a food and beverage manager, both of whom report to the "exec."

On the other hand, in the 100-unit inn diagrammed in Figure 10.2, the general manager may be responsible—with an executive housekeeper and perhaps a front-

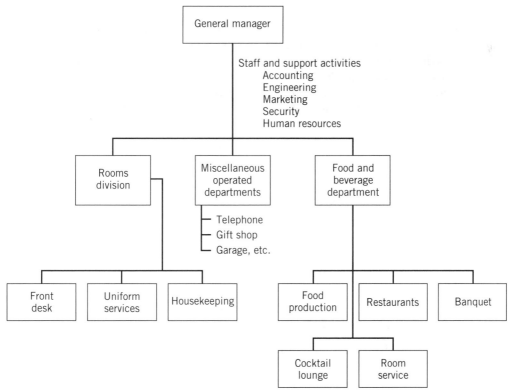

Figure 10.1 Major functional areas found in hotels and motor hotels.

Figure 10.2 Functional organizational chart for a small motor hotel.

office manager or chief clerk—for running the rooms and for supervising an assistant manager responsible for food and beverage. At one extreme, in the small property, the executive staff may consist of two or three persons supported by a few department heads and key employees. On the other hand, a large property requires a complex organization with several layers of authority.

It is important to note that a smaller property may have functional areas (food production, bar, dining room, dish, pot, receiving, and cleanup, for instance, in the food and beverage area) but no true department heads. The restaurant in a small inn may be run by a restaurant manager who directly supervises all the employees with help from lead employees in each functional area on each shift. For instance, the hostesses for the day and evening shifts may provide leadership to the dining room staff during their shifts; a head cook on each shift does the same for the kitchen staff. The manager may be responsible for hiring and discipline on both shifts, usually along with someone designated as an assistant when the manager is off duty. This arrangement is economical and convenient in small properties as long as the restaurant manager delegates enough responsibility to avoid becoming overcommitted.

𝒯HE ROOMS SIDE OF THE HOUSE

Room rental is a hotel's main business and its major source of profit. The day-to-day operations of the typical **rooms department,** in larger hotels, sometimes called the rooms division, yields a departmental income (the revenue remaining after the direct operating costs of the department) of 70 percent or more, compared with 15 to 20 percent for the food and beverage department. Thus, the people on the rooms side of the house are crucial to the operation's financial success.

The Front Office

More than any other group, the desk clerks represent the hotel to its guests. They greet the guests on their arrival and make them welcome (or not, depending on their manners). If something goes wrong, most guests will complain first to the front desk. When the guests leave, the desk clerk checks them out. If anything has gone wrong, this will be a good time to catch it. ("I hope you enjoyed your stay"— and then *listen* to the answer.) Although the duties of the desk overlap, they will differ with the work shift.

In the following discussion, a small inn serves as a model. The functions in a larger property may be broken down into specialties (reception desk, cashier, mail, and key clerk) performed by different persons. Our purpose is to describe the work of the **front office** and its functions. Your own observations will illustrate for you the variety of ways in which the work is organized.

The **morning clerk** works from 6:45 A.M. to 3:15 P.M. With a half-hour meal break, this is an eight-hour day. Because the evening crew comes in at 2:45 P.M. and the night auditor goes off duty at 7:15 A.M., all shifts overlap so as to ensure a

Whether at the Ritz or, as here, at a Microtel, lobbies create the first impression as the guest arrives.
Courtesy of U.S. Franchise systems

smooth transition from one shift to the next. Some properties maintain a logbook in which information or events with which later shifts should be familiar are noted. The new shift's first task on coming on duty is to check the logbook to make sure they're fully briefed.

The morning shift's work is concentrated in the early hours (from around 7:30 A.M. until midmorning) on checking out guests. At the same time, of course, the employees on this shift answer guests' questions and perform other routine tasks. However, their main responsibility is checking out guests.

When a guest is ready to leave, the clerk verifies the final amount of the bill, posts any recent charges, and assists the guest in settling with cash, check, or credit card, according to the house credit policy. This credit policy, which lays down guidelines for accepting checks and specifies the acceptable credit cards, is an important part of any clerk's training.

Although the technical aspects of the clerk's work are important, the courtesy a clerk accords a guest is at least as important. A departing guest must have an opportunity to register complaints if he or she has had problems. The morning clerk's work, thus, includes a special responsibility for ensuring that guests leave with the intention of returning to the hotel on their next visit to town.

As guests check out and their rooms become vacant, housekeeping is notified.

Courtesy is an important component of the desk clerk's job, as they represent the hotel to the guests.
Courtesy of U.S. Franchise Systems

This permits housekeeping to make up the rooms promptly so that they will be ready when new guests check in later that day. As the rooms are made up, housekeeping notifies the desk so that early arrivals can be accommodated in rooms that are ready to rent. Alternatively, the room status can be changed to ready to rent at housekeeping's computer terminal, when the room is made up.

Most properties now have computerized reservation systems that keep track of the balance between rooms available and reservation requests. The morning clerk and her or his supervisor, the guest services manager (or front-office manager), monitor this process and block any special reservation requests. In a property that does not have a computerized reservation system, they will block the day's reservations.

The **afternoon clerk's** work is shaped by the fact that the heaviest arrival time begins, in most transient houses, a little after 4:00 P.M. The afternoon clerk, therefore, takes over the reservation planning begun by the morning clerk and greets the guests as they arrive.

First impressions are crucial, and the desk clerk's warm welcome often sets the tone for the guest's entire stay. By remembering the names of repeat visitors, meeting special demands when possible (such as for a ground-floor room), and bearing in mind that the guest has probably had a hard, tiring day of work and travel, the desk clerk can convey the feeling that the guest is among friends at last. The clerk checks in the guest, which establishes the accounting and other records necessary for the stay.

The **night auditor** is a desk clerk with special accounting responsibilities. When things quiet down (usually by 1:00 A.M.), the auditor posts those charges not posted by the earlier shifts, including (most especially) the room charge. He or she then audits the day's guest transactions and verifies the total balance due the hotel from guests as of the close of the day's operations. The **auditing process** can be quite complicated, but simply stated, the auditor compares the balance owed to the hotel at the end of yesterday with today's balance. He or she verifies that the balance is the correct result of deducting all payments from yesterday's balance and adding all of today's charges. This process, summarized graphically in Figure 10.3, not only verifies today's closing balance of guest accounts owed to the hotel but also systematically reviews all transactions when an error in the balance is found. For this reason, the night auditor's job is important, requiring intelligence, training, and integrity.

Automation of the Front Office

Although the main element of personal service—a smile, a friendly greeting, and generally courteous treatment of the guest—cannot readily be automated, much of the clerical work has been greatly simplified in most hotels by the installation of a **property management system (PMS).** The PMS improves operational efficiency by eliminating repetitive tasks and improves service by providing information more quickly and accurately. At the same time, the PMS improves operational control. We need to understand the PMS in order to see how the front office functions.

ADD:
Yesterday's closing balance of accounts owed by
guests to the hotel

$64,217.91

LESS:
Payments received today against accounts
(say **$4,340.97**)

PLUS:
All charges made today to hotel or guest accounts
(say **$17,614.86**)

EQUALS:
Today's closing balance of accounts owed by guests
to the hotel

$77,491.80

Figure 10.3   A schematic view of the night audit process.

The computer program (or programs) that embody the PMS prompt the clerk to follow an appropriate work sequence for every task. For instance, when a guest checks into the hotel, the clerk begins by "telling" the computer that the guest has a reservation or not. If the guest has a reservation, the clerk need only type in the name and the computer will retrieve the reservation and automatically print out the necessary records. In most cases, the guest is simply asked to sign his or her name. If the guest doesn't have a reservation, the clerk gets the necessary information, following the format on the front-desk computer screen (depicted in Figure 10.4) and types it in.

When the guest checks out, the computer once again presents a screen with

```
┌─────────────────────────────────────────────────┐
│  GUEST INFORMATION        ROOM DESIGNATION       │
│  Name: Tom Farmer         Room Type: Dbl         │
│  Phone: 612-999-1212      Rack Rate:  86.00      │
│  Adress: 6199 Thorton Blvd  Folio Rate: 70.00    │
│        Minneapolis, MN    # Nights:    2         │
│  Special Request: Crib    Extras:    Crib–NC     │
│  Market: 12–15B                                  │
│  Credit:                                         │
│  Credit Card: Diners Club #99552211887712        │
│  Exp. 9/1/03                                     │
│  Folio Limit: $500                               │
│  ──────────────────────────────────────────     │
│  Guest Walk-In Display                           │
│  (1) Room Info  (2) Guest Info  (3) Additional Info │
│  (4) Post Charge or Credit  (5) Change or Update │
│  (6) Check In                                    │
│              02  27  15:07                        │
└─────────────────────────────────────────────────┘
```

Figure 10.4 The walk-in registration screen. Note the menu across the bottom of the screen that prompts the clerk as to the choices of activity appropriate to dealing with a walk-in.

prompts (note the menu at the bottom of the screen in Figure 10.4) that will help the clerk to move through the appropriate sequence, verifying the balance with the guest, posting any late charges, and accepting payment by credit card or cash or billing the account directly if prior arrangements have been made. Figure 10.5 shows the screen the clerk sees when checking out Mr. Farmer.

Where the front-desk computer is interfaced (i.e., electronically interconnected) to other systems, such as restaurant and bar point-of-sale (POS) terminals and a housekeeping-department terminal, front-office clerical routines are further simplified. When guests settle a dinner or bar check by charging it to their room number, the cashier in the food or beverage (F&B) outlet posts this entry on his or her POS, and that posting is automatically entered on the guest's bill at the front-office terminal. This system assures that all charges will be posted to the guest's bill immediately. Manual posting is required for any charges that are not automatically handled by the system. In properties that do not have departments such as F&B interfaced to the front-office system, those charges are also posted manually. This is more time consuming for both departments and it is also likely to lead to more mistakes.

In much the same way, when housekeeping is interfaced, at the time the guest checks out, the room shows up as vacant and ready to make up on the housekeeping terminal. When housekeeping personnel have cleaned the room, they make the appropriate entry and the room is automatically added to the ready-to-rent total in

```
┌─────────────────────────────────────────────┐
│  GUEST INFORMATION        ROOM DESIGNATION    │
│  Name: Tom Farmer         Room Type: Dbl      │
│  Phone: 612-999-1212      Rack Rate:  86.00   │
│  Adress: 6199 Thorton Blvd  Folio Rate: 70.00 │
│          Minneapolis, MN  # Nights:   2       │
│  Special Request: Crib    Extras:     Crib−NC │
│  Market: 12−15B                               │
│  ───────────────────────────────────────     │
│  Credit:                                      │
│  Credit Card: Diners Club #99552211887712     │
│            Exp. 9/1/03                         │
│  Folio Limit: $500  BAL 270.13                │
│  ───────────────────────────────────────     │
│  Guest Check Out Display                      │
│  (1) View Folio  (2) Posting  (3) Transfer  (4) Payment │
│  (5) Check Out  (6) Print Folio               │
│              02  29  11:42                     │
└─────────────────────────────────────────────┘
```

Figure 10.5   The check-out screen.

the front-office terminal. Where housekeeping is not interfaced, lists of "on change" and "ready-to-rent" rooms are usually communicated back and forth by phone.

Most chain or franchised properties interface their front office not only with other departments but also with their group's central reservation system (CRS). This permits the CRS to determine room availability directly and automatically from the individual property. This is an important time-saver for front-office staff and helps maximize the usefulness of the CRS to the individual property. The PMS can also be used to automate and integrate a number of other functions in the hotel, as shown in Figure 10.6.

Reservations and Yield Management

Traditionally, the hotel industry has looked at **occupancy** as a measure of success. Another indicator of operational success that we have always consulted is the **average rate** per rented room (the average daily rate, or ADR). Yield management puts these two together and, using forecasting based on the history of past sales, sets out to get the best combination of occupancy and ADR.[1] **Yield management,** then, involves varying room rates according to the demand for rooms in any given time period. The argument is that, when the hotel is going to be full, it makes no sense to sell any rooms at special discount rates. On the other hand, on a night when the hotel is definitely not going to fill, selling a room at a discounted price is better than not selling it at all. Going beyond maximizing rate, hotels are using yield management to take more multiple-night (instead of single-night) reservations during busy periods on the theory that a multiple-night reservation offers less proportionate risk of a vacant room following check-out.[2] As with so much in hotel

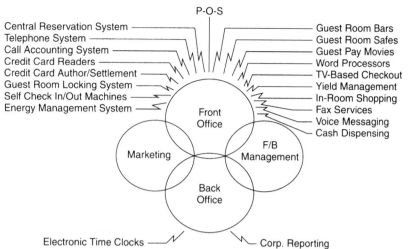

Figure 10.6 Hotel property management system interfaces.
(*Source:* Chervenak, Keane and Company.)

operations, careful employee training is essential to secure an effective yield management system that is operated in a way that will generate maximum revenue but that will not offend guests. Yield management is discussed further in Chapter 12.

Although yield management is still relatively new to lodging, it has been used in a number of other industries, most widely in the airline industry. It can also be used by car rental agencies, theme parks, sporting events, cruises, hospital facilities, and in selling advertising time and freight shipments.[3]

Security

In a hotel of any size, security is a major concern. In a large hotel, **security** may be a department but no matter what its organizational status, security has become the focus of top management attention.[4] Security came forcefully to the attention of hotel operators in 1976 when a well-known singer, Connie Francis, was raped at knifepoint in a Long Island motel. That such a terrible event could happen in a lodging property was enough to gain management's attention—but the $2.5 million awarded to the victim by the jury underlined that concern. The door in her room appeared to be locked but could be opened. In fact, security practice in many hotels had become lax. The jury found that the hotel had not exercised reasonable care. The question of **reasonable care** has been a continuing concern for operators since the Francis case. In recent years, a spate of bad publicity on television and in the newspapers has heightened hotel managers' attention to this problem.

The matter of security can be approached as a technical problem and as a management problem. Both approaches are probably necessary to reach a solution.

Technical Problems in Security.   The largest technical commitment on the part of hotel operators has been the replacement of the metal key with electronic or card-based locks, a practice that is now being mandated by many franchise systems. A new combination is electronically or mechanically encoded on the key with each guest registration. The lock in the guest room door is reset electronically by the first entry of the electronic or card key. In the case of an on-line system, the door is reset from the front desk at the time of registration. Where installation of new key systems is not economically feasible, removal of room numbers from the key to be replaced by coded letter or number identification systems is a minimum requirement. The guest room key and lock is an obvious and essential first line of defense for the guest's personal security.

Other security products being sold for use in hotels include room safes and improved peepholes that provide a fuller, less distorted view than the traditional means for guests to see who is knocking at their doors.[5] One intriguing new security product currently available is the biometric safe. To gain access to this safe, "the guest simply places his or her thumb on the safe's scanner. Thereafter, opening the safe involves just another quick thumb scan. No key or cards to be lost, stolen or duplicated. No codes to remember."[6]

Managerial Problems in Security.   Management's problem is not just to protect the guest; the question of high damage settlements must be weighed, too. A minimal approach to ensuring a hotel has exercised "reasonable care" for the guest's safety begins with a professional assessment, a broad overview of the hotel and its security for the guest's person and property. With this overview in hand, the hotel management can take the steps necessary to exercise its reasonable care. Actions range from installing new locks (about $250 per room or more), increasing lighting in parking lots and guest areas, uniformed guards, and installing closed-circuit-television surveillance. The guard service is useful in itself but the visibility of the guard also acts as a deterrent to crime. Similarly, closed-circuit television is a warning to intruders that they may be under surveillance. In some cases, dummy cameras are mixed with the real thing in a security system to enhance the impression of surveillance.

Telephone

Because the system of accounting for hotels recognizes telephone activity as a separate department for revenue purposes, one often hears about the **telephone department.** Only in the largest hotels, however, is there really a separate organizational unit to match this designation, and, in such hotels, it is headed by a chief operator. The telephone service in many properties is handled by a person who also serves as a second desk clerk. Many properties, particularly those of approximately 100 units with automatic phone systems, require the desk clerk to operate the switchboard as part of their regular duties.

The increasing availability of voice mail and automated systems in hotels has expanded the services provided to guests—and, increasingly, expected by them. It is now common to provide voice mail in each guest room. In addition to improving the level of service available in the hotel, this has the effect of reducing staffing requirements to take, record, and deliver guest messages.

Lighweight portable phones will, in time, diminish the importance of telephone service in hotels and reduce the size of the PBX system required to service hotels, according to Chervenak, Keane and Company, one of the world's leading hotel technology consulting firms. Pocket phones will be based on LEO (low earth-orbiting satellites) and will make it possible to reach people anywhere (including in their hotel room) using their personal number, which will work worldwide.[7]

Housekeeping

Housekeeping, that less-than-glamorous but essential department, is as much a production department of a hotel as the front desk and bell staff are service depart-

Housekeeping can be thought of as the "production department" of the hotel.
Courtesy of Holiday Inn Memphis East

*𝒥*ndustry
**Practice
Note 10.1**

The Concierge

In luxury hotels, the concierge offers the guests important services. He or she is expert in giving directions to local attractions, securing tickets to shows, and recommending local restaurants, tours and other entertainment. The concierge knows about local transportation, tour schedules, and nearly any other information a tourist might want. The concierge is most commonly found in North America in luxury hotels or in luxury floors in larger hotels.

When the concierge at the Phoenician Resort (**http://www.thephoenician.com/**) in Phoenix, Arizona, was asked to give his definition of the position, he replied,

> The closest thing you could find to a friend in a resort or hotel. Somebody a guest can turn to when they need something, somebody a guest can trust to help meet their requests and expectations. Concierges are in the business of making memories. We are not the people who know everything, we just know how to find everything.

This same concierge tells a story about lending the shoes off his feet to a guest who had forgotten to pack his dress shoes.[1]

In most hotels, the front desk and bell staff generally share the work that the concierge does in the luxury property. It is important, if there is no concierge in the property, to see that the guest (who is, after all, usually an outsider to the community) has some place in the hotel to turn for information. He or she is likely to need up-to-date information about airport limousine schedules; the hours of religious services and the locations of churches; and

Luxury hotels such as the Four Seasons offer round-the-clock concierge service.
Courtesy of Four Seasons Hotels

such entertainment possibilities as sporting events, movies, and the theater. Some hotels give employees special training in how to give directions and provide lists of local attractions.

1. *On the Camelback Corridor News,* August 1995, p. 10.

ments. It is clear that without clean rooms to rent, a hotel would have to close. For this reason, the management should always pay close attention to morale factors such as pay and worker recognition in the housekeeping department.

The housekeeping department is usually headed by an executive housekeeper. In a smaller property, a linen room assistant may double as an assistant housekeeper and inspector. In larger properties, the executive housekeeper will have at least one assistant and several supervisors, generally known as inspectors, who supervise room attendants in a designated area.

In some hotels, housemen take responsibility for cleaning the halls and heavy work such as moving furniture. These employees often form a separate subdepartment. Hotels with their own laundries often assign the supervision of that area to the housekeeping department. Generally, a working laundry supervisor or lead worker handles routine supervision under the executive housekeeper's general direction.

Uniformed Services Staff

Uniformed staff who perform personal services for the guests are part of the rooms division. These include the bell staff, concierge, security, valet, and garage. Of course, the property classification, size, and location determine whether there is a need for these positions. We will discuss the bell staff next and, in Industry Practice Note 10.1, the concierge.

The Bell Staff. Many motor hotels do without a bell staff because most of their guests prefer to "room" themselves. On the other hand, the **bell staff** plays an important role in the larger and more luxurious hotels. The process of **rooming a guest** includes more than just carrying luggage and showing a guest to a room. Rather, it begins when the clerk assigns a room. At this point, the bellman takes charge, welcoming the guest in both word and manner and, on entering the room, demonstrating its operations and features. He or she shows the guest how to operate the air conditioning and turn on room and bath lights. The bellman will usually turn on the television and run through the channels and networks available. The bellman may also indicate when the food service is open and provide other information the guest may need.

$\mathcal{F}$OOD AND BEVERAGE DEPARTMENT

Originally, the hotel restaurant was designed to give a traveler in a strange city a place to eat where the food would be good or at least palatable—and safe to eat. In recent years, however, the restaurant industry has grown in diversity of both concepts and menus. Moreover, that growth has meant the spread of restaurants into more and more locations, making restaurant food service readily available. Many successful chain restaurants carry well-known brand names to which travelers are accustomed. In the face of stiffening restaurant competition for the hotel guest's food and beverage patronage, some hoteliers have developed hotels, such as the economy and all-suite properties discussed in Chapter 9, that offer only very limited food service—usually a complimentary breakfast and, in all-suite operations, complimentary cocktails in the evening.

On the other hand, *in full-service hotels,* the food service operation continues to be not only a vital service but a key competitive weapon.[8] Many full-service hotels have several quite different food outlets. This extends the services available to the guest—and helps keep the guest's food business in the hotel. Although well-run restaurants and banquet departments are vital to full-service hotels, they are not by any means an easy thing to deliver. In fact, there's an old saying among hotel people that "if you can run the food, the hotel will run itself." Like most folklore, this exaggeration carries more than just a grain of truth. Perhaps a personal recollection by one of the authors will illustrate this point:

> My first job as an innkeeper was in a hotel with a leased food and beverage department. That is, the owners had leased the food and beverage department to a food service management company to "keep the food problems out of our hair," as they put it. This is sometimes a disastrous "solution," and it certainly was in this case.
>
> A banquet held in the hotel was fouled up, and I, as the innkeeper, was apologizing to a prominent automobile dealer for the problems he and others had had. I concluded my explanation by commenting that unfortunately, because the restaurant was leased, there was not much I could do about it. His reply has always stayed with me.
>
> "Tom," he said, "suppose you came down and bought a car from me and a few weeks later had mechanical trouble. Suppose my service department couldn't fix the trouble, and you came to me to complain and I told you, 'It's beyond my control. My service department is leased.' Would you ever buy another car from me? Your food and beverage department is your service department."

I was genuinely hard put to give any adequate answer to his question—because there wasn't any. The car dealer was right. Service in any part of the hotel is important. However, nothing seems to enrage guests quite so much as slow breakfast service, cold soup, or a tough steak.

Many hotels in recent years have emphasized the **food and beverage department's** role as a profit center, that is, a specifically identified, profitable part of the hotel's operation. The typical hotel food and beverage department in the United States creates about half as much in dollar sales as does the rooms department but generally only provides between 10 and 20 percent as much profit as that generated by the rooms department.

Many hotelkeepers still regard the food and beverage department as a key marketing activity whose main purpose is to secure guest patronage for the hotel and only secondarily to generate profits. These operations are not operated to lose money. However, they may price food and drink very reasonably and offer large portions or exceptionally good quality to attract patronage from the community. The reasoning is that this approach will build their reputation with guests and local

This restaurant's decor in Las Vegas' New York, New York Hotel seeks to capture the feel of Greenwich Village.
Courtesy of New York, New York Hotel, Las Vegas

people. In turn, this reputation attracts guests to stay (and referrals of guests by local people) in the hotel's rooms.

Restaurants

Many motor hotels offer coffee-shop service, a more or less formal dining room, and a cocktail lounge. The hotel restaurant's hours of operation are related to the guests' needs rather than just to food and beverage profits. For example, many hotels open at least one food room at 6:00 A.M. to serve those who are early risers because they have come from another time zone, have an early plane to catch, or want to beat the morning traffic. The few guests who turn up before 7:00 in the morning hardly ever warrant the added payroll hours for cooks, waitresses, and the cashier. If guests' schedules are accommodated, however, they are likely to return to the hotel and spend those rooms department dollars that provide a 70 percent plus profit margin.

Similarly, the dining room's sales volume falls off dramatically in most properties between 8:30 and 9:00 P.M., but many hotel dining rooms stay open to accommodate the few late-arriving guests. The bar, too, may serve only a few guests in the midafternoon or after 9:00 P.M., but, again, the full service a guest expects must be available.

Although management personnel need not always be present at opening or closing time, some lead employee, such as the cashier or first cook, must accept responsibility for unlocking and locking food storage areas, turning lights and equipment on at opening and off at closing, setting up the cash register or closing it out, and so forth.[9] Because of the long operating hours, one hostess is generally responsible for the day shift (from 7:00 A.M. to 3:00 P.M.), and a second is in charge of the evening shift (from 3:00 P.M. until closing). In smaller properties, one of these supervisors may be designated to act for management when the restaurant manager is not on duty.

Hotel menus, too, take on a special character related to the guests' needs. Breakfast and the evening meals are the most important to the transient hotel guest, who may not have arrived in time for lunch or may be away from the hotel for that meal. (This statement does not apply to destination properties such as resorts.) Once again, personal experience furnishes a good illustration of this point:

> At breakfast, I always provided freshly squeezed orange juice in the dining room where the guests could see that it really was fresh. This was foolishly expensive from the restaurant's standpoint, but I received enough guest comment slips saying "I stay at this hotel because of the fresh orange juice" to convince me that we weren't really being extravagant.
>
> At the evening meal, we offered, as a "Traveling Man's Special," one complete meal at a rock-bottom price featuring a low-cost appetizer, a wholesome but inexpensive entrée, salad, and dessert. In a freestanding restaurant, this would make no sense because it would reduce the check average, taking sales away from more expensive items on the menu. But many travelers are cost-conscious because they are paying their own expenses or, as with government employees (and professors!), they receive only limited reimbursement for their travel costs. A "bargain meal" thus attracts such customers to a hotel. Some guests told us they ate the inexpensive meal—but had a couple of cocktails before the meal and charged the whole amount on their expense accounts. The total cost was still within their company's travel allowance.

Banquets. Some large properties offer a catering department (or banquet department) headed by a catering manager who books and sells banquets. Smaller properties include this activity among the restaurant manager's duties. Larger properties have special full- and part-time banquet service staffs. Smaller properties draw banquet service personnel from their regular crew and often supplement them with part-time employees.

Banquets are often profitable but, once again, in many properties the banquet menus and banquet rooms are meant principally to serve the rooms department. Thus, a meeting may occupy one conference room all day. Perhaps the hotel supplies a coffee break and a luncheon in another room. It probably charges the businesspeople little, if anything, over what those meals and snacks would cost in the dining room. Moreover, it may not charge extra for the meeting facilities. If such a meeting accounts for 20 or 30 guest room rentals—or even only 10 or 15—the logic we have mentioned before clearly applies. The 70 percent profit on room sales makes this use of banquet space desirable.

Food Production.   In most properties, the person in charge of food production is called the *executive chef.* A chef is a person who has completed, either formally or informally, the training that qualifies him or her to be an excellent professional

Banquet space can be used to sell guest rooms by accommodating an organization's meeting needs.
Courtesy of Hotel Newfoundland, Montreal, Canada

cook. The chef should also be an effective manager who can purchase food; hire, train, and discipline employees; and plan appetizing meals priced to yield a profit. All too often, however, the title of chef is bestowed on somebody who is, at best, a head cook. True chefs are still in relatively short supply and are expensive to hire. (On the other hand, a good chef will usually help the success of the operation, thus offsetting the cost.)

An increasingly common title in American food service is food production manager. Although these managers are almost invariably accomplished cooks, they emphasize kitchen management and rely on strict adherence to written recipes, rather than on their craft skills, to ensure quality. The type of management chosen by a property generally reflects the dollar volume of food sales. More sales may permit the expense of a chef or food production manager. Smaller properties may have to content themselves with a head or lead cook. In this case, the restaurant manager generally works more closely with the kitchen.

With the greater availability of quality frozen prepared foods as well as the growing acceptance of limited menus, an approach to food service that requires limited culinary skills is becoming more and more common in hotels that don't try to reach the luxury standard.

Large convention properties may support a separate subdepartment, often made up largely of part-time workers who prepare only banquet food. Some properties even use a separate banquet kitchen.

Because of the hours of operation, a manager should clearly designate early and late supervision hours. This supervision may require a lead cook—or perhaps the restaurant manager or an assistant—to work as a supervisor.

Sanitation and Utility.   Sanitation is so important that many hospitality programs offer entire courses on the subject. Our purpose here is simply to repeat the point made in Chapter 4 regarding the importance of dishwashers, pot washers, and the cleanup crew. In Chapter 3, we noted that many students find that the only summer jobs available are in these areas. They may not be the most interesting jobs but, as we said earlier, they provide an ideal observation point for learning about how a food service operation functions.

There is another reason for mastering these jobs while a student. The assistant restaurant manager job includes responsibility for this function in most hospitality operations—restaurants, hotels, and institutions. It is most commonly assigned to people just out of management training programs. Success in this job often launches a successful career, and a good working relationship with subordinates is helpful in this entry-level position. Few things will help you toward that goal more than the ability to roll up your sleeves and help out when one of your crew gets "stuck." (Be careful, however, not to turn yourself permanently into a manager/dishwasher just to win popularity contests.) You need not plan to spend your life in the dishroom, but never be afraid to say you started there!

The Exceptional Case.   As a student of food service, you should be aware that in a few hotels—usually older and smaller ones—the food department actually generates more profit than the rooms department does. In these cases, the innkeeper or owner is an unusually talented foods person and devotes the greatest portion of time to the food department. In these properties, as in all the others, however, the success of the food department invariably increases room sales.

Leased Restaurants.   The practice of leasing restaurants has become increasingly common. At this point, we can summarize the arguments on the subject. By leasing a restaurant, a full-service property permits hotel management to focus its attention on the more profitable rooms guest instead of the time-consuming food service operation. In addition, that difficult operation is taken over by experts, often with a major franchised brand. On the other hand, the hotel's "service department" is put in the hands of another company, which is concerned with its own objectives and profits. This topic is discussed again in Chapter 12.

Staff and Support Departments

Some departments or activities in a hotel offer no direct guest services. Instead, they maintain systems for the property as a whole, such as sales, marketing, and engineering. Some of these activities do, however, service the departments that deal directly with the guests: Accounting and human resources immediately come to mind.

Sales and Marketing.   Marketing means designing a hotel's services and facilities to suit the needs and tastes of potential guests—or shaping the operations of an existing property to its most likely guests. A second marketing function is encouraging the guests to choose your property by emphasizing all of those service activities that make the property pleasant and convenient. Finally, marketing is promoting the property among various potential guests and groups of guests. (This duty is often thought to be all there is to marketing, but it actually comes after the first two.)

Marketing is a general-management function that involves all levels of the operation. One important day-to-day activity in this area is personal selling. In large properties, a sales manager and one or more sales persons are responsible for finding sales leads and following up on them with personal sales calls and booking functions. Some properties define the sales department's work as the national convention market. Others identify local firms as the principal place to concentrate their efforts. Determination of just which market to approach is a crucial top-management decision usually made by the general manager, the sales manager, and even the ownership. In chains, corporate policy may dictate these decisions, but most often the precise market for a particular property must be specifically designated by the local management. (Some properties hire outside sales firms called hotel representatives to undertake sales activities for them in key markets.)

In smaller hotels, the general manager is responsible for managing sales. He or she will commonly make the sales calls personally and entertain people from potential sales accounts in the hotel. In some properties, the general manager is assisted in this work by a full- or part-time sales representative.

Because marketing is essential, a major trade association, the Hotel Sales Marketing Association International (HSMAI), conducts educational and informational programs for both sales personnel and general management. This organization, which publishes excellent materials on sales and marketing, is a good one to join on graduation or as a student if there is a chapter on your campus.

Accounting. Sometimes referred to as the **back office** (in contrast with the front office or front desk), accounting is charged with two quite different duties, accounts receivable and financial reporting and control. In large hotels, the accounting department may be headed by a comptroller and consist of several skilled clerical workers. Chains generally develop sophisticated corporate accounting departments that supervise work at the individual property. In a small property, on the other hand, the work is usually done by some combination of the innkeeper's secretary, a chief clerk, and an outside accountant.

When guests check out, they may pay their bills with cash, but they often charge this expense instead. The accounts receivable (bills owed by guests) in a hotel are divided into two parts. First, a **house ledger** (or tray ledger), kept at the front desk, is made up of bills owed by guests in the house. Charges by guests posted after they have checked out and charges by other persons, such as restaurant patrons not in the hotel, are kept in what is often called the **city ledger.** The name is derived from an earlier time when charging hotel bills was not common. Instead, guests paid cash when they checked out, and any charge not in the house ledger was a charge from some local customer, someone "in the city" who had a charge account at the hotel rather than someone "in the house." Incidentally, the word ledger originally referred to a book on whose pages these records were kept. Today, records of charges are usually maintained "in memory" on a computer. The function, however, and even the terminology are the same.

The other, less routine accounting functions involve preparing operating statements, conducting special cost studies, and overseeing the hotel's cost control systems. In small properties, much of this work is done by an outside accountant, whereas the larger properties often have their own full-time accounting staff headed by a comptroller or chief auditor.

Human Resources. Lodging is a labor-intensive industry with a relatively high employee turnover. As a result, issues related to human resources are an important consideration in any hotel and are commonly placed under the staff supervision of a human resources department. This department may be responsible for any or all of the following functions: employment advertising and applicant searches, maintaining job descriptions, providing employees with orientation to the company and the hotel, designing and reviewing compensation patterns and benefit packages, and complying with government labor regulations. Although the human resources department, as noted previously, is closely involved with the employment process, the hiring decisions are usually made by the appropriate department head.

As we noted a moment ago, in large properties, a human resources department manages most of the processes just listed. In smaller properties, this work is done by the manager and his or her secretary.

Engineering. The engineering function is so important that many hospitality management programs have one or more courses devoted to the disciplines that support it. Once again, we will simply describe briefly the work of this area. Large- and medium-sized hotels usually employ a chief engineer who supervises an engineering staff. Together, they are responsible for operating the hotel's heating and air conditioning; for maintaining its refrigeration, lighting, and transportation (elevator) systems; and for overseeing all of the hotel's mechanical equipment. Breakdowns in these areas seriously inconvenience guests. And, of course, utility costs have always been significant and, in recent years, have been increasing at an alarming rate.

In small properties, the engineer is often little more than a handyman who carries out routine maintenance and minor repairs. Outside service people supply the more specialized maintenance skills. In these properties, the innkeeper often supervises the engineering (or maintenance) function.

In any property, large or small, general management should at least

1. Determine what periodic maintenance of equipment is required (oiling, filter changing, making minor adjustments, and the like)

2. Establish a schedule for accomplishing that work

3. Develop a reporting system and physical inspection system that assures management that this work is carried out properly and on time

$\mathcal{I}$NCOME AND EXPENSE PATTERNS AND CONTROL

As with so many subjects discussed in this chapter, whole courses are often devoted to the topic of this section. Our purpose here, therefore, is to provide you with an understanding of the control structure of a hotel and a limited introduction to the vocabulary of control in hotels and restaurants.

The Uniform System of Accounts

Hotel accounting is generally guided by the **Uniform System of Accounts for Hotels,** which identifies important profit centers in hotels as revenue departments.

The uniform system first arranges the reporting of income and expense so that the relative efficiency of each major department can be measured by the departmental income. Table 10.1 shows a typical rooms department schedule of income and expenses for a 250-room motor hotel, and Table 10.2 shows a food and beverage department schedule for such a property. The rooms departmental income and the food and beverage departmental income figures help the manager evaluate the performance of key department heads working in those areas.

To determine the property's overall efficiency, we deduct four categories of **undistributed operating expenses** from the total of the various departmental incomes. These costs—administrative and general expense, marketing and guest entertainment, property operation, and maintenance and energy costs—are judged to be costs that pertain to all departments in a way that cannot be perfectly assigned to any one department.

The amount remaining after deducting these four categories of expense from the total of departmental income is called **total income before fixed charges.** This figure is probably the best measure of the success not only of the total property but of the general manager as well. For this reason, many managers receive bonuses based on their performance as measured by this figure. It is fair to evaluate the manager without regard to the remaining costs, which can best be described as capital costs.

Table 10.1

Rooms Department
Schedule of Income and Expenses

	Expenses	
	In Dollars	In Percent
Room Sales	$4,343,825	100.0%
Departmental Expenses		
Salaries and Wages Including Vacations	551,665	12.7
Payroll Taxes and Employee Benefits	178,097	4.1
Total Payroll and Related Expenses	729,762	16.8%
Laundry, Linen, and Guest Supplies	130,315	3.0
Commissions and Reservation Expenses	43,346	3.3
Complimentary Food and Beverage Expenses	4,344	0.1
All Other Expenses	125,971	2.9
Total Rooms Expenses	$1,133,738	26.1%
Rooms Departmental Income	3,210,087	73.9

Source: Ratios in this table are based on *Trends in the Hotel Industry—1997,* PKF Consulting; Full Service Hotels, p. 73.

Table 10.2

Food and Beverage Department Schedule of Income and Expenses	In Dollars	In Percent
Food Sales	$1,112,019	80.0
Beverage Sales	278,005	20.0
Total Food and Beverage Sales	$1,390,024	100.0%
Cost of Sales		
Food Cost (after credit for employee meals)	331,382	29.8%
Beverage Cost	64,775	23.3
Total Food and Beverage Cost	396,157	28.5%
Food Gross Margin	993,867	71.5%
Other Income		
Public Room Revenue	66,721	4.8
Other Income	69,501	5.0
Gross Margin and Other Income	$1,130,089	81.3%
Departmental Expenses		
Salaries and Wages Including Vacations	487,898	35.1%
Payroll Taxes and Employee Benefits	170,973	12.3
Total Payroll and Related Expenses	658,871	47.4%
Laundry and Dry Cleaning	15,290	1.1
China, Glass, Silver, and Linen	19,460	1.4
Contract Cleaning	6,950	0.5
All Other Expenses	100,083	7.2
Total Food and Beverage Department Expenses	800,654	57.6%
Food and Beverage Departmental Income	329,435	23.7%

Source: Ratios in this table are based on *Trends in the Hotel Business—1997,* PKF Consulting; Full Service Hotels, pp. 70 and 73.

Almost all of these **capital costs**—rent, property taxes, insurance, interest, and depreciation—are a direct function of the cost of the building and its furnishings and fixtures. The responsibility for these costs lies with the owners who made the decisions when the property was first built and furnished. These costs, therefore, lie beyond the control of the manager. Table 10.3, a typical statement of income and expense for a 250-room midscale property, shows how all of these figures relate to net profit.

Table 10.3

The Full Service Hotel
Statement of Income and Expense
For Year Ending December 31, 200X

	In Dollars	In Percent
Revenue		
Rooms	5,647,513	69.8%
Food and Beverage	1,974,202	24.4
Telecommunications	210,366	2.6
Minor Operated Departments	169,910	2.1
Rentals and Other Income	89,001	1.1
Total Revenue	8,090,992	100.0
Departmental Expenses		
Rooms	1,417,526	25.1[a]
Food and Beverage	1,449,064	73.4[a]
Telecommunications	114,018	54.2[a]
Other Departmental Expenses	110,151	1.4[b]
Total Departmental Expenses	3,090,759	38.2%
Total Departmental Income	5,00,233	61.8
Undistributed Operating Expenses		
Administrative and General	784,826	9.7
Marketing	428,822	5.3
Franchise Fees	129,456	1.6
Utility Costs	372,185	4.6
Property Operations and Maintenance	396,458	4.9
Total Undistributed Operating Expenses	2,111,747	26.1%
Gross Operating Profit	2,888,486	35.7
Management Fees	299,367	3.7
Income Before Fixed Charges	2,589,119	32.0%
Property Taxes	242,730	3.0
Insurance	56,636	0.7
Reserve for Replacement	169,911	2.1
Amount Available for Debt Service and Other Fixed Charges	2,119,842	26.2%
Pretax Income	1,270,285	15.7

[a]Percentage of departmental revenue.
[b]Percentage of total revenue.
Source: Ratios in this table are based on *The Host Study: Hotel Operating Statistics—1997;* Smith Travel Research, p. 15.

Key Operating Ratios and Terms. In Chapter 4, we introduced some key ratios and food service terms, which are used in hotel food service, as well. In addition, the hotel industry has other indicators of an operation's results:

Occupancy is generally indicated as a percentage:

$$\text{Occupancy percentage} = \frac{\text{Rooms sold}}{\text{Total rooms available}}$$

Average rate is an indication of the front desk's success in gaining the full rate on rooms sold rather than discounting:

$$\text{Average rate} = \frac{\text{Dollar sales}}{\text{Number of rooms sold}}$$

The average rate is also a mix of the double-occupancy rooms sold (rooms with two or more guests). This is reflected by the ratio:

$$\text{Number of guests per occupied room} = \frac{\text{Number of guests}}{\text{Number of occupied rooms}}$$

Because housekeeping is the largest and most controllable labor cost in the rooms department, many hotels compute the average number of rooms cleaned in the following ratio:

$$\text{Average rooms cleaned per maid day} = \frac{\text{Number of rooms occupied}}{\text{Number of eight-hour maid shifts}}$$

All of these ratios are usually computed for the day, the month to date, and the year at year's end. Comparisons of these indicators with earlier operating results and with the budget provide important clues to an operation's problems or success.

Capital Structure. We will discuss some of the financial dimensions of the hotel business further in Chapter 11. At this point, however, we need to describe briefly the capital costs found on the hotel's income statement because they are a significant part of a hotel's cost structure. Capital costs include rent, depreciation, and interest. Related costs, property taxes and insurance, can be included here because these taxes or fees are dependent on the value of the land and the building.

Depreciation is a bookkeeping entry that reflects the assumption that the original cost of the hotel building, furniture, and fixtures should be gradually written off over their useful life. Interest, of course, is the charge paid to the lenders for the use of their funds.

The hotel industry is capital intensive. That is, it uses a large part of its revenue to pay for capital costs, including real estate taxes. Close to 20 cents of every sales dollar go to cover costs related to the hotel's capital structure.

Hotel development is attractive to some investors because it is highly leveraged. Leverage, as a financial term, refers to the fact that a small amount of an investor's capital can often call forth much larger amounts of money lent by banks or insurance companies on a mortgage. A fixed amount of interest is paid for this capital, and so if the hotel is profitable, the investor's earning power will be greatly magnified, but the investor's modest initial investment need not be increased. Earnings go up, but interest does not. Nor does investment—hence, the word leverage.

Leverage, as developers have discovered repeatedly, can be a double-edged sword. Operating profits boom in good times and cover fixed interest payments many times over. When times turn bad or the effects of overbuilding begin to be felt, revenues fall, but interest rates (and required repayments on the principal of the loan) do not. The result can be a wave of bankruptcies.

$\mathcal{E}$NTRY PORTS AND CAREERS

An old adage says that there are three routes to advancement in the hotel industry: sales and marketing, accounting, and food and beverage. According to this adage, sales and marketing is the best route to the top in good times, but accounting, with its mastery of cost control, is the surest route in bad times. These three routes do lead to advancement, but they are by no means the only places to start.

Front Office

Many people begin their careers in the lodging industry in the front office, the nerve center of the hotel and the place where its most important sales occur. The front office is an important area. With the growing importance of the limited-service property, moreover, it increases in prominence because in those properties it is a critical area of technical knowledge. On the other hand, we should note that front-office techniques can be mastered fairly quickly. Moreover, this still leaves a good many of the hotel's important operating functions outside the front office yet to be learned. Although some executives have risen to general manager from the front office, most of them are found in small properties. If your ambitions include advancement to general manager, you will want to think carefully about building on a successful front-office experience by adding experience in another area. In a limited-service property, this should probably be marketing.

Many people find front-office work, with its constant change and frequent contact with guests, the most rewarding of careers. Moreover, improved pay scales in this area in recent years have upgraded the long-term attractiveness of this work, as has the increasingly sophisticated use of the computer in the front office. Another advantage of working in this area is a more-or-less fixed work schedule, although the afternoon shift's hours (from 3:00 P.M. to 11:00 P.M.) and those of the night auditor (from 11:00 P.M. to 7:00 A.M.) are viewed by many as drawbacks to those specific jobs.

Accounting

It is certainly true that during the Great Depression of the 1930s, many of the successful managers were accountants. Today, however, accounting has become a specialized field, and successful training in this area can be so time consuming that it may be difficult to master the other areas of the operation. Although accounting may not offer as easy a route to the general manager's slot as it once did, it does offer interesting and prestigious work for those who like to work with numbers. Moreover, the hours in this area tend to be reasonably regular, the pay is usually good, and the position is prestigious.

Although accounting per se is not as common a route to general manager as it once was, a new offshoot of accounting, operations analysis, is quite a different story. Operations analysts conduct special cost studies either under the direction of the auditor or comptroller or as a special assistant to the general manager. Some operation analysts work in corporate headquarters. The operations analyst's job is such a good training ground for young managers that a regular practice of rotation through this job for promising managers has become, in some companies, a feature of management development.

Sales and Marketing

The key to the success of any property involves *having* sales. Thus, it is not surprising that many successful hotel operators have a sales background. On the other hand, salespeople often find that a grounding in front-office procedures and in food and beverage operations (with special emphasis, respectively, on reservations and banquet operations) leads to success in sales. Successful sales personnel are much in demand, and a career in sales offers interesting and financially rewarding work to the successful.

The importance of sales and marketing tends to increase when there is an oversupply of rooms in a market. Increasingly, the marketing manager for a hotel is asked to conduct market research or to analyze market research done by others. Indeed, a common requirement for senior positions in marketing is the ability to prepare a marketing plan. Such a plan evaluates the local environment and the competition, sets goals for the plan period (usually one to three years), and presents the strategy and tactics to fulfill the plan. A solid educational background is a great help to the modern hotel marketing manager.

Food and Beverage

Food and beverage is one of the most demanding areas of the hotel operation, and it is an area in which Murphy's law—If anything can go wrong, it will!—most often applies. Success calls for the ability to deal effectively with two separate groups of skilled employees—cooks and serving personnel. Along with mastering both product cost control techniques (for both food and alcoholic beverages) and employee-scheduling techniques, the food and beverage manager must also work in sanitation and housekeeping and master the skills of menu writing. He or she must complete all these duties against at least three unyielding deadlines a day: breakfast, lunch, and dinner.

Many general managers brag that "I'm basically a foods person." Their success probably can be traced to the factors we discussed earlier in the chapter: The food and beverage department is the service department of the full-service hotel and, in competitive markets, a successful food and beverage operation helps fill the hotel. Food and beverage managers may, however, find themselves stereotyped by firms as "foods people" and their advancement hindered because owners prefer to keep them in their specialty, in which qualified managers are so scarce. In cases in which advancement to general manager is blocked, however, qualified managers have not usually had trouble finding another job.

An advantage of careers in food and beverage is career progression flexibility. Accomplished management and supervisory people in the food and beverage field almost always enjoy the option of moving to work outside the hotel in restaurants, clubs, or institutions. Although food and beverage probably requires longer hours than does any other area in the business, it is typically a well-paid position and offers not only career flexibility but unusually solid job security as well. Finally, it forms a sound basis for advancement into general management.

Owning Your Own Hotel

Many students are attracted to the hospitality management field because they would like some day to own their own businesses. Whereas new hotels require large investments, existing operations can sometimes, under special circumstances of two different kinds, be purchased with little or no investment. First, after a wave of overbuilding and during economic recessions (and particularly when these two occur simultaneously), bankruptcies become common. In addition, when banks must take over a hotel, they need someone to handle operations. They are often willing to give an opportunity for an ownership interest to a person with the know-how to take the property off their hands.

Some older hotels in smaller cities offer another kind of opportunity. They may have lost their competitiveness as hotels, while still occupying prime downtown real estate in a good food and beverage location. Because of this fact, together with an older hotel's extensive banquet facility and liquor license, the property may be revitalized by a well-run and imaginatively promoted food operation. The profits of that food operation may then be plowed back into improving the hotel facilities. The improved facilities and the property's improved reputation, earned by its newly successful food and beverage operation, often result in a greatly improved rooms business. Examples of such operations can be found in many parts of the country. Where they are found, they always share these three characteristics: excellence in the food operation; unusually effective promotion, generally enhanced by the manager's community involvement; and very, very hard work by that manager, who seems to live and breathe the hotel and restaurant business.

The hotel business offers many rewarding careers in front office, accounting, marketing and sales, and food and beverage. For those whose ambition and temperament makes them want to extend themselves, the top job is within reach and ownership is in sight.

SUMMARY

The first topic we discussed in this chapter was the major functional areas of a hotel and who runs them. Although big hotels have true departments and department managers, smaller hotels would designate these as areas, supervised by lead employees.

We next examined the rooms side of the hotel. The front office is particularly important, as it is the guests' first real contact with the hotel. The front office generally has a morning clerk, an afternoon clerk, and a night auditor, all with both different and overlapping duties. All help in making reservations, generally through a computerized reservation system.

The property management system (PMS) makes the operation of the front office more efficient and usually links it electronically to the hotel's other departments and, more often than not, to the hotel chain's central reservation service. Reservation systems often make use of yield management systems that are designed to get the best total dollar revenue possible through a mix of occupancy and average daily rate. Security is a concern that can be addressed technically through improved door-locking systems and other devices. Managerially, security involves assuring that the hotel is exercising reasonable care for security of the guest's person and property by establishing an overall security system for the property. Other rooms-side departments are the telephone department, the housekeeping department, and the bell staff.

The food and beverage department is very important to the full-service hotel, as it may determine whether guests return to the hotel (or come in the first place). We described the kinds of restaurants that various types of hotels offer, banquet facilities (if any), food production, and sanitation and utility.

We next looked at hotels' staff and support departments: sales and marketing, engineering, and accounting. The accounting department is sometimes referred to as the back office. We explained the hotel departmental income and expenses, operating ratios and terms, and, finally, capital costs.

We finished the chapter with a look at the best routes to advancement in the hotel industry—front office, sales and marketing, accounting, and food and beverage—and the advantages and disadvantages of each. We also discussed the possibility of owning your own hotel.

◆ KEY WORDS AND CONCEPTS

Rooms department	Average rate
Front office	Yield management
Night audit	Security: reasonable care
Auditing process	Telephone department
Property management system	Housekeeping
(PMS)	Bell staff

Rooming a guest   City ledger
Food and beverage department   Uniform system of accounts
Staff and support departments   Undistributed operating expenses
Back office   Income before fixed charges
House ledger   Capital costs

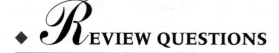

◆ REVIEW QUESTIONS

1. How does the organizational structure differ in large hotels and small?

2. Describe some of the duties of the morning clerk, the afternoon clerk, and the night auditor.

3. What are the benefits of a property management system? How does it make the front office run more smoothly?

4. What is the purpose of yield management? What problems does it pose?

5. What does the saying "If you can run the food, the hotel will run itself" mean?

6. Describe the different kinds of restaurants that a large hotel might have.

7. What are the advantages of the sanitation and utility area for a summer job?

8. What are capital costs? How important are they in hotels?

◆ INTERNET EXERCISES

1. **Site Name:** *TravelWeb*
   URL: http://www.travelweb.com/
   Background Information: Need a hand making on-line reservations? This is the place. You'll find help on searching for hotels and flights, booking your plans, and obtaining additional information.

   EXERCISE: You are going to attend the National Restaurant Association Convention in Chicago. Plan the complete trip to Chicago from your current location to include flight and hotel reservations on line using the dates provided by your instructor. Choose the appropriate flight and hotel information and submit your plan to your instructor.

   2. **Site Name:** *Successful Meetings*
      URL: http://www.successmtgs.com/
      Background Information: *Successful Meetings* magazine educates businesspeople about the meeting, convention, and incentive-travel industries. It offers news about industry events, issues and people, destination and package-deal updates, and how-to information for anyone who plans meetings.

      Site Name: *Meeting News*
      URL: http://www.meetingnews.com/
      Background Information: *Meeting News* is a professional journal that helps industry professionals in creating cost-effective, successful meetings. Use this web site to help plan meetings. It has a site selection interactive database with over 7000 meeting and event facilities on line. You may search for facilities that meet your specific needs.

      Site Name: *Meetings & Conventions*
      URL: http://www.meetings-conventions.com/
      Background Information: *Meetings and Conventions* provides similar information to the two sites listed previously.

      EXERCISE: Using the preceding sites, plan and organize a three-day meeting for 650 people in Nashville, Tennessee given the following information. The meeting participants are basically middle class with an average family income of $40,000. Approximately 60 percent of the attendees are female with 25 percent of the total being considered minorities. Choose an appropriate meeting hotel for the meeting and prepare a list of at least three outside tours that would be of interest to both participants and their spouses. Justify, in writing, your choice of arrangements.

 ◆ *N*OTES

---

1. Yield management is described more fully by one of its originators in lodging, Eric Orkin, in his article, "Boosting Revenues Through Yield Management," *Cornell Hotel and Restaurant Administration Quarterly,* February 1988, pp. 52–58. This article remains one of the clearest expositions of the principles and practices of yield management.

2. Remarks by Michael A. Levin during a workshop, "The Value of Branding," International Hospitality Industry Investment Conference, June 7, 1994.

3. Sheryl E. Kimes, "The Basics of Yield Management," *Cornell Hotel and Restaurant Administration Quarterly,* November 1989, p. 46.

4. I am indebted to Professor Anthony Marshall for much of the material in this section. Dr. Marshall is an attorney as well as Dean of the School of Hospitality Management at Florida International University and a leading authority on the legal aspects of hotel security.

5. CKC Report, March 1993, p. 8.

6. CKC Report, April 1997, p. 11.

7. CKC Report, March 1993, p. 10.

8. The reader may wish to review the section in Chapter 2 regarding restaurant operating ratios, as they are also used in the industry in discussing hotel food and beverage operations.

9. The responsibilities, tasks, roles, and supervisory concerns described for restaurants in Chapter 4 are sufficiently similar that we need not repeat that information here, except in a very general way.

Chapter 11

Courtesy of San Diego Marriott Hotel and Marina, Marriott International

Forces Shaping
the Hotel Business

The Purpose of This Chapter

Lodging is a capital-intensive business and so capital plays a major role in shaping the hotel business. In just the recent past, lodging has seen a major inflow of funds from sources that were not formerly available to most hotels. Lodging is a cyclical industry characterized by long lead times on projects. As a result, supply and demand changes are not always as related to each other as they ideally should be.

The argument for understanding the economics of lodging and its capital structure can be likened to the needs of someone walking through a forest in a high wind. It's not a bad idea to keep a sharp lookout to avoid falling branches—or at least to know what hit you!

This Chapter Should Help You

1. Describe how and why the hotel industry is cyclical

2. Discuss the impact of the securitization of the hotel industry on capital availability

3. Identify the major means of raising debt and equity capital used for hotel development and describe how debt has been securitized

4. Explain what a REIT is and what the advantages of the various kinds of REITs are

5. Describe the drawbacks of being a publicly owned company

6. Name and define the dimensions of the hotel investment decision
7. Discuss the relationship between segmentation and encroachment in hotel franchising
8. Assess management companies as a tool for owners and a vehicle for your own professional development

THE ECONOMICS OF THE HOTEL BUSINESS

Hotel developers build long-term assets on the basis of relatively short-term cycles. A hotel's lifetime is usually 30 or 40 years and often 100 years or more, but the cycle of hotel building is more like 10 to 20 years in length. The result, historically, has been periods of excess capacity followed sooner or later by periods of more or less frantic building.

The hotel business, then, is cyclical. It is also highly **capital intensive** and, in recent times, there has been a major increase of capital flowing into the industry. Although the industry has always been a highly competitive one, recent influxes of capital may mark the beginning of a change in the industry's competitive structure. We will consider each of these points, cyclicality, capital intensity, and the impact of capital flows into the industry, in the following sections. In the next chapter, we will consider competition in lodging.

Hotels, large or small, require major investments in land, physical plant, and equipment. As an industry that needs to borrow capital, its expansion is very sensitive to economic conditions.
Courtesy of Bally's Casino Hotel and Resort, Las Vegas

A Cyclical Business

The hotel business is **cyclical.** The demand for hotel rooms rises and falls with the business cycle. Generally, the demand for hotel rooms changes direction three to six months after the economy does.[1] This is not surprising, as both business and pleasure travel are easy expenditures to cut out in a declining economy and to restore when it improves. In any local market, the hotel business is likely to have its own cycle, related to the supply of hotel rooms, as well as the demand for them. However, the cycle generally starts with the demand for rooms, potential or actual. Perhaps the easiest way to see this cycle is to work through an imaginary, but quite realistic, example.

An Example of the Hotel Business Cycle. "Oldtown," a quiet city of 100,000, has been a stable community with a balanced economy for many years. Not long ago, during a period of general economic expansion, a large national company built a large factory complex in Oldtown. The ripple effect from this spread to the suppliers for the factory complex, as well as to a number of other companies that, when they heard about the factory complex, learned what an attractive site Oldtown was. Employment soared: Some people were transferred to Oldtown; others moved there seeking jobs.

Our study now shifts to Major Hotels' corporate offices where, in a meeting with the vice presidents of operations and real estate, the vice president for development suggests that Major ought to look into building a hotel in Oldtown. There is immediate agreement to do a preliminary study. Three months later, the preliminary study shows encouraging results, and so several lines of activity are set in motion. A consulting firm is hired to do a formal feasibility study, an architect is hired to do preliminary design work, and informal conversations with Major's bankers begin. Six more months pass. The results of the consultant's feasibility study confirm Major's preliminary study, the preliminary design is a beauty, and everybody agrees this could be a great hotel. The bankers, having looked at the studies and the design, decide to process Major's loan application quickly. (They have had a surge in deposits and need to get that money into interest-earning loans. They need to lend, just as Major needs to borrow.) Best of all, the ideal location has been found, and negotiations to acquire a site are going well.

At a meeting of Major's executive committee, a formal proposal to go ahead is presented. The discussion touches briefly on the competition, but everyone quickly agrees that Oldtown's existing hotels are tired and will be no match for the proposed property. When somebody asks, "Is anybody else going in there?" the answer is, "A few people have been nosing around, but there's nothing firm as far as we can tell." Everyone agrees that it is time to purchase the site and sign a design contract with the architect. Because this is a meeting, everybody's commitment is a public matter.

The same series of events is taking place at Magnificent Hotels, LowCost Lodges, Supersuites, and a couple of other companies. However, because each company keeps things fairly quiet until everything is settled, there are only vague rumors that others are also interested in Oldtown.

Finally, 18 months after the first vice-presidential meeting at Major, the company announces that a 300-room hotel will be built in Oldtown, and the ground breaking is set two weeks hence. The story is front-page news. Over the next six months, similar announcements from Magnificent, LowCost, and Supersuites make the front page, too.

At Major, these other companies' announcements cause quite a stir. At a meeting of the executive committee, they all shake their heads and agree that those other companies are crazy; they have no sense at all in overbuilding like this. One very junior vice president who is sitting in raises the possibility that Major should abandon the project, but he is quickly shouted down. Thousands of dollars have already been spent on feasibility studies and architectural work, a site has been purchased, and contracts have been signed for construction. "Besides," says the financial vice president, "what would our banks say if we pulled out now? Do you think we'd get another loan commitment as easily next time?" Because everybody has agreed to the project publicly, for any to admit that he or she was wrong would also be publicly embarrassing.

Eighteen months later, Major's beautiful new property opens, and the general manager hands the following situation report to the vice president of operations:

> Within four blocks of my office, there are a thousand rooms under construction. Every place my sales staff goes, they trip over our competitors' people. Magnificent is slashing its convention rates for next year; LowCost has announced a salespersons' discount when its hotel opens next month; and Supersuites is offering free cocktail parties every evening. I think we will do all right after the first couple of years because our operation is going to be stronger and of better quality, but don't expect much for our first two or three years until we are established.

There are no further announcements of lodging construction in Oldtown.

We have spent quite a bit of time looking at this cycle of events to illustrate the significance of factors such as the complexity of the decision to build a hotel, the lead time required, the preliminary expenditures, and the public corporate and individual commitment to the decision. This cycle shows that an increase in demand can set off a series of events that usually cannot be stopped even when it becomes clear that the market is or will be overbuilt.

In other markets, it takes years for the demand to catch up with the overbuilding. In some, however, the demand keeps increasing, and in three to five years another round of building starts, this time fueled by all the old faces plus some new ones—for those who didn't get in the first time. All have a need to be represented in the growth market.

Our example was of a local market, but this is usually part of a larger, national market. Different local events related to a general national period of prosperity set off building booms in many local markets because demand for hotel rooms is closely related to general economic conditions. When the national economy turns down, so does the hotel business. Hotel building tends to come in waves or cycles that end, much to everybody's surprise, in an overbuilt industry.

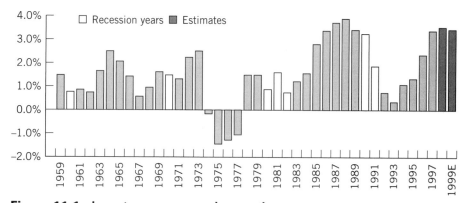

Figure 11.1 Long-term room supply growth.
(*Source:* John Rohs and Warren Gump, *Lodging Industry Annual Review*, February 25, 1998.)

Hotel Cycles and Financial Performance. Figure 11.1 shows the growth rate for room supply over a 40-year period, from 1959 to 1999. Three cycles are depicted there from peak to trough to peak. The cycles from 1964 to 1973 and from 1973 to 1988 are history, whereas the most recent cycle, which began at the 1988 peak, may well have 1998 or 1999 as its ending peak.

It is interesting to contrast the economic performance of the industry with the changes shown in its growth rate in Figure 11.1. In the 11-year period ending in 1993, the lodging business lost a staggering total of $33 billion.[2] Construction activity continued during this period, and, for most of those years, at a brisk pace. Until 1986, the growth was driven, to some degree, by tax considerations, which developers seemed to think made profit a secondary consideration. Another factor explaining hotel growth in the face of losses in operations was the increasing emphasis on segmented room products. Although the market as a whole in a city might have enough rooms to satisfy demand, if there was a shortage of one specific category, say limited service or all suite, then developers in that category saw that as an opportunity and new rooms were built to satisfy that specialized need. In some cases, rooms were built where there was no shortage of any kind, simply because of competitive pressure for major brands to be represented in an important market.

In spite of an oversupply in the market, generally, some segmented hotel products did well but many hotels went bankrupt. Indeed, some new properties opened to bankruptcy. The boom became a bust but the building continued—and the scenario we explored at the beginning of the chapter gives you an idea how this could happen. Much of the construction during the recession of 1990 and 1991 is accounted for by projects that were still in the developmental pipeline; that is, in construction or under contract.

Part of the meaning of a cyclical market is that there *are* good times as well as bad. The industry broke even in 1992 and had a profitable year in 1993. U.S. hotel pretax profits in 1997 are expected to exceed the record $12.5 billion earned in

Figure 11.2 Dollar change in hotel construction activity.
(*Source:* John Rohs and Warren Gump, *Lodging Industry Annual Review,* February 25, 1998; U.S. Department of Commerce.)

1996. As a result, investors continue to pour capital into hotel real estate.[3] Some, however, are already planning for the next downturn. Motel 6 has entered into sale and leaseback arrangements on $1 billion worth of real estate and one of its principal reasons was to free up cash for acquisitions in the next down cycle.[4]

Figure 11.2 focuses on changes in construction activity from 1990 to 1997. Figure 11.3 offers a different way of viewing the current lodging development cycle. Prepared by the research division of a hotel realty company, it characterizes the stages of the cycle from 1991 to 1997. In this view, the 1990–1991 period constituted an early recovery period, followed, in 1993, by a consolidation of that recovery, which continues. Late 1993 saw the beginning of a period of expansion, which also continues. The development cycle, according to these analysts, entered its mature phase in 1996.

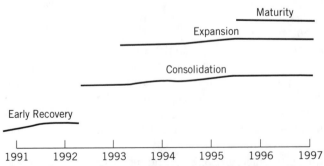

Figure 11.3 Lodging development cycle, 1991–1997.
(*Source: Lodging Econometrics,* February 1998.)

Table 11.1 Investments Raised from Public Sources, 1991–1997 (Millions of Dollars)

	1991	1992	1993	1994	1995	1996	1997	Total 1991–1997
Non-REIT IPOs	0.0	140.7	0.0	159.5	738.2	1,310.4	120	2,468.8
REIT IPOs	0.0	0.0	39.8	295.6	901.8	348.4	0.0	1,585.6
Secondary stock offerings	289.0	0.0	663.3	597.5	1,125.8	4,503.2	4,104.1	11,282.9
Debt offerings	800.0	0.0	419.5	1,082.5	2,076.0	4,338.6	2,796.9	11,513.5
Total flow of public funds	1,089.0	140.7	1,122.6	2,135.1	4,841.8	10,500.6	7,021.0	26,850.8

Source: Lodging Econometrics, February 1998.

The Securitization of the Hotel Industry

The **securitization** of the hotel industry[5] refers to the influx of funds into the industry in return for equity and debt securities issued by publicly traded hospitality companies. As a senior manager with the accounting firm of Arthur Anderson put it, "The story in the U.S. has been the emergence of Wall Street in hotel finance. There have always been the Marriotts, the Sheratons, the Hiltons, companies that obtained most of their financing from public markets."[6] However, the recent expansion of financing vehicles that are relatively new to the hotel industry such as commercial mortgage-backed securities (CMBSs) and real estate investment trusts (REITs) has led to an unprecedented growth in the funds from public markets invested in lodging. To understand this development, we will briefly consider these "new" forms of debt and equity capital. As a point of clarification, when speaking of debt we will be referring to borrowed funds such as mortgages, bonds, debentures, and the like. We will use the term equity to refer to ownership, here in the form of stock sold to individual and institutional investors. Table 11.1 provides a summary of investment in hotels through public markets from 1991 to 1997.

Debt Investments and Commercial Mortgage-Backed Securities. For many years, borrowing for hotel construction was limited to banks and insurance companies—except for a handful of public companies. Now, there is widely available another ready source of debt for that kind of construction. Hotel developers can access it through the "conduits" we will discuss in a moment. This wider availability of loans poses some real questions about the dangers of overbuilding. A **commercial mortgage-backed security (CMBS)** is "a security, often a bond rated by bond agencies, backed by a pool of commercial mortgages"[7] and the future income those mortgages will generate from payments of interest and principal.

CMBS debt is assembled by **conduit lenders** using their own funds to lend initially to the borrower. When a sufficient dollar amount has been assembled, the mortgages are "packaged" and sold to the public and institutional investors. There

Well-financed companies are especially well suited to carry out large complex hotel development.
Courtesy of Trump's Castle

are specialized firms such as Nomura Capital International that engage in this business. Banks, brokerage firms, and other financial institutions also have divisions that act as conduit lenders.[8] As Table 11.1 shows, over $11.5 billion dollars flowed into the hotel industry from public debt offerings between 1991 and 1997, close to half the capital raised from public markets.

Other Sources of Debt Financing. Owners may find that they can obtain at most a 65 percent first mortgage on a property. To decrease the amount of their own funds required, they resort to what is called **mezzanine financing.** Mezzanine[9] financing, sometimes referred to as **gap financing,** "bridges the gap between the first mortgage and the amount of equity committed to a project."[10] It is very much like a second mortgage. Mezzanine financing is not secured by a mortgage—or else is "subordinated" to a first mortgage. It carries a higher interest rate than mortgage financing because of its higher risk. In the previous example, however, if the owners could obtain 65 percent first-mortgage financing and another 20 percent mezzanine financing, the amount of their own capital required to build the property would be reduced from 35 percent to 15 percent of the cost, effectively increasing their power to expand.

Sources of Equity Investment. The principal sources of equity investment in lodging in the 1990s have been real estate investment trusts (REITs), initial public offerings (IPOs), and secondary stock offerings.

Real Estate Investment Trusts. A real estate investment trust (REIT) is a trust or corporation similar to a mutual fund but one that limits its investments to real estate. The REIT *pays no income tax* on its earnings provided that it pays 95 percent or more of its profit to its shareholders. Real estate investment trusts can invest in either debt or equity. The REIT provides the typical advantages of corporate ownership to shareholders, those of limiting shareholder liability and of providing shares that can be bought and sold on stock exchanges, along with the tax advantages mentioned previously.[11] Those tax advantages mean a larger portion of earnings can be passed on to investors. The requirement that earnings be paid out ensures that the earnings form the basis for higher dividends and, hence, a higher income yield. Finally, because the investment is in real estate, which is conventionally seen as a source of a steady flow of funds from rents, interest payments, and repayment of loan principal, REITs have often been viewed as investments paying a more *reliable* yield to their holders than is typical of other stocks or mutual funds. As a result of this combination of factors, REITs have become very attractive to many investors. Several different kinds of hotel REITs are discussed in Industry Practice Note 11.1

When a REIT buys a hotel or group of hotels, it can borrow money or issue stock to cover the transaction. Borrowed funds *require* payment of interest on the funds borrowed but funds raised from stock have no such requirement. Because of their popularity with the investment community, REITs have had no difficulty in raising capital from issuing stock. For instance, when Starwood, a "paired-share REIT" (see Industry Practice Note 11.1), purchased four former Ritz Carlton hotels for $334 million in 1998, more than half of the purchase price was paid in Starwood's stock.[12] That represents over $165 million of capital that did not have to be borrowed and, therefore, required no interest payments. As a result, the fixed costs associated with that purchase have been reduced substantially. On the other hand, there are the same $165 million worth of stock shares in the market, which are expecting an above average return on their investment, a subject to which we will return.

Real estate investment trusts have raised over $1.5 billion between 1991 and 1997 from **initial public offerings (IPOs).** Initial public offerings are first-time offerings of a company's stock to the public.

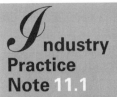

Industry Practice Note 11.1

There Are REITs . . . and Then There Are Paired-Share REITs and . . . Some Other Possibilities

Hotel and Motel Management listed 14 lodging REITs or real estate investment trusts in early 1998. Real estate investment trusts are essentially corporations that have met certain IRS requirements to avoid paying corporate-level taxes.

◆ Because 95 percent of taxable profits must be paid as dividends, there are limited funds for growth and *REITs must constantly return to the capital markets to sell additional stock or obtain new debt for additional capital to fund growth.* This makes traditional REITs highly vulnerable to changes in stock market sentiment.

◆ Traditional hotel REITs cannot operate properties. This results in "leakages" of profit. These leakages arise from payment of management fees and franchise fees. Because REIT regulations do

Figure 2 Integrated paired-share REIT structure. (*Source:* John Rohs and Warren Gump, *Lodging Industry Annual Review,* February 25, 1998.)

not permit lease payments from the hotel to the REIT to be based on the hotel's profitability, the REIT may also lose out on "extra" profits that arise when a hotel achieves an unusually high level of profitability. This is a third possible source of leakage.

Figure 1 shows the traditional REIT arrangement.

PAIRED-SHARE REAL ESTATE INVESTMENT TRUSTS

A paired-share REIT consists of a REIT and a hotel corporation (hereafter called a C Corp) whose shares are paired one for one and *traded together on the stock exchange as a single unit.* As Figure 2 indicates, the "leakage" of the traditional REIT is captured by the C Corp in a paired-share arrangement. Because the

Figure 1 Traditional REIT structure. (Source: John Rohs and Warren Gump, *Lodging Industry Annual Review,* February 25, 1998.)

paired shareholders own an equal stake in both the C Corp and the REIT, profits foregone by the REIT flow back to the stockholder via the C Corp and vice versa. Within what is permitted under government REIT regulations, management attempts to minimize C Corp profits through high lease payments because the C Corp's income *is* subject to taxes.

The 1984 revision to the tax code eliminated the ability to pair the shares of a REIT and an operating company *except for the few paired-share REITs then in existence.* At the time, this seemed like a small matter because the few paired-share companies were small and had insignificant operations. The potential that laid hidden until the recent expansion of paired-share REITs is suggested by some recent actions of the three paired-share REITs active in the hotel business:[1]

   *Starwood Capital (***http://www.starwoodlodging.com/***)* acquired Sheraton and Westin Hotels and Resorts for over $16 billion, giving it two franchise brands it can use to realign its branding practices and eliminate much of the "leakage" of franchise payments to other franchisors. With the two hotel chains Starwood acquired, it also got two very sophisticated management organizations.

   *Patriot American Hospitality (***http://www.patriotamerican.com/***)* acquired Interstate Hotels Corporation in 1997 for $2.1 billion, as well as Wyndham Hotel Company for $1.1 billion in cash and stock.[2] Interstate was North America's largest hotel management company, which gives that paired-share REIT the organizational strength to manage its growing inventory of hotels. Wyndham represents a hotel *brand* Patriot can use with its existing properties and in its continuing expansion.

   *Meditrust (***http://www.reit.com/***),* one of the world's largest owners of assisted-living centers, nursing homes, and retirement communities, entered the lodging field when it acquired La Quinta Inns for $3 billion in cash, stock, and assumed debt.

PAPER-CLIP REAL ESTATE INVESTMENT TRUSTS AND OTHER ARRANGEMENTS

Attempts to work within the existing tax code to gain some of the benefits of a paired-share REIT have led to the formation of so-called paper clip REITs. As *Hotel and Motel Management* put it, "the two organizations [making up the paper-clip REIT] are separate public companies that are . . . 'paper clipped' together through an inter-company agreement." The first paper-clip REIT, formed out of the merger of CapStar Hotel Company (**http://www.capstar.com/**) and American General Hospitality (**http://www.capstar.com/**) was *MeriStar*. MeriStar became the third-largest REIT in the United States, as well as the second-largest independent hotel management company. MeriStar's portfolio operates under the flags of Hilton, Westin, Radisson, Sheraton, Marriott, Doubletree, and Crowne Plaza. Under the "paper-clip" arrangement, "the operating company has the right of first refusal to lease and manage all future hotels acquired by the REIT, and provides the REIT with the right of first refusal to acquire hotels presented by the operating company."[3]

This is a looser connection than in a paired-share REIT. The C Corp and the REIT share common management control and have agreements to work together in the future but the two stocks trade separately. Over time, their shareholder bases are likely to be different and so more care must be taken with leases and other agreements so they don't unduly disadvantage either the REIT or the C Corp stockholder. Figure 3 shows the relationships in a paper-clip REIT.

Other recent arrangements involve agreements between REITs and management companies for the management company, such as Promus (**http://www.promus.com/**) to develop properties and immediately sell them to the REIT, retaining management contracts and franchise agreements. Host Marriott, to give another example, proposes to develop a REIT that would own 219 Courtyards, Fairfields, and Residence Inns, all of which would continue to be operated by Marriott International.[4]

Figure 3 Integrated paper-clip REIT structure. (*Source:* John Rohs and Warren Gump, *Lodging Industry Annual Review,* February 25, 1998.)

The paired-share structure is under attack by the Administration and Congress but many acquisitions have already taken place, which are unlikely to be reversed. Finally, as noted previously, Marriott is forming its own REIT, and a paper-clip REIT, Meri-Star, is one of the largest hotel companies in the United States. It seems clear that REITs will have a prominent place in the hotel business worldwide for the foreseeable future.

1. There are three other known paired-share REITs: First Union Real Estate Investment Trust, Hollywood Park, and privately held Corporate Properties Investors. Hollywood Park dropped its paired-share status some time ago and is now attempting to resurrect it.
2. *Hotels,* May 1997, pp. 5 and 57.
3. *Hotel and Motel Management,* April 6, 1998, pp. 1 and 60.
4. *Lodging,* February 1998, p. 13.

Source: This note is condensed from a significantly more extensive discussion by John Rohs and Warren Gump, *Lodging Industry Annual Review,* February 25, 1998, pp. 26–28, unless otherwise noted.

Other Publicly Held Companies.   As we noted earlier, companies like Hilton and Marriott have long been **publicly held,** that is, owned by stockholders whose shares are publicly traded. These and other publicly traded corporations are often referred to as **C Corps** to distinguish them from REITs, which are also corporations.[13] In addition to companies that have long traded publicly, a large number of companies have "gone public" through IPOs during the rising market in stocks that has marked the mid- and late 1990s. In fact, hotel companies that have gone public have raised nearly $2.5 billion in that way between 1991 and 1997.

Secondary Offerings.   When a company that is already publicly traded issues additional shares, they are referred to as a **secondary offering.** From 1991 to 1997, REITs and C Corps raised $11.5 billion dollars through secondary offerings.

Table 11.1 summarizes the total of investments raised from all public sources from 1991 to 1997. Including both debt and equity, that amount reached nearly $27 billion during the seven-year period, the vast majority of it in the last four years of that period.

Securitization and Competition.   Although we will defer most of our discussion of competition in the lodging business to the next chapter, this is a good point at which to consider the impact of the huge influx of capital on the hotel business and its competitive structure. With more funds coming into the industry, it becomes easier to build more rooms, increasing competition. As capital has become more readily available and, in a rising stock market, effectively less costly, mergers and acquisitions (M&A) activity has increased, as well. Figure 11.4 shows the number of times firms have acquired another firm or merged with one another. Mergers and

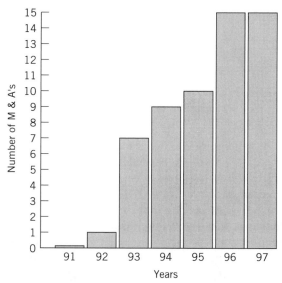

Figure 11.4 Hotel company mergers and acquisitions activity, 1991–1997.
(*Source: Lodging Econometrics,* February 1998.)

acquisitions increased from none in 1991 to an average of 15 in 1996 and 1997. In the last six years of the period, 57 such transactions took place, each of them tending to reduce the number of competitors and increase market concentration.

The merger of Promus and Doubletree, to give one illustration of the impact of M&A activity, created a company that rivals industry leaders like Marriott in its breadth of product offering, management depth, financial soundness, and growth prospects. The resulting company, Promus Hotel Corp., has strength in the franchises it offers, as well as in its record as a management company.

Real estate investment trusts have been active players in the mergers and acquisitions field, too. The financial power of the REITs is substantial. Because of their ready access to the public capital markets, they can manage large acquisitions with new stock issues. The stock either can be used to raise cash toward the purchase price or can be given to the seller as part of the purchase price. In effect, they have the power to virtually "coin money"—*as long as their stock market value holds up.*

An interesting example of financial muscle is the purchase by Starwood Lodging of two leading upscale international chains within a two-month period. In early September of 1997, Starwood purchased Westin Hotels and Resorts for just under $1.6 billion. Then, in October, the company announced the purchase of ITT Sheraton for a price of $14.6 billion.[14] With these transactions, Starwood Hotels' portfolio "includes more than 650 hotels and resorts located in over 70 countries worldwide, with additional hotel and resort projects under development around the world."[15] In assessing these and other purchases by Starwood, Rohs points out that

> Significant synergy and cost savings should develop from merging ITT Sheraton, Westin and Starwood into an industry juggernaut. Approximately 90% of the room base is in the most attractive upscale hotel segment. . . . [On the other hand] integrating three separate organizations and infrastructures could prove challenging. [The company is also] dependent on capital markets to fund acquisitions because of REIT payout requirements.[16]

Although it is appropriate to notice an increase in the concentration ownership of hotels as a result of the influx of capital and M&A activity, we need to realize that this still leaves us with a *very* highly competitive industry. A study by Prudential Real Estate Investors in August of 1997 reported that public ownership had grown to 17.3 percent.[17] Over 80 percent of the industry, then, is still held privately. It does seem clear, however, that ownership in some areas of the industry, particularly in the upscale segments, has become somewhat more concentrated. It is unlikely, on the other hand, that concentration is sufficient for any firm to exert market control (i.e., to control the price level).

The Hazards of Public Ownership

There are a number of factors that influence stock prices but there is wide agreement that the most powerful influence is a company's earnings—or the prospect of earnings. For this reason, management in publicly held companies is under constant pressure not only to maintain but to increase their earnings each quarter. In some cases, this pressure can encourage a short-term focus by managers. This relentless pressure has been characterized by an entrepreneur from the food service sector of the hospitality industry, Howard Schultz, founder and president of Starbucks.

> Alongside the exhilaration of being a public company is the humbling realization, every quarter, every month, and every day, that you're a servant of the stock market. That perception changes the way you live, and you can never go back to being a simple business again. We began to report our sales monthly including comps— "comparable" growth of sales at stores that have been open at least a year. When there are surprises, the stock reacts instantly. I think comps are not the best measure to analyze and judge the success of Starbucks. For example, when lines get too long at one store, we'll occasionally open a second store nearby. Our customers appreciate the convenience and the shorter lines. But, if, as often happens, the new store cannibalizes sales from the older store, it shows up as lower comps, and Wall Street punishes us.[18]

Case History 11.1 describes the experience of Sam Barshop, founder of La Quinta Inns, as that publicly held company became the target of a takeover.

There is a possibility, too, that having a significant portion of the industry in public hands, particularly those of REITs where shareholder expectations are often focused on dividend yields, may pose some long-term problems to the stability of the industry. As one knowledgeable observer put it,

The flow of public funds into lodging has been especially helpful to growth-oriented companies such as U.S. Franchise Systems, whose Microtel double room is shown here.
Courtesy of U.S. Franchise Systems

Historically, the hotel business has been cyclical in nature and characterized by widely dispersed ownership operating with a long-term development outlook. Considering Wall Street's preoccupation with quarter-to-quarter growth and ever-increasing yields for shareholders, [the hotel business] would seem an unlikely choice [for public shareholders]. Whether these interesting times are ultimately viewed as a blessing or a curse will depend on how effectively our industry's leadership responds to Wall Street and its fickle ways. A heavily consolidated industry may, in the end, prove a curse if the industry overextends itself and falls out of favor with the investment community.[19]

Growth in Lodging

Between 1987 and 1996, lodging demand grew by slightly more than 2 percent (2.2%), while supply grew just under 2 percent (1.9%).[20] Different segments of lodging, however, had quite different growth rates. As Table 11.2 shows, during the three years 1995 to 1997, different rate and service categories had quite different growth rates for both supply and demand. In 1997, urban and suburban hotels experienced healthy growth in market share of demand, while airport, highway, and resort hotels experienced a decrease in demand.[21] Similar contrasting performance can be found for different areas of the country and for different cities within those areas.[22] Accordingly, to speak of a growth rate for the industry can be some-

*C*ase History 11.1 Going Public: Some Good News and Some Bad

In 1968, the first two La Quinta Inns were built by Barshop Motel Enterprises in San Antonio, Texas, to serve visitors to the 1968 World's Fair, HemisFair.[1] Although he had not intended to start a chain, the limited-service concept of La Quinta was so successful that Sam Barshop was approached by developers and investors and soon his company began to expand. In 1973, in order to secure funds for expansion, the company went public. By 1978, 10 years after the first inn opened, there were 56 inns in operation with an occupancy of 90 percent. Another 19 inns were under construction. By the end of the 1980s, there were about 200 La Quinta Inns in operation.

In 1989, however, a Hong Kong firm, Industrial Equity, began to acquire shares of La Quinta and, by early 1990, controlled 10 percent of the outstanding shares. Shortly thereafter, a second group of investors headed by two Texas financiers, the Bass brothers, began to acquire shares. In January of 1991, La Quinta hired Goldman Sachs, a New York investment banking firm, to explore ways to "increase shareholder value"—including the sale of the company.

A contemporary La Quinta Inn
Courtesy of La Quinta Inns

However, at that time, mergers and acquisitions activity was depressed, as were La Quinta's shares, by a recessionary stock market. La Quinta, which had been as high as $26, was selling in the $11 to $15 range and a suitable buyer for the company could not be found. La Quinta's management spent an estimated $2 million in fees to attorneys, management consultants, advisors, and investment bankers fighting to retain control of the company. The company's operations and expansion were seriously compromised as executives spent time fending off what they saw as a hostile takeover bid.

Finally, in June of 1991, an accommodation between La Quinta's management and the dissident shareholders was reached. Five of La Quinta's eleven-person board were asked to resign and new directors representing the Bass-led group (which, by then, owned 14.9 percent of the company's shares) were elected in their place. Barshop's supporters on the board retained five seats and the eleventh seat on the board went unfilled. Working with the new board, the consulting firm of McKinsey and Company conducted a three-month management study of La Quinta. As a result, the company was restructured, reducing its workforce by 72 people, 50 of whom were at the corporate offices. The company also took a $7.95 million restructuring charge, including $3.94 million for severances. At that time and shortly thereafter, several senior executives resigned and then, in March of 1992, Barshop turned over the presidency of the company to a former executive vice president of Motel 6, remaining as chairman of

the board for another two years until he resigned in March of 1994.

In June of 1991, at the time of the first compromise with the Bass-led group, Barshop had these comments on being a publicly held company:

> There are a lot of advantages to not being a public company. You're not responsible to the Securities and Exchange Commission or a large number of shareholders. You run your own business. You can focus on cash flow rather than earnings per share. . . . It's been stressful. Business isn't as much fun as it used to be. I've never dealt with anything like this before. Things aren't done the way they used to be. I've learned more about proxies than I ever wanted to know. It's been an interesting experience. But I hope it's a one time experience.[2]

Mr. Barshop ultimately lost control of his company, a company that by that time had 220 inns in 29 states. He sold 80 percent of his shares for $17.4 million and was paid something on the order of a million dollars during the last two years he served as chairman. Finally, we should note that he will go down in hospitality history as the man who invented the limited-service hotel.

1. This note is based, except as noted, on news stories reported in the *San Antonio Express News,* the *San Antonio Light,* and the *San Antonio Business Journal,* between January 1990 and March 1994; the June 1988 issue of *Input,* an employee publication of La Quinta; and public statements by La Quinta Inns to its employees and the press. I would like to thank Ms. Mary Starling, secretary to Mr. Sam Barshop, for her assistance with the preparation of this note.
2. R. Michelle Brewer, "The Private Woes of Going Public," *San Antonio Light,* June 16, 1991, pp. A1–A2.

what deceptive unless the statement is properly qualified. Still, an overall growth rate of about 2 percent is slightly less than the long-term growth rate of 2.3 percent for the economy as a whole projected by the Bureau of Labor Statistics.[23]

*D*IMENSIONS OF THE HOTEL INVESTMENT DECISION

The decision to invest in a hotel has at least three dimensions involving **financing, real estate values,** and **operations.** Although all three are important, the weight each will receive varies with the particular merits of an individual decision and with economic conditions. In the first half of the 1980s, financial and tax considerations

Table 11.2 Share of Room Demand and Supply Growth by Rate and Service Category, 1995–1997

	Demand[a]	Supply[b]
Upper upscale	3.1%	11%
Upscale	4.8	15
Midscale with food and beverage	−0.8	−3
Midscale without food and beverage	12.6	44
Economy	6	37
Budget	1.5	7
Independents (all categories)	−0.5	Negative
Extended stay (all categories and included in above)	n.a.	19

[a]Compound average growth rate, 1995–1997.
1/[b]Proportion of total growth.
Source: John Rohs and Warren Gump, *Lodging Industry Annual Review*, February 25, 1998, pp. 18–21.

often led to building hotels whose profitability was uncertain. Depressed real estate played a very prominent role in the purchase of hotel properties in the early 1990s. Those of us whose chosen vocation is operations—*running* a hotel—need to be reminded that our own set of interests is only one leg of the hotel tripod.

Financial

As we have noted previously, hotels are capital intensive. Because most of the capital used in building a hotel—or buying one—is borrowed, it is not surprising that interest rates, availability of capital, taxation, and, in the international environment, exchange rates are all important considerations. Global Hospitality Note 11.1 discusses the impact of global exchange rate fluctuations on hotel valuations.

Interest Rates, Inflation, and Leverage. One of the reasons given for the popularity of hotel investments in the latter half of the 1990s has been unusually low interest rates. When there are fears of inflation, hotels have been seen as a good **inflation hedge.** Although the value of money decreases in inflationary periods, the value of hotel assets often increases enough to offset inflation and perhaps show a gain, even after deducting interest costs.

Leverage refers to the ability to invest some of your own capital and do most of the deal with borrowed capital. With a thousand dollars worth of debt attracting, say, four thousand dollars worth of mortgage money, the thousand dollars of equity is able to earn the profits, after fixed interest payments, provided by the full five thousand dollars. The debt is said to *leverage* earnings because all of the profit *after interest charges* goes to the owners. When times are good and profits high, leverage is looked on very favorably. When, however, profits fall, interest charges do not—and so leverage cuts two ways.

Global Hospitality Note 11.1

Exchange Rates and Hotel Valuations

Exchange rate fluctuations have made U.S. assets attractive to foreign buyers and foreign assets a good buy for U.S. companies, depending on whose currency is up and whose is down. For instance, in 1997, Southeast Asian and Korean currencies fell in value dramatically in international monetary markets. As a result, U.S. firms were widely reported to be shopping for major acquisitions in those parts of the world.

To illustrate just how these currency fluctuations affect value, let's assume two currencies, the dollar and the "bazoola," are each worth 1 unit of the other. Now, assume that, for any of a number of reasons, the bazoola falls over an 18-month period to the point where it is worth 50 cents. At that point, $1 is worth 2 bazoolas. From the point of view of the holder of dollars, a $1 million asset, which would have cost a like amount of bazoolas just a year and a half ago can now be purchased for only $500,000. For such a purchaser, the change in cost is about the same as if the price had gone from a million to half of that.[1]

Although hotel purchases in Asia have not been widely reported yet, there is a general recognition that "Real estate owners and developers, schooled as they are to think in cyclical terms, will ultimately hear opportunity knocking."[2] We do have the record of what happened when the shoe was on the other foot, however, and the yen soared against the dollar in the latter part of the 1980s. A hotel whose value remained at $100 million in the United States from 1984 to 1988 would have cost a Japanese buyer 24 billion yen in 1984 but only 13 billion yen in 1988.[3]

1. In a less simplified example, questions of future value, earning power, and related issues would come into play.
2. Tony Dela Cruz, "Adjusting to Reality," *Hotels,* April 1998, pp. 40–48.
3. Tadayuki Hara and James J. Eyester, "Japanese Hotel Investment: A Matter of Tradition and Reality," *Cornell Hotel and Restaurant Quarterly,* November 1990, pp. 98–104.

Taxes. As noted earlier, the U.S. tax laws of the early 1980s encouraged the construction of hotels by offering special tax credits that meant investors could sometimes make money on the project, even if the hotel was not profitable. Although those artificial inducements to construction are gone, the deductibility of interest on loans still constitutes a tax advantage. Take, for example, one corporation that paid interest of 9.2 percent on its debt; after paying taxes of about 40 percent, the cost of the loan, after taxes, was only 5.6 percent.[24] The "tax saving" arises because, although all of the interest must be paid, some 40 percent of it in this example is balanced by a reduction in income tax. In a capital-intensive business like hotels, this can lend an advantage to borrowers. Global Hospitality Note 11.2 shows how international tax considerations have affected sales of hotel companies in the past.

Global Hospitality Note 11.2

Globalization and Taxation

The increased globalization of the lodging industry has complicated valuation decisions by adding the impact of another country's tax laws to the purchase equation. The purchase of Holiday Inns some years ago by Bass, Ltd. (**http://www.bass.co.uk/**), an English firm, for instance, was facilitated by differences in British tax laws, which created a tax advantage for Bass that was not available to an American buyer.

Japanese investors in the 1980s, too, found advantages in the tax deductibility of foreign exchange "losses" that could be created by accelerating payments of debt between U.S. subsidiaries of Japanese companies and the Japanese parent when exchange rates favored this tactic.[1]

1. Tadayuki Hara and James J. Eyester, "Japanese Hotel Investment: A Matter of Tradition and Reality," *Cornell Hotel and Restaurant Administration Quarterly,* November 1990, pp. 98–104.

Real Estate

Hotels also may be built because an area or community development needs the property; that is, the hotel may be necessary to a larger project. Alternatively, the underlying value of the real estate and its appreciation may be a more important consideration to some investors than is the profitability of the hotel. For example, a number of foreign investors in North America have apparently, from time to time, been willing to invest money in hotel properties for their longer-term appreciation and as a safe haven for their funds.

Hotel pricing can make hotel real estate more attractive than other real estate, particularly in inflationary times, because of the ability to increase rates, literally, overnight. The ability to increase revenues is not as flexible in other real estate projects in which rents are generally fixed by long-term leases. As a result, hotels, although they have a higher risk than other real estate, find favor with investors, especially during the optimistic growth phase of the hotel industry cycle.

Hotel companies are highly active not only as operators and franchisors of hotels but as real estate developers. Promus and Marriott, for instance, sustain their growth in part by buying, developing, and then reselling land and hotel properties. Indeed, such companies have a real interest in continuing expansion of their brands to gain a greater share of the market and to ensure that their brands have a presence in the widest number of local markets. Naturally, they also want to gain the profits from development. These motives to expand, however sensible they may be from the individual company's vantage point, often lead to the "overbuilding" that has been such a bane to the hotel business generally.

An Operating Business

The hotel's profitable operation is often the first dimension of a hotel deal that students of hotel management consider. As we have just noted, however, hotel companies—and other developers—have significant business interests outside of operations in both development and franchising of hotels. This does not mean they are uninterested in operations, however. In fact, both Promus and Marriott require the buyer to sign a management contract on hotels they develop so that they retain the right to control the operation's quality and to profit from the management of the property while expanding their chain.

Segmentation: For Guests or Developers?

Much of the development of new product segments—economy, all suite, executive floors, superluxury—can be related to specific market segments. For example, economy segments are aimed at rate-conscious consumer groups such as retirees. (Days Inn reports that a significant proportion of its guests are seniors.) Residence Inns has a clearly targeted segment in mind as do other extended-stay properties, and

Segmentation in lodging seeks to develop a product for a specific customer segment, but it also gives the hotel company another brand to expand with. The TownePlace Suites hotel pictured here is Marriott's newest brand in the fast-growing extended stay market.
Courtesy of Marriott International

full-service hotels' upscale range of products, from executive floors to superluxury, is for the expense-account market. Transient all-suite hotels target upper-level executives on weekdays and upper-middle-income families on weekends. **Segmentation** certainly meets guest needs.

On the other hand, we have noted that many hotel companies are real estate developers, and a strategy of segmentation has also met their business needs as developers. Having several brands that appeal to different final consumers permits hotel companies to put more than one hotel in a market. Thus, if Promus had an Embassy Suite in a city, it could still quite legitimately develop its other brands for other segments—a Hampton Inn for the limited-service market and a Homewood Suite for extended-stay guests. This helps sell hotels and franchises to investors, as well as rooms to guests. As one observer put it,

> Most hotel companies are largely service companies that sell a product—a specific kind of hotel—to developers. . . . Today, hotel companies are offering developers a range of hotels so the company can match the hotel product to the site. Having multiple brands or chains allows hotel companies to provide a product to meet developer needs.[25]

As a result, hotel companies may be developing more than one property in the same city—a Hampton Inn and an Embassy Suite or perhaps a Marriott Courtyard and a Fairfield. Although the company's brands are not generally competitive with each other, there is, inevitably, a degree of overlap. It is not as clear, however, that all such development is noncompetitive. This is particularly a problem for companies such as Choice and Cendant, which are principally franchisors.

From an ethical point of view, there is nothing even faintly questionable about a company's developing two hotels that will compete with each other. The franchisor is in the business of selling franchises, the franchisee wants to invest in a property, and a developer needs a property to round out a project. Each pursues his or her own interest in an informed way. The resulting increase in competition is a business risk that should surprise no one. Nevertheless, such practices have led to serious problems between franchisors and franchisees.

Encroachment.   In the franchise business, the practice of loading additional franchisees into the same market with one or more existing franchisees is called **encroachment.** The new franchisee is seen as encroaching on the market area of the existing franchisee. (In the hotel business, encroachment is often referred to as **impact.** The sales and profits of the existing franchisee are said to be unfavorably "impacted.") One leading hotel investor has called encroachment "the issue of the 90s."[26] The problem is very clear when the additional property has the same brand name and shares the same reservation service. The problem is only slightly less difficult where the brand name is different but the market segment and reservation service are the same—as is the case, for instance, with Choice Hotels' Rodeway and Econolodge brands. What happens where impact is serious is that the property affected suffers a loss in occupancy and average rate. Although encroachment is difficult to prove in a court of law, it has been the frequent subject of negotiation for franchisees, who have often gained concessions in franchise fees to offset the impact of a new property.[27]

As a result of growing problems with encroachment, it is unlikely that any franchise would be written today without specific geographic protection. Michael Levin, when he was president of the Americas Division of Holiday Inn Worldwide, predicted that, in the future, arbitration will be used whenever a new franchise is granted in an area, even before any dispute arises.[28]

Management Companies *advantage Disadvantage*

The arrangement between the **management company** and the hotel owner, a **management contract,** is described by Professor James Eyester of the Cornell Hotel School:

> A management contract is a written agreement between a hotel motor inn owner and operator in which the owner employs the operator as an agent [employee] to assume full operational responsibility for the property and to manage the property in a professional manner. As an agent, the operator pays in the name of the owner, all property operating expenses from the cash flow generated from the operation; it retains its management fees, and remits the remaining cash flow, if any, to the owner. The owner provides the hotel or motor inn property to include land, building, furniture and fixtures, equipment, and working capital and assumes full legal and financial responsibility for the project.[29]

The first management company may have been the Caesar Ritz Group. Before the turn of the century, Ritz, with his famous chef, Escoffier, was "paid a retainer to appoint and oversee the managers of separately owned hotels. That arrangement allowed the hotel to advertise itself as a Ritz hotel."[30] The first U.S. "hotel management company" was the Treadway Hotel Company, which began operating small college inns in the 1920s.[31] During the 1930s, the American Hotel Corporation managed bankrupt hotels, but, as late as 1970, there were only three or four management companies in operation in the United States.

In the 1970s and 1980s, as the number of hotels expanded rapidly, much of the development was undertaken by people whose abilities and experience lay in finance and real estate rather than in hotel operations. To manage the hotels developed by these nonoperator owners, the number of hotel management companies expanded rapidly.

There are two kinds of management companies. First, most chain organizations such as Hilton, Marriott, or Promus serve as management companies for hotels under their franchises. Chains dominate the management contract field for properties with more than 300 rooms. Chains require a substantial minimum fee just to defray their central-office overhead. They have difficulty in working with smaller properties that don't generate enough revenue to cover the minimum fee. Accordingly, smaller management companies have an advantage in the under-300-room category. Independent management companies are able to operate smaller properties, often under different franchises. They offer owners more control over daily operations and more flexibility in contract terms.

Typically, a management contract fee is based on a modest percentage of sales and a larger percentage of gross operating profit. Management companies enjoyed their greatest growth following the boom in hotel construction in the 1980s when they assumed the management of distressed properties. Under those circumstances, contracts were short term and involved little, if any, ownership interest in the hotel on the part of the management companies. In 1998, in contrast, 30 to 40 percent of contracts being written require some form of equity or debt participation in the financing of the property by the management company, and one well-informed observer suggests that the time is coming when management companies without ownership interests in their properties will go out of business.[32] Moreover, there is pressure on management companies as more owner operators purchase properties to operate themselves[33] and some have speculated that the third-party management company is in decline.

On the other hand, the president of one medium-sized operating company, Sage Hospitality Resources, commented that,

> We've seen a remarkable swing in market opinion. There are an awful lot of owners out there who do not want their properties operated by large public companies. Those companies are not driven by people to whom owners have access, but unseen shareholders who are only concerned with the company meeting its numbers.[34]

Independent management companies offer several advantages to those starting a career in the hotel business. The company with a successful track record will have experienced and knowledgeable people in its senior ranks. Working with and under such well-qualified and broadly experienced managers can be an education in itself. Moreover, a larger company will probably have properties of varying sizes and franchise affiliations and, thus, offer both opportunities for career progression from smaller to larger properties and a broad variety of experiences.

The largest independent management company in terms of number of properties in 1998 was Tharaldson Property Management with 250 properties, principally Super 8 Motels, which Tharaldson owns and operates under franchise from Cendant. The revenue leader was Boyd Gaming Corp. with 1997 revenues of over $819 million.[35]

As with any company you are considering, it is a good idea to inquire about the company's reputation before signing on in a responsible position. And, again, as with any company, a good way to get to know a prospective long-term employer is through employment in the summer or part time during the school year.

Entrepreneurial Opportunities

We should pause here to note the significance of the management company's function for those who want to have ownership interest in a hotel. Management companies serve a need for mortgage holders and developers that can also be filled by individuals. Those individuals, who, through education and experience, prepare themselves to manage a hotel, can regard a time of economic reverses for the industry as a time of opportunity for themselves. In particular, with locally financed (i.e., mortgaged) properties that get into trouble, there is a real opportunity from time to time to secure an ownership position in return for assuming an existing mortgage. This kind of opportunity is more likely to occur with older properties, and so the importance of a good food background—in order to merchandise the property—is clear.

𝒮UMMARY

Lodging is capital intensive and cyclical. Because of long lead times, supply often continues to grow even after demand has stopped growing or begun to decrease. As a result, in the 11 years ending in 1993, the lodging industry lost $33 billion while construction continued throughout the period. In 1997, however, hotel profits were once again at a peak.

Securitization is selling an ownership or a debt instrument (such as a bond) in a property through the public security markets. The effect of securitization was to bring nearly $27 billion of the public's investment funds into the lodging industry between 1991 and 1997. Major developments have included the widening of lodging's access to debt through CMBSs, to equity through IPOs and secondary offerings, and to both equity and debt through REITs. The impact of securitization has been to enable a considerable boom in hotel building. Although securitization brings advantages in the availability of capital, it also has the inherent risks associated with a falling stock market. Mergers and acquisitions activity and the growth of paired-share REITs (see Industry Practice Note 11.1) has increased concentration of ownership marginally in the upscale market but the lodging industry remains a highly competitive one.

The hotel investment decision has three dimensions: financial, real estate, and operating. The large amount of debt associated with hotel construction gives leverage and, in the international market, changing currency values can also provide financial advantages. Low interest rates are especially advantageous to leveraged deals. Hotel real estate can provide an inflation hedge and the speed with which hotel rates can be raised gives a flexibility in rentals rates few other forms of real estate offer. Real estate development also offers profits to development companies, including hotel companies like Promus and Marriott, which are active developers. A final means of profiting from a hotel is by operating it profitably but this is not always the largest source of profit.

The tendency toward overbuilding in a cyclical industry is sometimes exaggerated by the segmentation strategies of major hotel companies. Segmentation can lead to a multibrand hotel company seeking to build one of each of its brands in a market. In some cases, the company may feel being represented in a major market is more important than the short-run profit potential. Building multiple brands can also lead to problems of encroachment where the same reservation network is divided between two or more properties and, in many cases, multiple properties with the same brand in a market can reduce the advantage of a franchise.

Management companies have grown up to serve nonoperator owners. In difficult economic times, these companies' services are especially in demand as lenders become "involuntary owners." These same difficult times, however, often offer those with operating know-how major entrepreneurial opportunities.

◆ *K*EY WORDS AND CONCEPTS

<table>
<tr><td>Capital intensive</td><td>Hotel investment dimensions</td></tr>
<tr><td>Cyclical</td><td>   financing</td></tr>
<tr><td>Securitization</td><td>   real estate</td></tr>
<tr><td>Commercial mortgage-backed</td><td>   operations</td></tr>
<tr><td>   security (CMBS)</td><td>Inflation hedge</td></tr>
<tr><td>Conduit lenders</td><td>Leverage</td></tr>
<tr><td>Mezzanine financing</td><td>Segmentation</td></tr>
<tr><td>Gap financing</td><td>Encroachment</td></tr>
<tr><td>Real estate investment trust (REIT)</td><td>Impact</td></tr>
<tr><td>Initial public offerings (IPOs)</td><td>Management company</td></tr>
<tr><td>Publicly held</td><td>Management contract</td></tr>
<tr><td>C Corps</td><td>Entrepreneurial opportunities</td></tr>
<tr><td>Secondary offering</td><td></td></tr>
</table>

◆ *R*EVIEW QUESTIONS

1. Match the *numbered term* to the appropriate *lettered description:*

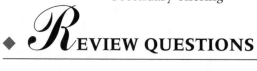

1. CMBS	A. Assembles individual hotel mortgages, packages them, and sells the resulting (debt) securities (bonds) to investors
2. REIT	B. Hotel company such as Hilton or Marriott
3. C Corp	C. Influx of funds from public securities markets into all levels of the hotel business
4. IPO	D. Bridges the gap between the funds available from a mortgage and the amount of equity investment available
5. Mezzanine financing	E. Borrowed funds such as represented by mortgages, bonds, or debentures
6. Conduit lender	F. Sale of stock for the first time by a company
7. Securitization	G. Ownership interest such as represented by stock in a company
8. Equity investment	H. Securities sold to investors made up of and backed by more than one mortgage
9. Debt	I. A company similar to a mutual fund but which limits its investment to real estate

2. How does the hotel business react to the business cycle? Explain why hotel building continues after demand turns down.

3. What does securitization mean? How is it affecting the hotel business?

4. What have been the major effects of securitization on competitive conditions in lodging?

5. What are the hazards of public ownership?

6. What are the main elements of a hotel investment decision?

7. Has segmentation contributed to encroachment? What are the effects of encroachment?

8. Why did hotel management companies come into existence?

9. What are the main differences between chain and independent management companies?

◆ NTERNET EXERCISES

1. **Site Name:** *Lodging Research Network*
   URL: http://www.lodgingresearch.com/lrn/pagebuilder2.asp
   Background Information: The Lodging Research Network was created to provide the most accessible and preeminent source of data, information, and research relating to the lodging industry. Designed as a sophisticated intranet/Internet site, the Lodging Research Network leverages the existing data resources and expertise of the Hospitality Consulting Group and incorporates carefully chosen content from reliable third-party sources.

   EXERCISE: Use the search engine on the preceding site to search for news on how the Internet is impacting the hotel industry. For example, how is the Internet impacting hotel bookings?

2. **Site Name:** *Hotel Online*
   URL: http://www.hotel-online.com
   Background Information: Hotel Online is the hospitality industry's on-line meeting place, providing the latest and most relevant news, trends, discussion forums, employment opportunities, classified advertising, and product pricing available anywhere.

   Exercise: Find at least two trends that are occurring in the hotel industry as defined by the consultants at this web site. Use the data they provide to present the trends in a class discussion.

3. **Site Name:** *Starwood Hotels and Resorts/Worldwide Inc.; Innkeepers USA Trust*
   URL: http://www.starwoodlodging.com/default.html
   http://www.inkeepersusa.com/
   Background Information: As the nation's largest and fastest growing hotel REIT, Starwood Hotels & Resorts' investment strategy is to acquire or develop full-service, upscale hotels at prices well below replacement cost in major urban markets. Innkeepers USA Trust is the only hotel REIT that specializes in the ownership of upscale, extended-stay hotels. Innkeepers' geographically diverse portfolio is concentrated primarily in states with the lowest amount of new construction.

   EXERCISES:

   a. Describe the difference between Starwood Hotels and Resorts and Starwood Hotels and Resorts Worldwide, Inc.

   b. Identify and discuss Starwood's mission and growth strategy.

   c. How much money does Starwood have invested in the hotel industry? How many properties are in Starwood's portfolio?

   d. Describe the new Starwood "W Hotels" concept to include the target marketing population, the amenities and the services provided?

   e. Surf the Innkeepers USA site. What are the similarities and differences between Innkeepers USA and Starwood?

 OTES

1. John J. Rohs, *Lodging: Light at the End of the Tunnel* (New York: Schroder and Co., 1991), p. 9.

2. Juergen Bartels, President, Carlson Hospitality Group, quoted in *Lodging,* January 1994, p. 30.

3. *Hotels,* September 1997, p. 44.

4. *Lodging,* March 1998, p. 44.

5. The phrase "securitization of the hotel industry" is used by Patrick Ford in his article, "Flood Tide," *Lodging,* May 1997, pp. 56–61. This section draws extensively on his work.

6. Steven Shundich, "The Art of the Deal," *Hotels,* September 1997, p. 44.

7. Ibid., p. 43.

8. Jun Hun, "To Securitize or Not to Securitize/The Future of Commercial Real Estate Debt Markets," *Real Estate Finance,* Summer 1996, pp. 71–79.

9. The original use of the word "mezzanine" was to designate the floor between the lobby floor and the first floor in a building.

10. Michael Cahill, "Lending a Hand," *Hotels,* May 1997, p. 62.

11. Michael J. Brody and David S. Raab, "A Primer on Real Estate Investment Trusts," *Real Estate Finance Journal,* Winter 1994, p. 36.

12. *Hotel and Motel Management,* February 2, 1998, p. 1.

13. The term C Corp is also derived from the classification of these corporations under Subchapter C of the IRS tax code. (See *Hotels,* September 1997, p. 43.)

14. The information is taken from "Timeline of Events–1997," which was issued by Starwood Hotels and Resort and Starwood Trust, n.d. The final purchase price for Sheraton is taken from the companies' press release of February 24, 1998. The months cited in the text are those of the announcement of the "definitive agreement" and not the closing date of the purchases.

15. Starwood press release of February 24, 1998.

16. John Rohs and Warren Gump, *Lodging Industry Annual Review* February 25, 1998, p. 54.

17. *Hotels,* September 1997, p. 44.

18. "Starbucks: Making Values Pay," excerpt from Howard Schultz and Dori Jones Yang, *Pour Your Heart Into It* (Hyperion, 1997); reprinted in *Fortune,* September 29, 1997, pp. 268–269.

19. Patrick Ford, "Flood Tide," *Lodging,* May 1997, p. 56. Mr. Ford is president of National Hotel Realty Advisors.

20. "Special Analysis: Ten Year Trend 1988–1997," *Lodging Outlook,* January 1998, chart 1.

21. *Lodging Outlook,* September 1997, chart 3.

22. Rohs and Gump, *Lodging Industry Annual Review,* pp. 8–9.

23. Ronald E. Kutscher, "Summary of BLS Projections to 2005," *Monthly Labor Review,* November 1995, p. 5. The measure used is gross domestic product.

24. Avner Arbel and Robert H. Woods, "Debt Hitchhiking: How Hotels Found Low Cost Capital," *Cornell Hotel and Restaurant Administration Quarterly,* November 1990, pp. 98–104.

25. Glenn Withian, "Hotel Companies Aim for Multiple Markets," *Cornell Hotel and Restaurant Administration Quarterly,* November 1985. In the argument cited here, Withian is quoting industry analyst Daniel Lee.

26. Allen J. Ostroff, Senior Vice President, Prudential Realty Group, Remarks made during a workshop, "The Franchise Impact Issue: The Value of Flag Conversion," Hospitality Industry Investment Conference, New York, June 6, 1994.

27. Peggy Berg, President, Highland Investment Advisors Group, Remarks made during a workshop, "The Franchise Impact Issue: The Value of Flag Conversion," Hospitality Industry Investment Conference, New York, June 7, 1994.

28. Michael Levin, Remarks made during a workshop, "The Value of Branding," Hospitality Industry Investment Conference, New York, June 7, 1994.

29. James J. Eyester, *The Negotiation and Administration of Hotel Management Contracts,* quoted in Robert M. James, "Management Companies," *Lodging,* June 1985, p. 105.

30. Daniel R. Lee, *Lodging* (New York: Drexel Burnham Lambert, 1984), p. 23.

31. Robert M. James, "Management Companies, *Lodging,* June 1985, p. 105.

32. Steven Rushmore, Remarks made during a presentation to the Hospitality Industry Investment Conference, June 7, 1994.

33. *Lodging,* January 1998, p. 19.

34. Robert A. Nozar, "Spotlight on Management Companies," *Hotel and Motel Management,* March 2, 1998, pp. 30–31.

35. Ibid., p. 30. I have excluded Interstate Hotels Co. from consideration because it was purchased by the REIT, Patriot American, and was no longer an independent entity.

Chapter 12

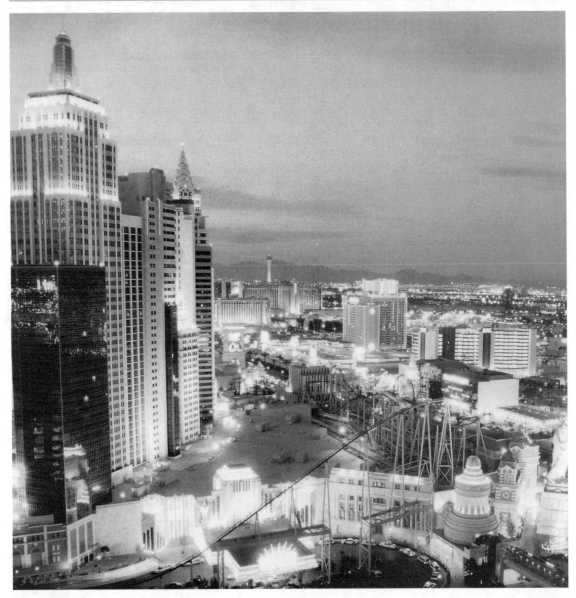

Courtesy of Las Vegas News Bureau

Competition in the Lodging Business

The Purpose of This Chapter

In this chapter, we will be concerned with competition in lodging. As we did when we considered the food service business, we will use the marketing mix as a framework for the analysis of competition. First, however, we must consider the somewhat special conditions in lodging under which this competition takes place. Then, it will be necessary to describe the way in which the marketing mix is applied to lodging. Finally, we will use this perspective to consider the competitive practices of the industry.

This Chapter Should Help You

1. Understand the conditions of competition in lodging and how they affect the hotel business

2. Apply the concepts of the marketing mix to lodging competition

3. Describe lodging segmentation in terms of the differing needs of customers being met

4. Assess the role of food service and other means for differentiation in lodging

5. Analyze the strengths and weaknesses of yield management in the hotel business

6. Determine the impact of travel intermediaries and channels of distribution on lodging

7. Discuss the importance of partnerships and frequent-guest programs to lodging marketing

THE CONDITIONS OF COMPETITION

The decade of the 1990s has been one of violent change for lodging. The losses the industry experienced in the late 1980s and early 1990s illustrate what overcapacity can do. In a fragmented market, with its many independent agents pursuing their own interests, overbuilding remains a constant threat. Indeed, the increasing role of public capital markets, which we discussed in the last chapter, increases the availability of capital for possible overbuilding. The low variable cost of the industry makes price cutting in the short run tempting—and price cutting is always tempting when overcapacity is a problem. Moreover, technological changes related to where, how, and when a hotel room is sold are changing the marketplace every day. In the following sections, we will discuss each of these **conditions of competition** briefly.

A Fragmented Market

The facts of the marketplace are that the ownership of hotel properties is spread among a wide number of individuals and corporations. The presence of national and regional hotel brands gives the appearance of a few dominant chains. Owner-

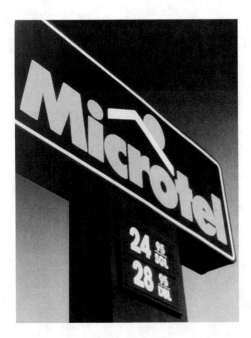

A chain brand has come to be called a "flag."
Courtesy of U.S. Franchise Systems

ship in the hotel business, however, is not highly concentrated; rather, it is highly **fragmented**.

A hotel brand or franchise has come to be called a "flag." Although it is not as easy for a hotel to drop a franchise as it is to take down a flag, the analogy is compelling. As Smith Travel Research put the matter,

> The total conversions [i.e., changes in "flag"] . . . during the ten year period [1987 to 1996] involved more than 60 per cent of the average number of properties and over 70 per cent of the average number of rooms available in that time span! . . . Brand loyalty is apparently fickle, at least among operators.[1]

As Table 12.1 shows, there was a fairly steady rate of conversions from one brand to another throughout the 10-year period. Brand conversions were at a higher rate for the last five years, however, than for the first five. Aside from a modest increase in concentration in the upper upscale segment, any appearance of "a few dominant chains" based on chain logos in front of hotels is deceptive because those signs can be changed fairly quickly. From a business planning perspective, a fragmented industry is relatively less predictable than is a more concentrated industry, such as automobile manufacturing. This increases risk.

In a market dominated by a few sellers, competition can be fierce but it is usually fairly predictable. Large firms have large stakes and are less likely to do something unpredictable. In a fragmented market, with many small firms seeking their own interests and survival, competition is much less predictable. When survival *is* at stake, as it often is in lodging, desperate measures taken by one or a few players can destabilize an entire market.

Table 12.1   Hotel Brand Conversions, 1987–1996 (Number of Hotels)

	Chain to Chain	Chain to Independent	Independent to Chain
1987	148	51	40
1988	661	228	211
1989	893	264	259
1990	1,181	316	403
1991	1,596	344	512
1992	1,487	410	549
1993	1,448	373	462
1994	1,444	444	518
1995	1,493	312	415
1996	1,464	268	416
TOTAL	11,815	3,010	3,835

Source: Lodging Outlook, June 1997.

A Cyclical Market

A second condition that shapes competition in lodging, as noted in Chapter 11, is that lodging is a **cyclical industry**, which has been characterized by periodic overcapacity. The immediate outlook for the industry depends, in large part, on where the industry is in the cyclical process. In 1998, "the limited service markets are close to the saturation point."[2] In the full-service category, one authoritative assessment is that, "Construction of full-service hotels has become economically feasible; but, full service projects still require *public* [i.e., government]/private financing in many markets due to their relatively high costs."[3]

This is another way of saying that, solely on the basis of customer demand, in the absence of any kind of government subsidy, building in this sector is often not economically feasible; that is, supply (capacity) is at or near the level of what people will willingly pay. Only in the *upper upscale sector* (just 12 percent of the industry) is demand still outgrowing supply. Problems of overcapacity in the industry, then, may not be far off, marking the possible end of a cycle. Generally, when overcapacity threatens an industry, pricing stability is undermined.

Cost Structure

A third critical competitive characteristic of the lodging business is that it has a **low variable cost** in relation to sales and a correspondingly high fixed cost.[4] A low variable cost means that there is very little cost associated with the sale of one more rooms. The variable cost can be as low as $5 per rented room, ranging up to $15 or $20, while the corresponding room rate might range from $30 to $120. This large margin over costs makes it easy to cut prices and still show a profit—in the short run. The temptation to cut prices is particularly strong in periods where supply exceeds demand, occupancies and revenues fall, and the need to meet the burden of high fixed costs becomes more pressing.

Securitization

Another pair of related conditions that are of relatively recent origin were also discussed in Chapter 11. They are the growth in **securitization** in the industry and the growing relative size of REITs. Securitization, by making capital more readily available to developers, makes overbuilding more of a threat. Real estate investment trusts establish new modes of financing whose impact is still difficult to gauge, but they clearly increase the total financing available for purchase of hotels and bring an increased number of firms with "deep pockets" (i.e., well-financed firms) to the hotel business in all of its segments.

Technological Revolution

A final factor is the **impact of technology** on the hotel business. Technology and the change it brings cuts across all areas of the hotel business: improving service, facilitating control of costs, heightening security, and the like. As a condition of competition, however, we need to note that, in the area of marketing, the techno-

Industry Characteristic	Impact
Fragmented ownership	Unpredictability, especially in down markets
Cyclical Periodic overbuilding	Overcapacity exerts downward pressure on prices
Low variable cost High fixed cost	Exerts downward pressure on prices
Increasing securitization	Makes capital more available for development
Technological revolution	Heightens role of travel intermediaries (travel agents, reservation services, airlines, etc) adding to marketing costs and reducing control over price

Figure 12.1 The conditions of competition in lodging.

logical revolution has fundamentally altered the way hotel rooms are offered for sale. The global distribution system (GDS) has heightened the role of intermediaries such as travel agents, airline reservation services, and others in selling hotel rooms. The use of the Internet, still in its infancy as a medium for reservations, appears likely to be an equally fundamental change in the way hotels do business. The Internet is already having a major impact on how properties communicate with customers. Finally, computerization of guest and customer prospect information makes possible the use of individualized information in planning and executing promotional plans.

These five conditions of competition are summarized in Figure 12.1. Collectively, they describe an industry that is, on a scale of competitive to monopolistic, highly competitive. Within the boundaries of these conditions of competition, we can use the marketing mix to analyze competitive practices in lodging.

THE MARKETING MIX IN LODGING[5]

The **marketing mix** is conventionally thought of as encompassing the *4Ps: product, price, place, and promotion.* In most cases, the application of these four terms varies somewhat as one moves from industry to industry. In lodging, then, we can hardly be surprised that we need to modify the 4Ps to make the concepts that underlie them in lodging clearer.

> *Product,* for instance, includes both physical goods and services. It also involves characteristics that are present in the individual property such as the guest room, lobby, or the amenities package and services offered by a hotel. However, product also refers to the lodging system's (i.e., chain, franchise group) services. Ultimately, the product the *guest consumes* is an *experience,* what happens to her or him, in its totality, during a visit.

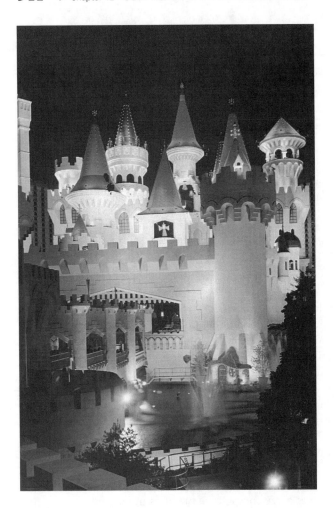

The lodging product consists of the guest's entire experience. In Las Vegas, the Excalibur and other huge resort hotels seek to capture the guest's imagination.
Courtesy of Excalibur Hotel and Casino

Price refers not to some fixed rate but a price that varies with levels of demand and with customer groups served. Because there is no inventory of yesterday's rooms, there is pressure to sell rooms each day. Alternatively, what is for sale is a fixed capacity and so price tends to rise in periods of high demand. The truth is "rack rate" (the listed price you might find in a directory) is paid by only a small percentage of guests, probably less than one-fifth. It is more realistic, therefore, to speak of *pricing policy* rather than just price. As noted previously, the industry is cyclical and fixed costs tend to exert downward pressure on prices in markets where there is overcapacity.

Place, referring to the *location* of an individual property, is a very important aspect of the lodging marketing mix, but the *places* where the hotel room is sold, such as, for instance, travel agents and other travel intermediaries, are

PRODUCT	Goods and services Lodging System and Individual Property Characteristics
PRICE	Pricing Policy: Varies with Demand and Customer
PLACE	Location of property Travel Intermediaries Used

PROMOTION	Marketing Communication
	    Mass Communication: Advertising, Sales Promotion, Public Relations
	    Individualized Communication and Rewards

Figure 12.2   The lodging marketing mix.

also extremely important. This latter aspect, we will find, is also a *system* characteristic in chains and other lodging groups.

Promotion refers to *marketing communication,* generally taken to include persuasive activities such as advertising, sales promotion, and public relations. We will also include, here, other persuasive activities such as frequent-traveler programs and other individualized means to reward customers for brand loyalty.

Figure 12.2 summarizes the lodging marketing mix as it is discussed in this chapter. In the next section, we will explore these concepts in detail in terms of market tactics.

𝒞OMPETITIVE TACTICS

The competitive strategies and tactics used in the lodging marketplace are implemented by using the elements of the marketing mix to target guest segments and to differentiate "our" offering from "theirs." The notion that "if you build a better mousetrap, the world will beat a pathway to your door" may have an element of truth in it. The success of the hospitality transaction does begin with the product, but in a competitive market it must be priced right and conveniently placed for the purchaser. Finally, the offer of the hotel must be persuasively communicated to the right public or publics.

𝒫RODUCT—IN A SEGMENTED MARKET

Lodging products are made up of both goods and services. By the term goods, we mean the tangible aspects of lodging such as a lobby or a guest room. Services, on the other hand, involve guest interactions with staff or hotel facilities. Both goods and services are crafted to meet the needs and preferences of particular target markets. At a very basic level, the industry is divided into properties that serve the "upstairs" guest and those that serve the "downstairs" guest.[6]

The needs and preferences of the "downstairs guests" mean that they are willing to pay for more than the minimum in services.
Courtesy of Marriott International

Upstairs guests are interested in what you find upstairs in a hotel, that is, guest rooms. They want comfortable, clean accommodations. This market is willing to give up "extra" services—that is, services that they don't want—for a lower price. The success of the limited-service segment clearly indicates that there is a large upstairs market that focuses on just the basics in the guest room. Fairfield, Comfort, or Hampton Inns represent a comparatively upscale version of the upstairs market, while many all-suite properties represent a deluxe approach to the upstairs market, just as Motel 6 aims at the economy minded. It is important to see how each focuses on guest preference in a different way.

The **downstairs market**, on the other hand, either needs the more extensive services of a full-service hotel or finds them desirable. Downstairs guests want the traditional lobby floor attractions of full-service hotels: dining rooms, cocktail lounges, meeting and banquet facilities, and the like. Downstairs guests are willing to pay for the additional services because they are necessary or because they can readily afford them. Generally, we would include not only full-service transient hotels but also convention hotels, conference centers, and resort properties in the service-intensive downstairs segment. One of the most basic service decisions involves food service. Another decision involves the level and kind of other services and amenities offered to the guest. We should note again that downstairs guests traveling on business during the week on an expense account may be upstairs guests seeking a lower price when traveling at their own expense on the weekend.

It is important to realize that the upstairs–downstairs segmentation represents basic strategies, active programs aimed at achieving customer patronage. The upstairs strategy reduces certain services to permit the property to operate profitably while offering the guest a superior guest room and a lower price. The downstairs strategy is more service intensive and is aimed at a guest who is willing to pay for more service.

Food Service

Hotels serving the upstairs market have chosen to eliminate or reduce drastically the food service available in the property. It is important, however, to realize that they have not ignored **food service.** Off-premise food service is almost invariably available nearby and basic guest needs—for breakfast—are often met in the property.

Bed and Breakfast—Plus. The practice of giving away a continental breakfast is certainly not new. It has been common in small motels for years. However, the *advertised, standardized* availability of a "free breakfast," that is, one covered by the price of the room, has a special appeal. In the economy market, for instance, a continental breakfast of juice, pastry, and coffee is generally all that is provided. In some all-suite properties, as well, a continental breakfast is the standard, but a number offer a full, cooked-to-order breakfast.

Many all-suite properties also provide a scaled-down, on-premise restaurant, but very few offer substantial meeting and banquet facilities. Residence Inns has a grocery shopping service available to its guests, and Homewood Suites provides an on-premise convenience store. Because long-stay suites provide a full kitchen, they do not offer any food service beyond a complimentary breakfast. Among all-suite properties, then, there is not the uniformity in curtailment of food service that is found among most budget properties. In general, however, elimination or at least simplification of food service is the rule. The purpose is to meet the preferences of the upstairs guest while maintaining a competitive rate.

Managing Food Service. For full-service hotels, the option of discontinuing food service—or limiting it to breakfast—just won't work. On the other hand, managing a food service operation presents many problems. Although food service profits in hotels in 1996 were at their highest level since 1988,[7] over the long run most hotel restaurants make little, if any, profit after capital costs and a fair share of undistributed operating expenses. Operating a restaurant that is not very profitable or even losing money presents some real problems. The most obvious is a poor or negative return on investment, but this is really the least of the problems. More serious is the fact that an unsuccessful operation is always facing pressure to reduce costs, to cut the losses. There is a point, however, beyond which cost cutting impairs service and annoys or offends the guest and risks high-profit rooms revenue.

Even if the cost-cutting pressure is manageable, food service demands a great

Limited-service hotels offer a free continental breakfast in pleasant surroundings, such as at Wingate Inns, shown here.
Courtesy of Cendant Corp.

deal of top-management attention. The food service operations people required for a restaurant are hard to find. Where top managers in a hotel lack food service experience, it is difficult for them to supervise the skilled people they have hired to run the restaurant. Even where the general managers have the experience, they may feel their time and attention should be spent elsewhere.

Our discussion to this point makes a good case for turning the hotel's restaurant over to a company more expert in food service. The practice of **leasing** the restaurant to an outside food service operator is becoming increasingly common, particularly in small to mid-sized full-service operations and in all-suites. Embassy Suites leases most of its restaurants and, because Embassy operates its own complimentary breakfast, basic services are assured for the rooms guest. Operators report good results for properties that have selected good operators. For instance, "At the Doubletree Hotel in Chicago 'Mrs. Park's Tavern' has a management agreement with the property and has doubled its F&B revenues."[8]

Unfortunately, although leasing can solve some restaurant problems, there are some real disadvantages to leasing a hotel's food service. The most fundamental problem is that there are now two companies running major parts of the hotel and each company has its own business objectives and priorities. In good times, the clash of interests is often not apparent. When business turns down, however, because of the restaurants' higher variable cost structure, the restaurant company has to cut costs—and services—to survive. However, this is just the point where the hotel needs its restaurant to be a "service department" if it is to be competitive. Maintaining service levels may benefit rooms sales—but there is no way for the restaurant to derive much benefit from the sale of a few more rooms. With this situation, it is no wonder that leased operations work out reasonably well until business goes through a bad patch, at which point disputes multiply.[9]

Limiting Food Service. One tactic operators can choose is to convert their kitchen to **sous vide,** a method of preserving prepared food. Food is prepared and then chilled and vacuum packed in airtight pouches. This work can be done by the main prep crew during a single shift with a smaller, less skilled crew to do reconstituting and plating during slower meal periods. Sous vide provides excellent quality frozen or chilled prepared food and good variety, though at a somewhat higher food cost. The offsetting advantages, in addition to quality control, are a substantial reduction in the skill level required to run the restaurant and a reduction in payroll, particularly in the kitchen.

A substantial number of Marriott Courtyard properties took a somewhat different tack. They found that, although they had strong breakfast and lunch sales, their dinner business was minimal—so they closed their restaurant at dinner.[10] This would once have been an unthinkable reduction in service for a hotel, but with the great expansion in mid-priced and upscale dinner houses, there are undoubtedly plenty of restuarants in the immediate area of these hotels to fill their guests' needs.

Brand Name Restaurants. At a minimum, the availability of some kind of food service in the immediate area is essential for most hotels that do not operate their own food service facilities. Probably the best-known company to rely on the **on-site franchised restaurant** is La Quinta Motor Inns. This limited-service hotel chain offers restaurant operators a build-to-suit leased restaurant on the motel site. It has used this arrangement with several restaurant companies, including Denny's, Cracker Barrel, Bob Evans Farms, Waffle House, and Shoney's. Because fast food has become so expert in breakfast service, La Quinta also works with companies such as McDonald's and Wendy's, which offer the fast breakfast service its rooms customers want. Generally, the lease specifies the minimum number of hours of operation and allows the guests to charge their food to their room.

Full-service hotels have begun to lease out their restaurants to franchisees of major food service chains. Alternatively, some hotel operators have become franchisees of these chains themselves. The names of chains now operating within a hotel, such as Denny's, Pizza Hut, Bennigan's, Bobby McGee's, Steak and Ale, and Restaurants Associates, are well known to the traveling public and, as such, serve as a draw for the hotel. In addition, as franchisees, these operations receive field support and advice from the franchise organization that can help smooth out some of the rough spots.

Leased Specialty Restaurants. Upscale operators such as Hilton are generally not prepared to give up their basic food service operations. They have found, however, that leasing some space to a well-known brand name operator will result not only in substantial revenue but will enhance the image of the hotel and act as a draw to rooms guests. One of the longest-standing examples of this tactic is Trader Vic's, a Polynesian restaurant, which, after an initial success in Hilton's Palmer House in Chicago, has gone on to lease and operate in other Hilton hotels. At the other end of the scale of complexity,

> ITT Sheraton decided to improve its coffee sales and "jump on the bandwagon for recognizability" with its new longterm relationship with Starbucks Coffee. Sheraton is taking a two tiered approach. Some hotels have run Starbucks outlets through licensing arrangements. Other locations have a leased Starbucks.[11]

Conventional Hotel Restaurants. A single direction for hotels' food services is by no means clear. Some hotel operators are finding that they can't compete successfully with local top-quality food service restaurants in attracting local trade and so are building smaller restaurants and reducing the number of food service outlets in the hotel from two or three to one. Some luxury hotels are opting for more casual outlets rather than formal dining rooms. A growing number of hotels are opening

Upscale full-service hotels generally provide a variety of restaurants.
Courtesy of Caesar's Palace, Las Vegas

European-style bistros and brasseries that combine a casual atmosphere with an upscale feel.

Upscale hotel companies such as Marriott and Hyatt, as well as luxury properties such as Four Seasons, continue to meet guest expectations for full service with a variety of restaurants in their properties, and these almost always include a top-of-the-line, luxury restaurant. The editor of *Hotels* put the case for hotel restaurants as follows:

> Hotel companies such as Sheraton, Shangri La, San Francisco's Kimpton Hotels, Disney, London's Savoy Group and many others run successful restaurants and, in some cases, enormously successful banquet and catering departments. The potential residual effect of a well-run F&B department is increased occupancy—in some cases by as much as 33 per cent—and support for your company's quality image.[12]

It is true that food service has been greatly simplified in the economy segment that serves the upstairs market. It has frequently been deemphasized or leased out in some midscale properties. Nevertheless, in the downstairs market of convention, resort, and big-city luxury hotels, a successful food service operation is absolutely essential.

Restaurants as a Competitive Strategy.   Hotel restaurants do not generally make a profit after all costs are considered. One hospitality consultant has estimated that, after allocation of all overhead, a hotel restaurant actually loses about 5 percent on sales.[13] This difficulty arises because food service is the hotel's "service department." The argument for devoting all the time and effort to food service, however, is fairly straightforward. Food service in many markets adds points to occupancy and secures local referrals. The resulting higher occupancies more than offset the lower profit on food service.

Properties serving the upstairs market have opted to offer limited services to guests—and, as a result, can offer attractive room rates. They know they can count on restaurants in their immediate area to supplement the complimentary services they offer in house. In both cases—upstairs and downstairs—product, service, and resulting price are being crafted as a means to serve the guests' needs and preferences and, thus, gain patronage in a highly competitive market.

Other Services and Amenities

A wide range of services, distinctive physical plant features, and products are used by hotels to **differentiate** a property from its competitors.

The Concierge and Superfloors.   As we noted in Chapter 10, the basic function of the **concierge** is to provide guest service and information. The cross keys, symbol of the concierge, is intended to convey a degree of expertise and knowledge significantly above that of the bell staff. The concierge knows the right restaurants, the best shows, and can probably get reservations or tickets if they are required. In many ways, the concierge acts as a friend to the stranger, giving service and rendering that "extra" in service that makes a stay a distinctive experience in hospitality.

Many hotels are adding a concierge to the lobby staff, whereas a number of companies associate the concierge closely or exclusively with their *superfloors,* that is, special areas such as executive floors and tower suites. On these floors, special lounges and other services are commonly provided.

Before concluding this discussion, we should comment again on the wide *variety* of practice. Luxury hotels, such as the Four Seasons or Dallas's Mansion at Turtle Creek, offer substantially the same services as those available on the executive floors, but to all their guests. Many hotels, although not offering concierge service, have established a business class service within their hotel that secures the guest upgraded amenities. Radisson business class, for instance, provides business guests amenities such as a full breakfast, daily newspaper, in-room movies, in-room coffee maker and coffee, local and toll-free phone access, a desk with a computer or laptop hookup, and fax receipt or delivery. A business class room averages $20.00 per night above the hotel's corporate rate.[14]

At the other extreme, limited-service operators, particularly in the economy

Fitness facilities, such as these at a Wingate Inn, meet the demands of health conscious travelers.
Courtesy of Cendant Corp.

and budget segments, have pared "extras" to the bone. As one well-known economy chain's advertising put it, "We don't have it because you don't want it."

Fitness Facilities.   Fitness has become a major concern for many North Americans. It is not surprising, therefore, that **fitness facilities** of some kind have become fairly standard in most hotels. Some provision for fitness is commonly found even in economy hotels. Fitness facilities, however, are a good example of a service and amenity that is not necessarily a powerful differentiator. Like free shampoo and shower caps, if one hotel adds an exercise machine or two, the competition can quite readily copy the effort.

Spas, on the other hand, if properly planned, are not as easy to duplicate because they embody a great deal of personal service. According to *Hotels,* "Resorts around the world are witnessing significant boosts in both group and leisure business associated with a growing interest in spa, fitness and recreational facilities."[15] Spas are generally found in upscale hotels and resorts, adjacent to a gym, and offer facilities such as treatment rooms, a beauty salon, a patio dining area, and lounges. Although spas appeal primarily to women, a growing number of men are using them, as well. Resorts have reported increased occupancies and average rates—as well as a significant operating profit—from the addition of a spa.[16]

Business Centers.   Business travelers expect and use a **business center.** The extent of the service, however, varies considerably. For instance, the Marriott World Center in Orlando, Florida, a resort and convention hotel, has typists available by the hour (or page), computers, copying equipment that can handle large-scale jobs, faxes, and even a bindery for books. In Seoul, South Korea, the Radisson Hotel has a business center with two conference rooms; workstations and Internet hookups; audiovisual equipment; and secretarial, translation, courier and shipping, and business card printing services. On the other hand, the typical Wingate Hotel offers a self-service center that includes a computer, a printer, and a fax machine. Even economy motels make business services available. Business travelers are on the road frequently and are potentially repeat guests. It makes sense to cater to their needs in order to gain their regular patronage.

Assessing Services and Amenities.   As a competitive tactic, what stands out is the ease with which many of the services and amenities we have been discussing can be copied. The first hotel or motel in a city that put in a television set undoubtedly had an advantage—but not for long. In addition, shampoo—once rarely seen in a hotel room—has now become commonplace. Indeed, in regard to personal-care amenities, it is becoming necessary to have them just to avoid damaging the property's reputation, but it is difficult to see them as offering any lasting competitive advantage. Similarly, exercise facilities are an easily duplicated service. However, finding or training a good concierge is almost as difficult as providing memorable food service. Again, food service is very difficult to do well, and its very complexity ensures that it will not be easy to copy. Although some property types may be able to dispense with food service and rely on restaurants in their neighborhood, it seems likely that they

Wingate Inns provide a self-service business center to their guests.
Courtesy of Cendant Corp.

will have greater difficulty in differentiating themselves from their competitors, especially as the number of properties multiply and properties age.

Another differentiator that is very difficult to copy is excellence in service across the board, in all departments. In this connection, it is interesting to note that it was limited-service chains that led the way with the 100 percent satisfaction guarantee. The guarantee, in turn, is based on an operating strategy of empowerment, that is, of giving employees the discretion to take care of the guests' needs or problems right away. The result has been very high consumer satisfaction ratings and a more motivated workforce. Reportedly, the guarantee itself costs very little (0.3 percent of sales) and fulfilling it gains much more favorable public relations and word of mouth than could be purchased for such a modest cost.[17] The degree to which service guarantees have been widely adopted, however, suggests that at least the *statement* of a guarantee is not difficult to copy. The development of a company culture that is really capable of fulfilling the promise of the guarantee, however, is something that cannot be easily duplicated.

System-Wide Services

In franchise organizations, the franchisor is responsible for the design of the basic business system. A successful franchise will be designed to provide the services its target market seeks. Moreover, routine services such as those provided by property management systems will ensure error-free operation of functions such as accounting, billing, and credit, which are important to the guest. Thus, the franchisor is responsible for establishing a mode of operations that is professional and leaves the guest feeling that he or she is in secure hands. This enhances the guest's experience.

The maintenance of quality in operations is a property-level responsibility, but **quality assurance** through inspection systems is a vital function of the franchisor. *You* can maintain *your* property but your reputation is really in the hands of all your fellow franchisees. Establishing an acceptable level of quality, assuring that quality through frequent inspections, and providing assistance when a problem remains persistent are all important activities of the *franchisor,* as is the encouragement of high operating standards. Some franchisors award ratings somewhat like the Mobil star rating system and publish those ratings in their directories. They also encourage franchisees to publicize their ratings in their advertising. Franchisors also arrange for mentoring of properties that are experiencing quality problems by teams from more successful franchise members.

Another important service rendered by the franchise or chain organization is a national or, more commonly, an international reservation service. This will be discussed in a following section.

Another aspect of product involves the *brand name* of the hotel. Brand is

One of the most important attributes of a successful franchise is an established brand name.
Courtesy of Marriott International

Table 12.2 The Cost of a Franchise

Budget Hotels		Midscale Hotels		First-Class Hotels	
Chain	1996 Total Cost as a Percentage of Total Rooms Revenue	Chain	1996 Total Cost as a Percentage of Total Rooms Revenue	Chain	1996 Total Cost as a Percentage of Total Rooms Revenue
Key West Inn	5.6	MainStay Suites	7.2	Homewood Suites	8.1
Rodeway	5.4	Best Western	1.7	Embassy Suites	7.7
Budget Host	0.9	InnSuites	4.5	Doubletree Hotels	7.4
Hampton Inn/Suites	8.4	Quality Inn/Suites	7.7	Doubletree Club	7.3
GuestHouse	3.3	Country Inn and Suites	8.0	Clarion	5.1
Americinn	8.8			Hilton Hotel	8.6
Budgetel Inns	7.2	Howard Johnson	8.7	Hilton Garden Inn	8.6
Comfort Inn	9.3	Park Inns	6.1	Hilton Suites	8.6
Sleep Inn	8.5	Days Inn	9.0	Omni	6.9
Econo Lodge	7.8	Ramada	8.7	Radisson	8.1
Shoney's Inn/Suites	7.0	Wingate Inn	8.7	Residence Inn	7.5
Shoney's Suites	8.5	Candlewood	7.5	Hawthorn Suites	7.6
Scottish Inns	4.9	Courtyard	9.5	Marriott	10.0
Downtowner Inns	5.4	Comfort Suites	8.7	Marriott Resorts	10.0
Passport Inn	4.9	Holiday Inn	8.5	Towne Place Suites	7.8
Red Carpet Inn	5.4	Holiday Inn SunSpree	9.0	Crowne Plaza	8.5
Master Hosts Inns/ Resorts	5.9			Four Points Hotel	8.0
Sundowner Inns	5.5			Sheraton	8.0
Best Inns/Suites	4.1			Westin	7.2
Motel 6	7.2				
Travelodge	8.9				
Thriftlodge	8.9				
Super 8	8.2				
Villager Lodge	7.2				
Microtel	8.2				
Signature Inns	4.0				
Fairfield Inn/Suites	8.9				
Howard Johnson Inns	8.9				
Ramada Limited	8.9				
Holiday Inn Express	9.3				

Source: Stephen Rushmore and Carolyn A. Malone, *Hotel Franchise Fees Analysis Guide—1997* (Mineola, NY: HVS International, 1997.)
For a comprehensive list of hotel chains, go the the following URL: **http://www.wku.edu/~hrtm/hotlrest.htm.**

thought of as an aspect of product because it affects the consumer's perception of the product. When you see a sign that says Motel 6, Howard Johnson, or Hilton, you undoubtedly have different images before you set foot in the property. We will be concerned with brands again when we discuss advertising.

Brand names are not inexpensive. Table 12.2 summarizes the cost of a year's franchise payments to several of the more prominent brands. Stephen Rushmore commented on the varying level of payments:

> Some of the lower franchise fee percentages belong to chains such as Budget Host and Best Western; technically these represent associations or referral organizations rather than franchises. These groups are structured for the benefit of their member hotels, so fees are oriented more toward covering operating costs rather than producing large profits. Consequently, their percentages are somewhat representative of the actual cost of operating a franchise organization and provide an indication of the margin of profit realized by other chains.[18]

*P*RICE AND PRICING TACTICS

Some would say that the goal of price is to maximize profit—and that may be the intention of many who set prices. However, in anything but the short term, the very competitive hotel market restrains price gouging. There is also a lower limit on rates set by cost—the cost of the property (capital cost); the cost of operating the property; and, finally, we should consider a part of "cost," a reasonable return for ownership. Otherwise, the hotel will go out of business. Thus, we can say that upper and lower boundaries for price are set by competition in the market and cost.

With a low **variable cost**—say $10 to rent one more room—and plenty of margin between that variable cost and a selling price of, say, $75, the decision to discount is not difficult. Add to that the fact that there are **fixed costs** (payroll for a minimum crew size, fixed overhead costs, a mortgage and interest or rent) that *must* be met to keep the doors open. Pricing is also subject to the fact that unsold rooms have no value the next day; that is, there is no inventory. As a result, during slow periods, whether a recession or just an off season, there is a tendency toward discounting when demand is slack.

On the other hand, in times of peak demand, prices tend to be at their maximum. Pricing is subject to the pressure of limited capacity—there are only so many rooms that can be sold on any given night and so "when the town is full," there is very little give in rates. Limited capacity supports and raises price in good times. Under these circumstances, there is a natural tendency for hotel prices to vary with demand: discounted during slow periods but at their upper limits when demand is strong.

In fact, however, hotels can't afford to drift at the mercy of these short-run currents. Hotel pricing, in practice, is *proactive;* that is, pricing, like other elements of the marketing mix, should be used to *attract customer's long-run patronage* not just to generate revenue for the short run. If a convention will bring in a thousand room nights (three days for 330 people), it may make sense to rent rooms with a regular rate of $75 for $65 to convention attendees in order to get the convention, especially considering the food and beverage, meeting room rental, and other spending such a large group will bring to the property. If there is a logic to reducing rates in order to attract a convention, a similar process of reasoning can be used to set a special corporate rate for companies that will use, say, 1000 room nights a year. The principle is that of a discount for a large-volume sale.

The regular rates may be too high for some types of customers who can't afford full rates or who have a low level of reimbursement: clergy, government employees and military personnel, sports teams, and, yes, even professors. These market segments might never consider the hotel if all that was available was the regular rate. Recall that a hotel has busy periods but also slow periods and it becomes clear that these groups of people, even at reduced rates, can add significantly to profit as customers during a slow weekend or off-season period. The alternative is to have the rooms stand empty, yielding no revenue.

We could add to the list of special cases but this should be enough to suggest why price is not some fixed figure but one that varies with conditions and with the customers being served. The question does arise, however, as to when special rates should be honored. Simple logic suggests that, during very slow periods, a hotel might be glad to have all the special cases described previously, even at rates discounted 25 to 50 percent. On the other hand, a hotel is not interested in selling a $75 room for $37.50 during a period when the hotel is certain to be full. In between peaks and valleys in demand, there are times when what rates should be charged are not quite so clear and may have to be decided on a day-by-day basis. To deal with this set of issues, the tool of *yield management* was adapted from a similar practice developed by the airlines.

Yield Management

One knowledgeable researcher defines **yield management** as follows:

> Yield Management is a method that can help a firm sell the right unit to the right customer at the right time and for the right price. It guides the decision of how to allocate undifferentiated units of limited capacity to available demand in a way that maximizes profit or revenue. The question is, how much should one sell at what price and to which market segment.[19]

The process of developing a yield management system begins with a study of room demand in a property over a period of some years. Based on this history, regular patterns of slow and peak periods—and those in between—are identified, and, using a computer, the information is modeled so as to give a theoretical forecast of demand. Managers then begin to plan their pricing tactics based on history *and a forecast of actual expected events*. The following conversation might take place during a hotel's planning session:

> Week A is theoretically a busy week but that's because that's when the Cattlemen's Association meeting is held. Since that piece of business has moved to another city, we'd better open up the special rate categories or we'll be in real trouble. On the other hand, week B has usually been slow but this year we have the Furniture Show and so we'll be full. Let's close out all special rates except to our best corporate accounts.

Yield management, then, is based on combining a history of room demand with a current forecast for demand. Normally, forecasts are made for a period of a year but reviewed quarterly, monthly, weekly, and, finally, daily. As demand shifts, apparent slow periods heat up, and forecasted busy days turn soft. Throughout this period, the rates are adjusted up and down to try to maximize revenue. Although a computer is not absolutely necessary for this activity, most hotels use a special computer program to manage yields and, indeed, many central reservation systems have a yield management function built into their programs for each property served.

The Problems of Yield Management.   Although yield management helps solve recurrent problems regarding day-to-day rate variations, its implementation presents some serious problems. From the customer's point of view, pricing may appear arbitrary and unfair. Guest A visiting with Guest B in the lobby may discover that the two of them have identical rooms but quite different rates. The rate listed in a chain's directory (often called the rack rate) may be charged to only a few unknowing customers. As *Fortune* magazine put it, "Except in rare circumstances—say in the event of a big convention or when a hotel has few rooms to begin with—a traveler needn't accept the advertised "rack" rate price foisted on those who don't know to ask for better."[20] That author detailed the widely differing rates he was able to get by (1) calling an 800 number, (2) calling the property front desk, and (3) through his travel agent. A perception of unfairness on the part of our customers is hardly surprising.

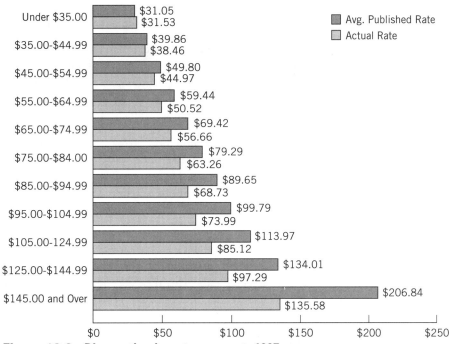

Figure 12.3 Discounting by rate segment, 1997.
(*Source:* Smith Travel Research.)

There is no question that there *is* discounting in lodging. Figure 12.3 shows discounting by rate segment in 1997.[21] The discounting shown there, however, took place in one of the strongest hotel markets in recent history. If the discounts for 1997 shown in Figure 12.3 are contrasted with discounts given in 1993, the sensitivity of the industry to down markets stands out. In 1993, discounts for the under-$55 rate categories were nearly double those of 1997 and roughly one and a half times greater for the rest of the rate categories.

Whatever public perception there may be of inconsistent discounts, the pressures on managers to yield profits, passed along to employees, suggests that efforts to maximize revenue based on yield management are there to stay. One researcher suggests four ground rules for implementing yield management in ways that are more acceptable to guests:

1. Disclosure of the rate structure and the concessions offered should be available to customers. "For example, a hotel can advertise the various rates available and the restrictions or benefits associated with each of these rates."

2. Cancellation restrictions can be offered along with a reduced rate so as to match the customer's benefit with one for the hotel. "For example, Marriott offers a substantially lower price for advance purchases."

3. Other reasonable restrictions such as a minimum length of stay may be offered in exchange for a favorable rate.

4. Different prices are offered for products that are perceived to be different. A room with a view or one on an "executive" floor may carry a higher price; lower prices are seen as fair where these guarantees are not required.[22]

Another area of problems for yield managers lies in staff training. If a customer stayed in a hotel for $75 last time and asks for the same rate, a well-trained reservationist can explain that that category of rooms is "sold out." An untrained (or disgruntled) reservationist might respond instead, "Sorry, we're almost full so we're only selling at our maximum rate."

The reservationist and desk clerk's jobs are to try to "sell up," to get the highest rate possible. Today's varying rate structures are complicated, however, and a poorly trained reservationist may not know the twists and turns of special rates and end up having them explained to him or her by a regular guest. Once the guest is in control of the transaction, minimum rate and maximum upgrade are the most likely outcome.

Rate Competition

Competition in lodging (within any single segment) is usually conducted on the basis of nonprice elements. This means product enhancement such as added services, as well as advertising and promotion. Price enters as an active element in large-scale sales—and during slow periods, when any sale looks attractive to some managers. The problem with price cutting in a down market is that it is generally matched by competitors and then everybody is doing the same business but at

While price is not the main competitive tactic within segments, multiconcept chains can use new lodging products, such as Marriott's TownePlace Suites, to enter other price segments.
Courtesy of Marriott International

lower prices! This down market problem has been with hotels for a long time and will probably continue to plague us because of the industry's competitive nature and the economic realities we discussed earlier.

$\mathcal{P}$LACE—AND PLACES

Location is a widely recognized factor in the success of a hotel and that is one aspect of place we need to consider. In today's hotel business, however, rooms are sold for individual hotels in many different *places* through travel intermediaries all over the world. This latter aspect of place is often referred to as the **channels of distribution.**

Location

Ideal hotel locations have long been at the center of travel networks and near destinations. Airport hotels and roadside motels come immediately to mind. Downtown hotels were once located downtown because they were near the railroad station, then the hub of the principal means of transportation. Today, downtown hotels' locations are advantageous because they are close to the business and cul-

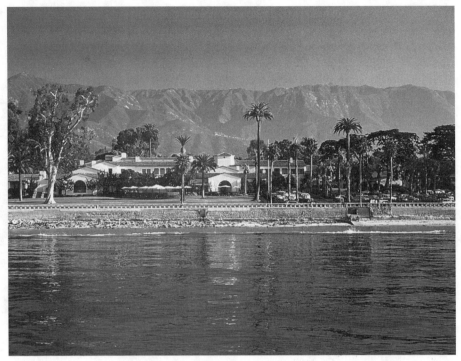

Location is a critical factor in the success of a hotel, inn, or resort.
Courtesy of Four Seasons Hotels

tural destinations their guests come to visit. The fastest-growing location type for hotels in 1998 is suburban,[23] serving the growing number of business-oriented destinations such as office parks and company headquarters that have moved out of the downtown area.

The decision to build a specific hotel in a particular location is generally based on a feasibility study. The contents of a feasibility study are outlined in Figure 12.4. The location of an individual hotel is of vital importance to that property but the individual hotel is, today, a part of a complex system for providing information and reservation services to travelers, a part of the channels of distribution.

Channels of Distribution

Businesses and other corporate entities that are active in the channels of distribution are referred to as channel members. These include hotel chains, franchise systems, and referral (membership) services such as Best Western, as well as hotel sales and representation companies such as Utell, described in Industry Practice Note 12.1. Travel agents are critical channel members—as are other agencies that make travel arrangements such as travel wholesalers and incentive houses. The latter put together packages to be used by companies to reward their employees and

Site Location	Relative to transportation systems and destinations
Demand Analysis	Demand in immediate area as well as in the wider (i.e., city or area wide) community
Market Characteristics	Trends in demographic and economic conditions; used to support demand projections
Analysis of the Competition	1) Quality of competitive operators 2) Number of competitive units relative to present and projected demand 3) Outlook for new competition
Financial Analysis	1) Projection of occupancy, average rate, total income, and expense 2) Commentary on feasibility of the project

Figure 12.4   Contents of a feasibility study.
(*Source:* Adapted from Stephen Rushmore, CRE, *How to Perform an Economic Feasibility Study of a Proposed Hotel/Motel.*)

dealers for outstanding performance. Although individual hotels are channel members and can influence other channel members to gain sales, the franchisor (or chain headquarters) takes the heaviest responsibility for determining and maintaining the group's relationship with the other channel members.

Hotel chains and franchise organizations maintain national and regional sales offices and provide central reservation services (CRSs) to hotels that are part of their system. One group of franchises, owned by Cendant, manages the eight different franchise brands shown in Figure 12.5. According to Cendant's chairman, Henry Silverman, his company accounts for 50 percent of franchised properties in the United States.

Franchising provides a brand with a means to move relatively quickly into many geographic markets. Although franchising is well established in the United States, it is still a fairly new business practice overseas, where conditions for franchising vary from one region to another. Global Hospitality Note 12.1 (page 366) summarizes the hotel franchising outlook in the world's major areas.

Travel agents have long played an important role in selling hotel rooms. Today,

Howard Johnson	Days Inn
Super 8	Villager Lodge
Knight's Inn	Travelodge
Ramada Inn	Wingate Inns

Figure 12.5   Cendant franchise brands.

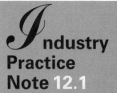

Industry Practice Note 12.1

Travel Intermediaries: REZolutions

"Reach" is a term used in marketing to describe how large the audience for a company's marketing is. From its headquarters in Phoenix, Arizona, REZolutions (**http://www.anasazi.com/**) is a company that provides solutions to the problem of representation that broadens the reach of small to medium-sized hotel chains and independent hotels. The company was formed in 1997 as a result of a merger between Utell International and Anasazi, now each divisions of the new company. Utell, although active in the United States, was best known for marketing and representation outside the United States. Anasazi's strengths were in the U.S. market and in technology.

First of all, through its Utell division, the company provides marketing and reservation services to over 7700 hotel properties in 180 countries and represents 1.25 million rooms worldwide, 10 percent of the hotel rooms in the world. Utell generated 4 million reservations worldwide in 1997, worth over $1.25 billion. Utell represents properties in most of the world's major cities including Paris (273 properties), London (205 properties), New York (82 properties), San Francisco (48 properties), and Miami (46 properties). Utell also has working relationships with over 150,000 travel agencies. Although the full complement of hotels it serves includes economy and mid-priced properties, Utell also represents 1500 luxury

(five-star) hotels. In addition to representing independent and brand name hotels worldwide, Utell markets four of its own brands, principally outside the United States.

Anasazi, the other component of REZolutions, has several specialties, all of them derived in one way or another from the company's unchallenged strength in technology. The first set of services revolves around its central reservation system, RezView, which it licenses to lodging companies. RezView users, including Utell clients, account for one-third of the world's hotel rooms.

Growing out of its reservations expertise, Anasazi through its ATRI division also establishes and operates "private label" central reservation systems and call centers for individual properties and about 40 chains, including Loews Hotels, Fairmont Hotels, Forte Hotels, and Shangri-la Hotels and Resorts.

Finally, because reservation systems are more and more frequently integrated into property management systems, Anasizi has developed a PMS that fully integrates both voice and GDS reservations, yield management, guest recognition, and group sales office systems.

Source: Lodging, November 1997, pp. 80–84. We would also like to acknowledge the assistance of Ms. Kristi Warren of Utell International in the preparation of this note.

however, they are only one kind of channel member, albeit a very important one. Figure 12.6 identifies a number of the main channel members and the arrows in the figure indicate how these members can interact with one another in the global distribution system (GDS). At the top of the figure are the three major sources of reservations: travel agents, business travel offices, and individual travelers. As the

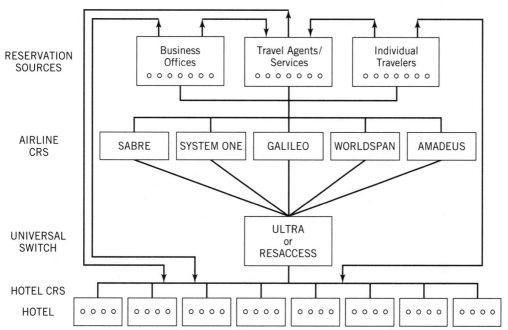

Figure 12.6   The global distribution system.
(*Source:* Chervenak, Keane and Company.)

diagram indicates, individuals and business travel offices may choose to make their arrangements through travel agents or they may call a hotel CRS directly through an 800 number. Another option, however, is for the individual to contact the property directly. This, in the past, has involved either delay through the mail or the expense of a long-distance call. Today, however, both may use the **Internet** to contact the hotel or CRS directly—and that communication is virtually instantaneous. Booking on the Internet is still in its infancy but it is interesting to note that Best Western says its 1997 Internet bookings were $4 million, up a remarkable 400 percent from the previous year.[25] A recent study, discussed in Industry Practice Note 12.2 (page 368), suggests that all forms of travel will experience major growth in Internet bookings.

Returning to Figure 12.6, another group of channel members identified there is the airline CRS. When making travel arrangements for a passenger, airlines can offer to place their room reservation for them, as well. The large car rental companies and virtually all travel agents are also interfaced to one or more of the airline CRSs. A moment's reflection suggests how many "virtual front desks" have been added to the hotel industry, not only through airline reservation systems but through all the other agencies interfaced to the airline systems. Unfortunately, however, none of them offers this service to the hotel free. Commissions are required for hotel reservations made through airline and other travel companies in very much the same way that they are for travel agents.

Franchising Worldwide

Global Hospitality Note 12.1

Mapping the state of hotel franchising worldwide is a tale of two very different models. One is rooted in North America, where most of the world's hotel franchising takes place. In the U.S., particularly, all the desirable elements for brand growth have flourished for generations. "The U.S. has one culture, one currency, no borders and everyone travels freely" commented the head of Cendant's Global Services Division. . . . Hotel franchising outside of North America requires much more of an entrepreneurial mindset. . . . The Head of Choice International commented, "Internationally, you need to have the local expertise on the ground to actually understand the nature of the [local] hotel business, ..."[1]

A number of problems confront international franchisors that they would not encounter in the United States. Many countries lack the infrastructure of roads, air terminals, and adequate air traffic control systems. What roads there are are often smaller and frequently poorly maintained. Countries' economies are often more centralized and people are less likely to drive between distant centers. Because automobile travel is not as well established in many countries, there are many fewer opportunities to develop roadside motor hotels, which have been the basic building block of franchise systems in the United States.

In the United States, locations around interstate highways are quickly bought up by developers but in many countries obtaining good locations is extremely difficult because of a morass of government regulation. Downtown locations, which are usually preferred, are often relatively more costly than hotel locations in the United States.

Hotel chains seeking to expand into a country very often pick a central point such as Buenos Aires

in Argentina as a "gateway" city. To establish their presence in the country, they begin by building a company-operated hotel, which permits them to maintain control of the operation and ensure a good reputation. It also gives the company a chance to set in place regulations to protect its trademarks. In making such investments, however, companies are subject to political, economic, and currency risks that would not be present in such an investment in North America.

LATIN AMERICA

Latin America has the advantage of a continental culture and one predominant language, Spanish. The second major tongue, Portuguese, however, is native to the largest country in the hemisphere, Brazil. Although political stability seems increasingly well established in Latin America, the region is still plagued by economic and currency instability, as evidenced recently by severe inflation in Brazil. A spokesman for Choice International (**http://www.hotelchoice.com/**) commented that the existing hotel properties are not of the kind that would draw significant tourism from Europe and so properties must be "tailored for the local market."

Cendant is making a master franchise for Argentina the focus of initial development in Latin America, with a 600-room Howard Johnson property slated for Buenos Aires. According to a Cendant spokesman, the company is following this model and is in negotiations for master franchises in 10 countries, most of which are developing countries. (A master franchise gives development rights for a large area, often a whole country, to one company.)

EUROPE

Europe offers greater political and economic stability than much of the rest of the world and, with free trade across its borders, the prospect for growth. On the other hand, economic growth rates have been slowed by government regulation and high taxes. Because of heavy taxes on wages, it is an expensive market in which to conduct business. The coming of a single currency is generally regarded as likely to have a favorable impact on currency risk.

The major franchising companies are taking quite different approaches to development in Europe. Cendant is negotiating national franchises in several countries. Choice, on the other hand, has a single master licensee, Friendly Hotels of London, in which Choice has purchased a controlling interest. Holiday Hospitality is limiting franchising and instead working to develop properties and then negotiate a management contract for the property. Radisson has relied on a combination of franchising and partnerships such as that which it has developed with Radisson SAS.

Franchising thrives in times when the hotel business is slow and when owners feel the need of a brand to stimulate reservations. Although the European hotel industry is presently prospering, only 30 percent of its hotels have a brand affiliation. Europe is a mature market in which there is no lack of facilities so "new builds" is not likely to be the source of great franchise growth. The low affiliation rate, however, suggests it could be a rich market for conversions in the next downturn.

ASIA

Asia has suffered from economic turmoil resulting from currency crises in several countries followed by severe declines in several national stock markets.

The price for hotel properties, however, remains inflated in spite of these declines and so, although acquisitions are likely to be attractive at some point in the future, there has been limited activity to date. Most franchisors are taking a long view. Holiday Hospitality's spokesman said, "Eventually you'll start to see some weakening of hotel [resale] prices which will give us the opportunity to accelerate in Asia." Choice's international vice president suggests that today's developers in Asia are more pragmatic and are likely to build hotels for the continent's emerging middle class when growth does resume.

Cendant's Days Inns, undiscouraged by recent developments, announced the opening of 10 franchised Day's Inns in China, a country as yet untouched by currency turmoil.

THE MIDDLE EAST AND AFRICA

Cendant is active in franchising in Israel where there are seven Days Inns and eight Howard Johnsons and has plans to expand into Egypt and Morocco. The first Days Inn in South Africa is under construction. Holdiay Hospitality's licensee in South Africa, Southern Sun, is reportedly expanding its development plans.

Nevertheless, the Middle East and Africa frequently experience what *Hotels* calls "geo-political stress, flashing caution signs to prospective franchisors."[2] An ITT Sheraton (**http://www.sheraton.com/**) executive indicated his company ranked the Middle East behind all other regions because potential franchisees lack capital of their own and have less access to capital markets.

1. Tony Dela Cruz, "Speed to Market," *Hotels,* February 1998, pp. 38–48.
2. Ibid.

Source: Adapted in part from *Hotels,* February 1998.

The growth in channels of distribution has the favorable effect for hotels of increasing distribution—the number of places their product is sold. Channels, however, ususally add marketing costs for the hotel and add, as well, another dimension to competition, putting added pressure on hotel prices. It is reasonable to assume that the growth in the power of channel members in lodging sales will reduce properties' control over pricing. One factor that makes the Internet appear so very

Travel Bookings on the Internet to Skyrocket

Travel products booked over the Internet will grow enormously between 1998 and 2001 as competition in the market heats up and millions of consumers learn how to book travel on line, according to a major study of travel technology commissioned by the Travel Industry of America (**http://www.tia.org**). Travel revenues from Internet bookings, including air travel, hotel rooms, car rentals, packaged vacations, and other travel products, totaled $276 million in 1996. In 1997, the number will skyrocket to $827 million, a 200 percent increase. The AAA (**http://www.aaa.com/**) web site offers on-line reservation booking.[1] By the year 2000, the size of the on-line travel industry will be over $4.7 billion and will reach $8.9 billion in the year 2002.

Some of the factors that account for the phenomenal growth in the use of the Internet in travel are:
1. More households will be coming on line.
2. Security for credit card transactions over the Internet will be improving.
3. Travelers will be using new electronic payment media such as smart cards.
4. Increasing competition among on-line travel sites will increase awareness and draw more consumers to the market.

1. Graeme R. Clarke, Address to the 1997 Travel Outlook Forum, October 6, 1997. Mr. Clarke is senior vice president of the AAA.

Source: Travel Industry of America, October 1997, except as noted.

attractive to hotel operators is that it offers the chance to minimize the payment of fees to travel intermediaries. The Internet is being used by hotels and customers for much more than individual travel. Sales and catering software vendors "are working on Internet integration because access will boost hospitality productivity and reduce costs,"[26] by giving a much broader access to potential customers for banquet department products. Holiday Hospitality has established a web site to help professional meeting planners find one or more properties that can fill their particular group and meeting needs. The web site includes a form the meeting planner can fill out to send a request for proposal (RFP) to potential meeting sites—via the Internet.[27] For the present, however, the Internet accounts for only a small though rapidly growing percentage of reservations.

*P*ROMOTION: MARKETING COMMUNICATION

Marketing communication is *persuasive* communication. It uses the tools of mass communication and individualized communication to encourage patronage of a hotel or a group of hotels such as a chain or franchise group. Until quite recently, individualized communication for hotels largely meant personal selling. Although personal selling is still a vital tool of hotel marketers, an increasingly important role is played by individualized communication based on information about customers (and people similar to them) captured in the databases of guest history systems and transaction records we will discuss in a moment.

Mass Communication

Advertising, sales promotion, and public relations are the principal mass-medium selling tools.

Advertising.   **Advertising** is paid communication. It uses print media (a favorite among hotels) such as newspapers and magazines, electronic media such as television and radio, and outdoor media such as billboards. Another mass medium is direct mail, but the possibilities for individualizing direct-mail offers have been multiplied so greatly by the databases mentioned earlier that we need to qualify its classification as a mass medium.

Advertising is carried out by the individual property—usually aimed at the local community but sometimes at potential guests in cities that serve as a major point of origin for visitors.

Brand Advertising.   Brand advertising is carried out by chains and franchise and membership organizations. Several of the largest advertisers in the hotel industry in 1996 are identified in Table 12.3. In addition to the companies listed there, we should also consider Marriott International and Cendant Corp. Marriott International spent over $44 million on advertising in 1996, but, in that year, nearly 50 percent of the company's sales came from its contract food service unit and so the entire amount cannot be treated as hotel advertising. Cendant (which was then called HFS) spent over $100 million on advertising, but it is in several other franchising businesses and it is impossible to determine from public records what part of its expenditure was for its eight hotel brands. The dollar amounts, in any case, are intended principally to make the point of how much companies spend nationally to keep their brand in the public eye. A brand is one of the principal valuables, along with a reservation service, that the franchising company brings to the individual franchisee or member.

Table 12.3   Lodging's Five Largest Advertisers, 1996 ($ millions)

Hilton Hotels	$27.3
Holiday Hospitality	24.8
ITT Sheraton	17.7
Hyatt	12.3
Best Western	11.4

Source: "Leading National Advertisers" (Competitive Media Reporting, 1997).

Advertising on the Internet.   In a study conducted by PKF Consulting, 70 percent of the hotels contacted had a presence on the World Wide Web (WWW) in the form of a web page. The most common features of web pages are photographs and information on the surrounding area. Over half said their web pages allow guests to make reservations.[28]

At Marriott's web site (**http://www.marriott.com**),

> Visiting customers can use a mapping system to locate any Marriott, Courtyard, Residence Inn, or Fairfield Inn in the U.S. Once the location is mapped, the visitor may zoom in or out for desired detail. Also, at the click of a button, the system can calculate estimated driving times and road by road directions to and from any location, including any of the 16 million businesses and attractions found in the data base.[29]

Boston's Convention and Visitors Bureau has a site (**http://www.meeting path.com**), where Boston-area hotels can post short-term guest room availability. New England hotels that participate in the site can display up to 29 pages of detailed text and graphics to describe their properties.[30]

The perception of some is that people who use the Web are mostly computer-literate youngsters. A survey of Internet shopping by the National Retail Federation's magazine, *Stores,* however, reaches a different conclusion. The survey found that 64 percent of Internet shoppers were "between 40 and 64 years old, well educated and have money to spend."[31] That sounds like a good target market for hotels.

Sales Promotion

Sales promotion is "a marketing communication activity which offers an incentive to immediate action."[32] Sales promotions, at the property level, are often special events or individualized rewards for frequent guests such as a "salesman's club."

At the chain level, special contests and games are used to increase call volume to reservation centers. Not surprisingly, although these were common during the industry's slower years—and reportedly very successful in achieving their goals— they are less commonly seen in the late 1990s when business is good.

One of the most common forms of sales promotion has as its target customers that are already patronizing the system's hotels. These are the frequent-traveler programs.

Partnerships and Reward Programs.   Frequent-guest clubs offer regular guests a reward for brand loyalty. According to *Lodging,* "Frequent stay programs are probably a hotel chain's biggest marketing expense. Yet they instill loyalty that helps drive business, and they also provide opportunities to collect more and better information about customers."[33]

The first hotel frequent-guest program was introduced in 1983 by Holiday Inns, followed quickly by Marriott. Early in the process, hotels learned that many guests

Brand	Program	Enrolled	Airline Partners	Reward Medium
Hilton	Honors	5 million	13	Points and miles
Holiday Inn	Priority Club; Crown Plaza Preferred	5 million	36	Points or miles
Hyatt	Gold Passport	3 million	11	Points or miles
Loews	Loews First	n.a.	3	Frequent-flyer miles
Marriott	Honored Guest; Marriott Miles	7.2 million	7; 11	Points; frequent-flyer miles
Radisson	Airline Partner Program	n.a.	17	Frequent-flyer miles
Ritz Carlton	None	n.a.		
Sheraton	Sheraton Club International	1.2 million	17	Transferable club miles
Super 8	V.I.P.	4.2 million	None	$3.50
Westin	Westin Premier	1 million	10	Points or miles

Figure 12.7 Hotel frequent-travel programs.
(*Source:* Adapted from *Lodging,* February 1997.)

preferred air miles to "hotel miles," which were exchangeable only for free hotel stays. As a result, hotels formed **partnerships** with airlines. Hotels purchased frequent-flyer miles at wholesale rates and offered their guests a choice between points good for hotel stays *or* airline miles. As airline partners, the hotels also receive favorable coverage in airline frequent-flyer publications. The partnership makes especially good sense for hotels because the largest hotel programs have between 5 and 7 million members while major airlines have more than 20 million members. As Figure 12.7 shows, most hotel programs offer either miles or "points." Points can either be converted into air miles or be used to purchase merchandise—or used for hotel stays. The merchandise programs were begun when hotels discovered that the *most frequent* travelers had more frequent-flyer miles than they could use and were interested in some other form of reward.[34]

Two "special cases" in Figure 12.7 deserve discussion. Note that the Ritz Carlton chain has no frequent-guest program. It found that its guests were not interested in the kinds of rewards offered by the typical frequent-guest programs and preferred instead personal attention. As a result, the chain launched a guest *recognition* program. Super 8, on the other hand, has no partnership with an airline because its guests arrive predominantly by car. Instead, Super 8 offers a discount either on the hotel rate or on car rentals. These are best suited to its guests' needs.[35]

Frequency Marketing and Databases. Frequent-traveler programs do more than reinforce customer loyalty. They provide a wealth of detailed information on customers. From membership information, hotels can learn about the demographics of their customer base, as well as where they come from. From transaction records, it is possible to build up a record of individual spending patterns and preferences. These databases permit hotels to learn who their *best* customers are. They also make it possible to custom design offers to guests, which can be delivered by direct mail or phone. Does a guest come most frequently in the fall? Perhaps he or she would like to see the area in the spring. Does the guest come regularly—and perhaps has not visited the property for some time? Is something wrong? What needs to be done to remedy the problem?

Moreover, once a profile of the hotel's best customers has been developed, it is possible to purchase other databases on people who have a similar profile:

> Many hotel companies overlay an on-line data base with information from credit card companies or transportation companies. Secondary overlays are available from geodemographic and psychographic information firms. In combination, the data from these external sources provide invaluable enhancement to a hotel's in-house records.[36]

$\mathcal{M}$ARKETING AND COMPETITION

Competition should be proactive, not reactive. In each element of the marketing mix, there is a tool for reaching and attracting guests. With the development of databased marketing, moreover, the appeal can be more carefully crafted to motivate our guests and people like them, and even to reach them individually with the appeal best suited to them.

$\mathcal{S}$UMMARY

The conditions of competition in the hotel business have five characteristics: a fragmented market, resulting in unpredictability and higher risk; a cyclical market, which makes for periodic overcapacity; a low variable cost, which makes discounting look easy; a recent inflow of investment capital, which has helped the industry to expand capacity; and a technological revolution, which has altered the way in which hotel rooms are offered for sale.

Our discussion of competitive practices was structured by the model of the marketing mix. Product is ultimately the guest's experience. Ways of improving that experience discussed include food service, other services and amenities, and system-wide services. Limited-service properties do not offer restaurant service to their "upstairs" guests but food service continues to be a major competitive tool in reaching the "downstairs" guests in full-service hotels. Food service is difficult to manage and some properties have leased their food service operations. This "solution" has built-in problems of giving up control of the "service department" of the hotel. Other hotels use franchised restaurants to gain a successful food service format, field supervision, and the power of an additional brand. Still others have sought to limit the problems and skills required by food service by simplifying their food service operations. The problem with most services and amenities is that many are easily copied and so do not offer differentiation. System-wide services provided by franchisors include quality assurance for the entire system, an international reservation service, and the establishment and maintenance of a brand name and image.

The low variable cost and consequent wide margin in room sales offers many opportunities for special rates. These are extended to volume customers, and during slow periods, to specially targeted customers such as sports teams. Rates can also vary according to demand as yield management dictates. The practice of yield management runs the risk of offending customers who are charged different rates for the same product at different times. Good practice in yield management dictates full disclosure of pricing to customers and restrictions on rooms sold at lower rates such as advance purchase or minimum stay.

Place refers not only to the property's location but to the channels of distribution. Travel intermediaries such as travel agents and the GDS are playing an increasing role in hotel sales. The Internet is expected to become a real force in the sale of hotel products in the near future.

Promotion or marketing communication uses mass advertising in the electronic and print media. Brand advertising in large chains involves very large expenditures to establish and maintain a brand name and image. The Internet is becoming increasingly prominent in advertising and interactive web sites make the Internet an additional channel of distribution. Although such mass promotion remains important, hotels are moving toward tighter targeting in their marketing, based on databases made up of information on customers and their transactions.

◆ 𝒦EY WORDS AND CONCEPTS

Conditions of competition
    Fragmented
    Cyclical industry
    Low variable cost
    Securitization
    Impact of technology
Marketing mix
Product as guest's experience
Upstairs guests
Downstairs market
Food service
Leased restaurants
Sous vide
On-site franchised restaurant
Differentiation

Concierge
Fitness facilities
Business center
Quality assurance
Variable cost
Fixed costs
Yield management
Location
Channels of distribution
Internet
Marketing communication
Advertising
Sales promotion
Partnerships
Frequency marketing

◆ *R*EVIEW QUESTIONS

1. What are the conditions of competition in the hotel business? What is their impact?

2. What is the difference between the upstairs and the downstairs market? How does this affect hotel marketing?

3. What is the role of food service in lodging? Be specific as to its impact on each lodging industry segment.

4. What means of differentiation other than food service were discussed in the text? What is your assessment of the effectiveness of each?

5. What is meant by low variable cost in the lodging industry? What is its effect on competition?

6. Discuss the pros and cons of yield management.

7. What is meant by channels of distribution? What are the established channels for hotels? What are the new channels? What is the outlook for travel intermediaries in lodging?

8. What is the effect of frequency marketing on advertising and promotion in lodging?

9. What is the impact of partnerships on hotel marketing?

◆ *I*INTERNET EXERCISE

1. **Site Name:** *Choice Hotels*
   URL: http://www.hotelchoice.com/
   Background Information: With more than 4000 hotels open and under development in more than 33 countries, Choice Hotels International is one of the world's leading hotel franchise company.

   Site Name: *Ramada Inn*
   URL: http://www.ramada.com/
   Background Information: Ramada has over 950 hotels and competes with Choice Hotels in many markets.

   EXERCISES:

   a. Review both of the preceding sites. How do Ramada and Choice Hotels position themselves to compete with one another?

   b. Surf both sites and determine what franchise information is provided by each company. Which company provides the most extensive information?

◆ *N*OTES

1. In Chapter 9, we spoke of "conversions" of properties from one segment (i.e., Midscale) to another (i.e., economy). In this quote, the STR spokesman is discussing conversions from one brand to another. *Lodging Outlook,* June 1997, n.p.

2. M. Chase Burritt, "Lodging Forecast," *Real Estate Newsline,* E & Y Kenneth Leventhal, Winter 1998, p. 14.

3. Ibid., p. 14. Emphasis added.

4. The discussion here focuses on rooms department performance. The food and beverage (F&B) department, where one is present, has a somewhat lower fixed cost and a higher variable cost but the argument that it, too, is a high-fixed-cost business was made in an earlier chapter. In a hotel, F&B is basically a service department. Although no longer as commonly run on a break-even basis, according the PKF Consulting, "Today's food and beverage operations are designed to meet the needs of the guest, and/or work as an attraction to enhance the overall image of the property" (*Trends in the Hotel Industry—1997,* p. 69).

5. There are a number of other ways of viewing the marketing mix. See, for instance, Leo Renaghan, "A New Marketing Mix for the Hospitality Industry," *Cornell Hotel and Restaurant Administration Quarterly,* August 1981, pp. 32–33. The present view is adopted less as an analytical device than as a means of exposition.

6. The upstairs–downstairs guest dichotomy originated, we believe, with the Marriott organization.

7. *Trends in the Hotel Industry—1997* (San Francisco: PKF Consulting), p. 69.

8. Judy Liberson, "Strategic Alliances Create Profitable Blend," *Lodging,* January 1997, p. 63.

9. *Nations Restaurant News,* February 18, 1991, p. 42. Field research both before and after this date support the stated conclusion.

10. *Hotel and Motel Management,* September 7, 1992, p. 1. This practice continued to be the policy and practice of Courtyard as of May 1998, according to Marian Carruthers, a spokesperson for the company.

11. Liberson, "Strategic Alliances Create Profitable Blend," p. 63.

12. Jeff Weinstein, "Don't Turn F&B Space into Guestrooms Just Yet," *Hotels,* May 1997, p. 17.

13. Bjorn Hansen, "Hotel Food Service: Where's the Profit?" *Cornell Hotel and Restaurant Administration Quarterly,* August 1984, p. 96. Although the article is somewhat dated, this statement continues to accurately describe the operating results of the vast majority of hotel restaurants.

14. Fact Sheet, Radisson Hotels Worldwide "Business Class," February 1998.

15. n.a., " 'Great Escapes' Marketing Becomes the Industry Norm," *Hotels,* August 1997, p. 68.

16. *Lodging,* April 1994, pp. 43–47 and 92–93.

17. David C. Sullivan, Executive Vice President, Promus, Remarks during a panel discussion, "Suite Hotels and Limited Service Hotels," Hospitality Industry Investment Conference, New York, June 7, 1994.

18. Stephen Rushmore and Carolyn A. Malone, *Hotel Franchise Fees Analysis Guide—1997* (Mineola, NY: HVS International, 1997), p. 10. Mr. Rushmore is founder and president of HVS International, an international hotel consulting service working in a broad area of disciplines related to hotel evaluation and management. The company is the primary source of information on the sale of hotel properties in North America.

19. Sheryl E. Kimes, "Perceived Fairness of Yield Management," *Cornell Hotel and Restaurant Administration Quarterly,* February 1994, pp. 22–29.

20. Richard S. Teitelbaum, "Sleep Like a Prince, Pay Like a Pauper," *Fortune,* February 19, 1996, pp. 114–115.

21. I would especially like to acknowledge my indebtedness to Mr. Randall A. Smith, founder and president of Smith Travel Research, for providing this figure for this text.

22. Kimes, "Perceived Fairness of Yield Management," pp. 28–29. In mid-1998, special rates for advance purchase reservations were still available from Marriott on a property-by-property basis.

23. *Lodging Outlook,* November 1997, chart 2.

24. Philip Hayward, "A Conversation with Henry Silverman of HFS," *Lodging,* May 1997, pp. 46–50.

25. *Hotel and Motel Management,* October 20, 1997, p. 25.

26. Susan Bard Hall, "Sales and Catering Software Hooks into Internet," *Hotel and Motel Management,* March 2, 1998, p. 53.

27. *Hotel and Motel Management,* October 6, 1997, p. 49.

28. Patrick Quek, " 'Net' Gains," *Lodging,* March 1998, p. 19.

29. Mike Pusateri and Jeff Manno, "Growing with the Web," *Lodging,* January 1997, p. 71.

30. Ruth A. Hill, "Electronic Partners," *Lodging,* February 1998, p. 73.

31. *Business Upshot* (Ernst and Young LLP, March 1998), p. 7.

32. Robert H. Marriott, "Promotions—A Key Piece in Your Marketing Puzzle," *Proceedings of the Chain Operators Exchange* (Chicago: International Foodservice Manufacturing Association, 1987.

33. Kathleen Cassidy, "Miles, Miles and More Miles," *Lodging,* February 1997, pp. 48–52.

34. Ibid.

35. Ibid.

36. Paula A. Francese and Leo M. Renaghan, "Data-Base Marketing: Building Customer Profiles," *Cornell Hotel and Restaurant Administration Quarterly,* May 1990, p. 62.

Part 4

Travel, Tourism, and the Hospitality Industry

*C*hapter *13*

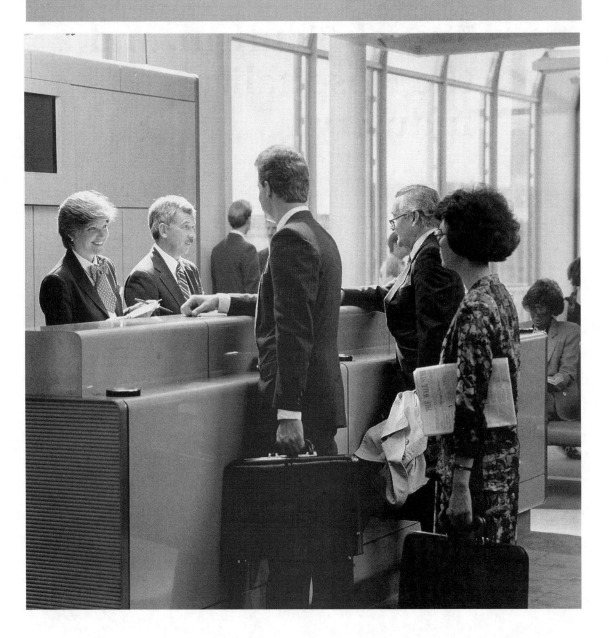

Tourism: Front and Center

The Purpose of This Chapter

Travel and tourism at the local, state, and even national levels are vital to the health of our economy, as well as to the hospitality industry. Indeed, tourism is big business and growing rapidly in North America and worldwide. The economic and social impacts of tourism are significant and this chapter discusses both of these dimensions.

This Chapter Should Help You

1. See the importance of tourism in local and national economies

2. Understand the factors that are supporting the growth of travel and tourism

3. Become familiar with current travel trends

4. Know the significance of the travel multiplier in assessing the economic significance of tourism

5. Recognize the importance of tourism in providing employment

6. Recognize the significance of tourism as a part of international trade and as a source of strength in the U.S. balance of payments

7. Become aware of the other major businesses that service travelers and the trends that are changing their business

8. Assess the noneconomic positive and negative impacts of tourism

𝒯HE IMPORTANCE OF TOURISM

Tourism's importance to the hospitality industry is obvious. Some parts of the industry, such as hotels, derive almost all of their sales from travelers. Even food service attributes roughly 25 percent of its sales to travelers. Moreover, many leisure-oriented businesses with a major food service and hospitality component, such as theme parks, are also dependent on travelers.

In the economy as a whole, the importance of tourism and the hospitality industry is increasing each year. As employment in "smokestack" industries—that is, manufacturing—falls, the service industries, including those businesses serving travelers, must take up the slack by providing new jobs. Tourism, then, is central not only to the health of the hospitality industry but also to the economy as a whole.

Tourism is the collection of productive businesses and governmental organiza-

Tourism is made up of highly varied businesses.
Courtesy of Vermont Travel Division

tions that serve the traveler away from home. According to the U.S. Travel Data Center, these organizations include restaurants, hotels, motels, and resorts; all facets of transportation, including rental cars, travel agents, and gasoline service stations; national and state parks or recreation areas; and various private attractions. The industry also includes those organizations that support these firms' retail activities, including advertising companies, publications, transportation equipment manufacturers, and travel research and development agencies.

Travel trends are significant to students of hospitality because they represent the way in which many of our guests arrive. This is where much of our business comes from. Beyond that, transportation companies—air, rail, and bus—are industries allied with the hospitality industry in tourism.

*F*ACTORS AFFECTING TRAVEL AND TOURISM

Travel and tourism are as American as baseball, hot dogs, apple pie, and the interstate highway system. Figure 13.1 illustrates the growth in total travel from 1986 to 1996 to a level of over 1.1 billion person trips. (A person trip is defined as one person taking one trip. If two persons go on that trip, that equals two person trips. A trip is any travel 100 miles or more away from home.) Although that is an increase of nearly 20 percent since 1991, the numer of trips did decrease about 1 percent from 1995.[1] The main component of travel is travel by auto and truck, which rebounded to a 4 percent gain in 1997.[2] Moreover, tourism growth continues to be fueled by more leisure time, rising family incomes, and the favorable demographic trends we have discussed in earlier chapters. We will look briefly at each of these factors.

Figure 13.1 U.S. resident travel volume, 1986–1996.
(*Source: Proceedings of the Travel Industry Association of America's 23rd Annual Marketing Outlook Forum*, 1998.)

Growing Leisure

There are several reasons for the increase in leisure time. People have more time off from work. Most companies' vacation policies have become more liberal. Moreover, the number of legal, paid holidays has increased and, significantly for tourism, more of these are timed so as to provide three-day weekends. Although the typical work week has stayed at 40 hours for many years, flexible scheduling arrangements have also added to people's leisure time.

Income Trends

The two-income family has become a major factor in travel. The majority of women today expect to work outside the home. A two-income family not only increases total family income but adds to the family's security. If one spouse loses a job, that does not eliminate all of the family's income.

Commonly, women leave the workforce for a period of time at the birth of a child, and many women return to work only on a part-time basis while young children are still at home. For those committed to a career outside the home, however, the ultimate intention is to return to full-time work. A further element of stability to family incomes today is the fact that if a husband loses his job or otherwise suffers an economic reversal, young mothers can and will expand their working commitment outside the home earlier than they may have originally intended.

There are many motives for women to work outside the home after marriage. Two common ones are career and necessity. Many women choose to be in the workforce for professional and career reasons and for the challenge, stimulation, and variety that working provides. Another reason, for many women, however, is to maintain the family income at a level that affords the family a comfortable and satisfying lifestyle. Income growth after inflation in most occupations has been slow in recent years, and, in some cases, family members have shifted from highly paid manufacturing work to less well-paid occupations, often in the service sector. Thus, some women work at least in part because they have to maintain their family income.

Two-income families, then, are not all well-to-do "yuppies" (young urban professionals). Many families pool two modest incomes to support a comfortable lifestyle. Because they are working to maintain a comfortable life, it is not surprising that they are disposed to spend their money on the goods and services they want. They are good customers—and even in bad times, they can usually maintain at least one income, making the stability of family spending in bad times greater today than it was a generation ago.

Almost all two-income families have time pressures. When both parents work, the household chores still need to be done and children must be cared for. This means that many people may have to sacrifice leisure time for household and family maintenance chores. Therefore, when they do get away, time is at a premium, and they seek "quality time." Though sensitive to price/value comparisons,

Two-income families and senior citizens are two growing demographic markets in travel and tourism.
Courtesy of Vermont Travel Division; courtesy of Carnival Cruise Lines

these travelers generally seek good value for their money rather than low-cost recreational experiences.

Demographics

Our earlier discussion of the "middle-aging of America" in Chapter 2 suggested the impact of demographic changes on tourism. Middle age generally means higher income and a greater propensity to travel. The age group that travels most, whether for business or pleasure, are those aged 35 to 44. This age group is most likely to use hotels and to take longer trips (1000 miles and over). Close behind them are the 45- to 54-year-olds.

Another significant demographic development for tourism is the growth in the mature market, that is, people over 55. The mature market will increase nearly 36 percent between 1995 and 2010. Growth in that population segment from 2000 to 2010 will be 27 percent.[3] Although this group represents a smaller share of household *income,* people 55 and over control over half of household *wealth.* In effect, their mortgages are paid and a large proportion of them have a nest egg of savings and retirement benefits on which to draw. This makes them good tourism customers.

The *pattern* of growth in the mature market suggests two subsegments that will be especially important.[4] The 55- to 65-year-old group, which will grow by a remarkable two-thirds from 1995 to 2010, as the first baby boomers move into their mature years, will be a very active group of consumers seeking new experiences and learning to deal with extended leisure, that is, the ability to take longer vacations as seniority increases vacation entitlements and as retirement approaches or as early retirement permits.

The other growth segment is at the other extreme of the mature market, that is, people over 85.[5] This segment will increase by over one-third (36.6 percent) from 1995 to 2010. The needs of people in this age group do suggest a major expansion in assisted-living facilities, but they also suggest opportunities for family travel that involve grandparents and grandchildren or all three generations, called "Grand Touring" by Lago and Poffley. Thus, this relatively small (5.67 million persons in 2010) but rapidly growing segment may give a further boost to the family travel market.

Moreover, a significant portion of those over 85 are still able to be quite active, and

> a sense of personal control is influential both in maintaining health status and in accomplishing goals. . . . Particularly as health impairment places severe constraints on functional independence, service packages and facilities that compensate for losses, but allow a person to retain a sense of control will be very desirable.[6]

TRAVEL TRENDS[7]

The most frequent reason for travel is to visit family and friends. Other pleasure travel, for outdoor recreation and entertainment, is just behind that. All **pleasure travel** accounted for 70 percent of 1.16 billion person trips taken in 1995.[8] Business and convention travel accounted for another 24 percent. As Figure 13.2 indicates, travel sales vary with the economy but have grown somewhat more rapidly than the economy in the mid-1990s. In Chapter 9, Figure 9.3 showed that, after solid growth in the 1980s, **business travel** exhibited no clear trend, rising and falling from year to year. The discussion in Chapter 9 makes clear that there are a number of reasons that business travel may not prove a consistent growth factor over the next few years. Travel growth, then, is likely to come from pleasure travel, which *has* grown at a modest but steady rate each year.

Mode of Travel

After automobiles, airlines are the second most common means of transportation and, as Table 13.1 shows, far and away the dominant common carrier. Although travel by private vehicle is still the dominant form of travel for Americans, it is interesting to note that air travel has shown steady growth throughout the 1990s, growing 25 percent during that time. Bus travel has grown 30 percent in the same period but still accounts for well under 2 percent of total travel. The increases in air and bus travel have increased those common carriers' share of the miles traveled by

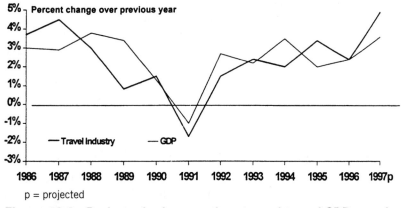

Figure 13.2 Real travel sales growth compared to real GDP growth, 1986–1997.
(*Source: Proceedings of the Travel Industry Association of America's 23rd Annual Marketing Outlook Forum*, 1998.)

nearly three percentage points as private vehicle travel share has declined by a like amount.

Trip Duration

As two working spouses in a family have become more common, vacations have become shorter. The typical vacation of the 1950s and 1960s was an annual event lasting 10 to 14 days. During the 1970s and 1980s, vacations, on average, were shortened to 5 to 7 days, and taken twice a year.[9] In the 1990s, the 2- to 3-day

Table 13.1   Intercity Transportation in the United States, 1990 and 1996

	1990		1996	
Mode of Transport	Billions of Passenger Miles	Percentage of Passenger Miles	Billions of Passenger Miles	Percentage of Passenger Miles
Common carriers				
Air	345.9	21.7	431.4	24.4
Bus	23.0	1.4	29.9	1.7
Rail	6.1	0.4	5.0	0.3
TOTAL	375.0	23.5	466.3	26.3
Auto, truck, and recreational vehicle	1217.7	76.5	1303.8	73.7
TOTAL, all modes	1592.7	100.0	1770.1	100.0

Source: Economic Review of Travel in America—1996, U.S. Travel Data Center.

"minivacation" has become increasingly popular. Although concentrated in the warmer months, this pattern offers people the chance for a break in fall and winter, too. The average length of stay for pleasure travelers using a hotel was 3.3 nights, while those who stayed with friends and relatives stayed 4.2 nights.[10]

The popularity of weekend vacations and shorter trips combining pleasure and business is more prevalent among younger travelers. Affluent travelers, with an average age of 50 or over, on the other hand, prefer vacations of a week or more.

THE ECONOMIC SIGNIFICANCE OF TOURISM

In total business receipts, tourism has consistently ranked second or third among all retail businesses. Only grocery stores—and in some years, automobile dealers—have greater sales. In 1996, the travel industry accounted for $452.5 billion in direct expenditures. Measuring the industry in terms of employment, as Figure 13.3 does, tourism provides more jobs than does any other industry except health care services. In 1996, tourism provided 6,750,000 people with employment and had a payroll of $121.6 million. Tourism also provided the various levels of government with tax receipts of over $67 billion.

Although tourism currently accounts for over $452 billion in receipts in the U.S. economy, that is only a superficial, first-order measurement of travel importance. A **travel multiplier** measures the effect of initial spending together with the chain of expenditures that result. (For example, when a traveler spends a dollar in a hotel, some portion of it goes to employees, suppliers, and owners, who, in turn, respend it—and so it goes.) Figure 13.4 illustrates how the multiplier works in practice. Although the precise computation of the travel multiplier need not concern us, the U.S. Travel Data Center estimates the final impact of the travel market for 1996 at just over $1 trillion dollars.

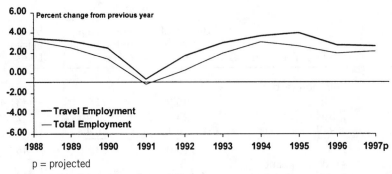

p = projected

Figure 13.3   Travel employment compared to total employment, 1988–1997.
(*Source: Proceedings of the Travel Industry Association of America's 23rd Annual Marketing Outlook Forum*, 1998.)

Tourist Spending for		Tourist Industry Expenses		Secondary Business Beneficiaries
Hotels	⇨	Wage, salaries, and tips	⇨	Employees
Restaurants		Payroll taxes		Government agencies
Entertainment and recreation		Food, beverages, and housekeep-		Food industry
Clothing		ing supplies		Beverage industry
Personal care		Construction and maintenance		Custodial industry
Retail		Advertising		Architectural firms
Gifts and crafts		Utilities		Construction firms
Transportation		Insurance		Repair firms
Tours		Interest and principal		Advertising firms
Museums and historical		Legal and accounting		News media
		Transportation		Water, gas, and electric
		Taxes and licenses		Telephone companies
		Equipment and furniture		Insurance industry
				Bank and investors
				Legal and accounting firms
				Air, bus, auto, and gas
				Taxi companies
				Government companies
				Wholesale suppliers
				Health care

Figure 13.4   The tourist dollar multiplier effect: tourist dollar flow into the economy.
(*Source:* Michael Evans, *Tourism: Always a People Business* (Knoxville: University of Tennessee, 1984).)

Tourism and Employment

Just over one in every twenty civilian employees is employed in an activity supported by travel expenditures, nearly seven million people. The travel industry contributes to job growth well in excess of its size. Employment in the last decade, as indicated in Figure 13.3, has consistently grown more rapidly than employment in the economy as a whole. Approximately one-quarter of food service employment can be traced to tourism and a much larger proportion of hotel and motel employment serves travelers away from home.

Publicity as an Economic Benefit

Communities often spend large sums of money to advertise their virtues to visitors and investors. They establish economic development bureaus to bring employers to town and even offer tax incentives and low-cost financing. Aside from its direct economic impact, tourism also offers a chance to achieve many of these same benefits. That is, a tourist attraction brings visitors to a city or area, and they can then judge for themselves the community's suitability as a place to live and work. A major tourist event in a city or region attracts huge numbers of visitors, often for their first visit to the area. Assuming the region has natural charms and man-made attractions, some visitors are likely to become interested in relocating there—or at least in making a return visit.

The travel industry provides jobs for about 7 million people.
Courtesy of Delta Airlines

THE UNITED STATES AS AN INTERNATIONAL TOURIST ATTRACTION

Tourism is the world's largest industry, accounting for over one-tenth of worldwide economic activity.[11] In fact, according to the World Travel and Tourism Council (WTTC), tourism now accounts for 10.7 percent of the world's gross domestic product, 11.9 percent of global capital investment, and 11.3 percent of worldwide consumer spending. In 1996, there were 593 million tourists worldwide[12] and world tourism spending was $3.6 trillion. Figure 13.5 shows worldwide tourism arrivals and their growth over the last 30 years. By 2006, the WTTC estimates that spending will have reached $7.1 trillion and attracted capital spending of $1.6 trillion. Such numbers boggle the mind, perhaps, as much as they enlighten it, but they are cited to help us grasp an important fact: International tourism is, indeed, a huge set of businesses whose effects are worth taking the time to understand. Global Hospitality Note 13.1 discusses some of the forces driving the growth of the world's largest industry.

What Makes Tourism Run?

Global Hospitality Note 13.1

A changing socioeconomic landscape, technology, competition, and modern marketing are combining to provide the driving forces behind the phenomenal growth of tourism to become the world's number one industry. First, as to demand and technology:

> The growth of tourism is due both to social factors that boost demand and to technology that makes travel possible. Demand for tourism is determined by wealth. Growing wealth will continue to produce new tourists as vast numbers of people in developing countries join the middle classes. [Consider] India's growing middle class and China's one billion keen consumers. But Latin America and Eastern Europe are coming aboard, too. Tourism thrives wherever politics allows it, and politics has recently caused many barriers to fall. . . .

The technology that sustains mass tourism is the jet plane. Air travel has opened up the world. In 1970, when Pan Am flew the first Boeing 747 from New York to London, scheduled planes carried 307 million passengers. Twenty five years later, the figure had risen to 1.15 billion. Cheaper and more efficient transport has been behind the development of tourism from the beginning.[1]

Tourism is not, however, growing just on the strength of demand and the technology needed to service it. Competition and the marketing efforts of competitors actively stimulate that demand.

> Like all consumer products, tourist destinations must persuade their customers that they have some combination of benefits which no one else can offer. Destinations are trying every bit as hard as airlines and hotels to establish themselves as brands, using all the razzmatazz of modern marketing. Every place tries to make the most of what it's got.[2]

1. "A Survey of Travel and Tourism," *The Economist*, January 10, 1998, p. 4.
2. Ibid., p. 10.

Figure 13.5   World tourism.
(*Source:* World Tourism Organization, U.S. International Trade Administration, 1997, e = estimate.)

Measuring the Volume

There are two different ways to measure the volume of international tourism. **Arrivals and departures** measure the volume of people traveling; **receipts and payments** measure money spent. Dollar figures have the disadvantage of being distorted by fluctuating currency values, but, to measure the *economic impact*, currency measures must be used. The best measure of *activity*, on the other hand, is the physical measure, arrivals and departures.

Arrivals and Departures in the United States. In the 1990s, total arrivals in the United States rose from just over 44 million in 1990 to 56 million in 1998, an increase of 26 percent. As shown in Figure 13.6, U.S. departures over the same period also increased, by 30 percent. Just over half of the total foreign arrivals are from Canada and Mexico. A large portion of these are very short stays, many less than a day. To focus on the richer long-stay market, Figure 13.7 shows the increase in travel by visitors from overseas to the United States. The number of overseas visitors has more than doubled since 1988.

The Travel Trade Balance. From the end of World War II until the mid-1980s, there was considerable concern about what was then called the "travel gap," the much larger number of persons—and travel dollars—leaving the United States than arriving here from foreign destinations. Even as recently as 1985, the number of Americans traveling outside the country were nearly nine and a half million more than the number of foreign visitors, and there was an unfavorable dollar **travel trade balance** of nearly $9 billion. The dollar balance of travel trade turned in favor of the United States by 1989. A travel gap represented a brake on economic growth in the United States. Today's favorable travel trade balance of nearly $29 billion, highlighted in Figure 13.8, is a stimulus to the economy. The U.S. Travel Data Center estimated that nearly a million jobs were generated by international tourism in the United States in 1996.[13]

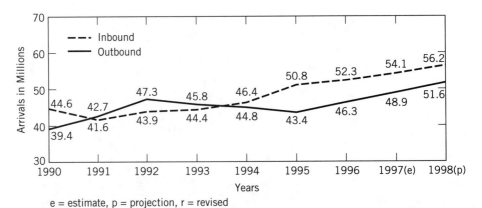

e = estimate, p = projection, r = revised

Figure 13.6 International arrivals to the United States versus U.S. travelers outside the United States.
(*Source:* U.S. International Trade Administration, 1997.)

Figure 13.7   Overseas arrivals in the United States.
(*Source:* U.S. International Trade Administration, 1998.)

Reasons for Growth of the United States as a Destination

One of the principal reasons for growth in travel to the United States is the world's rising standard of living, particularly in Western Europe, Asia, and Latin America. Moreover, the political changes in Eastern Europe led to a large percentage growth

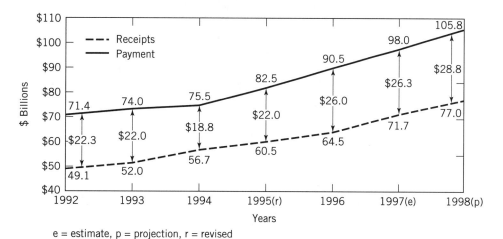

e = estimate, p = projection, r = revised

Figure 13.8   The travel trade surplus.
(*Source:* U.S. International Trade Administration, 1997.)

in travel, although from a very low starting point. Another factor appears to be increasing competition among international air carriers, which has held fares down. In addition, as more people travel, more people want to travel. People hear about places from friends and want to go there. The United States also has the destinations whether it be Disney World, natural attractions such as the Grand Canyon, or urban centers such as New York City. International travel is seen less as a venture into the unknown and more as something everybody's doing.

An important factor in international travel, and in the long-term growth of the United States as a destination, is currency fluctuation. Following World War II, the U.S. dollar was the strongest currency in the world. Other currencies were weak largely because those countries were recovering from war damage. By the 1970s, however, that recovery was complete and other currencies gained against the dollar. In the 1980s, economic growth in many of these countries accelerated the trend. The "cheaper dollar," then, made the United States a travel bargain and travelers to the United States and travel spending increased dramatically. On the other hand, this factor is a double-edged sword. When Asian currencies crashed in 1996 and 1997, the visitor flow from those countries to the United States slowed appreciably.

In the hotel industry, some properties in large cities with large numbers of

One of the major reasons for the success of the United States as a travel destination is that it has attractions the world wants to see.
Courtesy of New York Convention and Visitor's Bureau

foreign tourists attribute one-third or more of their occupancy to visitors from outside the country. Twenty-five percent of foreign visitors' budgets goes for lodging. Many hotels, responding to the needs of this market, are anxious to hire multilingual managers, clerks, and service personnel. Some hotels have also begun actively to promote foreign business through representation at travel trade fairs abroad and through solicitation of foreign tour business from travel agents. The importance of foreign visitors to restaurants is suggested by the fact that their second most popular leisure recreation activity (after shopping) was dining and food and beverage purchases. Nineteen percent of foreign visitors' expenditures is for food and beverage. Nearly half of the foreign visitors spending, then, is accounted for by the hospitality industry.

𝓑USINESSES SERVING THE TRAVELER

Passenger Transportation

Earlier, we looked at travel trends as a part of tourism. Here, our concern is to see travel as an allied industry that works with hospitality firms in serving travelers. You may recall that Table 13.1 showed growth in travel by **common carrier** (i.e.,

Amtrak operates intercity rail service throughout the United States, providing travelers an opportunity to view the countryside in comfort and safety.
Photo by Matt Van Hattem

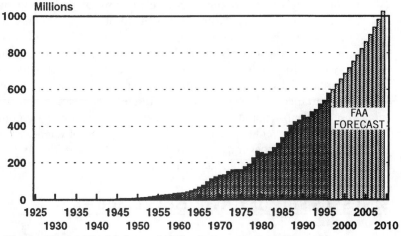

Figure 13.9 **The history of U.S. air transport traffic: revenue passenger miles.**
(*Source: Proceedings of the Travel Industry Association of America's 23rd Annual Marketing Outlook Forum,* 1998.)

air, rail, or bus) compared to travel by auto or other private vehicle. Bus travel has been increasing while rail travel has declined. Bus and rail, in any case, account for only a small share of travel. The growth component in common carrier travel, then, has been air.

Trends in Air Travel. The airlines have grown from an oddity in the transportation world of the 1920s, when only the daring flew, to the dominant common carrier worldwide. The growth of the airline industry is detailed in Figure 13.9. That figure also includes a Civil Aeronautics Administration forecast to 2010, when it is anticipated the billion-passenger mark will be reached. Figure 13.10 shows the growth *rate* history of airlines since 1950. Note that the average growth rate for the decade has fallen as the base against which the rate is computed has risen during this period of sustained growth. The dark vertical bars in the figure designate recessions. Notice that there are deep dips in airline sales volume that accompany a recession. Airlines, like most tourism industries, are very sensitive to the general economic climate.

Following deregulation in 1978, the number of airlines increased dramatically and competition became fierce on most routes. In order to achieve greater economies of scale, large airlines developed the **hub-and-spoke system** in the early 1980s.

Passengers are assembled at a central point—a hub—such as Chicago, New York, or Detroit by smaller aircraft that form commuter airlines. There, they board larger aircraft that fly to another hub from which passengers are disbursed to their final destinations by the same feeder system. If large aircraft fly with efficient load levels on high-volume routes, the hub-and-spoke system achieves the advantages of economies of scale. On the other hand, there are some offsetting disadvantages.

Figure 13.10 Air traffic growth rate history.
(*Source: Proceedings of the Travel Industry Association of America's 23rd Annual Marketing Outlook Forum,* 1998.)

Because of the complex schedules required to service the hub-and-spoke system, traffic control and weather delays can create serious problems. Delays multiply through the system, increasing costs because of idle aircraft and personnel time—to say nothing of passenger annoyance. Moreover, the large investment in people and equipment in hubs raises the fixed costs for operators using the centralized system.

An alternative to the hub-and-spoke system is the "short-haul" airline specializing in **point-to-point service**. In the mid-1990s, these short-haul airlines became more aggressive in both price and service. Point-to-point carriers manage short aircraft turnarounds, minimize staff, and hold down investment. As a result, they can offer lower fares and more frequent service, generally of the "no-frills" variety. As the point-to-point system has proved to have real competitive advantages, many of the larger carriers are launching no-frills, short-haul carrier subsidiaries that can duplicate the shorter routes, limited service, and lower fares offered by short-haul carriers. One of the first and still one of the most successful airlines using the point-to-point strategy is Southwest Airlines.

> Using either approach, however, commercial success is by no means guaranteed. Southwest's profitability, driven by relentless cost cutting, remains the exception. Of the new airlines that sprang up after the first flush of deregulation, as many died as survived. No-frills operators fly under half the internal routes in America.[14]

David Swierenga, chief economist of the Air Transport Association of America, comments on the impact of the hub-and-spoke and point-to-point alternatives:

> The hub and spoke system has been particularly beneficial to small communities because of the efficiency of being able to combine passengers going to many destinations on a single aircraft going to a spoke city. This has the societal advantage of connecting these small cities to a comprehensive transportation network.

At the same time, point to point service has generally not been successful in serving small communities because there are not enough passengers to fill an aircraft. Point to point airlines usually like to be able to provide five or six flights per day in a market in order to spread the terminal costs over many flights. Consequently, they have generally limited themselves to service in large to medium size cities where there are a sufficient number of passengers.[15]

Deregulation also had the effect of encouraging greater price competition. There are literally hundreds of thousands of special fares—many available only for a short period of time, ranging from a few minutes to a few days. (Special fares generally appear on the computer network used by airlines and travel agents and can be discontinued at will by the carrier.) Almost all of these special fares are discounted fares, and the impact of discounting has been to hold down the cost of travel. Most special fares, however, are structured so that they will not be attractive to the business traveler. Many, for instance, require travelers to stay over a Saturday night, a night when most business travelers would rather be home with their families. The effect of discounted fares has been to keep *personal* travel costs down while *business* travel costs rise. According to *The Economist,* "Although they fill only a

With point-to-point service, Southwest Airlines can offer lower fares on heavily traveled routes.
Courtesy of Southwest Airlines

fifth of the seats on scheduled flights, [business travelers] provide half the revenue. . . . On some routes they may be charged up to five times as much as another passenger on the same plane traveling in an economy seat."[16] As a result, the volume of personal travel has been more buoyant than business travel.

Another significant development in air travel has been the growth of partnerships between airlines, generally airlines with noncompetitive route structures. These partnerships offer advantages to both customer and airline. Partnerships permit airlines to share marketing and operating expenses over a route structure that is larger than either of their individual routes through "code sharing." As an example, consider the partnership between American Airlines and Air Canada. Through code sharing, both airlines can sell tickets on the same aircraft, whether it is operated by American or Air Canada. Each airline will have a flight number designating that flight, say American Flight 1 and Air Canada Flight 001. When the passenger goes to the terminal, he or she will be directed to the same aircraft by both airlines—with a simple explanation if the passenger has any questions. This permits the airlines to achieve a higher load factor. Load factor refers to the percentage of seats sold and is analogous to occupancy in the hotel business. Like the hotel business, airlines are a low-variable, high-fixed-cost industry. As a result, efforts that raise the efficiency of their use of resources have a pronounced favorable effect on profits. As Figure 13.11 makes clear, airline load factors have been increasing. The biggest factor in this improvement, however, has been the reduction of overcapacity that existed in the early 1990s.

Another aspect of partnerships is that, through code sharing, airlines can quote

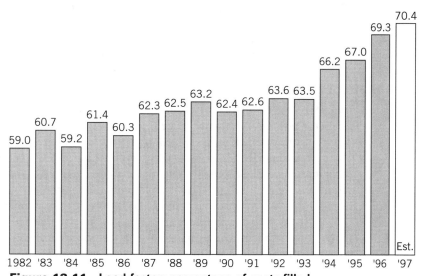

Figure 13.11   Load factor: percentage of seats filled.
(*Source: Proceedings of the Travel Industry Association of America's 23rd Annual Marketing Outlook Forum,* 1998.)

through fares, which are substantially less expensive than two separate tickets would be. Thus, Northwest can quote a fare from Minneapolis to Antwerp, Belgium, working with its partner KLM. In all probability, passengers will travel on both Northwest and KLM but with the same through ticket. This makes each airline more attractive in its own origination markets—while adding passengers to each other's aircraft to achieve higher load factors. Notice, too, that, because they can both advertise this "better deal" of a through fare, they share marketing expenses as well as aircraft. The increased efficiency is passed on, in part, to the customer with the lower through fare mentioned a moment ago. Another feature that is attractive to passengers is that frequent-flyer miles earned on both airlines can apply to the frequent-flyer program of the passenger's choice. Code sharing is under active consideration between airlines whose principal routes are in the United States but questions of antitrust regulation and acceptance by the unions must be resolved.

The Infrastructure Crisis. What is likely to interfere with the growth in air travel and ultimately retard or even halt it is the **infrastructure crisis.** As one authority put it,

> Air transport congestion is widely predicted in all parts of the world and is expected to be the single greatest impediment to the full realization of tourism growth potential during the coming decade. Most major hub airports in North America are at capacity levels and, by 2005, given current growth rates, the top 50 airports will be unable to accept new traffic.[17]

This overload is even worse in Europe and approaching critical proportions in much of Asia.

Infrastructure problems extend to the road system and to bridges as a result of "20 years of chronic underinvestment" by state and federal governments. These problems may well ultimately be resolved by the development of improved mass transit and restrictions in the use of highways but also by the development of high-tech "smart highways" that will speed traffic more efficiently.[18]

Channels of Distribution

In lodging, the development of **channels of distribution** as a significant factor is a relatively new development.[19] (See Chapter 12.) On the other hand, in other businesses, distribution channels have long been a basic ingredient. Those who manufacture consumer goods have several "layers of businesses" between the manufacturer and the final customer. Some of these intermediary businesses and agents are wholesalers, manufacturer's representatives, and brokers. Typically, these intermediaries move the product from the manufacturer to the retailer, who then sells to the final user, the retail customer. Although much of the hospitality industry is made up of retailers who provide goods and services directly to the customer, the travel agent and tour operators represent an important channel for many hotels, as well as for other tourism operators.

Travel Agents. The U.S. Travel Data Center defines **travel agents** as follows: "Travel agencies make travel reservations for the public and sell transportation,

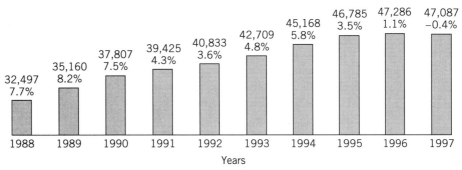

Figure 13.12 Growth in travel agency locations, 1988–1997.
(*Source: Travel Weekly Clipboard,* March 5, 1998, p. 19.)

lodging and other travel services on behalf of the producers of the services. They are retailers: they sell travel services provided by others directly to the final customer."

In 1996, there were 47,100 travel agency locations in the United States. Figure 13.12 shows the growth of travel agencies since 1988.

Although the large travel agencies are the most visible, the smaller agencies with gross billings (i.e., ticket and travel package sales) under $5 million annually still constitute the largest majority of agencies. Smaller agencies, however, have been hit especially hard by the airlines' actions in cutting back commissions they pay travel agencies from 10 to 8 percent.[20] Reportedly, this has been a major factor in a 6 percent reduction in the number of small agencies (gross billings under $2 million) between 1993 and 1995.[21] As Figure 13.12 indicates, in 1997, the number of agency locations showed its first decline.

Although airline commissions have been reduced, hotel, tour package, and cruise line commissions, which range from 10 to 15 percent, encourage travel agencies to devote more of their efforts to selling those products to travelers. Moreover, although commissions have been reduced for airline sales, travel agencies sold 10 percent more airline tickets in 1997 than in the previous year and their commission income rose 4 percent.[22]

Travel agents not only make reservations and sell tickets but also sell packaged tours. About one-fifth of their sales of leisure travel are packaged tours. It's clear that travel agents have considerable influence on the consumer and, thus, on the sales of other firms serving travelers. A majority of pleasure travelers, for instance, seek the advice of their travel agent on hotel selection, package tour choice, and car rental. Roughly 60 percent of business travelers use travel agents to make their travel arrangements.[23]

Travel wholesalers and tour brokers arrange to purchase space and services from all of the firms that serve travelers—carriers, hotels, restaurants, and attractions. Then, they sell the services of these firms to the consumer, generally through retail travel agents in return for a commission on those sales. Travel wholesalers such as American Express often retail their own tours, but they also work with the retail travel agencies that sell the tour package to customers in their local markets.

Carriers (such as airlines and bus and rail operators) also have their own tour operations and act as wholesalers of package tours. Tour wholesalers purchase services at deep discounts. They make their package attractive by offering a retail price that is still significantly less than the cost of all the package elements if the traveler purchased them separately. Even after this discount, both the tour broker and the retail travel agent have a margin for their operating costs and profit.

Hotels (especially resort hotels) often profit handsomely from associations with travel agencies. In return for the commissions they pay these agencies, the hotels have their properties represented in many communities. The travel wholesaler, too, can be important to hotels, because a listing in a wholesale package guarantees a listing with all of the wholesaler's retail affiliates. Some hotels, however, avoid travel agent representation and the accompanying commissions if it produces, on balance, relatively little income.

Reservation Networks

In the past, airline companies made airline reservations, and hotels and car companies made their own reservations. Travel agents called the appropriate reservation

Central reservation services play an important role in the travel industry.
Courtesy of United Airlines

system to inquire about or reserve a seat, room, or automobile. The revolutionary development in this area has been the linkup of these systems, as discussed in Chapter 12 (see Figure 12.6). All of these reservation systems can communicate with one another on virtually a worldwide basis. Because nearly all travel agents have computer terminals linked to one of the airline systems, the emerging system has literally thousands of instantaneous selling points. More and more of these companies are offering on-line booking systems to Internet users and more and more consumers are becoming not just acquainted with the Internet but comfortable with making purchases on line. What is emerging is an even more competitive travel marketplace. Offering to book tickets is no longer enough for survival. Travel agents, increasingly, must use the tools of their information-rich environment and their expertise to provide services to consumers they cannot readily provide for themselves. Although the information revolution is making a great deal possible, it is not necessarily making it easy—and the information environment of travel is becoming increasingly complex. Ultimately, travel agencies and other intermediaries who make it possible for the consumer to choose intelligently from the many options now available will survive. Those who simply book tickets may not.

NONECONOMIC EFFECTS OF TOURISM

So far, we have stressed the economic structure and impact of tourism. As we will see, however, tourism has other impacts, both unfavorable and favorable.

Crowding

A successful tourist attraction may, in effect, self-destruct from its own success. One of the major potential problems of tourism is **crowding**: So many people want to see the attraction that its own success destroys its charm.

At successful theme parks, this problem is addressed by designing places where guests will be waiting in line in "staging areas," with interesting views and even live or mechanized entertainment to distract the visitors. Another theme park tactic is to have lots of cleanup help, so that paper, cigarettes, and other trash never accumulates, thus reducing or eliminating some of the *evidence* of crowding.

Another example can be found in areas of scenic beauty such as popular national parks where trails often become more and more difficult as they progress. Indeed, most people turn around and return to the parking lot once the pavement ends. Even fewer continue once the unpaved trail actually becomes difficult to follow. In effect, reducing the amenities is a subtle form of unstated rationing of which the ultimate example is the wilderness area, where entrance is only on foot or by horse. Difficulty of access can thus reduce crowding. Another reaction to mass tourism and its impact is **ecotourism**, which is discussed in Industry Practice Note 13.1.

Along with crowding, tourism can result in noise, odors, and pollution. A special form of crowding is the traffic jam. In many areas, tourist traffic has increased but the local infrastructure—roads, bridges, and airports, for instance—has not kept up. The result is a serious traffic overload causing delays and, in some cases, accidents and injuries, as well. The traffic jam is equally annoying to visitors

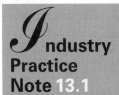

*I*ndustry
Practice
Note 13.1

Ecotourism

The fastest-growing theme in tourism today is the environment. So-called **ecotourism** has become a desirable label. It is jealously claimed by environmentalists who would like to reserve it for "low-impact" treks to observe animals in the wild, and for programs such as Belize's reef-monitoring project in which visitors are charged a considerable fee for scuba diving to collect data for scientific analysis. At the same time, the label is cheerfully appropriated by opportunists out to "greenwash" such offerings as glass-bottomed boat tours above coral reefs, or even "safaris" in which tourists pursue Zimbabwean elephants with paint guns.

The preferred definition of the Ecotourism Society in Virginia is, "Responsible travel that conserves natural environments and sustains the well-being of local people." James MacGregor, whose environmental consulting firm, ecoplan:net, prepared a report on sustainable tourism for the Bahamian government that was widely adopted as a model by other environmentally fragile destinations, offers three main criteria for ecotourism: There must be a direct return of a reasonable share of the revenues generated by the business to local people and to

conservation of the local environment; its operation must follow green principles; and the tourists must learn about what they are visiting, not just gawk at it.

That is probably rather stricter than would suit some of the 43 million Americans who, according to a survey by the Travel Industry Association of America, consider themselves ecotourists of a sort. However, it is a good yardstick by which to measure the great variety of nature-based tourism available worldwide. In places such as Central America and southern Africa, most visitors spend some time observing wildlife and probably learning about it, but even well-intentioned crowds can trample on a lot of plants and toes. Masai people in Kenya have accused their government of shoving them aside to make way for safari parks and lodges. Moreover, some wildlife reserves that lure the animals with food for a better view end up taming the beasts. True ecotourists find themselves in the age-old tourist bind: They want to see something "unspoiled," but help to spoil it just by being there.

Source: "Survey of Travel and Tourism," *The Economist,* January 10, 1998, p. 16.

and local inhabitants. This is an especially bad problem in the developing world where infrastructure was not highly developed in the first place. In the face of exploding traffic, the situation often becomes critical. Not surprisingly, people who live in a tourist attraction area may have mixed or hostile feelings about further development because of their concern for privacy, the environment, or just their ability to get safely to and from home on crowded highways.

Another possible impact of crowding is "crowding out." For example, a beach or other scenic area formerly used by local people may be bought and its use restricted to paying visitors. This has happened on several Caribbean islands and, in some cases, has resulted in the local populace's becoming unfriendly or even hostile as they found their beaches becoming inaccessible to "natives." This has led, in some cases, to sharp clashes between local people and visitors, an unfriendly environment, and a subsequent drop in the number of visitors.

These potentially unfavorable developments related to tourism give rise to the notion of "carrying capacity," that is, that an area can accept only a certain number of visitors without being hampered as a desirable destination. That carrying capacity can be seen in terms of the physical infrastructure we discussed in an earlier section of this chapter, but the notion extends to social institutions, as well.

Favorable Noneconomic Effects

Not all noneconomic effects, however, are necessarily unfavorable. Tourist success can often fuel local pride: Some tourist "events" such as festivals and fairs may be staged to celebrate some aspect of the local culture. Agricultural fairs, for instance, which draw thousands—and sometimes hundreds of thousands—of visitors, celebrate a region's agricultural heritage and its favored crops, as well as provide for important educational activities such as 4H meetings and contests.

In other cases, a local tradition may be observed. In a Portuguese community, it may be a blessing of the fishing fleet; in an area where many of German descent live, it could be "Oktoberfest." In these cases, adults are reminded of their background, and the young see their heritage dramatized as visitors come to admire it.

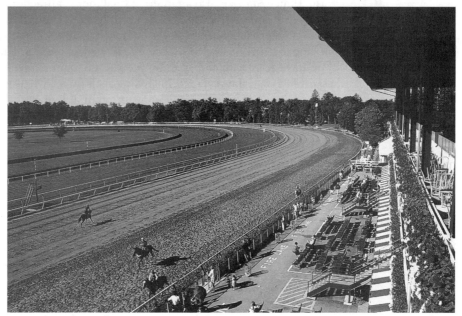

Annual events, such as the summer races in Saratoga Springs, NY, can draw visitors to a particular region or community.
Photo by Matt Van Hattem

Indeed, much early travel was for the purpose of pilgrimage, and religion still plays an important part in travel in some areas.

Because of its importance to the hospitality industry, tourism is significant to students of hospitality management. However, even if this weren't your field of study, it would be important for you to know about it. This is because whatever problems tourism raises, its positive impacts not only economically but also culturally and socially make it an important phenomenon of contemporary mass society.

$\mathcal{S}$UMMARY

This chapter opened with a discussion of the reasons that tourism is important to the hospitality industry. We then explained why people are traveling more: more leisure time, rising family incomes, and more middle-aged people who have the time and money to travel.

The most common reason for traveling is pleasure, followed by business. More people travel by car than by any other means. Travel by air increased over the last 10 years but fell somewhat when fares began to rise, suggesting that travel is price sensitive.

The economic significance of tourism is clear: Tourism ranks in the top three for total business receipts. Moreover, about one in twenty people is employed in an activity supported by travel expenditures. Indeed, communities seeking potential employers may profitably use tourism as an attraction.

The United States is also an international tourist attraction, its popularity often based on the value of the U.S. dollar versus that of other currencies, as well as a number of other factors. Foreign visitors to this country are an important means of improving the U.S. balance of payments, as well as the U.S. employment outlook.

We have also examined other businesses serving the traveler such as passenger transportation and travel agents. In looking at air travel, we considered the competition between hub-and-spoke and point-to-point airline systems and the strengths and weaknesses of both. While discussing channels of distribution, we noted the impact that technological change is having on this industry made up predominantly of small businesses. Finally, we closed the chapter by touching on the noneconomic effects of tourism, both unfavorable (such as crowding) and favorable (such as festivals, fairs, and the celebration of local traditions).

◆ $\mathcal{K}$EY WORDS AND CONCEPTS

Tourism	Business travel
Factors affecting travel and	Pleasure travel
tourism	Mode of travel
Leisure	Travel multiplier
Income	Tourism and employment
Demographics	Arrivals and departures

Receipts and payments
Travel trade balance
Common carrier
Hub-and-spoke system
Point-to-point service
Infrastructure crisis
Channels of distribution

Travel agents
Travel wholesalers
Reservation networks
Noneconomic effects of tourism
   Crowding
   Ecotourism

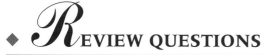

REVIEW QUESTIONS

1. What is tourism, and what organizations does it include?

2. What factors have caused the increase in tourism?

3. What are the main reasons that people travel?

4. Which age groups travel most, and what kinds of trips does each group take?

5. What are the recent trends in automobile and airline travel, and what are their causes?

6. Is tourism important economically to the United States? Explain.

7. What factors account for the improvement in the U.S. travel balance? What could threaten the favorable balance?

8. What are the relative advantages of hub-and-spoke and point-to-point airline systems? How does each work?

9. Describe some of the favorable and unfavorable noneconomic effects of tourism.

INTERNET EXERCISES

1. **Site Name:** *The Educational Institute of the American Hotel and Motel Association*
   URL: http://www.ei-ahma.org/webs/ahma/ahmahome.htm
   Background Information: The American Hotel and Motel Association (AH&MA) is the voice of the $80 billion U.S. lodging industry. The AH&MA, with headquarters in Washington, DC, offers communication, governmental affairs, marketing, hospitality operations, educational, convention, risk management, technology, information, and member relations services for hotels, motels, and lodging facilities throughout the world.

   EXERCISES: Go to the "Lodging Industry Profile" under the "Information Center" and find the following information: (a) List the ways tourism affects our economy. (b) Which country receives more tourists than any other country in the world?

(c) How many international travelers visited the United States in the last year? (d) How much money did visitors spend in the United States last year?

2. **Site Name:** *World Tourism Organization*
   URL: http://www.world-tourism.org/
   Background Information: The World Tourism Organization is the leading international organization in the field of travel and tourism. It serves as a global forum for tourism policy issues and a practical source of tourism know-how.

   EXERCISE: What services does the World Tourism Organization offer?

3. **Site Name:** *The World Travel and Tourism Council (WTTC)*
   URL: http://www.wttc.org
   Background Information: The World Travel and Tourism Council is the Global Business Leaders Forum for Travel and Tourism. Its members are chief executives from all sectors of the travel and tourism industry, including accommodation, catering, cruises, entertainment, recreation, transportation, and travel-related services. Its central goal is to work with governments to realize the full economic impact of the world's largest generator of wealth and jobs—travel and tourism.

   EXERCISES:

   a. What is Agenda 21 for the travel and tourism industry?

   b. What is WTTC's Millennium Vision?

4. **Site Name:** *The Air Transport Association (ATA)*
   URL: http://www.air-transport.org/
   Background Information: The Air Transport Association of America was founded by a group of 14 airlines meeting in Chicago in 1936. It was the first, and today remains, the only trade organization for the principal U.S. airlines. In that capacity, it has played a major role in all the major government decisions regarding aviation since its founding, including the creation of the Civil Aeronautics Board, the creation of the air traffic control system, and airline deregulation.

   EXERCISES:

   a. What data is provided by the ATA which would be of interest to the travel and tourism industry?

   b. Choose three graphs from the ATA Annual Report and discuss the importance of the graphs to the travel and tourism industry. (If you were a professional in this industry, why would you want or need this information?)

   c. Review the 10-year summary and track the "passenger load factor" for the last 10 years. What is the "passenger load factor" and what are the implications of the trend?

   d. What has been the trend for employment in the Air Transport Industry over the last 10 years?

   e. Overall, what has been the trend in the Air Transport Industry over the last 10 years?

◆ *N*OTES

1. "1998 Outlook for Travel and Tourism," *Proceedings of the TIA Marketing Outlook Forum* (Washington, DC: Travel Industry Association of America, December 1997).

2. Graeme R. Clarke, Address to the 1997 Travel Outlook Forum, October 6, 1997. Mr. Clarke is senior vice president of the AAA.

3. Paul R. Campbell, *Population Projections for States by Age, Sex, Race, and Hispanic Origin: 1995 to 2025*, U.S. Bureau of the Census, October 1996, pages 76–80.

4. Ibid.

5. Ibid. The population groups between the ages of 65 and 84 are projected to increase 12 percent during the same period.

6. Dan Lago and James Kipp Poffley, "The Aging Population and the Hospitality Industry in 2010: Important Trends and Probable Services," *The Hospitality Research Journal—The Futures Issue,* Vol. 17, No. 1, 1993, pp. 29–47.

7. Figures in this section are based on information from the U.S. Travel Data Center, except as noted. Time series data are, from time to time, in the words of the center, "revised to reflect a more accurate projection methodology." Accordingly, some statistics differ significantly from earlier editions of this text, which used Travel Data Center information based on the earlier methodology.

8. Travel Industry Association, *National Travel Study.* Figures are drawn from the period January to June 1996.

9. Kenneth E. Hornback, "Distributing Demand: Notes on a Space/Time Solution for the Outdoor Recreation Demand/Supply Problem," Paper delivered at the Southeastern Recreation Research Symposium, Asheville, NC, February 14–15, 1991.

10. *Tourism Works for America–1997 Report* (Washington, DC: Travel Works for America Council, 1997), p. 5.

11. *1996/7 WWTC Travel and Tourism Report,* World Travel and Tourism Council, pp. 34–37.

12. Helen Marano, "Outlook on International Travel to the U.S.," Presentation to the 1997 TIA Marketing Outlook Forum, October 5, 1997. The number of tourists is equated to the number of arrivals.

13. Ibid.

14. "Travel and Tourism Survey," *The Economist,* January 10, 1998, p. 6.

15. David A. Swierenga, personal communication, April 27, 1998.

16. Ibid.

17. J. S. Perry Hobson and Muzaffer Uysal, "Infrastructure: The Silent Crisis Facing the Future of Tourism," *Hospitality Research Journal,* Vol. 17, No. 1, p. 211.

18. George G. Fenich, "Localized Ground Transportation in the 21st Century and Its Impact on the Hospitality Industry," *Hospitality Research Journal,* Vol. 17, No. 1, p. 195.

19. Franchising can quite reasonably be seen as a channel of distribution in food service or it can be seen as a way of organizing a multiunit business. In food service, however, there are no significant intermediaries or resellers between the customer and the restaurant. For a discussion of channels in food service, see Tom Powers, *Marketing Hospitality,* Chapter 9, especially pp. 245–249 and 260–267.

20. "Travel and Tourism Survey," *The Economist,* January 10, 1998, p. 9.

21. William Niles, "Outlook for Travel Agencies," TIA 1996 Travel Outlook Forum, October 18, 1996.

22. Suzanne Cook, "Outlook on Domestic Tourism," TIA Marketing Forum, October 5–7, 1997.

23. *Travel Weekly Clipboard,* March 5, 1998, p. 19.

Chapter 14

Courtesy of New York, New York Hotel, Las Vegas

Destinations: Tourism Generators

The Purpose of This Chapter

Travel destinations (whether natural or created) are the magnets that set the whole process of tourism in motion. In this chapter, we look at the motivations of travelers, as well as the nature of mass-market travel destinations. Many of these are, to all intents and purposes, a part of the hospitality industry and offer attractive career prospects. You will need to be familiar with the economic and operating characteristics of destinations to round out your understanding of tourism.

This Chapter Should Help You

1. See the relationships between travelers' motives and the attractions of destinations

2. Distinguish between primary and secondary attractions

3. Understand the characteristics of the newer types of tourism destinations and their common elements

4. Know more about the kinds of activities theme parks offer to entice travelers

5. Understand some of the issues surrounding casino gambling, besides the entertainment factor

6. Become familiar with the significance of large- and small-scale urban play centers as a part of the tourism plant of any community

7. Evaluate the importance of temporary attractions, such as fairs and festivals

8. Understand the role that natural attractions play and their overall contribution to tourism

MOTIVES AND DESTINATIONS

If people had no place they wanted to go, tourism would be in jeopardy. However, people travel and they travel for many reasons—for instance, work and recreation. In this chapter, we will be concerned almost exclusively with travel for purposes of recreation. Even when people travel for this reason, however, their motives are varied, primarily because recreation is more than just play. Webster tells us that recreation also means reviving, giving new vigor, refreshing, and reanimating, as well as amusing, diverting, or gratifying.

Recreation has a function. It is not just the opposite of work; it is its counterweight. **Recreation** relates to relaxation but also to stimulation, to gaining renewed energy, as well as to playing. In short, it contributes to the attainment of balance in our lives. As a necessary and vital part of life, not surprisingly the things that attract different people are highly varied. For instance, perhaps the earliest motive for travel was religion and the sense of renewal of commitment that was and is experienced by the pilgrim. Today's pilgrimage attractions include Lourdes in France and Fatima in Portugal and, in the New World, Guadalupe in Mexico and Ste. Anne de Beaupre in Quebec.

Good health has always been of interest to people, and *health interests* have long been a major travel motive. In ancient times, the Romans were drawn to springs thought to have health-giving properties, which became fashionable again in the 18th century. Hot springs in the United States, such as Hot Springs, Arkansas, and French Lick Springs, Indiana, are less popular today than they were a few generations ago. While the recuperative power of natural springs are enough to attract some travelers, others seek to manage their health by different means—the Mayo Clinic, for instance, attracts so many people that its home in Rochester, Minnesota, has one of the highest ratios of hotel rooms per resident of any city in the United States.

Another reason that people travel is to be able to experience *scenic beauty,* especially the mountains and the seashore. Scenic beauty is often coupled with health-building activities: hiking, skiing, and swimming, for instance, so that both body and mind are refreshed by vistas and activities. A good example of this is the current popularity of state and national park systems, which are the most extensive response to these touring motives in history.

Sporting events have become big business but have long been popular—from the first Olympics in 776 B.C. to today's Final Four basketball tournament to the Kentucky Derby and the Superbowl. Events such as these have long attracted thousands of serious sports enthusiasts, as well as untutored onlookers. Indeed, sports arenas have become such big business that some institutional food service companies have created special divisions just to manage sports food service (as discussed in Chapter 8).

Culture, including history and art appreciation, are judged by some as not very interesting stuff, yet every year, yesterday's battlefields throng with thousands of visitors on guided tours. In the area of art appreciation, the Louvre is one of France's major cultural treasures. Closer to home, the Smithsonian museum complex is one of the biggest draws in Washington, DC. There are museums for almost everything—even museums that celebrate work and industry such as the Museum of Science and Industry in Chicago. Imagine a museum that focuses on work that people visit while on vacation! Other cultural events that attract tourists include the many music and theater festivals all across Europe and North America. Such events are often used by cities to celebrate and enhance the cultural life of the area, as well as to attract visitors' spending to strengthen the local economy.

Theater and spectacle, whether Broadway's *Cats* or Walt Disney's theme parks, are currently among the most significant tourist attractions. In addition, there are literally thousands of lesser known theaters and amusement parks that stimulate the local culture and economy by catering to the interests of people close to their homes.

Although we have been discussing the reasons that people travel, it should be noted that what these motives for travel also have in common is their focus on a

Visitors can climb to the top of historic Barnegat Lighthouse in New Jersey. Scenic beauty, health-building activities, and cultural appreciation are some of the major factors that motivate people to travel.
Photo by Matt Van Hattem

destination. Destinations can be of different types. Several years ago, Mill and Morrison distinguished between what they call primary, or touring, destinations and secondary, or stopover, destinations.[1] **Primary destinations** have a wide market and draw travelers from a great distance. These kinds of destinations, such as some of the religious and health-related destinations discussed previously (as well as more current examples such as Walt Disney World and Las Vegas) attract visitors from the entire North American continent and all over the world. Because such a high proportion of their visitors are away from home, these primary destinations can create a heavy lodging demand. Orlando, Florida, for instance, like Rochester, Minnesota (home to the Mayo Clinic), has a disproportionately high number of hotel rooms per capita.

Secondary destinations draw people from nearby areas or induce people to stop on their way by. Some secondary destinations may, in fact, have a higher number of visitors than do primary destinations. As a primary attraction, the Grand Canyon attracts fewer than 3 million visitors a year, although they come from all over the world. In contrast, many regional theme parks (as examples of secondary destinations) draw at least that many visitors. Atlantic City, for example, which is mainly a regional casino gambling center, attracts well over 10 times that many. In general, we can say that a primary attraction requires more services per visitor, but this does not detract from the importance of successful secondary attractions. Indeed, even smaller secondary attractions make important contributions to their locale.

The balance of this chapter will examine those destinations and attractions to which hospitality services are important enough that the attraction can usefully be thought of as part of the hospitality industry. We will consider primary destinations such as theme parks and casinos as well as significant secondary destinations in urban centers such as sports centers, zoos and aquariums, museums, and the like. We will then consider temporary destinations such as festivals and fairs. Finally, we will also look briefly at attractions in the natural environment such as national parks, seashores, and monuments. Our main interest will be in the impact of these kinds of destinations on opportunities in the hospitality industry, their significance for hospitality managers, and possible careers in such complexes.

*M*ASS-MARKET TOURISM

It was not so long ago that travel was the privileged pastime of the wealthy. The poor might migrate to move their homes from one place to another in order to live better or just to survive but only the affluent could afford travel for sightseeing, amusement, and business. That condition has not really changed; some affluence is still required for recreational travel and certainly one's level of affluence directly affects the number and types of vacations one can take. What has changed is the degree of affluence in our society. We have become what economists refer to as an affluent society.

When travel was reserved for the higher social classes, its model was the aristocracy. In hotels, for example, dress rules required a coat and tie in the dining room. As travel came within the reach of the majority of Americans, however, the facilities serving travelers adapted and loosened their emphasis on class. Many of the new establishments have, in fact, become mass institutions. Any discussion of such facilities would have to include Las Vegas and Walt Disney World in Orlando.

In Las Vegas casinos, mink-coated matrons play blackjack next to dungaree-clad cowboys. These are not social clubs that inquire who your parents are or which side of the tracks you live on. The color of your money is the only concern. Likewise, anybody with the money can buy a reserved seat in any of the new domed sports centers (such as Toronto's SkyDome) or stroll through one of the new mega-malls, which will be discussed later in the chapter. What we see developing (and continuing to evolve on larger and larger scales) are new "planned play environments," places, institutions, and even cities designed almost exclusively for play—that is, pure entertainment for the masses. Again, social class is meaningless in such places—Disney World has virtually no dress code for its guests. People come as they are. All comers are served and enjoy themselves as they see fit within the limits of reasonable decorum.

These essentially democratic institutions supply a comfortable place for travelers from all kinds of social backgrounds. Accordingly, as the popularity of these facilities increases, we see a new, more egalitarian kind of lodging and food service (and other hospitality-related) institution flourishing.

*P*LANNED PLAY ENVIRONMENTS

Recreation is as old as society itself. However, a society that can afford to play on the scale that Americans do now is new. Some anthropologists and sociologists argue that "who you are" was once determined by your work, what you did for a living, but that these questions of personal identity are now answered by how we entertain ourselves. Some years ago, futurist Alvin Toffler spoke of the emerging importance of "sub cults" whose lifestyles are built around nonwork activities. For these people, work exists as a secondary matter, as only a means to an end. Although there is some debate regarding the balance of work and play in this country, play is destined to serve an increasingly important role in our civilization. We are already seeing the pleasure principle being elevated to a higher level in our society.

To talk about a society in which leisure is the most important thing flies in the face of the work ethic and religious codes that have dominated our country, Japan, and many countries in Northern Europe for generations. It is becoming clear, however, that the new century will see a society in which leisure plays an increasingly dominant role.

Planned play environments have actually been around longer than one might believe. Fairs and festivals at which work (or trade) and play were mixed date back to the mid-1800s in the United States and to medieval times, or even earlier, in Europe. Amusement parks are anything but a 20th-century American phenomenon—the first amusement park was Vauxhall Gardens in England, built in the 1600s. In contrast, the first U.S. amusement park, Coney Island, is barely 100 years old (dating from 1895). What is new, however, is the sophistication that a television-educated public demands in its amusement centers today, and the scale on which these demands have been met since the first modern theme park opened at Disneyland. Disneyland, in effect, showed the commercial world that there was a way to entice a television generation out of the house and into a clean carnival offering live fantasy and entertainment. That television generation has now grown up and is busy raising a newer, younger television generation (who tend to be the same in this respect, only more so). Together, these two generations are shaping the scope and nature of today's tourism destinations.

There are a variety of leisure environments that have been artificially created for the enjoyment of tourists. These include theme parks, casinos, "urban entertainment centers," and fairs and festivals. We will discuss each of these in the following sections.

THEME PARKS

In the early 1970s, a number of old-style amusement parks closed their doors because they offered little more than thrill rides and cotton candy, as modern Americans began to demand more from their entertainment venues. Many of the old amusement parks fell in the face of more sophisticated competition from **theme parks** that catered more effectively to people's need for fun and fantasy.

According to industry sources, the United States has about 95 major themed attractions and 500 other, more traditional amusement parks. Although fewer in number, it is the theme parks that account for the lion's share of park receipts. The number of their visitors in 1997 was estimated at 300 million, the equivalent of more than one visit for every person in the United States.[2] These parks have clearly become an important part of both the national tourist market and the local entertainment market. In practice, though, about half the guests visit at least twice a year.

Themes

Just as restaurants are expected more and more to offer entertainment as well as food (note the popularity of the Hard Rock Cafe and Planet Hollywood), today's television-oriented traveler expects a park environment that stimulates and entertains in addition to offering rides and other amusements. One way to meet this demand is to build the park around one or more themes. An excellent example of this is Walt Disney World in Orlando, Florida, where there are themed areas within themed areas. Most people are familiar with the different theme parks at Disney World, which include the Magic Kingdom, Epcot Center, Disney–MGM Studios, and the newest park, Disney's Animal Kingdom. Within these different parks, however, are additional themed areas. For instance, the themed areas within the Magic Kingdom include Main Street USA, Adventureland, and Frontierland, among others.

Some parks, moreover, are built around one general theme. Busch Entertainment's Journey Through the Gardens, located near historic Williamsburg, Virginia,

Visitors can enjoy treats while strolling through Rhinefeld, a replica of a German village in Busch Gardens, Williamsburg, Virginia.
Courtesy of Busch Gardens, Williamsburg

uses a 17th-century European theme for the park as a whole and within that general theme offers eight areas themed to specific countries or regions: Banbury Cross and Hastings (England); Heatherdowns (Scotland); Aquitaine (France); Rhinefeld and Oktoberfest (Germany); New France (early North America); and Festa Italia and San Marco (Italy).

Whatever the theme, parks are known for their rides, among other things; one of the most popular being water rides. In fact, Busch has developed a separate theme park, adjacent to its Busch Gardens in Tampa, Florida, built around water and water rides. Adventure Island, as it is called, offers 25 acres of tropically themed lagoons and beaches featuring water slides and diving platforms, water games, a wave pool, a cable drop, and much more.

Although some parks cater to nostalgia (a romantic longing for the past), others recreate the past in a more realistic way. The Towne of Smithville, in New Jersey, for instance, has restored a mid-1800s crossroads community. It offers a Civil War museum and a theater, as well.

Some parks take their themes from animal life. Busch Gardens in Florida offers a 335-acre African themed park that includes the Serengeti Plain, home of one of the largest collections of African big game. It also serves as a breeding and survival center for many rare species. The animals roam freely on a veldtlike plain where visitors can see them by taking a monorail, steam locomotive, or skyride safari.

The sea offers enticing themes, as well. Mystic Seaport, in Mystic, Connecticut, is designed around a 19th-century seaport town complete with educational and recreational activities. A quite different type of experience (also based on the sea) can be found at Sea World (also owned by Busch Entertainment), which has been successful with parks in Florida; Ohio; San Antonio, Texas; and southern California. Sea World of Florida (in Orlando) features many different live shows including Cirque de la Mer, which is labeled as a "nontraditional circus"; the Shamu Adventure, featuring numerous killer whales; and additional shows, focusing on other sea life such as sea lions and otters. Like many theme parks, Sea World offers organized

The performing whales are an integral part of the Marine World theme.
Courtesy of Marine World Africa, USA

educational tours featuring the work of Sea World's research organization. A liberal amount of education-as-fun is found in its regular, entertainment-oriented shows. An official of the Disney organization summed up the theme parks' approach to education this way: Before you can educate, you must entertain. Theme parks do, indeed, constitute a rich educational medium.

Scale

Theme parks are different from the traditional amusement parks not only because they are based on a theme, or several themes, but also because of their huge operating scale. As in nearly everything else, Disney leads the way here. The entire Walt Disney World (WDW) in Florida comprises an amazing 47 square miles and offers four distinctly different theme parks, each with its own activities, food service operations, and retail stores. The original Magic Kingdom offers seven different lands or distinctively themed areas. The Epcot Center offers Future World, featuring high-tech pavilions, and the World Showcase, which boasts representative displays from nations around the world. Disney–MGM Studios gives visitors a firsthand look at backstage and the workings of a major film and video production facility. Disney's Animal Kingdom is the latest addition. The Animal Kingdom alone, which opened in early 1998, is five times the size of Disneyland (in Anaheim, California). It includes five themed areas and celebrates animal life—quite a different venue than the other three parks in the Disney complex. Walt Disney World also includes several smaller themed areas such as Pleasure Island, which offers after-dark excitement in its six nightclubs and five restaurants, mainly to young adults and couples without children. There are also two water parks, Typhoon Lagoon and River Country, which is part of the Fort Wilderness campground. Finally, there are 19 lodging facilities, including campgrounds and villas, on or adjacent to the parks that are operated by, or affiliated with, WDW. The career significance of WDW and similar enterprises is suggested by the fact that WDW is one of the largest private employers in the state of Florida. Clearly, WDW presents a good example of the huge scale on which theme parks may operate.

Themes and Cities[3]

By definition, theme parks are focused on a central theme or themes. Similarly, entire cities sometimes evoke a singular theme. Nashville, Tennessee, is hardly a one-theme town but it is closely associated with country-and-western music. Since 1925, it has been the site of the Grand Ole Opry, the wellspring from which has poured thousands of country songs and where many of the major country music stars have gotten their start.

The rise in country music's popularity in recent years is undisputed. The country music audience continues to increase; country music is estimated to hold a 10 percent market share nationally. In fact, country music is the number one music format on the radio today. The popularity of country-and-western music is probably a function of many factors, including the middle aging of the baby boomers. As baby boomers, with babies of their own, turned off hard rock and heavy metal, they

The Grand Ole Opry radio programs bring thousands of people to Nashville, Tennessee, to watch the show live.
Courtesy of Opryland USA

began to explore country music's more traditional themes. Country music saw a large increase in listeners with the emergence of Garth Brooks in the early 1990s and continues to maintain its popularity.

Although the Grand Ole Opry is the best known aspect of the country music scene centered in Nashville, it is only one part of the larger Opryland complex.

It should be noted that the complex, owned by Gaylord Entertainment, is undergoing significant remodeling at the time of this writing. The theme park, Opryland, is closed until 2000 when it will reopen as part of a total entertainment complex. The current configuration, minus the theme park, is described next.

On one side of the complex is the Cumberland River where the *General Jackson*, a giant, four-decked paddlewheel showboat, docks. On the other side is one of America's most successful convention hotel properties, the 2883-room Opryland Hotel. Finally, the Grand Ole Opry itself is housed in a 4400-seat auditorium, complete with its own radio station, which broadcasts to 30 different states.

Also associated with Opryland are the Nashville Network, which broadcasts both radio and cable television programs, and Country Music Television, a 24-hour country music video channel, which broadcasts not only in North America but in Europe, as well. All of this media activity and the longstanding reputation of Nashville as the Country Music Capital help support the growing popularity of the Opryland complex.

The complex has a lot to offer visitors, which is one of its draws. Another reason for Opryland's success in attracting visitors is that it actually targets three quite different markets. The theme park, until its closing, attracted half of its clientele from country music fans who live within 250 miles of Nashville. The other half were visitors from around North America and the world drawn by the Opryland reputation. Thus, in a way, Opryland is both a regional theme park (which are discussed later) and a national theme park.

The Opryland Hotel, on the other hand, draws from a quite different market. Eighty percent of the hotel's customers, an upscale market, are there to attend conventions, meetings, and trade shows. Although country-and-western music, and the fun that goes with it, is an important plus to this market, it is not the main draw. Rather, the key is the hotel's extensive facilities; the hotel claims more meeting, exhibit, and public space than any other hotel in the United States. The Opryland Hotel can accommodate 95 percent of U.S. trade shows and exhibitions, and the property's luxurious public facilities, guest rooms, and excellent service are another draw. The Opryland Hotel, itself, resembles a park, at times, complete with a conservatory, a water-oriented interior courtyard called the Cascades, and lots of indoor greenery. Within these areas, which are covered with acres of skylights, and elsewhere in the hotel, are situated numerous restaurants and lounges, 30 retail shops, 600,000 square feet of meeting space and various fitness facilities including swimming pools, a fitness center, and tennis courts.

The third market Opryland captures is drawn by the programs at the Grand Ole Opry every evening from 7 until midnight. Some of those filling the Opry's 4400-seat auditorium are visitors to the Opryland complex staying on for an evening's relaxation. Others are hotel guests but the main audience is a local one, drawn from communities within a few hours drive of Nashville by their love of country music and their admiration for the star-studded cast appearing at the Opry.

Opryland is a clear case of synergy between attractions and communications media that has created a major international tourist attraction. At the same time, it is a vital part of the local economy. When the entire complex is reopened, it will include the new theme park, the Grand Ole Opry and Opry Plaza, the hotel, the area encompassing the General Jackson, and a new "entertainment and retail" center to be called Opry Mills. Although Nashville and the Opryland complex are clearly leading the way, other cities that have made country music a major tourist attraction are Branson, Missouri, and Myrtle Beach, South Carolina.

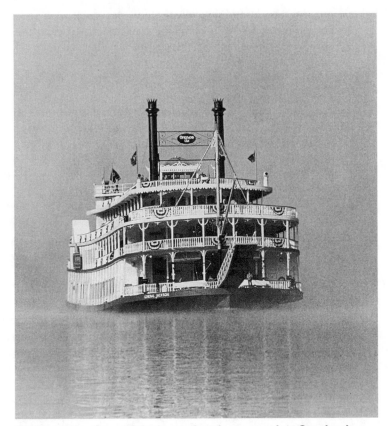

On board the General Jackson showboat, another Opryland attraction, passengers can enjoy dinner and a country music show.
Courtesy of Opryland USA

Regional Theme Parks

Theme parks catering to a regional rather than a national market have been grow-ing at a rapid pace in recent years. At least some of this development is attributable to the increasing cost of transportation and the pressure of economic insecurity and inflation on many incomes. The convenience, however, of nearby attractions and the fact that a visit can be included in a weekend or 3- or 4-day trip is probably an equally strong force. Not everyone can take the family on an extended trip to Disney World. Regional theme parks offer an alternative to many travelers.

Regional parks, aside from serving a smaller geographic area than parks such as Disney World, often target particular groups in their marketing. For instance, Six Flags Over Georgia offers special parties for high school graduating classes and presents an annual Christian Music Festival featuring top Christian talent that might not be as popular in other regions of North America. In Pigeon Forge, Tennessee, near Knoxville, Dollywood recreates the Smoky Mountains of the late 1800s through crafts and country music, as well as atmosphere, old-time home-cooked food, and rides. Country music and crafts are featured year round and also during special festivals held throughout the year. Regional parks such as Dollywood are clearly major sources of tourism: Dollywood attracts almost 2 million visitors each year.

Regional parks, though not as large as Walt Disney World, are not small either. Six Flags Over Georgia, for instance, offers over 100 rides, shows, and attractions. Rides in these parks are of impressive scale. Six Flags recently added its tenth themed area, called Gotham City. One ride in this area, Batman the Ride, is a fast-paced ride that takes passengers through parts of Gotham City. This single ride's carrying capacity is close to 1300 passengers per hour. Another ride, Splashwater Falls, is equally as spectacular and cost nearly $2 million to build. Although not on the same scale as Disney, Six Flags Over Georgia (and the other Six Flags parks) are on a scale that is large and impressive enough to draw very effectively from their respective regions.

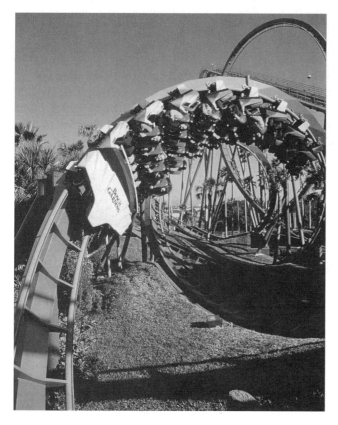

The popularity of regional theme parks has been growing at a rapid pace.
© Busch Entertainment Corp.

Employment and Training Opportunities

The growth of regional and even local theme parks and amusement centers is a favorable development for hospitality students because of the opportunities they offer for employment and management experience. Theme parks often operate year round, but on a reduced scale from their seasonal peak. Such business fluctuations can be extreme, as is the case at Paramount Canada's Wonderland (in Ontario), which has 3500 seasonal employees but only 150 permanent employees. Few parks experience such employment swings, however. During the months when school is out or when outside weather conditions favor park visitation, attendance soars. As it does so, food service volume (and demand for other support services) expands with it. Sometimes demand for these support services is quite large in proportion—Disney earns over 10 percent of its revenues from food service.[4] To meet these peaks, the crew expands each summer. To supervise this expanded crew, college-age people are chosen, usually from last year's crew, as supervisors, assistant managers, and unit managers. These positions are often quite well paid, but, more significantly, they offer a chance to assume responsible roles beyond those that most organizations offer to people early in their careers. Generally, these opportunities are accompanied by training and management development programs.

As a personal note: We have graded more summer field-experience papers than we care to recall, and consistently some of the best opportunities and training experiences we have encountered have been in regional theme parks. Take a close look at the regional and local theme park in your area as a possible summer employer.

In conclusion, theme parks, both regional and national, represent one type of man-made environment available to travelers. They are becoming increasingly popular and the market is becoming increasingly competitive. They only represent one type of such environments, however. Some very different types of tourist destinations are discussed next.

CASINOS AND GAMING

To move from the innocence of theme parks and country music to **casinos** and gaming may seem like a giant step, but they do have a good deal in common as tourism attractions—and they are becoming more similar all of the time. Just note the many similarities that are now drawn between two tourist destinations: Las Vegas and Orlando. In fact, many aging baby boomers, who once brought their children to theme parks such as Disney World, are being lured to casinos and gaming destinations (in some cases, they continue to go to both). We will begin by looking at two quite different gaming markets: Las Vegas and Atlantic City. First, however, some discussion of gambling in the United States is in order.

Gambling of all kinds has grown radically in the past decade. By 1998, 37 states (and the District of Columbia) had state/city-operated lotteries and others are considering offering a lottery. When all of the gaming opportunities are considered, it becomes clear that few states are unable to offer their residents the possibility of a legal wager.

Harrah's operates this riverboat casino on the Missouri River at North Kansas City. With a capacity of 1700 passengers, the North Star has 33 table games and over 800 slot machines.
Courtesy of Harrah's Casinos

The casino gambling environment is unique in that it combines not only the games usually associated with such operations, but also entertainment, food, and drink (and sometimes lodging). This makes it more of a total recreational experience, rather than a single, discrete activity conducted in isolation.

Casino gaming has exploded, driven by two developments, in particular. The first of these was the Indian Gaming Regulatory Act of 1988, requiring that any kind of gambling that was permitted anywhere, at any time, in a state be permitted on Indian reservations in that state once a compact between the state and the Indian tribe had been concluded. In 1998, 184 federally recognized tribes offered some sort of gaming on their land. This represents a significant increase, up from 81 in 1993. The facility that is generally believed to be the largest, as well as the most profitable, is the Foxwoods Casino—the Mashantucket Pequot–owned facility in Ledyard, Connecticut.

The other development, modern riverboat gambling, did not come into being until 1991 when Iowa legalized the first gaming riverboat. There were 40 boats operating in 1994. By 1997, there were 85 boats in operation (some riverboats are really just casinos at the river's edge with a moat around them) with gaming revenues of $6.4 billion dollars. Analysts expect the riverboat gaming market to continue to grow, albeit at a slower rate.[5] Figure 14.1 indicates some revealing riverboat revenue statistics for 1997.

Three primary forces appear to be driving the current growth in gaming. The

	Revenue	Admissions	Revenue/ Admission	Boats	Tax (a)
Illinois	$1,054,735,000	24,962,139	$42.25	9	15%–35%
Indiana	$950,323,262	24,392,584	$38.96	8	20%
Iowa	$441,902,926	12,226,277	$36.14	9	20%
Louisiana	$1,245,166,972	27,081,344	$45.98	13	19%
Mississippi	$1,984,508,089	65,341,082	$30.37	30	12%
Missouri	$746,791,087	38,045,667	$19.63	16	20%
Total:	$6,423,427,336	192,049,093		85	
Average:			$36.59		18.1%

(a) Excludes admissions tax. Illinois tax is graduated based on gross revenues.

Figure 14.1 Revenue and admission statistics for riverboat gaming in 1997.
(*Source:* John J. Rohs and Margaret Blaydes, *Schroder's Annual Gaming Review*, March 6, 1998. Published by Schroder and Co., Inc.)

first is a change in consumer tastes in which people have come to see gaming as a legitimate form of entertainment, rather than something that is done only by people of questionable background.

A second force that seems to be driving the industry is convenience. It is clear that the consumer's propensity to gamble is influenced by proximity to a gaming facility. Couple this with the estimate of there being a gaming facility no more than 300 miles way from every urban area in the country.[6] In short, most of the U.S. population is already within an easy day's drive of a casino and there are still many sites available for either gaming on a reservation or on a riverboat.

A third force that explains why gambling is now so widely permitted is the intense need state and local governments have for funds. New gambling establishments are usually subject to a relatively high level of taxation because of the potential for profit. Gaming, in effect, is a voluntary tax. A high proportion of the drop (the total amount wagered) becomes win (winnings by the house) and a high proportion of the win is taxed by the state. Even in states that may not tax gaming facilities as much as others, "gifts" to the state may be made—these "gifts" may often be in the tens of millions of dollars. It is important to recognize that, as the many taxation and employment benefits to gaming are recognized by civic and business leaders in areas that have not as yet legalized gambling, there is a strong inducement to legalize it in new jurisdictions. Figure 14.2 summarizes current gaming jurisdictions.

Las Vegas

The first settlement in Las Vegas can be traced back to 1829, but the town's formation dates from 1905, when it was a small desert railroad town. Casino gambling was legalized in 1931. Following World War II, Las Vegas grew more rapidly as large

	Land Based	Riverboat/ Dockside	Indian Gaming
Arizona			X
California			X
Colorado	X		X
Connecticut			X
Idaho			X
Illinois		X	
Indiana		X	
Iowa		X	X
Kansas			X
Louisiana		X	X
Michigan			X
Minnesota			X
Mississippi		X	
Missouri		X	
Montana			X
Nebraska			X
Nevada	X		X
New Jersey	X		
New Mexico			X
New York			X
N. Carolina			X
N. Dakota			X
Oregon			X
S. Dakota	X		X
Texas			X
Washington			X
Wisconsin			X
Totals	4	6	22

Figure 14.2 Current gaming jurisdictions with gaming operations.
(*Source:* Steve Bourle, *American Casino Guide.* Published by Casino Vacations, 1998.)

hotels were built, and, by the 1950s, Las Vegas had become an established tourist destination combining casinos, superstar entertainment, and lavish hotel accommodations. Today, the Las Vegas metropolitan area has over 1.2 million residents and over 100,000 hotel and motel rooms—roughly one room for every 12 inhabitants. The greater metropolitan area's annual occupancy rate averages around 80 percent. It remains to be seen how new hotel projects will affect citywide occupancy. In all, there are some 20,000 new hotel rooms projected to open between 1998 and 2000.

Las Vegas has a good deal more to offer than casinos. The city is also known for its incredible stage shows featuring such extravaganzas as Siegfried and Roy at the Mirage Hotel. This particular show features wild animals, including rare white lions and tigers, and a cast of some 90 men and women. Siegfried and Roy are large-scale illusionists who perform such high-tech feats of magic as turning a woman into a

The city that tourism built. The top picture shows Las Vegas just after the turn of the century, when it was a small railroad town in the desert. Pictured below is the famous Las Vegas "Strip" as it looks today.
Courtesy of Las Vegas News Bureau

600-pound white tiger and making an elephant disappear into thin air. At the nearby Excalibur, King Arthur's Tournament features medieval knights mounted on horseback, charging one another in the fashion of a joust. Down the street is the Tropicana's Folies Bergere, which brings a bit of Paris to Vegas, complete with showgirls and dancing. At the Luxor, which mimics an Egyptian pyramid, guests are transported by boat down the River Nile to the elevator that takes them to their rooms. The Luxor's floor show, In Search of the Obelisk, is essentially an archeological show—consistent with the main theme. In a very different vein, one of the newest attractions in Las Vegas is Star Trek: The Experience, located at the Las Vegas Hilton. A $70 million attraction, it is complete with theme restaurants, rides, and movie and television sets.

Hotel room rates in Las Vegas are among the most affordable in the resort industry, and eating inexpensively is no problem. Many hotels sell breakfast for as little as 99 cents and offer a buffet-style dinner for less than $5.00. Las Vegas also sports over 30 golf courses, many of them of championship caliber. In addition, there are numerous tennis and racquetball facilities, as well as other recreational facilities. Entertainment and sports facilities, as well as lodging and food service bargains, are used to attract visitors to the city and to play in the casinos.

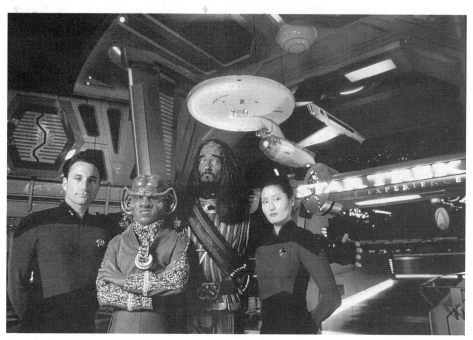

Star Trek: The Experience™ at the Las Vegas Hilton is one of the many new entertainment attractions in Las Vegas intended to draw visitors and families who are not primarily interested in gambling.
Copyright 1998 Paramount Pictures. All rights reserved.

Las Vegas literally is able to offer the tourist the "entire package." In addition to the activities and attractions listed previously, there are also natural attractions that enhance the city's image as a destination. The famous Hoover Dam and Lake Mead, with its 500 miles of shoreline, are less than a half hour away. Death Valley is a half-day's drive away, and the Grand Canyon is an easy day's drive from Las Vegas. Less well-known attractions within an hour's drive include the Valley of Fire, Red Rock Canyon, and a clutch of ghost towns.

Las Vegas is a fully developed tourist mecca, served by 60 major airlines—McCarron International Airport averages over 800 flights daily.

In addition to its recreational features, Las Vegas has a highly developed convention business, including a 1.9-million-square-foot convention center with another 2 million square feet available at major hotels in the area. More than 3.5 million conventioneers attended 3749 conventions held in the city in 1997, and another 27 million tourists pass through the city each year.

There is not a lot in Las Vegas except tourism, the businesses that serve the tourist, and the businesses that serve those businesses, and their employees. Las Vegas is the ultimate in destinations—the city that tourism built.

Although gambling continues to be Las Vegas' biggest business, the city is being repositioned as a place to go for entertainment, including gambling but certainly not limited to it. As more people across the country are exposed to gambling and consumers' perceptions of it evolve to a much wider acceptance, the kinds of people coming to Las Vegas are changing. There are many more first-time visitors and more families are making it a family destination. In addition, the city is now drawing a great many more international visitors than ever before—an increase from 10 percent in 1990 to 18 percent in 1996.[8]

Even with its entry into family entertainment, however, it is important to remember that gambling is the mainstay of the Las Vegas (and greater Clark County) economy. Casinos take in roughly $4.6 billion in Las Vegas each year and $5.7 billion in the county. Tourists spend over $400 each per visit, while conventioneers spend well over $700 and trade show attendees over $1000, all in addition to the sums spent on gaming—the average visitor spends close to $600 per visit on gambling. Between 1995 and 1997, the total visitor contribution increased from less than $21 billion to $25 billion.

Those newly acquainted with gambling, it seems, want to visit the big one. Las Vegas is a national, and increasingly international, center that probably stands to gain from the spread of gaming without suffering unduly from the proliferation of riverboat and Indian gaming competitors. On the other hand, it is likely that local and regional gaming centers will, in time, feel the effects of intensifying competition and some are even suggesting that the market is already saturated.[9]

Laughlin (Clark County)

Las Vegas statistics cover all of Clark County, which includes another gambling center, Laughlin. Its location, about 90 miles south of Las Vegas, may be part of its appeal. Casino gambling began there in a modest way in 1969. In 1984, Laughlin's population was only 95 people. Ten years later, it had risen to 8500 but, more significantly, the town had grown from one small casino and restaurant to a city sporting 10 major hotels along the Colorado River with 10,360 rooms, nearly 10,000 of them built in the past five years.

The dramatic growth of Laughlin, built in a mass market of visitors to whom gambling was just an activity rather than *the* activity, in some respects pointed the way for its larger neighbor, Las Vegas. Where Las Vegas' casinos are shut off from the outer world, in Laughlin picture windows are all the rage; everything is brightly lighted and open; and most casino employees wear Western dress, even the pit bosses. Much of the volume of traffic comes from nearby prosperous cities in Arizona such as Phoenix, while most of the rest are from southern California. In the winter, however, there is a significant number of snowbird customers who fill parking lots with recreational vehicles. A more "laid-back" atmosphere that is family friendly seems to account for the success of Laughlin. However, the area has been losing market share to other Nevada gaming areas. Although it bills itself as the "fastest growing entertainment area in the world," it experienced its fourth straight year of gaming win decline in 1997.

Atlantic City

Atlantic City has a lot to teach us about tourism, both good and bad. Atlantic City has always been a tourist city since its founding in the mid-1850s. It was once the premier resort city on the East Coast of the United States, famous for its boardwalk and its resort hotels, catering principally to prosperous upper-middle-class Americans. With the coming of automobiles, motels, cheaper travel, and changing tastes in leisure, however, Atlantic City began to deteriorate. From 1960 to 1975, the city's population declined by 15,000, the number of visitors fell to 2 million, the number of hotel rooms decreased by 40 percent, and Atlantic City became a case study in the difficulty of reviving a tourist center once it had gone downhill.

As one observer put it, Atlantic City was a tourist resort without any tourists.[10] From a peak tourist center for earlier generations, Atlantic City became virtually an abandoned hulk, rusting away at its moorings. Like many older, worn-out tourism centers, its plant was outmoded and in bad repair. Perhaps more serious, it no longer had any appeal in the market, and the revenue wasn't there to rebuild. Then, in 1976, gambling was approved, and in 1978 the first casino hotel opened.

The city's turnaround has been remarkable. Atlantic City is now drawing 37 million visitors each year, making it one of America's largest tourist attractions. Planning has also played a large role in its success. Atlantic City casinos are required to reinvest 1.25 percent of their gaming revenues in the community and state through the state-run Casino Reinvestment Development Authority. Literally billions of dollars have been invested in the city's infrastructure and housing stock. Atlantic City now boasts a new convention center and some 17,000 projected hotel rooms, which are in various stages of planning.

Atlantic City is quite different from Las Vegas. Although there are two major cities within a day's drive of Las Vegas, Los Angeles and San Diego, Atlantic City has one-quarter of the U.S. population within a 300-mile range. New York City, Philadelphia, and Washington, DC, are all within 150 miles. Approximately two-thirds of Atlantic city's visitors arrive by car, and just over one-fourth arrive by motorcoach. Few, in comparison, arrive by rail or air.

In contrast with Las Vegas' hotel and motel rooms, Atlantic City has only 16,000 rooms, although this number is expected to more than double in the next couple of years. With the large number of day-trippers, Atlantic City will never need as many overnight accommodations as does Las Vegas. On the other hand, Atlantic City hotel operators and tourism officials have recognized that overnight guests have a potentially greater impact on the economy. As a result, the agencies responsible for marketing Atlantic City and southern New Jersey have launched a collaborative effort to encourage longer-stay guests. Visitors are encouraged by this new regional program to see the historic and scenic attractions that abound in the area. New Jersey is, after all, one of the original 13 colonies, rich in history. Moreover, its beaches, which border the Atlantic Ocean, have long been famous as vacation spots.

Atlantic City's skyline was once a study in contrasts. Its new or renewed casino hotels are the latest word in casino glitter but between them, for a long time, were either run-down buildings where speculators had purchased property or open spaces where old buildings had been razed. Outside the boardwalk's immediate vicinity, much of the city was filled with dilapidated slum housing—an element that many often focused on when discussing Atlantic City. In recent years, however, the face of the city has begun to show the impact of the Casino Reinvestment Development Authority, as well as other private and public investment. Today, the city is benefiting from a $1 billion facelift. At its core is a new $250 million convention center as part of a corridor that was designed to create a spectacular entrance to the city. The corridor is a multiblock complex of enclosed shops, as well as an urban entertainment center that includes the new transportation center and connects the convention center to the famous boardwalk and several of Atlantic City's casino hotels. Further, new hotels are being built—some of the noncasino variety. Finally, much of the empty space on the other side of the main street has been filled with public parking garages to accommodate the many cars that visitors drive to Atlantic City.

The economic impact of Atlantic City is also being felt outside this city of 38,000 people, in the 125,000-person Atlantic County, and in the wider southern New Jersey area. Much of the tax revenue is dedicated to funding programs for the disabled, the disadvantaged, and senior citizens. Further, casinos in Atlantic City (still the only municipality in the state where casinos are allowed) employ about 50,000 state residents. Finally, regulatory savings are being used to develop new facilities such as a professional baseball park and aquarium.[11]

Casino Markets and the Business of Casinos

The business of casinos is gambling, at table games such as roulette, blackjack, and dice. In addition, a major and growing gambling pastime is the slot machine. From the casino's point of view, what matters in evaluating a customer is his or her volume of play, because the odds in every game clearly favor the house. Big winners are good news for the casino because of the publicity they bring. In the long run, however, the casino wins.

Casino markets can be divided into four general groups: tourists, high rollers at the tables, high rollers at the slot machines, and the bus trade. **Tourists** are those who visit the city to take in the sights, see a show, and try their hand at the games, but with modest limits in mind as to how much they are prepared to wager and lose, usually up to $100 but often as much as $250 or $500.

The **high roller**, as one Atlantic City casino executive put it, is a person who plays with black chips, that is, $100 chips. In Las Vegas, industry experts indicate that a high roller's average bet would be in the $150 to $225 range and that he or she would be expected to have a line of credit of $15,000 during a typical three-day visit to Las Vegas.

For high rollers, gambling is the major attraction, but they also thrive on the personal attention given to them by the casino and hotel staff and the **comps**, complimentary or no-charge services and gifts provided by the casino. Some high rollers wager more than the average and, a few, much more. In general, the level of comps is based on the volume of play, with some casinos prepared to provide free transportation, luxurious hotel suites, meals, and show tickets, for instance. More modest but still significant is the high roller slot player. In Atlantic City, a $500 gambling budget qualifies as a "slot high roller," but $2,000 is a closer figure in cash or line of credit for Las Vegas. Comps and special recognition are extended to these players, too, according to their level of play. Casinos issue cards with an electronic identification embedded in them. These cards are inserted into the machine to record the player's level of play, and comps are based on the volume of play (not losses). In fact, a $1 slot player is worth more to the house than a player who bets $100 in a table game. Because there is very little labor associated with slot machines, the house earns an 80 percent operating profit compared to 20 to 25 percent on table games.

Some areas depend greatly on such machines. The increasing proportion of casino space taken up by slot machines is explained, in good part, by a changing consumer base that includes a much wider spectrum of society than it did 20 or even 10 years ago. As you can see, however, the superior profit margins of slot machines probably enter into the calculation, too. On Las Vegas' Strip, slot revenue is 49 percent of the market, while table games account for 51 percent. In the newer gambling areas, however, such as riverboat and Indian-owned casinos, slots can account for as much as 75 percent of the wagering. In Atlantic City, slot machines represent 70 percent of gaming revenues.[12]

A final category of players, is the **bus trade**, effectively "low rollers." These are often retirees and, surprisingly, often people on unemployment compensation. They, too, come for the gambling but usually have a budget of only $35 to $70. They are often attracted by a bargain low price.

In Atlantic City, this bus trade still provides a substantial portion of the year-round volume of business but, as we have already noted, the city's casinos are

Interior of the casino in the New York, New York Hotel in Las Vegas.
Courtesy of New York, New York Hotel

deliberately reducing the significance of this segment while trying to build volume among more well-heeled players. Like their high-roller neighbors, the bus trade, too, are attracted by relatively generous comps. A bus deal, costing $10 to $12, might include round-trip bus transportation, a $5 meal discount coupon, and a $10 roll of quarters ("coin," as it's called in Atlantic City) to get them started.

Casino Staffing

The casino gaming staff is made up of dealers (and croupiers), a floor person who supervises several dealers, and a pit boss. (In craps, a boxman assists the dealer, handling the bank.) In the pit, a group of similar games, the pit boss is assisted by a pit clerk who handles record keeping.

The pit boss is really a technician, expert from years of experience in the practice of the game. He or she generally supervises the play, approves "markers," that is, approves the extension of credit (within house limits), approves in-house food and beverage comps for known players, and generally provides personal attention to high rollers.

The floor person supervises between two and five dealers, depending on the game, and never more than four games. He or she is also responsible for closely watching repeat customers to estimate their average bet, a figure that is crucial to the casino's marketing intelligence.

Slot machine areas are staffed by change people working under a supervisor. Change people and supervisors also offer recognition and personal contact for frequent visitors and slot high rollers.

Comps above a certain dollar level are generally approved by the casino's senior management. Comp services for a "junket" group are approved by the casino's marketing staff. Junkets are similar to tours that might be sold by a travel agent except that the sights are generally the casino and its hotel environment, and there may be no charge for any of the services because of the expectation of casino play by the visitor. Junkets are put together by the casino or, more commonly, by junket brokers in distant cities.

Dealers need to be alert to players' attempts at cheating, and they themselves are constantly scrutinized by supervisors and security personnel because of the temptation of dishonesty where so much cash is changing hands. The security systems that exist in casinos are incredibly sophisticated and unlike anything that exists in other segments of the hospitality industry. After tours of casinos, students inevitably comment on the security before anything else.

Working in casinos is very challenging. It requires a quick mind and an ability to work with people who are under considerable pressure. Players sometimes become abusive and unreasonable, and staff are expected to avoid, whenever possible, a difficult scene and permanently alienating a player and his or her friends. Not surprisingly, the higher the roller is, the greater will be the patience that may be expected of the staff. As is true with other segments of the hospitality industry, the casino industry is not for everyone. However, for those who like the excitement and the challenge, the segment provides great opportunities.

The authors would be uncomfortable if they did not close this section with a personal observation:

> Gambling does raise serious moral and social questions for many, including us. Often gamblers exceed the limit of what they can afford, damaging their ability to care for their families. Under the present conditions of the chaotic and unrestrained growth of gambling in many parts of the country, the probability of a scandal of major proportions is heightened. Our observations, moreover, are that gambling creates an environment that often degrades people and raises money and material things to a higher level than they deserve. A real and somewhat scary question, though, is whether this emphasis on money and things and the deemphasis of people are a result of gambling or whether gambling is a reflection of those traits in our society at large. Whatever our views on the moral and social aspects of casinos and gambling, however, we feel that any serious student of the hospitality industry needs to be aware of this large and growing part of our industry.

*U*RBAN ENTERTAINMENT CENTERS

When traveling for recreational purposes, people do not just limit their visits to theme parks and casinos. The term **urban entertainment centers** means just that—destinations located in cities (or even the cities, themselves), which offer a variety of tourist-related activities. Urban entertainment centers vary widely. Some are designed on a smaller scale as a draw for local traffic and an enhancement to the local environment. Others are on a scale nearly as grand as those we considered in regard to theme parks, and there are many that fall between these two extremes.

Sports stadiums, one type of urban entertainment center, have been with us since the time of Rome's Colosseum, but the latest variety of such centers is the covered superdome, such as those in Houston, Toronto, and New Orleans. Publicly owned stadiums and arenas are becoming essential to gaining the status of big-league cities—not only do the stadiums draw in the fans but they also help pay off the stadium bonds and create jobs.

These facilities host not only sports events but various types of entertainers, rock concerts, and circuses, and may also double as a convention center of sorts, such as the Superdome in New Orleans. Further, they provide gathering places that entertain residents or attract visitors to a city.

A close relative to such sports centers are downtown convention centers, which allow for a mixture of business and pleasure. The visitors to a convention or trade show are on business. However, many of these gatherings are more social than professional, and even the most business-oriented meetings are, in large part, devoted to having a good time. Conventions bring major influxes of people and spending. Chicago, for instance, attracted 4 million delegates who were attending various conventions, trade shows, and corporate meetings in 1997 (see Case History 14.1).

Convention, trade show, and sports centers were once largely the preserve of great metropolitan centers such as New York with its Jacob Javits Convention Center and Chicago with McCormick Place. Increasingly, however, cities such as Seattle and San Jose, California, large but of second rank in size, have developed urban entertainment centers as a means of challenging established travel patterns and increasing the travel business in their markets. It should be noted that many cities, including New Orleans, are currently in the midst of expansion projects that will allow them to compete more effectively with cities such as New York, Las Vegas, and Chicago.

Although medium-sized cities cannot bid in the national convention market for the very large conventions, they often can attract smaller national meetings and regional conferences. For this reason, many cities successfully sell bond issues to build civic meeting centers that improve a community's ability to compete for its share of the travel market. That travel market, more and more city leaders are learning, means more sales for local businesses, increased employment, and more tax revenues.

Whether the results of these civic efforts always justify such an investment is subject to debate. In any case, though, somebody must operate these centers, and the skills involved (dealing with various travelers, providing food service, and managing housekeeping and building operations, to name only a few) clearly fall within the hospitality management graduate's domain. The significance of this new area of hospitality management may be measured by the fact that ARAMARK has a special division to manage conference centers.

ℭase History 14.1 The National Restaurant Association Restaurant Show

The annual National Restaurant Association (**http://www.restaurant.org/**) Restaurant Show held in Chicago should interest students from both a supply and a demand perspective. Celebrating its 80th anniversary in 1999, it is the food service industry's largest gathering of people, exhibitors, and products/supplies. One hundred thousand conventioneers converge on Chicago each May to be a part of this show. In order to appreciate the sheer magnitude of the show, consider the following:

◆ Attracts over 100,000 attendees

◆ Offers almost 2000 exhibits, which include anything and everything having to do with the restaurant industry

◆ Shows the latest products and services available to the industry

◆ Covers 1.3 million square feet of exhibit space

◆ Offers culinary competitions, speakers, and activities for attendees, including the "Salute to Excellence" to which select hospitality students are invited

The show should be of interest to hospitality students for a variety of reasons: It represents a "destination" for people either in or affiliated with the restaurant industry; it is a good example of a mega-convention/trade show as discussed in the chapter; and it is a major industry event that every hospitality student should attend at least once. About 60 hospitality programs were represented at the 1998 show. Each of these programs managed a booth on the show floor where they were able to promote their schools. In most cases, the booths were staffed by both faculty and students of the program. Those that go each year already know what a valuable learning experience the show provides. Additional information about the show is available from the NRA office.

Increasingly, urban planners are including in their developments plazas designed to accommodate amusements, dining, and other leisure activities. One is also likely to find fine arts, gardens, and other visually appealing items adorning the area. The prototype of this kind of plaza is Rockefeller Center in the heart of New York City. Rockefeller Center takes up all of 11 acres of prime real estate, which represents a combination of leisure/tourist and business activities. Among other things, it has fine shops, restaurants (including the world-famous Rainbow Room), and tourist attractions, such as tours of NBC. The 6000-seat Radio City Music Hall is also located in the complex. It even has ice-skating rinks (in winter), horse shows, karate demonstrations, and model airplane contests in milder seasons.

Of the more recently constructed plazas, the First National Plaza in front of the First Chicago Building is a model for plazas to come. A computer controls the fountain, so that visitors won't get splashed on windy days. From May to October, the plaza features free noontime entertainment, late afternoon concerts, and an outdoor cafe. It also has, year round, a restaurant, a bar, a legitimate theater, and retail shops.

City waterfront redevelopment projects, too, have become centers that attract visitors and enrich the lives of the local people. Both Boston's and Baltimore's efforts have received a lot of attention over the last couple of decades. Both projects literally changed the image and demeanor of those cities. Other cities, albeit with different types of waterfronts, include New Orleans and San Antonio. These cities have done an effective job of using waterways as a central focus of their cities.

Restoration and revitalization of aging sections of a city require the involvement of hospitality industry operations. Dallas Alley (in Dallas, Texas) was built in what was a half-forgotten place, which housed freight cars, warehouses, and factories. In an old Sunshine Biscuit factory and an adjoining building that was once a Coca Cola bottling plant, a group of private investors built Dallas Alley, an aggregation of nine nightclubs. The center is located near a $25 million festival marketplace housed in a former cracker and candy factory. Dallas Alley, alone, attracts over a million visitors annually. Similarly, the old Jax Brewery in New Orleans was converted and now houses retail shops and restaurants.

Zoos and Aquariums

Zoos and aquariums can also be major tourism generators. For instance, each year roughly 5 million people visit the San Diego Zoo. The zoo also operates an 1800-acre wildlife preserve 30 miles north of San Diego. The zoo and preserve, like so many other tourist destinations, have a substantial educational mission. The preserve, for instance, is visited by 40,000 elementary and secondary schoolchildren each year. Aquariums, too, are becoming ever more popular. Fine aquariums exist in Baltimore, Boston, New Orleans, Chicago, and Vancouver, as well as some smaller cities.

As with other attractions discussed earlier in the chapter, zoos and aquariums must also provide food service to their visitors. Also, like other attractions, the number of visitors to these destinations expands when school is out. As a result, these operations can offer summer employment opportunities to students, with a decent chance at getting into a supervisory position.

Shopping Centers

Shopping centers are usually thought of as catering principally to local shoppers. Even so, such centers can be more than a little ambitious. The St. Louis Centre suggests the scale of a large, locally centered mall and the often close relationship of such centers to the hospitality industry. The Centre was begun as an urban renewal project in 1972 and was completed 13 years later at a total cost of $17.5 million. Comprising a two-block stretch of downtown St. Louis, the Centre serves about 10 million people each year, comprising a mix of locals, conventioneers, and tourists. The Centre has a mix of retail shops, sit-down restaurants and a food court. Other cities that have established similar retail attractions include New Orleans and Boston, among many others.

Finally, let's look briefly at two **mega-shopping centers**, one in western Canada and the other in Minnesota, both built on the grandest scale yet undertaken. In the case of the West Edmonton Mall, the aim from the very beginning was to attract tourists, as well as local residents, to the center, as Edmonton, Alberta, a city of 560,000, could not support a mall of this scale by itself.

The scale quite literally boggles the mind. Consider its total indoor area of 5.2 million square feet, equivalent to 28 city blocks. It is a combination mega-mall/amusement park/food court/hotel/recreation center/museum/casino. In fact, it combines all of the elements already discussed in this chapter! Malls are also sup-

A shopping center with a difference. Canada's West Edmonton Mall is both a mall and a theme park. Among its attractions are four submarines.
Courtesy of Triple 5 Corp.

posed to have stores and it has 800 of them, along with restaurants, miniature golf, an aquarium, movie theaters, and much more. The ceiling peaks at 16 stories with a mile-long, two-level main concourse. The interior plantings include $3 million worth of tropical plants, which includes a grove of 50-foot palm trees! The mall houses an amusement park and a water park with a 5-acre pool where you can surf on 6-foot waves, water-ski, ride the rapids, and get a suntan, even when the outside temperature is well below zero. The sights include a dolphin show, a Spanish galleon, an 18-hole miniature golf course, a 50,000-gallon aquarium, and four submarines. The 33-foot-long computer-controlled subs will seat 24 people. The mall is dedicated to the idea that shopping is more than just a utilitarian chore and can be an opportunity for fun.

About a third of the visitors to the mall are from Edmonton and its trading area. Nearly a fifth are from Alberta outside the 60-mile trading area. The other half comes from the rest of Canada and the United States. Half of these Canadian visitors and 75 percent of the Americans come specifically to visit the West Edmonton Mall. Visitors from the United States average a four-day stay. Visitors, interestingly enough, spend as much or more money outside the mall as they do inside.

In Bloomington, Minnesota, just outside Minneapolis, is another mega-mall only slightly smaller than the West Edmonton Mall. The Mall of America covers 4.2 million square feet (about 78 acres). An indoor seven-acre theme park, Knotts Camp Snoopy, at the heart of the mall, offers 50 rides, shows, and other attractions. The mall also includes over 400 retail outlets as well as an 18-hole miniature golf course, over 50 restaurants, nightclubs, and bars, several offering live entertainment. Twelve thousand people are employed at the Mall of America. The mall drew 35 million visitors during its first year and it continues to draw between 35 and 40 million people each year.[13] The mall even has its own newspaper to keep its faithful properly informed of current and upcoming events. Although a description of the mall cannot begin to do it justice, readers might want to visit its web site and take the virtual tour (**http://www.mallofamerica.com**).

*T*EMPORARY ATTRACTIONS: FAIRS AND FESTIVALS

Fairs date from the Middle Ages when they served as important centers for economic and cultural revival. **Festivals** also have their roots in early history and were originally religious events. Towns both large and small have long hosted such events.

World Expositions (World's Fairs) are year-long attractions, but even a local fair such as the agricultural fair in Duquoin, Illinois, which annually attracts a quarter of a million people to this town of 7000, can have a major impact on a city. Some fairs celebrate local industry, whereas others have cultural, religious, and historical roots, as is the case with Mardi Gras in New Orleans (Mardi Gras could perhaps be best characterized as a citywide celebration, rather than a festival, per se). Tradition is not enough, however. A successful event must attract tourists, whether local, regional, national, or international.[14] Indeed, a festival or fair is a quasi-business activity. Its success is measured by its ability to attract visitors, to cover its costs, and to maintain sufficient local support to keep it staffed, usually almost entirely with unpaid volunteers.

Winter festivals reposition the season of slush and rust as a community asset. The growing popularity of winter sports fits well with ice carnivals. The one in St. Paul, Minnesota, which dates all the way back to 1886, includes events such as concerts, skiing, sleigh rides, ice sculptures, hot-air balloon rides, parades, a royal coronation, car racing, and a softball tournament on ice. Quebec's winter carnival, begun in 1954 to energize a stagnant economy, is now the city's third largest industry and generates revenues of $30 million a year. Summer festivals in warmer climates may accomplish similar objectives.

Events such as these clearly affect the economy of the cities and regions that sponsor them. Local patrons spend money from their family entertainment budget that might have left the community. Visitors spend in food, lodging, souvenirs, gasoline, public transportation, and the like. In most cases, the event itself makes purchases that contribute to the local economy.

The economic effects of fairs and festivals can have a major impact on the community and especially on its hospitality industry. For this reason, hospitality industry managers are often prominent sponsors and backers of such events. In some instances, festivals and events may actually be organized by the local industry. This was the case with the French Quarter Festival in New Orleans, which was established in an effort to draw locals back into the downtown area.

We ought not lose sight of the fact, however, that, like so many other aspects of tourism, fairs and festivals also bring important social and cultural benefits to their communities: They celebrate the local heritage and bring members from all parts of the community together to work as volunteers. A good example of this comes, again, from New Orleans. The New Orleans Jazz and Heritage Festival, known worldwide for its music, actually brings together several elements of local and international cultures into one big festival. It has grown from a small local event that drew several hundred people to one that attracted almost 500,000 people over seven days in 1998 (see Case History 14.2). Money from the event also goes to support the local community radio station, fund grants, and provides numerous other community benefits.

In some cases, a festival may even be used to help in the regeneration of a community. In New Haven, Connecticut, the Office of Housing and Neighborhood Development uses neighborhood festivals as a centerpiece in its Commercial Revitalization Program. The effect of a festival on a neighborhood's turnaround is described as follows:

> The signs of change are now visible to the community. The investment climate has improved substantially and outside interest has emerged. There may be a desire to show off improvement. Many new characters are involved and the character of the area is changing.[15]

Large or small, then, these kinds of events can be a vital part of the life of a community, city, or region. In some cases, they may help to define, or reinforce, a community. They clearly serve a variety of functions and, like other entities discussed earlier, offer opportunities for graduates of hospitality programs.

𝒞ase History   The New Orleans JazzFest
14.2

Many festivals have music as their primary focus: the Newport Jazz Festival, the Chicago Blues Festival, and (once upon a time) Woodstock. Internationally, there are such renowned annual musical events such as the Montreaux Jazz Festival (Switzerland) and Sunsplash (Jamaica). One festival that stands out in the United States, however, is the New Orleans Jazz and Heritage Festival (or JazzFest, to locals). New Orleans, itself, is a melting pot of culture, which is one of the reasons the city is such a unique American city and JazzFest is uniquely New Orleans.

JazzFest celebrates all that is New Orleans (as well as cultures that have a direct connection to New Orleans). Over 4000 artists (musicians as well as crafts and culinary practitioners) participate in the festival each year. Imagine a festival with eight major music stages and several smaller ones; three crafts areas, each representing a different genre of crafts; and over 70 food booths offering the best food that New Orleans (and the rest of the world) has to offer; plus interviews, cooking demonstrations, exhibits, activities for the kids, and much more. It's a music festival, culinary event, and crafts fair all rolled into one. This past year, in addition to the usual offerings, the country of Panama was celebrated with exhibits, performances, and dances from that country.

JazzFest grew from a small gathering, where there were actually more performers than attendees, to a major event, which drew an excess of 450,000 people in 1998. In a city that is known for its Mardi Gras, JazzFest has become the preferred event for a lot of people and a good example of a festival that truly has a positive impact on its host city.

𝒩ATURAL ENVIRONMENTS

Urban entertainment centers may be the epitome of man-made tourism attractions. Not everything, however, that contributes to tourism is man made. In the public sector, national and state parks, forests, and waters should interest hospitality students just as much. These uniquely American recreation areas have been copied the world over. As far as hospitality innovation goes, they are, in fact, relatively new. The first park created by Congress, Yosemite, was established toward the end of the Civil War, in 1864.[16] The National Park Service itself was not established until 1916.

The number of visits to national parks grew rapidly in the 1950s and 1960s, expanding roughly to four times the 1950 total by 1965 and doubling again by 1980. As Figure 14.3 indicates, growth slowed during the first half of the 1980s and even showed a modest decline during some years.[17] The early 1980s, saw both a serious recession and an energy crisis. Because the largest number of parks and other reserved areas under National Park Service (NPS) administration are located in areas distant from population centers in the midwestern and eastern United

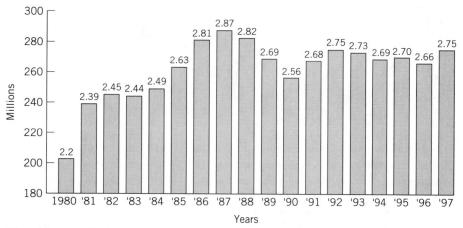

Figure 14.3   National Park Service recreation visits.
(*Source:* National Park Service.)

States, national park visits are sensitive to economic conditions and to the price and availability of gasoline. The most recent recession, however, does not appear to have retarded the growth in park visitation. Total annual park visits (for recreation purposes) exceeded 275 million in 1997. Nonrecreation visits added another 143 million visits.[18] Interest in nature and environmental experiences continues to grow—beyond visits to national parks. This is reflected in Global Hospitality Note 14.1.

In 1997, there were almost 16 million overnight stays in national parks. Lodging in park concession hotels accounted for 22 percent of those stays, and recreational vehicle stays accounted for another 17 percent. Tent camping accounted for almost 23 percent, while backpacking accounted for about 14 percent. The balance is largely accounted for by organizational group camping and overnight boating trips.[19]

The National Parks Service Act of 1916 established the National Parks System with the clear intention of providing recreation and, at the same time, preserving the parks for the enjoyment of future generations. The increased crowding of existing facilities has led those interested in preservation as well as recreation, including the National Park Service itself, to propose drastic limitations on the use of private automobiles within the parks. The National Parks and Conservation Association (NPCA), a private group that supports a conservationist view of natural parks, has suggested that such accommodations as hotels, cabins, and campgrounds be restricted or even reduced within these parks.

The NPCA does not argue that hospitality facilities and services should be unavailable. Instead, it proposes that staging areas with lodging and other services be established in nearby communities and that these staging areas be connected to the parks by low-cost transportation. Proposals like this would reduce private auto use and help preserve the natural beauty, a park's principal attraction and reason

Ecotourism in Other Countries

𝒢lobal Hospitality Note 14.1

The hospitality and tourism industries, as well as tourists themselves, have long been accused of being environmentally unfriendly. Much has changed recently, though, and there seems to be a movement toward a "greening" of the industry. Many hotels are doing what they can to cut down on their waste streams and some major restaurant chains are converting to more biodegradable materials. Perhaps the greatest changes that are taking place, however, are in the area of tourism.

The environmental viability of certain tourism destinations is becoming a growing concern to both users and suppliers. Ecotourism has arrived, though. Ecotourism is, simply defined, tourism and related activities that are not only friendly toward the natural environment but that also serve to promote enjoyment of the natural environment.[1] The hope is that ecotourism is where education and preservation of the environment can coexist and where resource conservation can be achieved while servicing tourists.

Although the concept of ecotourism has been around since the beginning of time, the label has only recently been coined. Travelers have always had the option of striking out on their own to

experience any number of activities including camping, hiking, canoeing, and so on. The new genre of ecotourism, however, presents travelers with a host of available choices. Tourists may now visit such international destinations as Belize, Costa Rica, Laos, and Kenya to interface with the local culture and natural environment. It is believed that the whole ecotourism movement began in the tiny country of Belize where it both served to protect the country from becoming spoiled and, at the same time, promote what the country had to offer in the way of its natural resources.[2]

Travelers, or ecotourists, can now participate in organized tours of jungles and rainforests, go on safaris (where guns are replaced with cameras), or even stay at an "eco resort" such as the Lapas Rios resort in Costa Rica. So called "eco resorts" have even emerged that offer travelers many of the comforts of home in an environmentally friendly setting. Ecotourism has truly become an international phemonena.

1. Patricia Wright, "Paradise Preserved," *Massachusetts Magazine,* Summer 1994.
2. Larry Krotz, *Tourists* (Faber and Faber, 1996).

for being. It might also create major new commercial recreation areas and opportunities for hospitality firms and graduates of hospitality management programs. Moreover, given the leadership of the national parks in the field of recreation, this pattern might well extend to state parks and forests in future years if it is accepted by Congress and the people.

This huge tourism activity has created many opportunities for tourism enterprises serving the areas that surround natural recreation sites. Although park management is a specialized field addressed in professional education programs in parks and recreation management at colleges and universities, the management of the auxiliary services in and around parks—particularly food services, hotels, and

Canoeing inside Santa Elena Canyon in Big Bend National Park, Texas.
Courtesy of National Park Service/photo by M. W. Williams

motels—lies within the hospitality management career area. Park lodging and food service concessions hire large numbers of students and, in fact, are staffed largely by students during peak periods. People who work for the same concessionaires for several summers have a good opportunity of gaining supervisory experience and of seeing some beautiful country.

$\mathcal{S}$UMMARY

In this chapter, we discussed recreation, its motives and different types of destinations. After explaining why people travel, we divided destinations into primary or touring and secondary or stopover. Then we talked about planned play environments, such as national and regional theme parks, casinos (as exemplified by Las Vegas and Atlantic City), urban entertainment centers such as sports stadiums and mega-shopping centers, and, finally, the natural environment, especially national parks.

Along the way, we pointed out the possible employment opportunities for both temporary jobs and permanent careers. Destination attractions are often big hospitality businesses in themselves and act as magnets that keep the flow of tourism not only going but also growing.

◆ $\mathcal{K}$EY WORDS AND CONCEPTS

Recreation	Planned play environments
Primary destinations	Theme parks
Secondary destinations	Casinos

Casino markets	Fairs
Tourists	Festivals
High rollers	Urban entertainment centers
Bus trade	Mega-shopping centers
Comps	Natural environments

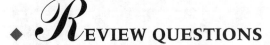REVIEW QUESTIONS

1. What are some of the reasons that people travel?

2. What is the difference between primary and secondary destinations?

3. What do country music, theme parks, and casinos have in common as tourist attractions? How are they different?

4. Briefly describe a theme park that you have visited, and explain why you think it is popular.

5. How do national theme parks, such as Disney World, differ from regional theme parks, such as Six Flags?

6. Besides gambling, what advantages does Las Vegas offer?

7. What are comps and why are they important to casinos?

8. Describe how mega-shopping centers combine different tourism elements.

9. What is a staging area, and why is it important?

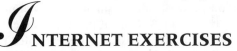INTERNET EXERCISES

1. **Site Name:** *The U.S. State Department*
   URL: http://www.state.gov/index.html
   Background Information: The Department of State is the leading U.S. foreign affairs agency. It advances U.S. objectives and interests in shaping a freer, more secure, and more prosperous world through formulating, representing, and implementing the President's foreign policy. The Secretary of State, the ranking member of the Cabinet and fourth in line of presidential succession, is the President's principal advisor on foreign policy and the person chiefly responsible for U.S. representation abroad.

   EXERCISES

   a. What international travel services/information does the U.S. State Department provide?

b. Given two countries such as Colombia and Germany, determine the safety issues/warnings issued by the U.S. State Department for traveling in these countries.

2. **Site Name:** *Theme Park Interest Group*
   URL: http://pages.prodigy.com/alpha/themecoi.htm
   Background Information: A guide to theme parks around the world featuring sections on attractions, carousels, ferris wheels, and roller coasters.

   Site Name: *Travel-Finder Directory for "Amusement and Theme Parks"*
   URL: http://www.travel-finder.com/search/Amusement__and__Theme__ Parks.html
   Background Information: Search for amusement and theme parks by activity, state, country, region, and/or continent.

   EXERCISE: Choose a theme park in the United States and one overseas. In a class discussion, describe the overall theme, rides/attractions/shows, prices, job opportunities, etc. for each theme park.

3. **Site Name:** *The Online Gaming Guide*
   URL: http://www.gaming-guide.com/
   Background Information: This web site indexes hotel casino resorts, on-line casinos, on-line sports betting, sports handicapping, interactive lotteries, interactive bingo, and many more interesting web destinations.

   Site Name: *Casino Links Online*
   URL: http://www.casinolinks.com/
   Background Information: CasinoLinks.com is a web site that indexes casino resorts and hotels, Internet casinos and gaming, as well as gambling tips and merchandise.

   EXERCISE: Find info on the Trump Taj Mahal Casino. What information is provided about the casino on the web site?

 ◆ *N* OTES

1. Robert Christie Mill and Alastair M. Morrison, *The Tourism System* (Upper Saddle River, NJ: Prentice–Hall, 1985), Chapter 8.

2. Susan Mosdale, Director of Association Relations, International Association of Amusement Parks and Attractions, personal communication, April 7, 1998.

3. We would like to acknowledge the assistance of Tom Adkinson of Gaylord Entertainment who provided us with the information in this section and was more than generous with his time in expanding on the factual material.

4. *Nations Restaurant News*, December 6, 1993, p. 7.

5. John J. Rohs and Margaret Blaydes, *Schroder's Annual Gaming Review*, March 6, 1998.

6. Karl Titz, "Casino Marketing," *Casino Management: Past, Present, Future*, p. 245.

7. Brad Farner, Smith Travel Research, personal communication, June 8, 1998.

8. Rohs and Blaydes, *Schroder's Annual Gaming Review*.

9. Ibid.

10. David Gardner, Executive Vice President, Atlantic City Casino Association, personal communication. Mr. Gardner was employed as a city planner in Atlantic City during the 1960s.

11. Casino Gambling in New Jersey: A Report to the National Gambling Impact Study Commission, January 1998.

12. Rohs and Blaydes, *Schroder's Annual Gaming Review.*

13. Mall of America Web Site (www.mallofamerica.com), May 14, 1998.

14. Donald Getz, *Festivals, Special Events and Tourism,* (New York: Van Nostrand Reinhold, 1991).

15. *A Promotion Guide to Commercial Revitalization* (New Haven, CN: Office of Housing and Neighborhood Development, n.d.), p. 9.

16. The first national park was Yellowstone, established in 1872. Yosemite was originally a California state park created by the U.S. Congress. It became a national park in 1890.

17. National Park Service (NPS) statistics have undergone a substantial revision. The Statistical Abstract published by the NPS shows figures adjusted to the revised basis only back to 1980, making direct comparison to earlier periods difficult.

18. Public Use Statistics Office, National Park Service, personal communication, May 13, 1998.

19. Public Use Statistics Office, National Park Service, personal communication, May 13, 1998.

Part 5

Management in the Hospitality Industry

Chapter 15

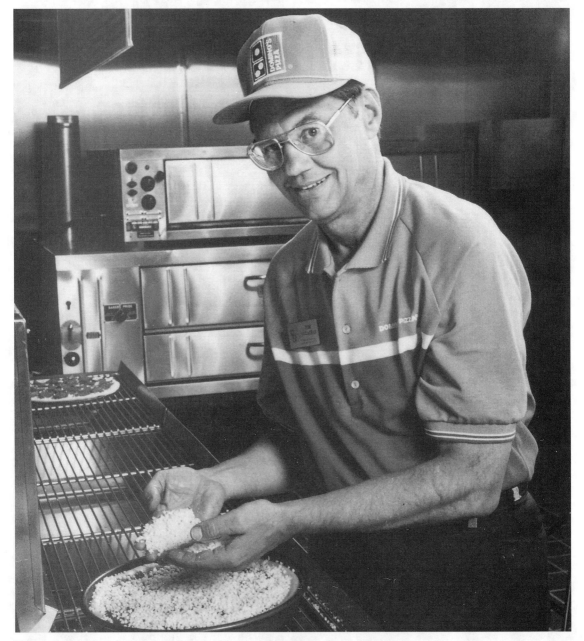

Thomas S. Monaghan, founder and president of Domino's Pizza, Inc.

Management: A New Way of Thinking

The Purpose of This Chapter

We modern North Americans are so management conscious that we often forget how new a field of thought and kind of work management actually is. Like any growing idea, management is still moving toward maturity. As a student, therefore, you would be wise to be skeptical about any "eternal truths" or unchanging principles you may hear associated with the field of management. One useful way to develop a sense of management as a growing and changing field is to review its brief history. This chapter conducts that tour.

Management innovations have had a profound impact on the hospitality industry. In this chapter, we examine closely organizations that pioneered the development and application of modern management in the hospitality industry.

This Chapter Should Help You

1. Discuss the importance of the recent emergence of management as a field of work and study

2. Describe the contributions of some of the early 20th-century management thinkers and associate them with later management developments

3. Discuss the significance of the contributions E. M. Statler, Vernon and Gordon Stouffer, Howard Johnson, Harland Sanders, Ray Kroc, Kemmons Wilson, and Sam Barshop made to the development of management in the hospitality industry

449

4. Understand how modern franchised systems have helped the hospitality industry grow

5. Describe how the customer, not the operator, ultimately defines a business

6. View management as supervisory and managerial work that uses a marketing approach and innovation to define the organization's purpose and the purpose of those it employs

$\mathcal{M}$ANAGEMENT AND SUPERVISION

Students considering a career in hospitality supervision and management naturally want to understand the hospitality profession in general and the various kinds of opportunities it offers. It is equally important for them to understand the work that supervisors and managers do. We have devoted a major portion of this text to discussions of this work.

Supervision is derived from two Latin words that, taken together, mean "to oversee." As such, **supervision** involves principally the direction and leadership functions of management. (These two functions will receive special attention in Chapter 20.) Supervisors are also involved in the other functions of management that we will soon be discussing. They must plan, and they must understand the plans made by senior management that they will follow in their operations. They must understand and come to function effectively within a complex organization. The staffing function, which we will discuss in Chapter 18, is at the heart of a hospitality supervisor's work, and the control function cannot be carried out without supervisors becoming sources of information and of the corrective action indicated by control systems.

There is some difference between supervision and management. The supervisor's work occurs at the operating level; that is, he or she works directly with the employees as they do their work. **Management,** on the other hand, is concerned with the totality of the organization's problems. Managers engaged in long-range planning may well discover a need, for example, to redesign the organization structure or the control system. Very often, especially in large organizations, managers direct the work of supervisors, who, in turn, direct the employees' actual tasks. Most hospitality managers, however, must also do a good deal of supervision.

This distinction between management and supervision is not of major importance early in a management career. In the hospitality industry, nearly all managers begin as supervisors, and able supervisors usually advance to more senior ranks. Moreover, "managers" often perform work that some might call supervisory—the actual direction of employees in productive tasks. As a practical matter, then, management and supervision are so closely intertwined as to make distinguishing them a theoretical exercise with little practical value for us. To be sure, we will often refer to supervision and management, but by itself the term *management* usually includes *supervision.*

In the next five chapters, we will explore the work of managers and supervisors. In this chapter, we will define management and address its development as a body of knowledge used by managers.

Although managing—both the overseeing and the designing and organizing of work—is as old as civilization, management as an organized body of thought is only about 100 years old. Indeed, until recent times, the way that society was organized made it unlikely (useless, really) to consider management as a field of study and thought.

In this and the following chapters, we will use the term *business.* In fact, modern management has been mainly a development of the private sector, the business community. However, students whose interests lie in nonbusiness areas such as administrative dietetics or community food service programs should not feel at all left out, because nonprofit and government-funded food service programs now widely use these same techniques. In fact, minor adjustments make modern business management relevant to almost any managerial task.

$\mathcal{T}$HE ECONOMIZING SOCIETY

The economist Robert Heilbroner identified three means of organizing a society and dealing with its economic problems: tradition, command, and the market system.[1] The two means with the longest history are tradition and command, whereas the market system, by contrast, emerged from medieval Europe along with our modern age.

Tradition embodies the wisdom of experience, gained through trial and error, in a set of social customs regarded as nearly unchangeable. Primitive societies are traditional societies. Primitives regard the idea of change with fear, and so their whole society is based on the absence of change. For this reason, tradition offers only poor direction in the modern world.

Command—imposed authority—is a solution to society's problems often associated with traditional society. Command was the mode of social control of such ancient empires as the ones the Egyptians and Romans built, and it is the means by which modern dictatorships rule.

The **market system,** however, emphasizes the free choice of individuals. In theory, consumer decisions govern the allocation of resources, and competition sets the prices in the marketplace. In practice, critics point out, there are many imperfections in the market system, but we must recognize it as a system that offers consumers—and workers—more choice than does any other system the world has ever seen.

One central idea of the market economy completely foreign to most other cultures (including that of medieval Europe, out of which our society developed) is the idea of individual gain or profit seeking as not just a legitimate activity but also as a cornerstone of our civilization. Traditional societies are based principally on community interests, but the market system encourages, indeed exalts, individual interest.

Management, therefore, focuses on the problems of large organizations, though it is used in smaller organizations, as well. In premodern times, such management thought as there was served the church and the military. As royal power and ancient tradition were displaced by an economizing society and the market system, the creative energies of businesspeople began to occupy a more central place in Western civilization, particularly in the United States. In the 19th century, large business organizations came into being, and with them came a need to develop theories to deal with the complex problems associated with those organizations. The field of management was born.

Management is struggling to deal with a greater consciousness of community values regarding matters such as the environment as well as individual gain as joint determinants of economic action. Because management's values derive from the changing values of the society in which it works, we can expect that a change in society's consensus on the importance of individual choice in the marketplace will have a major impact on management in the future. Management, still barely 100 years old, has already passed through a number of changes. In the changing society out of which management arises, there is bound to be further development.

*M*ANAGEMENT: A NEW VIEW OF PROBLEMS

The problems that management deals with weren't really problems at all in the traditional and command economies. People worked at what their parents had worked at; they did what they were told to do. The problem of motivation was largely solved by the fact that the worker's alternative to following orders was starvation. Even in early modern times, when democracy was still growing in the political realm and had little to do with our economic way of life, people worked for low wages. More applicants were always standing at the door if any employee wanted to leave.

Under these circumstances, work was accomplished by masses of poorly paid people using brute strength. They gathered for long hours in factories where they were treated pretty much as though they were machinery. Skilled artisans performed another kind of work. Their skills moved from parent to child—traditional means of dealing with traditional problems.

In the late 1800s, however, Frederick Taylor initiated a new way of thinking about work. It was called scientific management, and it focused on finding the best way to accomplish the task at hand. A few years later, a Frenchman, Henri Fayol, reflected on the problems of organizing large-scale enterprises. These two men set the directions that management thought was to follow for over a generation, focusing at one level on the task and, at a higher level of abstraction, on the organization of work in complex organizations. These concerns continue to be central to our studies today.

In the late 1920s, the work of Elton Mayo brought a more conscious concern with workers as people. Thus, in not much more than 30 years, a whole new field of study began and moved from a concern with work to a preoccupation with the worker. A number of other points of view have developed within management since then, but these three original concerns—task, organizational design, and the worker—although considerably refined by later thinkers, remain at the heart of hospitality management today.

Management, then, is a very modern institution; indeed, it is a new way of viewing the problems of work in an expanding and increasingly wealthy society. This new way of viewing problems has become one of the strongest forces in the last 100 years of our civilization's development. Because its development has been so rapid, our view of management problems has changed dramatically during that period. Management continues to change with the dynamic society in which it operates, and those entering a career in management must prepare themselves for a constantly changing career. It is useful, therefore, for us to examine briefly the contributions of the early management theorists to see the power of their ideas and how this young field of ours grew.

THE MANAGERIAL REVOLUTION

The two thinkers generally credited with laying the foundation of modern management are Frederick Taylor and Henri Fayol. As we will learn, they were concerned with quite different problems. Taylor formulated industrial engineering principles and a wholly new way of organizing tasks. Fayol voiced the first ideas underlying what has come to be called organizational theory.

Taylor: The Work Process Focus

Frederick Taylor founded the scientific management movement. He believed that "the most prominent single element in modern scientific management is the task idea." Taylor argued that instead of "herding men in large groups" and relying on brute strength of numbers, a careful study of the work to be done and the worker would result in greatly increased productivity, that is, in more units of output per unit of labor input. Although the Industrial Revolution achieved a revolution in productivity through the use of machines, Taylor offered a further revolution through improved work planning. Here is Taylor's own summation:

> Scientific management consists of a certain philosophy which results in a combination of four underlying principles of management: first, the development of a true science; second, the scientific selection of the workman; third, his scientific education and development; and fourth, intimate, friendly cooperation between management and men.

Let us briefly consider each of Taylor's points. His "true science," based on time-and-motion studies, eventually became the new field of industrial engineering. His idea was to make management's study and planning of the work, rather than numbers and strength (or traditional skill), the controlling factor in work. It was a revolutionary proposal. His method of studying and planning the work meant analyzing each task and developing the "one best way" to do them.

Moreover, his approach replaced the artisan shop, based on traditional skills, with the *controlled shop,* a productive process in which management planning rather than worker skill or strength directs the enterprise.

This idea of management planning reappears in Taylor's second notion—the scientific (we might say "studied") selection of the worker. Rather than relying on the low wages of the time to offset low productivity, Taylor wanted employers to choose the right person for the job. Such an obvious idea hardly seems revolutionary to us, but most of the managers of his time resisted this approach.

The "scientific education" of the workers is a third factor in the controlled-shop notion. Having planned the work and hired someone qualified to do it, Taylor advocated training the worker in the one best way to accomplish each task. He also advocated supervising workers closely so that no other method inadvertently entered the process. Management and the methods it prescribed, rather than the worker's skill or brawn, controlled the productive process.

Finally, Taylor wanted to achieve "friendly cooperation between management and men," principally through giving workers "what they most want, namely high wages." Taylor proposed using some of the increased profitability of the now more productive business to improve the workers' wages.

Taylor's ideal worker was "Schmidt," a laborer whom he introduced to work and his foreman in this way: "When this man tells you to walk, you walk—and don't talk back to him." Taylor called Schmidt a **"high-priced man"** because Schmidt would receive much more than the going wage if, by obedience to Taylor's methods, he achieved greater productivity.

It is easy to criticize Taylor for his extreme emphasis on pay as "what they want most" and for expecting unfailing obedience. What critics forget is the dramatic social change that has taken place in the world of work in the short time since the days of Schmidt, the "high-priced man."

In Taylor's time, the workforce was ill educated, largely immigrant, and in a poor bargaining position with its powerful employers. Today, social legislation such as unemployment insurance has removed the fear of starvation from the employer–employee equation. Most employers eagerly seek employees, and these employees are far better educated and more conscious of their own worth. Largely as a result of enormously improved productivity, the American employee works shorter hours for enormously improved pay. However, at least two key ideas of Taylor's remain as centerpieces in the American work scene: the **task idea** and the **controlled shop.**

The Task Idea.   We learned, through Frederick Taylor, that there is a one best way to do work. Thus, the study of layout and design in a hospitality curriculum usually involves finding the most efficient means of laying out the workplace. Using outside experts to lay out the work and design the workplaces in a way that fails to take account of human social needs, however, is coming increasingly under challenge. Nevertheless, no one is ready to give up the control idea of work design through the close study of the task to achieve maximum productivity, for such a move would be costly to employer and employee alike.

The Controlled Shop.   Taylor brought a shift away from achieving productivity through the skill of the artisan or unskilled brawn "herded in groups." The shift has been toward achieving productivity through work methods designed by management and work performance tightly controlled by supervision. As we will see shortly, Vernon and Gordon Stouffer, in developing the recipe kitchen, brought the controlled shop to food service. (McDonald's and other fast-food operators, through systems design and planning, have extended it even further.)

The notion of the controlled shop, too, is under challenge. Workers in some places now demand (and often receive) greater participation in the control of the workplace. Our discussion of this issue in Chapter 21 will reveal that no one challenges the notion that some agreed-upon system should be developed and followed. The discussion, rather, seems to focus on how the system should be designed and the amount of worker involvement in that design. Neither labor nor management wants to give up the high wages and profits that come from the high productivity bequeathed to us by Taylor and his successors.

Other Contributors.   Our brief discussion may encourage you to explore further the development of management thought. Among other things, you would learn of the many contributions made to scientific management by Taylor's colleagues and those who came after. We note in passing three other pioneers. Frank and Lillian Gilbreth advanced the study of the task by developing the *therblig* ("Gilbreth" spelled backward), defined as the smallest unit of human movement that can be measured. Developing standardized therbligs for all work motions speeds and simplifies the task of the industrial engineer.

H. L. Gantt, like Frederick Taylor, insisted on the close supervision of the work and the worker. He developed a system of charting work operations that relies on the now-familiar Gantt charts. These charts have been adapted for use in hospitality employee scheduling. The discussion of staff planning in Chapter 18 includes a brief description of their use.

Although a changing world challenges and alters the early work of the scientific management movement, in many ways the movement's contributions continue to have a lasting impact on our lives.

Fayol: Administrative Management

Whereas Taylor and his colleagues focused on the task and the shop, Henri Fayol focused on the organizational problems of departmental division and work coordination. The discussion in the next five chapters of this book is organized around management functions. This frame of analysis was originally advanced by Fayol in 1916, albeit in a somewhat different form. However, his conceptual scheme for viewing the work of managers has had a profound, shaping effect on the development of management thought

Fayol was French and his work, written in French, had limited circulation in English-speaking countries until 1929. It did not reach print in the United States until 1949. For this reason, it is difficult to trace Fayol's influence precisely. Doubtless, however, some scholars, students, and managers heard his work discussed. In any case, his ideas gained wide acceptance, which they still enjoy today.

Beyond describing management as a common set of activities—now called management functions—Fayol was among the first civilians to rationalize the staff role. He contrasted it with the role of line management and offered a clear statement of staff limitations. Our discussion of these topics in Chapter 17 owes a great debt to his early formulations of these issues.

Fayol first suggested two bases for dividing work into departments: functional and geographic. (An Englishman, L. H. Gulick, expanded his notion into four bases for departmentalization: function, process, clientele, and location.)

Fayol was concerned, too, with the number of people a manager could efficiently supervise, and his ideas on this subject were expanded by V. A. Graicunias into the notion of **span of control.** Departmentalization and span of control, too, are discussed in Chapter 17.

Human Relations: Work as a Social Process

In the late 1920s, the Western Electric Company conducted a series of tests to study the effect of light levels on worker productivity. The researchers raised the level of light in the factory, and, each time they did, productivity rose. Then, to test their results, they lowered the level of light, but productivity increased again. They lowered it still further, and, again, productivity rose! Here was a puzzle. What was going on?

The researchers gradually formed a hypothesis that the way the workers felt about their work was significant. The experimental process, the attention that the researchers paid to the workers, seemed to stimulate their productivity. The research was, thus, expanded to include a close study of the human interaction in the work groups being observed. The researchers discovered that social pressures in the work group were at least as important as was pay in determining level of effort and output of workers.

This work was begun under the direction of Elton Mayo and carried out largely by Fritz Roethlisberger and W. J. Dickson, all famous names in management thought. It set in motion a process of research and controversy that continues to be a lively area of debate among management theorists as well as managers and supervisors. Although there is wide disagreement over exactly how to interpret and put into practice the findings of the human relations school (or as it has more recently been termed, **organizational behavior**), few would argue today that pay is all that counts. Most managers are much more sensitive to the human and social needs of workers than they were just a few years ago.

The Agenda for Managers

We have noted the influence of the early theorists, Taylor, Fayol, and Mayo, and the practical uses to which their theories are put to this day. By way of a summary, we should note that the basic issues in hospitality management for the foreseeable future are embodied in the work of these three men and those who followed them. From Taylor, we get a concern with efficient production methods. Fayol set us to thinking about the design of the working organization. And Mayo and his followers alerted us to a concern for the worker as an individual and as a social being.

*M*ANAGEMENT: A DYNAMIC FORCE IN A CHANGING INDUSTRY

The hospitality industry, too, has had its managerial pioneers. Although we cannot, in the space allotted here, discuss them all, we will offer a brief description of the work of E. M. Statler and Vernon and Gordon Stouffer, and describe the development of modern hospitality franchise systems as exemplified in the work of Howard Johnson, Harland Sanders, Ray Kroc, and Kemmons Wilson. The contribution of another conceptual pioneer, Sam Barshop, founder of La Quinta and inventor of the limited-service hotel, is detailed in Case History 15.1. These sketches will help demonstrate the impact of management ideas on the evolution of the hospitality industry.

Statler: The First "National" Hospitality System

Ideas, especially as textbooks present them, often appear neat and tidy. However, they are usually the result of complicated development. The central perception of **E. M. Statler**—that a national market existed for quality accommodations for the growing American middle class—probably evolved from his experience in serving that market as his hotel holdings grew from the original Buffalo Statler to a chain serving many of the nation's major cities. After developing and operating two "temporary" hotels for the Pan American Exposition in Buffalo in 1901 and the World's Fair in St. Louis in 1904, Statler opened his first permanent hotel in Buffalo in 1908, where he had already made a name for himself with a successful, popular-priced restaurant. His hotel featured all the amenities of a luxury hotel, but both its plant and organization were designed for maximum efficiency. His slogan—A Room with a Bath for a Dollar and a Half—shook an industry that associated the luxury of a bath with high prices. Statler's became the first popular-priced, full-service hotel. In the hotel business of that day, a substantial portion of the hotel rooms were *plain rooms*, that is, rooms without a bath. All of the popular-priced rooms were of this variety. Thus, A Room with a Bath for a Dollar and a Half represented a major social innovation.

As the size of the Statler organization grew, the company developed central staff services in control, architectural design, and personnel. Statler produced, then, the first centralized corporate staff (as opposed to line management, a concept we will discuss in Chapter 17) in the hospitality industry. The enforcement of uniform standards in all Statler hotels provided a guest with the assurance of a familiar quality level wherever he or she went. Moreover, Statler was the first hotelier to perceive the power of the American middle-class market, and his was probably the first true hospitality chain with common operating standards for all properties.

It would take a much fuller discussion of Statler's many contributions—including his important role as the first influential backer of hospitality education—to give full credit to this pioneer. Fortunately, such a discussion is available in a full-length book published by the Statler Foundation.[2]

Stouffer's Modern Management Techniques

Vernon and Gordon Stouffer were sons of the owners of a successful family restaurant. In the early 1920s, they attended the Wharton School of Finance, where they studied the ideas of Frederick Taylor and the other management pioneers. As a result of that experience, the Stouffers introduced ideas that transformed the artisan- and craft-based field of restaurateuring into a modern American restaurant industry. In short, the Stouffers adapted the thinking of Taylor and Fayol to the restaurant.

The Recipe Kitchen: A Controlled Shop.   Their mother oversaw the original kitchen, but the Stouffer brothers could not build a chain on the skills of one person approaching retirement age. On the other hand, they did not want a chef, because (they argued) when you lose the chef and replace him or her, your food could change and your organization might fall apart. With this insight into the weaknesses of the craft-based kitchen, the Stouffers sought to achieve management control over the kitchen by developing a set of recipes that would produce a standard product. For many years, the Stouffers hired only women for work in the kitchen or pantry because (they argued) women were accustomed to following recipes, whereas men were inclined "to become chefs," making things their own way and destroying the uniformity of product for which Stouffers ultimately became famous.

The food production supervisor and her assistants were called managers: They planned the work; organized that work around stations; staffed the kitchens with the right people, properly trained for the right job; and controlled food costs through yield checks and portion control devices. Finally, the food production manager, while leading and directing her crew, placed great emphasis on following the recipes and methods specified by management.

The introduction of the management-controlled **recipe kitchen** greatly improved productivity over the traditional kitchens of the day. Closer management control also ensured remarkably low food costs. The result was a highly competitive price. As Statler had done with hotels, the Stouffers brought the amenities of fine dining within reach of the American middle-class mass market.

The organization of the traditional restaurant centered on the traditional roles associated with traditional work stations; the relations among workers and between work groups reflected the old chef–maître d'–steward pecking order. The Stouffers, however, adopted a modern system of departmentalization. Reporting to the general

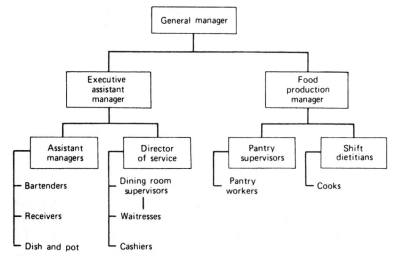

Figure 15.1 **The Stouffer restaurant organization (circa 1960).**

manager were the executive assistant manager and his or her assistants, a director of service, and the dietitian (or food production manager). Although these formally prescribed relationships changed somewhat from time to time, Figure 15.1 is a reasonably accurate description of the way the typical Stouffers unit was arranged.

Within the organization, ranks with the rigidity and symbolic trappings of an almost military organization were developed, complete with titles of address (Mr., Miss, Mrs. for supervisors and managers; first names for workers) and uniforms that clearly differentiated management from worker.

The Stouffers pioneered, as well, in the area of personnel management. They offered fringe benefits such as paid vacations, paid holidays, and group insurance long before these practices became widespread. The Stouffers were among those who supported the pioneering work of William Foote Whyte, which finally took the form of his study, *Human Relations in the Restaurant Industry.*

Thus, the three kinds of ideas that constituted then—and still do now—the agenda of management thought had a profound effect in shaping the Stouffer organization: the controlled shop focused on the task, a rational organization design, and concern for the worker as an individual human being.

The Building of Complex Hospitality Systems

No one person can take credit for the development of hospitality systems. In fact, these multiunit organizations have evolved over a number of years. One of the key foundations on which these organizations is based, however, is franchising and the pioneer in hospitality franchising was **Howard Johnson.** He began to build a franchise organization around a standard, restaurant-operating format in the

1920s. A generation or so later, Harland Sanders and Ray Kroc were the entrepreneurs most clearly associated with the development of franchised fast food. Kemmons Wilson made unique contributions to the development of modern lodging **franchise systems.** Each of these people had an idea that solved a consumer problem.

To make those ideas widely available, they needed to develop an operating system and an organization that could finance its own expansion; this meant giving up the owner-hired management pattern on which hospitality organizations had been previously based. It meant developing a whole new basis for organization based on shared interests and acceptance of authority on a voluntary basis. That acceptance, in turn, was motivated by a desire to share in a unique idea, that is, to share in the knowledge of the central organization. Moreover, the franchisee shared in the power of a large organization in marketing, purchasing, and operating system design. Much of that power related to the collective knowledge of the franchising organization. Finally, each of these men created a powerful consumer acceptance for his product and service that outlived its initial corporate organization and its founder.

Howard Johnson.   In the 1920s, as automobile ownership became more common and people began to travel more, travelers confronted the problem of finding a safe, reliable place to eat. **Howard Johnson,** whose initial success was in manufacturing ice cream, hit upon the idea of a restaurant with a standard appearance and menu and quality standards that would be immediately recognizable to travelers. Anyone who has ever driven into a strange town and wondered where to eat without risking food poisoning will know how critical Johnson's idea was to travelers of that day.

Although his idea was excellent, Johnson did not have the funds to expand his operation. He decided to franchise his operating system to others, following the method of expansion first pioneered by Singer Sewing Machines and used very successfully in Johnson's time by soft drink companies and automobile manufacturers to achieve rapid expansion in a growing national marketplace.

At one point, Howard Johnson's was the largest restaurant "chain" in the United States. We put "chain" in quotes here because until that time, as in Statler's day, the word chain implied common ownership. The restaurants in Johnson's "chain" were owned by many local operators (and investors), all of whom followed the same pattern in menu, decor, and operating procedure, not because of the legal force of common ownership but because of their compelling common interest.

Harland Sanders: Kentucky Fried Chicken.   **Harland Sanders** operated a very successful restaurant that was bypassed by a new highway. He needed a new idea to regain his customers' patronage so he developed a method of frying chicken quickly under pressure. This method permitted frequent small-batch cooking to ensure freshness and flavor. He also developed a batter that was flavored by a "secret recipe of herbs and spices." (This recipe, although changed a number of times since, is still "secret.") Finally, he coined the term Kentucky Fried Chicken that was "finger lickin' good." His slogan caught people's fancy. Customers came flocking back to his store, but he could make only limited use of his combination of operating idea, equipment innovation, and sloganeering in one town in Kentucky. Rather than try to build an organization based on ownership, he took to the road, presenting his business system to other restaurateurs and offering them a chance to share in it in return for a royalty. Those who were interested were licensed to use his system—and many of them became millionaires several times over. Once again, a "chain" emerged based on shared interests and mutual agreement rather than on the force of property rights.

Ray Kroc: McDonalds. **Ray Kroc** was a manufacturer's representative who sold milk shake machines very successfully. One restaurant that he sold to, which was owned by the McDonald brothers, bought an unusually large number of machines and Kroc went to see what made that restaurant so successful. What he saw so impressed him that he acquired the rights to license the operating system to others and eventually bought the McDonald brothers out.

What the McDonald system offered was the solution to two problems. The first was a customer need and the second was an operating problem. The customer problem involved the needs of the parents of the baby boomers. While the boomers were still little children and families were larger than they are today, these young parents needed a place to feed the whole family without spending a lot of money they didn't have. The McDonald's restaurant offered the most popular foods in America—hamburgers, french fries, and milk shakes—and promised change from a dollar for a whole meal. Moreover, there was no problem in serving little children. Even after McDonald's evolved out of its early drive-in and take-out format, McDonald's restaurants were places where everybody could come dressed for play or work and where kids could run around and not have to "be good." Not just the children loved it—McDonald's was a place for the whole family.

The operating problem that fast foods solved—and this is nearly as true for Sanders as for Kroc—was that of delivering food service at a price that made it such an attractive buy. The first key to achieving this goal was the limited menu. Menu limitation meant economies of scale in both purchasing and preparation. The second key was to take the idea of the controlled shop to its extreme. Every procedure was spelled out in detail, and work methods were designed that removed virtually all skill. Because quality was based on procedure rather than skill, it could be ensured with minimum-wage workers—and uniformity could be ensured in many outlets, eventually worldwide.

Kroc brought all the talents of the modern corporation to bear on developing and redeveloping his products and services. His redevelopment of the company's french fried potato product, for instance, has been compared to the systems engineering that the National Aeronautics and Space Administration first made famous in the space program. More than anyone before him, Kroc was able to tap the talents that were drawn into his growing organization of franchisees. Most of the new products, such as the Egg McMuffin and the Big Mac, were ideas initially developed by franchisees. Moreover, Kroc built an organization that was at once uniform and yet flexible enough to change with its markets and respond to competitive pressure.

McDonald's did not build its early success on advertising; but, as fast food became more competitive in the 1970s, Kroc oversaw the development of the awesome advertising muscle that has made McDonald's a household word around the world. The campuslike headquarters in Oak Park, Illinois, resembles nothing so much as the Versailles of Louis XIV. There, not only does the job of governance of this vast, largely voluntary (i.e., franchise) organization get accomplished, but visitors are awed with the massiveness of the resources and the restrained splendor of the setting. The author, during one of his visits to McDonald's headquarters, watched two new franchisees, one from Southeast Asia and the other from Germany, arriving at these headquarters. They were so visibly impressed that any idea they might have had that this "hamburger stand" company was anything other than all-competent was quickly banished. Hamburger University, a supertraining school, is one of the major tools that the organization Kroc built uses to secure uniformity in product, commitment in operation, and enthusiasm in management. Detailed training rather than strict discipline is the cement of the McDonald's organization. It is, ultimately then, knowledge rather than discipline that holds the organization together.

Kemmons Wilson: Holiday Inns. **Kemmons Wilson,** with his close associate Wallace Johnson, applied the idea of franchising to the lodging industry in the early 1950s in a way that swiftly built a national organization that set the pace for change in the lodging industry for 20 years. Seeing a need based on his own travels on business and with his family, Wilson developed a motor hotel, the Holiday Inn, that met the needs of both businesspeople and vacationing families. The system needs for reservation interchange, a well-known brand name, and standardized services were successfully surmounted and made his Holiday Inns a popular favorite. It was this consumer preference that made Holiday Inns the major and then dominant force in the lodging industry of the 1950s, 1960s, and 1970s. The rapid expansion of his idea was possible because of Wilson's success in enlisting ownership financing through many local investors in local projects—and these local people were usually able to find local mortgage money to complete the capital needs of these new Holiday Inns. Once again, a successful idea that solved consumer problems was expanded through the power of mutual self-interest, through a network of franchisees who conformed to the system because of their own self-interest. The development of another lodging innovation, the limited-service midscale hotel, is discussed in Case History 15.1.

The common elements that these pioneers share form the basis not only of the organizations that still bear their names but also of the many other organizations that have learned the lessons their success taught. One significant cornerstone is the largely voluntary nature of these organizations.[3] While not all hospitality chains today are franchised, the power of multiunit systems was first demonstrated by franchise organizations, and the dominant forces in mass-market hospitality today generally involve a significant proportion of franchised units.

Franchise organizations multiply the center of authority rather than concentrating it. Because the owner is generally closely involved with the unit, a number of advantages are secured. First, the owner's capital and credit are used to secure financing. Each franchised operation is a manageable small business investment; however, in the aggregate, they create a huge capital plant that spreads into every attractive location across the continent and eventually around the world. The national organization they build is one with local roots, tying local needs to a national program and vice versa.

The management within a franchised unit is not much different from that in any other hospitality unit. Above the unit level, however, the functioning of the organization is quite different. The owner's self-interest and the franchising corporation's knowledge are the cement of the organization rather than the legal force of central ownership. Franchise systems are really a means for the dissemination of ideas. The voluntary joining together of these organizations also secures for each of the participants economies of scale in research, development, purchasing, and, most significantly, marketing.

As we said at the outset, no one person can take credit for this development, but we can certainly recognize the seminal contributions of Howard Johnson, Harland Sanders, Ray Kroc, and Kemmons Wilson and try to learn from them.

$\mathcal{W}$HAT IS MANAGEMENT?

In the next five chapters, we will examine the work of managers, and we will organize that examination around the five functions of management. Before we turn to that discussion, let us look at the basic work of a business (or any other organization, be it a hospital, nursing home, or school lunch program). Peter Drucker, the economist and management consultant, stated that the basic purpose of business is to "create a customer," that is, to determine unfulfilled consumer needs and find a way to fill them. Drucker argued that the customer determines what a business is and that the central functions of a business are innovation and marketing.[4]

Before discussing Drucker's theory and applying it to our industry, we should pause for a moment to consider whether his line of reasoning applies to all of us in management and supervision. Some, for instance, would argue that marketing is an activity of the sales department. However, marketing is, basically, determining what the customer wants and then providing it in a way that makes it reasonably easy for the customer to obtain, while pricing it to recover the cost and make a profit. The specific work of marketing is usually handled by a separate department. Marketing, however, also includes a way of thinking about problems that is often the hallmark of the successful manager. Drucker put it this way:

$\mathcal{C}$ase History 15.1 — Where Does a Concept Come From?

Sam Barshop, founder of La Quinta Inns and originator of the limited-service motor hotel concept.
Courtesy of LaQuinta Inns

One of the most significant innovations in the lodging business in the last half of the 20th century has been the development of the midscale limited-service hotel, a concept that includes first-class guest rooms but very few of the other services of the full-service hotel. The man who first developed this concept is **Sam Barshop,** the founder of La Quinta Inns (**http://www.laquinta.com/**).

The interesting thing about the development of this concept is that it is a good example of learning from experience. The successful development of La Quinta was certainly no accident—but it was also not a blinding flash of inspiration.

Sam Barshop[1] and his brother Philip began building and leasing Ramada Inns in the early 1960s and then switched to a new franchisor, Rodeway Inns. As Barshop Enterprises, they obtained the exclusive franchise from Rodeway for the states of Texas, Oklahoma, Kansas, and Arkansas. Between 1961 and 1968, they built 20 Rodeway Inns.

The World's Fair, "HemisFair 68," was sited in San Antonio and Sam and Philip[2] decided to build two properties there to accommodate visitors to the fair. With their experience with Ramada and Rodeway under their belts, they tried to buy out their franchisor. That proved not to be possible and so "La Quinta" was born. They chose the name La Quinta—which means country place—to match the Spanish motif of the buildings. No one had any notion of building a chain of La Quintas. To quote Sam Barshop, "We were going to build two motels in San Antonio and that would be that."[3] Early success, however, was an important learning experience and the chain began to take form.

One of the basics of the La Quinta concept, and, indeed, the limited-service concept in general, was to avoid the operational headaches and costs of a restaurant operation—but the first five La Quintas did have restaurants, which Sam and Phil later characterized as "the biggest mistake we ever made." They learned from that mistake, however, and the La Quinta operating concept soon included a *freestanding, leased* restaurant operated by a successful franchise company such as Denny's, Cracker Barrel, or Shoney's.

Another important element of the concept was value. A critical aspect of that value was *price,* which was set at 20 to 25 percent below that of the competition. Eliminating the capital and operating costs of a restaurant made that room rate possible. The other aspect of the La Quinta value was *quality.* La Quinta provided a room that had all the features, quality, and cleanliness of the industry standard of the time, Holiday Inns. La Quinta targeted the business traveler and one measure of its success was that 65 percent of its customers were businesspeople, a large proportion of them repeat customers. Inns were located so they had easy access to the interstate highway system, airports, and business destinations such as office complexes, industrial parks, medical centers, and universities, yet were outside the downtown core where real estate prices were too costly for their rate structure.

Barshop described the La Quinta concept in this way:

Try not to make things too complicated. You can't be everything to everybody. We've got a simple concept, and we're going to cookie cut, and cookie cut, and cookie cut, until there aren't any more cookies left to cut.[4]

As we all know now, the cookie-cutter formula was one others could copy but, for something like 15 years, La Quinta had its concept to itself. Then, along came Hampton Inns, Fairfield Inns, and a number of other similar concepts. In time, too, came other investors, proxy fights, and Barshop's eventual retirement.[5] The fact of Barshop's innovation, however, is that it changed the face of lodging.

1. The following discussion is based, except as noted, on articles from the June 1988 anniversary issue of *INNPUT,* a monthly publication for the employees of La Quinta Motor Inns. We would like to acknowledge our indebtedness to Ms. Mary Starling, secretary to Mr. Barshop, in preparing this case history.
2. Philip Barshop left La Quinta in 1977 to run the family real estate business.
3. Christopher H. Lovelock, "La Quinta Motor Inns," Management Case (Boston: Harvard Business School, 1980), p. 1.
4. Ibid., p. 6.
5. For a discussion of the takeover of La Quinta, see Case History 11.2.

> Marketing is so basic that it cannot be considered a separate function (i.e., a separate skill or work) within the business, on a par with others such as manufacturing or personnel. Marketing requires separate work and a distinct group of activities. But it is first a central dimension of the entire business. It is the whole business seen from its final result, that is, from the customer's point of view. Concern and responsibility for marketing must, therefore, permeate all areas of the enterprise.[5]

This marketing viewpoint can actually guide us not only in dealing with guests but in dealing with employees, as well. Employees are, after all, "customers" who "buy" jobs from employers with their time and effort.

We might also hear the argument that innovation is really a function of top management only. Surely opportunities for innovation exist, however, on a smaller scale and at all levels of the organization. Indeed, it is almost "un-American" to attribute all the opportunity for creative work to some "top group." The supervisor or junior manager who does not try to develop his or her own solutions to problems will be less useful to an organization than if he or she sees innovation as part of the work. Our earlier discussion of franchising underlines the importance of bringing ideas up through the organization.

The marketing and innovation work of junior managers must take place on a smaller scale and lower level, and it will be subject to the policy of the organization. Nevertheless, thinking your work through in terms of the needs and wants of those you deal with—employees and guests—and trying to find a new solution when old ways seem ineffective will make your work more fulfilling for you and more valuable to your operation. Finally, an understanding of the significance of marketing and innovation should make you more ready to support the efforts of others in these areas.

Indeed, Drucker pointed to what he called "the fallacy of the *unterneymer.*" (Unterneymer is German for "top man.") He noted that the definition of business purpose is most often thought of as the concern of the owner or, at most, a few people at the top of the organization. In the German tradition of the unterneymer, Drucker said,

> the top man and especially the owner-manager, alone, knows what the business is all about and alone makes all the entrepreneurial decisions. Everybody else is a technician who carries out prescribed tasks. . . .
>
> [T]his may have been adequate in the nineteenth century business in which a few men at the top who alone made decisions, with all the rest manual workers or low level clerks. It is a dangerous misconception of today's business enterprise.
>
> In sharp contrast to the organization of the past, today's business enterprise [also today's hospital or government agency] brings together a great many men of high knowledge and skill, at practically every level of the organization. But high knowledge and skill also means decisions impact on how the work is to be done and on what work is actually tackled. They make, by necessity, risk-taking decisions, that is, business decisions, whatever the official form of the organization.[6]

The continuing definition of what a business is remains important to managers at all levels of an organization.

What Is Our Business?

To answer this question, Drucker posed a series of additional questions:

◆ Who is the customer?

◆ What is value to the customer?

◆ What will our business be?

◆ What should our business be?

We have seen how Statler and the Stouffer brothers, in different areas, thought through the needs of the emerging American middle-class market—a market that really constituted a "new" customer. The developers of franchise systems, Johnson, Sanders, Kroc, and Wilson, established organizations that harnessed the interests of ownership to serve a common organizational purpose. Each of these pioneers then used the field of management to serve that market efficiently.

Let's illustrate Drucker's frame of analysis with some examples from the hospitality industry: community nutrition programs, the community hotel, and franchised hospitality chains.

Who Is the Customer?   The answer to this question is complicated by the fact that there are usually at least two customers, and generally more. Recall that the school lunch program got its start as a national program not only to fill the needs of hungry students but also to use up surplus farm commodities and help solve the nation's unemployment problem during the Great Depression.

Although we can't trace the process exactly, we know that the great expansion in the school lunch program was a response to the growing participation of women in the workforce. Indeed, the development of preschool feeding and the school breakfast program are more recent innovative responses to the twin problems of working mothers and poor families. Although the customer is the child who eats and the parents who need no longer remain home to prepare a meal, the buying decision is made by Congress and other state and local funding agencies, and the ultimate customer is the American people. Much the same can be said for congregate feeding programs for the aging.

It is hardly possible to identify the single "entrepreneur" responsible for the growth of community nutrition programs. They have resulted from the work of many people, both within and outside the school lunch program and other food service programs. This revolution in the way that social obligations are arranged to provide nutrition is still going on—a dramatic example of identifying customer needs and innovating to fill those needs with people at all levels of many operations involved in the work. Neither community nutrition programs nor any of its elements—school lunch, preschool feeding, congregate meals—are the work of an unterneymer!

On a smaller scale, community hotel promoters discover every generation or so that town leaders in smaller communities can benefit from a small first-class hotel. The guest is also an important customer, but as the discussion in Chapter 9 suggested, many community hotels would never have been built were it not for the positive influence (expected or real) of these hotels on real estate values, employment, and community growth in a small town. Thus, community leaders are important customers for community hotel developers, in many ways as important as are the guests the hotel is built to serve.

The franchise systems we discussed earlier illustrate the notion of multiple levels of customers. The guest who buys the product or service is an important customer, but so is the potential franchisee. The franchise organization must not only satisfy the guest but also develop a system that fills the needs of local investors and entrepreneurs who want to run a successful business in their community.

What Is Value to the Customer?   Each customer has different values to be fulfilled. The guest at a Holiday Inn values a standard level of product and service, conveniently located, and priced within his or her means. (These means are defined by "the American middle class," to which the guest almost invariably belongs.) The franchise holder, on the other hand, buys a familiar hospitality brand name, national advertising, and a referral system.

Value to the guest in a community hotel is clean, comfortable accommodations. Value to the local investors, however, results from factors such as improved property values and a community that can more readily attract other employers with new local job opportunities.

The value of community nutrition programs to students, young children, and senior citizens is adequate nutrition and a palatable meal. Government supports these programs for these reasons. However, we can speculate that perhaps even more significant is the fact that these programs solve other problems. They fill the needs of families in which the mother works and can no longer serve a midday meal (or sometimes even breakfast). Congregate feeding for the elderly also supplies services that families no longer provide for their aging members. The obverse is true: Congregate feeding often frees the elderly from a dependence on their children.

What Will Our Business Be?   This question recognizes the simple fact that "the only constant is change"—that, for organizations to survive in a changing environment, they must change with it. Holiday Inns was originally and for many years a company of roadside inns located on the outer edges of cities, along expressways, or near airports. As urban renewal began to revitalize downtowns, and as many downtown hotels continued to deteriorate or even closed their doors, a large new market began to emerge. Accordingly, Holiday Inns developed prototype properties to serve urban centers and changed from strictly a motel company to a hotel–motel company.

In the mid-1980s, as segmentation became more widespread, Holiday Corporation—its name changed to recognize the company's broadened commitments—evolved into a multibrand company represented in nearly every significant area of lodging: Hampton Inns in the economy market, Holiday Inns in the conventional motor hotel market, and the Crowne Plaza properties and the Embassy Suites in upscale markets. Holiday recognized, as well, the significance of its destination activities and high profits in the casino business and expanded its commitment to its Harrah's division. Then, in 1990, Holiday sold off what had once been its flagship brand, Holiday Inns, to another company. This reflected management's judgment that the casino business and the newer, more segmented lodging concepts, Hampton, Embassy, and Homewood, offered the company's stockholders the best return. The successor company to Holiday Corporation's non–Holiday Inn assets, Promus, in time split Harrah's gambling business from its hotel operations and, even more recently, Promus Hotel Corporation merged with Doubletree to form one of the most powerful hotel corporations in North America. (See Chapter 11 for a discussion of this merger.)

What *Should* Our Business Be?   Drucker began his discussion of the question in this way:

> "What *will* our business be?" aims at adaptation to anticipated changes. It aims at modifying, extending, developing the existing, ongoing business.
>
> But there is a need also to ask "What should our business be?" What opportunities are opening up or can be created to fulfill the purpose and mission of the business by making it a different business?[7]

The school lunch program began by serving children in public schools. As public food service programs expanded to include preschool children and the elderly, however, many officials of the school lunch program started to wonder whether their organization could be expanded to embrace such other community food service programs as congregate meals for the elderly. The school lunch program in every community already has a production plant. Moreover, it maintains central service facilities in lunchrooms unused except during the noon recess (and, perhaps, the early morning). It also has skilled workers and managerial and nutritional savvy, and it is genuinely community based. Thus, the question, "What should our business be?" is properly raised by school lunch leaders. It will be interesting to watch how food service answers these four questions in the next generation.

McDonald's began as a drive-in restaurant on the outskirts of a city, serving hamburgers, french fries, and shakes, principally at lunch and dinner. Because of its great success, McDonald's might have been content. Instead, management constantly asked what its business should be, and today's McDonald's features dining facilities attractively decorated where guests can sit and eat their meals rather than carrying them to the car. McDonald's has also moved aggressively and successfully into the breakfast market and, more recently, became a major factor in downtown food service. Instead of resting on its laurels as the country's most successful drive-in chain, McDonald's management continually looks for new opportunities. "What should our business be?" asks McDonald's. The answers account for McDonald's steady expansion and its place as the world's largest restaurant system, serving all three meals and available in most market areas in North America and throughout the world.

In Business for Yourself?

Some students certainly plan to enter business for themselves. Those who succeed will remember the key questions we have just reviewed. Students whose careers involve working as supervisors and mangers for others must realize that they are also in business for themselves—selling their services and making a career based on their reputation for effectiveness. The analysis we have just offered serves them, too.

Who are your customers, and what is value to them? The patrons of your operation are obviously customers, and their needs and wants must be satisfied. The employer is your customer, and, in an important way, especially for junior managers and supervisors, the employees you direct are also your customers. If they were not there, there would be no need for a supervisor. The balancing of the needs of all these "customers," properly done, will require creative marketing and innovation on your part.

What will your business be? And what should it be? Career change is so common in North America that we all should consider the possibilities together. Is there an area of the industry that might offer greater opportunities? Or shorter hours? Or higher pay? At some point in a career, you may want to change the nature of your business: for instance, from supervisor in a large operation to unit manager. As these changes arise, you should ask yourself questions about your ability to "change your business." Perhaps additional work in accounting, a human relations training program, or some other specialized work or study would help you supply value to your proposed new customers.

Success—defined as income, advancement, or more work satisfaction—will come from taking a creative approach to the work of management. In the next five chapters, we will consider just what kind of work supervisors and managers do. We emphasize here, though, that even during that time when you prepare for managerial duties, by working as a server or a dishwasher, you can use an understanding of management functions. Servers, cooks, and bartenders are "in business for themselves," building knowledge through experience, building a reputation for effectiveness, and deriving personal satisfaction and self-confidence from work well done. This "business" is worth managing, and more success will come from having managed it well.

The functions of management summarized in the next five chapters are presented separately for our convenience in analyzing the work of managers. You should realize, as each of the next five chapters repeats, that none of these functions is accomplished separately. Management is really a continuous process involving, in varying degrees, all the functions nearly all the time.

𝒮UMMARY

This chapter began our discussion of management. First, we defined management and supervision. Second, we outlined the history of coping with economic problems: tradition, command, and the market system.

We turned then to three pioneers in management theory: Taylor and his work process focus, the task idea, and the controlled shop; Fayol and administrative management; and Mayo and his concern with the worker.

We moved to a discussion of pioneers in the hospitality industry. Statler introduced the idea of a popular-priced, full-service hotel, as well as uniform standards in all his hotels. He was perhaps the first to recognize the power of the middle-class market in regard to the hospitality industry. The Stouffers adapted Taylor's and Fayol's ideas to their restaurants. They used a recipe kitchen—a controlled shop—which standardized the management and organization of their restaurants. Johnson, Sanders, Kroc, and Wilson all played key roles in developing franchise organizations based on voluntary adherence, mutual interest, and shared knowledge. They offer a national organization a local focus in every market they serve.

The last section of this chapter was devoted to a study of Drucker's theories of management and how they apply to the hospitality industry. We considered several questions: What is management? Who is the customer? What is value to the customer? What will our business be? and What should our business be?

◆ *K*EY WORDS AND CONCEPTS

Supervision	Organizational behavior
Management	E. M. Statler
Tradition	Vernon and Gordon Stouffer
Command	Recipe kitchen
Market system	Complex hospitality systems
Work process focus	Howard Johnson
High-priced man	Franchise systems
Task idea	Harland Sanders
Controlled shop	Ray Kroc
Span of control	Kemmons Wilson
Administrative management	Sam Barshop

◆ *R*EVIEW QUESTIONS

1. How do management and supervision differ?

2. Compare tradition, command, and the market system.

3. Describe Taylor's principal contributions to management theory.

4. What were Statler's main contributions to hospitality management? The Stouffers' contributions?

5. What are the forces that bind modern franchise organizations together?

6. According to Drucker, what *should* our business—the hospitality industry—be?

◆ 𝒥NTERNET EXERCISES

1. **Site Name:** *Search Engines*
   URL: Alta Vista (http://www.altavista.digital.com/),
   HotBot (http://www.hotbot.com/),
   Mamma (http://www.mamma.com/),
   Excite (http://www.excite.com/)
   Background Information: Many current management philosophers differentiate management from leadership skills. As a manager in the hospitality industry, you will be using both management and leadership skills throughout your career. The key is to determine how they differ and when to use them appropriately.

   EXERCISES:

   Use your favorite search engine, or one listed above, and search for articles/ information on management versus leadership.

   a. Determine what characteristics differentiate a manager from a leader.

   b. Lead a class discussion on which is more important—managers or leaders.

   c. When is it most appropriate to use management skills and/or leadership skills?

2. **Site Name:** *Search Engines*
   URL: Alta Vista (http://www.altavista.digital.com/),
   HotBot (http://www.hotbot.com/),
   Mamma (http://www.mamma.com/),
   Excite (http://www.excite.com/)
   Background Information: There have been many leaders in the hospitality industry such as Ray Kroc, Howard Johnson, Harland Sanders, Kemmons Wilson, Vernon and Gordon Stouffer, and Sam Barshop. There are also many current leaders. All of these individuals have made significant contributions in changing the hospitality industry.

   EXERCISES:

   Chose a current or past leader and search for information on that individual using your favorite search engine or one of the search engines listed above.

   a. Discuss the contributions this individual has made to the hospitality industry and how the industry changed as a result of his or her actions.

   b. Where do you see your chosen individual using management skills and/or leadership skills most effectively?

◆ 𝒩OTES

1. Robert L. Heilbroner, *The Making of Economic Society,* 4th ed. (Englewood Cliffs, NJ: Prentice–Hall, 1972).

2. Floyd Miller, *Statler, America's Extraordinary Hotelman* (Buffalo: The Statler Foundation, 1968).

3. Nothing said here should be interpreted to imply that franchise organizations are perfect, necessarily more humane, or free of error, politics, and the arbitrary exercise of power than are independently owned operations. In fact, no human organization achieves perfection and neither do franchise organizations. They do, however, have the substantial advantages set forth.

4. Peter Drucker, *Management: Tasks, Responsibilities, Practices* (New York: Harper & Row, 1974), p. 61. The discussion in this section takes many of its ideas from Chapters 6 and 7 of Drucker's book.

5. Ibid., p. 63.

6. Ibid., p. 76.

7. Ibid., p. 92.

$\mathscr{C}$hapter *16*

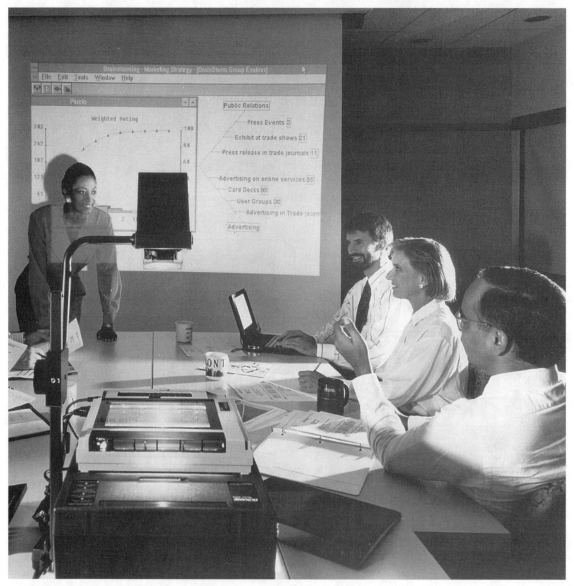

Courtesy of Xerox Corporation

Planning in Hospitality Management

The Purpose of This Chapter

Planning is a necessary everyday activity both in life and in managing. Planning should go on at every level of the organization, from dishwasher to the chairman of the board. Unfortunately, it often gets overlooked at all these levels. Planning for your life's work is as essential as planning today's menu. Accordingly, this chapter presents planning as an active process related to long-range organizational goals and to day-to-day work, as well. Although the concepts we present are most clearly related to planning in organizations, they need only be adapted to be useful to students considering their career goals.

This Chapter Should Help You

1. View planning as an organizational process that goes on at all levels

2. View yourself as a supervisor or manager who plans and as an organization member who is affected by organizational plans

3. Define and use the key planning concepts discussed in this chapter

4. Explain how planning is related to and arises from goal setting that begins with a guest or client

5. State the relationship between plans and evaluation

6. Describe planning as a general management function (strategic planning), as an operation management function (tactical planning), and as work done by individuals for the organization and for themselves

7. Explain the need for policy and long-range planning, and describe and use some selected tools developed in this chapter for this purpose.

WHY STUDY PLANNING?

Planning is something that everybody agrees is important. Planning, however, is often neglected, probably because it requires hard thinking and involves the uncomfortable work of dealing with uncertainty.

An absence of conscious planning leads to two related kinds of problems. First, because employees must know what their employers expect of them, an absence of management planning leads to confusion at work. Second, to settle that confusion, employees often plan for themselves. Their plans may be aimed at goals completely unrelated to the organization's goals. For example, if management fails to develop a seating chart for the dining room, the waitresses will almost certainly work out their own system. Such a system may or may not be good for guest service, but you can bet it will suit the convenience of the waitresses.

Failure to plan invites trouble. Three different kinds of examples illustrate why planning is necessary at all levels of the organization. Consider, first of all, the waitress who does not plan her next trip to the dining room in the light of the needs of her entire station. She will probably have to run back and forth to get one or two items that she could have brought all at once. In this way, she wastes two of her most precious resources: time and energy. By the end of the day, she has worked harder than her co-workers and probably has earned less in tips from those customers who had to wait for her to complete those extra trips. Planning by individual workers, then, is important.

If you have ever been in a restaurant that ran out of eggs at breakfast or bread during a rush on the sandwich station, you have seen our second example—the results of poor operational planning. And you know its costs: dissatisfied guests, upset employees, the loss of some of those inconvenienced customers, and perhaps some of the people they talk to. In general, the operation's reputation suffers.

Notice in the third example that the higher the level of decision making, the more widespread the effects of poor planning. In Chapter 11, the decision-making process for building new hotels is discussed. That process is one that leads to periodic overcapacity even while building continues. As noted there, the hotel industry lost $33 billion in the 11-year period ending in 1993 but, for most of that time, building continued at a brisk pace. (See Figure 11.1.)

The failure to plan entails serious risks at any level. Your own plans are most important to you. Just as the waitress wasted time and the restaurant that ran out of eggs lost profit opportunities, you may waste a good deal of effort and miss opportunities if you fail to plan in these two ways.

Case History 16.1 Planning on an Olympic Scale at ARAMARK

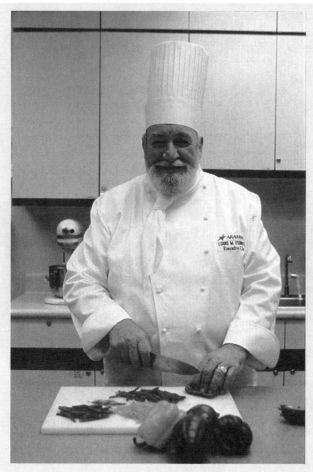

Louis Ferretti, ARAMARK's Senior Executive Chef, led a team of six executive chefs working with 35 managers and 66 supervisors in ARAMARK's 1996 Olympics Games contract.
Courtesy of ARAMARK

In the ancient Greek Olympics, athletes confined themselves to vegetables, figs, nuts, barley, and porridge—and after the games, in celebration, they ate roasted oxen. No such simplicity was possible, however, in Atlanta where the '96 Olympics Games were held.

ARAMARK had provided food service at 10 Olympic Games and another 8 Olympic-related games in the previous 25 years so the '96 Games were not a new experience for the company. Even when you know how, though, such a complex undertaking calls for a lot of planning. In fact, ARAMARK estimates its managers spent 100,000 hours in planning before the first meal was served!

Consider the nature of the challenge: 15,000 athletes, coaches, staff, and officials from 197 countries would be served 5 million meals over the course of the 17 days. The main service area and the location of the central kitchen were a parking lot and garage at Georgia Tech, which were in use for those purposes right up to the end of May! When ARAMARK took them over on June 1, it had only until July 6 to be in operation. Round-the-clock dining had to be provided in the Olympic Village and food service was also needed in eight other Olympic venues with more than 1900 points of service.

The planning process started, of course, with the needs of the customer. Meals had to provide for the nutritional needs of athletes and, at the same time, offer diners a taste of home and choices that suited their religious and ethnic preferences. Executives could and did call upon the ARAMARK Culinary Center in Philadelphia, the company's research and development arm, for help in this massive project. ARAMARK's managers compiled data on Olympic meals served since 1968, their popularity, and potential production problems and, moreover, took into account nutrition, flavor, texture, color, and variety. From this planning process came a five-day rotating selection of over 550 recipes that suited people from all corners of the globe—from Russian borscht to Japanese miso soup and Korean kim chee, Moroccan fish tangine, and Greek moussaka. To suit the Atlanta location, southern fried chicken, black-eyed peas, and Georgia peach cobbler were added to the international menu. In advance of the Olympics, recipes were tested in 26 cities. These "preview dinners" also gave ARAMARK opportunities to train members of the Olympic staff in diverse locations.

To deal with the need for erecting a large food service facility more or less overnight, off-site construction of a modular kitchen was begun in August 1995. Use of a huge crane solved problems of "moving in" and an above-ground dining tent was installed to provide air-conditioned dining in the Georgia summer weather, as well as space to install

Senior executive chef
5 executive chefs
35 managers
66 supervisors
105 lead staff
275 chefs and prep persons
382 servers and waitpersons
308 utility and warehouse workers

Figure 1 Olympic food service staffing requirements.

the additional electrical, plumbing and gas lines a food service operation requires. In total, the plant erected by ARAMARK provided a 150,000-square-foot food service operation including a tented seating and serving area of 75,000 square feet, a modular kitchen measuring 25,000 square feet, and an additional 50,000 square feet for food storage, employee services, and office space. Figure 1 gives a summary of the staff that made up the Olympic food service team.

To provide the "carbo-loading" that nonstop events of 90 minutes or more call for, three made-to-order pasta stations were constructed. The menu also offered a wide selection of vegetarian and high-protein foods, available around the clock—as well as rich desserts for those in a mood to indulge or celebrate. To manage production efficiently, ARAMARK

1 Menu planning
2 Forecasting customer portions
3 Establishing needs
4 Purchasing
5 Receiving and food storage
6 Production
7 Service
8 Accountability

Figure 2 ARAMARK Eight Step program.

instituted its Eight Step program. At each step in the cycle, the Eight Step program ensures that particulars about inventory, recipes, menus, and nutrition are addressed. The steps are summarized in Figure 2.

To manage this complex process from a standing start was a challenge for ARAMARK. Of course, its experience in managing food service at previous Olympic events stood them in good stead but, in the end, the task would have been impossible without detailed, meticulous planning. Indeed, the company's broad experience in all kinds of food service had long ago convinced its management of the vital importance of planning.

We would like to acknowledge the assistance of Joan Rice and John Wannenberg of ARAMARK's Public Information Office in the preparation of this case history.

First, you need to plan for yourself at several levels:

1. Whatever work you do (desk clerking, college homework, or motel house-keeping), your work will be easier and quicker if you can plan it.

2. As a supervisor or manager, you must learn to plan the work of others. (Moreover, senior-level managers must not only plan work—how to do—but must also plan on the grander scale of organizational goals—what to do.)

3. In addition to planning the work you do for others, you must think of your own career as a business (because you sell services to your employer). Thus, your career development means planning for the kinds of services you want to be selling at some future point—banquet manager, sales representative, food production supervisor, general manager, and so forth—and then planning how to achieve that position within a reasonable period.

Second, you will probably have to accept that, as a member of an organization, you are part of somebody else's plans. The point is that understanding the planning process helps you understand the need of a well-managed company for carefully developed plans. As an understanding participant in planning, you should be a more effective employee and find greater meaning in your work.

The following discussion should help you work effectively by improving your readiness to plan your work and the work of others. Moreover, the basic approach to business can be applied to your own career planning. Case History 16.1 gives an example, from Aramark's experience, of planning in action in operations.

$\mathcal{P}$LANNING IN ORGANIZATIONS

Planning is the work that managers [and workers] do to visualize the future in a concrete way and to determine courses of action that will achieve the organization's goals over a definite period.

As we have noted, planning at the different levels of the management hierarchy has different characteristics. The pyramid in Figure 16.1 provides a convenient

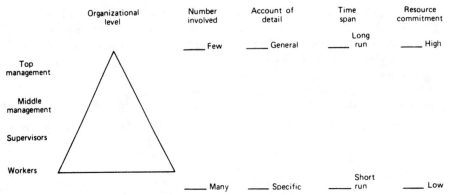

Figure 16.1 Dimensions of planning in organizations.

way of symbolizing some of these characteristics. The higher in the organization the planning activity takes place, the fewer persons will be involved in the planning, and the more general the nature of the plan and commitment will be. At lower levels, the planning involves more people and more detail.

For example, the waitress's work plans might cover a period of one meal or, perhaps, just a *turn* on her station (the time it takes to serve a party—to "turn" her table). Purchasing at the operating level seldom covers a period of more than a week, and usually just a day or two. These are good examples of short-range planning.

Although short-range planning is absolutely essential, it differs from long-range planning, in which resources are committed on a much larger scale. Not surprisingly, specialized tools for long-range planning have been developed to assist managers at that level. We will examine these long-range planning tools at the end of this chapter.

Formalized business planning is increasingly common in multiunit chains. A survey of chain food service executives revealed that nearly three-quarters of their companies made annual strategic plans with five-year future projections.[1]

A full-fledged plan is complex. A marketing plan, for instance, will contain a research summary, a statement of marketing goals, a statement of both strategy and tactics for achieving the plan's goals, and provision for measuring progress toward the plan's goals and for revising the plan if conditions change. It is important to remember, though, that the banquet manager's plan of how to serve tomorrow's banquet is no less a plan even if it is more straightforward.

Some Planning Concepts

The term *planning* denotes anticipating several different sets of circumstances for different purposes. Several other key terms will help you fill out the idea of the planning process.

Policies are general guidelines for dealing with the future. They don't tell what to do; they indicate how to reach a decision. Policies leave much to the discretion of the decision maker. However, they provide a predetermined, agreed-upon basis for decisions.

> The unit manager of a large chain of restaurants is approached every week for small contributions to local charities. The company's policy does not say what to give or whom to give to. Policy does say what general kinds of organizations can be considered and what the limits on the manager's discretion are and what the maximum amount is that can be given each year. (The manager may be able to give, for instance, as much as $100 to a single organization without approval—but only if the total budget has not already been spent.) It is still up to the unit manager to gauge the situation and decide whether to make any particular donation and how much to give up to the maximum set by the guidelines of policy.

A **plan** is a reasoned means of moving toward some selected goal. A plan reflects policy and may include rules, methods, procedures, standards, and budgets. A plan may have both strategic and tactical elements.

> The most comprehensive of plans may not be written down in one place. On the other hand, the operations manual of a well-run company is a useful example of a group of plans. Some companies, particularly larger ones, develop strategic plans over a long period; these plans express management's vision of the organization's future and elaborate goals, methods, budgets, and the like. Both these examples suggest that a full-fledged plan is complex. But your plan for tackling the week's work is no less a plan just because it is straightforward.

> Thus, a plan describes future events of whatever complexity in a way that shows how they will be ordered to achieve the organization's goals.

Rules state what must be done (or must not be done) in a given situation. Rules leave no discretion in their execution.

> "Food production employees must wear hair nets in the kitchen" answers a question about one aspect of an employee's future behavior. Most companies have a rule that the "paperwork" must be done before a new employee can go to work, receive a paycheck, or take a vacation.

Methods and procedures resemble rules. Methods indicate how a standard job is to be done. Procedures are really a sequential set of rules.

> The method for performing a repetitive task may be determined by a food service operator with the help of industrial engineers. As a result of these studies, waste motions are minimized, and the time required is reduced to a minimum and standardized.

> Most hotels have a procedure that specifies the process that a guest's records should go through during his or her stay—just as most health care institutions have a similar procedure for patient records.

Standards specify not procedures but outcomes. Some standards pertain to cost control, and many relate to quality control.

Quality standards determine, for instance, how food should taste or what quantity of nutrition should be present, as in the approved plan school lunch. Standards might also specify how many seconds it should take for a phone operator to respond to a guest or to place an outside call; or the length of time a bellhop requires to "room" a guest.

Cost standards indicate an acceptable cost for some activity. Thus, the preceding method specifies a standard time for stripping a turkey. Similarly, most hotels have a standard number of rooms that should be cleaned per eight-hour maid day (usually between 12 and 18).

A **budget** is a numerical plan, generally expressed in dollars, although sometimes units of weight or time may be used, as well. The budget specifies the dollar results expected from a plan of operation.

Most well-run operations prepare budgets that express in dollars the results they expect. Those budgets may be supported (in their estimates for housekeeping payroll, for instance) with a statement about hours budgeted at various levels of occupancy as a base for departmental payroll projections.

Strategy and **tactics** are terms borrowed from the military to denote level of importance and time dimensions in plans. Strategy implies large-scale, high-level, and long-term commitment. In Figure 16.1, strategy would lie at the upper end of the pyramid. Tactics are often of great importance, but they are intended to implement the strategy. To give one set of examples of the difference between strategy and tactics, Taco Bell embarked on a diversification strategy. A further strategic decision Taco Bell took was that diversification would be accomplished by acquiring successful companies whose concepts were already a proven success rather than develop new concepts themselves. Finally, they determined that, once acquired, the companies (such as the drive-through chain Hot 'n Now or Chevys, a Tex-Mex chain) would be expanded aggressively.[2] These were strategic decisions and, as such, concerned with overall goals (diversification and expansion) and the general means of achieving them (buy companies and grow them). Tactics, on the other hand, are specific, relating methods to individual circumstances. In this example, the question of where to expand a new concept or when and where to open a new store first would be tactical decisions.

$\mathscr{G}$OAL SETTING: MANAGEMENT BY OBJECTIVES

How do we go about setting goals in organizations? Some traditionalists insist that we should already know what our goals are. "A great hotel is . . ." and generally they fill in the blanks with a description of "the way we've always done it." If we press them, however, we find they really don't intend to offer the same level of service as the "great hotel" offered a generation or two ago. In most operations, anyway, this goal is just not possible. Costs, particularly labor costs, have risen astronomically, and the supply of labor for some jobs has decreased to the vanishing point. So, it turns out, what the traditionalist really proposes is for us to come as close as we can to "what we've always done."

The traditionalist's eyes, you see, are set firmly in the past. He or she defines what's to be done in terms of the standards derived from past experience. We, of course, do not argue that we can't learn from experience; we can and we must. The past, however, is not where one begins goal setting in a consumer-oriented society.

The logical place to begin goal setting is with the person who really sets the goals: the guest. Accordingly, we should take a marketing approach to our operations.[3] If the needs and wants of the guests aren't met, they will take their business elsewhere. (If guests in a congregate meals program, on the other hand, don't like what they are served, they will complain to the agency, to their representative in congress, or to the newspaper.)

Examine these examples of goals and see how they relate to the guests' needs and wants: Elaborate service requires highly skilled waitresses and waiters, an attentive maître d', and a large backup staff. This is "great" service, most restaurateurs would agree. However, we would never put it in a truck stop. The reasons are obvious, but revealing.

Our guest at the truck stop wants a hearty meal of the kind of food he or she is used to. Correct classical service would seem "snooty." This guest wants friendly and fast service, simple food, and modest prices. Here is another example from the experience of one of the authors.

> Not long ago, my wife and I were talking to a professor in another field of study who had just come back from New York. He was describing in great detail a really "fine restaurant" he had eaten in. After he left, my wife turned to me and said, "Do you realize what he was saying? He was describing as a 'fine restaurant' a place in which he doesn't like to eat!" As I thought about it, I realized he had intended to praise the restaurant but had, for the most part, been commenting on how snobbish he had found the place. Without saying so, he had indicated that the formality of the place made him uncomfortable.

Traditional forms of formal service may still be effective in some operations, but we can no longer assume uncritically that the traditional way is the only way. Moreover, we certainly cannot uncritically accept traditional forms of service as goals to strive for.

Health care presents an unusually interesting example of shaping products and services to guests' needs—and wishes. For example, most hospitals now realize that the meals they serve their patients can, to an extraordinary degree, raise or lower the morale of those patients. For some, the meal may be nearly the only pleasant thing that happens to them all day. For this reason, many hospitals have begun to spend more effort and money on food service than would ordinarily be necessary. Providing special diets is, of course, an even more obvious example of the guests' needs in determining service.

Guests' needs may, however, be only one of the goals to be met. Our society has made the school systems largely responsible for feeding children their noon meal.

In specifying the approved plan lunch requirements, the Food and Nutrition Service amplifies the young guest's goal (a good lunch) to include the need for the lunch to contain an adequate and balanced diet. The agency has yet a further goal mandated by Congress: nutrition education. A school must use the approved plan lunch to help teach young people what a balanced diet is. However, the school lunch manager must still design a menu that will appeal to the students, or else he or she will face complaints from the students and their parents.

Characteristics of Well-Thought-Out Goals

"Our goal is better service." That is the kind of statement to be wary of. Specifically, what does it mean? In the process of setting goals, we might better ask ourselves, "How will I know when I get there?"

Some people suggest a checklist nicknamed the "Five Ws and an H" to help a manager make sure that the issues have been examined from every angle:

WHO

WHAT

WHERE

WHEN

WHY

HOW

Perhaps most important, though, is to set objective and measurable goals. "How will I know when I get there?"

The front-desk staff of a motor hotel in the middle of a large city were criticized for being cold and impersonal. A number of unsuccessful "courtesy campaigns" were tried but had little effect. (This front desk was very busy, and the clerks felt themselves under pressure because of waiting lines, and the like.) Finally, a clerk suggested that everybody adopt a rule: *Always* smile at the guest during your first words. Then a "policeman" was appointed to remind those who forgot. Within a week, the smile had become habit and—just as that clerk thought—many of the guests responded with a smile and the interchange became much friendlier.

> *Goal.* Be friendlier.
>
> *Objective behavior.* Smile.
>
> *Measure.* Informal inspection.

A hotel that served mainly a business clientele felt that a fast breakfast service would attract guests. The guests at this hotel generally had appointments to keep and planes to catch. When management began to talk about "fast service," though, it specified that "fast enough" was:

- ◆ The guest gets a menu when he or she takes a seat.
- ◆ The guest gets water and is offered coffee within two minutes.

◆ The order is taken within three minutes (of seating) if he or she is in a hurry.

◆ A "jiffy breakfast" will be served within six minutes (of seating) if a guest orders it.

From this list of specific goals, the hotel established seating procedures that tried to ensure that a waitress would arrive on the station or one of the two adjoining stations at the time of seating. (If there was no waitress, the hostess would detail a busboy to get water or coffee or get it herself.) Waitresses were prepared to take orders on the station next to theirs and turn over those orders to the appropriate person later. A special serving point (and procedure) was established in the kitchen for the jiffy breakfast.

Goal. Fast service.

Objective behavior. Follow schedule.

Measure. Management could (and did) time the service.

Neither of these useful approaches would fit in *every* operation. In a small-town motor hotel with a fairly slow pace, the extreme effort on the part of employees to get a smile out of themselves wouldn't be needed. It might even make a nice friendly person look like a windup doll! In a resort hotel where guests come to relax, attentive service may be appropriate, but the hurry-up breakfast pattern would make them feel rushed. Our examples do not represent solutions; they represent goal-setting procedures that solve problems in such a way that we can tell when we have, in fact, reached a solution.

Goal Congruence

In setting its goals, an organization should be realistic. If a service goal requires a waitress to lose tip income, we can expect her, one way or another, to resist the goal. For example, restaurants sometimes promote their wine sales. Management reasons that the increased beverage check will increase the waitresses' tips. It urges them: "You really ought to want to sell wine." However, their procedure makes it difficult for a waitress to obtain a bottle of wine quickly for the guest because of inadequate stocking (and staffing) of the bar where the wine is kept. The waitress finds she loses more in slow turnover and guest dissatisfaction because of delays in getting the wine she has sold. Management cannot understand why the waitresses don't try to sell wine—"they really ought to." When people don't do what they "ought to," though, management should look at the system design to see what went wrong, rather than urge compliance because "you ought to want to. . . ."[4]

Management scholars often use the term **goal congruence.** This term refers to the need to design and present an organization's goals in such a way that organizational goals and individual employee goals mesh rather than clash. Goals of different people in an organization should also fit the goals of the organization if maximum harmony and efficiency are to be achieved.

Goals and Policies

Once an organization has established its goals, it is ready to develop policies to implement them. Policies, you may recall, are general guidelines for dealing with the future. They leave much to the decision maker's discretion while providing a basis for reaching decisions.

There are goals at all levels of the organization, of course, but policies address goals that affect the entire organization; they have, in short, a significantly broad effect. In the hospitality industry, one major policy issue centers on guest self-service, an idea that arises largely from the goal of holding down costs and menu prices as much as possible in spite of rising wages, food costs, and utility bills. Eliminating or reducing the bell staff in motor hotels is one example of a policy decision; so is the increasing use of buffets and self-service salad bars. Once a company has established its policy in self-service, decisions on individual issues become clearer.

Companies often regard policies on unionization as especially important. Some companies set a goal of avoiding unionization and resist it by every legal means available, whereas others are indifferent to an organizing drive. A few companies actually encourage union representation. We take no position here on the pros and cons of a union. We merely point out that this illustrates policy as a guide for action. In the three instances just cited, an incipient union-organizing drive would trigger three quite different reactions: a hurried and worried call to the home office, a yawn, or a friendly greeting.

As policies evolve, they call forth programs of action, strategies, and tactics to implement policy and achieve goals through action.

$\mathscr{P}$LANNING IN OPERATIONS

When management establishes goals and determines policies, its planning work has only begun. It needs a plan of action to specify how the policy will be implemented. Those two terms borrowed from the military, *strategy* and *tactics,* distinguish between levels of plans. Strategy tells you where you want to go and why you want to get there. Tactics deal with *how* to get there.

Strategic Issues

Strategy concerns long-range basic plans. Our discussion will focus on examples in three strategic areas out of many that could be chosen: product and service strategy, personnel strategy, and community relations. These three areas conveniently illustrate how policy guides decisions and is implemented by both planning and action.

Product and Service Strategies. In food service, a menu is a plan; the general pattern of an operation's menus represents a strategy; and the customer you intend to reach dictates the strategy you will develop. Consider a steakhouse such as Steak and Ale. The menu reflects a policy of limited selection. This limited selection simplifies production and service. A strategy of self-service for salads represents a decision to give up portion control in return for the advantage of having the guests serve themselves. The advantages of the self-service are (1) the server has one less course to serve and (2) the guests can eat salad while their steaks are being cooked. A server can carry a larger station, and so fewer servers are needed. Moreover, the guest begins to eat sooner; the wait between courses is shorter; consequently, table turns are more rapid. With faster turns, a restaurant can serve more guests during peak meal periods. The trade-off for portion control on salads is more than worth the advantages gained.

The recipe kitchen strategy that the Stouffers adopted years ago permitted them to dispense with highly skilled chefs. The rule at the Stouffers' restaurants was that everything was prepared from a recipe. A recipe is, of course, a kind of procedure. This recipe kitchen strategy helped the Stouffers train unskilled cooks, and, as long as precisely the same procedures were followed, it ensured constant quality in several cities. In much the same way, McDonald's and other fast-food operators have chosen a menu strategy that dictates much of the rest of what happens in their operation. Similarly, the economy motel's product and service strategy defines the market it will aim for, the kind of building it will construct, and the size of its staff.

Personnel Strategies.   We will briefly examine two important personnel-related issues to suggest the policies and strategies they dictate. Many companies wishing to avoid unionization use a compensation strategy that offers pay and fringe benefits well above union scale. In other cases, an aggressive compensation strategy may be adopted by a company not because of unionization but simply to help it hire the cream of the crop in its labor market.

Such a strategy dictates the rule that whenever the wage level in the local labor market rises, the company raises its wages. To follow this strategy, the company must initiate a procedure of regular wage surveys in the area.

Community Relations Strategies.   Not surprisingly, different sectors of the hospitality industry court community favor in different ways. Let us look briefly at policy—and resulting strategy—in the commercial restaurant business, in the hotel business, in health care, and in school food service.

The traditional way to offer the goods and services of a fast-food chain is to buy advertising in the various media. Although a hotel or a local, independent, high-quality restaurant may also purchase advertising, many of these kinds of operations rely more on public relations activities. Thus, a local innkeeper may devote a great deal of time to public service activities in order, through such involvement, to build a favorable public image for the inn. This active public relations strategy may differ from that of a nearby fast-food operation that depends on advertising to bring the public through the door. The fast-food manager must spend his or her working time closely supervising operations; public relations may well be a minor part of the job.

In health care, it is usually just proprietary facilities that advertise, and, even then, that advertising tends to be low keyed. On the other hand, community hospitals actively involve themselves in public relations. Although they do not generally seek sales per se, hospitals do rely on periodic fund drives to raise capital for expansion or improvements. Thus, a favorable image in the community is helpful to them, too.

In recent years, the school lunch program has discovered that an active, interested group of supporters in the community can help them obtain the financial and moral support of the school board and school administrators. Consequently, a strategy of community involvement for school lunch managers dictates their being active with parent groups and other influential groups, especially those interested in nutrition in the community.

Each of these institutions—fast food, restaurant, hotel, hospital, and school lunch—needs financial support from the community in the form of sales, donations, or appropriations. Each has a policy of seeking community support, but their strategies differ according to the operational circumstances of each and the guests or clients they serve.

From Strategy to Tactics

Tactical issues are generally concerned more with short-range and localized actions. Like strategies, however, tactics are plans, the means of implementing policy.

In one high-occupancy chain motor hotel in a busy city, the property's marketing strategy was dictated by its franchise affiliation. This affiliation attracted the middle-income traveler who wanted comfortable accommodations but could not afford a luxury hotel. The property's downtown location gave it a special appeal to businesspeople. The manager realized, however, that a very large number of hotel rooms were being built in this market area. It became apparent that when all the properties under construction opened, the area would have an oversupply of rooms for several years to come. To prepare for this future marketing problem, the manager developed what was dubbed "FIRM Service."

A list of the largest firms in the area was compiled, and the hotel's sales representatives' work concentrated almost exclusively on these firms. At each of these firms, one or more contacts who placed rooms business was established and given a special number to call for reservations.

Furthermore, the manager instructed the front-office staff to hold a small number of rooms each day for FIRM Service accounts and to release them only as the house was filled. Only in exceptional circumstances was a FIRM Service request refused, and FIRM Service reservations were never "pulled" (canceled in the evening on the assumption the guest would not arrive).

The manager was too shrewd to assume that the property could keep business simply out of loyalty or gratitude; customers can be pretty fickle. What the manager did think—and rightly so—was that, when the market became more competitive, the hotel's sales personnel would be in a good position to reach key people at important accounts in the community. This tactic cost practically nothing, and it dealt with the problem of heavy future competition by gaining an advantage in that local market, which seemed most promising.

ℒONG-RANGE PLANNING TOOLS

You can often plan for today and tomorrow "in your head." The situation may be simple enough for you to grasp intuitively. However, when you make decisions that will have an effect for months or years, you need more sophisticated planning tools. These tools are usually considered at some length in courses on management accounting and finance. Moreover, we might properly include them in a later chapter on control. We will discuss them here, however, in order to emphasize the *quantitative* side of planning.

Return on Investment

When an organization makes an investment, it generally expects to earn that investment back within some definite period. Take the following simple situation: A new vacuum sweeper for use in public areas costs $2000. The larger machine is more efficient, and it reduces the number of hours required to vacuum the area from 100 a month to 90. If the operator's time costs $6 per hour, we can calculate two crude measures of value, and these measurements are common, simple decision aids. They are called the **payback period** and the **return on investment.** A useful formula is

$$P = \text{Payback period}$$
$$OS = \text{Operating savings}$$
$$NI = \text{Net investment}$$
$$P = \frac{NI}{OS}$$

For our problem:

$$OS = 10 \text{ hours} \times \$6 = \$60$$

and

$$P = \frac{\$2000}{\$60} = 33.3 \text{ months}$$

Notice that we have specified the *monthly* savings, so the payback period is also expressed in months. These calculations tell us whether we can plan on this investment paying for itself in a reasonable period of time.

Another way of analyzing this problem is to determine the **return on investment** (ROI). Here, we just invert our formula, but the results are usually expressed in annual terms, and so the monthly savings in the previous problem are multiplied by 12.

$$ROI = \frac{OS}{NI} \quad \frac{\$720}{\$2000} = 0.36 \text{ or } 36\%$$

In a business in which money to invest is at a premium and many departments require funds for new equipment, these techniques give us the means to establish investment priorities. Most organizations have specific rules for investments that relate to return on investment. Thus, these calculations help to consider the purchase in the context of those rules, sometimes called *hurdle* rates. (The word *hurdle* is adopted from the track-and-field sports scene. The "hurdle" is something you have to be able to reach or surpass, much as a runner must clear the hurdle in a race.)

In more complex cases, a *time-adjusted* rate of return may be used as the hurdle. This tool recognizes that a dollar today is worth more, by the interest it can earn in a bank, than a dollar will be a year from now. The interest rate (called in these problems the *discount rate*) can be changed to reflect varying costs of capital and risk assumptions.

Another common quantitative planning tool is the *break-even point computation.* This technique is similar to the payback period method. Suppose a new banquet room is proposed. Management expects the banquet check average to be $9.00 and the banquet check food costs to be 33 percent. All other costs of the proposed banquet department are fixed. If the fixed costs (the monthly payroll; heat, light, and power; depreciation; and so forth) for this room amount to $15,000, how many banquet covers must be sold per month to *cover* the cost of the banquet room (in other words, to break even)? Our new formula follows:

BEP = Break-even point
MR = Marginal revenue   (revenue less variable cost)
FC = Fixed costs   (the costs that will occur regardless of volume of sales if the decision is made to go ahead)
S   = Sales
VC = Variable cost

$$MR = S - VC = \$9.00 - \$3.00 = \$6.00$$

$$BEP = \frac{FC}{MR} = \frac{\$15,000}{\$6} = 2500 \text{ meals}$$

Thus, 2500 meals per month will cover all costs for this room. Management can now plan whether or not to build this room on the basis of its judgment about the number of meals it will probably serve.

Cost–Benefit Analysis

In business, the measure of dollar profit earned is not just useful—it is the principal decision-making guide. In school lunch or congregate feeding, however, such a measure is not enough. To begin with, revenue from guests is not always a significant factor, because the cost of the program is covered by government funds. The program's goal is not to earn a profit. Moreover, the decisions cannot always be measured in dollars. (In school lunch, how much is a hungry child worth?)

Although the variables cannot all be measured in dollars, a first step in **cost–benefit** (or cost-effectiveness) **analysis** is to make explicit those costs and savings that can be identified.

Suppose a congregate meals program is trying to decide whether to use 20 small feeding sites distributed throughout the county or to transport all its clients to a central point. The costs and savings to be specified would include the savings in food production and service staff in the central location and the reduction in food distribution expense (trucking food to 20 sites), in contrast with the cost of transporting clients to a central site.

Once this "homework" is done, however, it is still necessary to weigh the possibility that some aged clients might not feel up to the long trip and that others might feel uncomfortable in a strange neighborhood. For these reasons, participation might decline. These problems would actually reduce costs and subsidies, but that is hardly what the staff wants! Planning in the public sector is sometimes more complicated than in private business, because not all costs and benefits have dollar values. Public programs, however, must still do their homework so they can report what cost effects result from changes in plans.

Goals and policies provide the basis for developing plans, both strategic and tactical. As the goals addressed relate to longer periods, however, those responsible for planning cannot rely on intuition. They must use more formal and often complex means of analysis.

𝒯HE INDIVIDUAL WORKER AS PLANNER

If an operation is to be successful, individual workers must begin to consider themselves as planners. Notice the planning that a server automatically engages in as she moves from kitchen to dining room and back. As she steps out of the kitchen, she quickly sums up the situation on her station: One of her three tables (Table A) has just been seated. A second party has finished its main course (Table B) since she left the dining room. A third party (Table C) is waiting for the dessert she is carrying. She plans her next moves in order of priority:

1. Serve dessert (Table C).

2. Greet and assure return while serving water (Table A).

3. Take dessert order (Table B).

4. Take appetizer and main course orders (Table A).

5. Return to kitchen.

As she carries out this plan and heads back to the kitchen, she realizes that she also must plan her movements in the pantry to minimize wasted time and effort. On the way out of the dining room, she asks the busperson if he can clear Table B. With his assurance on that, she plans her moves in the kitchen:

1. Call dinner orders (for Table A).

2. Pick up appetizer (for Table A).

3. Pick up dessert (for Table B).

4. Return to dining room.

Her pattern is not necessarily the right way to handle a three-table station, and an actual situation would certainly not be this neat. The point is that a waitress relies heavily on planning, whether or not she is conscious of it.

When the head cook arrives at work at 8:00 A.M., she realizes that three meals confront her with immediate problems:

> Breakfast is now in progress and unusually busy. The short-order cook is in trouble because he's running out of his setup (raw food stored in a nearby refrigerator). The turkey on the menu for dinner needs to come out of the freezer right away. A roast round has to go in the oven immediately to be ready for an early banquet.

A great many different steps, the cook realizes, must be taken later in the day, but these immediate matters are of pressing concern. She takes these steps in order or priority and with a view to saving time and effort:

> She enters the walk-in with a cart, steps into the adjacent freezer (which can be reached only from the walk-in), and places the turkeys on the cart. Back in the walk-in, she places the round on her cart. These actions delay her only a minute. Now she loads the bacon, sausage, and eggs the short-order cook needs and proceeds to the kitchen, giving the supplies to the short-order cook, . . . and so on.

Her solution here may not be absolutely correct, but the incident should illustrate how essential planning is for that cook.

> Grab cart so you can carry everything. Take one minute while you're in the walk-in to get the two other things you need from there. While you are there, solve the breakfast cook's problem. It's going to be a busy day, so don't make three trips when one will do.

Not surprisingly, the hospitality industry rejects those management "experts" who assert that planning is exclusively a management function. Planning obviously pervades the well-run hospitality operation at all levels, from the maid who checks the stock on her cart to the general manager who orchestrates all the planners he or she works with.

Planning as a Personal Process

In Chapter 1, we discussed the notion of knowledge as retained earnings. We suggested that someone interested in a hospitality career can begin to accumulate useful learning experiences in the earliest, least-skilled jobs. Now, it is time to reinforce that concept with the conviction that personal career goals need to be identified as early as possible (without an artificial forcing).

These goals may well dictate a policy of putting skill learning first and income second in choosing jobs while in college and perhaps for those first years out of college, as well. This "learn first, earn second" strategy ensures "practice." If income is more important (or essential), however, you may have to alter your strategy. Planning, policy, and strategy are not something somebody else does. No plan is more important to you than is your own plan for yourself.

SUMMARY

Planning in organizations was the principal topic of this chapter. We first explained the reasons for planning and its different levels.

We defined and described several planning concepts: policies, plans, rules, methods, procedures, standards, budgets, strategies, and tactics.

Next, we discussed goal setting or management by objectives, and, after defining and illustrating it, turned to some of the subsets of goals. These included the characteristics of well-thought-out goals, goal congruence, and goals and policies.

Planning in operations requires strategy and tactics. We considered product and service strategies, personnel strategies, and community relations strategies. We then gave an example of successful tactics.

The long-term planning tools we explored were return on capital and cost–benefit analysis.

The last section covered the individual worker as a planner, which we illustrated with examples of a waitress and a cook. We ended with a short discussion of planning as part of career preparation.

◆ KEY WORDS AND CONCEPTS

Policies	Goal setting
Plan	Management by objectives
Rules	Goal congruence
Methods and procedures	Return on investment (ROI)
Standards	Payback period
Budget	Rate of return
Strategy	Cost–benefit analysis
Tactics	

◆ REVIEW QUESTIONS

1. Outline some of the reasons why you should study planning.

2. Define policies, plans, rules, methods, procedures, standards, budgets, strategies, and tactics.

3. What are the five questions that might be asked when setting goals?

4. What does goal congruence mean?

5. Is planning part of your study habits? Explain.

◆ NTERNET EXERCISES

1. **Site Name:** *The Ritz-Carlton Hotel Company*
   URL: http://www.ritzcarlton.com/toc.htm
   Background Information: The Ritz Carlton Hotel Company has 34 hotels world-wide (24 city hotels and 10 resorts) in Australia, Canada, Hong Kong, Indonesia, Malaysia, Japan, Korea, Mexico, Singapore, Spain, U.S. Virgin Islands, and the United States. It won the Malcolm Baldrige National Quality Award in 1992 for quality service.

   EXERCISES:

   a. What are the goals and objectives of the Ritz Carlton?

   b. What are some of the policies of the Ritz Carlton?

   c. Is there goal congruence (organizational goals and individual employee goals mesh rather than clash) at the Ritz Carlton?

2. **Site Name:** *The Four Seasons*
   URL: http://www.fourseasons.com/
   Background Information: Founded in 1960 by Isadore Sharp, chairman and chief executive officer, Four Seasons Hotels and Resorts is a Toronto-based company engaged in the management and ownership of medium-sized, luxury urban hotels and resort properties.

   EXERCISES:

   Compare the Ritz Carlton and the Four Seasons web sites.

   a. Which company provides more information on its goals and objectives?

   b. For a luxury hotel chain, which company embodies the luxury theme more completely? Why?

◆ OTES

1. Bryan G. Herron, "Strategic Planners or Restaurateurs . . . One and the Same?" *Proceedings of the 12th Annual Chain Operators Exchange* (Chicago: International Foodservice Manufacturers Association, 1985).
2. *Wall Street Journal*, May 14, 1993, p. B4 and May 19, 1994, p. B6.

3. For the best statement of this point of view, see Peter Drucker's work, particularly *Management: Tasks, Responsibilities, Practices* (New York: Harper & Row, 1974).

4. For an excellent and witty discussion on this point, see Robert Mager and Peter Pipe, *Analyzing Performance Problems or You Really Oughta Wanna* (Belmont, CA: Fearon Publishers, 1970).

Chapter 17

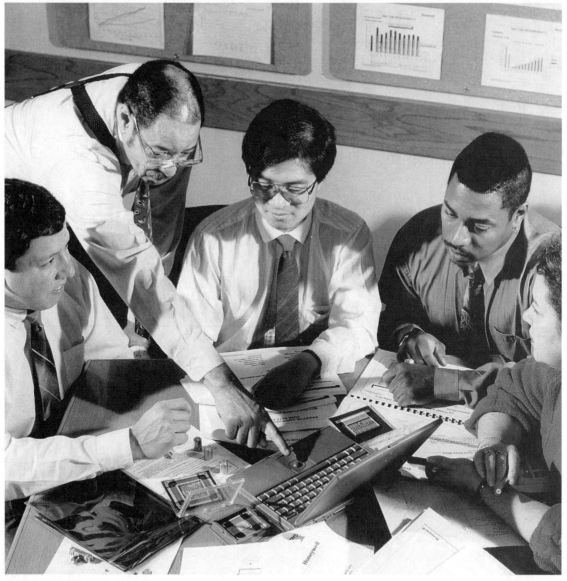

Courtesy of Honeywell, Inc.

Organizing in Hospitality Management

The Purpose of This Chapter

This chapter discusses the way people come together to work, an enjoyable and interesting subject. In a "society of institutions," knowing how institutions get "put together" can also help guide both work and life. Working relationships are rarely arbitrary. Moreover, an understanding of the limits of authority—and the limits on accepting authority—is essential to someone building a career in managing and supervising others. We are all on the receiving end of organizational decisions and the exercise of authority from time to time. So the basic argument is that understanding how management organizes will help you polish your hospitality management skills.

This Chapter Should Help You

1. Describe organization as a problem that is often solved informally in small operations

2. Distinguish between the various sources of authority and the limits of each in the workplace

3. Explain how work is allocated among organizational units (departments, for instance)

4. Trace the line-and-staff functions and explain the differences in the kinds of authority each exercises

5. Discuss the pros and cons of such organizational issues as the role of committees, the problems of bureaucracy, the "one boss" theory, and emerging approaches to organization in the modern hospitality industry

What is a real emergency? Except in organizations set up specifically to deal with them (fire companies and ambulance crews, for example), emergencies are nonroutine, serious situations, in which nobody knows for certain what to do. Some people shout orders; others run toward the door; others do whatever seems best to deal with the problem. To try to achieve results without organization is to invite a permanent emergency.

Small food service operators often appear to have established no real organization. A small restaurant needs only the simplest of organizations. You may recall from Chapter 5, however, that small restaurants have been declining in significance in the market. (The same is true of small motels.) Motor hotels, schools, colleges, and hospitals (even the small ones) are all, in reality, complex organizations. Your future, therefore, will probably involve work in an organization of some complexity.

Moreover, although we will discuss organizing principally from the perspective of the larger organizations in our industry, our discussion applies in a general way to the smallest organizations, as well. When we feel special solutions to organizing problems are useful, we will identify and discuss these solutions.

Before we begin, here is a definition of the organizing function in management:

Organizing is the work managers do to bring order to the relations between people and work as well as among the various people at work.

UTHORITY: THE CEMENT OF ORGANIZATIONS

Organization charts sometimes give the impression that the company just fits together in that way. In fact, for any group to function, it must have **authority** at several levels to make it come together and stay together.

The Bases of Authority

Formal authority has its basis in law, but there are limits placed on that authority by the way that people in the work group perceive the organization and their relation to it.

The Legal Basis for Authority. Laws and the legal system imply a community's potential use of force to maintain order. In our society, private property is a central social institution; in the business firm, the basic rationalization for management has been ownership. In the small firm, in effect, authority is often based on this notion: "I own this company and have the right to control my property. If you want to work here, you'll have to do as I say."

In the large corporation, the line of reasoning is more complex (stockholders elect a board, the board hires a top manager, the top manager delegates authority to subordinates). However, the essence of it is simply "I represent ownership" instead of "I own."

Franchise organizations present a more complicated case. The franchisor undoubtedly has a legal right to enforce agreed-upon procedures and quality standards with its franchisees. Franchise organizations, however, rely more on persuasion, advice, and peer pressure (from other franchisees) to maintain standards. In fact, only a very small proportion of franchisees have their franchises terminated for unsatisfactory operations. Moreover, *introducing change* in a franchise organization, except in matters clearly spelled out in the franchise agreement, is possible only through negotiation and persuasion. Often, the persuasion is based on the fact that the franchisee would be better off with whatever change is desired. As you can see, the mutual interest of all franchisees is a strong force that parallels the legal rights inherent in the franchisor's authority.

In governmental activities such as school lunch programs and congregate feeding, the basis of authority is legislative activity exercised by the duly elected representatives of the people. The enabling legislation authorizes the activity, together with periodic appropriation legislation that specifies the amount of money available and how it can be spent.

In either the company or a public agency, there lies behind the manager's order the ultimate force of authority of the **law.** When the boss says, "You're fired," he or she can call on public authority to back up this position. The same is ultimately true for a franchisor's regulation: Failure to comply will result in termination of the franchise. Although the law is the ultimate basis of formal authority (and some such fundamental basis is undoubtedly necessary to give stability to social institutions), constant resort to the law is not an effective tool for getting people to do things on an everyday basis. A sure sign of a weak, inadequate manager is the repeated use of social force ("You do it or I'll fire you").

Acceptance as a Basis for Authority. Subordinates can undermine a manager's authority in all kinds of subtle ways. In a rich society, the simplest way is to quit and get another job. Of course, an employee can stay and simply ignore orders whenever the manager's back is turned. These two approaches are by no means rare in the hospitality industry. Thus, to gain the employees' support, a supervisor or manager must win their acceptance of his or her authority and the employees' recognition that he or she is a person qualified for responsibility. In the hospitality industry, this acceptance generally means, first of all, credibility as a person qualified in the work the employees themselves do. An illustration from the personal experience of one of the authors may help:

> Unfortunately, I can't cook. This hasn't usually been a problem, as I've generally had a qualified food production supervisor to work with. I was once hired, however, as general manager to replace a man who had been promoted. On arriving at work, I learned that

1. The restaurant manager had just been fired.

2. The general manager was staying on "for a while."

3. I was the new restaurant manager.

4. I could take over as general manger as soon as the restaurant, which had been losing $16,000 on average each month since it opened, became profitable.

All of this came as a surprise, but I wasn't too concerned, as much of my experience had been in food service management. The problem I did have, however, was that there was no kitchen organization—just some cooks, with no one in particular in charge! I knew there was no way I could supervise those cooks because I didn't know enough about their work to be credible to them. I'd have been laughed out of the kitchen.

Fortunately, I was able to find a retired chef willing to help me out for a few weeks. I could explain to him what results I wanted—hours of service, menus, price ranges, and so forth—and he could interpret this need into specific directions for the cooks. Without the necessary credibility, in short, I needed an intermediary.

Aside from being another good argument for wide professional experience, this story illustrates the need, in a complex organization, for supervisors whose authority is acceptable to the work group. It would be equally difficult to supervise a front-office staff's work without any understanding of the technical aspects of what clerks do. Supervisors don't have to be experts, but they do require a sufficient familiarity with the work to "speak the language" and understand what is happening.

This principle does not apply just to the skilled work stations. Anyone who has ever seen an executive housekeeper whom the maids thought of as "too good to get her hands dirty," or a restaurant manager who couldn't, in an emergency, help out in the dishroom or bus a few dishes, knows how difficult this detachment makes their work with their subordinates.

Informal Organizations. Sociologists who study work groups note that right alongside the formal organization established by management is an informal social organization that grows up within the work groups. This **informal organization** usually has a leader consciously or unconsciously recognized by the group. The group develops its own expectations (norms) on what constitutes a fair day's work. And it develops an informal way of ranking its members (a status system). An insecure manager can feel threatened by an informal work group like this. The experienced manager or supervisor comes to accept the work group as a part of the natural order of things, like sunrise and sunset. He or she should establish working relations with this informal structure to ensure that the work at hand gets done. Most of all, the experienced manager realizes that the informal group constitutes a real limitation on his or her formal authority.

Authority and Responsibility   *limit on authority define limit of responsibility*

It is an axiom of organizational theory that the manager can be rightly held responsible for results only as far as his or her effective authority extends. For instance, you may recall from Chapter 10 that the uniform system of accounts for hotels records income and costs so that each manager is held responsible for results in the area that he or she controls. The innkeeper, for instance, is not responsible for capital costs because these costs reflect decisions made by the owners at the time of the construction or purchase of the property.

Authority: A Summary

The effective manager seeks to establish authority on the basis of competence acknowledged by the people he or she works with. The experienced manager accepts the social nature of a work group and learns to work effectively with its informal leaders. The ultimate basis of authority, however, lies in the legal reality of ownership or legislative authorization. The effective manager, though, has little need to rely on these fundamental sources of authority.

Authority that is based on competence and the acceptance of others is the strongest kind of authority.
Courtesy of the National Restaurant Association

Case History 17.1 Reorganization in a Multibrand Company

When Tom Oliver was appointed the new president of the Holiday Corporation, one of the first things he did was to change the company's name to Holiday Inn Worldwide (HIW) (**http://www.holiday-inn.com/**). Another early move, however, had more than symbolic content. He named brand presidents to take charge of each of its brands. A year earlier, the Crowne Plaza Group had been given its own president and separated from the Holiday Inn brand to seek a four-star image internationally and one distinct from the Holiday Inn brand. In the 1997 reorganization, the Holiday Inn Group and the Express/Leisure Group became separate divisions. As one franchisee put it, "Appointing a leader for those groups is good because now the distinction can be made clearer to the public and the franchisees." The same franchisee pointed out that the Select Holiday Inn and Suites brands need the most work because "no one knows what they are."

This new organizational framework is but one of many that has been adopted since Holiday Inns was acquired by the British brewing company, Bass PLC (**http://www.bass.co.uk/**). Indeed, even earlier, before the Holiday Inns flagship brand was sold off, the company fluctuated back and forth between a centralized and decentralized form of organization.

This latest reorganization reminds us that a company's form of organization is, in many ways, a management tool and, as such, open to change to achieve a particular result. In this case, each brand needs its own development and so a centralized organization is less appropriate than one which gives the people responsible for each brand more opportunity to innovate.

Overall direction of the company is in the hands of a nine-member board, which includes the three brand presidents, two international presidents, and the heads of finance, human resources, legal, and information technology.

Source: Adapted from Jeff Weinstein, "Oliver Tries to Refresh HIW Brands," *Hotels,* July 1997, p. 23.

DEPARTMENTALIZATION

For work to be done in complex organizations, these organizations must divide authority according to some logical basis. One manager cannot, after all, do everything. This division of authority is called **delegation.** Sometimes, as in Case History 17.1, it becomes necessary to rearrange authority relationships to meet new circumstances.

We turn now to a discussion of delegation, which is necessary before we can properly understand departmentalization.

The Delegation of Authority

In formal organizations, authority must be shared. Management scholars assert, in the *scalar principle,* that authority must extend in an uninterrupted *scale,* or series of steps, from the top to the bottom of an organization. Responsibility is accepted at each level, and, in turn, some authority is delegated to the next lower level. Although authority certainly can be delegated, most management scholars agree that responsibility cannot. That is, if something goes wrong because of a subordinate's error, the boss still must take responsibility along with the subordinate.

The scalar principle has been defined in one authoritative text as follows:

> The more clear the line of authority from the ultimate authority for management in an enterprise to every subordinate position, the more effective will be responsible decision making and organized communication.[1]

The delegation of authority may not be particularly important in small organizations in which management works closely with workers and can exercise control through actual participation. However, in larger, more complex organizations such as a hotel or hospital, a large restaurant, or a school district made up of many lunch programs, delegation becomes *necessary* just to get the work done. For instance, a hotel manager cannot simultaneously direct housekeeping, the front office, and the kitchen. Thus, senior managers must delegate authority to subordinate managers, that is, managers below them in the scale.

Authority is generally delegated in the context of agreed-upon policies and procedures. For instance, the chairman of ARAMARK described how decentralized authority works in that very large contract company:

> The operation of our business lines is more or less left to the division presidents but we do have explicit operating policies and strict financial controls that they must adhere to. However, the execution or how you satisfy the customer is strictly up to the individual [executive in charge].[2]

Delegation is necessary to get the work done. A second, less obvious reason for delegating authority is to develop management talent in the organization. As people leave for other jobs or enter retirement, the organization must keep up with the turnover. New positions are created, too, because organizations seek to expand. Most companies like to draw on their own employees to fill these openings. A third, related benefit that comes from having junior management and supervisory jobs in an organization is to keep bright, eager employees engaged and excited about their work by assigning them increased responsibility.

Unfortunately, many people have trouble delegating authority. This is especially true of people, such as chefs or dining room supervisors, who may have begun their working life as skilled workers, in this case as a cook or waitress. They are used to doing the job themselves, and they find it difficult to turn the work over to somebody else.

The fact is that, when a manager delegates a task, it is sometimes done incorrectly. The newly promoted supervisor who is skilled in the work at hand becomes very frustrated. He or she may feel "it's easier to do it myself." In the very short run—dealing with just one task—the supervisor is correct in that feeling. The reason for delegation, though, is the multiplicity of tasks that confront the work group for which the supervisor is responsible. Although any one task may be easier to do oneself, it's literally impossible for one person to do all of them. To get all the work done (with high average standards but probably some tolerance for error), the supervisor must delegate and concentrate his or her efforts on developing the competence of the work group.

Span of Control

You may recall from Chapter 15 that one of the early management scholars, V. A. Graicunias, attempted to develop a mathematical approach to determine how many people a manager can supervise directly. This **span of control,** Graicunias thought, was stretched taut by the increasing number of relationships between manager and subordinate, between subordinate and subordinate, and between the manager and the various combinations of subordinates. The number of relationships rises rapidly, as Table 17.1 shows.

Although the number of subordinates reporting to a manager cannot really be stated precisely, some management scholars assert that the ideal lies between three and eight subordinates. The exact number that a manager may supervise depends on the complexity of the work itself, the ability and training level of the subordinates, and the ability of the manager.

This concept of span of managerial responsibility is related to Graicunias's span of control, which refers to the number of people the manager supervises directly. The **span of managerial responsibility,** on the other hand, refers to the number of persons with whom the manager routinely interacts, that is, the number who have direct and unhindered access to the manager. For instance, a hotel manager

Table 17.1   Increase in Relationships

Number of Subordinates	Number of Relationships
1	1
2	6
3	18
4	44
5	100
6	222
7	490
8	1080
9	2376
10	5210

may have a food and beverage manager, a rooms department manager, a sales manager, a chief engineer, and a comptroller, all of whom report directly to him or her. In addition to these five, the manager may routinely consult with supervisors one or two levels below. He or she might discuss problems with a hostess, or the banquet chef, or one of the housekeeping inspectors. These people may feel quite free to consult with the general manager personally if a problem arises. Even at the top of a very large organization, consultation and interaction extend beyond the span of control. To quote the chairman of ARAMARK again, "I spend a lot of time on the road surveying both employees and customers to get suggestions or listen to complaints. So, I am aware of what is going on out in the field."[3]

For most hospitality organizations, span of managerial responsibility is as important a concept as is span of control. Span of control refers to formal reporting relationships, but hospitality organizations tend to develop important informal supervisor–subordinate relationships that don't fit the narrow span-of-control concept.

The principle of *unity of command* dictates that everyone has just one boss. This notion is generally sound, but, as the discussion in the preceding paragraph indicates, reality is a good deal more complicated. In the hospitality industry, unity of command generally means that a manager does not routinely interfere in the workings of a subordinate's department. Rather, he or she discusses problems with the department head and lets that person take any remedial action necessary. When a serious problem of guest satisfaction or some other emergency arises, however, rules often are put aside, and the manager may intervene directly.

Bases for Departmentalization

There are five common bases for dividing the work (and the authority over the work) into departments: function, product or service, geographical, customers, and process. The hospitality industry uses each of these departmental divisions. Function and product are the most common bases of departmentalization at the operating level, whereas territory and customer are the most common at the corporate level. A short discussion of each basis follows:

Function. The clearest example of functional departmentalization is found in food service, in which each functional department performs a different kind of work. Thus, the restaurant may be divided into service, food preparation, and sanitation. The kitchen may be further divided into such stations as meats, salads, and desserts. The organization of a restaurant, which we discussed earlier, is a good example of a functional organization at the unit level.

Product or Service. Hotels are divided into quite different product–service units, each with its own expertise. The most obvious divisions are between rooms, food and beverage, telephone, and other departments (for instance, garage). Below that level, however, functional division is the rule.

Geographical. In restaurant and hotel chains, it is common to assign supervisory responsibility for the operations in a particular region to a single manager. For example, Shoney's area supervisors have a geographic area of responsibility. In school lunch, in which each lunch program is located in a separate school, geographic divisions make one manager responsible for each unit.

Customers. Some companies that operate in several different hospitality business areas divide their operations by customer type. For instance, ARAMARK groups much of its food service by customer. The Business Service Group serves B&I dining, vending, and coffee services accounts. The Education Dining Group is further divided between college and university food service and school food service. A third division is devoted to health care, while a fourth, Leisure Services, specializes in stadiums, arenas, convention centers, and national and state parks.

Process. Many large hotels divide their food and beverage activities into a restaurant department, a bar department, and a banquet department because the preparation and service in these three areas can involve such different processes.

No one set of these departments represents the "best" means of division. What is important is that authority and responsibility be divided in a way that suits the particular needs of the market being served and the organization doing the work. We should note, too, that smaller organizations may not identify formal departments at all. In a small motor hotel, for example, the manager may serve as sales manager and personnel manager and take operational responsibility in the rooms or food and beverage department, as well. Nevertheless, as different functions are performed, the manager—and other "double-duty" management people—realize the need to shift gears and call different skills and styles into play. Organizational people who serve in multiple roles sometimes lament their unpredictable existences. However, they also tend to enjoy the recognition that attends their ability to get several different jobs done.

LINE AND STAFF

Line Management

Line authority is closely related to the ideas inherent in the scalar principle. **Line authority** passes from one operations person to another in a direct line from the top to the bottom of the organization. The rooms manager reports to the general manager. The hostess, food production manager, and banquet manager report to the food and beverage manager and, in turn, oversee subordinate supervisors and workers, as shown in Figure 17.1. A direct, unbroken line of authority runs from, say, a banquet waiter to the general manager. The work of line people directly affects guest service at all levels. Moreover, line management is the preponderant managerial role in the hospitality industry.

Figure 17.1 Line organization in a hotel.

Staff Assistance

Staff roles were originally limited to providing specialized assistance to line managers. Staff people, in effect, service the people who serve the guest. The staff person's special *expertise* is important, but a number of related kinds of staff *activities* have also become common.

The Advisor.   The personnel manager and comptroller are two good examples of advisory staff positions in the hospitality industry. They have specialized knowledge about their area of work—wage-and-hour laws or accounting procedures, for instance—that the line manager they report to can and should call upon. Each of these persons also acts for the manager in his or her area of specialty; that is, these staff people not only give a manager their expert advice, but they also act for him or her and for other line people by interviewing and screening applicants or maintaining accounting records. In these acts, however, they function as *representatives* of the manager, and they amplify the manager's ability in a specialized field.

Staff Service.   The purchasing manager, like other staff people, renders a service to the line departments rather than directly to the guests. Similarly, the engineering department assists the line departments in maintaining the physical systems necessary to the guests' comfort.

The "Assistants To."   In large properties or at the corporate level, senior executives commonly designate a person as, for instance, the assistant to the manager. This person has no authority, but he or she assists the manager with any project requiring special attention. Persons in such jobs are not mere "errand runners." The "assistant to" slot is often used to train rising young managers, and they are commonly given fairly wide ranging (if temporary) authority for completing any project to which they are assigned. Because people in this position are usually junior to those with whom they are working, while at the same time they represent high authority, the "assistant to" position requires great tact. Its advantage is that it expands the capacity of the senior executive because it equips him or her with a trusted, able assistant who can pursue details closely and report back. Moreover, as we just suggested, it can be a valuable training slot.

The Staff as Boss.   A staff person exercises authority in two kinds of situations. When the comptroller or chief engineer directs his or her subordinates in tasks, the authority exercised is clearly identical with line authority. Beyond that, as we shall see shortly, staff people are sometimes given "functional authority" over line people. Thus, the comptroller may direct the dining room cashiers (who regularly report to the hostess) in how to complete a new form. Similarly, the personnel manager may issue a directive to all departments laying out the procedures for handling grievances. This functional authority amplifies the competence of the line, but it sometimes creates confusion.

The Staff in the Small Organization.   In a small organization, the staff work may consist of part-time jobs assigned to regular employees, or it may be handled by outside specialists who provide services as needed. For instance, a 100-room motor hotel probably cannot afford a comptroller, chief engineer, or personnel manager. That property will, however, probably retain a firm of auditors to inspect its books regularly and develop an internal controls manual. Maintenance may consist of routine work done by a handyman. The expert service of plumbers, refrigeration specialists, heating contractors, and so forth will be called in as needed. Finally, the general manager, his or her secretary, or some other key person probably handles the personnel work.

$\mathcal{I}$SSUES IN ORGANIZING

Lest the student consider organization a cut-and-dried matter, we should examine some of the areas of organization theory that are, more than most, unsettled. Because each of these areas also sheds light on special problems in hospitality organizations, this section will serve the dual purpose of explaining theory and increasing your understanding of practice.

Functional Staff Authority

We mentioned that organizations sometimes authorize staff people to "give orders" across the entire organization within their special field of expertise. To illustrate the value—and some of the problems—of this practice, consider the problems of a chain hotel organization.

Figure 17.2 illustrates the organization of this chain at the corporate level and the organization of a typical unit within the chain at the operating level. As the figure shows, one vice president is "in the line." The vice president for operations is

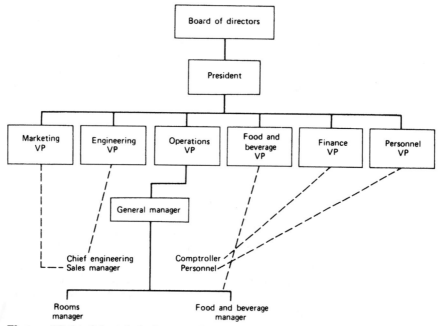

Figure 17.2 A hotel chain organizational chart.

charged with overseeing all properties, and the general manager of each hotel reports to him or her directly. There are five other vice presidents. These officers are specialists in the field of marketing, engineering, food and beverage, finance, and personnel; each is responsible for developing programs in his or her respective area.

The work of the corporate marketing vice president, for instance, includes developing the company's advertising program and directing its national sales office. The engineering vice president develops energy conservation measures and commands a small, highly technical staff. The vice president for food and beverage is an expert in that area of operation. He or she serves as a combination inspector, troubleshooter, and consultant in matters pertaining to food and beverage. The financial vice president oversees the company's accounting. The personnel officer is concerned with companywide compensation and fringe-benefit policies and monitors changes in legislation affecting employment and work practices.

Notice that each of these staff vice presidents is connected by a dotted line to a function of management at the unit level. This line indicates that each exercises staff supervision or **functional staff authority** over his or her special fields of work at the unit level. Now, who does the hotel's accountant work for? Does he or she have two bosses? The answer to this question for each of these "dotted line relationships," as they are sometimes called, depends on a number of factors.

First, the relationship is essentially technical. A new financial reporting procedure may be developed, and directions for implementing it may come from the vice president. Notice, however, that it is a fairly narrow, specialized exercise of authority.

Second, the staff supervisory activity varies in intensity with both the function and the circumstance. The engineering vice president, for instance, probably interacts with the chief engineer at the property only infrequently, as, for example, when some new piece of equipment is installed or a new energy control procedure is developed. Most of the chief engineer's work in a hotel is routine, although the work of the vice president is almost entirely specialized and technical. On the other hand, if a major renovation of the hotel is undertaken, the engineering vice president would work much more closely with the property.

The personnel vice president does not tell the local personnel manager whom to interview or hire. That is the work of the line managers at the property. On the other hand, the vice president will take an interest in the hiring process as it relates to complying with law, as in fair-employment practices.

The possibilities of mixed loyalties on the general manager's staff and of clashes between general manager and staff vice presidents are remote, but clearly these relationships call for tact. The disadvantages that accompany these blurred lines of authority are more than offset by the top-quality expertise made available. The hospitality industry is becoming too complex a business to do without such an expert staff.

One area in which staff supervision has proved uncommonly difficult is food and beverage. This area really involves a line function; therefore, a number of companies have eliminated staff supervision in this area, leaving it entirely in the hands of the general manager.

Independent operators avail themselves of various kinds of expert advice. We noted some of them earlier: an accountant, an attorney, specialized engineering people. The manager of the operation must often achieve the necessary expertise to act as a staff specialist in some areas, particularly marketing. Many a general manager has been heard to remark, "I'm wearing my sales manager's hat today." In fact, hotel general managers often join the Hotel Sales and Marketing Association International specifically for this reason.

Increasing the Span of Control: Empowering Managers

Only a generation ago, a leading French management writer, Jean Jacques Servan-Schreiber,[4] pointed out that one of the major factors in the success of American companies was their more fully developed organization structure. Companies in the United States had more supervisors and more levels of supervision and, as a result, they had better control over quality. Now this pattern is reversing itself and the "flat organization" (i.e., one without a hierarchical, many tiered management structure) is becoming the norm. Many multiunit companies are reducing dramatically the number of levels of field supervision, with the result that the remaining supervisors oversee more units.

Taco Bell and Pizza Hut have been prominently associated with restructuring their organization to eliminate intermediate layers of management. This increases the responsibilities of the remaining managers. The span of control for field supervisors, such as area managers at Taco Bell, went from one area manager for every "five-plus stores to one for every 20-plus stores."[5] Pizza Hut did away with one whole level of management, the district managers. District managers used to supervise five to seven stores. Now, area managers supervise 11 or more stores.[6] The difference between the span of control at these two Tricon subsidiaries is probably accounted for, in large part, by the greater complexity of the Pizza Hut operation.

The reduction in middle managers and the increase in span of control has more than one effect. It cuts out an expensive layer of managers, complete with salaries, fringe benefits, expenses, clerical support, and office space. More important, perhaps, the role of the multiunit manager changes.

The remaining area managers now have about twice as many stores to oversee. They obviously can't spend as much time with each store. That means the *individual store manager has more responsibility* for her or his own operation. The kind of supervision, moreover, that an area manager can give 20 or 12 stores is different from that which one district manager used to give 5 or 6 stores. There is much less time for detail and personal involvement in the operation. We might expect the role to be more that of a consultant than of a "boss," and the nature of the interaction to be more that of one who gives expert advice than of one who gives detailed orders. This makes the store manager much more responsible for the success or failure of his or her own unit. No doubt, that sometimes feels like "sink or swim."

The evidence to date suggests that increasing the span of control works. We see it being done by more and more companies. Domino's eliminated a number of middle-management positions by consolidating eight regional offices into five. The lodging company, Promus, put it this way:

> As we reduce layers of management, we improve communications and allow each employee to expand his or her responsibilities. This is our commitment to empowerment—allowing our employees to grow and assume more responsibility to provide excellent service to every customer every time. . . .

Empowerment requires an environment of teamwork and cooperation with minimal layers of supervision and maximum individual responsibility.[7]

Committees

Complex organizations that make decisions that involve several departments, or disciplines, need methods for communicating and involving different kinds of specialized expertise. Although "management by committee" is really a contradiction in terms, **committees** often serve as management devices in health care, education, and all kinds of governmental activities, such as congregate feeding and school lunch programs. Although the role of committees is not so prominent at the unit operating level in the private sector, many properties find committees useful in a number of areas, particularly in energy conservation and environmental manage-

[handwritten margin note: disadvantage: time limit avoid action shift responsibility compromise]

ment and recycling programs. Most companies make extensive use of committees at the headquarters level.

Committees allow a number of different interests to gain representation. In health care, the dietary department often prepares food that is delivered to the nursing-care staff which, in turn, delivers the food to the patients. The food may be purchased for the dietary department by a separate purchasing office, which may also receive the deliveries and handle bulk product storage. The staff cafeteria is sometimes intended as a fringe benefit to employees, providing subsidized meals to the staff below cost. This makes the dietary department important to the personnel officer, just as the need for cafeteria and other accounting procedures makes the dietary department important to the accounting office. The nature of the dietary department's work might well require an advisory committee, to help it react to proposed operating or policy changes.

Such a committee offers all the advantages usually advanced for committees: It helps coordinate plans and transfer information. Committee membership by junior management provides an opportunity for management development as the junior members come to learn how the organization functions. Occasionally, the committee also builds morale: When everyone is consulted, no one is offended, or so the argument goes.

The disadvantages of committees can offset their advantages to some degree. Committees tend to consume a great deal of time. A "short," one-hour meeting of six people consumes six labor hours. Moreover, committees often avoid action rather than take it, and they can be used to avoid or shift responsibility for unpopular or risky decisions. In addition, because committees are supposed to give a hearing to many views, they often encourage compromise.

The case for consultation in the hospital dietary department does not necessarily call for a committee. A committee will regularize consultation, but the same consultation could take place informally among the interested parties. This approach might take a little more time for the person seeking the consultation, but it would almost certainly take less time for all the participants.

Committees are unquestionably useful where the purpose served warrants their use. For example, in energy and recycling management, many hospitality organizations find the committee approach unusually effective in communicating technical information across the organization and in funneling practical suggestions to management. In these cases, committees also serve as a motivational tool by allowing all participants to be involved.

[handwritten margin note: Compare w/ ad hocracy]

Bureaucracy

Bureaucracy is a bad word to most Americans. It is curious, therefore, to realize that Max Weber, the German sociologist who invented the term, developed his theory of **bureaucracy** as an ideal type of large organization and an ideal way of how it should be run. The following characteristics are those that Weber identified as part of a large hierarchical organization:

1. The organization's work is embodied in statements of fixed official duties.

2. Decisions are governed by abstract, rational rules that are the only proper basis for decision.

3. The bureaucratic official avoids emotionalism and is impersonal.

4. Technical qualification in the appropriate field is the basis for entry and advancement in a bureaucracy.

Weber's model of bureaucracy seeks the most efficient solution to problems on strictly impersonal, rational grounds. Bureaucracy is a means of avoiding the arbitrary exercise of power as in an absolute monarchy, in which people exercise power because of their relationship to the monarch or some other person in power. It also seeks to avoid the problem of political organizations in which the "in" clique holds sway over everyone. In sum, then, it seeks to replace personal relationships—with their possibility for favor and lack of fairness—with an impersonal, rational, efficient organization.

As large organizations have come to play a more and more important role in our society, we have discovered that *bureaucratic politics* (a notion that Weber would have abhorred) has become a problem and that bureaucrats can, in fact, be arbitrary and unfair, bending rules to their own purposes. Bureaucracies, moreover, can seek "efficient" solutions in ways that are wildly wasteful.[8]

Weber's contribution, however, remains. He asserted (and subsequent management scholars have confirmed) that large organizations have special problems. The special organizational rules along the lines that Weber suggested, although far from perfect, clearly constitute a useful starting point for solutions to organizational design problems in an increasingly complicated society.

Ad Hocracy

In his book *Future Shock,* Alvin Toffler pointed to a significant development in organizations that began in the aerospace industry and other science- and engineering-related activities. Toffler dubbed this new approach to management **ad hocracy.** The word is derived from the Latin phrase *ad hoc,* meaning "to this." The idea is that of an organization responding forcefully to particular situations in an environment that constantly changes. In these situations, the work to be done, rather than a traditional organizational structure, dictates who is in charge. The structure can best be described as a team with changeable captains. If the problem to be solved involves engineering, the team leader will be an engineer with the skills necessary to the current need. If the problem lies in another area, the person with the necessary abilities will take the reins.

Although most hospitality organizations follow the traditional line or line-and-staff organization, operations whose problems resemble those of the aerospace industry are emerging, especially among the new, large resort and casino operations.

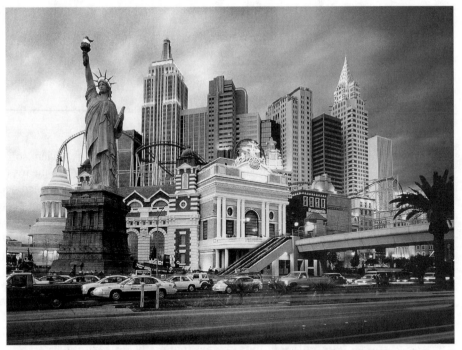

Large casino resorts have such a complex customer mix that they've had to develop flexible organization structures to be able to respond to all of them.
Courtesy of New York, New York Hotel, Las Vegas

Casino Resort Hotels. A large casino resort hotel is actually involved in five different businesses in a big way (and a few other businesses less closely connected to its operating format and organizational structure). First, casino resort hotels are among the world's largest hotels. Second, they are among the world's largest gambling centers. Third, many are a major factor in the convention business in North America, with numerous meeting and banquet rooms ranging in capacity from 75 to thousands. Fourth, they are large centers for entertaining and dining, boasting numerous restaurants, each with a distinctive menu and atmosphere. Finally, they usually feature large and extravagant stage shows.

Operating these businesses for one common clientele would be challenge enough. The hotel's situation is complicated, however, by the fact that it caters to three different markets: the casual visitor, who comes alone or with family for a Las Vegas vacation; the convention guest; and the junketeer.

These hotels serve the first market, the traditional class of guest, with the traditional departments that operate according to an organization structure similar to that of any other hotel. The other two kinds of guests, however, present special cases, because each has been attracted by a specific marketing activity in a highly competitive area.

The national convention market receives the attention of literally hundreds of top hotel sales organizations. As a result, when a convention is sold, the hotel's marketing department must follow up on the service. If, for instance, the sales department has promised a special registration procedure on arrival or has agreed to some special service for a banquet, sales must have the means of seeing to it that the special agreement is met. Moreover, if a problem develops for the convention group, the group's contact person will probably want to turn for help to the sales representative with whom he or she first dealt. That sales representative needs the organizational means to solve problems.

Junket guests are gamblers (with *good* credit ratings) who visit Las Vegas as guests of the hotel with all expenses paid, often including transportation both ways. Although some of these visitors win at the gambling tables, the perfectly legitimate casino percentages favor the house more than enough to cover the cost of visits over the long run. Many of Las Vegas's major hotels solicit junket business. This solicitation is principally directed by the marketing department. Once again, when junket guests get to the hotel, these "high rollers" must receive excellent treatment so that the marketing department's efforts to secure return visits remain fruitful.

To solve the problem of these special markets, many Las Vegas hotels have evolved an unusual organization structure. In the typical hotel, a simple organization structure might look like the one in Figure 17.3. The marketing department sells, and the operating departments service the sale. The convention guest might have some contact with the sales representative, but this contact is probably just either a quick, friendly visit or some limited liaison with the operating department.

Many casino hotels, however, have built a somewhat different structure, as illustrated in Figure 17.4. When an individual guest arrives, the organization functions much as it does in traditional hotels. When a convention arrives, however, the marketing department stations a representative at the front desk during registration. This representative has the authority to intervene and settle any problems

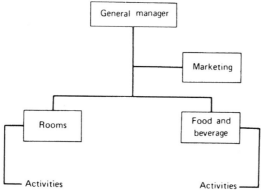

Figure 17.3 Traditional hotel organization.

Figure 17.4 Ad hocracy in a casino resort.

related to servicing the sale. Similarly, a representative of the marketing department is present at convention banquets, working right along with the food and beverage department's supervisors—again to guarantee the service sold by the marketing department. A similar, though less formalized system operates for junket guests.

For this reason, we have to draw solid lines in Figure 17.4, indicating *authority* between the marketing department and the operating department activities.

Although confusion undoubtedly arises from time to time, this organization functions smoothly. People who work in complex organizations learn to live with more complex relationships. Casino hotels must determine authority by the task at hand.[9]

Walt Disney World. Walt Disney World (WDW) is another highly complex resort organization comprising several distinct businesses, including a theme park, food service, hotel operations, outdoor camping, and sports. The problems at WDW are twofold. First, the park is constantly changing and growing, and will be for many years to come. This problem of growth and change is complicated by dramatic swings in volume that see the workforce at WDW more than double during the summer's peak season.

During a visit to WDW, we were impressed by one small but interesting fact: The food service organization chart was drawn on a large metallic blackboard. Departments and organizational units were connected by chalk lines, and all the names on the board were on small magnetized plaques that could easily be moved around on the board. Conversation confirmed the impression suggested by the board: The organization structure changed so fast at WDW that the only way management could keep up with it was to use a medium on which changes could be made often and easily.

We do not intend to imply that blackboards are better than paper for organization charts; rather, the point is that dynamic organization forms are increasingly required in growing, changing, complex hospitality firms.

$\mathcal{S}$UMMARY

Our description of organization began with a discussion of authority, its legal basis and its acceptance by those supervised as a basis. The latter led us to touch on the informal organization and then authority and responsibility.

We then turned to departmentalization and the delegation of authority. Span of control is an approach used to determine the number of people that a manager can supervise directly, and span of managerial responsibility refers to the number of people with whom a manager routinely interacts. The five bases for dividing work (and authority over it) are function, product or service, geography, customer, and process. Authority also refers to line management and staff assistance, which we also described.

We considered some of the issues in organization theory: functional staff authority, committees, bureaucracy (as defined by Weber), and ad hocracy (as defined by Toffler). We finished with two examples of flexible organizations, those of the large casino resort hotels in Las Vegas and of Walt Disney World in Orlando, Florida.

◆ $\mathcal{K}$EY WORDS AND CONCEPTS

Authority	Span of managerial responsibility
Legal basis for authority	Line management
Law	Line authority
Acceptance as a basis for authority	Staff
Informal organization	Functional staff authority
Departmentalization	Committees
Delegation	Bureaucracy
Span of control	Ad hocracy

◆ $\mathcal{R}$EVIEW QUESTIONS

1. Does an effective manager often use his or her legal basis for authority? Explain.

2. Describe how informal organizations in work groups operate.

3. What is the scalar principle?

4. Differentiate between span of control and span of managerial responsibility.

5. What are the five common bases for dividing work? Briefly describe each in regard to the hospitality industry.

6. What are some of the advantages of committees?

7. Outline Weber's definition of bureaucracy.

8. What is an ad hocracy?

◆ INTERNET EXERCISE

1. Site Name: *Hotel, Restaurant and Tourism Online Professional and Trade Journals*
URL: http://www.wku.edu/~hrtm/journals.htm
Background Information: This web page provides links to hospitality professional journals on line and serves as a launchpad to retrieve information from these journals.

EXERCISES:

a. Choose several of the on-line journals and serach for recent articles on authority, informal organizations, departmentalization, delegation, span of control, re-organization, line-and-staff relationships, or any topic deemed appropriate by the instructor. Read the articles and lead a class discussion on the topic you have chosen.

b. Describe how the articles supplement the information contained in the textbook. Be sure to provide the other students with the name of the journals where the information was found.

◆ NOTES

1. Harold Koontz and Cyril O'Donnel, *Management: A Systems and Contingency Analysis of Managerial Functions*, 6th ed. (New York: McGraw–Hill, 1976), p. 379.
2. *Nations Restaurant News*, December 17, 1990, p. 58.
3. *Nations Restaurant News*, December 17, 1990, p. 58.
4. Jean Jacques Servan-Schreiber, *The American Challenge* (New York: Atheneum, 1968).
5. Leonard A. Schlesinger and James L. Heskett, "The Service Driven Company," *Harvard Business Review*, September–October, 1991, p. 77.
6. *Cornell Hotel and Restaurant Administration Quarterly*, May 1991, p. 94.
7. Michael G. Muller, *Restaurant Industry Review* (San Francisco: Montgomery Securities, January 1994), p. 48.

8. For a witty but telling analysis of the problems of "dysfunction" of bureaucracies, see C. Northcoat Parkinson's book, *Parkinson's Law* (Boston: Houghton Mifflin, 1957).

9. This example was originally based on a 1976 interview at what was then the MGM Grand. More recent interviews in 1989, 1991, 1994, and 1997, however, indicate that what was true at the Grand over 20 years ago has now become a widely observed practice in casino resort hotels.

$\mathscr{C}$hapter *18*

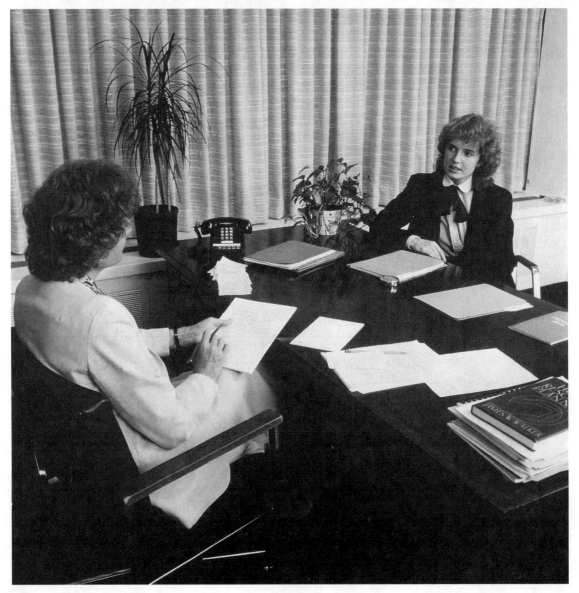

Photo by Ken Karp

Staffing: Human Resource Management in Hospitality Management

The Purpose of This Chapter

One of the major contributions made by Taylor and the scientific management theory was the principle of fitting the right person to the job rather than hiring just whoever came along. Accordingly, modern hospitality management has developed effective procedures for selecting its employees. This trend has been helpful because personal service—and personal interaction with a guest—are crucial to our field. Since a hospitality firm spends somewhere between 20 and 40 percent of its revenue on direct and indirect wage costs, an understanding of the management function concerned with managing human resources has become essential to the education of managers in our industry.

This Chapter Should Help You

1. Discuss the importance of job specifications and describe how they are prepared

2. Name the major sources for new employees and the advantages of each source

3. Describe the selection and employment process and its major component activities of information gathering, induction, and training

4. Outline the general procedure of staff planning, and identify and describe the major tools in that process

Some management scholars argue that "staffing" is not a separate function but is actually part of organizing. But everyone in the hospitality industry believes that human resource management at all levels is one of the major concerns of management.

During the 1970s, when the hospitality industry's growth was fastest, there was also a continuing influx of young people into the workforce as the baby boomers entered their teenage and college-age years. By the beginning of the 1980s, however, the number of young workers began to decline, a decline that has continued steadily and one that will continue through the late 1990s. Because the industry has continued to expand, a growing shortage of workers has developed in more markets, reaching, for some operators, crisis proportions. Although the shortage will not worsen seriously, it will be late in this decade before it gets better and then only slowly.

As early as 1985, more than 80 percent of fast-food managers surveyed by *Nations Restaurant News* reported their operation to be understaffed, and, even when we have faced recession, most labor markets have continued to report periodic scarcity. We have noted, too, in earlier chapters that competition for workers from sectors like health care is fierce now and likely to grow more so. Fast food has felt the shortage of young workers more severely than have some other hospitality businesses, but virtually all segments are significant employers of young people, and all draw from roughly the same total labor pool. When one part of that pool is in short supply, it doesn't take long for others to feel it, too.

Operators have found that where labor shortages have been severe, it meant that managers often had to work stations to cover for absent crew members. Moreover, when not working to cover missing employees, they had to spend an excessive amount of time on recruiting. We'll look at what they and others have done to address the labor shortage later in the chapter. Even if there weren't periodic labor shortages, human resource management would be a major concern for two good reasons.

First, and most important, in a field whose stock in trade is **personal service,** the success of the whole enterprise often rests on the kind of employee and how he or she performs a certain job. In particular, the public contact employee—the waiter or waitress, counterperson, or desk clerk—must be chosen with special care. The back-of-the-house employee must also have definite qualifications. If the cook that the waitress must deal with in the back of the house is a tempermental plate-thrower or a foul-mouthed grouch, it will be hard for her, regardless of how pleasant she may be, to show her good side in the dining room.

A second reason for the importance of staffing is the significance of its cost. Few hospitality firms spend less than 25 percent of their sales on payroll costs, and some hotel food service departments spend as much as 40 percent of food and beverage sales on payroll and related costs. Moreover, wages had been rising rapidly in the hospitality industry even before there was a labor shortage. With wages rising rapidly at all levels of operation, you can be sure that **wage cost** will be a major concern for the rest of your career.

Aside from wage rates, one of the major contributors to the high cost of labor is high turnover. There are definite costs associated with hiring and training an employee. If that employee leaves just when he or she is about to become productive, the turnover will be both expensive and wasteful. Reducing turnover, then, is a primary goal of the human resource function. This reduction involves some key ideas: matching the person to the job; giving the new employee a favorable first impression of the company; stressing the importance of the job; and providing enough training to make the new employee feel able to do the work required.

Actually, human resource management involves, at one time or another, all the other components of the management process. As you will see in the last section of this chapter, staff planning is crucial, and staffing reflects management's organizing efforts at controlling labor costs. The process of induction and training is closely tied to the function of directing and leading. Because of the importance of people in our industry, however, we must isolate the staffing work of managers for the purposes of study. We can define staffing—or human resource management—in this way:

> Staffing is the work that managers and supervisors do to determine the specific personnel needs of their operations—to attract qualified applicants and to choose from these the best suited for employment and training. The manager accomplishes the human resource management function by using specialized staff planning tools.

𝓕ITTING PEOPLE TO JOBS

Although most managers have always tried to choose the right person for the job, particularly in responsible positions, until Frederick Taylor's time, there was no general awareness of the importance of this practice. In some places, tradition determined who would take a job. Labor was often so poorly paid that people were chosen for the jobs on the basis of how little payment they would accept. Thus, although it may seem obvious to us, the modern practice of matching person to job has been the general practice for only about a hundred years.

We should note that some people in hospitality management still don't have an organized notion of the human resource function, and an even larger group sometimes appears not to understand it. Some managers are constantly surprised when work does not get done, even though they have not staffed their positions so that it will get done. Such people hire whoever comes in the door and put him or her to work with little or no training. Either hospitality managers who proceed in this way fail or they succeed in spite of their staffing weaknesses because of some other special strengths. Just because some operators do not understand the principle of wise staffing, however, is no reason to follow their lead and ignore these principles.

Many successful, independent operators appear to follow no formal staffing procedures but achieve effective staffing results anyway. Although they may ignore formal procedures, these operators generally follow informal procedures picked up through experience, in talking with competitors, at trade shows and industry meetings, and so forth. In practice, these informal procedures may come close to more formalized programs. These operators, by and large, are the "old pros." Although their results are good, beginners would probably do better to start with proven

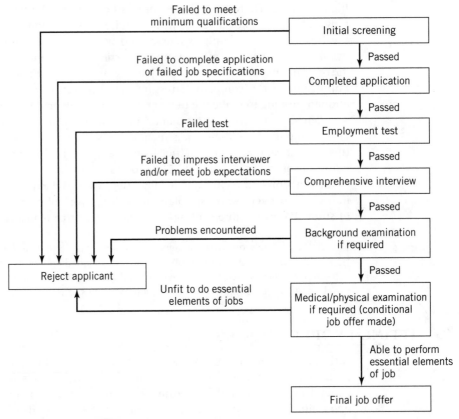

Figure 18.1 Steps in the job selection process.
(*Source:* David A. De Cenzo and Stephen P. Robbins, *Human Resource Management,* 5th ed., New York: John Wiley & Sons, 1996, p. 171. Reprinted with permission.)

fundamentals. Figure 18.1 spells out those fundamentals as a set of steps managers should follow in the selection process.

Job and Person Specifications

If a company has no formal staffing procedure, the first step in adopting one will be to identify each job being done. For each job identified, the company prepares a **job description.** (Job descriptions for workers are often based on formal task analyses prepared by someone with industrial engineering training.) Figures 18.2 and 18.3 illustrate management job descriptions.

The logic of the job description should be obvious. We can hardly hire the right person for the job until we have a good idea of what the job is. Once a job is analyzed carefully, some minimum standards for an applicant should emerge. Sometimes these standards are broken down into physical requirements, mental ability, and emotional or attitudinal characteristics.

NAME: _____		DATE: __ / __ / __ Page __ of __		
POSITION TITLE: Food Service Manager	JOB CODE:	EFFECTIVE DATE:		
REPORTS TO: Food Service Director	LOCATION: East			
DIVISION: Educational	AREA GROUP	REGION/DEPT	DIST/SEC/UNIT	

Basic Function:
  Handle all assigned responsibilities in a professional manner.

Scope:
  1. Responsible for all phases of unit as designated by FSD.
  2. Responsible for all phases of the cafeteria.
  3. Responsible for all catered events.
  4. Responsible for expanding business volume in the above listed areas.

Principal Duties (by Key Result Area):
  1. Training and developing staff to full potential.
  2. Ordering, using competitive bids and approved suppliers.
  3. Manning/pricing.
  4. Developing two specials per month as per schedule forwarded to FSD and DM; that is, "monotony breakers."
  5. Determining pre- and postcost to attain a financial success.
  6. Maintaining records for following year reference.
  7. Attaining financial goals.
  8. Maintaining a high level of satisfaction.

Position Specifications:
  1. Must be able to work as an integral part of a management team.
  2. Must be able to maintain a rapport with superiors and subordinates.
  3. Must be able to cope with work pressures.
  4. Must be innovative and willing to take the initiative.
  5. Must maintain a professional appearance as deemed necessary to satisfy the client.
  6. Must have the ability to plan and organize.

Where/How to Obtain Training:
  1. Second-Phase Management Development Program.
  2. On-the-job training.
  3. Company-initiated programs and films.
  4. Management meetings.

Figure 18.2 Job description—manager.

NAME: _____ DATE: __ / __ / __ Page __ of __

POSITION TITLE: Chief Dietitian	JOB CODE: FO 6	EFFECTIVE DATE:	
REPORTS TO: Food Service Director	LOCATION: East		
DIVISION: Health Care	AREA GROUP	REGION/DEPT	DIST/SEC/UNIT

Basic Function:
  To obtain or improve nutritional status of patients

Scope:
  To be responsible for high-quality nutritional patient care and instruction.
  To be responsible for overseeing the activities of one other dietitian.

Principal Duties (by Key Result Area):
  1. Visiting and instructing patients and recording in medical charts.
  2. Supervising diet-aides and insuring that all patients are visited within 24 hours of admission.
  3. Working closely with in-service department orienting new hires and students to procedures of dietary department.
  4. Operating an outpatient diet instruction clinic.
  5. Supervising proper preparation and distribution of tube feedings and nourishments.

Position Specifications:
  BS degree in Foods and Nutrition.
  1 year ADA accredited internship.
  ADA membership.
  ADA registration.

Where/How to Obtain Training:
  Local monthly dietitian's journal club.
  State and national dietetic association meetings.
  Local and state diabetes association meetings.

Figure 18.3 Job description—dietitian.

Physical Requirements. The person hired must be able to do the job. If a waitress must reach across a booth, the applicant may have to conform to some minimum height requirement (five feet is used by some companies). A receiver's job may require someone able to lift 100 pounds and generally be able to do heavy physical work. Many public contact jobs carry requirements for personal appearance and for personal hygiene habits. Cocktail waitresses, for instance, are often chosen for their attractiveness, as well as their serving ability. Recent federal regulations have complicated this process, however, often making the hiring process more dependent on unwritten rules. An employer, however, still has the need to fit the person to the job.

Mental or Intellectual Abilities.   Some jobs require specific intellectual abilities. Desk clerks and other public contact employees must speak reasonably clear English. (In Quebec, they will need English and also are required to be fluent in French. In some parts of the United States, Spanish is helpful.) Waitresses and waiters must have sufficient arithmetic ability to total a check. Cooks and bartenders must be able to convert recipes from one quantity to another.

Emotional or Attitudinal Characteristics.   Once again, public contact employees should express by their manner a reasonably pleasant disposition. Those who are hired to work under pressure, such as waitresses and bartenders, should not project a nervous or irritable disposition. An increasing number of companies are concerned, as well, with an employee's ability to get along with fellow workers and to work in a team.

Handicapped Employees.   In some jobs, physical or mental disabilities are not a drawback. Food service is a major employer of handicapped workers. The number of people with physical, emotional, and mental disabilities who were employed during the 1980s, declined by 23 percent. In the same period, however, the food service industry actually increased employment of handicapped people by nearly 12 percent. Among operators who employ handicapped workers, 90 percent reported that disabled workers' performance was excellent or good when compared to nondisabled workers.[1]

$\mathcal{R}$ECRUITING

Once we know what kind of people we want for each job we've identified, we must try to attract a pool of applicants that permits us to select the best qualified. Indeed, we will shortly argue that, in the face of labor shortages, it has become as necessary to segment the labor market as it has been to target the appropriate customer group. The major sources of prospective employees are the operation itself (the internal source) and various outside sources. Each has its special strengths and problems.

It is interesting to see what steps are taken in the search process in a severe labor shortage such as the one we mentioned earlier. What one company did was to appoint a special task force of personnel and operations people to lead a crash recruiting program in the area. The task force compared the company's operating, pay, and personnel practices with those of its competitors. As a result, wages and benefits were adjusted as appropriate; an incentive program was introduced for suggestive selling; and the employee food discount and vacation programs were improved. Moreover, the task force used mobile recruiting vans and developed a reward program for referrals of new employees by those already on staff.

As you can see, **recruiting** involved thinking through the job the company had to offer in much the same way it might have looked at a product for sale.

Increasingly, employers are seeing themselves as having, in effect, "jobs for sale," with their prospective employees as their customers. Day in and day out, crisis or not, recruiting follows the same general pattern.

Internal Sources

Employees often recommend their friends and relatives for work. Many employers, such as Friendly's, pay a bonus to employees who refer applicants who take a job and stay in it for a specified period of time. Hiring people who come with the recommendation of reliable employees increases the chances that the new employee will fit in with the existing organization. Because the person recommending the new employee has to go on record not only with the boss but also with fellow employees, he or she is likely to make recommendations cautiously. Besides, they'll have to work with the new hire, too.

A second **internal source** is the pool of former employees. Some may have left to raise children or pursue further schooling; others may have changed employers for what looked like a better opportunity. Because former employees are a known quantity—and because they know the company and its practices—they have an advantage over a new applicant. Many firms make a practice of using former employees, particularly waitresses, on a part-time basis for parties and banquets or for an extra busy day like Mother's Day or a football weekend.

Although internal sources offer the advantages of a known quantity, these sources may not supply enough people in a tight labor market. If an operation requires a major addition to its workforce—for example, after expansion—these sources are often inadequate, and so the operation must look outside.

External Sources

The two major means of contacting employees are through advertisements and employment agencies. Also, some applicants "walk in." Finally, operations that are organized by a union can call the hiring hall and ask that members be referred for employment.

Advertising.   The strengths and weaknesses of **advertising** lie in the number of applicants it generally yields. In a newspaper help-wanted ad, you direct your request to a large readership. People who read help-wanted ads are usually searching for a job or thinking of changing jobs. From this large number of readers, a good number of people are likely to apply. Thus, the employer can choose those who appear to be best qualified from among a large pool of applicants. When several positions must be filled or when a new operation is being started, the large numbers of applicants offer obvious advantages.

On the other hand, those large numbers can be a disadvantage. Dealing with a great number of applicants is time consuming. Each must be given an application and must be told how to complete it, and then each application must be processed. These clerical duties are compounded by management's time-consuming commitment to interview the applicants. Because applicants are members of the public—that is, members of the community from which the customers come—each applicant must receive courteous attention, or management risks losing their patronage or that of their relatives and acquaintances. Because of the time commitment necessary, many employers use newspaper advertising only if they have a number of positions to fill or if the labor market is especially tight.

Some firms have found job fairs and open houses an effective approach to mass recruiting. Job fairs provide a neutral atmosphere where job seekers and employers can meet informally. The setting lends itself to brief, informational exchanges that also offer the employer an opportunity to screen applicants and call back those who seem interesting. An open house functions in much the same way but gives the company an opportunity to acquaint applicants with its operation.

Employment Agencies.   Each state maintains employment offices in or accessible to all communities in the state. The agencies are operated with tax revenue; thus, they require no placement charge from either the employer or the employee. Because people must register with the employment service when they are out of work in order to qualify for unemployment compensation, this office remains constantly in touch with job seekers.

Many employers make it a point to become personally acquainted with the state employment office's manager and counselors. If the employment office staff knows an employer's applicant standards, the office can save a great deal of time by screening applicants for the employer. Then, too, these staff people are often contacted by people they have helped before who are considering a change of employer. The experienced counselor often helps employers make hiring choices, and the counselor's recommendation can also influence a capable employee's choice of employer.

Private employment agencies charge a fee, which is sometimes paid by the employer. Although some private agencies handle hourly personnel in the hospitality industry, the authors' experience suggests that the greatest users of private employment agencies in our field are supervisory and executive personnel.

Segmenting the Employee Market

Each segment—teens, working mothers, or older workers—has special needs. For teens, part-time and weekend work is important. Many mothers are interested in working while their children are in school. Older workers have quite different perceptions of the hiring process and do not respond well to newspaper advertising. Rather, they are more likely to respond to specialized employment organizations and state, city, and local agencies. They, too, prefer part-time employment and flexible scheduling.

In today's workforce, an educated and often discriminating employee decides where to work: Under the circumstances, recognizing recruiting as more like selling just makes sense.

$\mathscr{S}$ELECTION AND EMPLOYMENT

To this point, we have explored ways to determine what kinds of employees we need and ways to contact potential employees. We turn our attention now to the process of selecting and "breaking in" new workers. The first step, *employee selection,* is followed by *orientation* and then by *training.* Each step is crucial to developing productive workers.

Selection

Rich Melman's Lettuce Entertain You has one of the hospitality industry's lowest turnover rates (47 percent). Suzie Southgate-Fox, the company's vice president for human resources, sums up the secret of Lettuce's success: "We hire carefully. We look for people with things we can't teach." She uses words such as "aware, caring, sweet, giving and team player to describe the traits they want."[2]

The **selection** process involves gathering, classifying, and analyzing information available from several sources. An **application** often tells more than an applicant realizes. For instance, if an applicant cannot follow the simple directions on the form, a manager is entitled to wonder if he or she will be able to learn the job. If an applicant does not bother to fill it out completely, he or she may be unwilling to do assigned work. If the open position—say, that of a desk clerk—involves writing, an application filled out in an illegible scrawl may disqualify the applicant.

A properly completed application should account for the applicant's work over the period specified on the application. Any "blanks" or "extended vacations" should be carefully checked. (The cashier you're about to hire may have spent some time in jail for embezzlement!)

The application form usually helps screen out applicants, retaining the ones that management is interested in interviewing. The application can also help start the **interview.** During the first part of the interview, an interviewer should clarify any ambiguous information on the application. The interviewer will also want to give the applicant information about the company and the job. This interchange helps most interviewers begin the process of sizing up the applicant, determining what kind of a person he or she is and how he or she would get along with the present employees. Interviewing should also focus on the applicant's background and indicate whether he or she is, in fact, qualified (or what is sometimes a bigger problem, overqualified) for the job and whether he or she would actually like the job and be likely to continue in it. A form that suggests one company's approach to summarizing an interview and an applicant evaluation is shown in Figures 18.4 and 18.5.

Applicants should list their references and former employers on the application blanks, and these entries should be checked. Most references are selected because the applicant thinks he or she will receive a good review, and so it is important to check with the employers to verify the employment history and, where possible, to learn how the applicant performed. At the end of the interview, the applicant should be told (if possible) whether or not he or she is to be hired. If several people are being considered, an applicant should be told when a decision is to be made. Those applicants who are not hired should be notified promptly so they can continue their search for employment. Most employers maintain a file of applications from people who were not hired. Thus, a person not chosen at one time may be contacted later. (Incidentally, a file like this helps establish that management has followed fair-employment practices.)

Although the object of the selection process is to find the right people, that, in part, means avoiding the wrong people. One group most employers want to avoid are people who use drugs. Estimates of drug users range as high as 30 percent of the workforce—and 75 percent of drug users use drugs on the job, so this is not a small problem. Experience indicates that drug users have five times as many workers' compensation cases and draw three times as much in health claims, thus impacting insurance premiums unfavorably. Absenteeism among drug users is two and a half times that of nondrug users and people with this problem are 25 percent less productive than the rest of the workforce. The drug user looks pretty much like the rest of the workforce. Three-quarters are white and nearly 90 percent are over 18. Accordingly, many employers have begun to use preemployment drug testing as a means of excluding these undesirable prospects.[3]

Marriott's Fairfield Inns claims to offer "the cleanest room at any price" and so the hiring of housekeepers is important to that company. *Restaurants and Institutions* reports that

> Marriott interviewed as many as 27 people for each housekeeper it hired for hotels in Detroit. This defines the question: Are you going to hire the first person you interview 27 times or are you going to go through 27 people to get to the one you need. The second approach requires a special level of discipline; it forces management to rethink the entire hiring process.[4]

Orientation

It's an old saying—and a true one—that first impressions are lasting impressions. It is surprising, then, how often new employees are told to sign some papers, given directions to the locker room, and then promptly forgotten! Such casual procedures destroy the golden opportunity to start a new employee off on the right foot. Common sense should suggest that the new employee be enthusiastically and cheerfully introduced to the operation, to fellow workers, and to the new job.

Ritz Carlton Hotels puts heavy emphasis on **orientation** of new employees because it is the company's experience that the first three or four days are crucial in determining the outlook an employee will have in his or her work.[5]

The Operation. Your restaurant or hotel or dietary department is old ground to established employees. However, it is unmapped territory to a newcomer. For this reason, a guided tour by a member of management helps make an employee's first day comfortable. Basic information, such as where the employees enter the building, where and when smoking is permitted, and where personal belongings are kept, should be provided. Some employees report spending a very uncomfortable

TO: _____

FROM: _____

INTERVIEW REPORT

NAME OF APPLICANT: _____

DATE OF THIS
INTERVIEW: _____

ADDRESS _____ PHONE _____

CANDIDATE FOR: _____
(Job Title)

INTERVIEWER: _____

PLEASE REPORT YOUR INTERVIEW IMPRESSIONS BY CHECKING THE ONE MOST APPROPRIATE BOX IN EACH AREA.

1. APPEARANCE				
☐	☐	☐	☐	☐
Very untidy; poor taste in dress.	Somewhat careless about personal appearance.	Satisfactory personal appearance.	Good taste in dress; better than average appearance.	Unusually well groomed; very neat; excellent taste in dress.

2. FRIENDLINESS				
☐	☐	☐	☐	☐
Appears very distant and aloof.	Approachable; fairly friendly.	Warm; friendly sociable.	Very sociable and outgoing.	Extremely friendly and sociable.

3. POISE-STABILITY				
☐	☐	☐	☐	☐
Ill at ease; is "jumpy" and appears nervous.	Somewhat tense; is easily irritated.	About as poised as the average applicant.	Sure of himself; appears to like crises more than average person.	Extremely well composed; apparently thrives under pressure.

4. PERSONALITY				
☐	☐	☐	☐	☐
Unsatisfactory for this job.	Questionable for this job.	Satisfactory for this job.	Very desirable for this job.	Outstanding for this job.

5. CONVERSATIONAL ABILITY				
☐	☐	☐	☐	☐
Talks very little; Expresses himself poorly.	Tries to express himself but does fair job at best.	Average fluency and expression.	Talks well and "to the point."	Excellent expression; extremely fluent; forceful.

6. ALERTNESS				
☐	☐	☐	☐	☐
Slow to "catch on."	Rather slow; requires more than average explanation.	Grasps ideas with average ability.	Quick to understand; perceives very well.	Exceptionally keen and alert.

7. INFORMATION ABOUT GENERAL WORK FIELD				
☐	☐	☐	☐	☐
Poor knowledge of field.	Fair knowledge of field.	Is as informed as the average applicant.	Fairly well informed; knows more than average applicant.	Has excellent knowledge of the field.

8. EXPERIENCE				
☐	☐	☐	☐	☐
No relationship between applicant's background and job requirements.	Fair relationship between applicant's background and job requirements.	Average amount of meaningful background and experience.	Background very good; considerable experience.	Excellent background and experience.
9. DRIVE				
☐	☐	☐	☐	☐
Has poorly defined goals and appears to act without purpose.	Appears to set goals too low and to put forth little effort to achieve these.	Appears to have average goals; puts forth average effort to reach these.	Appears to strive hard; has high desire to achieve.	Appears to set high goals and to strive incessantly to achieve these.
10. OVERALL				
☐	☐	☐	☐	☐
Definitely unsatisfactory.	Substandard.	Average.	Definitely above average.	Outstanding.

THIS IS:
1st INTERVIEW ☐
2nd INTERVIEW ☐
3rd INTERVIEW ☐

Figure 18.4 Analysis of requirements for a food service director.

first day because they were too embarrassed to ask strangers directions to the restrooms.

Are you proud of your operation? Are there certain dining rooms that are especially nice, certain views especially attractive? Let the newcomer share in these high points, too.

Certainly, a part of this orientation should be a statement of the standards of the operation, with regard to both quality of product and service and personal conduct and hygiene. Such a statement should be made in a friendly way by a member of management, and it may also be presented to the new employee in the form of an orientation handbook. Such a "postinterview" conversation also gives management an opportunity to restate its policies on wages, fringe benefits and working conditions, days off, and so forth, as well as to make sure any questions the new employee may have are answered.

Fellow Workers. Don't assume a new worker is a gregarious person who quickly strikes up friendships. Introduce the new employee to the others in the work group and to others with whom he or she will come into contact. Thus, for instance, the host or hostess should introduce a new server not only to the other servers but to cooks, pantry workers, and dishwashers, as well.

The Job. Finally, the new employee (1) should be shown exactly where he or she will work, (2) should receive a full description of the job, and, if possible, (3) should get an opportunity to observe the work in action. Such an experience can be brief,

Applicant _____

Job considered for _____ Grade _____

Evaluated by: _____ Date _____

SUMMARY
APPLICANT EVALUATION
CONFIDENTIAL

| Rating Overall | ☐ Matches Requirements | ☐ Exceeds Requirements | ☐ Below Requirements | Recommend Hire? _____ |

Major Strong Characteristics _____

_____

Major Weak Characteristics _____

_____

FACTOR EVALUATIONS FOR THIS POSITION
See Management Employment Program for definitions.

SKILLS, KNOWLEDGE, ABILITIES

	✔ Check	The Applicant in Relation to This Position		
	Matches	Almost Matches	Exceeds	Fails To Meet
Appearance and presentation				
Education				
Mental ability				
Mobility				
Experience				
Physical condition				
Special skills and knowledge				
Relationships background				

HABITS, AMBITIONS, DRIVES

Leadership				
Perseverence				
Stability				
Self-reliance				
Energy				
Maturity				
Ability to get along with others				
Need for income				
Need for status and power				
Need to serve				

SFS 0121-0567

Figure 18.5 Applicant evaluation form.

but it gives the employee an overview of the work and lays a good foundation for training.

TRAINING

Some operations—especially independent operations that do not feel they can afford a continuing **training** program—prefer to hire trained employees. Even when experienced workers take a new job, they must still receive enough training to orient them to the operation's special procedures. Many companies prefer to hire people with no experience at all. These companies argue that it is easier to train from scratch than to hire someone who has to unlearn what the employer, at least, views as a satchel of bad habits. An employee who knows only one way to do the work is unlikely to stray from approved practice.

Training is unquestionably costly. Employees must be paid for the time when they are learning but not yet productive, and trainees also consume a good deal of the trainer's valuable time. This is why the selection process we discussed earlier is so important. There is no point in spending time, money, and effort on somebody who turns out to be unqualified for or uninterested in the job.

The alternative to training—not training—may be even more expensive. Training does cost a lot; but the cost of not training is poor service and lost customers, and a lost customer may never return. Thus, the lost revenue from poor service far exceeds the cost of training a worker properly.

Not only does management lose customers by not training, but it is liable to lose the employee, as well, at just about the time he or she becomes productive. An employee who is thrown into a job that he or she does not know is bound to feel inadequate, to say the least, and is likely to begin looking for other work.

Steven Hickey, senior vice president of T.G.I. Friday's, notes that "training is probably the most important aspect of reduced turnover because it minimizes mistakes and that minimizes a lot of reasons for turnover."

Training and retraining can be the key to maintaining quality in products and, at the same time, reducing turnover. At Ritz Carlton, for instance, training leads to certification for quality performance—and then to periodic retraining for recertification.[6]

Industry Practice Note 18.1 explores the newest medium for training, the Internet, and some of its advantages. Global Hospitality Note 18.1 reports on training problems presented by other cultures.

Management Training

Companies, particularly those planning to expand, often develop large entry-level training programs for new or promotable management employees. Companies may accelerate their management training activity in advance of a major expansion drive to have a pool of assistant managers to draw from as new unit managers are needed. Some chains cooperate with local educational institutions, using both their facilities and staff to handle a surge in training needs. Some companies, too, are

*I*ndustry Practice Note 18.1 — Training and the Internet

The Internet is having a dramatic impact on hospitality training, according to Kathy Kennedy and the American Hotel and Motel Association's Educational Institute. Ms. Kennedy indicates that many major companies are getting ready to provide training to students wherever they may be: at home, in the office, or at other work-related locations. One advantage claimed for Internet training is cost effectiveness. The saving for one hotel company in printing and distribution costs alone is estimated at $7.5 million. Higher completion rates are also expected for these courses because of the "synchronized multimedia content." The best instructors available can be used without regard to their location—or the student's. Finally, content and corporate culture can be communicated consistently to all participants.

Source: Kathy Kennedy, "The Internet: Training's New Power Tool," *Hotels,* February 1998, p. 26.

finding that management training helps reduce turnover. Such courses include content relating to both people skills and new technical skills needed on the job. Managers are often encouraged, too, to continue their training by means of company correspondence courses, local continuing education courses, as well as through professional reading.

Because managers are responsible for the productivity of all their employees, it makes good sense for companies to concentrate their efforts on preparing productive managers. For the future hospitality manager, management training programs may offer a shortcut to acquiring practical management know-how. Looking into your prospective employer's training program is just enlightened self-interest.

A note of caution about what to expect, however, may be in order. William Lombardi, vice president of Olive Garden, said of his company's management training program:

> We lose a lot of people, sometimes in the first few weeks of our management training program because they want a rule book and they want 50 policies or 500 policies. They want to know what they are supposed to do in every situation. And we say, "Do the right thing. Do the thing that's going to get you a happy guest. Do the thing that's going to keep your employee motivated." And a lot of people struggle with that![7]

On-the-Job Training

The most common method of training in the hospitality industry is pairing the new employee with an experienced worker. Unfortunately, this pairing is often done haphazardly: A new worker is assigned to whichever experienced worker may be

Global Hospitality Note 18.1

Training in a Global Hospitality Industry

Some examples from an international trainer's notebook suggest that training in different cultures requires a trained sensitivity to the culture and to local secular and even religious norms of conduct.

◆ When a trainer in Indonesia asked training class participants to critique each other's presentations orally, "One man burst into tears and ran out of the room sobbing uncontrollably" according to Carol Sage-Robin, a trainer for Westin. In Indonesian culture, she discovered, criticizing someone else's work publicly was unacceptable. Thereafter, participants used written critiques.

◆ Training schedules in Muslim countries need to build in regular prayer breaks.

◆ In China and Bahrain, unmarried men and women would be embarrassed to work together without supervision.

◆ In some countries, the accustomed pace is slower than in North America. During a training class for restaurant servers in Sumatra, Ms. Sage-Robin indicates, "I was having a hard time getting the employees to move as fast as I needed them to. I tried playing fast rock music but that did not work." Then she noticed the outdoor swimming pool. She took the class outside where it was hot as blazes and asked everyone to follow her—and to keep up with her as she walked at a fast pace around the pool. Those who didn't keep up were not allowed to return to the air-conditioned restaurant until they did keep up. In this way, she communicated to the class the speed at which food servers had to move to give satisfactory service.

◆ Another trainer had great success in the Caribbean with an exercise in which employees rewrote the company song and then sang their version. In Bahrain, however, the exercise was a repeated flop and the trainer realized what the problem was when she discovered that to the Shiite Muslims in her class, singing in this way was forbidden.

Source: Elizabeth Johnson, "Training in an International Setting," *Hotels,* May 1997, p. 32.

handy. A "market research" study of restaurant employees' views on training found that many felt their training had not been formal enough and that it lacked manager involvement. Employees prefer to train with a training specialist or a manager instead of "just another employee."[8]

Although the details of developing an actual training program extend beyond our concern here, we can note that the basic elements involve developing trainers who (1) know—and will show—the approved way of doing the task and (2) are trained in training as well as in the job. Both the National Restaurant Association and the American Hotel and Motel Association Educational Institute offer excellent "Train the Trainer" courses.

Task analyses that spell out in writing the steps necessary in each job greatly facilitate training. The learner can be given them to study, and the trainer can use them to be ready to give instruction.

During the beginning of World War II, a huge number of war plant workers had to be trained for new jobs in a hurry. At that time, management experts identified a four-step procedure as the best way to go about this rapid training:

1. *Tell me.*   Explain the task to the worker. Include why it needs to be done and why it must be done in just this way.

2. *Show me.*   Demonstrate the job, explaining as you go along. Continue demonstrating until the worker is ready to try it.

3. *Let me do it.*   Let the worker perform the task slowly, asking questions as needed. Not until trainer and trainee are comfortable with the trainee's independent performance should he or she be allowed to do it alone.

4. *Follow up.*   Once the new employee achieves enough proficiency to be able to perform independently, he or she should receive close supervision to be sure that shortcuts or bad habits don't don't grow gradually to mar performance.

Notice that an employee is not generally trained in a job but in tasks. Thus, training for a new dishwasher might involve the following:

1. Scraping—removing garbage from plates

2. Racking—putting dirty dishes in racks

3. Feeding—feeding dirty dish racks into the dishwasher

4. Catching—receiving dish racks from the "clean end" of the machine

5. Stacking—removing clean dishes from the rack and stacking them in a temporary storage place

6. Transporting—moving clean dishes back to where they are used, often in special carts or lowerators

Each of these (and the list could be extended a great deal further) is a separate task, and, for each, "one best way" will permit the greatest possible speed and the least breakage and injury. Teaching tasks separately, one at a time, may seem slow, but it is really the best way to prepare a new employee for the complete dishwasher job.

Everybody Gets Trained

A final point is worth noting here. Training never stops! When a new employee comes to work, management can take charge of that learning process or leave it to whatever influences come along. Either way, the employee will be trained. Clearly, however, common sense sides with a planned, management-controlled training effort.

ℛETAINING EMPLOYEES

Because so much effort goes into recruiting qualified people, and so much time and trouble goes into training them, there is a clear need to hold onto good people once they come on board. We can hardly solve so complex a problem here, but this may be a good place to review some key provisions that some companies are finding helpful. Several factors are crucial to **retaining employees.** As we've already indicated, taking the effort to get the right people is an important first step.

Second, the way people are treated makes a great difference. Praise in public for a good job, but reprimand in private when things don't go right. Efforts to improve two-way flow of information are important, too. In smaller units, face-to-face conversation may be enough. In larger companies, company newspapers can recognize employees' accomplishments. At some companies, employees fill out an "employee comment slip" reporting what customers say, evaluating the food they served, and commenting on what was good or bad on their shift. Managers read these carefully. Even more companies use periodic employee surveys to assess employee morale and managers' effectiveness in dealing with people.

Offering opportunities for advancement is important. Companies that promote from within find most of their management trainees from their own hourly ranks. They offer an opportunity for advancement that is an added inducement to performance.

Bonus and incentive programs are another method that companies use to retain employees. For example, in 1997, Buffets Inc. introduced a new incentive program designed to help them retain restaurant managers. If the unit manager signs a commitment letter and agrees to remain at his or her assigned restaurant for three years, he or she will receive a $20,000 bonus, which is in addition to the manager's base salary and annual bonus. The unit managers then receive an additional $30,000 bonus for every 3-year period they remain at their assigned restaurants. Buffets Inc. feels that the new program will actually save them money. The company estimates that it loses more than $20,000 in sales after a good unit manager leaves a restaurant.[9]

Many companies pride themselves on offering competitive pay and good benefits. A growing fringe benefit intended to reduce both turnover and absenteeism is a company-sponsored day-care program. Some employers subsidize day care. A spokesman for a 300-unit Hardee's franchisee, for instance, noted that his company did this because it employed a lot of single parents. One Burger King franchisee found that, since it started to subsidize its hourly employees' day-care costs, its turnover rate fell to one-third the industry average.

Companies are approaching their employees' child-care problems in several different ways. Some offer subsidies to the employees' child-care costs, while others provide flexible hours and make information on local day-care services available to employees. Still others make special arrangements with a national day-care provider. For instance, one company negotiated a 10 percent discount for its employees and then offered them another 10 percent subsidy. Finally, some employees pool their resources with neighboring businesses to establish a joint child-care effort or establish a center themselves, on site.

*S*TAFF PLANNING

Hospitality managers concentrate on **staff planning** not only because of the high proportion of income they spend on salaries and wages but also because of the great importance they attach to adequate coverage—that is, always having sufficient staff in the appropriate jobs to meet the operation's needs. Anyone who has seen a hotel coffee shop flounder when the key breakfast cook failed to show up, or a kitchen where the pot washer walked out in the middle of a meal, knows the chaos caused by the absence of just one key person. On the other hand, you may have noticed some food service operations that both open at 7:00 A.M. and bring in a full dishroom crew at 7:00 A.M. The crew then sits around with nothing to do until the dirty dishes gradually start to collect a half-hour or 45 minutes later. Proper staff planning ensures coverage, but it would avoid superfluous, wasteful coverage like this.

Because staff planning is so important, most hospitality curricula devote at least a large part of one course, and sometimes more than that, to it. In our brief discussion, we can only introduce this form of planning and some of its key tools.

Job and Work Needs

Staff planning begins by identifying each work station in the operation. Next, a **schedule** showing the number of persons needed at these stations in the course of each day, by time period, is prepared. This analysis usually follows the graphic pattern shown in Figure 18.6. This kind of chart shows at a glance where there is double coverage for a job and what, if any, rest periods are provided.

Because the volume of business may vary from one day to another, many operations prepare a separate schedule for each day of the week and sometimes separate sets for different seasons. Comparing actual coverage needs with staffing schedules results in a constant revision of these schedules. A dollar of unneeded labor cost at one station can, at a moment's notice, be moved to reinforce the coverage someplace else.

Once management prepares schedules of its **operating needs** for each day, and thereby ensures adequate coverage for each job, it can draw up a weekly schedule providing for day-off relief. The schedule for the dish, pot, and receiving crew shown in Figure 18.7 is primarily a management tool (1) to analyze seven-day schedule needs (the problem is simpler but similar in six- or five-day operations), (2) to ensure adequate coverage for each job each day, and (3) at the same time, to be sure that each employee receives the appropriate time off.

A schedule like the one shown in Figure 18.7 is also a communication tool. When posted, this schedule shows employees which person works what job for which hours each day of the week. Managers who keep their schedules in their heads and rely on simply telling people when they are to work are almost bound

Figure 18.6 Typical daily schedule.

occasionally to have two people showing up for the same job at times and no people on other days! The result is increased cost, inadequate coverage, poor service, and low morale.

Part-Time Employees

To complete our discussion of staff planning, we should offer a word about **part-time employees.** An operation often needs a position covered for only part of a shift, and it sometimes needs extra people on a job only on busy days. To hire a full-time person would obviously be an expensive solution; instead, the hospitality industry is using more part-time employees to avoid overstaffing.

Some added costs and problems result from relying on part-time people. First, an operation that uses part-time help extensively carries more people on its payroll. The same (and often a lesser) number of labor days can be worked, but more people will fill the jobs. This means more payroll records and more recruiting, interviewing, hiring, and training. Moreover, a part-time employee usually works part time

	Mon.	Tues.	Wed.	Thurs.	Fri.	Sat.	Sun.
Receiver- 6–2:30 John						off / N.R.	off / N.R.
Ass't. Receiver- 8–4:30 Pete						off / N.R.	off / N.R.
Head Potwasher- 8–4:30 Al	off / Hal	off / Hal					
P.M. Potwasher- 4:30–1:00 Monty						off / N.R.	off / N.R.
Part-time Potwasher- 5–9:00 Joe					off / Hal		
A.M. Dishwasher 7:30–4:00 Hubert	off / Mac	off / Mac					
Part-time Dishwasher 11:30–2:30 Murray						off / N.R.	off / N.R.
P.M. Dishwasher- 4:00–12:30 Lou			off / Mac	off / Mac			
P.M. Dishwaser #2 5:30–2:00 Jake					off / Mac	off / Mac	
Dish-(split) Ron 11:30–3:30 & 5:30–9:30			off / Hal	off / Hal			
Part-time Dish-P.M. 6:30–9:00 Art						off / N.R.	off / N.R.
Dish. Relief- Mac	A.M. Dish 8–4:30	A.M. Dish 8–4:30	P.M. Dish 4–12:30	P.M. Dish 4–12:30	P.M. Dish #2 5:30–2:00	off / N.R.	off / N.R.
Pot.-Dish. Relief- Hal	Head Pot. 8–4:30	Head Pot. 8–4:30	Dish Split 11:30–3:30 & 5:30–9:30	Dish Split 11:30–3:30 & 5:30–9:30	Part-time Pot 4:30–1:00	off / N.R.	off / N.R.
Pot.-Relief/ Part-time Noah						P.M. Pot. 4:30–1:00	P.M. Pot. 4:30–1:00
Dish. Relief Part-time Norm					P.M. Dish. 4:00–12:30		

Figure 18.7 Weekly posted schedule.

because he or she has a main commitment elsewhere. (Part-timers are usually housewives, students, or "moonlighters" taking a part-time job in addition to their main employment.) Scheduling people with responsibilities outside your establishment creates special problems: to name only a few, a spouse's vacation; exams, semester breaks, or graduation; and fatigue.

One significant cost advantage of part-timers is that they receive fewer fringe benefits and, in many companies, virtually none. This advantage, however, is under political attack and may well disappear as future wage-and-hour legislation is enacted at the state or national level.

Although part-time employees present some problems, greater flexibility and lower payroll costs often make them economically attractive. You can expect that the work of hospitality managers in future years will be even more involved with supervising and motivating part-time employees than it is today, as the industry's labor shortage continues.

Computerized Scheduling

Computer programs to schedule employees are increasingly common. However, people can schedule at least as well as computers can, and so scheduling programs don't generally seem to reduce payroll hours. Rather, their great advantage is their speed. By using a computer, managers can complete their scheduling work in roughly one-third the time that doing it by hand takes. Computerized scheduling is especially helpful when there is a change in managers in a unit. Much of the experience of the manager who has been there a while is programmed into the computer: work stations, staffing reqirements, employee availability and work preferences, and peak-and-valley days and time periods. When the new manager comes in, he or she doesn't have to learn who everyone is and what their job is. Thus, the computer offers a real convenience to managers and is a time-saver for them.

This chapter, more than the other management function chapters, has focused on the "nuts and bolts" of hospitality management. Staffing in hospitality management is obviously a nuts-and-bolts function, but one that is vital to the success of an operation.

Our nuts-and-bolts approach in this chapter illustrates another important fact about hospitality management: the importance of attention to detail. It is important for management to develop sources of good employees, to look at the details found on an application, to check references carefully, to pay special attention to a new employee's introduction to work, to base that employee's training on individual task analysis, and to undertake painstaking staff planning. As one of the earliest hospitality educators, Bernard R. Proulx, the first head of the School of Hotel, Restaurant and Institutional Management at Michigan State University, used to tell his students, "The secret to success in the service industry is attention to detail."

$\mathcal{S}$UMMARY

In a service-oriented field such as the hospitality industry, human resource management is especially important. Also, because the hospitality industry usually spends so much of its income on wages, choosing the right employees is essential.

First, the right person must be chosen for the job, in terms of both physical and mental abilities. Second, those kinds of persons must be recruited for the job, using internal and external sources to find them. When a pool of applicants has been gathered, some must be selected, by means of the application, an interview, and a reference check. Then comes the employee's induction, or orientation to the job and to fellow employees. Training is necessary and generally involves on-the-job training.

Retaining people and planning staffing needs are also important. In regard to the latter, we talked about using part-time employees and computerized scheduling.

KEY WORDS AND CONCEPTS

Personal service	Application
Wage cost	Interview
Job and person specifications	Orientation
Job description	Training
Recruiting	Retaining employees
Internal sources	Staff planning
External sources	Scheduling
Advertising	Job and work needs
Employment agencies	Operating needs
Selection	Part-time employees

REVIEW QUESTIONS

1. What has given rise to the current labor shortage?

2. What kinds of qualifications should be considered when recruiting an employee for the dishroom? As a waiter or waitress? As a supervisor?

3. Describe some of the internal and external sources that employers use to find employees.

4. What does orientation to a job involve, and why is it important?

5. Why do some companies prefer to hire people with no experience?

6. Explain why management training is especially important before opening a new operation.

7. What are the advantages of hiring part-time employees? The disadvantages?

INTERNET EXERCISES

1. **Site Name:** *Hotel, Restaurant and Tourism URL Directory*
   URL: http://www.wku.edu/hrtm/hotlrest.htm
   Background Information: This directory lists the URLs for numerous hotel and restaurant chains.

EXERCISES:

Select a hotel and a restaurant from the list and surf their web sites. Determine if they offer employment opportunity information on their web pages.

a. What job opportunities are listed on their web pages?

b. What training do they offer?

c. Do they list job requirements?

d. Do you consider this an effective method for recruiting employees? Why or why not?

e. What is the difference between the recruiting efforts of the hotel versus the recruiting efforts of the restaurant?

2. **Site Name:** *News, Newspapers and Magazines on the Net*
   URL: http://www.wku.edu/~hrtm/news.htm
   Background Information: This site is a directory for major newspapers, magazines, and news agencies on line. There is also a link for Newspapers Online, which lists the major newspapers in each state as well as links to most of the smaller newspapers.

EXERCISES:

Choose a newspaper, perhaps a newspaper from your hometown or state. Search the classified advertisements for hotel and/or restaurant management jobs.

a. Did you find the advertisements informative?

b. What did you like and dislike about the job ads?

c. Print the best and worst advertisements you found for class discussion.

c. Based on what you have seen, what information would you have included in a classified advertisement to attract potential candidates for management positions?

 ◆ *N*OTES

1. *Restaurants USA,* June–July 1992, p. 36.

2. Margaret Sheriden, "Head Count," *Restaurants and Institutions,* January 1, 1998, p. 62.

3. *Restaurants and Institutions,* March 15, 1993, p. 121.

4. *Restaurants and Institutions,* May 15, 1993, p. 120.

5. Remarks during a panel discussion at the Council on Hotel, Restaurant, and Institutional Education Annual Conference, Chicago, August 1993.

6. Panel discussion, 1993 Annual Conference on Hotel, Restaurant, and Institutional Education, Chicago.

7. *Restaurants and Institutions,* April 1, 1993, p. 94.

8. Joan Viewager, "Research Summary: Exploring the Effectiveness of Hourly Employee Training," *Proceedings of the 21st Annual Chain Operators Exchange* (Chicago: International Foodservice Manufacturers Association, 1994).

9. Amy Zuber, "Buffets Inc. Aims to Keep Managers with $20K Incentive Program," *Nation's Restaurant News,* Vol. 31, N. 43, October 27, 1997.

Chapter 19

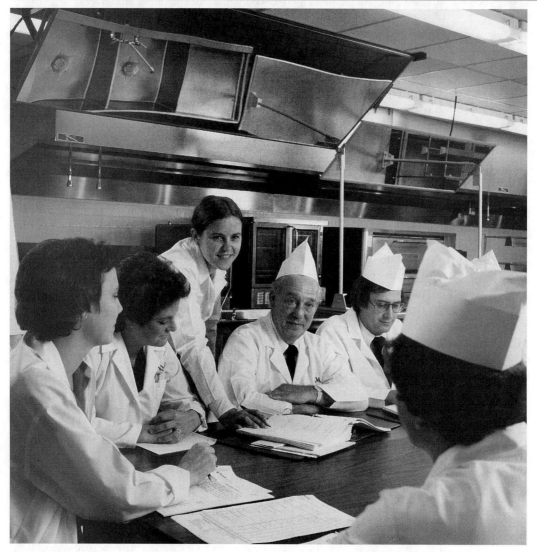

Courtesy of Marriott International

Control in
Hospitality Management

The Purpose of This Chapter

If you've ever found yourself working on too many projects at once and suddenly felt the need to sit down and "figure out just what I'm getting done," you will understand how important it is to control projects before they begin to control you. A hospitality system has so many varied activities that the control function is absolutely essential to its efficiency and success. In this chapter, therefore, we will explore the ways in which organizations measure their results against goals—how they appraise exactly what they are getting done.

Control is too often thought of as exclusively "something for the accountants to worry about." However, nothing could be further from the truth! The information from control systems really exists, first and foremost, to guide management action. In fact, in hospitality operations, control information often does not even enter the accounting stream; it may not even be numerical. Although whole courses—indeed, entire curricula, such as accounting—are devoted to a detailed study of control, our purpose here is more basic: We want you to see control as the heart of hospitality management.

This Chapter Should Help You

1. Explain the relationship of control to the other functions of hospitality management

2. See control (a) as future oriented and (b) as a basis for management action

3. Describe the characteristics of an effective control system

4. Recognize the principal financial accounting statements and explain their managerial purpose

5. Identify and describe the principal tools of managerial accounting used by the hospitality industry

6. Explain the concept known as decision accounting

Because specialized courses are taught in the area of control, hospitality students sometimes get the impression that control is separate, something located "over there" in the accounting office. However, we will see in this chapter, **control** is an integral part of every manager's and every supervisor's work:

> Control is the work that managers and supervisors do to measure performance against standards, detect and analyze variances from target performance, and initiate corrective action.

Control affects and is affected by all the other functions. For instance, the standards that result from planning are meaningless without some way of measuring performance, just as a set of numbers measuring performance are meaningless without some idea of the results desired (i.e., some standard). Similarly, a major function of organizing is to fix responsibility for results. Once again, if we have a measure that can tell us something is wrong but no means of saying who takes responsibility for corrective action, the purpose of control will by stymied.

In Chapter 18, we saw that proper staffing is necessary to achieve the productivity that allows us to meet payroll cost targets and that staff planning is the basis for that control. As you read Chapter 20, on the directing and leading function, you will want to remember that control information is an important basis for management action. If control systems yield nothing but numbers, they will be useless. Perhaps an illustration from the personal experience of one of the authors can demonstrate this point best:

> I once was hired to relieve a man—let's call him Mr. Brower—who was the food and beverage manager in a hotel whose food operation was losing money badly. Mr. Brower had received his early training in a well-established hotel company with several operations.
>
> When I was introduced to Mr. Brower, he took me into his office and pulled out a set of ledger books. As he opened the first, he said, "We've got a terrific control system. All our food is issued from the storeroom only on requisitions, and the storeroom man sends the requisition slips up to me and I post them. As you can see, we have a daily food cost in 18 categories!"
>
> As I talked further with Mr. Brower, I learned that most of his early experience had been as a "food controller"—someone responsible for maintaining the food cost accounting system for the hotel where he worked. What he had done was to come as close to duplicating the elaborate control system at the hotel where he used to work, and then he labored long and hard to maintain the system.

Unfortunately, he had produced a system that told him in great detail that his operation was going broke. He didn't know what to do about it, so he sat in his office and kept his records straight! The process of untangling the mess involved getting rid of the storeroom man who really wasn't needed in an operation of that size (and who had been regularly stealing the food), establishing food and payroll cost standards, and then correcting performance on specific work stations and food products.

*C*ONTROL AND THE "CYBERNETIC LOOP"

The word *cybernetic* is derived from the ancient Greek word for the steersman on a ship. In early times, the steersman would aim the ship toward some point on the horizon. If the ship's course varied to the left, he'd move the tiller to steer a bit to the right and vice versa.

In modern management, control systems fill a similar function. As an operation progresses, various information about the progress is collected and presented to management in a usable form. If the report indicates that the food cost is on target, management can turn its attention elsewhere. If the food cost is off, however, it's up to the manager to "move the tiller" and to take corrective action on the basis of the information, just as the steersman reacted when he saw the bow of the ship moving off the point to which he was steering. The term *loop* is used in conjunction with *cybernetic* because the process is continuous. Action constantly takes place, and information about that action must constantly pass through the loop to indicate either that the process is on course or that corrective action is required. This constant vigilance results in more information being sent through the loop, and so on.

A simple example of the **cybernetic loop** in action—a cashier's report—is shown in Figure 19.1. A simple diagram of the cybernetic loop appears in Figure 19.2.

Mary, a cashier, starts her shift with a $100 bank. Throughout her eight-hour shift she accepts cash from customers who are paying for their meals or making change. As necessary, Mary rings up each sale on a cash register. At the end of her shift, she prepares a report that shows

1. The amount of sales rung up on the register

2. The amount of money she is depositing (which is always the amount of money in her cash drawer, less her $100 bank)

Cashier's Report

Shift: A.M.
Cashier: Mary

Sales	319.72
Cash Deposit	319.87
Over (Short)	.15

Figure 19.1 Cashier's report.

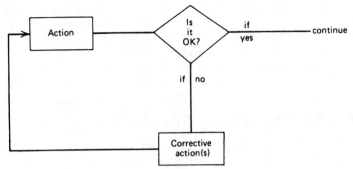

Figure 19.2 The cybernetic loop.

3. The difference between the sales she has collected and her deposit, or the amount she is over or short

Most cashiers make small errors, and so they may be over or short a few cents. However, if the error is greater than 50 cents (or some other prescribed amount), management approval of the report may be required.

Notice what this procedure accomplishes. If Mary's report indicates she's "on course," no management action will be needed. If she makes an error over the prescribed amount, management must be informed. Depending on the circumstances, management can accept the error or initiate corrective action. The corrective action is not intended so much to correct an error that has already occurred as it is to find the cause of the error and take steps to avoid it in the future. Once management locates the error that Mary has been making, it can help her avoid it. Thus, control is future oriented and forward looking. Control, in effect, records and studies what has happened, not principally to place the blame on someone, but to discover what went wrong so the error can be avoided in the future. We study the past not for itself but for what it can teach us for the future.

This example also provides a good illustration of a term we've already used a good deal: **information system.** An information system collects, transcribes, and summarizes information about transactions or other events and provides management with a summary for analysis and action. Figure 19.2 shows a simple version of the information system as a cybernetic loop. An action is followed by some test against standards. If the performance is acceptable, the process will continue; if it is not, some corrective action or actions will be taken, and then we will try again.

Information systems are concerned with more than just financial data. For instance, some information systems involve personnel and marketing. Many states have developed nutritional audits for the custodial and health care institutions they operate. These nutritional audits measure not so much the cost of food as the nutritional adequacy of the diets being served.

The key to designing an information system is to determine just what information is needed or, to use the language of the systems analyst, just what *information output* is required of the system. An information system, then, is any means of collecting information (cash register tapes, meat yields, guest counts) and translating the raw information into an intelligible, usable summary form. Examples shown in Figure 19.3 are a cashier's report, a meat yield report, and a summary of guest arrivals per 10-minute time segment.

The final element is that the report must go to the right management person to be useful. Figure 19.3 illustrates this simplified concept of a **control system** using the three examples cited.

Lest the term *information system* discourage a student with its apparent complexity, let us look at some examples of control through management action based on exceedingly simple information systems.

Control Through Management Action

Many food service operators have found that the recipe itself can be one key to controlling food quality and reducing waste. At some food service operations, the food production director and other members of the management taste samples of all the food that has been prepared to be sure that it has been prepared correctly. Because these managers are trained to taste (and have tasted the same recipe many times before), what better way to be sure that quality standards have been met?

Recipes also specify portion sizes, but it takes skill to portion correctly when carving a roast, for example, and errors are common. To aid a carver, many operations use the over-and-under portion scale. This scale is actually a simple information system that permits a carver to correct over- or underportioning and to know when his or her carving hand has grown a little heavy or a little light. If the person portioning the meat keeps a simple record of how many portions are served from a cut of meat, at the end of the meal a supervisor can prepare a yield report and compare the results (portions served) with the standard that has been established for that product.

Indeed, some food production managers actually study the garbage can! By periodically raking through the garbage, they can see what kind of food and how much of it is being left on plates. If one item consistently becomes waste, it can indicate either poor quality or overportioning. Further study of the information serves as the basis for management action. In short, regular garbage inspection can be part of an information system!

In large- and medium-sized hotels, housekeeping supervisors below the executive housekeeper level are often called inspectors. Their supervisory duties include not only assigning work and issuing supplies but also physically inspecting each room as it is finished to be sure it has been made up to the hotel's standards and reporting the results to the housekeeper and front desk.

Many hospitals (and other hospitality institutions, as well) collect patient comments and tally them. If the dietary department complaint rate suddenly goes up, the dietitian knows there is a problem and can begin the necessary study to correct it. These complaints can become the focus, again, of an information system.

Data	Source	Report (Sample Format)	User (Person who Receives Report)
1 *Amount of Sales*	*Cash Register Tape*	*Cashier's Report*	*Restaurant Manager Accounting Department*

Date 7/1/97	Shift AM
Sales	252.00
Cash deposit	251.70
Over (short)	(.30)
Cashier	SW

Data	Source	Report	User
2 *Pounds of Meat and Price*	*Invoice*		*Food Production Manager Shift Supervisor*

Yield report

Product	Inside rd
Purveyor	Eastern
Raw weight	18
Cost	1.80/32.40
Cooked weight	16.5
Number of servings	39
Cost/serving	.83

Data	Source	Report	User
3 *Guest Count*	*Cash Register Tape (number of sales)*		*Store Manager Shift Supervisor*

Time/Sales Volume Report

Day of Week	Monday	Shift AM

Reading#	10:00 to 11:00
	Guest count
1	7
2	12
3	18
4	23
5	32
6	25

	11:00 to 12:00
1	27
2	32
3	35
4	33
5	31
6	30

Figure 19.3 Illustrations of simple information systems.

Characteristics of Control Systems

We can conclude our discussion of control systems by identifying four of their common characteristics:

1. Control systems are *continuous*. Data are collected and stored on a continuing basis so that if something goes wrong, the data can be carefully analyzed to direct management's corrective action.

2. Reports must be *timely*. Data must be collected and reported so that management can act to correct a problem before there is too great a loss. Thus, many food service operators compute their food costs weekly or every 10 days, rather than monthly, in order to catch and correct promptly any unfavorable food cost patterns that develop.

3. Control is aimed at some *key point*, and no action is called for unless a problem is detected. This approach is sometimes called *management by exception*. Thus, a food cost is computed periodically because it is a key cost in a food service operation. If the food cost is out of line, further study and action will be initiated. If no problem is detected in the routine report, no action will be taken.

4. Control is *action oriented*. At the risk of belaboring this point, we repeat that nothing really is controlled until somebody does something about the problem. Thus, control systems and information systems are similar, but a control system not only includes the information but also provides for corrective action, if it is required.

$\mathcal{T}$OOLS FOR CONTROL

Managers use two somewhat different kinds of tools to achieve control: *financial accounting* and *managerial accounting*. Although each form of accounting has significant similarities, each is designed to meet particular needs.

Financial Accounting

Students will recognize financial accounting as the subject routinely taught in their first college accounting course. **Financial accounting** is based on a series of conventions adopted by the accounting profession to ensure a common basis of reporting the results of business operations. Financial accounting is principally designed for outsiders: for bankers who may be asked to lend money or for stockholders or potential investors who want to evaluate the firm's performance in comparison with other investments.

The principal financial reports used in financial accounting are the **balance sheet** and the **statement of income and expense.** The balance sheet is simply a statement of the firm's value and ownership. On one side, it lists the firm's assets, and, on the other, the claims against those assets by those to whom the firm owes money and by the owners. Table 19.1 provides an example of a hospitality industry

Table 19.1   Travel-On Motel Balance Sheet as of December 31, 200x

Assets		
Current assets		
Cash	$ 10,000	
Accounts receivable	15,000	
Inventories	12,000	
		$ 37,000
Fixed assets		
Building	$1,000,000	
Less depreciation	250,000	
		750,000
Furniture and fixtures	$ 110,000	
Less depreciation	55,000	
		55,000
TOTAL ASSETS		$842,000
Liabilities and Capital		
Current liabilities		
Accounts payable	$ 15,000	
Accrued expenses	7,000	
Mortgage payable (within one year)	10,000	
		$ 32,000
Long-term liabilities		
Mortgage		600,000
Capital		
Common stock	$ 100,000	
Retained earnings	110,000	
		210,000
TOTAL LIABILITIES AND CAPITAL		$842,000

balance sheet. The balance sheet offers a great deal of information to financial analysts, but its use in day-to-day operations is limited.

The statement of income and expenses, on the other hand, is used by operations people both to evaluate performance on a month-to-month basis and, as we shall see, to prepare budgets for future periods.

Each segment of the hospitality industry has a uniform system of accounts that tells accountants how to classify the various kinds of income and expenses. The uniform systems of accounts serve two purposes. First, they present income and cost information so that results in one operation can be compared to those in other operations or with industry averages. Second, uniform systems of accounts collect information in a way that pinpoints performance against responsibility. In a restaurant, the chef or food production manager is responsible for the food cost; the people responsible for certain groups of workers (cooks, waitstaff, dishwashers) are responsible for their component of payroll cost; and the restaurant manager is responsible for the restaurant's overall operating performance. The accounting profession has developed the term **responsibility accounting** to describe this means of classifying and reporting financial information. This form of accounting is not, however, new to the hospitality industry. The hotel industry (with its own uniform system of accounts) has long pioneered responsibility accounting.

Income and expenses are divided among departments—in hotels, these departments include rooms, food and beverage, and telephone—and a departmental net income is derived by subtracting the departments' expenses from the revenue it generates. Each departmental net income represents an accurate reflection of the department head's performance. The general manager's performance is assessed by total income before fixed charges, which is the total of all departments' net operating incomes less certain unallocated expense items.

Just as the American Hotel and Motel Association periodically updates and publishes a *Uniform System of Accounts for Hotels,* the National Restaurant Association publishes a *Uniform System of Accounts for Restaurants.* The American Hospital Association supplies similar guidance in health care, and the Food and Nutrition Service publishes guidelines for school lunch accounting.

One major purpose served by following the appropriate industry accounting system is that it permits your operation to compare its results with industry averages. For the hotel–motel industry, the accounting firm of Pannel, Kerr, Forster, and Company publishes an extensive study of hotel industry performance based on the uniform system of accounts. Smith Travel Research publishes an annual summary of hotel operating statistics, *The Host Report,* which reviews income, cost, and profit performance of hotels according to the categories introduced in Chapter 10. The National Restaurant Association publishes a similar statistical study for restaurants called *Restaurants Operations Report.* The American Hospital Association supplies similar data in health care.

Managerial Accounting

Financial accounting is prepared according to accounting conventions that enable outsiders to evaluate performance. Financial accounting statements, particularly the statement of income and expenses, *are* useful to managers as well as to outsiders, we should note, but they must always follow the conventional form prescribed by the accounting profession. **Managerial accounting,** on the other hand, is prepared by and for insiders, that is, management. For that reason, it can take any form that is helpful to managers. The principal concerns of managerial accounting in the hospitality industry are food and beverage cost control and payroll control. Some operators pay fairly close attention to such miscellaneous direct operating costs as cleaning and guest supplies as well as utilities, but much less time and effort are generally spent on these. The information these control systems yield, in turn, is used in the budgeting process.

Food and Beverage Cost Control.   **Food and beverage cost control** can be divided, in turn, into two general areas: *precost* and *postcost* control. **Precosting** refers to the process of determining in advance the cost of a portion of food or drink (or of a whole meal). The best way to do this is to work from standard recipes and determine the cost of the recipe ingredients. Then, if standard portions are used, the recipe cost can be divided by the yield to determine the cost per portion. The cost developed in this process becomes an important selling price determinant. Once (1) the cost, (2) the selling price, and (3) the numbers of each item sold are known, an operator can predict food or beverage cost with reasonable accuracy—if nothing goes wrong!

Postcost control, sometimes called *historical control,* focuses on what has happened so that if something does go wrong, management will know about it at the earliest possible moment and will have the information necessary to find out specifically what did go wrong. The purpose of postcontrol, then, is not so much to remedy errors that have already taken place but, as we noted earlier, to provide a basis for steps to prevent the same mistake from being repeated.

Payroll Control.   Our discussion in Chapter 18 showed that the principal technique for controlling payroll costs is staff planning that includes a tight, analytical scheduling process to ensure adequate coverage for each station and to avoid wasted coverage. Scheduling may be likened to precost control. For each payroll period, the payroll cost (i.e., the ratio of payroll cost to sales) is computed and compared with the target that management has established for that cost. When costs are out of line, management can institute special reporting systems for overtime hours (hours in excess of 40, for which time and a half must generally be paid) and for "extra" hours (hours in excess of those budgeted for the period).

Specialized Controls.   Some operations develop special reporting procedures to control such other direct operating costs as cleaning supplies. These procedures generally take the form of issuing systems that permit management to monitor closely the use of supplies such as soap, cleanser, and paper towels.

Some restaurants control china, glass, and silver breakage costs by taking a periodic inventory to determine the number of pieces broken or lost. This figure is then related to sales in a ratio called "the number of guests per broken piece." This kind of information can be tabulated simply by noting breakage as it happens. If management notes who broke each piece (usually by sorting the broken pieces into bins for each worker group), it then becomes possible to categorize daily breakage by worker group. Management can then focus attention on those who are most responsible for the breakage.

Budgeting.   The process of operating the controls described here yields a great deal of information about the business patterns that can be expected in the future. A **budget** is basically a plan of action spelled out in dollars, and it is usually based on information provided by the management accounting systems. Sales for some future period are estimated; then, applying the percentage for each expected cost (food cost, payroll cost, supplies cost, and the like), management can prepare an expense budget. Because cost patterns change, expense budgets may be based in part on past experience and in part on expected future cost trends.

The procedure for preparing budgets in many hospitality operations, especially at the unit level, need not be especially complicated: On a copy of a current or recent statement of income and expenses, write the estimate for the budget period alongside the figures for the past period. Base the new figures on experience and expected future trends (as shown in Table 19.2). These estimates may then be formalized after discussion with key department heads.

In multiunit companies, budgets are sometimes drawn up at the company's headquarters using computerized records of past performance and are then "rolled down" to the district and unit levels. At that point, the process reverses itself, with the units forwarding the revised unit budgets to the district level. Once approved at that level, the district totals its unit budgets and sends them to the control office as the district budget. As you can imagine, this process often involves a good deal of negotiation among the different levels of a multiunit firm.

Whereas business firms base their budgets on sales, public-sector food service operators (such as school lunch programs) must use appropriations as a basis for starting the budget process. Thus, for school lunch, the local school board may supply some operating funds; the state is another source of funding; and the federal government supplies a certain amount for each lunch served, and an additional amount for each free and reduced-price lunch. Finally, most students pay a certain amount for each meal. The income portion of the budget is basically a reflection of the number of meals served (student payments and the federal subsidy) and, thus, is similar to the sales item in a commercial operation. In some cases, additional sources of revenue may also be identified.

In health care, sales (except in the pay cafeteria) are not the determining figure for budgeting. That figure is, rather, some budgeted amount based on (1) the number of patient days expected and (2) the budgeted cost per patient day for food service. Although sales, as such, are not the key, the starting point in the budget is the number of physical units (i.e., meals) that management expects will be consumed—a concept fundamentally quite similar to the sales estimate of a commercial operation.

Expense items in nonprofit budgets are prepared in much the same way as in the commercial sector—that is, they are based on past experience and adjusted for expected change. In some cases, the expenses themselves are different. For instance, public institutions may receive commodities donated by the federal government. These donations change the cost of some items, but the budgeting procedure remains basically the same.

A budget should be the basis for management's cybernetic action: Actual results are compared with budgeted results, variances from budget target are analyzed to determine causes, and corrective action is initiated.

Table 19.2 Mid-Town Restaurant Statement of Income and Expenses, Year Ending December 31, 200x

	$	$	
Sales			
Food	757,251	77.0	848,000
Beverage	226,507	23.0	252,700
Total	983,758	100.0	1,100,700
Cost of Sales			
Food	326,375	43.1	356,100
Beverage	61,116	27.0	66,000
Total	387,491	39.4	422,100
Gross Profit	596,267	60.6	678,600
Other Income	14,756	1.5	66,000
Total Income	611,023	62.1	744,600
Controllable Expenses			
Payroll	252,286	25.6	290,600
Employee Benefits	46,237	4.7	53,900
Direct Operating Expenses	54,107	5.5	60,500
Music and Entertainment	5,902	.6	6,600
Advertising and Promotion	15,740	1.6	17,600
Utilities	20,659	2.1	23,100
Administrative and General	59,025	6.0	66,000
Repairs and Maintenance	16,724	1.7	18,700
Total	470,680	47.8	539,000
Income before Occupation Costs	140,343	14.3	207,600
Occupation Costs			
Rent, Property Taxes, and Insurance	45,253	4.6	48,000
Interest	5,998	.6	5,000
Depreciation	19,651	2.0	19,600
Total	70,902	7.2	72,600
Net Income before Other Deductions	69,441	7.1	135,000
Other Deductions	4,918	.5	5,000
Net Income before Taxes	64,523	6.6	130,000

Decision Accounting

Both financial accounting and management accounting are basically cyclical and repetitive. Budgets, for instance, can be prepared monthly, quarterly, and annually. As a month elapses, statements of results are reflected on accounting statements and compared with the budget. Then the whole cycle begins again next month.

Financial accounting statements, moreover, embody the conventions accepted by the accounting profession. For instance, when an asset is acquired, a *useful life* for that kind of an asset is assumed, and the cost of the item is *written off* by means of an accounting entry reflecting its depreciation. Thus, a motor hotel valued at $1 million with a 20-year useful life will charge $50,000 a year to depreciation on its accounting statements. At the end of five years, following accounting conventions, the motor hotel will be valued at $750,000. Quite clearly, these conventions are convenient and permit standard treatment (or one of several standard treatments) to be applied in a way that helps make the resulting accounting statement understandable to insiders and outsiders alike. However, although accounting conventions are necessary, they often distort what is really happening. For instance, if the motel just described has been bypassed by an expressway, its value may have dropped far more than the depreciation entry indicates; by contrast, if a new office park has been built across the street, the motel's value may have doubled instead of depreciating.

Decision accounting, which is often related to *strategic planning,* differs from financial and management accounting in that it is not cyclical. The information for a decision is assembled in numerical form on a one-time basis.

Also, the conventions of accounting play no part in decision accounting. The assumptions made are those deemed appropriate to the analysis of the particular decision at hand. For instance, decision accounting tends to focus on direct variable costs such as food cost and payroll. It tends to ignore bookkeeping entries such as depreciation. Some examples of decision accounting tools—the payback period, rate of return, and break-even point computation—were presented in Chapter 16.

$\mathcal{S}$UMMARY

Control is the means by which management measures performance, detects and analyzes variances, and initiates corrective action. In this context, we defined a cybernetic loop and gave an example of it, a cashier's report.

Most control is carried out through an information system of some sort, and we also illustrated this with some examples: food portion sizes, inspections of cleaned rooms, and patients' comments on hospital service.

We then enumerated the characteristics of control systems and examined the principal tools to achieve control: financing accounting and managerial accounting. In regard to managerial accounting, we discussed food and beverage cost control, payroll control, specialized controls, and budgeting. Finally, we considered decision accounting.

◆ $\mathcal{K}$EY WORDS AND CONCEPTS

Control	Control system
Cybernetic loop	Financial accounting
Information system	Balance sheet

Statement of income and expense	Postcost control
Responsibility accounting	Payroll control
Managerial accounting	Specialized controls
Food and beverage cost control	Budget
Precosting	Decision accounting

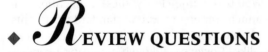

◆ REVIEW QUESTIONS

1. What is a cybernetic loop? How is it used in connection with cash control?

2. Give some examples of information systems in the hospitality industry.

3. What are the four characteristics of a control system?

4. How is managerial accounting used in food and beverage costs?

5. Describe decision accounting.

◆ INTERNET EXERCISES

1. **Site Name:** *The Hilton Hotels Corporation*
   URL: http://www.hilton.com/
   Background Information: The Hilton Hotels Corporation is one of the world's leading lodging and casino gaming companies. It is the world's largest gaming company with 15 hotel and riverboat casinos. The Hilton provides gaming entertainment in three of the world's largest gaming centers—Las Vegas, Atlantic City, and Australia.

   EXERCISES:

   Surf the Hilton web site and find the page with the annual and quarterly reports. Compare the current quarter's performance with that of the same quarter the previous year. For example, compare 2nd quarter 2000 with 2nd quarter 1999.

   a. Identify and describe the financial indicators used in these reports.

   b. Did the Hilton perform better or worse? What are its reasons for doing better or worse?

   c. What are its financial goals for the future?

2. **Site Name:** *Cooker Bar and Grill*
   URL: http://www.cookers.com/index.html
   Background Information: The Cooker Restaurant Corporation owns and operates 52 full-service Cookers restaurants under the Cooker concept in 10 states. Restaurants average approximately 7900 square feet and 255 seats, and are de-

signed to provide traditional and comfortable dining experiences rather than a theme atmosphere or menu.

EXERCISES:

Surf Cookers' web site and find the page with financial information. Compare the current quarter/year's performance with that of the same quarter/year the previous year. For example, compare 1999's performance with 2000's performance.

a. Identify and describe the financial indicators used in these reports.

b. Did Cookers perform better or worse? What are its reasons for doing better or worse?

c. What are its financial goals for the future?

Chapter 20

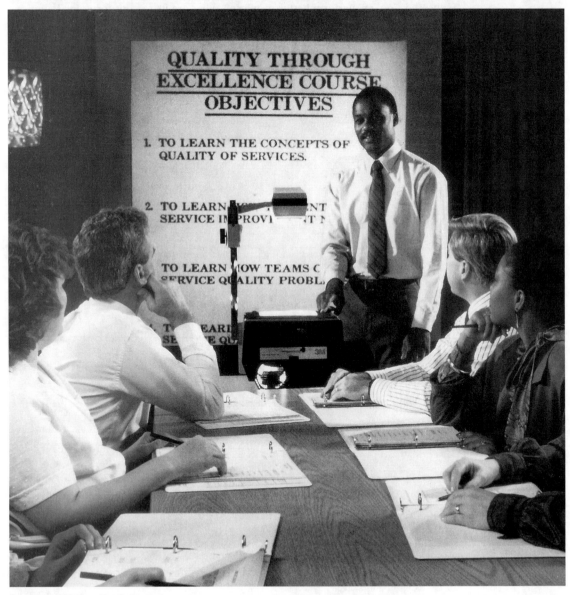

QUALITY THROUGH
EXCELLENCE COURSE
OBJECTIVES

1. TO LEARN THE CONCEPTS OF
QUALITY OF SERVICES.

2. TO LEARN   NT
SERVICE IMPROV   T

TO LEARN OW TEAMS
SERVICE QU ALITY PROBL

Courtesy of Hershey Foods Corp.

Leadership and Directing in Hospitality Management

The Purpose of This Chapter

The most visible work the manager does is to function as the leader of the work group: giving orders and instructions to employees, checking employee performance, and commending or correcting that performance. This chapter describes this work first as a function of worker needs and then as a function of the manager and his or her abilities. We intend this chapter to help you develop a style of leadership that suits you personally.

This Chapter Should Help You

1. Explain the relationship of leadership and directing to the other work that managers do

2. Discuss the various incentives that motivate people to accept direction

3. Associate your thinking about leadership and directing to a coherent body of action-oriented theory so that you can continue the process of learning this crucial subject *after* you finish this course

4. List the factors discussed in this chapter that inhibit and support communication in the workplace

5. Describe the factors that underlie management authority and the kinds of behaviors managers engage in when directing

6. Develop your management style in a way that is flexible enough to meet the variety of situations you will encounter as a manager

THE "CONCLUSIONS" OF SOCIAL SCIENCE RESEARCH

Management scholars and other social scientists have devoted a great deal of attention to the study of leadership. This attention is appropriate because leadership is clearly an important activity in what Peter Drucker calls "a society of institutions." Unfortunately, these scholars have raised more questions than they have been able to answer to everyone's satisfaction. Indeed, one sometimes gets the impression that those in the knowledge industry who concern themselves with management earn a living by disproving one another's theories.

In fact, social science research models itself on the kinds of definitive, quantitative proofs found in the physical sciences, but it may never reach definitive conclusions about such subjective concepts as leadership. Fortunately, our purpose is less ambitious than that of scholars. To be sure, we want a theory that will guide practice, but we can accept some ambiguity in both our analysis of this subject and the conclusions we draw from it. Because leadership remains an "open subject," we all have a great deal more to learn about it.

Some management scholars differentiate between *directing*—a management function—and *leadership*. **Leadership** is seen as a kind of influence, a way of bringing people to work willingly toward the company's goals. In this view, employees *will* respond to the boss's authority alone but this response will likely be just enough to get by. Leadership is seen as an art, that of involving people's full voluntary cooperation. We can have no quarrel with this description of leadership and, indeed, will have more to say on the subject later in the chapter.

The distinction between authoritative directing and leadership may be theoretically valid, but it does little to guide practice. Implicitly, managers lead when they simply direct. If the leadership is effective, the results will be raised above the minimum; if it is ineffective, the results will remain at some minimal norm or may even be pushed below a norm by personal antagonism.

As a practical matter, however, a manager's act of directing can never be separated from his or her leadership. Thus, we will use the terms interchangeably: When we use the word **direction,** we imply *leadership,* because, for better or worse, it is always present and in action.

Social science research has given us numerous insights into the process of leading and directing, and it has identified the key factors that managers must take into account as they go about building their leadership style. A brief review of some of these conclusions is useful in itself; moreover, it will help round out your understanding of the other management functions.

Relationship to Other Management Functions

Perhaps the clearest way to show how closely the management functions are interrelated is to try to imagine leading without fulfilling the other functions. The results would be at once chaotic, dictatorial, and apathetic.

Without planning, work becomes chaotic. The order in which things are to be done, the quality of work deemed acceptable, and how much work must be done all would be determined by individual judgment and on the spur of the moment. The manager would be reduced to direction based on guess, and only the simplest or most stable operations would survive. Consider, as an example, the problems of staffing and staff planning: Without a clear plan of the work to be done, and a plan that provides the right people to do it, an operation would be paralyzed.

Without organization—without some reasonable and coherent means of structuring authority relationships so that the work gets done—the authority of the strongest (power) becomes the only basis for directing. This is never the best approach to directing in any society, and it simply will not work in our affluent, educated society. In any case, only small and simple enterprises can operate on this authoritarian basis. We occasionally see operations in which direction is based solely on the authority of the owner ("Do it or I'll fire you"), but the employees rarely stay there for long.

Without control, employees begin to believe that nobody cares because nobody detects and corrects deviations from standards. Employees become apathetic about standards. Without feedback, no organism (let alone human employees) can learn. Once again, we are reduced to a chaos in which nobody really knows what to do or who is in charge.

Your leadership must be informed by understanding the plans of your organization, as well as the plans you make for yourself. Moreover, leadership must be exercised within the bounds of authority, implicit or explicit, in an organization. Finally, you must base your continuing acts of leadership both on measures of your own performance and on the performance of the units and the people under your direction.

*W*HY PEOPLE FOLLOW

People enter an organization and perform their work, as directed by a manger with definite plans, for several good reasons, all of them selfish. Understanding in a general way what people expect from their work will permit you to base your directing activities on their needs and wants. This understanding is the essence of leadership. Our subject in this section, then, is really **motivation.** You will come to understand employees' motives first through study and observation and later, as a new manager, through practice. This growing understanding will permit you to shape your management activities to reflect the motives of the people working with you.

Necessity as Work Motivation

The time-honored and most basic reason that people work is to provide themselves and their dependents with food, shelter, and clothing. When human labor was in excess supply and society's attitude was less protective of the disadvantaged, this motive was indeed powerful. When the alternative was between work and starvation, the threat of a job loss was terrifying, and this fear maintained a society based on wages.

Economic and social policy in our society today has greatly eroded the power of an employer. To be fired or laid off is certainly an inconvenience and may often involve severe hardship. Economic policy in most Western countries, however, is committed to maintaining high employment levels. Moreover, unemployment compensation provides sufficient income to stave off disaster, and the government employment service facilitates placement in another job. Besides, the majority of families today have two incomes. If husband or wife is laid off, the other family member's income, along with unemployment compensation, will help most households cope. Thus, the manager's threat to fire (which would, in any case, be a last resort) has much greater limitations as a motivator than it did in earlier times.

Advantage as Work Motivation

In a positive way, people seek not just enough money to live but also an income to satisfy the many aspirations now taken for granted in an affluent society. Thus, people work not only for money but also for "more money." Many employees are motivated to work harder to keep a good job, to gain a raise, or to earn a bonus.

As ambitious people repeatedly demonstrate, workers will often put forth extra effort to secure promotion in rank. They do this not only for the increased income but often for the increased social status, as well. We are social animals, and once we have taken care of our basic needs, we begin to pursue socially recognized rewards other than money. Not everyone, however, chooses to pursue such goals at work. Rather, recognition in their other reference groups—family, church, neighborhood, fraternal organizations—may be more important to them. Thus, personal ambition often, but not universally, spurs increased effort at work.

Personal Satisfaction as Work Motivation

We all know people who love their work, and work hard because they enjoy what they do. Such people may include the chef whose whole life is centered on preparing delicious food, the hostess or waitress who enjoys her contacts with people so much she seems to bubble, or (significantly) the mentally challenged dishwasher who is devoted to his or her work. In some cases, the work itself may not be so interesting, but the job may provide other rewards of a social nature. For example, many people enjoy coming to work because that is where their friends are.

Independence as Work Motivation

Many people are motivated toward self-direction and independence. The idea of "being your own boss" as a unit manager entices many managers and employees. Waitresses and cooks often find that an important part of their work satisfaction is that they are good enough at what they do to require almost no direct supervision. However, this is by no means a universal motivation. Hardly anyone wants a work situation in which he or she is "hassled," but not everyone seeks independence. Some prefer or need clear company (or work group) norms and the frequent encouragement to achieve them. Indeed, for many employees, encouragement, praise, and personal recognition outweigh independence as motivation.

Encouragement, Praise, and Recognition as Work Motivation

We have to recognize that many unskilled jobs in our industry are filled by people who find the work itself dull and unrewarding. We can do a great deal to reduce that dullness by fostering a friendly climate at work, praising good performance, and recognizing the worker as a person who makes an important contribution. We set unrealistic goals, however, if we expect everyone to respond warmly to these managerial efforts. In the final analysis, people are hired to do a job, not to be cheerful. (Being—or at least appearing—cheerful should, however, be part of the job of public contact employees.) It is much more pleasant for everyone if workers are happy in their work, but the essential need is to have the work done according to the approved standards.

Money as Work Motivation

Social science research has focused largely on the significance of nonmonetary rewards. That research, however, also provides ample evidence that pay is important. Money is, of course, an economic reward, but workers and managers often see it as a form of social recognition, as well. For some people, a fancy title is important, whether a young manager is called "assistant vice president" or the dishwashers are renamed "sanitation specialists." Most people, however, expect and want utilitarian rewards for superior effort.

Company Policy as Work Motivation

Company policy regarding such important matters as fringe benefits and working conditions can be an extremely important motivator. Some social scientists maintain that these conditions are taken for granted by workers. They argue that their absence would cause dissatisfaction but that their presence is not positively motivating. In the hospitality companies the authors have studied, however, it seems clear that these factors are important positive forces *for the long-term employees,* for those who stay with the company. Because these loyal employees are especially valuable, we should view company policies as important motivators in our industry.

Fringe benefits include, among other things, vacation; sick leave; paid holidays; free or reduced-price employee meals; uniforms; group health, accident, and life insurance; educational benefits; child-care assistance; and pension plans. Some fringe benefits, such as social security and unemployment insurance, are required by law. Fringe benefits took their name originally from the fact that they were a minor part—only the "fringes"—of an employee's compensation. Today, however, fringe benefits account for up to one-third or more of some employers' wage bills. As they become a more significant part of compensation, employees consider them in choosing which jobs to take and, especially, in deciding whether to stay with an employer or to change jobs.

Working conditions is a term that refers to both the physical and the social aspects of the workplace. One employer may offer an air-conditioned, clean, well-lighted kitchen, employee lockers and restrooms, and an acceptable employee dining area. The employee who can choose will prefer this place (other things being equal) to a hot, dingy workplace where the employee's personal belongings are unprotected and where he or she must take meal breaks in a remote corner or eat standing up.

Similarly, people prefer to work in a friendlier environment in which they feel accepted and respected by their co-workers and by management. People generally like to work with other people much like themselves. This means that the employee selection process should take into account whether or not a prospective employee is likely to fit in and to accept the kind of work and interpersonal norms management and the work group expect.

Our discussion to this point suggests many different motives for working. An operation that recognizes that the motives for working vary from one worker to another will train its managers to respond to each worker as an individual. This means not only respecting the individuality of each worker but also shaping a manager's directing activities as much as possible to call forth the best effort from each worker.

Does Happiness Lead to Productivity?

Morale is the attitude a worker or work group feels or expresses toward the work. However, inexperienced managers often assume, incorrectly, that if morale is high, the work will automatically go well. In fact, research results find little direct correlation between high morale in the workplace and productivity. People may be happy at work and spend a good deal of their effort visiting with one another and in other ways expressing their happiness instead of working. Certainly, then, a manager's efforts to improve morale must include a clear expression of quality and quantity work standards. Just as we cannot expect every worker to be cheerful, we cannot settle for cheerfulness in place of adequate work.

In service organizations, however, employee morale (attitude and outlook) may be more important than it is in most other work. An employee with "guest contact" can hardly separate his or her attitude from the work, because work effectiveness depends on his or her manner toward the guests. The guests, in turn, do not recognize the physical service (a waitress brings the food) as separate from the way that service is performed (with a smile and a friendly word or with a frown and a snarl).

Moreover, employees in service systems are highly interdependent. Therefore, at least one criterion for acceptable employee performance has to be an ability to work with others. An irritable, unpleasant employee in a key position—whether or not the position deals with customers—can upset the other employees. If employees are irritated with one another, that irritation is bound to be sensed by the guest. So employee morale is especially important in service organizations.

𝓛EADERSHIP THEORIES

Douglas MacGregor suggested that there are two different ways in which we can look at workers' attitudes toward work.[1] Each of these views, which MacGregor labeled *Theory X* and *Theory Y,* has implications for management.

Theory X.   According to **Theory X,** people do not really like to work, so they must be "coerced, controlled, directed, threatened with punishment" to get them to work. The average worker, this theory argues, avoids responsibility, is unambitious, and wants security more than anything else.

Management based on Theory X is paternalistic at best and, at the very least, authoritarian. Rewards and punishment, the "carrot and stick," are assumed in this theory to be the key to employee productivity.

Theory Y.   In contrast with Theory X is a more generous view of human nature. It sees "physical and mental effort in work to be as natural as play or rest," and it recognizes self-direction instead of external control as the principal means of securing effort. According to **Theory Y,** under the proper conditions people will, indeed, accept and even seek responsibility. Employees have (says Theory Y) a much greater capability for problem solving than most organizations realize.

Management based on Theory Y relies on a worker's achievement-oriented motives and his or her desire for self-fulfillment rather than on sheer managerial authority. Theory Y calls for developing organizations in which employees can best fulfill their goals by working toward the success of the organization.

Who's Right?   The best answers to the question, Who's right? are "both of them" or "it depends." The question addresses but does not answer the central problem of management in a democratic society. Although we don't have any absolute and final answers, we can identify and consider the issues better in the light of the two theories just discussed.

Three Important Elements of Modern Leadership

To exercise leadership in our modern society, you must understand the nature of authority, both formal and informal, and the realistic limits on managers' use of authority. One of the most important limits on authority is the psychology of the individual worker, and an equally strong factor is that of informal group pressures. Leadership, then, is a result of the interaction of authority with the limits placed on management action by the psychology of the individual worker and the work group.

Authority.   Authority in organizations is based on legal rights derived from business ownership and, in governmental organizations, from legislative acts. In franchise organizations, the leadership style franchisors use in their relationships with their franchisees is generally based on developing a consensus, but the underlying basis of authority is still the legal fact of the franchise agreement that spells out the authority of the franchisor.

A somewhat different kind of authority may be conferred on a leader by a group. The term "informal group," a topic we discuss in more detail later in the chapter, refers to the social organization of the workplace that happens as a social process, in each work group. This distinction between formal and informal organization sets the ground for us to make the crucial distinction between a *formal leader*

Setting standards is an important part of leadership
Courtesy of the National Restaurant Association

and an *informal leader*. The **formal leader** is in charge because of legal rights. Nevertheless, the formal leader can and should seek to supplement this legal authority with recognition by the group of his or her professional competence. A formal leader may also win acceptance as the group's informal leader or, more commonly, establish a productive relationship with the informal group structure.

An **informal leader** exercises a more subtle but very real kind of influence. Effective managers strive to work whenever possible with the person or persons that a group chooses (more or less unconsciously) as leader.

Authority is accompanied by the right and ability to reward or punish. Although MacGregor and others see modern business relying less and less on formal authority, nobody expects it to disappear. To get results, however, authority must be tempered, in a relatively affluent society, in both substance and style. Your directing must be as fair as you can make it, and you should issue your directions in a manner that does not offend. Workers are entitled to their opinions, and employee turnover is too expensive to permit indulgence in arbitrary or offensive directing behavior. Theory X may not be altogether wrong, but certainly it is no longer enough.

The Psychology of the Worker—and the Work. The strength of Theory Y is in recognizing that many workers attempt to achieve personal goals and to find self-fulfillment in their work. For these workers, a clear communication of the organization's standards and goals during their training period is the most welcome form of direction. Workers who perfectly fit this pattern are not as common in our industry as we could wish, but persons who come close and require a minimum of supervision are not hard to find. The manager who is secure in his or her own competence will avoid unnecessary supervision and the appearance of harassment without losing sight of the need to assert the organization's standards when necessary.

A word about praise may be in order here. Most people thrive on encouragement, but praise is difficult to bestow graciously and may be subject to inflation. If an employee is competent and hardworking, a pat on the back from the manager may look like condescension. When you say, "You're doing a good job, Jane," she may say (to herself), "I know that. Who asked you?" Moreover, just as too much money in an economic system can lead to inflation and devalued currency, praise given too often and too easily loses its value.

The best kind of praise is your respect for the worker and your appreciation of work well done. This respect and appreciation usually comes through in consulting with workers and in attending to their advice, solicited or unsolicited. This attention makes what *they do,* not what *you say,* important.

The work that people do may not really be important to them. For instance, a part-time waitress who sees herself principally as a wife, a mother, and a member of the PTA and her church group is unlikely to see her work as her principal means of self-fulfillment, even though she may take considerable pride in that work. Motivating her will thus require a different approach from, for instance, your boss's approach to motivating you, an ambitious, rising manager.

People in many unskilled jobs, such as dishwashers, simply do not find the satisfaction that Theory Y suggests they should be receiving. For that to happen, we need to redesign our organizations—and society itself, for that matter. Although such a grand redesigning is an interesting subject, it goes beyond the scope of this chapter and, to be frank, the realistic limits of hospitality managers today.

The Work Group as a Social Unit. Leadership and directing must use the authority that a manager derives from the formal organization, and it must take into account the various individual motivations—from pay to praise to self-fulfillment—normally found within a **work group** made up of individual employees. A third significant force is the work group itself as a social unit. When people come together to work, they develop a social organization with its own leadership, its own norms of work and social conduct, and, very often, a cliquish structure.

In a waitress or waiter work group, for instance, managers find strong feelings about how work should be distributed (including the number of guests that should be seated on a station). Some restaurants actually use a *turn system* in which each waitress serves a party seated at her station in rotation. The object is to be sure each server gets a fair share of the business. Variations from the order of turns can create a great deal of trouble for a supervisor.

In practice, however, some waiters or waitresses can handle more parties than others can. Following the turn system can, therefore, hold back the more able and place some guests at stations in which a slower server is actually overloaded. The result is that the fast service person may seek another employer and the guest who gets stuck with an overloaded, slow server may seek another restaurant. The turn system of seating, however, is most significant as an example of the power of a work group over a weak or indifferent management.

In responding to the norms that workers develop among themselves, no manager should surrender the formal authority inherent in their position. Neither can a manager, however, afford to ignore a force as strong as social pressure. One way to deal with this force is exemplified by an incident from one of the authors' experience as a manager dealing with an informal work group leader:

> When they encounter the person whom a work group has chosen (very informally, sometimes subconsciously) as their leader, many managers regard that person as a threat to their authority. But an alternative way to approach the situation is to view the informal group leader as a communication link to the work group. When I was a young manager, I met a waitress, Ethel, who was an unusually competent person and had the respect of all the other waitresses. She was also a very strong-willed person who often opposed steps I wanted to take in managing the restaurant. At one point, I wanted to fire her. But the man I worked for just laughed and said I could fire her "when you've learned what she knows." It took me a good deal of time to find out that if I consulted Ethel instead of ordering her, I could get not only her cooperation but often some good advice. Building on this realization, I found that instead of announcing "policy," I could discuss a problem or goal with Ethel, indicating what I thought but remaining open to her reactions. Generally, the results of our discussions would make the rounds and, in a few days, become adopted as policy both by the house and the waitresses—without any fuss. Moreover, the new policy carried force because it had been accepted voluntarily. Also, my own role as the formal leader was reinforced by my acceptance of the work group's social values.

Within larger work groups, subgroups or **cliques** often form. Sometimes relations between these cliques are friendly or neutral; sometimes they become unfriendly or downright hostile. Management cannot do away with clique formation, but knowledgeable managers can arrange their directing activities so that they take these strong forces into consideration.

We do not present these few words on the informal group as a full discussion of this complex subject. Rather, we intend to offer only a few examples to illustrate the meaning of this third force bearing on the manager's directing and leading activities.[2] This discussion sets a useful background, too, for the subject of worker participation in management.

Participation

In a democratic society composed of educated and relatively affluent workers, the influence of the worker and the work group is increasing. However, this increase in power need not be seen as a threat to management. A manager secure enough to invite and accept participation in decision making can harness strong forces for obtaining results. The level of worker participation, however, may vary with the circumstances.

Information.   Keeping employees informed about matters that affect their work represents only the minimum level of consideration for a prudent manager. Employees whose assignments must be changed deserve an adequate explanation of what changes are to be made and why they must be made. When changes affect an entire group, the group should receive enough information to understand what is going on. Many managers use regular staff and department meetings to accomplish this function.

Consultation.   Before a decision must be made, a manager can prevent hard feelings by consulting the workers who will be affected by that decision, as well as others who are knowledgeable in the area. Because of their familiarity with the activity in question, workers often see problems that managers may miss. Technical issues aside, this consultation often eases tensions associated with change and increases its chances of acceptance. As the previous section suggests, it is particularly important to consult workers who have the respect of their fellow workers and whose support may be crucial in gaining acceptance. Consultation should not be viewed as relinquishing management's responsibility and authority for decisions based on the prerogatives of ownership or some other legally constituted authority.

Involvement.   Managers often see a problem, develop a variety of solutions with the workers, and then present these alternatives to the employees themselves for their decision. If the first solution they choose does not work, further discussion and change are obviously in order. Often, however, the best way to gain acceptance of change is to involve those affected in the decision. Moreover, the solution to some problems probably belongs to and should be undertaken by the work group.

Thus, for instance, a group of waitresses may be asked to help management develop the best means for assigning sidework (housekeeping chores in the dining room such as stocking side stands or filling salt and pepper shakers). Management cannot really ask whether or not this work should be done; it must be done. The issue is how. Implicitly, if the solution offered does not work in practice, management must confer again with the affected workers and arrive at another solution.

*C*OMMUNICATION

For directions to be followed, they must be understood. The best thought-out plan will fail if it is not communicated in a way that can be comprehended.

Barriers to Communication

Factors that inhibit clear communication pertain to the language we use, the differing backgrounds of the sender and the receiver, and the circumstances in which the communication takes place.

Semantic Barriers.   Different people attach different meanings to words. The phrase "my work" may have quite a different meaning to a manager and to a busboy. To one, it refers to a life's work; to the other, a part-time job after school.

The word "management" also conjures up different images for the manager and the person responsible for busing the dishes. To the manager, it may mean "responsible execution of carefully studied company policy." By contrast, the busboy or busgirl may think of the fact that "the boss docked my pay because I was late." A communicator must, therefore, choose words that convey the meaning of the sender in such a way that the receiver understands that meaning. *Loaded words* with strong emotional meanings—*free enterprise, the system, right to work*—may do more to confuse than to clarify discussion.

Social Background.   Social background is closely related to the problem just considered. The values of the middle-class American, the background typical among managers, carry certain assumptions that may not strike the expected response among some employees. A good example is the idea of ambition.

People brought up in middle-class families that encourage striving for success take ambition for granted. By contrast, people raised in poverty, who have acquired only limited schooling and who see themselves as "never having had a chance," may look at ambition quite differently. When the middle-class manager assumes, as he or she communicates, that the pot washer shares this enthusiasm for achievement, the manager may be in for some unpleasant surprises. It is important to consider exactly where (in the current vernacular) the other person "is coming from."

Immediate Environment.   The place where communication occurs can have an important effect on what gets understood. If a worker has been late, calling that person into the office to discuss the tardiness may be taken as a signal of a serious offense. If that signal is appropriate, fine; but if the tardiness is a first offense, it may be better to mention the matter to the worker privately in the immediate work area at a time when he or she is not busy.

On the other hand, a reprimand in front of other workers has quite a powerful negative impact. (There's an old and good rule to remember: Praise in public, reprimand in private.) Similarly, discussion of complicated matters at the wrong time results in confusion. Let's suppose the broiler operator asked you about a problem on his or her withholding tax form at a time when you couldn't answer and you said, "I'll get back to you later." To try to answer that question in the middle of the rush hour when he or she is under considerable pressure will probably inhibit understanding and increase annoyance.

Gateways to Communication

Listening.   One of the most important acts in telling somebody something—paradoxically—is for you to listen. Communication is not a one-way street; it is an interchange. When you speak to people, they reply either in words or with *body language*—the way they hold themselves, the look on their faces, a shrug of the shoulders. Listening and observing these body language cues will tell you a great deal about how your message has been received.

Empathy.   Your ability to put yourself in the other person's shoes in a conversation can be crucial to understanding and dealing with his or her reaction.

*E*LEMENTS OF LEADING AND DIRECTING

Leading and directing are really continuous processes, but we can break them down into some key activities in which managers typically engage. In fact, the actions (or elements) we discuss here portray the diversity of leading and directing and how they can vary from situation to situation. They include (1) telling someone what to do, (2) providing information on how to do it, (3) seeing that he or she has learned how to do it, (4) making the performance of the work as appealing and comfortable as possible, and (5) conferring specific rewards or punishments for performance. Now, we will examine these elements of leading and directing in more detail.

1. *Orders* obviously tell someone to do something. They are acts of authority—authoritative directions.

2. *Instruction* provides information, for our purposes, about some hospitality work-related activity.

3. *Training* involves guiding employees toward the mastery of often complex activities. Thus, a manager may give new employees a week's training to qualify her or him to begin work as a waitress or waiter. Properly executed, training involves not only telling and showing the trainees how to do the work but also evaluating later—for the benefit of both the trainees and the trainer—the quality of that learning. Trainees are permitted to do the work under supervision and to repeat the process until they achieve an adequate mastery.

4. *Motivating* moves beyond ensuring that the worker knows how to do something; motivating makes the employee eager, or at least willing, to do the work. A manager who motivates employees tailors the whole array of inducements—pay, recognition and status, self-fulfillment—in a way appropriate to the needs and wants of each worker (within, of course, the limits of what is possible).

5. *Sanctions* may be either positive or negative, *rewards or punishments.* Although motivation generally may be thought of as continuous and positive, individual acts of sanction can be either a raise or promotion on the one hand or a fine or reprimand on the other.

If a manager has done his or her job correctly, the employees will know what to do and how to do it, and they will have a sufficient mastery of the work to accomplish it properly. Managers must continually respond to the individual needs and wants of workers to gain their willing commitment to work. Finally, managers are expected to recognize outstanding performance and, when necessary, to penalize those who do not perform adequately. Case History 20.1 describes one manager's responsibilities in the food service industry.

*C*ase History
20.1

What Does a Leader Do for a Living?

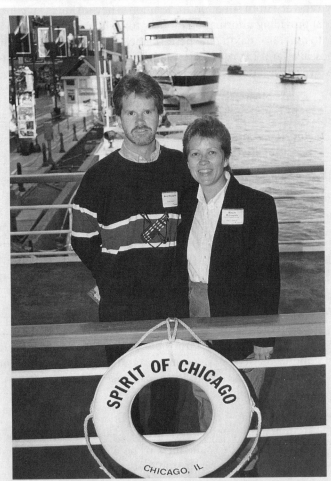

Mary Jo McLoughlin

Mary Jo McLoughlin was born and grew up on Chicago's south side where she was very active in sports. She traces the development of her leadership style, in part, to those experiences. She began her education with an associate's degree from Wilbur Wright Community College and then earned her bachelor's degree as a transfer student at Northern Illinois University. After graduation in 1980, she worked as a clinical staff dietitian at the Rehabilitation Institute of Chicago. After five years in this position, she joined Szabo Food Service as a food service manager in business services.

Soon after ARAMARK purchased Szabo in 1986, she became a district human resources director for ARAMARK's Business Services. Among her principal responsibilities were overseeing recruiting, management development, and training. She also served as a human resources consultant for line managers and was the district's affirmative action officer. During this busy time, she also managed to earn her MBA at De Paul University—one or two courses at a time in the evening over a four and a half year period.

Mary Jo thoroughly enjoyed the staff position as human resources director but she missed being in the line "where the action is," as she put it. So, in late 1996, when she was offered the position of regional manager in school support services, she was delighted to accept. In this position, her greatest responsibility—and one she feels keenly—is to the 30,000 students in the hundred schools that make up the 13 school districts in her region.

At the level of the individual school, a supervisor or lead employee, depending on the size of the operation, is in charge. These people report to the Support Services Director of that school district who, in turn, reports to Mary Jo.

Mary Jo's work can be seen from many perspectives but we will concentrate our attention on just three of them: directing operations, developing people, and client contact. First of all, although she can delegate operational authority for the 13 districts, she continues to be responsible for outcomes in those 100 schools. She makes regular visits to each school district every month but she also has the help of ARAMARK's management systems and audit staff. As well as her own visits, ARAMARK audit staff may undertake unannounced visits. Sometimes these audit visits are made by a Support Services Director from another school district (as a part of training that person for broader responsibility). However, Mary Jo usually makes these audit visits herself. In these unannounced inspections, financial records are checked but other records are reviewed, as well, to ensure compliance with school district and ARAMARK operational guidelines and standards.

Developing other people is another big part of Mary Jo's job. The individual employees in the school are certainly interested in how much they are paid and so wage surveys have to be made periodically to ensure competitive pay levels. The most important motivation for most hourly employees, however, is that the job provides the enjoyment that comes from being around kids and from the socialization of the workplace. From among these people come the local supervisors who can and often do ultimately rise to management positions. Keeping in touch with operations and the people in them is an important and rewarding part of her work.

ARAMARK has developed its own "Career Management System," which helps structure Mary Jo's efforts in working with others to develop their careers. Each year, she talks with her directors as they set goals for the coming year. Employees have personal development goals of their own but they also need to meet corporate goals in areas such as profit, safety, and nutrition. In an annual review, the work of the past year is assessed against the goals set a year earlier. Out of this comes a development plan, which involves continuous learning, as well as a program of individually planned actions and outcomes. Incentives for managers are paid on the basis of performance as compared with the plan for the previous year.

When a promising supervisor is identified for further development, he or she begins a 13-week, structured on-the-job training program and then may serve for a year or so as an assistant support services director. This could also be the path followed by someone who had graduated from college and joined ARAMARK. School districts vary from 1 to 15 or more schools and the smaller districts are an ideal assignment for a newly promoted assistant support services director for further development. An able young manager with a two- or four-year degree might be given this kind of responsibility.

A third area of responsibility Mary Jo relishes is client contact. In meetings with principals and school business managers, as well as with school boards, Mary Jo represents ARAMARK and her employees to the client. In fact, her regular schedule calls for attendance at school board meetings to present issues pertaining to the food service program.

Mary Jo has technical support on line via her laptop computer and fax in an office in her home but her real office is wherever she is—in effect, in her head. She says she got spoiled when she was in human resources and had a full-time administrative assistant. Although there is some clerical assistance available from the ARAMARK district office, she handles much of her correspondence via E-mail and fax. She has become very comfortable with technology.

Mary Jo lives with her husband, Mark, and their two sons, Mark and Luke, in Chicago where the regional manager's job keeps Mary Jo more than occupied, although she also manages to coach Little League baseball in her free time. Figure 1 gives a typical day's schedule. She finds that the challenge and responsibility—and the work with people—are her greatest rewards in her job as a leader.

6:30 A.M.	Good Morning!
7:00 to 7:30 A.M.	At work in her office at home.
8:30 A.M. to 2:00 P.M.	Visit to a school district Visit may include site inspection(s), client meetings, training, "hands on" involvement in the operation, or an audit.
2:00 to 6:00 P.M.	Possible stop at an adjacent district to work with the director.

Figure 1 A typical day's schedule.

Leadership and Change

To this point, we have been discussing leadership and directing as two aspects of the same management function. Moreover, we have been discussing that function as a part of everyday ongoing activity in an operation. In an organizational crisis such as in a company that is losing money, however, the leadership needs of that organization emerge as critical.

In an organization that needs to make *fundamental changes,* the work of the leader has three basic elements[3]:

1. *Establishing direction.* Seeing where an organization needs to go and expressing that vision in a way that people can understand is vital. Moreover, the strategies for producing the necessary changes must be spelled out. Thus, the vision must be one that can be acted on effectively.

2. *Aligning people.* Getting the appropriate people in the organization not just involved but committed to achieving the new goals is a necessity. This involves "lining up" coalitions in the informal organization who will support the program of change. Some might call this "selling" the vision.

3. *Motivating and inspiring.* In effect, this involves keeping people sold, keeping them moving in the right direction, often against obstacles that come from inside the organization from people who are threatened by the needed changes.

We might consider the case of a new hotel manager who takes over an operation that has been completely demoralized.[4] The hotel is at a very busy airport in a booming city. For its first few years, the hotel had both high occupancy and profits, but management neglected both the physical plant and the organization's morale, that is, its people. Management turnover was high and employee turnover disastrously so. As new hotels were added in the area, the market became overbuilt at about the same time the city's boom ended. Occupancy in the hotel dropped from over 85 percent to below 65 percent, then to less than 60 percent, and profit turned to loss. Bill Wayle was hired as Food and Beverage Director but the General Manager (GM) quit two days after he arrived. The company asked Bill to take the GM's job. He took over the operation but found almost immediately that the man he reported to was not prepared to make some key expenditures. Bill's response was to decline the GM's job unless he had the necessary support. He was given the modest financial support he requested, finally, and so the turnaround could begin.

The first thing Bill did was to make some cosmetic changes in the lobby, replacing soiled and damaged furniture and light fixtures. The next thing he did was to announce a long-range improvement plan. He met regularly and frequently with department heads, attended department meetings, and spent a lot of his time moving around the hotel, talking with employees. Everywhere his message was the same: "We can't fix everything at once but we *can* improve our service *now.* Will you help?"

Bill reexamined operating procedures, pruned unnecessary payroll from politically powerful departments, and spent that money where it really affected service. He spent a lot of time on the phone selling *his* boss on the need to replace items such as worn-out bedspreads and lampshades and to begin the long-term improvement plan he had already promised the employees.

Almost at once, the employee turnover dropped and people bought into Bill's program to improve service *now.* As service improved and the property began to look less shabby, occupancy improved. In less than a year, the hotel was profitable again. With these results, it became easier to sell his company on the need for major investment. We can look at Bill Wayle's activities in the context of our description of leadership for change.

Establishing Direction. "Better service—now" was a vision everybody could be a part of. The few very visible changes Bill made helped employees feel that things were getting better and enabled them to respond to comments about worn facilities positively. "We're working on it. It's going to get better" is a more effective response—to both employee and guest—than "Gee, I'm sorry it's such a mess."

Aligning People. Bill's frequent attendance at department meetings and his almost daily meetings with department heads in the early days established a new attitude—that somebody *cared* about the property. The consistent, *realizable* vision of improving service was repeated in every conversation and sold people on the idea that the hotel *could* be turned around. People either left the organization or began to take responsibility for their actions with the guests. Significantly, Bill had to sell his boss and the corporate headquarters on every investment in the property. From the beginning, he took a serious career risk in refusing to continue without support. In the longer run, he used effective operating results to line up support both above and below for his vision of returning the hotel to first-class status.

Motivating and Inspiring.   Effective employees were recognized. Virtually all supervisory positions were filled by promotions from within. Effective performance was rewarded with public and highly visible praise, and effective people found their salaries raised as much as company policy permitted. These actions supported the growing enthusiasm for the turnaround program.

In a time of crisis, when change is needed, leadership becomes especially crucial. Good solid management needs to accompany leadership, but leadership has to tell managers where they are going (direction), line up support for new direction (alignment), and keep everybody sold and enthusiastic (motivating and inspiring). All of these are important in everyday leadership, too, but especially so in a time when an organization needs dramatic change.

DEVELOPING YOUR OWN LEADERSHIP STYLE

As we have argued earlier, a manager's leadership role in directing the work ultimately stems from his or her formal authority. To direct work effectively, managers must take into account at least three factors. The first is the work that needs to be done. The second is the person or persons who are to do the work—and their individual characteristics. The third is the informal socializing group structure of the work group in question.

In fact, then, leadership is not an inflexible behavior pattern. **Leadership styles** will vary from situation to situation and place to place. If you are a junior manager just out of training and working with a group of senior workers, you will conduct yourself more tentatively than you might later as a general manager dealing with a similar group. If your employees' work is exciting and highly profitable, as might be the case for a waitress group in a top-flight restaurant yielding generous tips, your leadership conduct might be different from what it would be toward the night cleanup crew that arrives as the restaurant is closing.

The dictionary provides several meanings for the word *style*. One of the meanings is a synonym for fashion—the way "everybody" is doing something. When we speak of management style, however, we certainly do not mean the current fashion. The definition that suits our needs better is "the manner or tone assumed in a discussion." The way leadership is carried out reflects the person who does the leading. Some leaders are flamboyant and confident; others, more reserved and (at least at first) unsure. The important point is that leadership in our industry is not some mysterious thing one is born with or without. Rather, it is a set of learned abilities. Just as people's personalities differ, so each person is likely to behave differently in directing the work of others. The difference, however, is usually in style, in manner and tone, not in substance. The basic goal of directing, as in all management functions, is achieving the desired results.

It will be up to you, finally, to determine how you best achieve results. Your success, however, will depend not only on the strength of your formal position, on the workers and work you direct, and on the work group, but also on who you are and what manner and tone, what style, works best for you in the situations you face.

You can begin to form your leadership style now, and you should. In field experiences, summer jobs, and part-time employment, you can observe the management style of others, even though you may not at first be given managerial responsibility. You can analyze the situations that managers confront and the people in those situations. Then you can decide for yourself how well you think the situations were handled, how they might have been handled better, and how you might feel most comfortable in handling similar situations.

You should certainly consider the process of learning to act as a leader and directing the work of others as continuous and lifelong. The most accomplished artists, after years of practice, will still speak of how much they have left to learn. Management, as it is implemented by individual managers, is definitely an art based on understanding and practice. It is a fascinating art one can learn through both study and practice. The fascination can last a lifetime, and the process has already begun for you.

$\mathcal{S}$ UMMARY

First, we defined leadership, differentiated it from direction, and explained the reasons that it is important.

Our second subject was people's motivations for working: necessity; advantage; personal satisfaction; independence; encouragement, praise, and recognition; money; and company policy. This led us to consider whether happiness, or high morale, results in high productivity.

We discussed MacGregor's Theory X and Theory Y, plus three elements of modern leadership: authority, psychology of the worker, and the work group. Worker participation was also described as important.

Good communication between managers and workers is important as well, and so we talked about possible barriers (semantic, social background, and immediate environment) and possible gateways (listening and empathy) to effective communication.

The last topics were an enumeration and description of the elements of leading and directing, the special requirements of leadership in times of crisis, as well as ways to develop your own leadership style.

KEY WORDS AND CONCEPTS

Leadership
Direction
Motivation
Fringe benefits
Working conditions
Morale
Theory Y

Theory X
Formal leader
Informal leader
Work group
Cliques
Leadership styles

REVIEW QUESTIONS

1. What is the difference between leadership and direction?

2. Describe what would happen at a Burger King without leadership.

3. List and briefly discuss the motivations for working.

4. How do Theory X and Theory Y fit with your management style—or intended style? Would you lean toward X or Y or some other position?

5. Using the three basic elements of leadership discussed in this chapter, analyze a critical situation you have encountered, either at work or as a student. How did the leaders involved respond? How should they have responded? What would you have done?

6. Describe the informal structure of a work group to which you have belonged.

7. Describe a manager or boss you have admired, and explain why.

8. Do you think you would be a good leader? Why or why not?

INTERNET EXERCISES

1. **Site Name:** *Hotel, Restaurant and Tourism Online Professional and Trade Journals*
   URL: http://www.wku.edu/~hrtm/journals.htm
   Background Information: This web page provides links to hospitality professional journals on line and serves as a launchpad to retrieve information from these journals.

EXERCISE: Choose several of the on-line journals and search for recent articles on employee motivation, communication within an organization, leadership, facilitating change, or any topic deemed appropriate by the instructor. Read the articles and lead a class discussion on the topic you have chosen. How do the articles supplement the information contained in the textbook? Be sure to provide the other students with the names and URLs of the journals where the information was found.

 OTES

1. Douglas MacGregor, *The Human Side of Enterprise* (New York: McGraw–Hill, 1960).
2. An excellent discussion of this subject is found in George C. Homans, *The Human Group* (New York: Harcourt Brace and World, 1950).
3. John P. Kotter, *A Force for Change* (New York: The Free Press, 1990).
4. This incident is adapted from a case provided by the executive described and is chronicled in more detail there. See Thomas F. Powers, *The Royal Hotel* (Guelph, Ontario: School of Hotel and Food Administration, 1987).

Part 6

Hospitality:
A Service Industry

Chapter 21

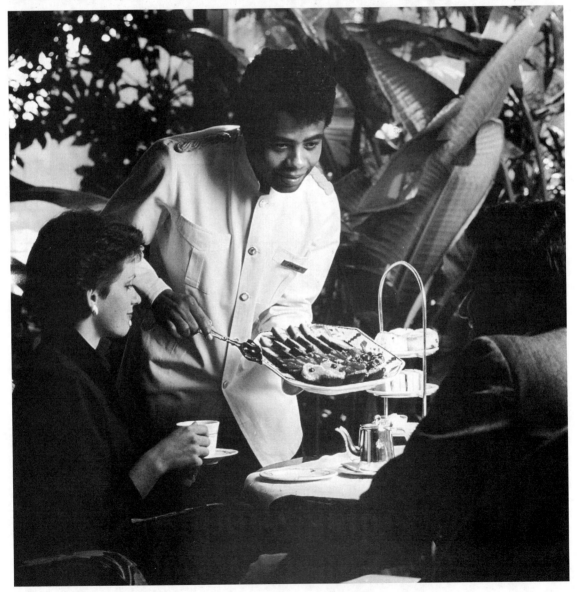

Courtesy of Four Seasons Hotels

The Role of Service in the Hospitality Industry

The Purpose of This Chapter

While details differ, the tangible side of the hospitality industry is surprisingly similar. Fast-food operations resemble one another within food categories, one budget motel offers pretty much the same as another, and so forth. Whether it's Big Mac vs. the Whopper, or Hampton Inns vs. Fairfield Inns, company offerings look a lot alike. Increasingly, companies are realizing that *service* is the best way to achieve differentiation and is what can give an operation a competitive edge. This chapter examines service as a process, considers the work of rendering service as a personal experience, and, finally, considers how companies manage service.

This Chapter Should Help You

1. Define service both in terms of guest experience and the operation's performance

2. Describe the principal characteristics of service

3. Recognize service as having task and interpersonal aspects

4. Become familiar with the two views of managing the service process

5. Learn how companies organize for service

6. See service as a basis for successful competition

"Dear Mr. Wilson," the letter from Mortimer Andrews to the company president began, "Yesterday I arrived at your hotel in Chicago with a confirmed reservation guaranteed by my credit card only to be told that no room was available. I was furious and let the desk clerk know how I felt in no uncertain terms. The clerk, John Boyles, handled the situation so well that I wanted to write and tell you about it.

"John responded to my very angry tirade about my reservation by admitting the mistake was the hotel's. He said that he had made reservations for me at a nearby Sheraton and that your hotel would take care of the difference in the room rate. When I reluctantly agreed, he called a cab—after letting me know your hotel would pay the cab fare, too.

"What struck me was John's real concern for my situation, his professional manner, and the fact that he didn't give me any excuses. 'It was our mistake and we're anxious to do everything we can to make it right.' John carried my bags out and put me in the cab, convincing me that somebody really cared about this weary traveler.

"I travel a lot and it's hard work without the extra hassles and foul-ups. On the other hand, everybody makes mistakes. John's concern and assistance make a big difference in the way it feels when one of them happens to you. I thought you should know about this young man's superior performance. He is a real asset to your company. He restored my faith in your hotel and I'll be back."

This incident may not seem like a major event, but consider for a moment just what the stakes are. Mr. Andrews is a frequent traveler. If we assume that he is on the road an average of two days a week, at the end of the year his business would be the equivalent of a meeting for 100 people. If we assume an average rate (in all cities he visits, large and small) of $65 per night, the room revenue involved is $6500. Using industry averages, he is likely to spend an additional $3250 on food and beverage. In other words, the receipts from this one guest amount to a $10,000 piece of business—and there is no shortage of other hotels he could stay at if he doesn't like yours.

The rule of thumb, moreover, is that a dissatisfied customer will tell the story of his or her problem to 10 others. The possibility for bad word of mouth and potential loss of other sales makes the problem of the dissatisfied guest even more serious.

In fact, a study of 2600 business units in all kinds of industries, conducted by the Strategic Planning Institute, has been summarized in this way: "In all industries, when competitors are roughly matched, those that stress customer service will win."[1] If this is true in manufacturing and distribution, how much more true must it be for those of us whose business *is* service.

The population group that has dominated the hospitality industry (and most of the rest of the economy) are the baby boomers. Over the next 15 years, this group will continue to move into the relatively affluent middle years. They are the best-educated consumers, quite literally, in history. These relatively affluent, sophisticated consumers (as we have noted elsewhere in this text) can afford and will pay for good service. Moreover, competitive options give them plenty of other places to go if they don't receive the kind of service they seek. It is not too much to say that excellence in service will be a matter of survival by the year 2000.

The role that John Boyles played in keeping Mr. Andrews' business illustrates how important the service employee is in hospitality. That incident invites us to consider just what service is, how it is rendered in hospitality companies, and how companies can organize for and manage service. These are the subjects of this chapter.

$\mathscr{W}$HAT IS SERVICE?

"Service," according to one authority, "is all actions and reactions that customers perceive they have purchased."[2] In hospitality, **service** is performed for the guest by people (a waitress serves a meal, for instance) or by systems such as the remote guest check-out operated through a hotel's television screen. The emphasis in our

From the guest's point of view, service is the performance of the organization and its staff.
Courtesy of Resorts International Casino Hotel, Atlantic City, NJ

definition is on the guest's total **experience**. Indeed, from the guest's point of view, service is the **performance** of the organization and its staff.

The guest and the employee are personally involved in the service transaction. If a customer purchases a pair of shoes or a car, he or she takes the finished product away with no concern about who made it or how. On the other hand, in hospitality, to give one example, a lunch is served. The service is produced and consumed at the same time. The service *experience* is an essential element in the transaction. If the server is grumpy and heavy-handed, likely the guest is unhappy. A cheerful and efficient server enhances the guest experience.

Notice we say *enhances*. The tangible side of the transaction must be acceptable, too. All the cheerfulness in the world will not make up for a bad meal or a dirty guest room. At the same time, it is also true that a good meal can be ruined by a surly server, just as a chaotic front office or poor bell-staff service can ruin a stay in a hotel that is physically in excellent shape. The hospitality *product*, then, includes both *tangible* goods (meals, rooms) and *intangible* services. Both are essential to success.

The server's behavior is, in effect, a part of the product. Because servers are not the same every day—or for every guest—there is a necessary variability in this "product" that would not be encountered in a manufactured product. The guest is also a part of the service transaction. A guest who is not feeling well or who takes a dislike to a member of the staff may have a bad experience in spite of all efforts to please.

Because service *happens to somebody,* there can be no recall of a "defective product." It is now a guest's experience. For this reason, there is general agreement that the only acceptable performance standard for a service organization is **zero defects**. *Defects*, however, should be defined in terms of the type of operation and the guest's expectations. At a McDonald's, waiting lines can be expected during the rush hour and will be accepted as long as they move with reasonable speed. However, a dirty or cluttered McDonald's, even in a rush period, represents a "defect," an emergency that needs to be remedied right away. On the other hand, a waiting line at a restaurant in a Four Seasons Hotel is, by Four Seasons' own definition, a defect. It is an emergency that needs to be remedied by a hostess or manager offering coffee or soft drinks and apologizing for the delay. Zero defects is the goal for which both organizations design their systems but the meaning of defect varies according to company goals and customer expectations. While neither company is perfect, both have standards and dictate emergency action, such as management stepping in to help out until the defect is remedied, when a defect occurs.

Because the consumption of the service and its production occur simultaneously, there is no inventory. An unused room, as the old saw goes, can never be sold again. A dining room provides not only meals but the capacity of a certain number of seats. While unused food remains in inventory at the end of the day, unused *capacity*—an unused table today—has no use tomorrow. This puts pressure on hospitality businesses to operate at as high a level of capacity as possible, offering special rates to quantity purchasers. A hotel's corporate rate structure is one example of such quantity pricing.

Let us summarize the **characteristics of service** that we have identified to this point. Service is experience for the guest, performance for the server. In either case, it is intangible, and the guest and server are both a part of the transaction. This personal element makes service quality control difficult—and quite different from manufactured products. Because there is no recall of the guest's experience, to repeat, the standard for service operations must be zero defects. Finally, production and consumption are simultaneous. Thus, there is no inventory.

Types of Service

There are three general types of service transactions: electronic–mechanical, indirect personal, and face-to-face transactions.[3]

Electronic–mechanical transactions in hospitality range from vending machines to such services as automated check-in and check-out. Other examples are the in-room well-stocked refrigerator that takes over much of the room service department's work in a hotel and a hotel's automatic-dial telephone system. Electronic–mechanical transactions are generally acceptable and sometimes even preferred by the guest where they eliminate inconvenience, such as waiting lines. On the other hand, as frequently vandalized vending machines eloquently testify, electronic and mechanical failures often infuriate people. There is a premium on correct stocking, maintenance, proper programming, and adequate capacity so that breakdowns in service will not occur when no person is there to speak personally for the operation.

Indirect personal transactions include telephone contacts such as hotel reservation services, the reservation desk at a restaurant, or the work of a room service order taker. Some indirect transactions such as those just mentioned are generally repetitious in nature and, thus, subject to careful "scripting." That is, because most of these interactions follow a few very similar patterns, the employee can be trained in considerable detail as to what to say and when to say it. Some indirect contacts, however, are nonstandard. For instance, a guest calls the maintenance or housekeeping department directly from his or her room with a problem. An individual response to the particular guest problem is necessary, but the general procedure in such cases can be clearly specified in advance. Training in telephone manners—and careful attention to just who answers the phone in departments that don't specialize in guest contact work—is essential to maintaining the guest's perception of the property.

Face-to-face transactions have the most power to make an impression on the guest. Here, the guest can take a fuller measure of people—their appearance and manner. People whose work involves frequent personal contact with guests must be both selected and trained to be conscious, effective representatives of the organization. Because an increasing part of the services in modern organizations are automated, the personal contact that does take place must be of a superior quality. It is also important that public contact employees be prepared to deal sympathetically with complaints about automated services. As John Naisbitt has pointed out, the more people have to cope with "high tech," the more they require a sympa-

Face-to-face service transactions have the most power to make an impression on the guest.
Courtesy of ARAMARK

thetic human response from the people in organizations. Naisbitt calls it "high touch."[4]

We must continue to be interested in all kinds of service transactions, whether personal or not. The work of designing computerized systems or scripting standardized indirect transactions, however, is generally specialized and done by experts. Virtually all of us, on the other hand, will have to deal with guests face to face. Accordingly, much of our attention in the balance of this chapter will focus on personal service. Figure 21.1 summarizes the characteristics, while Table 21.1 shows the three types of service interactions.

RENDERING PERSONAL SERVICE

Service involves "helpful, beneficial, or friendly action or conduct."[5] As we have just noted, some of these actions are provided by mechanical or computerized devices or involve only indirect personal contact, usually by phone. The most challenging service area involves helping that is performed person to person. Indus-

Service is
- an experience that happens to the guest.
  No recall of defects is possible.

- performance for the organization
  Zero defects is the service system design goal.

- a process whose production and consumption are simultaneous.
  Unsold "inventory" has no value.

Because the employee is so much a part of the guest's experience, the employee is part of the product.

Figure 21.1   Characteristics of service.

try Practice Note 21.1 discusses some of the personal costs of service, stress in particular, and considers how the industry has begun to remedy them.

There are two basic **aspects to the personal service act**: that of the **task**, which calls for technical competence, and that of the **personal interaction** between guest and server, which requires what we can sum up for now as a helpful or friendly attitude (Figure 21.2).

Task

As recently as the late 1970s, the hospitality industry's ideas on personal service as expressed in training programs and waiter–waitress manuals focused principally on procedure.[6] The following is a representative sample from the classic, *Essentials of Good Table Service:*

> *The Correct Way to Hold Plates:* Plates should be held with the thumb, index finger, and the middle finger. The upper part of the plate's rim should not be touched; this prevents fingers from getting into the soup or leaving marks on the plate.[7]

Table 21.1   Three Types of Service Transactions

Type of Interaction	Example	Key Points
Mechanical— electronic	TV check-out	Acceptable if eliminates inconvenience. Failure unacceptable to guest. Plan to be error free.
Indirect	Telephone contacts room service housekeeping	Detailed scripting desirable for many transactions. General procedure specified.
Face-to-face	Guest registration	Person represents the organization to the guest.

Industry Practice Note 21.1

Service and Stress

Consider for a moment how outsiders portray the food service workplace. In a famous scene from the film *Five Easy Pieces,* actor Jack Nicholson nearly reduces a hapless waitress to tears when she repeatedly attempts to explain that she isn't allowed to make substitutions in his order. Anyone who has served in a restaurant would agree that the scene is not particularly far-fetched. Servers are forced to deal with frustrated or aggravated customers daily—a task virtually any psychologist would label as being intensely stressful. When confronted with anger or adversity, our first reaction can be reduced to two fundamentals: fight or flight. To stand there and try to reason the problem out with a total stranger almost runs counter to our basic human nature.

Historically, stress was simply accepted as a given in restaurant work; it tended to go along with the territory. Fortunately, however, times are changing.

One way the industry is beginning to deal with the problems of stress is to limit the number of hours employees are expected to work. The old 60-hour work week is gradually beginning to fade into history as it becomes increasingly apparent that more humane shifts help prevent employee burnout.

Improved training methods are another way the industry is helping employees deal with daily stress. New employees—particularly servers—are exposed in role-playing scenarios to the types of interpersonal encounters they can expect to meet on the job and, if they are prepared for the inevitable confrontations, they will be able to deal with them more easily.

Clearly, however, with the industry's appetite for new workers growing—and its struggle to overcome deeply rooted perceptions of employee mistreatment accelerating—other, more sweeping responses should also be considered. One of the more constructive actions that could be taken is to ensure that management understands how to handle stress in a constructive manner.

The seemingly treasured European traditions of tossing heavy pieces of kitchenware at errant employees or demeaning them loudly in front of their colleagues does little to foster loyalty or job satisfaction. Bullies in management positions are usually only successful at stroking their own egos and heightening already high levels of tension. A little restraint, a little understanding, a little humane thinking can go a long way toward reducing anxiety in an already tense situation.

Source: Excerpted from the editorial, "As Workplace Stress Heats Up, Help Simmer Tempers with a Little Patience, Understanding," *Nations Restaurant News,* December 1, 1997, p. 23.

Functional task competence is still an essential element in any service action. Guests don't want a thumb in their soup any more than they want a bellman to get lost rooming them—or a front desk that can't find their reservation.

In modern service organizations, the task side of service is controlled by management through carefully developed systems that are supported by written procedures. Procedures of this kind control work in very much the same way that a carefully designed assembly line controls the way goods are manufactured.[8]

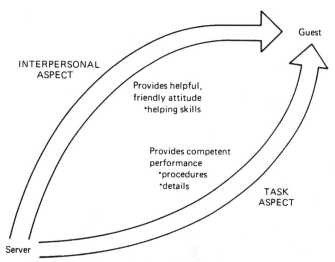

Figure 21.2 Two aspects of service.

As one authority on the study of services put it, "In real estate, the three components of successful investing have always been *location, location and location*. In service encounter management, the components for success might be stated as *details, details, details.*"[9] If a service organization is failing, blaming the employee is a "cop out." Getting the procedures right and a proper system functioning is the task of management.

Although there is no substitute for accomplishing the task of service competently, that alone is seldom enough to secure repeat business in a highly competitive marketplace.

Interpersonal Skills

The other aspect of personal service involves the way in which the server—waitress, bellman, or desk clerk—approaches and deals with the guest. Perhaps the best model for thinking about the kind of behavior that secures a favorable response from the guest is that of "helping skills." These were originally derived from studying the working techniques of psychotherapists. The **helping skills** have now been simplified into a technique for anyone whose work involves interacting with people. In fact, methods for its use have been developed for a wide variety of "people workers," ranging from police to college residence hall proctors to nurse's aides. All have in common that they are "people helpers" and provide services to people.

The core conditions of a friendly and helpful attitude can be spelled out more fully. Servers need to be able to put themselves in the other person's shoes; in a word, they need empathy. They need to present a friendly face to the guest and to do so in a way that is not going to be seen as just an act; they need to be (or at least appear) sincere.[10]

Trainers in the skills that underlie successful interpersonal behavior assume

Both technical competence and good interpersonal skills are important to personal service.
Courtesy of United Airlines

that things like eye contact, facial expression, hand movements, and body language, generally, are *learned skills* and, hence, readily teachable. For instance,

> Good eye contact consists of looking at another individual when he is talking to you or when you are talking to him. Eye contact should be spontaneous glances which express an interest and desire to communicate further.

> Poor eye contact consists of never looking at another individual; staring at him constantly and blankly; and looking away from him as soon as he looks at you.[11]

Thus, employees must learn not just to have an attitude that is helpful and friendly to the guest but to convey that attitude to the guest by their behavior. Excellent interpersonal behavior is characterized by warmth and friendliness and a manner that imparts a sense of being "in control" to the guest—or the sense of being in the charge of someone who knows very well what he or she is doing.[12]

MANAGING THE SERVICE TRANSACTION

Most work done in the hospitality industry has the focused activity of a single process and can be supervised by someone who can keep track of what is going on. For instance, food preparation in a kitchen is organized around the process of cooking, usually following written or unwritten recipes. If the food is acceptable, the process is being managed correctly. Hospitality *service,* on the other hand, is made up of transactions that are numerous, diverse, and often private. In a dining room each interaction between a server and a guest is really something just between the two of them—or, at most, between the server and the guest's party at that table. A multitude of these transactions are taking place in the dining room over the period of a single meal. The problems of managing this process are made more complex by the fact that the product is the guest's experience. The problem of producing a favorable feeling about an operation in numerous guests is too complex for any management to control in any detail.

Two somewhat different basic approaches to this challenge of managing service have developed.[13] The most common, which we can call the *product view of service,* focuses on controlling the tasks that make up the service. An increasingly important alternative is the *process view of service,* which concentrates on the guest–server interaction. The two views are not necessarily mutually exclusive. In practice, some of the elements of control that underlie the product view are found in any well-run service unit. In addition, attention to the way we treat people, that is, a process orientation, is necessary in any operation.

Hospitality service is made up of numerous transactions, some private, which create a total experience for the guest.
Courtesy of Four Seasons Hotels

The Product View of Service

The **product view** looks at service as basically just another product that businesses sell to customers. The product view concentrates on rationalizing the service process to make it efficient and cost effective—as well as acceptable to the guest. The focus is on *controlling* the accomplishment of the tasks that make up the service. Employee behaviors that are part of that task are prescribed, often in considerable detail.

Perhaps the best example of the product view of service is McDonald's and fast food, generally.[14] Theodore Leavitt has described old-style, European service as a process anchored in the past, "embracing ancient, pre-industrial modes of thinking," involving a servant's mentality and, often, excessive ritual. Leavitt contrasts this with the rationale of manufacturing, where the orientation is toward efficiency and results—and where relationships are strictly businesslike. Leavitt sees the key to McDonald's success as "the systematic substitution of equipment for people, combined with the carefully planned use and positioning of technology."

The fast-food formula for success is a simplified menu matched with a productive plant and operating system designed to produce just one specific product line. Leavitt suggests that giving employees choices in their tasks "is the enemy of order, standardization, and quality." The classic example of this simplification and automation is the McDonald's french fry scoop, which permits speed of service and accurate portioning with no judgment or discretion on the part of the employee. A McDonald's unit, Leavitt says, "is a machine that produces, with the help of totally unskilled machine tenders, a highly polished product."[15]

Detailed control of procedures and process is, however, not limited to fast food. Carol King, the president of QualityService Group, a quality-assurance consulting firm, advocates setting measurable "service levels [as] the equivalent of setting manufacturing product standards," which, in turn, must "be related to the customer's requirements and the properties' desired image." As examples of service standards, she suggests,

> one might limit to five minutes the maximum amount of time a guest should wait in a check-out line. Human needs can be met by such performance standards as "every guest is greeted on arrival"; "eye contact is made at least once during the transaction"; "when guests give their names, as when checking in or claiming a reservation, they are subsequently addressed by name." . . . Procedures must be thoroughly defined and documented, specifying how each task should be performed.

Measurement of the system's performance, King advocates, should include guest evaluations, operating audits, and inspection.[16]

The product view faces obstacles on two different fronts. First, the pool of employees that hospitality service firms draw from has been shrinking for several years. In the light of this scarcity, employers have begun to look for means to make service jobs more attractive. Because many employees prefer to be able to use their own judgment rather than just follow the rules, the close control of behavior required by the product view is increasingly called into question. Perhaps even more significant are guest reactions, particularly in upscale markets.

Widespread application of the product view of service has led guests to "ask where the *service* has gone from the service industries," as one writer put it.

> They [i.e., the hospitality industry] have perfected training methods to provide the guest with adequate but impersonalized attention and unvarying hamburgers. . . . Especially in the hospitality industry, some managers and customers feel that the loss of the personal touch is too severe a penalty to pay for productivity gains through "production line" approaches.[17]

The Process View: Empowerment

The product view of service, as we have just noted, sees service as a product that can be controlled efficiently in a production process that is typical of manufacturing. The **process view**, on the other hand, focuses on the interaction between the service organization and the guest.[18] The key contrast between the two approaches, as we will view them, is between *control* and *empowerment*. The process view of service calls for satisfying the guest's desires as the first priority. Service employees increasingly are being given the discretion—that is, **empowered**—to solve problems for the guest by making immediate decisions on their own initiative and discussing these later with management. Three examples from the experience of

Empowerment is especially important in situations where the service employee is expected to exercise judgement and discretion.
Courtesy of Marriott International

Four Seasons, a premier hotel chain, illustrate the kind and degree of impact this approach is having on hospitality companies.[19]

♦ A guest ordered a dinner of linguini and clams. When the order came, the dish was divided into white and black (squid ink) linguini. The guest ate the white linguini but left the black half untouched on the plate. The server inquired if the dinner was all right, and the guest responded, "I just don't like squid ink linguini." The incident came to light because the guest was a "spotter" employed by a firm retained by Four Seasons to "shop" its hotels and report on the quality of service.

In reviewing the incident, management learned that the description "squid ink linguini" was not indicated on the menu. As the guest had no way of knowing that something she didn't like was going to be served, the waiter should have removed the charge for this item from the guest's bill even though she didn't complain. The waiter did not do so, however, because the property's accounting procedure would have required a lengthy process and management authorization for taking the charge off the guest check.

As a result of this incident, the property's accounting rules were changed to make it possible for a server to void an item on a bill immediately and account for that action later. (The menus were also reprinted to identify the squid ink linguini specifically.)

♦ A guest called the desk and asked to have a fax machine installed in his room. The property did not have a fax machine available for this purpose but the clerk undertook to rent one from an equipment supply house. Because the supply house required a sizable cash deposit, the clerk asked the guest for the cash.

When the front-office manager learned of this, she told the clerk to pay the deposit out of hotel funds and charge the guest's account for the "paid out." She then used this incident to teach not only this clerk but the whole front office as part of the hotel's constant retraining process to heighten everyone's sensitivity to the need to *solve the guest's problem* with a minimum of inconvenience to the guest and clean up the paper work later. (The property also added fax machines to the equipment available for guest use.)

♦ A guest's reservation had identified a preference for a club floor room with a king-sized bed and an ocean view. When the guest arrived, he found the room had all the requested features but was too small for his working needs. He called the concierge and told him of his problem. Looking at room availability, the concierge indicated he could meet all of the guest's requirements only with a room that was not on a club floor. That would mean the guest would not have concierge services available. The guest decided to stay where he was. A few minutes later, however, the concierge called the guest back. After studying his reservations, the concierge had been able to juggle some arrivals so as to make a room on the club floor available, one that had the ocean view and adequate space. The concierge offered the guest the room at the same rate although it was an executive suite, which normally carried a higher rate. The concierge was able to do this because of a recent change in procedure giving him the authority to make decisions to satisfy guests—and account for them later. The guest accepted the concierge's offer and, not surprisingly, later wrote to compliment the hotel's management on its superb service.

In these examples, we have seen how one luxury hotel group is trying to make its employees more concerned for the guest. It is changing operating and accounting rules and procedures to help employees do what they have to do to satisfy guests. This is precisely what is meant by the term *empowering*.

We can take another example—a training program developed by the Marriott Corporation to provide greater discretion to waitresses and waiters.[20] The new program was substantially different in both content and procedure from more traditional programs.

Training was built around working groups of three or four employees who began by discussing key questions such as, What does good service to kids mean? What would be the best way of serving coffee? When do you think the check should be presented? Who should get it? Discussion questions often covered a wide variety of service situations ranging from taking orders to handling criticisms and complaints. Results from the small groups were then brought to the whole departmental group to serve as a basis for general discussion by the department.

Procedures, too, were viewed differently from more conventional programs.

> There is no formula for greeting guests or introducing yourself. Servers are encouraged to come up with their own way of meeting the customer. The guideline is how to make the customer feel welcome. How you do it is your choice. The trainer emphasizes that how you do things is more important than what you do. There are no rigid rules or routines because the idea is to avoid routines.[21]

Production or Process View?

Some kinds of operations are ideally suited to the "production line" approach to service. Fast-food restaurants, amusement parks, and budget motels come to mind as having the need for the cost efficiency of the production approach. Patrons of upscale operations, however, demand the personal attention and individualized service that is facilitated by the process view of service, and midmarket operations are increasingly interested in empowering employees to achieve the competitive advantage that comes from committed service people.

As we noted at the outset of this discussion, some attention must be paid to the quality of personal interchanges in the most bare-bones economy operation. Similarly, basic tasks must be accomplished with competence and dispatch in the most luxurious of operations. It is not a matter of choosing between two different approaches but of adapting each approach to the needs of particular operations. The reliance on rule setting and the product approach is associated with mass-market

PRODUCT VIEW OF SERVICE		PROCESS VIEW OF SERVICE
Emphasizes service as a task		Emphasizes interaction with the guest
Controls		Empowers employee
employee behavior	vs.	to satisfy guest's needs and desires
cost of transaction/process		to solve guest's problem
objective, measurable standards		
Concentrates on what we do		Concentrates on what the guest wants

Figure 21.3 Managing the service transaction: two approaches.

operations, but we should note that several limited-service hotel chains have built "satisfaction guaranteed" programs for guests around employee empowerment with excellent results. Figure 21.3 summarizes key characteristics of the two views of service discussed.

HOW COMPANIES ORGANIZE FOR SERVICE

Early in this chapter, we defined what service was. In the section we just finished, we were concerned with two approaches to managing numerous and diverse service transactions. These approaches were based on either control of the tasks or empowerment of individual servers to solve problems for guests. In this final section, we will consider the steps necessary on a companywide basis to achieve excellence in service.[22] To do this, we will consider what underlies a service strategy, the development of a service culture, the importance of people to service organizations, and the development of a service system as a competitive advantage.

Service Strategy

The basis of a **service strategy** is market segmentation. **Market segmentation** identifies groups of customers and prospects who share sufficient characteristics in common that a product and service can be designed and brought to market for their needs.[23] A wide variety of service levels and types are available in hospitality. In food service, these range from fast food to coffee shop to dinner house to haute cuisine. Each of these levels of service denotes a different style—counter service; fast, a simple table service; informal, unhurried table service with multiple courses; and, with haute cuisine, most probably formal European-style service. Each level denotes a particular price level and, most probably, a distinctive ambience, as well.

We said earlier that zero defects is the standard that service organizations must set. This very high standard, however, is set in the context of **customer expectations** for a particular segment and operation type. The *level of service* is an intrinsic part of the service segmentation strategy. A leading management book on customer service points out, "*Segmenting by customer service*, rather than by customer, often reveals that it is possible to give great service to a wide range of people who share a narrowly defined set of expectations."[24]

At STAR TREK: The Experience™ at the Las Vegas Hilton, guests can sit down and have a drink with their favorite Star Trek characters. Successful hospitality service should fit the setting and meet guests' needs and expectations.
Copyright 1998 Paramount Pictures. All rights reserved.

A rising young executive may take clients to an haute cuisine restaurant, his or her spouse to a casual dinner house, and the kids to a quick-service restaurant. When alone, the executive may lunch at a nearby family restaurant because it is convenient, fast, and offers a suitable selection. The needs of the same person and that person's expectations of the operation vary according to occasions.

Similarly, different people in each of these situations will have different needs. The primary business of a restaurant is serving food. Second only to that, however, restaurants are in the business of providing guests with experiences that meet their expectations. Rather than targeting guests solely by demographic and lifestyle factors—though these are important, too—restaurants can target guests by the kind of dining occasion a guest is seeking. Quick-service restaurants fit relatively few kinds of dining *occasions*—though they fit a whole variety of demographic or lifestyle segments—depending, of course, on the occasion. Thus, restaurants are designed with particular occasions and dining experiences in mind as much as they are with particular groups of people in mind.

A point to consider is that there is no intrinsically "better" kind of service: only service that fits the setting and is designed to meet guest needs and expectations. With service level, of course, go other factors such as price, atmosphere, and location. Indeed, these are crucial to the zero-defect goal of a service operation. A Four Seasons room rate is roughly 10 times that charged by Motel 6—and that rate differential is necessary to fulfill the luxury guest's expectations. On the other hand, Motel 6 customers are not disappointed by the service level they encounter. It is what the budget guest expects.

Earlier, in the lodging chapters, we segmented the market broadly into two groups, "upstairs" and "downstairs" customers. The upstairs customer is seeking a guest room (i.e., upstairs) for the night and minimal supporting service. For this customer, Marriott offers the Courtyard concept, with limited food and beverage facilities in the property, and Fairfield Inns, which have no food and beverage facilities but are located near other restaurants. Courtyard and Fairfield both offer top-flight guest rooms and highly competitive rates for their segment. These properties have eliminated some services but, because of that, have been able to provide attractive rates. Most significantly, the service level they do offer fits the guest's expectation for that kind of property.

On the other hand, some guests do want the "downstairs" services of a full-service hotel. These include the luxurious lobby and a range of restaurants and bars as well as shops. Meeting and banquet facilities are important to the downstairs guest, too. Marriott targets the downstairs guest with its Resorts and Hotels Division—and a quite different price range. For each price and service range, operating standards are set to meet the target segment's expectations.

It is important to pay careful attention to the *level of expectation* your advertising arouses in your customer and not to overpromise. "Embassy Suites ads feature Garfield, a plump, scruffy cartoon cat known for his self-indulgence, to send the message that the 'suite life' costs no more than staying in a traditional hotel."[25] By poking a little fun at itself with Garfield, Embassy Suites avoids evoking images of grand luxury and Old World service and adjusts its guests' expectations to the fairly narrow range of services it actually offers.

Strategy in service, then, involves picking a distinct segment and crafting facilities and services specifically to fit the expectations of those guests. Care must be taken not to overpromise because anything less than the service your guest expects will result in disappointment, lost sales, and unfavorable word-of-mouth reputation. Figure 21.4 gives an overview of setting a service strategy.

Service Culture

A company's culture can be defined

as a set of assumptions or an ideology shared by members of an organization. These assumptions are used by people to identify what is important and how things work in

- Choose market segment or segments.
- Determine appropriate service level and standards.
- Don't overpromise
- Fulfill expectations

Figure 21.4   Setting a service strategy.

that company. When these assumptions become formalized, rules for behavior are established so that people know how to act.[26]

To establish a strong **service culture**, an absolute prerequisite is top-management commitment.

"There's a sign on my desk that reads 'What have you done for your customer to-day?' " says Hervey Feldman, President of Embassy Suites. "I worship at my sign every day, and all my hotel managers worship at theirs"—Bill Marriott writes thank you letters to his hotels' best guests, volunteering to fix anything they're unhappy with, and so do the managers of Marriott Hotels.[27]

The visible commitment of top management to the service culture sets the tone for the rest of the organization. The following conversation, overheard in a restaurant's dining room just after the breakfast rush, between a young trainee and the restaurant manager, illustrates the logic of management commitment to service. During the rush, the restaurant manager had been on the floor almost continuously, generally pouring coffee and water refills for guests and occasionally even busing dirty dishes.

TRAINEE (jokingly): Hey! I thought you said managers weren't supposed to work stations. You looked like one of the bus boys out there this morning.

MANAGER (smiling): Well, I know what you mean but you have to understand an-other truth. We want our customers to be happy with our service so they'll come back—and send their friends here, too. So, when there's a big rush like that I like to pitch in and please a few customers. When the rest of the service staff sees me hus-tling, they know what I think is important and they tend to reach a little harder to please people, too.

Say It and Mean It.   Research on company culture in the hospitality industry suggests that where there is a wide divergence between what company officials say and what they do, employees will be cynical and indifferent to the quality of service. On the other hand, where there is a close relationship between what the company publicly claims its service policies are and the way things actually happen within the organization, employees' ratings of managerial competence tend to be high. The evidence suggests "that there is a higher profitability in restaurants where what should happen [according to company policy] is happening."[28]

Communication. Top management must not only take a position but must communicate it to employees. Department meetings and general employee meetings are important.

> A popular tool in companies that have many low wage employees in constant contact with customers is the employee council. Employees from each department elect a representative and the representatives meet weekly with the general manager. He updates them on everything he's doing; they ask questions, offer suggestions, voice opinions, and then go back to their departments to explain what's going on.[29]

Other media such as employee newsletters, posters, or even the "Annual Report to Employees" that ARAMARK publishes help create and maintain a climate of enthusiasm for service.

Manager as Helper. *Service America!* made famous the motto, "If you're not serving the customer, you'd better be serving someone who is."[30] This approach sees employees as internal customers whose needs must be met. In effect, managers treat the employees as they'd like to have them treat the guests. The intention is that employees follow management's example. The philosophy underpinning this view is that "a manager's main responsibility is to remove obstacles that keep people from doing their jobs."[31] To quote an often-restated position of J. Willard Marriott, the Marriott Corporation's founder, "You can't make happy guests with unhappy employees."

Restraining Bureaucracy. *Bureaucracy* is a "bad word" for most North Americans, but it is actually a name for the kind of structure necessary to serve any large organization. In other words, in large companies, a certain amount of bureaucratic structure is needed. Nevertheless, a consistent effort needs to be made to resist the bureaucracy's tendency to achieve internal efficiencies by making rules that, in their total effect, can strangle the service out of a service organization. With too

---

Developing a service culture in a company requires:

- Commitment of top management
  In word and policy
  In action

- Policy and practice to be the same
  High profitability is achieved when what *should* happen *does* happen

- Constant, clear communication, up as well as down the organization

- Employees to be treated as customers
  Manager's job: service to employees

- Restraining bureaucratic tendencies
  Customer is more important than rules.

Figure 21.5 Developing a service culture.

Service employees represent an organization to the guest. They are an important component of the hospitality product.
Courtesy of Buffets Inc.

much bureaucracy, employees quote the rules of the operation rather than satisfy the customers' requests.

It is useful to recall, here, the experiences cited earlier at Four Seasons. That company decided to reformulate a lot of its rules to make it possible for servers to make exceptions to the rules to satisfy guests based on their own judgment—and account for their decisions later.

Figure 21.5 summarizes the development of a service culture.

The Employee as Product: The Importance of People

Because the service employee (and often the back-of-the-house employee, too) is involved personally in transactions with the guest, the employee usually comes to represent the operation to the guest. Managing, it has been said, is getting results through people, and that is doubly true of managing service. The tools that are being used to undertake this job at the company level are employee selection, training, motivation, and employee "award and reward programs." Each will be discussed briefly.

Selection.   Employee recruiting has become, for many firms, a marketing activity. In spite of vigorous recruiting to fill positions, operations have to choose their hires with care, especially in public contact service jobs. At Four Seasons, all employees hired must first be interviewed by the general manager or the executive assistant manager, as well as division and department heads. As we noted earlier, in Detroit, Marriott interviewed 27 applicants for each one hired. At Guest Quarters, prospective employees pass through four interviews, one of which is with the general manager. The key point for each company is the fit of the person with the company and the particular service team he or she will be working on.[32]

Training.   Companies that lead their industries in service tend to share two unusual characteristics. First, most such companies emphasize cross-training. Embassy Suites, for instance, encourages employees to master several jobs. The wider training not only gives the property a more flexible employee but also heightens the employee's understanding of the total operation. Moreover, the increased training can add to the interest and excitement of the work.

A second characteristic is that all employees share certain core training experiences. McDonald's Hamburger University has a special four-day program through which staff, head office, and other nonoperations employees gain an understanding of the company's operations, products, and policies. Thus, all responsible employees pass through some Hamburger University orientation to the company. Virtually all senior executives at McDonald's, too, have store-operating experience. Similarly, "Everyone at Embassy Suites understands how to inspect a room for cleanliness."[33]

Motivation.   Embassy Suites has a system called Skills Based Pay (SBP), which encourages all employees to learn the 10 basic jobs that are necessary to operate the hotel. After being in a job for a probationary period of 90 days, an employee can apply for certification that is based on a written test and a work sample. The work sample is passed on by both supervisor and the employee's co-workers. Certification means a pay increase and the chance to train for a different job one day a week. In time, this permits the employee to win further certification and pay increases. The result is increased job interest and a clear career path. In fact, half of the people in Embassy Suites' management training program came up through the ranks through SBP.[34]

Embassy also has a bonus program called Success Sharing. When a hotel meets or exceeds targets that are set quarterly for occupancy, customer satisfaction, and cleanliness, employees get a bonus that amounts to about $100 per month based on the number of hours worked and their hourly rate. Roughly 90 percent of Embassy's properties achieve the levels of performance necessary to receive the bonus.[35]

Like many companies, Embassy Suites also has an employee-of-the-month award to recognize outstanding performance. Moreover, workers get frequent feedback on their performance in terms of how they are contributing to the property's success. The Success Sharing and SBP programs link individual and corporate success in a way that reinforces team building.

Employee Awards.   Awards programs "are formal expressions of encouragement and praise that effective frontline supervisors mete out continually. By creating service heroes and service legends, the programs charge up all employees, not just the winners." To succeed, programs must have "credibility, frequency and psychic significance" to the employee. The process of selecting winners, if it is to have that credibility and significance to employees, must be "careful, obviously meritocratic and tightly linked to customer perceptions of service quality." Awards need to be made soon after the performance they are intended to recognize so that the linkage is clear; to have tangible value like a day off; and to involve active recognition and applause, "not just a name on a plaque." Otherwise, nobody will care.[36]

Participation in Planning.   Workers must have "ownership" of service standards and procedures if the standards and procedures are to be accepted in the workplace. The necessary step to secure acceptance is to involve employees in planning either by consulting them fully in the planning process or by asking them to actually do the planning themselves.

When Rusty Pelican Restaurants set out to improve sales per employee hour without hurting service quality, for instance, work groups in the restaurants were asked to set targets for themselves. Productivity improvements were seen almost at once, partly because the employees wanted to see how much improvement they could bring about. Management's original targets for productivity improvements were easily met and sustained. In informal interviews, customers also rated the service quality as being higher.[37] The process of making the employee a key part of the product is summarized in Figure 21.6.

Service as a Sustainable Competitive Advantage

The products sold in hospitality are strikingly similar. One hotel room is very much like another. Although there are important differences among food service segments, within each segment there is considerable similarity—often, almost unifor-

---

REQUIREMENTS

Employees selected who fit the team.

Training emphasizes
 cross training,
 basic shared experience

Motivation offers
 reward for desired performance,
 frequent feedback for team building.

Awards provide
 formal public recognition based on guest service.

Participation in standard setting creates "ownership" of standards.

Figure 21.6   Making the employee the product.

Businesses that stress customer service are generally the most successful.
Courtesy of Hyatt Hotels

mity. Service offers the most important opportunity to differentiate one product from another. When a service system is established at the chain level, the ability to operate multiple units across a wide territory successfully gives the company an advantage over newcomers to the field. The company's reputation for a dining experience or night's (or week's) stay is an invaluable resource. Almost certainly, it is based on personal interaction with company employees. That is, the company's reputation, its sustainable competitive advantage, is most likely based on its service—and that means, its service employees.

UMMARY

Service is an intangible experience of performance that the guest receives along with the tangible side of the product purchased. Because the service is performed and consumed at the same time, there is no inventory—such as, for instance, of unused rooms from last night—that can be sold at a future date. Both server and guest are a part of the transaction, which complicates quality control. Service quality has two sides: the task and the interpersonal interaction. Different planning and control problems arise for mechanical, indirect, and personal service transactions, with personal service the most difficult to manage.

The service transaction is the heart of service in hospitality. Controlling the details of task performance fits well with a product view of service, while a process view focuses more on the personal interaction between guest and server. In the process approach, servers are empowered to solve problems for the guest.

The basis of service strategy is market segmentation, largely based on consumer service expectations. Successful service companies develop a service culture based on top-management commitment, consistency between policy and practice, and well-developed channels of communication. Because service people are a part of the product, a good service team is essential. Service teams are based on careful selection and training and built on motivational programs that include rewards and involvement in service planning. Because most hospitality products are strikingly similar, service is the most significant sustainable competitive advantage.

◆ 𝒦EY WORDS AND CONCEPTS

Service as	Personal interaction
customer's experience	Helping skills
operation's performance	Product view
Zero defects	Process view
Characteristics of service	Empowering
Electronic–mechanical transactions	Service strategy
	Market segmentation
Indirect personal transactions	Customer expectations
Face-to-face transactions	Service culture
Aspects of service	Employee as product
Task	

◆ ℛEVIEW QUESTIONS

1. What does zero defects mean in service? Does it mean perfection?

2. Discuss the three types of service transactions. What are the considerations managers need to take into account in planning for them?

3. What are the two aspects of service? Which is more important in your opinion?

4. What are the two views of managing the service transaction? Can you think of examples from your own experience where each was appropriate?

5. How is a service strategy designed? What is its basic determinant? What other considerations are important?

6. What do companies need to do to develop a service culture?

◆ INTERNET EXERCISES

1. Site Name: *National Institute of Standards and Technology (NIST)*
URL: http://www.quality.nist.gov/
Background Information: To assist U.S. businesses and nonprofit organizations in delivering ever-improving value to customers, resulting in marketplace success, and in improving overall company performance and capabilities utilizing the Malcolm Baldrige National Quality Award framework core values and methods.

EXERCISES:

a. Go to the NIST site and determine which hospitality organizations have won the Malcolm Baldrige National Quality Award.

b. Do you think this award has any impact on the hospitality industry? Why or why not?

2. Site Name: *Hotel, Restaurant and Tourism URL Directory*
URL: http://www.wku.edu/~hrtm/hotlrest.htm
Background Information: This directory lists the URLs for numerous hotel and restaurant chains.

EXERCISES:

a. Choose several hotel and restaurant chains. Which companies provide quality assurance information to their customers?

b. Which organizations provide a guarantee of some sort to their customers?

c. How difficult was it to find the guarantees?

◆ NOTES

1. William H. Davidow and Bro Uttal, *Total Customer Service: The Ultimate Weapon* (New York: Harper & Row, 1989), p. 40.

2. Christopher H. Lovelock, *Services Marketing* (Englewood Cliffs, NJ: Prentice–Hall, 1984), p. 3.

3. This discussion draws on G. Lynn Shostock, "Planning the Service Encounter," in John A. Czepiel, Michael R. Solomon, and Carol F. Surprenant, *The Service Encounter* (Lexington, MA: Lexington Books, 1985), p. 248. Shostock's terminology (remote, indirect, and direct) is slightly different.

4. John Naisbitt, *Megatrends: Ten New Directions Transforming Our Lives* (New York: Warner Books, 1982).

5. *Webster's Unabridged Dictionary.*

6. For a fuller discussion, see Thomas F. Powers, "Service: An Institution in Transition," *Cornell Hotel and Restaurant Administration Quarterly,* May 1979, pp. 61–69.

7. *The Essentials of Good Table Service* (Ithaca, NY: Cornell Hotel and Restaurant Administration Quarterly, 1971), p. 22.

8. Carol A. King, "Service-Oriented Quality Control," *Cornell Hotel and Restaurant Administration Quarterly,* November 1984, pp. 92–98.

9. Shostock, "Planning the Service Encounter," p. 253.

10. Two of the popularizers of interpersonal skill training put this more formally: "empathetic understanding, positive regard, and genuineness." See Steven J. Danish and A. L. Hauer, *Helping Skills: A Basic Training Program; Leader's Manual* (New York: Behavioral Publications, 1973), p. 1.

11. Ibid.

12. King, "Service-Oriented Quality Control," p. 97. I have used a somewhat different choice of words.

13. Peter G. Klaus, "Quality Epiphenomenon: The Conceptual Understanding of Quality in Face-to-Face Service Encounters," in Czepiel, Solomon, and Surprenant, *The Service Encounter.*

14. Theodore Leavitt, "Production Line Approach to Service," *Harvard Business Review,* September–October 1972, reprinted in *Service Management* (Cambridge, MA: Harvard University, n.d.), pp. 20–31.

15. Ibid., pp. 22–25.

16. King, "Service-Oriented Quality Control," pp. 95–97.

17. D. Daryl Wyckoff, "New Tools for Achieving Service Quality," *Cornell Hotel and Restaurant Administration Quarterly,* November 1984, p. 78.

18. Klaus, "Quality Epiphenomenon," p. 21.

19. James Brown, Senior Vice President, Four Seasons Hotels, personal communication, May 31, 1990.

20. The discussion of training in the process view of service is based on David L. Romm, "The Quiet Revolution at Allies," *Cornell Hotel and Restaurant Administration Quarterly,* August 1989, pp. 26–34. Subsequent to the publication of this article, Marriott sold its restaurant division.

21. Idib., p. 31.

22. This section draws extensively on Davidow and Uttal, *Total Customer Service.*

23. For an extended discussion of market segmentation for the hospitality industry, see Thomas F. Powers, *Marketing Hospitality,* 2d ed. (New York: John Wiley & Sons, 1997), especially Chapter 3.

24. Davidow and Uttal, *Total Customer Service,* p. 70. Emphasis added.

25. Ibid., p. 114.

26. Kareen H. Tidball, "Creating a Culture Adds to Your Bottom Line," *Cornell Hotel and Restaurant Administration Quarterly,* May 1988, p. 63.

27. Ibid., pp. 64 and 67.

28. Ibid., pp. 64–67.

29. Davidow and Uttal, *Total Customer Service,* p. 103.

30. Karl Albrecht and Ron Zempke, *Service America!* (Homewood, IL: Dow Jones–Irwin, 1985), p. 96.

31. Davidow and Uttal, *Total Customer Service,* p. 106.

32. Ibid., p. 123.

33. Ibid., pp. 128–129.
34. Ibid., p. 116.
35. Ibid., p. 117.
36. Ibid., p. 131.
37. Wyckoff, "New Tools for Achieving Service Quality," p. 79.

Index